THE TWEETS
OF PRESIDENT
DONALD J. TRUMP

The Tweets of President Donald J. Trump

The Most Liked and Retweeted Tweets from the Inauguration through the Impeachment Trial

Published by Forefront Books.

For information and pricing on Bulk orders, please email info@forefrontbooks.com

Cover Design by Bruce Gore, Gore Studio Inc.
Interior Design by Bill Kersey, KerseyGraphics

Print Trade Paper: 978-1-948677-56-1
E-Book: 978-1-948677-57-8

THE TWEETS
OF PRESIDENT
DONALD J. TRUMP

★★★★★★★★★★★★★★★★★★★★★★★★★★

THE MOST LIKED AND RETWEETED TWEETS FROM THE INAUGURATION THROUGH THE IMPEACHMENT TRIAL

Forefront
BOOKS

INTRODUCTION

★★★★★★★★★★★★★★★★★★★★★★★★★★★

From the first president of the United States all the way to the current occupant of the White House, the ability to communicate with the American people effectively has always been of monumental importance. During the days of George Washington, Thomas Jefferson, Theodore Roosevelt, and Woodrow Wilson, newspapers were the primary vehicle used by presidents to connect with the voting public. During each administration, some newspapers supported the governing administration while others opposed it.

Then during the Great Depression, President Franklin D. Roosevelt, making use of modern technology, changed everything. Harnessing the popularity of the radio as his medium, he communicated directly with the American people via his "Fireside Chats." At the time, this innovation was groundbreaking. Along with newspapers, radio remained the primary communications vehicle until the 1960 presidential election. During his campaign, John F. Kennedy masterfully used the medium of television for the first time to communicate his new vision for America. Achieving an upset, he won the presidential election by defeating Richard M. Nixon.

The effective use of television, particularly with campaign ads, has dominated the political landscape ever since—that is, until Donald J. Trump arrived in 2016. He used the internet to communicate instantly and effectively with the American people on their cellphones. But Twitter was (and remains) his preferred social media vehicle. Establishing his political positions by tweeting numerous times a day, Trump pulled a major upset by defeating Hillary Rodham Clinton to become the 45th president of the United States.

Once in office, Trump did not abandon his penchant for tweeting. Instead, he doubled down on it, making it his primary means of communicating with the American people. As one can imagine, this has not set well with reporters and news anchors in the media who consider themselves to be the primary disseminators of what is newsworthy and what is not.

Nevertheless, this has not dissuaded Trump in the least. Knowing how effective sending a tweet could be, he once wrote, "Boom. I press it and within two seconds we have breaking news."

Since the establishment media has been predominantly hostile toward President Trump, he has used his Twitter account to bypass them completely, other than to criticize them for spreading "fake news." Instead, he has gone to the American people directly. Despite the fact that nearly 70 percent of Americans believe the president tweets too often, he continues to tweet daily.

His tweets, which often set policy, have become an important part of not only his legacy but also of the permanent presidential record. A decade earlier, such a thing would not have seemed possible. But that was then, and this is now. Tweeting has become the natural progression for communication from newspapers to radio to television to the internet. His tweets have become a permanent part of American history.

Wall Street keeps its eye on President Trump's Twitter feed so keenly that the Dow Jones average rises and falls based on what Trump tweets. World leaders consistently look to what President Trump tweets, especially where foreign policy is concerned. Politically, Trump's followers and political enemies react, almost instantaneously, to what Trump tweets about this and that.

He tweets so often that the role of press secretary has diminished significantly in his administration. What is important is the content of Trump's tweets. Based on what Trump says, he sets policy, announces initiatives, and hires and fires people, all while simultaneously scolding the media and the "deep state" for their attempts to undermine his administration.

With a massive Twitter following of 75.2 million by the spring of 2020, Trump's direct impact upon the American population cannot be dismissed, nor can the value of his tweets as an essential part of the historical record be denied. To put the enormous impact of his tweets into perspective, Trump won the White House with 63 million votes—a number significantly lower than his massive Twitter following.

The Tweets of President Donald J. Trump is a primary document—not a secondary resource where others recount what Trump's tweets contain. There are Trump's own words. Because of this, the reader will know exactly what President Trump thought about myriad issues based in his tweets, making this book far more valuable than what his friends or enemies have to say about what he wrote. As you will come to learn by reading *The Tweets of President Donald J. Trump*, the difference is staggering.

JANUARY 2017 - MARCH 2017

★★★★★★★★★★★★★★★★★★★★★★★★★★

Entering office with enthusiasm and boundless energy, the Trump administration begins with the president tweeting shortly after midnight of his first day in office. Anticipating a peaceful transition of power, as protestors march in the street in opposition to him and Democrats in Congress unite to resist him, Trump is faced with a united front of opposition against him from day one, and he tweets about it.

It all begins today! I will see you at 11:00 A.M. for the swearing-in. THE MOVEMENT CONTINUES - THE WORK BEGINS! **1/20/2017 12:31**

Today we are not merely transferring power from one Administration to another or from one party to another - but we are transferring... (1/2) **1/20/2017 17:51**

power from Washington D.C. and giving it back to you the American People. #InaugurationDay (2/2) **1/20/2017 17:51**

What truly matters is not which party controls our government but whether our government is controlled by the people.
1/20/2017 17:52

January 20th 2017 will be remembered as the day the people became the rulers of this nation again. **1/20/2017 17:53**

The forgotten men and women of our country will be forgotten no longer. From this moment on it's going to be #AmericaFirst **1/20/2017 17:54**

We will bring back our jobs. We will bring back our borders. We will bring back our wealth - and we will bring back our dreams! **1/20/2017 17:54**

We will follow two simple rules: BUY AMERICAN & HIRE AMERICAN!#InaugurationDay #MAGA **1/20/2017 17:55**

THANK YOU for another wonderful evening in Washington D.C. TOGETHER we will MAKE AMERICA GREAT AGAIN https://t.co/V3aoj9RUh4 **1/21/2017 4:56**

A fantastic day and evening in Washington D.C.Thank you to @FoxNews and so many other news outlets for the GREAT reviews of the speech! **1/21/2017 11:53**

Had a great meeting at CIA Headquarters yesterday packed house paid great respect to Wall long standing ovations amazing people. WIN! **1/22/2017 12:35**

Watched protests yesterday but was under the impression that we just had an election! Why didn't these people vote? Celebs hurt cause badly. **1/22/2017 12:47**

Wow television ratings just out: 31 million people watched the Inauguration 11 million more than the very good ratings from 4 years ago! **1/22/2017 12:51**

Peaceful protests are a hallmark of our democracy. Even if I don't always agree I recognize the rights of people to express their views.

1/22/2017 14:23

Busy week planned with a heavy focus on jobs and national security. Top executives coming in at 9:00 A.M. to talk manufacturing in America. **1/23/2017 11:38**

Will be meeting at 9:00 with top automobile executives concerning jobs in America. I want new plants to be built here for cars sold here! **1/24/2017 11:11**

Great meeting with automobile industry leaders at the @WhiteHouse this morning. Together we will #MAGA! https://t.co/OXdiLOkGsZ **1/24/2017 17:04**

Great meeting with Ford CEO Mark Fields and General Motors CEO Mary Barra at the @WhiteHouse today. https://t.co/T0elgO6LP8 **1/25/2017 0:46**

Congratulations to @FoxNews for being number one in inauguration ratings. They were many times higher than FAKE NEWS @CNN - public is smart! **1/25/2017 2:16**

If Chicago doesn't fix the horrible "carnage" going on 228 shootings in 2017 with 42 killings (up 24% from 2016) I will send in the Feds! **1/25/2017 2:25**

Big day planned on NATIONAL SECURITY tomorrow. Among many other things we will build the wall! **1/25/2017 2:37**

I will be asking for a major investigation into VOTER FRAUD including those registered to vote in two states those who are illegal and.... (1/2) **1/25/2017 12:10**

even those registered to vote who are dead (and many for a long time). Depending on results we will strengthen up voting procedures! (2/2) **1/25/2017 12:13**

I will be making my Supreme Court pick on Thursday of next week.Thank you! **1/25/2017 12:17**

Beginning today the United States of America gets back control of its borders. Full speech from today @DHSgov:... https://t.co/8aDaHsAhg9 **1/26/2017 0:03**

As your President I have no higher duty than to protect the lives of the American people. https://t.co/o7YNUNwb8f **1/26/2017 2:14**

Ungrateful TRAITOR Chelsea Manning who should never have been released from prison is now calling President Obama a weak leader. Terrible! **1/26/2017 11:04**

The U.S. has a 60 billion dollar trade deficit with Mexico. It has been a one-sided deal from the beginning of NAFTA with massive numbers... (1/2) **1/26/2017 13:51**

of jobs and companies lost. If Mexico is unwilling to pay for the badly needed wall then it would be better to cancel the upcoming meeting. (2/2) **1/26/2017 13:55**

Miami-Dade Mayor drops sanctuary policy. Right decision. Strong! https://t.co/MtPvaDC4jM **1/26/2017 23:53**

Look forward to seeing final results of VoteStand. Gregg Phillips and crew say at least 3000000 votes were illegal. We must do better! **1/27/2017 13:12**

Mexico has taken advantage of the U.S. for long enough. Massive trade deficits & little help on the very weak border must change NOW! **1/27/2017 13:19**

The #MarchForLife is so important. To all of you marching --- you have my full support! **1/27/2017 16:27**

.@VP Mike Pence will be speaking at today's #MarchForLife -- You have our full support! https://t.co/1jb53SEGV4 **1/27/2017 16:30**

Congratulations Secretary Mattis! https://t.co/mkuhbegzqS **1/27/2017 22:00**

I promise that our administration will ALWAYS have your back. We will ALWAYS be with you! https://t.co/D0aOWhOH4X **1/27/2017 23:46**

The failing @nytimes has been wrong about me from the very beginning. Said I would lose the primaries then the general election. FAKE NEWS! **1/28/2017 13:04**

...dwindling subscribers and readers.They got me wrong right from the beginning and still have not changed course and never will. DISHONEST **1/28/2017 13:16**

Today we remember the crew of the Space Shuttle Challenger 31 years later. #NeverForget https://t.co/OhshQsFRfl **1/28/2017 15:42**

Somebody with aptitude and conviction should buy the FAKE NEWS and failing @nytimes and either run it correctly or let it fold with dignity! **1/29/2017 13:00**

Our country needs strong borders and extreme vetting NOW. Look what is happening all over Europe and indeed the world - a horrible mess! **1/29/2017 13:08**

Christians in the Middle-East have been executed in large numbers. We cannot allow this horror to continue!

1/29/2017 15:03

The joint statement of former presidential candidates John McCain & Lindsey Graham is wrong - they are sadly weak on immigration. The two... (1/2) **1/29/2017 21:45**

...Senators should focus their energies on ISIS illegal immigration and border security instead of always looking to start World War III. (2/2) **1/29/2017 21:49**

Only 109 people out of 325000 were detained and held for questioning. Big problems at airports were caused by Delta computer outage..... (1/2) **1/30/2017 12:16**

protesters and the tears of Senator Schumer. Secretary Kelly said that all is going well with very few problems. MAKE AMERICA SAFE AGAIN! (2/2) **1/30/2017 12:20**

There is nothing nice about searching for terrorists before they can enter our country. This was a big part of my campaign. Study the world! **1/30/2017 12:27**

If the ban were announced with a one week notice the "bad" would rush into our country during that week. A lot of bad "dudes" out there! **1/30/2017 13:31**

I have made my decision on who I will nominate for The United States Supreme Court. It will be announced live on Tuesday at 8:00 P.M. (W.H.) **1/30/2017 13:43**

Where was all the outrage from Democrats and the opposition party (the media) when our jobs were fleeing our country? **1/30/2017 14:23**

The Democrats are delaying my cabinet picks for purely political reasons. They have nothing going but to obstruct. Now have an Obama A.G. **1/31/2017 0:45**

Nancy Pelosi and Fake Tears Chuck Schumer held a rally at the steps of The Supreme Court and mic did not work (a mess)-just like Dem party! **1/31/2017 11:21**

When will the Democrats give us our Attorney General and rest of Cabinet! They should be ashamed of themselves! No wonder D.C. doesn't work!

1/31/2017 11:27

Getting ready to deliver a VERY IMPORTANT DECISION! 8:00 P.M. **2/1/2017 0:31**

Hope you like my nomination of Judge Neil Gorsuch for the United States Supreme Court. He is a good and brilliant man respected by all. **2/1/2017 3:45**

Everybody is arguing whether or not it is a BAN. Call it what you want it is about keeping bad people (with bad intentions) out of country! **2/1/2017 12:50**

Iran is rapidly taking over more and more of Iraq even after the U.S. has squandered three trillion dollars there. Obvious long ago! **2/2/2017 3:06**

Do you believe it? The Obama Administration agreed to take thousands of illegal immigrants from Australia. Why? I will study this dumb deal! **2/2/2017 3:55**

If U.C. Berkeley does not allow free speech and practices violence on innocent people with a different point of view - NO FEDERAL FUNDS? **2/2/2017 11:13**

Congratulations to Rex Tillerson on being sworn in as our new Secretary of State. He will be a star! **2/2/2017 11:18**

Attending Chief Ryan Owens' Dignified Transfer yesterday with my daughter Ivanka was my great honor. To a great and brave man - thank you! **2/2/2017 11:25**

Iran has been formally PUT ON NOTICE for firing a ballistic missile.Should have been thankful for the terrible deal the U.S. made with them! **2/2/2017 11:34**

Iran was on its last legs and ready to collapse until the U.S. came along and gave it a life-line in the form of the Iran Deal: $150 billion **2/2/2017 11:39**

Yes Arnold Schwarzenegger did a really bad job as Governor of California and even worse on the Apprentice... but at least he tried hard! **2/3/2017 11:24**

Iran is playing with fire - they don't appreciate how "kind" President Obama was to them. Not me! **2/3/2017 11:28**

Thank you to Prime Minister of Australia for telling the truth about our very civil conversation that FAKE NEWS media lied about. Very nice! **2/3/2017 11:34**

Meeting with biggest business leaders this morning. Good jobs are coming back to U.S. health care and tax bills are being crafted NOW! **2/3/2017 11:41**

Professional anarchists thugs and paid protesters are proving the point of the millions of people who voted to MAKE AMERICA GREAT AGAIN! **2/3/2017 11:48**

A new radical Islamic terrorist has just attacked in Louvre Museum in Paris. Tourists were locked down. France on edge again. GET SMART U.S. **2/3/2017 12:51**

We must keep "evil" out of our country! **2/3/2017 23:08**

Countries charge U.S. companies taxes or tariffs while the U.S. charges them nothing or little.We should charge them SAME as they charge us! **2/4/2017 3:07**

When a country is no longer able to say who can and who cannot come in & out especially for reasons of safety &.security - big trouble! **2/4/2017 12:59**

Interesting that certain Middle-Eastern countries agree with the ban. They know if certain people are allowed in it's death & destruction! **2/4/2017 13:06**

The opinion of this so-called judge which essentially takes law-enforcement away from our country is ridiculous and will be overturned! **2/4/2017 13:12**

After being forced to apologize for its bad and inaccurate coverage of me after winning the election the FAKE NEWS @nytimes is still lost! **2/4/2017 13:39**

MAKE AMERICA GREAT AGAIN! **2/4/2017 14:26**

What is our country coming to when a judge can halt a Homeland Security travel ban and anyone even with bad intentions can come into U.S.? **2/4/2017 20:44**

Because the ban was lifted by a judge many very bad and dangerous people may be pouring into our country. A terrible decision **2/4/2017 21:44**

Why aren't the lawyers looking at and using the Federal Court decision in Boston which is at conflict with ridiculous lift ban decision? **2/4/2017 23:37**

The judge opens up our country to potential terrorists and others that do not have our best interests at heart. Bad people are very happy! **2/5/2017 0:48**

Just cannot believe a judge would put our country in such peril. If something happens blame him and court system. People pouring in. Bad! **2/5/2017 20:39**

I have instructed Homeland Security to check people coming into our country VERY CAREFULLY. The courts are making the job very difficult! **2/5/2017 20:42**

Enjoy the #SuperBowl and then we continue: MAKE AMERICA GREAT AGAIN! **2/5/2017 22:49**

What an amazing comeback and win by the Patriots. Tom Brady Bob Kraft and Coach B are total winners. Wow! **2/6/2017 3:36**

Any negative polls are fake news just like the CNN ABC NBC polls in the election. Sorry people want border security and extreme vetting.

2/6/2017 12:01

I call my own shots largely based on an accumulation of data and everyone knows it. Some FAKE NEWS media in order to marginalize lies! **2/6/2017 12:07**

The failing @nytimes writes total fiction concerning me. They have gotten it wrong for two years and now are making up stories & sources! **2/6/2017 16:32**

The failing @nytimes was forced to apologize to its subscribers for the poor reporting it did on my election win. Now they are worse! **2/7/2017 2:33**

The threat from radical Islamic terrorism is very real just look at what is happening in Europe and the Middle-East. Courts must act fast! **2/7/2017 2:49**

I don't know Putin have no deals in Russia and the haters are going crazy - yet Obama can make a deal with Iran #1 in terror no problem!

2/7/2017 12:11

It is a disgrace that my full Cabinet is still not in place the longest such delay in the history of our country. Obstruction by Democrats! **2/8/2017 1:04**

If the U.S. does not win this case as it so obviously should we can never have the security and safety to which we are entitled. Politics! **2/8/2017 12:03**

My daughter Ivanka has been treated so unfairly by @ Nordstrom. She is a great person -- always pushing me to do the right thing! Terrible! **2/8/2017 15:51**

Big increase in traffic into our country from certain areas while our people are far more vulnerable as we wait for what should be EASY D! **2/8/2017 17:41**

Thank you Brian Krzanich CEO of @Intel. A great investment ($7 BILLION) in American INNOVATION and JOBS!... https://t.co/oicfDsPKHQ **2/8/2017 19:22**

Immigration Ban Is One Of Trump's Most Popular Orders So Far' https://t.co/wAelwuQ4BE **2/8/2017 19:39**

Majority in Leading EU Nations Support Trump-Style Travel Ban' Poll of more than 10000 people in 10 countries... https://t.co/KWsIWhtC9o **2/8/2017 21:46**

Trump administration seen as more truthful than news media'https://t.co/6LmsR5JOSW **2/8/2017 22:07**

Congratulations to our new Attorney General @ SenatorSessions! https://t.co/e0buP1K83z **2/9/2017 1:05**

Sen.Richard Blumenthal who never fought in Vietnam when he said for years he had (major lie)now misrepresents what Judge Gorsuch told him? **2/9/2017 11:57**

Sen. McCain should not be talking about the success or failure of a mission to the media. Only emboldens the enemy! He's been losing so.... **2/9/2017 13:26**

..Ryan died on a winning mission (according to General Mattis) not a "failure." Time for the U.S. to get smart and start winning again! **2/9/2017 13:52**

SEE YOU IN COURT THE SECURITY OF OUR NATION IS AT STAKE! **2/9/2017 23:35**

LAWFARE: "Remarkably in the entire opinion the panel did not bother even to cite this (the) statute." A disgraceful decision! **2/10/2017 13:15**

The failing @nytimes does major FAKE NEWS China story saying "Mr.Xi has not spoken to Mr. Trump since Nov.14." We spoke at length yesterday! **2/10/2017 13:35**

Heading to Joint Base Andrews on #MarineOne with Prime Minister Shinzō earlier today. https://t.co/4JFhyYdeHO **2/10/2017 23:24**

Our legal system is broken! "77% of refugees allowed into U.S. since travel reprieve hail from seven suspect countries." (WT) SO DANGEROUS! **2/11/2017 12:12**

...design or negotiations yet. When I do just like with the F-35 FighterJet or the Air Force One Program price will come WAY DOWN! **2/11/2017 13:24**

Melania and I are hosting Japanese Prime Minister Shinzo Abe and Mrs. Abe at Mar-a-Lago in Palm Beach Fla. They are a wonderful couple! **2/11/2017 13:33**

Having a great time hosting Prime Minister Shinzo Abe in the United States! https://t.co/Fvjsac89qS... https://t.co/hKqbMB2aQ9 **2/11/2017 18:28**

I am so proud of my daughter Ivanka. To be abused and treated so badly by the media and to still hold her head so high is truly wonderful!

2/11/2017 23:00

Played golf today with Prime Minister Abe of Japan and @TheBig_Easy Ernie Els and had a great time. Japan is very well represented! **2/11/2017 23:15**

A working dinner tonight with Prime Minister Abe of Japan and his representatives at the Winter White House (Mar-a-Lago). Very good talks! **2/11/2017 23:24**

The crackdown on illegal criminals is merely the keeping of my campaign promise. Gang members drug dealers & others are being removed! **2/12/2017 11:34**

While on FAKE NEWS @CNN Bernie Sanders was cut off for using the term fake news to describe the network. They said technical difficulties! **2/12/2017 12:14**

After two days of very productive talks Prime Minister Abe is heading back to Japan. L **2/12/2017 13:04**

Congratulations Stephen Miller- on representing me this morning on the various Sunday morning shows. Great job! **2/12/2017 15:41**

Just leaving Florida. Big crowds of enthusiastic supporters lining the road that the FAKE NEWS media refuses to mention. Very dishonest! **2/12/2017 22:19**

Welcome to the @WhiteHouse Prime Minister @JustinTrudeau! https://t.co/WKgF8Zo9ri **2/13/2017 16:59**

Wonderful meeting with Canadian PM @JustinTrudeau and a group of leading CEO's & business women from Canada... https://t.co/wAoCOaYeZ6 **2/13/2017 18:50**

The real story here is why are there so many illegal leaks coming out of Washington? Will these leaks be happening as I deal on N.Korea etc? **2/14/2017 14:28**

Obamacare continues to fail. Humana to pull out in 2018. Will repeal replace & save healthcare for ALL Americans. https://t.co/glWEQ0INR4 **2/14/2017 22:50**

The fake news media is going crazy with their conspiracy theories and blind hatred. @MSNBC & @CNN are unwatchable. @foxandfriends is great! **2/15/2017 11:40**

This Russian connection non-sense is merely an attempt to cover-up the many mistakes made in Hillary Clinton's losing campaign. **2/15/2017 12:08**

Crimea was TAKEN by Russia during the Obama Administration. Was Obama too soft on Russia? **2/15/2017 12:42**

The real scandal here is that classified information is illegally given out by "intelligence" like candy. Very un-American! **2/15/2017 13:13**

Stock market hits new high with longest winning streak in decades. Great level of confidence and optimism - even before tax plan rollout! **2/16/2017 11:34**

Leaking and even illegal classified leaking has been a big problem in Washington for years. Failing @nytimes (and others) must apologize! **2/16/2017 11:58**

The spotlight has finally been put on the low-life leakers! They will be caught! **2/16/2017 12:02**

FAKE NEWS media which makes up stories and "sources" is far more effective than the discredited Democrats - but they are fading fast! **2/16/2017 14:10**

The Democrats had to come up with a story as to why they lost the election and so badly (306) so they made up a story - RUSSIA. Fake news! **2/16/2017 14:39**

Trump signs bill undoing Obama coal mining rule' https://t.co/yMfT5r5RGh **2/16/2017 23:44**

Despite the long delays by the Democrats in finally approving Dr. Tom Price the repeal and replacement of ObamaCare is moving fast! **2/17/2017 10:13**

Going to Charleston South Carolina in order to spend time with Boeing and talk jobs! Look forward to it. **2/17/2017 11:38**

Thank you for all of the nice statements on the Press Conference yesterday. Rush Limbaugh said one of greatest ever. Fake media not happy! **2/17/2017 11:43**

The FAKE NEWS media (failing @nytimes @NBCNews @ ABC @CBS @CNN) is not my enemy it is the enemy of the American People! **2/17/2017 21:48**

One of the most effective press conferences I've ever seen! says Rush Limbaugh. Many agree.Yet FAKE MEDIA calls it differently! Dishonest **2/17/2017 23:15**

Looking forward to the Florida rally tomorrow. Big crowd expected! **2/18/2017 0:02**

Don't believe the main stream (fake news) media.The White House is running VERY WELL. I inherited a MESS and am in the process of fixing it. **2/18/2017 13:31**

Will be having many meetings this weekend at The Southern White House. Big 5:00 P.M. speech in Melbourne Florida. A lot to talk about! **2/18/2017 13:51**

My statement as to what's happening in Sweden was in reference to a story that was broadcast on @FoxNews concerning immigrants & Sweden. **2/19/2017 21:57**

Give the public a break - The FAKE NEWS media is trying to say that large scale immigration in Sweden is working out just beautifully. NOT! **2/20/2017 14:15**

HAPPY PRESIDENTS DAY - MAKE AMERICA GREAT AGAIN!

2/20/2017 14:33

Just named General H.R. McMaster National Security Advisor. **2/20/2017 21:00**

Congratulations to our new National Security Advisor General H.R. McMaster. Video: https://t.co/BKn9r225Kk https://t.co/VBXcJ1b6Pv **2/21/2017 0:38**

Americans overwhelmingly oppose sanctuary cities' https://t.co/s5QvsJWA6u **2/21/2017 20:46**

The so-called angry crowds in home districts of some Republicans are actually in numerous cases planned out by liberal activists. Sad! **2/21/2017 23:23**

Very much enjoyed my tour of the Smithsonian's National Museum of African American History and Culture...A great job done by amazing people! **2/22/2017 12:50**

Seven people shot and killed yesterday in Chicago. What is going on there - totally out of control. Chicago needs help! **2/24/2017 0:01**

find the leakers within the FBI itself. Classified information is being given to media that could have a devastating effect on U.S. FIND NOW **2/24/2017 12:36**

Trump vows to fight 'epidemic' of human trafficking https://t.co/oDLZ2NdrtA **2/24/2017 17:04**

FAKE NEWS media knowingly doesn't tell the truth. A great danger to our country. The failing @nytimes has become a joke. Likewise @CNN. Sad! **2/25/2017 3:09**

Maybe the millions of people who voted to MAKE AMERICA GREAT AGAIN should have their own rally. It would be the biggest of them all! **2/25/2017 12:25**

The media has not reported that the National Debt in my first month went down by $12 billion vs a $200 billion increase in Obama first mo.
2/25/2017 13:19

Great optimism for future of U.S. business AND JOBS with the DOW having an 11th straight record close. Big tax & regulation cuts coming! **2/25/2017 13:27**

I will not be attending the White House Correspondents' Association Dinner this year. Please wish everyone well and have a great evening! **2/25/2017 21:53**

Congratulations to Thomas Perez who has just been named Chairman of the DNC. I could not be happier for him or for the Republican Party! **2/25/2017 22:02**

The race for DNC Chairman was of course totally "rigged." Bernie's guy like Bernie himself never had a chance. Clinton demanded Perez! **2/26/2017 11:33**

For first time the failing @nytimes will take an ad (a bad one) to help save its failing reputation. Try reporting accurately & fairly! **2/26/2017 11:42**

Russia talk is FAKE NEWS put out by the Dems and played up by the media in order to mask the big election defeat and the illegal leaks! **2/26/2017 18:16**

Big dinner with Governors tonight at White House. Much to be discussed including healthcare. **2/26/2017 20:13**

I will be interviewed on @foxandfriends at 6:00 A.M. Enjoy! **2/28/2017 2:43**

THANK YOU! **3/1/2017 13:38**

Since November 8th Election Day the Stock Market has posted $3.2 trillion in GAINS and consumer confidence is at a 15 year high. Jobs! **3/2/2017 11:00**

Jeff Sessions is an honest man. He did not say anything wrong. He could have stated his response more accurately but it was clearly not.... (1/4) **3/3/2017 2:22**

...intentional. This whole narrative is a way of saving face for Democrats losing an election that everyone thought they were supposed..... (2/4) **3/3/2017 2:27**

...to win. The Democrats are overplaying their hand. They lost the election and now they have lost their grip on reality. The real story... (3/4) **3/3/2017 2:35**

...is all of the illegal leaks of classified and other information. It is a total "witch hunt!" (4/4) **3/3/2017 2:38**

It is so pathetic that the Dems have still not approved my full Cabinet. **3/3/2017 12:19**

We should start an immediate investigation into @ SenSchumer and his ties to Russia and Putin. A total hypocrite! https://t.co/Ik3yqjHzsA **3/3/2017 17:54**

We must fix our education system for our kids to Make America Great Again. Wonderful day at Saint Andrew in Orlando. https://t.co/OTJaHcvLzf **3/3/2017 20:48**

I hereby demand a second investigation after Schumer of Pelosi for her close ties to Russia and lying about it. https://t.co/qCDljfF3wN **3/3/2017 21:02**

MAKE AMERICA GREAT AGAIN! https://t.co/kuQiZDz4rA **3/3/2017 22:13**

The first meeting Jeff Sessions had with the Russian Amb was set up by the Obama Administration under education program for 100 Ambs...... **3/4/2017 11:26**

Terrible! Just found out that Obama had my "wires tapped" in Trump Tower just before the victory. Nothing found. This is McCarthyism! **3/4/2017 11:35**

Just out: The same Russian Ambassador that met Jeff Sessions visited the Obama White House 22 times and 4 times last year alone. **3/4/2017 11:42**

Is it legal for a sitting President to be "wire tapping" a race for president prior to an election? Turned down by court earlier. A NEW LOW! **3/4/2017 11:49**

I'd bet a good lawyer could make a great case out of the fact that President Obama was tapping my phones in October just prior to Election! **3/4/2017 11:52**

How low has President Obama gone to tapp my phones during the very sacred election process. This is Nixon/Watergate. Bad (or sick) guy!

3/4/2017 12:02

Arnold Schwarzenegger isn't voluntarily leaving the Apprentice he was fired by his bad (pathetic) ratings not by me. Sad end to great show **3/4/2017 13:19**

Is it true the DNC would not allow the FBI access to check server or other equipment after learning it was hacked? Can that be possible? **3/5/2017 11:32**

Who was it that secretly said to Russian President "Tell Vladimir that after the election I'll have more flexibility?" @ foxandfriends **3/5/2017 11:40**

Thank you for the great rallies all across the country. Tremendous support. Make America Great Again! **3/5/2017 17:30**

45000 construction & manufacturing jobs in the U.S. Gulf Coast region. $20 billion investment. We are already winning again America! **3/6/2017 21:22**

There is an incredible spirit of optimism sweeping the country right now—we're bringing back the JOBS! https://t.co/BNSLvKiEVj **3/6/2017 23:49**

Buy American & hire American are the principles at the core of my agenda which is: JOBS JOBS JOBS! Thank you @ exxonmobil. **3/7/2017 3:49**

Thank you to @exxonmobil for your $20 billion investment that is creating more than 45000 manufacturing & construction jobs in the USA! **3/7/2017 3:50**

122 vicious prisoners released by the Obama Administration from Gitmo have returned to the battlefield. Just another terrible decision! **3/7/2017 12:04**

I am working on a new system where there will be competition in the Drug Industry. Pricing for the American people will come way down! **3/7/2017 13:46**

Don't let the FAKE NEWS tell you that there is big infighting in the Trump Admin. We are getting along great and getting major things done! **3/7/2017 14:14**

I have tremendous respect for women and the many roles they serve that are vital to the fabric of our society and our economy. **3/8/2017 11:12**

On International Women's Day join me in honoring the critical role of women here in America & around the world. **3/8/2017 11:13**

LinkedIn Workforce Report: January and February were the strongest consecutive months for hiring since August and September 2015 **3/8/2017 12:11**

Great news. We are only just beginning. Together we are going to #MAGA! https://t.co/BSp685Q9Qf https://t.co/K7yeBZsf6r **3/8/2017 23:54**

Despite what you hear in the press healthcare is coming along great. We are talking to many groups and it will end in a beautiful picture! **3/9/2017 17:01**

We are making great progress with healthcare. ObamaCare is imploding and will only get worse. Republicans coming together to get job done! **3/11/2017 14:39**

It is amazing how rude much of the media is to my very hard working representatives. Be nice you will do much better! **3/13/2017 12:52**

JOBS JOBS JOBS! https://t.co/wAkQMKdPXA **3/14/2017 15:00**

Does anybody really believe that a reporter who nobody ever heard of "went to his mailbox" and found my tax returns? @NBCNews FAKE NEWS! **3/15/2017 10:55**

Can you imagine what the outcry would be if @SnoopDogg failing career and all had aimed and fired the gun at President Obama? Jail time! **3/15/2017 11:02**

Will be going to Detroit Michigan (love) today for a big meeting on bringing back car production to State & U.S. Already happening! **3/15/2017 11:13**

Looking forward to a big rally in Nashville Tennessee tonight. Big crowd of great people expected. Will be fun! **3/15/2017 11:29**

In Nashville Tennessee! Lets MAKE AMERICA GREAT AGAIN! https://t.co/m5UR4vv6UH **3/16/2017 0:03**

North Korea is behaving very badly. They have been "playing" the United States for years. China has done little to help! **3/17/2017 13:07**

Despite what you have heard from the FAKE NEWS I had a GREAT meeting with German Chancellor Angela Merkel. Nevertheless Germany owes..... (1/2) **3/18/2017 13:15**

...vast sums of money to NATO & the United States must be paid more for the powerful and very expensive defense it provides to Germany! (2/2) **3/18/2017 13:23**

The Democrats made up and pushed the Russian story as an excuse for running a terrible campaign. Big advantage in Electoral College & lost! **3/20/2017 10:49**

Just heard Fake News CNN is doing polls again despite the fact that their election polls were a WAY OFF disaster. Much higher ratings at Fox **3/20/2017 12:35**

Congratulations Eric & Lara. Very proud and happy for the two of you! https://t.co/sOT3cTQc40 **3/20/2017 17:15**

Big day for healthcare. Working hard! **3/22/2017 13:09**

Spoke to U.K. Prime Minister Theresa May today to offer condolences on the terrorist attack in London. She is strong and doing very well. **3/23/2017 1:33**

Just watched the totally biased and fake news reports of the so-called Russia story on NBC and ABC. Such dishonesty! **3/23/2017 12:18**

A great American Kurt Cochran was killed in the London terror attack. My prayers and condolences are with his family and friends. **3/23/2017 15:16**

Today I was thrilled to announce a commitment of $25 BILLION & 20K AMERICAN JOBS over the next 4 years. THANK YOU... https://t.co/nWJ1hNmzoR **3/24/2017 17:59**

ObamaCare will explode and we will all get together and piece together a great healthcare plan for THE PEOPLE. Do not worry! **3/25/2017 14:37**

Thanks you for all of the Trump Rallies today. Amazing support. We will all MAKE AMERICA GREAT AGAIN!
3/25/2017 22:37

General Kelly is doing a great job at the border. Numbers are way down. Many are not even trying to come in anymore. **3/27/2017 1:04**

Why isn't the House Intelligence Committee looking into the Bill & Hillary deal that allowed big Uranium to go to Russia Russian speech.... **3/28/2017 1:26**

Big announcement by Ford today. Major investment to be made in three Michigan plants. Car companies coming back to U.S. JOBS! JOBS! JOBS! **3/28/2017 10:36**

Why doesn't Fake News talk about Podesta ties to Russia as covered by @FoxNews or money from Russia to Clinton - sale of Uranium? **3/28/2017 22:41**

If the people of our great country could only see how viciously and inaccurately my administration is covered by certain media! **3/29/2017 12:21**

APRIL 2017 - JUNE 2017

★★★★★★★★★★★★★★★★★★★★★★★★★★★

Focusing on deregulating the economy to stimulate faster growth, signs of financial prosperity become increasingly evident in the markets and with the addition of new jobs. Nevertheless, Trump's political opposition continues to plague his presidency. Signs of bitterness become manifest with the shooting of Rep. Steve Scalise (R-LA). The Russian collusion narrative gains momentum with the appointment of Special Counsel Robert Mueller.

It is the same Fake News Media that said there is "no path to victory for Trump" that is now pushing the phony Russia story. A total scam! **4/1/2017 13:02**

The real story turns out to be SURVEILLANCE and LEAKING! Find the leakers. **4/2/2017 13:34**

Melania and I are honored to light up the @WhiteHouse this evening for #WorldAutismAwarenessDay. Join us & #LIUB.... https://t.co/tR3hqqyWvv **4/3/2017 0:58**

Did Hillary Clinton ever apologize for receiving the answers to the debate? Just asking! **4/3/2017 11:21**

JOBS JOBS JOBS!https://t.co/XGOQPHywrt https://t.co/B5Qbn6llzE **4/6/2017 2:12**

Congratulations to our great military men and women for representing the United States and the world so well in the Syria attack. **4/8/2017 14:54**

Judge Gorsuch will be sworn in at the Rose Garden of the White House on Monday at 11:00 A.M. He will be a great Justice. Very proud of him! **4/8/2017 19:58**

Happy Passover to everyone celebrating in the United States of America Israel and around the world. #ChagSameach **4/10/2017 23:56**

North Korea is looking for trouble. If China decides to help that would be great. If not we will solve the problem without them! U.S.A. **4/11/2017 12:03**

Had a very good call last night with the President of China concerning the menace of North Korea. **4/12/2017 12:22**

One by one we are keeping our promises - on the border on energy on jobs on regulations. Big changes are happening! **4/12/2017 23:10**

Jobs are returning illegal immigration is plummeting law order and justice are being restored. We are truly making America great again! **4/13/2017 0:32**

I have great confidence that China will properly deal with North Korea. If they are unable to do so the U.S. with its allies will! U.S.A. **4/13/2017 13:08**

Things will work out fine between the U.S.A. and Russia. At the right time everyone will come to their senses & there will be lasting peace! **4/13/2017 13:16**

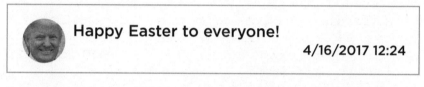

Happy Easter to everyone!

4/16/2017 12:24

Someone should look into who paid for the small organized rallies yesterday. The election is over! **4/16/2017 13:13**

Our military is building and is rapidly becoming stronger than ever before. Frankly we have no choice! **4/16/2017 13:41**

The Fake Media (not Real Media) has gotten even worse since the election. Every story is badly slanted. We have to hold them to the truth! **4/17/2017 12:17**

I am committed to keeping our air and water clean but always remember that economic growth enhances environmental protection. Jobs matter! **4/22/2017 21:49**

Don't let the fake media tell you that I have changed my position on the WALL. It will get built and help stop drugs human trafficking etc. **4/25/2017 12:36**

HAPPY BIRTHDAY to our @FLOTUS Melania! https://t.co/rYYp51mxDQ https://t.co/np7KYHglSv **4/26/2017 14:53**

North Korea disrespected the wishes of China & its highly respected President when it launched though unsuccessfully a missile today. Bad! **4/28/2017 23:26**

The Democrats without a leader have become the party of obstruction.They are only interested in themselves and not in what's best for U.S. **4/30/2017 12:09**

...Trump/Russia story was an excuse used by the Democrats as justification for losing the election. Perhaps Trump just ran a great campaign? **5/3/2017 3:06**

Cryin' Chuck Schumer stated recently "I do not have confidence in him (James Comey) any longer." Then acts so indignant. #draintheswamp **5/10/2017 2:42**

Dems have been complaining for months & months about Dir. Comey. Now that he has been fired they PRETEND to be aggrieved. Phony hypocrites! **5/10/2017 19:23**

The Democrats should be ashamed. This is a disgrace!#DrainTheSwamp https://t.co/UfbKEECm2V **5/11/2017 0:14**

We finally agree on something Rosie. https://t.co/BSP5F3PgbZ **5/11/2017 19:55**

Russia must be laughing up their sleeves watching as the U.S. tears itself apart over a Democrat EXCUSE for losing the election. **5/11/2017 20:34**

China just agreed that the U.S. will be allowed to sell beef and other major products into China once again. This is REAL news! **5/12/2017 13:20**

Wishing @FLOTUS Melania and all of the great mothers out there a wonderful day ahead with family and friends! Happy #MothersDay **5/14/2017 15:13**

This is the single greatest witch hunt of a politician in American history! **5/18/2017 11:52**

With all of the illegal acts that took place in the Clinton campaign & Obama Administration there was never a special counsel appointed! **5/18/2017 14:07**

Getting ready for my big foreign trip. Will be strongly protecting American interests - that's what I like to do!
5/19/2017 14:24

Great to be in Riyadh Saudi Arabia. Looking forward to the afternoon and evening ahead. #POTUSAbroad https://t.co/JJOra0KfyR **5/20/2017 9:44**

We stand in absolute solidarity with the people of the United Kingdom. https://t.co/X6fUUxxYXE **5/23/2017 12:04**

All civilized nations must join together to protect human life and the sacred right of our citizens to live in safety and in peace. **5/23/2017 15:58**

Bringing hundreds of billions of dollars back to the U.S.A. from the Middle East - which will mean JOBS JOBS JOBS! **5/27/2017 17:19**

Just returned from Europe. Trip was a great success for America. Hard work but big results! **5/28/2017 12:10**

The Fake News Media works hard at disparaging & demeaning my use of social media because they don't want America to hear the real story! **5/29/2017 0:20**

Honoring the men and women who made the ultimate sacrifice in service to America. Home of the free because of the brave. #MemorialDay **5/29/2017 12:11**

Today we remember the men and women who made the ultimate sacrifice in serving. Thank you God bless your families & God bless the USA! **5/29/2017 12:35**

I look forward to paying my respects to our brave men and women on this Memorial Day at Arlington National Cemetery later this morning. **5/29/2017 12:36**

We have a MASSIVE trade deficit with Germany plus they pay FAR LESS than they should on NATO & military. Very bad for U.S. This will change **5/30/2017 10:40**

Russian officials must be laughing at the U.S. & how a lame excuse for why the Dems lost the election has taken over the Fake News. **5/30/2017 11:04**

Despite the constant negative press covfefe **5/31/2017 4:06**

Who can figure out the true meaning of "covfefe" ??? Enjoy!

5/31/2017 10:09

Kathy Griffin should be ashamed of herself. My children especially my 11 year old son Barron are having a hard time with this. Sick! **5/31/2017 11:14**

Crooked Hillary Clinton now blames everybody but herself refuses to say she was a terrible candidate. Hits Facebook & even Dems & DNC. **6/1/2017 0:40**

The big story is the "unmasking and surveillance" of people that took place during the Obama Administration. **6/1/2017 11:05**

My job as President is to do everything within my power to give America a level playing field. #AmericaFirst ➡ ... https://t.co/hL7OwbWzyi **6/1/2017 22:50**

MAKE AMERICA GREAT AGAIN! **6/2/2017 1:00**

We need to be smart vigilant and tough. We need the courts to give us back our rights. We need the Travel Ban as an extra level of safety!

6/3/2017 23:17

Whatever the United States can do to help out in London and the U. K. we will be there - WE ARE WITH YOU. GOD BLESS! **6/3/2017 23:24**

We must stop being politically correct and get down to the business of security for our people. If we don't get smart it will only get worse **6/4/2017 11:19**

At least 7 dead and 48 wounded in terror attack and Mayor of London says there is "no reason to be alarmed!" **6/4/2017 11:31**

Do you notice we are not having a gun debate right now? That's because they used knives and a truck! **6/4/2017 11:43**

People the lawyers and the courts can call it whatever they want but I am calling it what we need and what it is a TRAVEL BAN! **6/5/2017 10:25**

In any event we are EXTREME VETTING people coming into the U.S. in order to help keep our country safe. The courts are slow and political! **6/5/2017 10:44**

Pathetic excuse by London Mayor Sadiq Khan who had to think fast on his "no reason to be alarmed" statement. MSM is working hard to sell it! **6/5/2017 13:49**

That's right we need a TRAVEL BAN for certain DANGEROUS countries not some politically correct term that won't help us protect our people! **6/6/2017 1:20**

The FAKE MSM is working so hard trying to get me not to use Social Media. They hate that I can get the honest and unfiltered message out. **6/6/2017 11:58**

Sorry folks but if I would have relied on the Fake News of CNN NBC ABC CBS washpost or nytimes I would have had ZERO chance winning WH **6/6/2017 12:15**

Today we remember the courage and bravery of our troops that stormed the beaches of Normandy 73 years ago. #DDay... https://t.co/zhR24dMzYB **6/6/2017 17:47**

Senate passed the VA Accountability Act. The House should get this bill to my desk ASAP! We can't tolerate substandard care for our vets. **6/7/2017 1:07**

I will be nominating Christopher A. Wray a man of impeccable credentials to be the new Director of the FBI. Details to follow. **6/7/2017 11:44**

Getting ready to leave for Cincinnati in the GREAT STATE of OHIO to meet with ObamaCare victims and talk Healthcare & also Infrastructure! **6/7/2017 12:17**

Despite so many false statements and lies total and complete vindication...and WOW Comey is a leaker! **6/9/2017 10:10**

Great reporting by @foxandfriends and so many others. Thank you! **6/9/2017 10:54**

The #FakeNews MSM doesn't report the great economic news since Election Day. #DOW up 16%. #NASDAQ up 19.5%. Drilling & energy sector... (1/2) **6/11/2017 12:22**

...way up. Regulations way down. 600000+ new jobs added. Unemployment down to 4.3%. Business and economic enthusiasm way up- record levels! (2/2) **6/11/2017 12:23**

I believe the James Comey leaks will be far more prevalent than anyone ever thought possible. Totally illegal? Very 'cowardly!' **6/11/2017 12:29**

The Democrats have no message not on economics not on taxes not on jobs not on failing #Obamacare. They are only OBSTRUCTIONISTS! **6/11/2017 12:49**

Great numbers on the economy. All of our work including the passage of many bills & regulation killing Executive Orders now kicking in! **6/12/2017 2:14**

We will NEVER FORGET the victims who lost their lives one year ago today in the horrific #PulseNightClub shooting.... https://t.co/7IZGgDJkxZ **6/12/2017 16:58**

The Fake News Media has never been so wrong or so dirty. Purposely incorrect stories and phony sources to meet their agenda of hate. Sad! **6/13/2017 10:35**

A.G. Lynch made law enforcement decisions for political purposes...gave Hillary Clinton a free pass and protection. Totally illegal! **6/13/2017 12:45**

Fake News is at an all time high. Where is their apology to me for all of the incorrect stories??? **6/13/2017 12:48**

2 million more people just dropped out of ObamaCare. It is in a death spiral. Obstructionist Democrats gave up have no answer = resist! **6/13/2017 13:56**

Just got back from Wisconsin. Great day great people! **6/14/2017 2:53**

Rep. Steve Scalise of Louisiana a true friend and patriot was badly injured but will fully recover. Our thoughts and prayers are with him. **6/14/2017 12:48**

Happy birthday to U.S. ARMY and our soldiers. Thank you for your bravery sacrifices & dedication. Proud to be your Commander-in-Chief! **6/14/2017 14:07**

Just left hospital. Rep. Steve Scalise one of the truly great people is in very tough shape - but he is a real fighter. Pray for Steve!

6/15/2017 1:41

They made up a phony collusion with the Russians story found zero proof so now they go for obstruction of justice on the phony story. Nice **6/15/2017 10:55**

You are witnessing the single greatest WITCH HUNT in American political history - led by some very bad and conflicted people! #MAGA **6/15/2017 11:57**

Why is that Hillary Clintons family and Dems dealings with Russia are not looked at but my non-dealings are?
6/15/2017 19:43

Crooked H destroyed phones w/ hammer 'bleached' emails & had husband meet w/AG days before she was cleared- & they talk about obstruction? **6/15/2017 19:56**

After 7 months of investigations & committee hearings about my "collusion with the Russians" nobody has been able to show any proof. Sad! **6/16/2017 11:53**

The Fake News Media hates when I use what has turned out to be my very powerful Social Media - over 100 million people! I can go around them **6/16/2017 12:23**

Despite the phony Witch Hunt going on in America the economic & jobs numbers are great. Regulations way down jobs and enthusiasm way up! **6/16/2017 12:54**

I am being investigated for firing the FBI Director by the man who told me to fire the FBI Director! Witch Hunt
6/16/2017 13:07

Back from Miami where my Cuban/American friends are very happy with what I signed today. Another campaign promise that I did not forget! **6/17/2017 1:30**

The MAKE AMERICA GREAT AGAIN agenda is doing very well despite the distraction of the Witch Hunt. Many new jobs high business enthusiasm.. (1/2) **6/18/2017 10:38**

...massive regulation cuts 36 new legislative bills signed great new S.C.Justice and Infrastructure Healthcare and Tax Cuts in works! (2/2) **6/18/2017 10:46**

The new Rasmussen Poll one of the most accurate in the 2016 Election just out with a Trump 50% Approval Rating. That's higher than O's #'s! **6/18/2017 11:02**

Camp David is a very special place. An honor to have spent the weekend there. Military runs it so well and are so proud of what they do! **6/18/2017 21:51**

The Dems want to stop tax cuts good healthcare and Border Security.Their ObamaCare is dead with 100% increases in P's. Vote now for Karen H **6/19/2017 12:27**

While I greatly appreciate the efforts of President Xi & China to help with North Korea it has not worked out. At least I know China tried! **6/20/2017 18:38**

Thank you @FoxNews "Huge win for President Trump and GOP in Georgia Congressional Special Election." **6/21/2017 2:33**

Congratulations to Karen Handel on her big win in Georgia 6th. Fantastic job we are all very proud of you! **6/21/2017 2:41**

Well the Special Elections are over and those that want to MAKE AMERICA GREAT AGAIN are 5 and O! All the Fake News all the money spent = 0 **6/21/2017 3:48**

Democrats would do much better as a party if they got together with Republicans on HealthcareTax CutsSecurity. Obstruction doesn't work! **6/21/2017 10:32**

By the way if Russia was working so hard on the 2016 Election it all took place during the Obama Admin. Why didn't they stop them? **6/22/2017 13:22**

...Why did the DNC REFUSE to turn over its Server to the FBI and still hasn't? It's all a big Dem scam and excuse for losing the election! **6/22/2017 14:08**

I certainly hope the Democrats do not force Nancy P out. That would be very bad for the Republican Party - and please let Cryin' Chuck stay! **6/22/2017 14:15**

Mexico was just ranked the second deadliest country in the world after only Syria. Drug trade is largely the cause. We will BUILD THE WALL! **6/22/2017 22:15**

I've helped pass and signed 38 Legislative Bills mostly with no Democratic support and gotten rid of massive amounts of regulations. Nice! **6/23/2017 10:39**

Just out: The Obama Administration knew far in advance of November 8th about election meddling by Russia. Did nothing about it. WHY? **6/24/2017 0:43**

Since the Obama Administration was told way before the 2016 Election that the Russians were meddling why no action? Focus on them not T! **6/24/2017 20:28**

Obama Administration official said they "choked" when it came to acting on Russian meddling of election. They didn't want to hurt Hillary? **6/24/2017 20:44**

I cannot imagine that these very fine Republican Senators would allow the American people to suffer a broken ObamaCare any longer! **6/24/2017 20:50**

MAKE AMERICA GREAT AGAIN!
6/24/2017 21:23

Hillary Clinton colluded with the Democratic Party in order to beat Crazy Bernie Sanders. Is she allowed to so collude? Unfair to Bernie! **6/25/2017 12:00**

The Democrats have become nothing but OBSTRUCTIONISTS they have no policies or ideas. All they do is delay and complain.They own ObamaCare! **6/26/2017 12:30**

The reason that President Obama did NOTHING about Russia after being notified by the CIA of meddling is that he expected Clinton would win.. **6/26/2017 12:37**

..under a magnifying glass they have zero "tapes" of T people colluding. There is no collusion & no obstruction. I should be given apology! **6/26/2017 13:05**

Very grateful for the 9-O decision from the U. S. Supreme Court. We must keep America SAFE! **6/26/2017 18:25**

Great day for America's future Security and Safety courtesy of the U.S. Supreme Court. I will keep fighting for the American people & WIN! **6/27/2017 2:31**

Wow CNN had to retract big story on "Russia" with 3 employees forced to resign. What about all the other phony stories they do? FAKE NEWS! **6/27/2017 10:33**

Fake News CNN is looking at big management changes now that they got caught falsely pushing their phony Russian stories. Ratings way down! **6/27/2017 12:30**

So they caught Fake News CNN cold but what about NBC CBS & ABC? What about the failing @nytimes & @ washingtonpost? They are all Fake News! **6/27/2017 12:47**

I just finished a great meeting with the Republican Senators concerning HealthCare. They really want to get it right unlike OCare! **6/27/2017 22:27**

The failing @nytimes writes false story after false story about me. They don't even call to verify the facts of a story. A Fake News Joke! **6/28/2017 10:49**

Some of the Fake News Media likes to say that I am not totally engaged in healthcare. Wrong I know the subject well & want victory for U.S. **6/28/2017 10:58**

New Sugar deal negotiated with Mexico is a very good one for both Mexico and the U.S. Had no deal for many years which hurt U.S. badly. **6/29/2017 12:27**

I heard poorly rated @Morning_Joe speaks badly of me (don't watch anymore). Then how come low I.Q. Crazy Mika along with Psycho Joe came.. **6/29/2017 12:52**

Good news House just passed #KatesLaw. Hopefully Senate will follow. **6/29/2017 21:37**

Good news out of the House with the passing of 'No Sanctuary for Criminals Act.' Hopefully Senate will follow.
6/29/2017 22:28

Just finished a very good meeting with the President of South Korea. Many subjects discussed including North Korea and new trade deal! **6/30/2017 1:44**

If Republican Senators are unable to pass what they are working on now they should immediately REPEAL and then REPLACE at a later date! **6/30/2017 10:37**

Crime and killings in Chicago have reached such epidemic proportions that I am sending in Federal help. 1714 shootings in Chicago this year! **6/30/2017 10:48**

Watched low rated @Morning_Joe for first time in long time. FAKE NEWS. He called me to stop a National Enquirer article. I said no! Bad show **6/30/2017 12:55**

JULY 2017 - SEPTEMBER 2017

★★★★★★★★★★★★★★★★★★★★★★★★★★★

As the NYSE continues to set new records of growth routinely in the summer of 2017, in the nation's capital, the focus of the media's attention remains squarely on the Mueller investigation, the firing of FBI Director James Comey, and Russian collusion. With Sarah Huckabee Sanders replacing Sean Spicer as press secretary, the conflict between the White House and the press corps continues to escalate.

Numerous states are refusing to give information to the very distinguished VOTER FRAUD PANEL. What are they trying to hide? **7/1/2017 13:07**

I am extremely pleased to see that @CNN has finally been exposed as #FakeNews and garbage journalism. It's about time! **7/1/2017 13:12**

Crazy Joe Scarborough and dumb as a rock Mika are not bad people but their low rated show is dominated by their NBC bosses. Too bad! **7/1/2017 13:20**

The FAKE & FRAUDULENT NEWS MEDIA is working hard to convince Republicans and others I should not use social media - but remember I won.... (1/2)

7/1/2017 22:02

....the 2016 election with interviews speeches and social media. I had to beat #FakeNews and did. We will continue to WIN! (2/2) **7/1/2017 22:02**

I am thinking about changing the name #FakeNews CNN to #FraudNewsCNN! **7/1/2017 22:08**

My use of social media is not Presidential - it's MODERN DAY PRESIDENTIAL. Make America Great Again! **7/1/2017 22:41**

#FraudNewsCNN #FNN https://t.co/WYUnHjjUjg **7/2/2017 13:21**

The dishonest media will NEVER keep us from accomplishing our objectives on behalf of our GREAT AMERICAN PEOPLE!... https://t.co/EwnwCeuGMv

7/2/2017 20:04

Stock Market at all time high unemployment at lowest level in years (wages will start going up) and our base has never been stronger! **7/2/2017 23:55**

Spoke yesterday with the King of Saudi Arabia about peace in the Middle-East. Interesting things are happening!
7/3/2017 11:19

At some point the Fake News will be forced to discuss our great jobs numbers strong economy success with ISIS the border & so much else! **7/3/2017 12:10**

If we can help little #CharlieGard as per our friends in the U.K. and the Pope we would be delighted to do so.
7/3/2017 14:00

Really great numbers on jobs & the economy! Things are starting to kick in now and we have just begun! Don't like steel & aluminum dumping! **7/3/2017 20:54**

Dow hit a new intraday all-time high! I wonder whether or not the Fake News Media will so report? **7/3/2017 21:10**

North Korea has just launched another missile. Does this guy have anything better to do with his life? Hard to believe that South Korea..... **7/4/2017 2:19**

....and Japan will put up with this much longer. Perhaps China will put a heavy move on North Korea and end this nonsense once and for all! **7/4/2017 2:24**

#HappyIndependenceDay #July4 #USA https://t.co/NsFsIPEFrp **7/4/2017 10:38**

Getting ready to celebrate the 4th of July with a big crowd at the White House. Happy 4th to everyone. Our country will grow and prosper! **7/4/2017 19:49**

Gas prices are the lowest in the U.S. in over ten years! I would like to see them go even lower. **7/4/2017 19:55**

#HappyIndependenceDay #USA https://t.co/9pfqnRsh1Z

7/5/2017 2:19

Getting ready to leave for Poland after which I will travel to Germany for the G-20. Will be back on Saturday. **7/5/2017 10:51**

The United States made some of the worst Trade Deals in world history.Why should we continue these deals with countries that do not help us? **7/5/2017 11:14**

Trade between China and North Korea grew almost 40% in the first quarter. So much for China working with us - but we had to give it a try! **7/5/2017 11:21**

On behalf of @FLOTUS Melania and myself thank you Poland! #ICYMI watch here ➡ https://t.co/COpVXnn8YG #POTUSinPoland https://t.co/ylU3wLZV2H **7/6/2017 14:02**

America is proud to stand shoulder-to-shoulder with Poland in the fight to eradicate the evils of terrorism and extremism. #POTUSinPoland https://t.co/MHxRmVvtsh **7/6/2017 16:02**

THE WEST WILL NEVER BE BROKEN. Our values will PREVAIL. Our people will THRIVE and our civilization will TRIUMPH! https://t.co/sozuVgdp5T **7/6/2017 17:21**

A strong Poland is a blessing to the nations of Europe and a strong Europe is a blessing to the West and to the world. https://t.co/vHzPwMtJSm **7/6/2017 20:45**

My experience yesterday in Poland was a great one. Thank you to everyone including the haters for the great reviews of the speech! **7/7/2017 6:59**

Everyone here is talking about why John Podesta refused to give the DNC server to the FBI and the CIA. Disgraceful! **7/7/2017 7:40**

I look forward to all meetings today with world leaders including my meeting with Vladimir Putin. Much to discuss.#G20Summit #USA **7/7/2017 7:42**

I will represent our country well and fight for its interests! Fake News Media will never cover me accurately but who cares! We will #MAGA! **7/7/2017 7:44**

Great first day with world leaders at the #G20Summit here in Hamburg Germany. Looking forward to day two! #USA https://t.co/bLKgZKQemw **7/7/2017 23:33**

We will fight the #FakeNews with you! https://t.co/zOMiXTeLJq **7/8/2017 18:17**

The #G20Summit was a wonderful success and carried out beautifully by Chancellor Angela Merkel. Thank you! **7/8/2017 18:20**

Law enforcement & military did a spectacular job in Hamburg. Everybody felt totally safe despite the anarchists. @PolizeiHamburg #G20Summit **7/8/2017 18:50**

Leaving Hamburg for Washington D.C. and the WH. Just left China's President Xi where we had an excellent meeting on trade & North Korea. **7/8/2017 18:55**

I strongly pressed President Putin twice about Russian meddling in our election. He vehemently denied it. I've already given my opinion..... **7/9/2017 11:31**

...We negotiated a ceasefire in parts of Syria which will save lives. Now it is time to move forward in working constructively with Russia! **7/9/2017 11:37**

Putin & I discussed forming an impenetrable Cyber Security unit so that election hacking & many other negative things will be guarded.. **7/9/2017 11:50**

...have it. Fake News said 17 intel agencies when actually 4 (had to apologize). Why did Obama do NOTHING when he had info before election? **7/9/2017 12:06**

Sanctions were not discussed at my meeting with President Putin. Nothing will be done until the Ukrainian & Syrian problems are solved! **7/9/2017 12:31**

MAKE AMERICA GREAT AGAIN!
https://t.co/NVDVRrWLs4 **7/9/2017 12:57**

For years even as a "civilian" I listened as Republicans pushed the Repeal and Replace of ObamaCare. Now they finally have their chance! **7/9/2017 20:07**

Syrian ceasefire seems to be holding. Many lives can be saved. Came out of meeting. Good! **7/9/2017 20:09**

The fact that President Putin and I discussed a Cyber Security unit doesn't mean I think it can happen. It can't-but a ceasefire can& did! **7/10/2017 0:45**

James Comey leaked CLASSIFIED INFORMATION to the media. That is so illegal! **7/10/2017 10:40**

I cannot imagine that Congress would dare to leave Washington without a beautiful new HealthCare bill fully approved and ready to go! **7/10/2017 10:47**

When I left Conference Room for short meetings with Japan and other countries I asked Ivanka to hold seat. Very standard. Angela M agrees! **7/10/2017 11:31**

If Chelsea Clinton were asked to hold the seat for her motheras her mother gave our country away the Fake News would say CHELSEA FOR PRES! **7/10/2017 11:47**

The Senate Democrats have only confirmed 48 of 197 Presidential Nominees. They can't win so all they do is slow things down & obstruct! **7/11/2017 10:59**

Working hard to get the Olympics for the United States (L.A.). Stay tuned! **7/11/2017 11:46**

Marine Plane crash in Mississippi is heartbreaking. Melania and I send our deepest condolences to all! **7/11/2017 12:09**

Big wins against ISIS! **7/11/2017 12:23**

My son Donald will be interviewed by @seanhannity tonight at 10:00 P.M. He is a great person who loves our country! **7/12/2017 0:24**

My son Donald did a good job last night. He was open transparent and innocent. This is the greatest Witch Hunt in political history. Sad! **7/12/2017 10:19**

Remember when you hear the words "sources say" from the Fake Media often times those sources are made up and do not exist. **7/12/2017 10:32**

ISIS is on the run & will soon be wiped out of Syria & Iraq illegal border crossings are way down (75%) & MS 13 gangs are being removed. **7/12/2017 11:05**

Why aren't the same standards placed on the Democrats. Look what Hillary Clinton may have gotten away with. Disgraceful! **7/12/2017 13:27**

The W.H. is functioning perfectly focused on HealthCare Tax Cuts/Reform & many other things. I have very little time for watching T.V. **7/12/2017 13:39**

Getting rdy to leave for France @ the invitation of President Macron to celebrate & honor Bastille Day and 100yrs since U.S. entry into WWI. **7/12/2017 22:35**

Honored to serve as Commander-in-Chief to the courageous men and women of our U.S. Armed Forces. A grateful nation thanks you! https://t.co/wERNV7J4oO **7/15/2017 1:34**

Stock Market at new all-time high! Working on new trade deals that will be great for U.S. and its workers! **7/15/2017 16:21**

Stock Market hit another all-time high yesterday - despite the Russian hoax story! Also jobs numbers are starting to look very good! **7/15/2017 16:30**

HillaryClinton can illegally get the questions to the Debate & delete 33000 emails but my son Don is being scorned by the Fake News Media? **7/16/2017 10:35**

Thank you to all of the supporters who far out-numbered the protesters yesterday at the Women's U.S. Open. Very cool! **7/16/2017 10:51**

Thank you to former campaign adviser Michael Caputo for saying so powerfully that there was no Russian collusion in our winning campaign. **7/16/2017 11:04**

With all of its phony unnamed sources & highly slanted & even fraudulent reporting #Fake News is DISTORTING DEMOCRACY in our country! **7/16/2017 11:15**

Heading back to Washington D.C. Much will be accomplished this week on trade the military and security! **7/17/2017 0:24**

Most politicians would have gone to a meeting like the one Don jr attended in order to get info on an opponent. That's politics! **7/17/2017 14:07**

Republicans should just REPEAL failing ObamaCare now & work on a new Healthcare Plan that will start from a clean slate. Dems will join in! **7/18/2017 2:17**

As I have always said let ObamaCare fail and then come together and do a great healthcare plan. Stay tuned! **7/18/2017 11:58**

Fake News story of secret dinner with Putin is "sick." All G 20 leaders and spouses were invited by the Chancellor of Germany. Press knew! **7/19/2017 0:53**

The Fake News is becoming more and more dishonest! Even a dinner arranged for top 20 leaders in Germany is made to look sinister! **7/19/2017 0:59**

I will be having lunch at the White House today with Republican Senators concerning healthcare. They MUST keep their promise to America! **7/19/2017 12:30**

Melania and I send our thoughts and prayers to Senator McCain Cindy and their entire family. Get well soon. https://t.co/fONWVlmYyz **7/20/2017 2:33**

I am asking all citizens to believe in yourselves believe in your future and believe once more in America. #AmericaFirst https://t.co/NOnhJyWp4J **7/20/2017 20:08**

Sean Spicer is a wonderful person who took tremendous abuse from the Fake News Media - but his future is bright! **7/22/2017 1:46**

So many people are asking why isn't the A.G. or Special Council looking at the many Hillary Clinton or Comey crimes. 33000 e-mails deleted? **7/22/2017 11:44**

...What about all of the Clinton ties to Russia including Podesta Company Uranium deal Russian Reset big dollar speeches etc. **7/22/2017 11:47**

My son Donald openly gave his e-mails to the media & authorities whereas Crooked Hillary Clinton deleted (& acid washed) her 33000 e-mails! **7/22/2017 12:00**

The Republican Senators must step up to the plate and after 7 years vote to Repeal and Replace. Next Tax Reform and Infrastructure. WIN! **7/22/2017 12:17**

ObamaCare is dead and the Democrats are obstructionists no ideas or votes only obstruction. It is solely up to the 52 Republican Senators! **7/22/2017 12:23**

To every PATRIOT who will serve on the #USSGeraldRFord: ✅ Keep the watch ✅ Protect her ✅ Defend her ✅ LOVE HER Good Luck & Godspeed! https://t.co/shcz5GQkCh
7/23/2017 0:50

As the phony Russian Witch Hunt continues two groups are laughing at this excuse for a lost election taking hold Democrats and Russians! **7/23/2017 20:09**

It's very sad that Republicans even some that were carried over the line on my back do very little to protect their President. **7/23/2017 20:14**

If Republicans don't Repeal and Replace the disastrous ObamaCare the repercussions will be far greater than any of them understand! **7/24/2017 0:01**

Thank you to @LOUDOBBS for giving the first six months of the Trump Administration an A+. S.C.reg cuttingStock M jobsborder etc. = TRUE! **7/24/2017 0:23**

Drain the Swamp should be changed to Drain the Sewer - it's actually much worse than anyone ever thought and it begins with the Fake News! **7/24/2017 10:40**

After 1 year of investigation with Zero evidence being found Chuck Schumer just stated that "Democrats should blame ourselvesnot Russia." **7/24/2017 10:52**

So why aren't the Committees and investigators and of course our beleaguered A.G. looking into Crooked Hillarys crimes & Russia relations? **7/24/2017 12:49**

Republicans have a last chance to do the right thing on Repeal & Replace after years of talking & campaigning on it. **7/24/2017 13:18**

So great that John McCain is coming back to vote. Brave - American hero! Thank you John. **7/25/2017 10:44**

Jared Kushner did very well yesterday in proving he did not collude with the Russians. Witch Hunt. Next up 11 year old Barron Trump! **7/25/2017 10:52**

After consultation with my Generals and military experts please be advised that the United States Government will not accept or allow...... (1/3) **7/26/2017 12:55**

....Transgender individuals to serve in any capacity in the U.S. Military. Our military must be focused on decisive and overwhelming..... (2/3) **7/26/2017 13:04**

....victory and cannot be burdened with the tremendous medical costs and disruption that transgender in the military would entail. Thank you (3/3) **7/26/2017 13:08**

IN AMERICA WE DON'T WORSHIP GOVERNMENT - WE WORSHIP GOD!🎥 https://t.co/jlejSgVnnA **7/26/2017 17:21**

Thank you Foxconn for investing $10 BILLION DOLLARS with the potential for up to 13K new jobs in Wisconsin! MadeInTheUSA https://t.co/jJghVeb63s **7/27/2017 0:01**

Come on Republican Senators you can do it on Healthcare. After 7 years this is your chance to shine! Don't let the American people down! **7/27/2017 11:24**

Big progress being made in ridding our country of MS-13 gang members and gang members in general. MAKE AMERICA SAFE AGAIN! **7/27/2017 18:37**

3 Republicans and 48 Democrats let the American people down. As I said from the beginning let ObamaCare implode then deal. Watch! **7/28/2017 6:25**

I am pleased to inform you that I have just named General/ Secretary John F Kelly as White House Chief of Staff. He is a Great American.... **7/28/2017 20:49**

If a new HealthCare Bill is not approved quickly BAILOUTS for Insurance Companies and BAILOUTS for Members of Congress will end very soon! **7/29/2017 16:27**

U.S. Stock Market up almost 20% since Election! **7/29/2017 17:04**

Unless the Republican Senators are total quitters Repeal & Replace is not dead! Demand another vote before voting on any other bill! **7/29/2017 20:36**

I love reading about all of the "geniuses" who were so instrumental in my election success. Problem is most don't exist. #Fake News! MAGA **7/29/2017 23:15**

I am very disappointed in China. Our foolish past leaders have allowed them to make hundreds of billions of dollars a year in trade yet... (1/2) **7/29/2017 23:29**

...they do NOTHING for us with North Korea just talk. We will no longer allow this to continue. China could easily solve this problem! (2/2) **7/29/2017 23:35**

Don't give up Republican Senators the World is watching: Repeal & Replace...and go to 51 votes (nuke option) get Cross State Lines & more. **7/30/2017 11:37**

If ObamaCare is hurting people & it is why shouldn't it hurt the insurance companies & why should Congress not be paying what public pays? **7/31/2017 12:16**

Highest Stock Market EVER best economic numbers in years unemployment lowest in 17 years wages raising border secure S.C.: No WH chaos! **7/31/2017 12:28**

A great day at the White House! **7/31/2017 22:19**

Stock Market could hit all-time high (again) 22000 today. Was 18000 only 6 months ago on Election Day. Mainstream media seldom mentions! **8/1/2017 12:49**

Only the Fake News Media and Trump enemies want me to stop using Social Media (110 million people). Only way for me to get the truth out! **8/1/2017 13:55**

I love the White House one of the most beautiful buildings (homes) I have ever seen. But Fake News said I called it a dump - TOTALLY UNTRUE **8/3/2017 1:29**

Business is looking better than ever with business enthusiasm at record levels. Stock Market at an all-time high. That doesn't just happen! **8/3/2017 12:08**

I am continuing to get rid of costly and unnecessary regulations. Much work left to do but effect will be great! Business & jobs will grow. **8/3/2017 12:12**

Our relationship with Russia is at an all-time & very dangerous low. You can thank Congress the same people that can't even give us HCare! **8/3/2017 12:18**

Toyota & Mazda to build a new $1.6B plant here in the U.S.A. and create 4K new American jobs. A great investment in American manufacturing! **8/4/2017 10:02**

West Virginia was incredible last night. Crowds and enthusiasm were beyond GDP at 3% wow!Dem Governor became a Republican last night. **8/4/2017 10:35**

Excellent Jobs Numbers just released - and I have only just begun. Many job stifling regulations continue to fall. Movement back to USA! **8/4/2017 12:45**

Prosperity is coming back to our shores because we are putting America WORKERS and FAMILIES first. #AmericaFirst https://t.co/4kTc6Om308 **8/5/2017 16:00**

Working in Bedminster N.J. as long planned construction is being done at the White House. This is not a vacation - meetings and calls! **8/5/2017 22:36**

The United Nations Security Council just voted 15-0 to sanction North Korea. China and Russia voted with us. Very big financial impact! **8/5/2017 22:44**

After many years of LEAKS going on in Washington it is great to see the A.G. taking action! For National Security the tougher the better! **8/5/2017 22:58**

United Nations Resolution is the single largest economic sanctions package ever on North Korea. Over one billion dollars in cost to N.K. **8/5/2017 23:14**

MAKE AMERICA GREAT AGAIN! https://t.co/g4ELhh9joH
8/6/2017 13:15

The Fake News refuses to report the success of the first 6 months: S.C. surging economy & jobsborder & military securityISIS & MS-13 etc. **8/7/2017 1:18**

Just completed call with President Moon of South Korea. Very happy and impressed with 15-0 United Nations vote on North Korea sanctions. **8/7/2017 1:22**

The Trump base is far bigger & stronger than ever before (despite some phony Fake News polling). Look at rallies in Penn Iowa Ohio……. **8/7/2017 10:58**

The Fake News Media will not talk about the importance of the United Nations Security Council's 15-0 vote in favor of sanctions on N. Korea! **8/7/2017 20:15**

I think Senator Blumenthal should take a nice long vacation in Vietnam where he lied about his service so he can at least say he was there **8/7/2017 20:48**

After many years of failurecountries are coming together to finally address the dangers posed by North Korea. We must be tough & decisive! **8/8/2017 11:17**

E-mails show that the AmazonWashingtonPost and the FailingNewYorkTimes were reluctant to cover the Clinton/ Lynch secret meeting in plane. **8/8/2017 18:00**

After 200 days rarely has any Administration achieved what we have achieved..not even close! Don't believe the Fake News Suppression Polls! **8/8/2017 18:10**

My first order as President was to renovate and modernize our nuclear arsenal. It is now far stronger and more powerful than ever before.... **8/9/2017 11:56**

...Hopefully we will never have to use this power but there will never be a time that we are not the most powerful nation in the world! **8/9/2017 12:03**

Senator Mitch McConnell said I had "excessive expectations" but I don't think so. After 7 years of hearing Repeal & Replace why not done? **8/9/2017 18:14**

#GodBlessTheUSA https://t.co/Fkq2gJQOKk **8/9/2017 21:36**

Can you believe that Mitch McConnell who has screamed Repeal & Replace for 7 years couldn't get it done. Must Repeal & Replace ObamaCare! **8/10/2017 10:54**

Mitch get back to work and put Repeal & Replace Tax Reform & Cuts and a great Infrastructure Bill on my desk for signing. You can do it! **8/10/2017 16:40**

.@IvankaTrump will lead the U.S. delegation to India this fall supporting women's entrepreneurship globally.#GES2017 @ narendramodi **8/10/2017 20:18**

Military solutions are now fully in placelocked and loadedshould North Korea act unwisely. Hopefully Kim Jong Un will find another path! **8/11/2017 11:29**

We ALL must be united & condemn all that hate stands for. There is no place for this kind of violence in America. Lets come together as one!

8/12/2017 17:19

We must remember this truth: No matter our color creed religion or political party we are ALL AMERICANS FIRST. https://t.co/FesMiQSKKn **8/12/2017 21:19**

Deepest condolences to the families & fellow officers of the VA State Police who died today. You're all among the best this nation produces. **8/12/2017 22:50**

Condolences to the family of the young woman killed today and best regards to all of those injured in Charlottesville Virginia. So sad! **8/12/2017 23:25**

The Obstructionist Democrats have given us (or not fixed) some of the worst trade deals in World History. I am changing that fast! **8/14/2017 10:54**

Now that Ken Frazier of Merck Pharma has resigned from President's Manufacturing Councilhe will have more time to LOWER RIPOFF DRUG PRICES! **8/14/2017 12:54**

Made additional remarks on Charlottesville and realize once again that the #Fake News Media will never be satisfied... truly bad people! **8/14/2017 22:29**

Feels good to be home after seven months but the White House is very special there is no place like it... and the U.S. is really my home! **8/15/2017 3:06**

For every CEO that drops out of the Manufacturing Council I have many to take their place. Grandstanders should not have gone on. JOBS! **8/15/2017 15:21**

Kim Jong Un of North Korea made a very wise and well reasoned decision. The alternative would have been both catastrophic and unacceptable! **8/16/2017 11:39**

MAKE AMERICA GREAT AGAIN! **8/16/2017 12:39**

Memorial service today for beautiful and incredible Heather Heyer a truly special young woman. She will be long remembered by all! **8/16/2017 14:58**

Rather than putting pressure on the businesspeople of the Manufacturing Council & Strategy & Policy Forum I am ending both. Thank you all! **8/16/2017 17:14**

The public is learning (even more so) how dishonest the Fake News is. They totally misrepresent what I say about hate bigotry etc. Shame! **8/17/2017 10:32**

Great to see that Dr. Kelli Ward is running against Flake Jeff Flake who is WEAK on borders crime and a non-factor in Senate. He's toxic! **8/17/2017 10:56**

Sad to see the history and culture of our great country being ripped apart with the removal of our beautiful statues and monuments. You..... (1/3) **8/17/2017 13:07**

...can't change history but you can learn from it. Robert E Lee Stonewall Jackson - who's next Washington Jefferson? So foolish! Also... (2/3) **8/17/2017 13:15**

...the beauty that is being taken out of our cities towns and parks will be greatly missed and never able to be comparably replaced! (3/3) **8/17/2017 13:21**

The United States condemns the terror attack in Barcelona Spain and will do whatever is necessary to help. Be tough & strong we love you!

8/17/2017 18:00

Study what General Pershing of the United States did to terrorists when caught. There was no more Radical Islamic Terror for 35 years! **8/17/2017 18:45**

Homeland Security and law enforcement are on alert & closely watching for any sign of trouble. Our borders are far tougher than ever before! **8/18/2017 12:31**

The Obstructionist Democrats make Security for our country very difficult. They use the courts and associated delay at all times. Must stop! **8/18/2017 12:55**

Radical Islamic Terrorism must be stopped by whatever means necessary! The courts must give us back our protective rights. Have to be tough! **8/18/2017 13:06**

Heading to Camp David for major meeting on National Security the Border and the Military (which we are rapidly building to strongest ever). **8/18/2017 14:09**

My thoughts and prayers are with the @KissimmeePolice and their loved ones. We are with you!#LESM **8/19/2017 4:59**

I want to thank Steve Bannon for his service. He came to the campaign during my run against Crooked Hillary Clinton - it was great! Thanks S **8/19/2017 11:33**

Important day spent at Camp David with our very talented Generals and military leaders. Many decisions made including on Afghanistan. **8/19/2017 11:47**

Steve Bannon will be a tough and smart new voice at @ BreitbartNews...maybe even better than ever before. Fake News needs the competition! **8/19/2017 17:47**

Looks like many anti-police agitators in Boston. Police are looking tough and smart! Thank you. **8/19/2017 19:22**

Great job by all law enforcement officers and Boston Mayor @Marty_Walsh. **8/19/2017 19:29**

Our great country has been divided for decades. Sometimes you need protest in order to heal & we will heal & be stronger than ever before! **8/19/2017 20:41**

I want to applaud the many protestors in Boston who are speaking out against bigotry and hate. Our country will soon come together as one! **8/19/2017 20:41**

Heading back to Washington after working hard and watching some of the worst and most dishonest Fake News reporting I have ever seen! **8/20/2017 23:22**

Thoughts & prayers are w/ our @USNavy sailors aboard the #USSJohnSMcCain where search & rescue efforts are underway. https://t.co/DQU0zTRXNU **8/21/2017 3:01**

Thank you the very dishonest Fake News Media is out of control! https://t.co/8J7y900VGK **8/21/2017 13:32**

Was with great people last night in Fort Myer Virginia. The future of our country is strong! **8/22/2017 10:46**

THANK YOU to all of the great men and women at the U.S. Customs and Border Protection facility in Yuma

Arizona & around the United States! https://t.co/tjFx8XjhDz **8/23/2017 0:20**

Not only does the media give a platform to hate groups but the media turns a blind eye to the gang violence on our streets! https://t.co/Mau0B1qYIP **8/23/2017 5:32**

Phoenix crowd last night was amazing - a packed house. I love the Great State of Arizona. Not a fan of Jeff Flake weak on crime & border! **8/23/2017 13:20**

Last night in Phoenix I read the things from my statements on Charlottesville that the Fake News Media didn't cover fairly. People got it! **8/23/2017 13:40**

The only problem I have with Mitch McConnell is that after hearing Repeal & Replace for 7 years he failed!That should NEVER have happened! **8/24/2017 13:42**

General John Kelly is doing a fantastic job as Chief of Staff. There is tremendous spirit and talent in the W.H. Don't believe the Fake News **8/25/2017 10:40**

Storm turned Hurricane is getting much bigger and more powerful than projected. Federal Government is on site and ready to respond. Be safe! **8/25/2017 22:12**

At the request of the Governor of Texas I have signed the Disaster Proclamation which unleashes the full force of government help! **8/26/2017 1:46**

I am pleased to inform you that I have just granted a full Pardon to 85 year old American patriot Sheriff Joe Arpaio. He kept Arizona safe! **8/26/2017 2:00**

Wonderful coordination between Federal State and Local Governments in the Great State of Texas - TEAMWORK! Record setting rainfall. **8/26/2017 22:57**

I will be going to Texas as soon as that trip can be made without causing disruption. The focus must be life and safety. **8/27/2017 12:59**

With Mexico being one of the highest crime Nations in the world we must have THE WALL. Mexico will pay for it through reimbursement/other. **8/27/2017 13:44**

We are in the NAFTA (worst trade deal ever made) renegotiation process with Mexico & Canada.Both being very difficultmay have to terminate? **8/27/2017 13:51**

Major rescue operations underway! **8/27/2017 14:39**

HISTORIC rainfall in Houston and all over Texas. Floods are unprecedented and more rain coming. Spirit of the people is incredible.Thanks! **8/27/2017 23:01**

Leaving now for Texas! **8/29/2017 12:10**

The U.S. has been talking to North Korea and paying them extortion money for 25 years. Talking is not the answer! **8/30/2017 12:47**

After witnessing first hand the horror & devastation caused by Hurricane Harveymy heart goes out even more so to the great people of Texas! **8/30/2017 13:12**

After reading the false reporting and even ferocious anger in some dying magazines it makes me wonder WHY? All I want to do is #MAGA! **8/30/2017 13:27**

Will be leaving for Missouri soon for a speech on tax cuts and tax reform - so badly needed! **8/30/2017 13:42**

Texas & Louisiana: We are w/ you today we are w/ you tomorrow & we will be w/ you EVERY SINGLE DAY AFTER to restore recover & REBUILD! https://t.co/YQb82K2VSB **8/30/2017 19:38**

First responders have been doing heroic work. Their courage & devotion has saved countless lives - they represent the very best of America! https://t.co/I0gvCQLTKO **8/31/2017 1:00**

THANK YOU to all of the incredible HEROES in Texas. America is with you! #TexasStrong https://t.co/8N4ABo9lhp **8/31/2017 20:06**

Wow looks like James Comey exonerated Hillary Clinton long before the investigation was over...and so much more. A rigged system! **9/1/2017 11:56**

Texas is healing fast thanks to all of the great men & women who have been working so hard. But still so much to do. Will be back tomorrow! **9/1/2017 12:58**

Stock Market up 5 months in a row! **9/1/2017 23:47**

I will be going to Texas and Louisiana tomorrow with First Lady. Great progress being made! Spending weekend working at White House. **9/2/2017 0:03**

TEXAS: We are with you today we are with you tomorrow and we will be with you EVERY SINGLE DAY AFTER to restore recover and REBUILD! https://t.co/p1Fh8jmmFA **9/2/2017 16:56**

Together we will prevail in the GREAT state of Texas. We love you!GOD BLESS TEXAS & GOD BLESS THE USA https://t.co/1rzmEenQlb **9/3/2017 1:55**

Just got back to the White House from the Great States of Texas and Louisiana where things are going well. Such cooperation & coordination! **9/3/2017 2:57**

Remember Sunday is National Prayer Day (by Presidential Proclamation)! **9/3/2017 3:02**

North Korea has conducted a major Nuclear Test. Their words and actions continue to be very hostile and dangerous to the United States..... **9/3/2017 11:30**

..North Korea is a rogue nation which has become a great threat and embarrassment to China which is trying to help but with little success. **9/3/2017 11:39**

South Korea is finding as I have told them that their talk of appeasement with North Korea will not work they only understand one thing! **9/3/2017 11:46**

I will be meeting General Kelly General Mattis and other military leaders at the White House to discuss North Korea. Thank you. **9/3/2017 16:07**

The United States is considering in addition to other options stopping all trade with any country doing business with North Korea.

9/3/2017 16:14

We are building our future with American hands American labor American iron aluminum and steel. Happy #LaborDay! https://t.co/lyvtNfQ5IO **9/4/2017 16:38**

Big week coming up! **9/5/2017 2:49**

Congress get ready to do your job - DACA! **9/5/2017 12:04**

I am allowing Japan & South Korea to buy a substantially increased amount of highly sophisticated military equipment from the United States. **9/5/2017 12:36**

I look forward to working w/ D's + R's in Congress to address immigration reform in a way that puts hardworking citizens of our country 1st. **9/5/2017 20:45**

Congress now has 6 months to legalize DACA (something the Obama Administration was unable to do). If they can't I will revisit this issue! **9/6/2017 0:38**

Will be going to North Dakota today to discuss tax reform and tax cuts. We are the highest taxed nation in the world - that will change. **9/6/2017 10:47**

Watching Hurricane closely. My team which has done and is doing such a good job in Texas is already in Florida. No rest for the weary! **9/6/2017 10:51**

Our incredible U.S. Coast Guard saved more than 15000 lives last week with Harvey. Irma could be even tougher. We love our Coast Guard! **9/8/2017 12:37**

Churches in Texas should be entitled to reimbursement from FEMA Relief Funds for helping victims of Hurricane Harvey (just like others). **9/9/2017 0:56**

The U.S. Coast Guard FEMA and all Federal and State brave people are ready. Here comes Irma. God bless everyone! **9/10/2017 2:56**

May God Forever Bless the United States of America. #NeverForget911 https://t.co/erycJgj23r **9/11/2017 18:35**

Fascinating to watch people writing books and major articles about me and yet they know nothing about me & have zero access. #FAKE NEWS! **9/12/2017 12:56**

The devastation left by Hurricane Irma was far greater at least in certain locationsthan anyone thought - but amazing people working hard! **9/12/2017 13:11**

Congratulations to Eric & Lara on the birth of their son Eric "Luke" Trump this morning! https://t.co/Aw0AV82XdE **9/12/2017 18:41**

I will be traveling to Florida tomorrow to meet with our great Coast Guard FEMA and many of the brave first responders & others. **9/13/2017 11:34**

With Irma and Harvey devastation Tax Cuts and Tax Reform is needed more than ever before. Go Congress go! **9/13/2017 12:36**

Crooked Hillary Clinton blames everybody (and every thing) but herself for her election loss. She lost the debates and lost her direction! **9/14/2017 2:47**

The "deplorables" came back to haunt Hillary.They expressed their feelings loud and clear. She spent big money but in the end had no game! **9/14/2017 2:52**

The WALL which is already under construction in the form of new renovation of old and existing fences and walls will continue to be built. **9/14/2017 10:20**

Does anybody really want to throw out good educated and accomplished young people who have jobs some serving in the military? Really!..... **9/14/2017 10:28**

Another attack in London by a loser terrorist.These are sick and demented people who were in the sights of Scotland Yard. Must be proactive! **9/15/2017 10:42**

Loser terrorists must be dealt with in a much tougher manner.The internet is their main recruitment tool which we must cut off & use better! **9/15/2017 10:48**

The travel ban into the United States should be far larger tougher and more specific-but stupidly that would not be politically correct! **9/15/2017 10:54**

We have made more progress in the last nine months against ISIS than the Obama Administration has made in 8 years.Must be proactive & nasty! **9/15/2017 11:00**

ESPN is paying a really big price for its politics (and bad programming). People are dumping it in RECORD numbers. Apologize for untruth! **9/15/2017 11:20**

Frank "FX" Giaccio-On behalf of @FLOTUS Melania & myself THANK YOU for doing a GREAT job this morning! @ NatlParkService gives you an A+! https://t.co/135DxuapUI **9/15/2017 16:49**

HAPPY 70th BIRTHDAY to the @USAirForce! The American people are eternally grateful. Thank you for keeping America PROUD STRONG and FREE! https://t.co/DYxkh3gj0R **9/15/2017 23:54**

A great deal of good things happening for our country. Jobs and Stock Market at all time highs and I believe will be getting even better! **9/16/2017 22:40**

I spoke with President Moon of South Korea last night. Asked him how Rocket Man is doing. Long gas lines forming in North Korea. Too bad! **9/17/2017 11:53**

The US has great strength & patience but if it is forced to defend itself or its allies we will have no choice but to totally destroy #NoKo. https://t.co/P4vAanXvgm **9/19/2017 17:22**

God bless the people of Mexico City. We are with you and will be there for you.
9/19/2017 20:05

Puerto Rico being hit hard by new monster Hurricane. Be careful our hearts are with you- will be there to help!
9/20/2017 2:23

I was saddened to see how bad the ratings were on the Emmys last night - the worst ever. Smartest people of them all are the "DEPLORABLES." **9/20/2017 2:41**

After allowing North Korea to research and build Nukes while Secretary of State (Bill C also) Crooked Hillary now criticizes. **9/20/2017 10:40**

Kim Jong Un of North Korea who is obviously a madman who doesn't mind starving or killing his people will be tested like never before! **9/22/2017 10:28**

The Russia hoax continues now it's ads on Facebook. What about the totally biased and dishonest Media coverage in favor of Crooked Hillary? **9/22/2017 10:44**

The greatest influence over our election was the Fake News Media "screaming" for Crooked Hillary Clinton. Next she was a bad candidate! **9/22/2017 11:26**

John McCain never had any intention of voting for this Bill which his Governor loves. He campaigned on Repeal & Replace. Let Arizona down! **9/23/2017 10:42**

Going to the White House is considered a great honor for a championship team.Stephen Curry is hesitatingtherefore invitation is withdrawn! **9/23/2017 12:45**

If a player wants the privilege of making millions of dollars in the NFLor other leagues he or she should not be allowed to disrespect.... (1/2) **9/23/2017 18:11**

...our Great American Flag (or Country) and should stand for the National Anthem. If not YOU'RE FIRED. Find something else to do! (2/2) **9/23/2017 18:18**

Very proud of our incredible First Lady (@FLOTUS.) She is a truly great representative for our country! https://t.co/yFv0WIjgby **9/23/2017 21:16**

Iran just test-fired a Ballistic Missile capable of reaching Israel.They are also working with North Korea.Not much of an agreement we have! **9/23/2017 21:59**

Democrats are laughingly saying that McCain had a "moment of courage." Tell that to the people of Arizona who were deceived. 116% increase! **9/23/2017 22:20**

Roger Goodell of NFL just put out a statement trying to justify the total disrespect certain players show to our country.Tell them to stand! **9/23/2017 22:25**

Just heard Foreign Minister of North Korea speak at U.N. If he echoes thoughts of Little Rocket Man they won't be around much longer! **9/24/2017 3:08**

If NFL fans refuse to go to games until players stop disrespecting our Flag & Country you will see change take place fast. Fire or suspend! **9/24/2017 10:44**

...NFL attendance and ratings are WAY DOWN. Boring games yes but many stay away because they love our country. League should back U.S. **9/24/2017 11:13**

Great solidarity for our National Anthem and for our Country. Standing with locked arms is good kneeling is not acceptable. Bad ratings! **9/24/2017 18:20**

Please to inform that the Champion Pittsburgh Penguins of the NHL will be joining me at the White House for Ceremony. Great team! **9/24/2017 18:24**

Courageous Patriots have fought and died for our great American Flag --- we MUST honor and respect it! MAKE AMERICA GREAT AGAIN! **9/24/2017 19:32**

Sports fans should never condone players that do not stand proud for their National Anthem or their Country. NFL should change policy!

9/24/2017 22:25

Making America Safe is my number one priority. We will not admit those into our country we cannot safely vet. https://t.co/KJ886okyfC **9/24/2017 23:49**

So proud of NASCAR and its supporters and fans. They won't put up with disrespecting our Country or our Flag - they said it loud and clear! **9/25/2017 11:25**

Many people booed the players who kneeled yesterday (which was a small percentage of total). These are fans who demand respect for our Flag! **9/25/2017 11:31**

The issue of kneeling has nothing to do with race. It is about respect for our Country Flag and National Anthem. NFL must respect this! **9/25/2017 11:39**

The White House never looked more beautiful than it did returning last night. Important meetings taking place today. Big tax cuts & reform. **9/25/2017 11:44**

#StandForOurAnthem **9/25/2017 13:02**

General John Kelly totally agrees w/ my stance on NFL players and the fact that they should not be disrespecting our FLAG or GREAT COUNTRY! **9/25/2017 22:28**

Tremendous backlash against the NFL and its players for disrespect of our Country.#StandForOurAnthem **9/25/2017 22:29**

Ratings for NFL football are way down except before game starts when people tune in to see whether or not our country will be disrespected! **9/26/2017 10:28**

The booing at the NFL football game last night when the entire Dallas team dropped to its knees was loudest I have ever heard. Great anger **9/26/2017 10:35**

But while Dallas dropped to its knees as a team they all stood up for our National Anthem. Big progress being made-we all love our country! **9/26/2017 10:47**

The NFL has all sorts of rules and regulations. The only way out for them is to set a rule that you can't kneel during our National Anthem! **9/26/2017 13:06**

Even Usain Bolt from Jamaica one of the greatest runners and athletes of all time showed RESPECT for our National Anthem! https://t.co/zkenuAP9RS **9/27/2017 1:15**

Congratulations to Roy Moore on his Republican Primary win in Alabama. Luther Strange started way back & ran a good race. Roy WIN in Dec! **9/27/2017 2:17**

Spoke to Jerry Jones of the Dallas Cowboys yesterday. Jerry is a winner who knows how to get things done. Players will stand for Country! **9/27/2017 11:09**

..But the people were Pro-Trump! Virtually no President has accomplished what we have accomplished in the first 9 months-and economy roaring **9/27/2017 13:41**

The electric power grid in Puerto Rico is totally shot. Large numbers of generators are now on Island. Food and water on site. **9/28/2017 14:01**

GDP was revised upward to 3.1 for last quarter. Many people thought it would be years before that happened. We have just begun! **9/29/2017 2:22**

The Fake News Networks are working overtime in Puerto Rico doing their best to take the spirit away from our soldiers and first R's. Shame! **9/30/2017 12:07**

Very important that NFL players STAND tomorrow and always for the playing of our National Anthem. Respect our Flag and our Country! **9/30/2017 22:26**

Because of #FakeNews my people are not getting the credit they deserve for doing a great job. As seen here they are ALL doing a GREAT JOB! https://t.co/1ltW2t3rwy
9/30/2017 22:46

OCTOBER 2017 - DECEMBER 2017

★★★★★★★★★★★★★★★★★★★★★★★★★★

With the potential for conflict with North Korea's "Rocket Man" escalating, making the unwanted likelihood of war on the Korean Peninsula increasing probable, domestically, the nation's attention as well as the president's turn to the NFL and players taking a knee during the national anthem. As jobs increase and unemployment decreases, with the nation's GDP rising, Trump initiates a massive tax cut for the American people. In the Middle East, the president's resolve to destroy ISIS remains as firm as his determination to renegotiate more favorable trade agreements for the USA. In December, President Trump formally recognized Jerusalem as the capital of Israel.

19000 RESPECTING our National Anthem! #StandForOurAnthem https://t.co/czutyGaMQV **10/1/2017 2:08**

I told Rex Tillerson our wonderful Secretary of State that he is wasting his time trying to negotiate with Little Rocket Man... **10/1/2017 14:30**

Being nice to Rocket Man hasn't worked in 25 years why would it work now? Clinton failed Bush failed and Obama failed. I won't fail. **10/1/2017 19:01**

My warmest condolences and sympathies to the victims and families of the terrible Las Vegas shooting. God bless you!
10/2/2017 11:11

I am so proud of our great Country. God bless America! **10/3/2017 11:40**

It is a "miracle" how fast the Las Vegas Metropolitan Police were able to find the demented shooter and stop him from even more killing! **10/4/2017 0:20**

A great day in Puerto Rico yesterday. While some of the news coverage is Fake most showed great warmth and friendship. **10/4/2017 10:25**

Wow so many Fake News stories today. No matter what I do or say they will not write or speak truth. The Fake News Media is out of control! **10/4/2017 11:29**

NBC news is #FakeNews and more dishonest than even CNN. They are a disgrace to good reporting. No wonder their news ratings are way down! **10/4/2017 14:47**

I will be landing in Las Vegas shortly to pay my respects with @FLOTUS Melania. Everyone remains in our thoughts and prayers. **10/4/2017 15:49**

WE LOVE YOU LAS VEGAS! https://t.co/nxRWeR1gEz
10/4/2017 23:36

On behalf of a GRATEFUL NATION THANK YOU to all of the First Responders (HEROES) who saved countless lives in Las Vegas on Sunday night. https://t.co/ZxuMYWnNHv **10/5/2017 1:08**

So wonderful to be in Las Vegas yesterday and meet with people from police to doctors to the victims themselves who I will never forget! **10/5/2017 10:44**

Why Isn't the Senate Intel Committee looking into the Fake News Networks in OUR country to see why so much of our news is just made up-FAKE! **10/5/2017 10:59**

Stock Market hits an ALL-TIME high! Unemployment lowest in 16 years! Business and manufacturing enthusiasm at highest level in decades! **10/5/2017 11:09**

Ralph Northamwho is running for Governor of Virginiais fighting for the violent MS-13 killer gangs & sanctuary cities. Vote Ed Gillespie! **10/6/2017 1:58**

More and more people are suggesting that Republicans (and me) should be given Equal Time on T.V. when you look at the one-sided coverage? **10/7/2017 12:04**

I asked @VP Pence to leave stadium if any players kneeled disrespecting our country. I am proud of him and @ SecondLady Karen. **10/8/2017 18:16**

Our country has been unsuccessfully dealing with North Korea for 25 years giving billions of dollars & getting nothing. Policy didn't work! **10/9/2017 10:50**

The trip by @VP Pence was long planned. He is receiving great praise for leaving game after the players showed such disrespect for country! **10/9/2017 11:05**

A big salute to Jerry Jones owner of the Dallas Cowboys who will BENCH players who disrespect our Flag."Stand for Anthem or sit for game!"

10/10/2017 1:51

Why is the NFL getting massive tax breaks while at the same time disrespecting our Anthem Flag and Country? Change tax law! **10/10/2017 10:13**

The problem with agreeing to a policy on immigration is that the Democrats don't want secure bordersthey don't care about safety for U.S.A. **10/10/2017 10:18**

Since Congress can't get its act together on HealthCare I will be using the power of the pen to give great HealthCare to many people - FAST **10/10/2017 10:30**

With Jemele Hill at the mike it is no wonder ESPN ratings have "tanked" in fact tanked so badly it is the talk of the industry! **10/10/2017 10:42**

The Democrats want MASSIVE tax increases & soft crime producing borders.The Republicans want the biggest tax cut in history & the WALL! **10/11/2017 10:36**

It is about time that Roger Goodell of the NFL is finally demanding that all players STAND for our great National Anthem-RESPECT OUR COUNTRY **10/11/2017 10:47**

With all of the Fake News coming out of NBC and the Networks at what point is it appropriate to challenge their License? Bad for country! **10/11/2017 13:55**

Happy to announce we are awarding $1M to Las Vegas - in order to help local law enforcement working OT to respond to last Sunday's tragedy. **10/11/2017 19:49**

Network news has become so partisan distorted and fake that licenses must be challenged and if appropriate revoked. Not fair to public! **10/12/2017 0:09**

People are just now starting to find out how dishonest and disgusting (FakeNews) @NBCNews is. Viewers beware. May be worse than even @CNN! **10/13/2017 0:12**

Hard to believe that the Democrats who have gone so far LEFT that they are no longer recognizable are fighting so hard for Sanctuary crime **10/13/2017 11:51**

Health Insurance stocks which have gone through the roof during the ObamaCare years plunged yesterday after I ended their Dems windfall! **10/14/2017 11:18**

Very proud of my Executive Order which will allow greatly expanded access and far lower costs for HealthCare. Millions of people benefit! **10/14/2017 11:27**

Since Election Day on November 8 the Stock Market is up more than 25% unemployment is at a 17 year low & companies are coming back to U.S. **10/16/2017 12:54**

The U.S. has gained more than 5.2 trillion dollars in Stock Market Value since Election Day! Also record business enthusiasm. **10/16/2017 12:57**

I was recently asked if Crooked Hillary Clinton is going to run in 2020? My answer was "I hope so!" **10/16/2017 13:12**

BORDER WALL prototypes underway! https://t.co/arFNO80zmO **10/17/2017 23:03**

As it has turned out James Comey lied and leaked and totally protected Hillary Clinton. He was the best thing that ever happened to her! **10/18/2017 10:56**

The NFL has decided that it will not force players to stand for the playing of our National Anthem. Total disrespect for our great country! **10/18/2017 11:06**

Democrat Congresswoman totally fabricated what I said to the wife of a soldier who died in action (and I have proof). Sad! **10/18/2017 11:25**

.@NFL: Too much talk not enough action. Stand for the National Anthem. **10/18/2017 20:42**

46% of Americans think the Media is inventing stories about Trump & his Administration. @FoxNews It is actually much worse than this! **10/19/2017 3:03**

Uranium deal to Russia with Clinton help and Obama Administration knowledge is the biggest story that Fake Media doesn't want to follow! **10/19/2017 11:17**

Workers of firm involved with the discredited and Fake Dossier take the 5th. Who paid for it Russia the FBI or the Dems (or all)? **10/19/2017 11:56**

The Fake News is going crazy with wacky Congresswoman Wilson(D) who was SECRETLY on a very personal call and gave a total lie on content! **10/20/2017 2:53**

Just out report: "United Kingdom crime rises 13% annually amid spread of Radical Islamic terror." Not good we must keep America safe! **10/20/2017 10:31**

I hope the Fake News Media keeps talking about Wacky Congresswoman Wilson in that she as a representative is killing the Democrat Party! **10/21/2017 12:07**

Subject to the receipt of further information I will be allowing as President the long blocked and classified JFK FILES to be opened.

10/21/2017 12:35

Stock Market hits another all time high on Friday. 5.3 trillion dollars up since Election. Fake News doesn't spent much time on this! **10/21/2017 13:14**

Officials behind the now discredited "Dossier" plead the Fifth. Justice Department and/or FBI should immediately release who paid for it. **10/21/2017 19:59**

Keep hearing about "tiny" amount of money spent on Facebook ads. What about the billions of dollars of Fake News on CNN ABC NBC & CBS? **10/21/2017 20:06**

Crooked Hillary Clinton spent hundreds of millions of dollars more on Presidential Election than I did. Facebook was on her side not mine! **10/21/2017 21:21**

Wacky Congresswoman Wilson is the gift that keeps on giving for the Republican Party a disaster for Dems. You watch her in action & vote R! **10/22/2017 12:02**

It is finally sinking through. 46% OF PEOPLE BELIEVE MAJOR NATIONAL NEWS ORGS FABRICATE STORIES ABOUT ME. FAKE NEWS even worse! Lost cred. **10/22/2017 12:08**

There will be NO change to your 401(k). This has always been a great and popular middle class tax break that works and it stays! **10/23/2017 11:42**

Two dozen NFL players continue to kneel during the National Anthem showing total disrespect to our Flag & Country. No leadership in NFL! **10/23/2017 11:53**

I had a very respectful conversation with the widow of Sgt. La David Johnson and spoke his name from beginning without hesitation! **10/23/2017 12:30**

Bob Corker who helped President O give us the bad Iran Deal & couldn't get elected dog catcher in Tennessee is now fighting Tax Cuts.... **10/24/2017 12:13**

Stock Market just hit another record high! Jobs looking very good. **10/24/2017 14:35**

So nice being with Republican Senators today. Multiple standing ovations! Most are great people who want big Tax Cuts and success for U.S. **10/24/2017 22:20**

Working hard on the biggest tax cut in U.S. history. Great support from so many sides. Big winners will be the middle class business & JOBS **10/25/2017 11:35**

The long anticipated release of the #JFKFiles will take place tomorrow. So interesting! **10/25/2017 19:56**

Big news - Budget just passed! **10/26/2017 15:05**

JFK Files are being carefully released. In the end there will be great transparency. It is my hope to get just about everything to public! **10/27/2017 11:38**

It is now commonly agreed after many months of COSTLY looking that there was NO collusion between Russia and Trump. Was collusion with HC! **10/27/2017 13:33**

Very little reporting about the GREAT GDP numbers announced yesterday (3.0 despite the big hurricane hits). Best consecutive Q's in years! **10/28/2017 12:22**

Just read the nice remarks by President Jimmy Carter about me and how badly I am treated by the press (Fake News). Thank you Mr. President! **10/28/2017 12:28**

While not at all presidential I must point out that the Sloppy Michael Moore Show on Broadway was a TOTAL BOMB and was forced to close. Sad! **10/28/2017 22:19**

JFK Files are released long ahead of schedule! **10/28/2017 23:15**

Never seen such Republican ANGER & UNITY as I have concerning the lack of investigation on Clinton made Fake Dossier (now $12000000?).... (1/3) **10/29/2017 13:53**

...the Uranium to Russia deal the 33000 plus deleted Emails the Comey fix and so much more. Instead they look at phony Trump/Russia.... (2/3) **10/29/2017 14:02**

...are now fighting back like never before. There is so much GUILT by Democrats/Clinton and now the facts are pouring out. DO SOMETHING! (3/3) **10/29/2017 14:17**

All of this "Russia" talk right when the Republicans are making their big push for historic Tax Cuts & Reform. Is this coincidental? NOT! **10/29/2017 14:48**

Report out that Obama Campaign paid $972000 to Fusion GPS. The firm also got $12400000 (really?) from DNC. Nobody knows who OK'd! **10/30/2017 11:37**

Sorry but this is years ago before Paul Manafort was part of the Trump campaign. But why aren't Crooked Hillary & the Dems the focus????? **10/30/2017 14:25**

....Also there is NO COLLUSION! **10/30/2017 14:28**

In NYC looks like another attack by a very sick and deranged person. Law enforcement is following this closely. NOT IN THE U.S.A.! **10/31/2017 21:30**

We must not allow ISIS to return or enter our country after defeating them in the Middle East and elsewhere. Enough! **10/31/2017 22:31**

My thoughts condolences and prayers to the victims and families of the New York City terrorist attack. God and your country are with you! **10/31/2017 22:57**

I have just ordered Homeland Security to step up our already Extreme Vetting Program. Being politically correct is fine but not for this! **11/1/2017 1:26**

The terrorist came into our country through what is called the "Diversity Visa Lottery Program" a Chuck Schumer beauty. I want merit based. **11/1/2017 11:24**

We are fighting hard for Merit Based immigration no more Democrat Lottery Systems. We must get MUCH tougher (and smarter). @foxandfriends **11/1/2017 11:30**

Wouldn't it be great to Repeal the very unfair and unpopular Individual Mandate in ObamaCare and use those savings for further Tax Cuts..... **11/1/2017 14:59**

The United States will be immediately implementing much tougher Extreme Vetting Procedures. The safety of our citizens comes first! **11/2/2017 2:19**

NYC terrorist was happy as he asked to hang ISIS flag in his hospital room. He killed 8 people badly injured 12. SHOULD GET DEATH PENALTY!

11/2/2017 3:43

...There is also something appropriate about keeping him in the home of the horrible crime he committed. Should move fast. DEATH PENALTY! **11/2/2017 11:54**

Donna Brazile just stated the DNC RIGGED the system to illegally steal the Primary from Bernie Sanders. Bought and paid for by Crooked H.... **11/3/2017 0:39**

....This is real collusion and dishonesty. Major violation of Campaign Finance Laws and Money Laundering - where is our Justice Department? **11/3/2017 0:48**

My Twitter account was taken down for 11 minutes by a rogue employee. I guess the word must finally be getting out-and having an impact. **11/3/2017 10:51**

Everybody is asking why the Justice Department (and FBI) isn't looking into all of the dishonesty going on with Crooked Hillary & the Dems.. **11/3/2017 10:57**

....People are angry. At some point the Justice Department and the FBI must do what is right and proper. The American public deserves it! **11/3/2017 11:11**

Pocahontas just stated that the Democrats lead by the legendary Crooked Hillary Clinton rigged the Primaries! Lets go FBI & Justice Dept. **11/3/2017 11:55**

I always felt I would be running and winning against Bernie Sanders not Crooked H without cheating I was right. **11/3/2017 14:29**

The rigged Dem Primary one of the biggest political stories in years got ZERO coverage on Fake News Network TV last night. Disgraceful! **11/3/2017 16:09**

The decision on Sergeant Bergdahl is a complete and total disgrace to our Country and to our Military. **11/3/2017 16:54**

Getting ready to land in Hawaii. Looking so much forward to meeting with our great Military/Veterans at Pearl Harbor! **11/3/2017 22:44**

Unemployment is down to 4.1% lowest in 17 years. 1.5 million new jobs created since I took office. Highest stock Market ever up $5.4 trill **11/4/2017 12:35**

Just gave a speech to the great men and women at Yokota Air Base in Tokyo Japan. Leaving to see Prime Minister Abe. https://t.co/6LRAgojvDB **11/5/2017 2:59**

Playing golf with Prime Minister Abe and Hideki Matsuyama two wonderful people! https://t.co/vYLULeOo2K **11/5/2017 6:25**

May God be w/ the people of Sutherland Springs Texas. The FBI & law enforcement are on the scene. I am monitoring the situation from Japan. **11/5/2017 20:06**

...Americans do what we do best: we pull together. We join hands. We lock arms and through the tears and the sadness we stand strong... https://t.co/qkCPgtKGkA **11/6/2017 4:48**

I have great confidence in King Salman and the Crown Prince of Saudi Arabia they know exactly what they are doing.... **11/6/2017 23:03**

....Some of those they are harshly treating have been "milking" their country for years! **11/6/2017 23:05**

NoKo has interpreted America's past restraint as weakness. This would be a fatal miscalculation. Do not underestimate us. AND DO NOT TRY US. https://t.co/4llqLrNpK3 **11/8/2017 15:15**

Congratulations to all of the "DEPLORABLES" and the millions of people who gave us a MASSIVE (304-227) Electoral College landslide victory! https://t.co/7ifv5gT7Ur **11/8/2017 18:17**

President Xi thank you for such an incredible welcome ceremony. It was a truly memorable and impressive display! 📷 https://t.co/J9x51h1LBe https://t.co/g4Z7mO5cV9 **11/9/2017 7:08**

In the coming months and years ahead I look forward to building an even STRONGER relationship between the United States and China. https://t.co/mK3SB7t3EV **11/9/2017 13:58**

I don't blame China I blame the incompetence of past Admins for allowing China to take advantage of the U.S. on trade leading up to a point where the U.S. is losing $100's of billions. How can you blame China for taking advantage of people that had no clue? I would've done same! **11/9/2017 23:39**

My meetings with President Xi Jinping were very productive on both trade and the subject of North Korea. He is a highly respected and powerful representative of his people. It was great being with him and Madame Peng Liyuan! **11/9/2017 23:44**

On behalf of an entire nation Happy 242nd Birthday to the men and women of the United States Marines!#USMC242 #SemperFi https://t.co/ecgoSJP5Uc **11/10/2017 12:57**

On this wonderful Veterans Day I want to express the incredible gratitude of the entire American Nation to our GREAT VETERANS. Thank you! https://t.co/GhQbCA7yIl **11/11/2017 12:11**

When will all the haters and fools out there realize that having a good relationship with Russia is a good thing not a bad thing. There always playing politics - bad for our country. I want to solve North Korea Syria Ukraine terrorism and Russia can greatly help! **11/12/2017 0:18**

Does the Fake News Media remember when Crooked Hillary Clinton as Secretary of State was begging Russia to be our friend with the misspelled reset button? Obama tried also but he had zero chemistry with Putin. **11/12/2017 0:43**

Why would Kim Jong-un insult me by calling me "old" when I would NEVER call him "short and fat?" Oh well I try so hard to be his friend - and maybe someday that will happen!

11/12/2017 0:48

After my tour of Asia all Countries dealing with us on TRADE know that the rules have changed. The United States has to be treated fairly and in a reciprocal fashion. The massive TRADE deficits must go down quickly!

11/14/2017 5:20

I will be making a major statement from the @WhiteHouse upon my return to D.C. Time and date to be set. **11/14/2017 6:23**

THANK YOU ASIA! #USA https://t.co/FziKSbrzcu

11/14/2017 17:39

Just returned from Asia after 12 very successful days. Great to be home! **11/15/2017 4:42**

Our great country is respected again in Asia. You will see the fruits of our long but successful trip for many years to come! **11/15/2017 10:30**

While in the Philippines I was forced to watch @CNN which I have not done in months and again realized how bad and FAKE it is. Loser! **11/15/2017 10:45**

Do you think the three UCLA Basketball Players will say thank you President Trump? They were headed for 10 years in jail! **11/15/2017 15:11**

...They should realize that these relationships are a good thing not a bad thing. The U.S. is being respected again. Watch Trade! **11/15/2017 16:39**

Why are Democrats fighting massive tax cuts for the middle class and business (jobs)? The reason: Obstruction and Delay! **11/16/2017 2:11**

To the three UCLA basketball players I say: You're welcome go out and give a big Thank You to President Xi Jinping of China who made..... (1/2) **11/16/2017 11:30**

....your release possible and HAVE A GREAT LIFE! Be careful there are many pitfalls on the long and winding road of life! (2/2) **11/16/2017 11:34**

China is sending an Envoy and Delegation to North Korea - A big move we'll see what happens! **11/16/2017 12:43**

The Al Frankenstien picture is really bad speaks a thousand words. Where do his hands go in pictures 2 3 4 5 & 6 while she sleeps? **11/17/2017 3:06**

.And to think that just last week he was lecturing anyone who would listen about sexual harassment and respect for women. Lesley Stahl tape? **11/17/2017 3:15**

If Democrats were not such obstructionists and understood the power of lower taxes we would be able to get many of their ideas into Bill! **11/17/2017 11:00**

Put big game trophy decision on hold until such time as I review all conservation facts. Under study for years. Will update soon with Secretary Zinke. Thank you! **11/18/2017 0:47**

Crooked Hillary Clinton is the worst (and biggest) loser of all time. She just can't stop which is so good for the Republican Party. Hillary get on with your life and give it another try in three years! **11/18/2017 13:31**

Now that the three basketball players are out of China and saved from years in jail LaVar Ball the father of LiAngelo is unaccepting of what I did for his son and that shoplifting is no big deal. I should have left them in jail! **11/19/2017 17:42**

Shoplifting is a very big deal in China as it should be (5-10 years in jail) but not to father LaVar. Should have gotten his son out during my next trip to China instead. China told them why they were released. Very ungrateful! **11/19/2017 23:36**

Border Patrol Officer killed at Southern Border another badly hurt. We will seek out and bring to justice those responsible. We will and must build the Wall! **11/20/2017 1:29**

Marshawn Lynch of the NFL's Oakland Raiders stands for the Mexican Anthem and sits down to boos for our National Anthem. Great disrespect! Next time NFL should suspend him for remainder of season. Attendance and ratings way down. **11/20/2017 11:25**

It wasn't the White House it wasn't the State Department it wasn't father LaVar's so-called people on the ground in China that got his son out of a long term prison sentence - IT WAS ME. Too bad! LaVar is just a poor man's version of Don King but without the hair. Just think.. (1/2)
11/22/2017 10:25

...LaVar you could have spent the next 5 to 10 years during Thanksgiving with your son in China but no NBA contract to support you. But remember LaVar shoplifting is NOT a little thing. It's a really big deal especially in China. Ungrateful fool! (2/2) **11/22/2017 10:33**

The NFL is now thinking about a new idea - keeping teams in the Locker Room during the National Anthem next season. That's almost as bad as kneeling! When will the highly paid Commissioner finally get tough and smart? This issue is killing your league!..... **11/22/2017 10:48**

I have long given the order to help Argentina with the Search and Rescue mission of their missing submarine. 45 people aboard and not much time left. May God be with them and the people of Argentina! **11/22/2017 21:32**

HAPPY THANKSGIVING your Country is starting to do really well. Jobs coming back highest Stock Market EVER Military getting really strong we will build the WALL V.A. taking care of our Vets great Supreme Court Justice RECORD CUT IN REGS lowest unemployment in 17 years....!

11/23/2017 11:28

MAKE AMERICA GREAT AGAIN! **11/23/2017 11:44**

HAPPY THANKSGIVING! https://t.co/nQhi7XopMW **11/23/2017 15:35**

ObamaCare premiums are going up up up just as I have been predicting for two years. ObamaCare is OWNED by the Democrats and it is a disaster. But do not worry. Even though the Dems want to Obstruct we will Repeal & Replace right after Tax Cuts! **11/23/2017 23:18**

After Turkey call I will be heading over to Trump National Golf Club Jupiter to play golf (quickly) with Tiger Woods and Dustin Johnson. Then back to Mar-a-Lago for talks on bringing even more jobs and companies back to the USA! **11/24/2017 12:10**

Horrible and cowardly terrorist attack on innocent and defenseless worshipers in Egypt. The world cannot tolerate terrorism we must defeat them militarily and discredit the extremist ideology that forms the basis of their existence! **11/24/2017 15:27**

Will be calling the President of Egypt in a short while to discuss the tragic terrorist attack with so much loss of life. We have to get TOUGHER AND SMARTER than ever before and we will. Need the WALL need the BAN! God bless the people of Egypt. **11/24/2017 18:49**

Time Magazine called to say that I was PROBABLY going to be named "Man (Person) of the Year" like last year but I would have to agree to an interview and a major photo shoot. I said probably is no good and took a pass. Thanks anyway!
11/24/2017 22:40

.@FoxNews is MUCH more important in the United States than CNN but outside of the U.S. CNN International is still a major source of (Fake) news and they represent our Nation to the WORLD very poorly. The outside world does not see the truth from them! **11/25/2017 22:37**

The last thing we need in Alabama and the U.S. Senate is a Schumer/Pelosi puppet who is WEAK on Crime WEAK on the Border Bad for our Military and our great Vets Bad for our 2nd Amendment AND WANTS TO RAISES TAXES TO THE SKY. Jones would be a disaster! **11/26/2017 13:52**

Since the first day I took office all you hear is the phony Democrat excuse for losing the election Russia RussiaRussia. Despite this I have the economy booming and have possibly done more than any 10 month President. MAKE AMERICA GREAT AGAIN! **11/26/2017 21:29**

Back in D.C. big week for Tax Cuts and many other things of great importance to our Country. Senate Republicans will hopefully come through for all of us. The Tax Cut Bill is getting better and better. The end result will be great for ALL! **11/27/2017 1:47**

We should have a contest as to which of the Networks plus CNN and not including Fox is the most dishonest corrupt and/or distorted in its political coverage of your favorite President (me). They are all bad. Winner to receive the FAKE NEWS TROPHY! **11/27/2017 14:04**

The Tax Cut Bill is coming along very well great support. With just a few changes some mathematical the middle class and job producers can get even more in actual dollars and savings and the pass through provision becomes simpler and really works well! **11/27/2017 14:24**

At least 24 players kneeling this weekend at NFL stadiums that are now having a very hard time filling up. The American public is fed up with the disrespect the NFL is paying to our Country our Flag and our National Anthem. Weak and out of control! **11/28/2017 12:45**

Melania our great and very hard working First Lady who truly loves what she is doing always thought that "if you run you will win." She would tell everyone that "no doubt he will win." I also felt I would win (or I would not have run) - and Country is doing great! **11/28/2017 13:00**

Meeting with "Chuck and Nancy" today about keeping government open and working. Problem is they want illegal immigrants flooding into our Country unchecked are weak on Crime and want to substantially RAISE Taxes. I don't see a deal! **11/28/2017 14:17**

After North Korea missile launch it's more important than ever to fund our gov't & military! Dems shouldn't hold troop funding hostage for amnesty & illegal immigration. I ran on stopping illegal immigration and won big. They can't now threaten a shutdown to get their demands. **11/29/2017 1:45**

Looks like another great day for the Stock Market. Consumer Confidence is at Record High. I guess somebody likes me (my policies)! **11/29/2017 12:03**

Wow Matt Lauer was just fired from NBC for "inappropriate sexual behavior in the workplace." But when will the top executives at NBC & Comcast be fired for putting out so much Fake News. Check out Andy Lack's past! **11/29/2017 12:16**

So now that Matt Lauer is gone when will the Fake News practitioners at NBC be terminating the contract of Phil Griffin? And will they terminate low ratings Joe Scarborough based on the "unsolved mystery" that took place in Florida years ago? Investigate! **11/29/2017 14:14**

Just spoke to President XI JINPING of China concerning the provocative actions of North Korea. Additional major sanctions will be imposed on North Korea today. This situation will be handled! **11/29/2017 14:40**

.@Theresa_May don't focus on me focus on the destructive Radical Islamic Terrorism that is taking place within the United Kingdom. We are doing just fine! **11/30/2017 1:02**

Funny to hear the Democrats talking about the National Debt when President Obama doubled it in only 8 years! **11/30/2017 2:23**

Stock Market hits new Record High. Confidence and enthusiasm abound. More great numbers coming out! **11/30/2017 13:05**

The Dow just broke 24000 for the first time (another all-time Record). If the Dems had won the Presidential Election the Market would be down 50% from these levels and Consumer Confidence which is also at an all-time high would be "low and glum!" **11/30/2017 15:46**

Today is a day that I've been looking very much forward to ALL YEAR LONG. It is one that you have heard me speak about many times before. Now as President of the United States it is my tremendous honor to finally wish America and the world a very MERRY CHRISTMAS! https://t.co/cTvdlUkfHV **12/1/2017 0:36**

A disgraceful verdict in the Kate Steinle case! No wonder the people of our Country are so angry with Illegal Immigration. **12/1/2017 3:30**

The Kate Steinle killer came back and back over the weakly protected Obama border always committing crimes and being violent and yet this info was not used in court. His exoneration is a complete travesty of justice. BUILD THE WALL! **12/1/2017 11:03**

The jury was not told the killer of Kate was a 7 time felon. The Schumer/Pelosi Democrats are so weak on Crime that they will pay a big price in the 2018 and 2020 Elections. **12/1/2017 11:13**

The media has been speculating that I fired Rex Tillerson or that he would be leaving soon - FAKE NEWS! He's not leaving and while we disagree on certain subjects (I call the final shots) we work well together and America is highly respected again!https://t.co/FrqiPLFJ1E **12/1/2017 20:08**

Biggest Tax Bill and Tax Cuts in history just passed in the Senate. Now these great Republicans will be going for final passage. Thank you to House and Senate Republicans for your hard work and commitment! **12/2/2017 12:54**

I had to fire General Flynn because he lied to the Vice President and the FBI. He has pled guilty to those lies. It is a shame because his actions during the transition were lawful. There was nothing to hide! **12/2/2017 17:14**

62 years ago this week a brave seamstress in Montgomery Alabama uttered one word that changed history... https://t.co/eOvCBcMIKX **12/2/2017 21:07**

So General Flynn lies to the FBI and his life is destroyed while Crooked Hillary Clinton on that now famous FBI holiday "interrogation" with no swearing in and no recording lies many times...and nothing happens to her? Rigged system or just a double standard? **12/3/2017 2:06**

Many people in our Country are asking what the "Justice" Department is going to do about the fact that totally Crooked Hillary AFTER receiving a subpoena from the United States Congress deleted and "acid washed" 33000 Emails? No justice! **12/3/2017 2:13**

Congratulations to @ABC News for suspending Brian Ross for his horrendously inaccurate and dishonest report on the Russia Russia Russia Witch Hunt. More Networks and "papers" should do the same with their Fake News! **12/3/2017 2:22**

I never asked Comey to stop investigating Flynn. Just more Fake News covering another Comey lie! **12/3/2017 11:15**

Tainted (no very dishonest?) FBI "agent's role in Clinton probe under review." Led Clinton Email probe. @ foxandfriends Clinton money going to wife of another FBI agent in charge. **12/3/2017 12:42**

After years of Comey with the phony and dishonest Clinton investigation (and more) running the FBI its reputation is in Tatters - worst in History! But fear not we will bring it back to greatness. **12/3/2017 13:00**

People who lost money when the Stock Market went down 350 points based on the False and Dishonest reporting of Brian Ross of @ABC News (he has been suspended) should consider hiring a lawyer and suing ABC for the damages this bad reporting has caused - many millions of dollars! **12/3/2017 13:15**

Report: "ANTI-TRUMP FBI AGENT LED CLINTON EMAIL PROBE" Now it all starts to make sense! **12/3/2017 13:36**

Democrats refusal to give even one vote for massive Tax Cuts is why we need Republican Roy Moore to win in Alabama. We need his vote on stopping crime illegal immigration Border Wall Military Pro Life V.A. Judges 2nd

Amendment and more. No to Jones a Pelosi/Schumer Puppet! **12/4/2017 11:17**

Putting Pelosi/Schumer Liberal Puppet Jones into office in Alabama would hurt our great Republican Agenda of low on taxes tough on crime strong on military and borders...& so much more. Look at your 401-k's since Election. Highest Stock Market EVER! Jobs are roaring back! **12/4/2017 12:00**

With the great vote on Cutting Taxes this could be a big day for the Stock Market - and YOU! **12/4/2017 12:03**

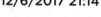

MAKE AMERICA GREAT AGAIN!
12/6/2017 15:00

I have determined that it is time to officially recognize Jerusalem as the capital of Israel. I am also directing the State Department to begin preparation to move the American Embassy from Tel Aviv to Jerusalem... https://t.co/YwgWmTOO8m **12/6/2017 21:14**

National Pearl Harbor Remembrance Day - "A day that will live in infamy!" December 7 1941 **12/7/2017 15:04**

I fulfilled my campaign promise - others didn't! https://t.co/bYdaOHmPVJ **12/8/2017 5:41**

Fines and penalties against Wells Fargo Bank for their bad acts against their customers and others will not be dropped as has incorrectly been reported but will be pursued and if anything substantially increased. I will cut Regs but make penalties severe when caught cheating! **12/8/2017 15:18**

Fake News CNN made a vicious and purposeful mistake yesterday. They were caught red handed just like lonely Brian Ross at ABC News (who should be immediately fired for his "mistake"). Watch to see if @CNN fires those responsible or was it just gross incompetence? **12/9/2017 13:02**

CNN'S slogan is CNN THE MOST TRUSTED NAME IN NEWS. Everyone knows this is not true that this could in fact be a fraud on the American Public. There are many outlets that are far more trusted than Fake News CNN. Their slogan should be CNN THE LEAST TRUSTED NAME IN NEWS!
12/9/2017 13:21

.@daveweigel of the Washington Post just admitted that his picture was a FAKE (fraud?) showing an almost empty arena last night for my speech in Pensacola when in fact he knew the arena was packed (as shown also on T.V.). FAKE NEWS he should be fired. **12/9/2017 23:14**

Great Army - Navy Game. Army wins 14 to 13 and brings home the COMMANDER-IN-CHIEF'S TROPHY! Congratulations! **12/9/2017 23:47**

No American should be separated from their loved ones because of preventable crime committed by those illegally in our country. Our cities should be Sanctuaries for Americans – not for criminal aliens! https://t.co/CvtkCG1pln **12/10/2017 2:17**

Things are going really well for our economy a subject the Fake News spends as little time as possible discussing! Stock Market hit another RECORD HIGH unemployment is now at a 17 year low and companies are coming back into the USA. Really good news and much more to come! **12/10/2017 13:30**

Getting closer and closer on the Tax Cut Bill. Shaping up even better than projected. House and Senate working very hard and smart. End result will be not only important but SPECIAL! **12/10/2017 13:35**

Very little discussion of all the purposely false and defamatory stories put out this week by the Fake News Media. They are out of control - correct reporting means nothing to them. Major lies written then forced to be withdrawn after they are exposed...a stain on America!
12/10/2017 21:18

Another false story this time in the Failing @nytimes that I watch 4-8 hours of television a day - Wrong! Also I seldom if ever watch CNN or MSNBC both of which I consider Fake News. I never watch Don Lemon who I once called the "dumbest man on television!" Bad Reporting. **12/11/2017 14:17**

Despite thousands of hours wasted and many millions of dollars spent the Democrats have been unable to show any collusion with Russia - so now they are moving on to the false accusations and fabricated stories of women who I don't know and/or have never met. FAKE NEWS!

12/12/2017 12:10

Lightweight Senator Kirsten Gillibrand a total flunky for Chuck Schumer and someone who would come to my office "begging" for campaign contributions not so long ago (and would do anything for them) is now in the ring fighting against Trump. Very disloyal to Bill & Crooked-USED!

12/12/2017 13:03

Consumer Confidence is at an All-Time High along with a Record High Stock Market. Unemployment is at a 17 year low. MAKE AMERICA GREAT AGAIN! Working to pass MASSIVE TAX CUTS (looking good). **12/12/2017 14:23**

Congratulations to Doug Jones on a hard fought victory. The write-in votes played a very big factor but a win is a win. The people of Alabama are great and the Republicans will have another shot at this seat in a very short period of time. It never ends! **12/13/2017 4:08**

Wow more than 90% of Fake News Media coverage of me is negative with numerous forced retractions of untrue stories. Hence my use of Social Media the only way to get the truth out. Much of Mainstream Meadia has become a joke! @foxandfriends **12/13/2017 13:02**

If last night's election proved anything it proved that we need to put up GREAT Republican candidates to increase the razor thin margins in both the House and Senate.

12/13/2017 14:45

Thank you Omarosa for your service! I wish you continued success. **12/13/2017 23:58**

Republican Tax Cuts are looking very good. All are working hard. In the meantime the Stock Market hit another record high! **12/14/2017 12:59**

In 1960 there were approximately 20000 pages in the Code of Federal Regulations. Today there are over 185000 pages as seen in the Roosevelt Room.Today we CUT THE RED TAPE! It is time to SET FREE OUR DREAMS and MAKE AMERICA GREAT AGAIN! https://t.co/teAVNzjvcx **12/14/2017 20:35**

Congratulations to two great and hardworking guys Corey Lewandowski and David Bossie on the success of their just out book "Let Trump Be Trump." Finally people with real knowledge are writing about our wonderful and exciting campaign! **12/16/2017 14:52**

Remember Republicans are 5-0 in Congressional Races this year. The media refuses to mention this. I said Gillespie and Moore would lose (for very different reasons) and they did. I also predicted "I" would win. Republicans will do well in 2018 very well! @foxandfriends **12/18/2017 11:23**

The train accident that just occurred in DuPont WA shows more than ever why our soon to be submitted infrastructure plan must be approved quickly. Seven trillion dollars spent in the Middle East while our roads bridges tunnels railways (and more) crumble! Not for long! **12/18/2017 18:41**

My thoughts and prayers are with everyone involved in the train accident in DuPont Washington. Thank you to all of our wonderful First Responders who are on the scene. We are currently monitoring here at the White House. **12/18/2017 18:51**

70 Record Closes for the Dow so far this year! We have NEVER had 70 Dow Records in a one year period. Wow!
12/18/2017 22:25

DOW RISES 5000 POINTS ON THE YEAR FOR THE FIRST TIME EVER - MAKE AMERICA GREAT AGAIN! **12/19/2017 11:04**

A story in the @washingtonpost that I was close to "rescinding" the nomination of Justice Gorsuch prior to confirmation is FAKE NEWS. I never even wavered and am very proud of him and the job he is doing as a Justice of the U.S. Supreme Court. The unnamed sources don't exist! **12/19/2017 15:07**

Congratulations to Paul Ryan Kevin McCarthy Kevin Brady Steve Scalise Cathy McMorris Rodgers and all great House Republicans who voted in favor of cutting your taxes! **12/19/2017 20:18**

The United States Senate just passed the biggest in history Tax Cut and Reform Bill. Terrible Individual Mandate (ObamaCare)Repealed. Goes to the House tomorrow morning for final vote. If approved there will be a News Conference at The White House at approximately 1:00 P.M. **12/20/2017 6:09**

I would like to congratulate @SenateMajLdr on having done a fantastic job both strategically & politically on the passing in the Senate of the MASSIVE TAX CUT & Reform Bill. I could have not asked for a better or more talented partner. Our team will go onto many more VICTORIES! **12/20/2017 16:39**

We are delivering HISTORIC TAX RELIEF for the American people!#TaxCutsandJobsAct https://t.co/lLgATrCh5o
12/20/2017 18:09

WE ARE MAKING AMERICA GREAT AGAIN! https://t.co/HY353gXV0R **12/20/2017 21:44**

The Massive Tax Cuts which the Fake News Media is desperate to write badly about so as to please their Democrat bosses will soon be kicking in and will speak for

themselves. Companies are already making big payments to workers. Dems want to raise taxes hate these big Cuts!
12/21/2017 12:24

Was @foxandfriends just named the most influential show in news? You deserve it - three great people! The many Fake News Hate Shows should study your formula for success!
12/21/2017 12:45

Home Sales hit BEST numbers in 10 years! MAKE AMERICA GREAT AGAIN **12/21/2017 13:56**

House Democrats want a SHUTDOWN for the holidays in order to distract from the very popular just passed Tax Cuts. House Republicans don't let this happen. Pass the C.R. TODAY and keep our Government OPEN! **12/21/2017 14:52**

Our big and very popular Tax Cut and Reform Bill has taken on an unexpected new source of "love" - that is big companies and corporations showering their workers with bonuses. This is a phenomenon that nobody even thought of and now it is the rage. Merry Christmas! **12/22/2017 12:47**

At some point and for the good of the country I predict we will start working with the Democrats in a Bipartisan fashion. Infrastructure would be a perfect place to start. After having foolishly spent $7 trillion in the Middle East it is time to start rebuilding our country! **12/22/2017 13:05**

"The President has accomplished some absolutely historic things during this past year." Thank you Charlie Kirk of Turning Points USA. Sadly the Fake Mainstream Media will NEVER talk about our accomplishments in their end of year reviews. We are compiling a long & beautiful list.
12/22/2017 14:17

With all my Administration has done on Legislative Approvals (broke Harry Truman's Record) Regulation Cutting Judicial Appointments Building Military VA TAX

CUTS & REFORM Record Economy/Stock Market and so much more I am sure great credit will be given by mainstream news? **12/22/2017 15:04**

Will be signing the biggest ever Tax Cut and Reform Bill in 30 minutes in Oval Office. Will also be signing a much needed 4 billion dollar missile defense bill. **12/22/2017 15:07**

95% of Americans will pay less or at worst the same amount of taxes (mostly far less). The Dems only want to raise your taxes! **12/22/2017 16:46**

The United Nations Security Council just voted 15-0 in favor of additional Sanctions on North Korea. The World wants Peace not Death! **12/22/2017 20:47**

Remember the most hated part of ObamaCare is the Individual Mandate which is being terminated under our just signed Tax Cut Bill. **12/22/2017 22:11**

How can FBI Deputy Director Andrew McCabe the man in charge along with leakin' James Comey of the Phony Hillary Clinton investigation (including her 33000 illegally deleted emails) be given $700000 for wife's campaign by Clinton Puppets during investigation? **12/23/2017 20:27**

The Stock Market is setting record after record and unemployment is at a 17 year low. So many things accomplished by the Trump Administration perhaps more than any other President in first year. Sadly will never be reported correctly by the Fake News Media! **12/23/2017 22:44**

Remember the Republicans are 5-0 in Congressional races this year. In Senate I said Roy M would lose in Alabama and supported Big Luther Strange - and Roy lost. Virginia candidate was not a "Trumper" and he lost. Good Republican candidates will win BIG! **12/23/2017 22:57**

.@FoxNews-FBI's Andrew McCabe "in addition to his wife getting all of this money from M (Clinton Puppet) he was using allegedly his FBI Official Email Account to promote her campaign. You obviously cannot do this. These were

the people who were investigating Hillary Clinton."
12/24/2017 12:25

The Fake News refuses to talk about how Big and how Strong our BASE is. They show Fake Polls just like they report Fake News. Despite only negative reporting we are doing well - nobody is going to beat us. MAKE AMERICA GREAT AGAIN! **12/24/2017 13:48**

The Tax Cut/Reform Bill including Massive Alaska Drilling and the Repeal of the highly unpopular Individual Mandate brought it all together as to what an incredible year we had. Don't let the Fake News convince you otherwise...and our insider Polls are strong! **12/24/2017 20:35**

People are proud to be saying Merry Christmas again. I am proud to have led the charge against the assault of our cherished and beautiful phrase. MERRY CHRISTMAS!!!!!

12/25/2017 2:56

MERRY CHRISTMAS!! https://t.co/xa2qxcisVV **12/25/2017 3:51**

MERRY CHRISTMAS!!! https://t.co/mYtV5GNdLl
12/25/2017 13:36

I hope everyone is having a great Christmas then tomorrow it's back to work in order to Make America Great Again (which is happening faster than anyone anticipated)! **12/25/2017 23:33**

Based on the fact that the very unfair and unpopular Individual Mandate has been terminated as part of our Tax Cut Bill which essentially Repeals (over time) ObamaCare the Democrats & Republicans will eventually come together and develop a great new HealthCare plan! **12/26/2017 11:58**

WOW @foxandfrlends "Dossier is bogus. Clinton Campaign DNC funded Dossier. FBI CANNOT (after all of this time) VERIFY CLAIMS IN DOSSIER OF RUSSIA/TRUMP COLLUSION. FBI TAINTED." And they used this Crooked Hillary pile of garbage as the basis for going after the Trump Campaign! **12/26/2017 13:24**

All signs are that business is looking really good for next year only to be helped further by our Tax Cut Bill. Will be a great year for Companies and JOBS! Stock Market is poised for another year of SUCCESS! **12/26/2017 22:17**

Just left West Palm Beach Fire & Rescue #2. Met with great men and women as representatives of those who do so much for all of us. Firefighters paramedics first responders - what amazing people they are! **12/27/2017 23:11**

"Arrests of MS-13 Members Associates Up 83% Under Trump" https://t.co/70iPHy2Yqn **12/28/2017 2:46**

Retail sales are at record numbers. We've got the economy going better than anyone ever dreamt - and you haven't seen anything yet! **12/28/2017 16:18**

Caught RED HANDED - very disappointed that China is allowing oil to go into North Korea. There will never be a friendly solution to the North Korea problem if this continues to happen! **12/28/2017 16:24**

In the East it could be the COLDEST New Year's Eve on record. Perhaps we could use a little bit of that good old Global Warming that our Country but not other countries was going to pay TRILLIONS OF DOLLARS to protect against. Bundle up! **12/29/2017 0:01**

While the Fake News loves to talk about my so-called low approval rating @foxandfriends just showed that my rating on Dec. 28 2017 was approximately the same as President Obama on Dec. 28 2009 which was 47%...and this despite massive negative Trump coverage & Russia hoax! **12/29/2017 12:46**

Why is the United States Post Office which is losing many billions of dollars a year while charging Amazon and others so little to deliver their packages making Amazon richer and the Post Office dumber and poorer? Should be charging MUCH MORE! **12/29/2017 13:04**

The Democrats have been told and fully understand that there can be no DACA without the desperately needed WALL at the Southern Border and an END to the horrible Chain Migration & ridiculous Lottery System of Immigration etc. We must protect our Country at all cost! **12/29/2017 13:16**

Many reports of peaceful protests by Iranian citizens fed up with regime's corruption & its squandering of the nation's wealth to fund terrorism abroad. Iranian govt should respect their people's rights including right to express themselves. The world is watching! #IranProtests **12/30/2017 3:42**

I use Social Media not because I like to but because it is the only way to fight a VERY dishonest and unfair "press" now often referred to as Fake News Media. Phony and non-existent "sources" are being used more often than ever. Many stories & reports a pure fiction!

12/30/2017 22:36

Jobs are kicking in and companies are coming back to the U.S. Unnecessary regulations and high taxes are being dramatically Cut and it will only get better. MUCH MORE TO COME! **12/30/2017 22:42**

Big protests in Iran. The people are finally getting wise as to how their money and wealth is being stolen and squandered on terrorism. Looks like they will not take it any longer. The USA is watching very closely for human rights violations! **12/31/2017 13:03**

Why would smart voters want to put Democrats in Congress in 2018 Election when their policies will totally kill the great wealth created during the months since the Election. People are much better off now not to mention ISIS VA Judges Strong Border 2nd A Tax Cuts & more?

12/31/2017 13:36

What a year it's been and we're just getting started. Together we are MAKING AMERICA GREAT AGAIN! Happy New Year!! https://t.co/qsMNyN1UJG **12/31/2017 19:06**

Iran the Number One State of Sponsored Terror with numerous violations of Human Rights occurring on an hourly basis has now closed down the Internet so that peaceful demonstrators cannot communicate. Not good!

12/31/2017 22:00

As our Country rapidly grows stronger and smarter I want to wish all of my friends supporters enemies haters and even the very dishonest Fake News Media a Happy and Healthy New Year. 2018 will be a great year for America! **12/31/2017 22:18**

HAPPY NEW YEAR! We are MAKING AMERICA GREAT AGAIN and much faster than anyone thought possible!

12/31/2017 23:43

JANUARY 2018 - MARCH 2018

★★★★★★★★★★★★★★★★★★★★★★★★★★

As the president begins his second year in office, the mainstream media's attention remains solidly focused on Russian collusion, with President Trump tweeting repeatedly about this being "fake news." While companies continue to return manufacturing jobs to the U.S., seizing an opportunity, non-citizens from Central America begin to cross the border at an accelerating rate. Reacting strongly to this, the conflict over immigration between the Republicans and the Democrats becomes a daily topic for Trump's tweets. Unemployment for minorities continues to decrease, while tensions with Kim Jong-Un in North Korea begin to abate.

The United States has foolishly given Pakistan more than 33 billion dollars in aid over the last 15 years and they have given us nothing but lies & deceit thinking of our leaders as fools. They give safe haven to the terrorists we hunt in Afghanistan with little help. No more! **1/1/2018 12:12**

Iran is failing at every level despite the terrible deal made with them by the Obama Administration. The great Iranian people have been repressed for many years. They are hungry for food & for freedom. Along with human rights the wealth of Iran is being looted. TIME FOR CHANGE!

1/1/2018 12:44

Will be leaving Florida for Washington (D.C.) today at 4:00 P.M. Much work to be done but it will be a great New Year!

1/1/2018 13:37

The people of Iran are finally acting against the brutal and corrupt Iranian regime. All of the money that President Obama so foolishly gave them went into terrorism and into their "pockets." The people have little food big inflation and no human rights. The U.S. is watching! **1/2/2018 12:09**

Crooked Hillary Clinton's top aid Huma Abedin has been accused of disregarding basic security protocols. She put Classified Passwords into the hands of foreign agents. Remember sailors pictures on submarine? Jail! Deep State Justice Dept must finally act? Also on Comey & others

1/2/2018 12:48

Companies are giving big bonuses to their workers because of the Tax Cut Bill. Really great! **1/2/2018 13:49**

Since taking office I have been very strict on Commercial Aviation. Good news - it was just reported that there were Zero deaths in 2017 the best and safest year on record!

1/2/2018 14:13

Democrats are doing nothing for DACA - just interested in politics. DACA activists and Hispanics will go hard against Dems will start "falling in love" with Republicans and their President! We are about RESULTS. **1/2/2018 15:16**

It's not only Pakistan that we pay billions of dollars to for nothing but also many other countries and others. As an example we pay the Palestinians HUNDRED OF MILLIONS OF DOLLARS a year and get no appreciation or respect. They don't even want to negotiate a long overdue... (1/2)

1/2/2018 22:37

...peace treaty with Israel. We have taken Jerusalem the toughest part of the negotiation off the table but Israel for that would have had to pay more. But with the Palestinians no longer willing to talk peace why should we make any of these massive future payments to them? (2/2) **1/2/2018 22:37**

North Korean Leader Kim Jong Un just stated that the "Nuclear Button is on his desk at all times." Will someone from his depleted and food starved regime please inform him that I too have a Nuclear Button but it is a much bigger & more powerful one than his and my Button works!

1/3/2018 0:49

I will be announcing THE MOST DISHONEST & CORRUPT MEDIA AWARDS OF THE YEAR on Monday at 5:00 o'clock. Subjects will cover Dishonesty & Bad Reporting in various categories from the Fake News Media. Stay tuned! **1/3/2018 1:05**

"President Trump has something now he didn't have a year ago that is a set of accomplishments that nobody can deny. The accomplishments are there look at his record he has had a very significant first year." @LouDobbs ShowDavid Asman & Ed Rollins **1/3/2018 4:03**

Such respect for the people of Iran as they try to take back their corrupt government. You will see great support from the United States at the appropriate time! **1/3/2018 13:37**

Stock Market had another good day but now that the Tax Cut Bill has passed we have tremendous upward potential. Dow just short of 25000 a number that few thought would be possible this soon into my administration. Also unemployment went down to 4.1%. Only getting better! **1/4/2018 2:11**

MAKE AMERICA GREAT AGAIN! **1/4/2018 2:13**

Many mostly Democrat States refused to hand over data from the 2016 Election to the Commission On Voter Fraud. They fought hard that the Commission not see their records or methods because they know that many people are voting illegally. System is rigged must go to Voter I.D. **1/4/2018 11:02**

As Americans you need identification sometimes in a very strong and accurate form for almost everything you do..... except when it comes to the most important thing VOTING for the people that run your country. Push hard for Voter Identification! **1/4/2018 11:11**

With all of the failed "experts" weighing in does anybody really believe that talks and dialogue would be going on between North and South Korea right now if I wasn't firm strong and willing to commit our total "might" against the North. Fools but talks are a good thing! **1/4/2018 11:32**

Dow just crashes through 25000. Congrats! Big cuts in unnecessary regulations continuing. **1/4/2018 15:48**

Thank you to the great Republican Senators who showed up to our mtg on immigration reform. We must BUILD THE WALL stop illegal immigration end chain migration & cancel the visa lottery. The current system is unsafe & unfair to the great people of our country - time for change! **1/4/2018 23:53**

MAKING AMERICA GREAT AGAIN!
https://t.co/iONbr1DkVk **1/5/2018 0:11**

I authorized Zero access to White House (actually turned him down many times) for author of phony book! I never spoke to him for book. Full of lies misrepresentations and sources that don't exist. Look at this guy's past and watch what happens to him and Sloppy Steve! **1/5/2018 3:52**

The Fake News Media barely mentions the fact that the Stock Market just hit another New Record and that business in the U.S. is booming...but the people know! Can you imagine if "O" was president and had these numbers - would be biggest story on earth! Dow now over 25000. **1/5/2018 4:04**

Dow goes from 18589 on November 9 2016 to 25075 today for a new all-time Record. Jumped 1000 points in last 5 weeks Record fastest 1000 point move in history. This is all about the Make America Great Again agenda! Jobs Jobs Jobs. Six trillion dollars in value created! **1/5/2018 11:35**

Well now that collusion with Russia is proving to be a total hoax and the only collusion is with Hillary Clinton and the FBI/Russia the Fake News Media (Mainstream) and this phony new book are hitting out at every new front imaginable. They should try winning an election. Sad! **1/5/2018 14:32**

Good idea Rand! https://t.co/55sqUDiC0s **1/6/2018 4:19**

Michael Wolff is a total loser who made up stories in order to sell this really boring and untruthful book. He used Sloppy Steve Bannon who cried when he got fired and begged for his job. Now Sloppy Steve has been dumped like a dog by almost everyone. Too bad! https://t.co/mEeUhk5ZV9 **1/6/2018 4:32**

The African American unemployment rate fell to 6.8% the lowest rate in 45 years. I am so happy about this News! And in the Washington Post (of all places) headline states "Trumps first year jobs numbers were very very good." **1/6/2018 11:49**

Brian Ross the reporter who made a fraudulent live newscast about me that drove the Stock Market down 350 points (billions of dollars) was suspended for a month but is now back at ABC NEWS in a lower capacity. He is no longer allowed to report on Trump. Should have been fired! **1/6/2018 11:57**

Now that Russian collusion after one year of intense study has proven to be a total hoax on the American public the Democrats and their lapdogs the Fake News Mainstream Media are taking out the old Ronald Reagan playbook and screaming mental stability and intelligence..... (1/3) **1/6/2018 12:19**

....Actually throughout my life my two greatest assets have been mental stability and being like really smart. Crooked Hillary Clinton also played these cards very hard and as everyone knows went down in flames. I went from VERY successful businessman to top T.V. Star..... (2/3) **1/6/2018 12:27**

....to President of the United States (on my first try). I think that would qualify as not smart but genius....and a very stable genius at that! (3/3) **1/6/2018 12:30**

I've had to put up with the Fake News from the first day I announced that I would be running for President. Now I have to put up with a Fake Book written by a totally discredited author. Ronald Reagan had the same problem and handled it well. So will I! **1/7/2018 14:40**

Jake Tapper of Fake News CNN just got destroyed in his interview with Stephen Miller of the Trump Administration. Watch the hatred and unfairness of this CNN flunky! **1/7/2018 15:15**

The Fake News Awards those going to the most corrupt & biased of the Mainstream Media will be presented to the losers on Wednesday January 17th rather than this coming Monday. The interest in and importance of these awards is far greater than anyone could have anticipated! **1/7/2018 20:35**

The Stock Market has been creating tremendous benefits for our country in the form of not only Record Setting

Stock Prices but present and future Jobs Jobs Jobs. Seven TRILLION dollars of value created since our big election win! **1/7/2018 20:42**

"His is turning out to be an enormously consequential presidency. So much so that despite my own frustration over his missteps there has never been a day when I wished Hillary Clinton were president. Not one. Indeed as Trump's accomplishments accumulate the mere thought of... (1/2) **1/8/2018 3:23**

...Clinton in the WH doubling down on Barack Obama's failed policies washes away any doubts that America made the right choice. This was truly a change election — and the changes Trump is bringing are far-reaching & necessary." Thank you Michael Goodwin! https://t.co/4fHNcx2Ydg (2/2) **1/8/2018 3:24**

African American unemployment is the lowest ever recorded in our country. The Hispanic unemployment rate dropped a full point in the last year and is close to the lowest in recorded history. Dems did nothing for you but get your vote! #NeverForget @foxandfriends **1/8/2018 14:20**

We are fighting for our farmers for our country and for our GREAT AMERICAN FLAG. We want our flag respected - and we want our NATIONAL ANTHEM respected also! https://t.co/16eOLXg6Fi **1/8/2018 23:19**

On behalf of the American people THANK YOU to our incredible law enforcement officers. As President of the United States - I will fight for you and I will never ever let you down. Now more than ever we must support the men and women in blue! #LawEnforcementAppreciationDay https://t.co/Qb4uxB4JRm **1/9/2018 17:11**

As I made very clear today our country needs the security of the Wall on the Southern Border which must be part of any DACA approval. **1/10/2018 0:16**

It just shows everyone how broken and unfair our Court System is when the opposing side in a case (such as DACA) always runs to the 9th Circuit and almost always wins before being reversed by higher courts. **1/10/2018 14:11**

The fact that Sneaky Dianne Feinstein who has on numerous occasions stated that collusion between Trump/Russia has not been found would release testimony in such an underhanded and possibly illegal way totally without authorization is a disgrace. Must have tough Primary! **1/10/2018 15:00**

The single greatest Witch Hunt in American history continues. There was no collusion everybody including the Dems knows there was no collusion & yet on and on it goes. Russia & the world is laughing at the stupidity they are witnessing. Republicans should finally take control! **1/10/2018 15:14**

Cutting taxes and simplifying regulations makes America the place to invest! Great news as Toyota and Mazda announce they are bringing 4000 JOBS and investing $1.6 BILLION in Alabama helping to further grow our economy! https://t.co/Kcg8IVH6iA **1/10/2018 23:37**

Good news: Toyota and Mazda announce giant new Huntsville Alabama plant which will produce over 300000 cars and SUV's a year and employ 4000 people. Companies are coming back to the U.S. in a very big way. Congratulations Alabama!
1/11/2018 4:29

In new Quinnipiac Poll 66% of people feel the economy is "Excellent or Good." That is the highest number ever recorded by this poll. **1/11/2018 11:43**

"45 year low in illegal immigration this year." @foxandfriends **1/11/2018 13:11**

Chrysler is moving a massive plant from Mexico to Michigan reversing a years long opposite trend. Thank you Chrysler a very wise decision. The voters in Michigan are very happy they voted for Trump/Pence. Plenty of more to follow! **1/12/2018 2:53**

Democrat Dianne Feinstein should never have released secret committee testimony to the public without authorization. Very disrespectful to committee members and possibly illegal. She blamed her poor decision on the fact she had a cold - a first! **1/12/2018 3:01**

The Democrats seem intent on having people and drugs pour into our country from the Southern Border risking thousands of lives in the process. It is my duty to protect the lives and safety of all Americans. We must build a Great Wall think Merit and end Lottery & Chain. USA! **1/12/2018 4:42**

Reason I canceled my trip to London is that I am not a big fan of the Obama Administration having sold perhaps the best located and finest embassy in London for "peanuts" only to build a new one in an off location for 1.2 billion dollars. Bad deal. Wanted me to cut ribbon-NO! **1/12/2018 4:57**

The so-called bipartisan DACA deal presented yesterday to myself and a group of Republican Senators and Congressmen was a big step backwards. Wall was not properly funded Chain & Lottery were made worse and USA would be forced to take large numbers of people from high crime..... (1/3) **1/12/2018 11:59**

....countries which are doing badly. I want a merit based system of immigration and people who will help take our country to the next level. I want safety and security for our people. I want to stop the massive inflow of drugs. I want to fund our military not do a Dem defund.... (2/3) **1/12/2018 12:09**

....Because of the Democrats not being interested in life and safety DACA has now taken a big step backwards. The Dems will threaten "shutdown" but what they are really doing is shutting down our military at a time we need it most. Get smart MAKE AMERICA GREAT AGAIN! (3/3) **1/12/2018 12:20**

The language used by me at the DACA meeting was tough but this was not the language used. What was really tough was the outlandish proposal made - a big setback for DACA! **1/12/2018 12:28**

Sadly Democrats want to stop paying our troops and government workers in order to give a sweetheart deal not a fair deal for DACA. Take care of our Military and our Country FIRST! **1/12/2018 12:50**

Never said anything derogatory about Haitians other than Haiti is obviously a very poor and troubled country. Never said "take them out." Made up by Dems. I have a wonderful relationship with Haitians. Probably should record future meetings - unfortunately no trust! **1/12/2018 13:48**

Today it was my great honor to proclaim January 15 2018 as Martin Luther King Jr. Federal Holiday. I encourage all Americans to observe this day with appropriate civic community and service activities in honor of Dr. King's life and legacy. https://t.co/samlJsz1Nt **1/12/2018 17:56**

Yesterday was a big day for the stock market. Jobs are coming back to America. Chrysler is coming back to the USA from Mexico and many others will follow. Tax cut money to employees is pouring into our economy with many more companies announcing. American business is hot again! **1/13/2018 13:13**

The Democrats are all talk and no action. They are doing nothing to fix DACA. Great opportunity missed. Too bad! **1/13/2018 13:14**

AMERICA FIRST! **1/13/2018 13:14**

I don't believe the Democrats really want to see a deal on DACA. They are all talk and no action. This is the time but day by day they are blowing the one great opportunity they have. Too bad! **1/13/2018 14:20**

So much Fake News is being reported. They don't even try to get it right or correct it when they are wrong. They promote the Fake Book of a mentally deranged author who knowingly writes false information. The Mainstream Media is crazed that WE won the election! **1/13/2018 22:08**

The Wall Street Journal stated falsely that I said to them "I have a good relationship with Kim Jong Un" (of N. Korea). Obviously I didn't say that. I said "I'd have a good relationship with Kim Jong Un" a big difference. Fortunately we now record conversations with reporters… (1/2) **1/14/2018 12:58**

…and they knew exactly what I said and meant. They just wanted a story. FAKE NEWS! (2/2) **1/14/2018 13:01**

DACA is probably dead because the Democrats don't really want it they just want to talk and take desperately needed money away from our Military. **1/14/2018 13:09**

I as President want people coming into our Country who are going to help us become strong and great again people coming in through a system based on MERIT. No more Lotteries! #AMERICA FIRST

1/14/2018 13:19

"President Trump is not getting the credit he deserves for the economy. Tax Cut bonuses to more than 2000000 workers. Most explosive Stock Market rally that we've seen in modern times. 18000 to 26000 from Election and grounded in profitability and growth. All Trump not O… (1/2) **1/14/2018 13:50**

…big unnecessary regulation cuts made it all possible" (among many other things). "President Trump reversed the policies of President Obama and reversed our economic decline." Thank you Stuart Varney. @ foxandfriends (2/2) **1/14/2018 13:59**

Statement by me last night in Florida: "Honestly I don't think the Democrats want to make a deal. They talk about DACA but they don't want to help..We are ready willing and able to make a deal but they don't want to. They don't want security at the border they don't want..... (1/2) **1/15/2018 12:57**

...to stop drugs they want to take money away from our military which we cannot do." My standard is very simple AMERICA FIRST & MAKE AMERICA GREAT AGAIN! (2/2) **1/15/2018 13:02**

Senator Dicky Durbin totally misrepresented what was said at the DACA meeting. Deals can't get made when there is no trust! Durbin blew DACA and is hurting our Military. **1/15/2018 20:28**

We must have Security at our VERY DANGEROUS SOUTHERN BORDER and we must have a great WALL to help protect us and to help stop the massive inflow of drugs pouring into our country! **1/16/2018 13:54**

The Democrats want to shut down the Government over Amnesty for all and Border Security. The biggest loser will be our rapidly rebuilding Military at a time we need it more than ever. We need a merit based system of immigration and we need it now! No more dangerous Lottery. **1/16/2018 14:07**

Do you notice the Fake News Mainstream Media never likes covering the great and record setting economic news but rather talks about anything negative or that can be turned into the negative. The Russian Collusion Hoax is dead except as it pertains to the Dems. Public gets it! **1/16/2018 14:19**

Unemployment for Black Americans is the lowest ever recorded. Trump approval ratings with Black Americans has doubled. Thank you and it will get even (much) better! @ FoxNews **1/16/2018 14:30**

New report from DOJ & DHS shows that nearly 3 in 4 individuals convicted of terrorism-related charges are foreign-born. We have submitted to Congress a list of resources and reforms.... **1/16/2018 23:19**

I promised that my policies would allow companies like Apple to bring massive amounts of money back to the United States. Great to see Apple follow through as a result of TAX CUTS. Huge win for American workers and the USA! https://t.co/OwXVUyLOb1 **1/17/2018 23:28**

During the campaign I promised to MAKE AMERICA GREAT AGAIN by bringing businesses and jobs back to our country. I am very proud to see companies like Chrysler moving operations from Mexico to Michigan where there are so many great American workers! https://t.co/hz2q9UTfnF **1/17/2018 23:32**

Despite some very corrupt and dishonest media coverage there are many great reporters I respect and lots of GOOD NEWS for the American people to be proud of! **1/18/2018 1:05**

ISIS is in retreat our economy is booming investments and jobs are pouring back into the country and so much more! Together there is nothing we can't overcome--even a very biased media. We ARE Making America Great Again!
1/18/2018 1:11

The Wall is the Wall it has never changed or evolved from the first day I conceived of it. Parts will be of necessity see through and it was never intended to be built in areas where there is natural protection such as mountains wastelands or tough rivers or water..... (1/2) **1/18/2018 11:15**

....The Wall will be paid for directly or indirectly or through longer term reimbursement by Mexico which has a ridiculous $71 billion dollar trade surplus with the

U.S. The $20 billion dollar Wall is "peanuts" compared to what Mexico makes from the U.S. NAFTA is a bad joke! (2/2) **1/18/2018 11:25**

Will be going to Pennsylvania today in order to give my total support to RICK SACCONE running for Congress in a Special Election (March 13). Rick is a great guy. We need more Republicans to continue our already successful agenda! **1/18/2018 12:53**

We need the Wall for the safety and security of our country. We need the Wall to help stop the massive inflow of drugs from Mexico now rated the number one most dangerous country in the world. If there is no Wall there is no Deal! **1/18/2018 13:16**

A government shutdown will be devastating to our military... something the Dems care very little about! **1/18/2018 13:49**

AMERICA will once again be a NATION that thinks big dreams bigger and always reaches for the stars. YOU are the ones who will shape America's destiny. YOU are the ones who will restore our prosperity. And YOU are the ones who are MAKING AMERICA GREAT AGAIN! #MAGA https://t.co/f2abNK47Il **1/18/2018 21:04**

House of Representatives needs to pass Government Funding Bill tonight. So important for our country - our Military needs it! **1/18/2018 23:39**

Government Funding Bill past last night in the House of Representatives. Now Democrats are needed if it is to pass in the Senate - but they want illegal immigration and weak borders. Shutdown coming? We need more Republican victories in 2018! **1/19/2018 12:04**

Today I was honored and proud to address the 45th Annual @March_for_Life! You are living witnesses of this year's March for Life theme: #LoveSavesLives. https://t.co/DMST4qhDmp **1/19/2018 18:39**

Just signed 702 Bill to reauthorize foreign intelligence collection. This is NOT the same FISA law that was so wrongly abused during the election. I will always do the right thing for our country and put the safety of the American people first! **1/19/2018 20:53**

Not looking good for our great Military or Safety & Security on the very dangerous Southern Border. Dems want a Shutdown in order to help diminish the great success of the Tax Cuts and what they are doing for our booming economy. **1/20/2018 2:28**

Democrats are far more concerned with Illegal Immigrants than they are with our great Military or Safety at our dangerous Southern Border. They could have easily made a deal but decided to play Shutdown politics instead. #WeNeedMoreRepublicansIn18 in order to power through mess! **1/20/2018 11:17**

This is the One Year Anniversary of my Presidency and the Democrats wanted to give me a nice present. #DemocratShutdown **1/20/2018 11:33**

For those asking the Republicans only have 51 votes in the Senate and they need 60. That is why we need to win more Republicans in 2018 Election! We can then be even tougher on Crime (and Border) and even better to our Military & Veterans! **1/20/2018 11:44**

#AMERICA FIRST! **1/20/2018 11:47**

Democrats are holding our Military hostage over their desire to have unchecked illegal immigration. Can't let that happen! **1/20/2018 14:27**

Beautiful weather all over our great country a perfect day for all Women to March. Get out there now to celebrate the historic milestones and unprecedented economic success and wealth creation that has taken place over the last 12 months. Lowest female unemployment in 18 years! **1/20/2018 18:51**

Unprecedented success for our Country in so many ways since the Election. Record Stock Market Strong on Military Crime Borders & ISIS Judicial Strength & Numbers Lowest Unemployment for Women & ALL Massive Tax Cuts end of Individual Mandate - and so much more. Big 2018! **1/20/2018 22:31**

The Trump Administration has terminated more UNNECESSARY Regulation in just twelve months than any other Administration has terminated during their full term in office no matter what the length. The good news is THERE IS MUCH MORE TO COME! **1/21/2018 0:47**

Great to see how hard Republicans are fighting for our Military and Safety at the Border. The Dems just want illegal immigrants to pour into our nation unchecked. If stalemate continues Republicans should go to 51% (Nuclear Option) and vote on real long term budget no C.R.'s!

1/21/2018 12:35

Thank you to Brad Blakeman on @FoxNews for grading year one of my presidency with an "A"-and likewise to Doug Schoen for the very good grade and statements. Working hard! **1/22/2018 1:21**

The Democrats are turning down services and security for citizens in favor of services and security for non-citizens. Not good! **1/22/2018 13:07**

Democrats have shut down our government in the interests of their far left base. They don't want to do it but are powerless! **1/22/2018 13:15**

End the Democrats Obstruction! https://t.co/tzBXilvW1b **1/22/2018 15:13**

Big win for Republicans as Democrats cave on Shutdown. Now I want a big win for everyone including Republicans Democrats and DACA but especially for our Great Military and Border Security. Should be able to get there. See you at the negotiating table! **1/23/2018 4:30**

Even Crazy Jim Acosta of Fake News CNN agrees: "Trump World and WH sources dancing in end zone: Trump wins again...Schumer and Dems caved...gambled and lost." Thank you for your honesty Jim! **1/23/2018 11:31**

In one of the biggest stories in a long time the FBI now says it is missing five months worth of lovers Strzok-Page texts perhaps 50000 and all in prime time. Wow! **1/23/2018 11:55**

Nobody knows for sure that the Republicans & Democrats will be able to reach a deal on DACA by February 8 but everyone will be trying....with a big additional focus put on Military Strength and Border Security. The Dems have just learned that a Shutdown is not the answer! **1/23/2018 13:34**

Thank you to General John Kelly who is doing a fantastic job and all of the Staff and others in the White House for a job well done. Long hours and Fake reporting makes your job more difficult but it is always great to WIN and few have won more than us! **1/23/2018 14:16**

Where are the 50000 important text messages between FBI lovers Lisa Page and Peter Strzok? Blaming Samsung! **1/24/2018 3:54**

Cryin' Chuck Schumer fully understands especially after his humiliating defeat that if there is no Wall there is no DACA. We must have safety and security together with a strong Military for our great people! **1/24/2018 4:07**

Tremendous investment by companies from all over the world being made in America. There has never been anything like it. Now Disney J.P. Morgan Chase and many others. Massive Regulation Reduction and Tax Cuts are making us a powerhouse again. Long way to go! Jobs Jobs Jobs! **1/24/2018 11:58**

Earlier today I spoke with @GovMattBevin of Kentucky regarding yesterday's shooting at Marshall County High School. My thoughts and prayers are with Bailey Holt Preston Cope their families and all of the wounded victims who are in recovery. We are with you! **1/24/2018 20:26**

Will soon be heading to Davos Switzerland to tell the world how great America is and is doing. Our economy is now booming and with all I am doing will only get better...Our country is finally WINNING again! **1/25/2018 0:27**

Today Americans everywhere remember the brave men and women of @NASA who lost their lives in our Nation's eternal quest to expand the boundaries of human potential. https://t.co/clBsJTGz8B https://t.co/jTJkusdBQA **1/25/2018 22:38**

Heading back from a very exciting two days in Davos Switzerland. Speech on America's economic revival was well received. Many of the people I met will be investing in the U.S.A.! #MAGA **1/26/2018 17:12**

DACA has been made increasingly difficult by the fact that Cryin' Chuck Schumer took such a beating over the shutdown that he is unable to act on immigration! **1/26/2018 17:16**

Thank you to Brandon Judd of the National Border Patrol Council for his strong statement on @foxandfriends that we very badly NEED THE WALL. Must also end loophole of "catch & release" and clean up the legal and other procedures at the border NOW for Safety & Security reasons. **1/27/2018 11:55**

On Holocaust Remembrance Day we mourn and grieve the murder of 6 million innocent Jewish men women and children and the millions of others who perished in the evil Nazi Genocide. We pledge with all of our might and resolve: Never Again! https://t.co/PfHM7UiZOC https://t.co/25W0SZHTOu **1/27/2018 19:30**

Taliban targeted innocent Afghans brave police in Kabul today. Our thoughts and prayers go to the victims and first responders. We will not allow the Taliban to win!

1/27/2018 22:59

I have offered DACA a wonderful deal including a doubling in the number of recipients & a twelve year pathway to citizenship for two reasons: (1) Because the Republicans want to fix a long time terrible problem. (2) To show that Democrats do not want to solve DACA only use it!

1/28/2018 3:58

Democrats are not interested in Border Safety & Security or in the funding and rebuilding of our Military. They are only interested in Obstruction! **1/28/2018 4:08**

Somebody please inform Jay-Z that because of my policies Black Unemployment has just been reported to be at the LOWEST RATE EVER RECORDED!

1/28/2018 13:18

Our economy is better than it has been in many decades. Businesses are coming back to America like never before. Chrysler as an example is leaving Mexico and coming back to the USA. Unemployment is nearing record lows. We are on the right track! **1/28/2018 13:18**

Congratulations to America's new Secretary of @HHSGov Alex Azar! https://t.co/Y9inQaCt7o **1/29/2018 20:12**

Heading to beautiful West Virginia to be with great members of the Republican Party. Will be planning Infrastructure and discussing Immigration and DACA not easy when we have no support from the Democrats. NOT ONE DEM VOTED FOR OUR TAX CUT BILL! Need more Republicans in '18. **2/1/2018 11:43**

March 5th is rapidly approaching and the Democrats are doing nothing about DACA. They Resist Blame Complain and Obstruct - and do nothing. Start pushing Nancy Pelosi and the Dems to work out a DACA fix NOW! **2/1/2018 11:51**

Thank you for all of the nice compliments and reviews on the State of the Union speech. 45.6 million people watched the highest number in history. @FoxNews beat every other Network for the first time ever with 11.7 million people tuning in. Delivered from the heart! **2/1/2018 12:02**

The Democrats just aren't calling about DACA. Nancy Pelosi and Chuck Schumer have to get moving fast or they'll disappoint you again. We have a great chance to make a deal or blame the Dems! March 5th is coming up fast. **2/2/2018 3:32**

The top Leadership and Investigators of the FBI and the Justice Department have politicized the sacred investigative process in favor of Democrats and against Republicans - something which would have been unthinkable just a short time ago. Rank & File are great people! **2/2/2018 11:33**

"You had Hillary Clinton and the Democratic Party try to hide the fact that they gave money to GPS Fusion to create a Dossier which was used by their allies in the Obama Administration to convince a Court misleadingly by all accounts to spy on the Trump Team." Tom Fitton JW

2/2/2018 11:49

With 3.5 million Americans receiving bonuses or other benefits from their employers as a result of TAX CUTS 2018 is off to great start! ✅ Unemployment rate at 4.1%. ✅ Average earnings up 2.9% in the last year. ✅ 200000 new American jobs.✅ #MAGA https://t.co/upqSvBhRqJ

2/2/2018 18:05

Rasmussen just announced that my approval rating jumped to 49% a far better number than I had in winning the Election and higher than certain "sacred cows." Other Trump polls are way up also. So why does the media refuse to write this? Oh well someday! **2/3/2018 14:40**

This memo totally vindicates "Trump" in probe. But the Russian Witch Hunt goes on and on. Their was no Collusion and there was no Obstruction (the word now used because after one year of looking endlessly and finding NOTHING collusion is dead). This is an American disgrace! **2/3/2018 14:40**

Great jobs numbers and finally after many years rising wages- and nobody even talks about them. Only Russia Russia Russia despite the fact that after a year of looking there is No Collusion! **2/4/2018 0:26**

"The four page memo released Friday reports the disturbing fact about how the FBI and FISA appear to have been used to influence the 2016 election and its aftermath....The FBI failed to inform the FISA court that the Clinton campaign had funded the dossier....the FBI became.... **2/4/2018 0:40**

...a tool of anti-Trump political actors. This is unacceptable in a democracy and ought to alarm anyone who wants the FBI to be a nonpartisan enforcer of the law....The FBI wasn't straight with Congress as it hid most of these facts from investigators." Wall Street Journal **2/4/2018 0:53**

My thoughts and prayers are with all of the victims involved in this mornings train collision in South Carolina. Thank you to our incredible First Responders for the work they've done! **2/4/2018 16:58**

Congratulations to the Philadelphia Eagles on a great Super Bowl victory! **2/5/2018 3:54**

The Democrats are pushing for Universal HealthCare while thousands of people are marching in the UK because their U system is going broke and not working. Dems want to greatly raise taxes for really bad and non-personal medical care. No thanks! **2/5/2018 12:11**

Thank you to @foxandfriends for exposing the truth. Perhaps that's why your ratings are soooo much better than your untruthful competition! **2/5/2018 12:17**

Little Adam Schiff who is desperate to run for higher office is one of the biggest liars and leakers in Washington right up there with Comey Warner Brennan and Clapper! Adam leaves closed committee hearings to illegally leak confidential information. Must be stopped! **2/5/2018 12:39**

Any deal on DACA that does not include STRONG border security and the desperately needed WALL is a total waste of time. March 5th is rapidly approaching and the Dems seem not to care about DACA. Make a deal! **2/5/2018 14:36**

Representative Devin Nunes a man of tremendous courage and grit may someday be recognized as a Great American Hero for what he has exposed and what he has had to endure! **2/5/2018 15:08**

Thanks to the historic TAX CUTS that I signed into law your paychecks are going way UP your taxes are going way DOWN and America is once again OPEN FOR BUSINESS! https://t.co/GISFbDDGXX **2/5/2018 20:42**

So disgraceful that a person illegally in our country killed @Colts linebacker Edwin Jackson. This is just one of many such preventable tragedies. We must get the Dems to get tough on the Border and with illegal immigration FAST! **2/6/2018 13:32**

My prayers and best wishes are with the family of Edwin Jackson a wonderful young man whose life was so senselessly taken. @Colts **2/6/2018 13:37**

Polling shows nearly 7 in 10 Americans support an immigration reform package that includes DACA fully secures the border ends chain migration & cancels the visa lottery. If D's oppose this deal they aren't serious about DACA-they just want open borders. https://t.co/XDMcDOr9vM **2/6/2018 16:00**

We need a 21st century MERIT-BASED immigration system. Chain migration and the visa lottery are outdated programs that hurt our economic and national security. https://t.co/rP9Gtr2E5N **2/6/2018 16:05**

HAPPY BIRTHDAY to our 40th President of the United States of America Ronald Reagan! https://t.co/JtEglBhm4c **2/7/2018 0:48**

Congratulations @ElonMusk and @ SpaceX on the successful #FalconHeavy launch. This achievement along with @ NASA's commercial and international partners continues to show American ingenuity at its best! https://t.co/ eZfLSpyJPK

2/7/2018 3:05

In the "old days" when good news was reported the Stock Market would go up. Today when good news is reported the Stock Market goes down. Big mistake and we have so much good (great) news about the economy! **2/7/2018 14:59**

NEW FBI TEXTS ARE BOMBSHELLS! **2/7/2018 16:10**

The Budget Agreement today is so important for our great Military. It ends the dangerous sequester and gives Secretary Mattis what he needs to keep America Great. Republicans and Democrats must support our troops and support this Bill! **2/7/2018 22:36**

Will be heading over shortly to make remarks at The National Prayer Breakfast in Washington. Great religious and political leaders and many friends including T.V. producer Mark Burnett of our wonderful 14 season Apprentice triumph will be there. Looking forward to seeing all! **2/8/2018 11:08**

Our founders invoked our Creator four times in the Declaration of Independence. Our currency declares "IN GOD WE TRUST." And we place our hands on our hearts as we recite the Pledge of Allegiance and proclaim that we are "One Nation Under God." #NationalPrayerBreakfast https://t.co/zukP40Ezpo **2/8/2018 17:13**

As long as we open our eyes to God's grace - and open our hearts to God's love - then America will forever be the land of the free the home of the brave and a light unto all nations. #NationalPrayerBreakfast https://t.co/1cwxs3l0uK **2/8/2018 20:10**

Time to end the visa lottery. Congress must secure the immigration system and protect Americans. https://t.co/yukxm48x9X **2/8/2018 23:26**

Wow! -Senator Mark Warner got caught having extensive contact with a lobbyist for a Russian oligarch. Warner did not want a "paper trail" on a "private" meeting (in London) he requested with Steele of fraudulent Dossier fame. All tied into Crooked Hillary. **2/9/2018 3:22**

Just signed Bill. Our Military will now be stronger than ever before. We love and need our Military and gave them everything — and more. First time this has happened in a long time. Also means JOBS JOBS JOBS! **2/9/2018 13:39**

Without more Republicans in Congress we were forced to increase spending on things we do not like or want in order to finally after many years of depletion take care of our Military. Sadly we needed some Dem votes for passage. Must elect more Republicans in 2018 Election! **2/9/2018 13:47**

Costs on non-military lines will never come down if we do not elect more Republicans in the 2018 Election and beyond. This Bill is a BIG VICTORY for our Military but much waste in order to get Dem votes. Fortunately DACA not included in this Bill negotiations to start now! **2/9/2018 13:59**

The Democrats sent a very political and long response memo which they knew because of sources and methods (and more) would have to be heavily redacted whereupon they would blame the White House for lack of transparency. Told them to re-do and send back in proper form! **2/10/2018 14:20**

According to the @nytimes a Russian sold phony secrets on "Trump" to the U.S. Asking price was $10 million brought down to $1 million to be paid over time. I hope people are now seeing & understanding what is going on here. It is all now starting to come out - DRAIN THE SWAMP! **2/10/2018 15:20**

Peoples lives are being shattered and destroyed by a mere allegation. Some are true and some are false. Some are old and some are new. There is no recovery for someone falsely accused - life and career are gone. Is there no such thing any longer as Due Process? **2/10/2018 15:33**

"My view is that not only has Trump been vindicated in the last several weeks about the mishandling of the Dossier and the lies about the Clinton/DNC Dossier it shows that he's been victimized. He's been victimized by the Obama Administration who were using all sorts of....... **2/10/2018 18:16**

Republicans want to fix DACA far more than the Democrats do. The Dems had all three branches of government back in 2008-2011 and they decided not to do anything about DACA. They only want to use it as a campaign issue. Vote Republican! **2/10/2018 18:50**

My thoughts and prayers are with the two police officers their families and everybody at the @WestervillePD. https://t.co/AoingY77Ky **2/10/2018 21:18**

My Administration has identified three major priorities for creating a safe modern and lawful immigration system: fully securing the border ending chain migration and canceling the visa lottery. Congress must secure the immigration system and protect Americans. https://t.co/xV1lgfhjBU **2/10/2018 23:34**

So many positive things going on for the U.S.A. and the Fake News Media just doesn't want to go there. Same negative stories over and over again! No wonder the People no longer trust the media whose approval ratings are correctly at their lowest levels in history! #MAGA **2/11/2018 18:21**

4.2 million hard working Americans have already received a large Bonus and/or Pay Increase because of our recently Passed Tax Cut & Jobs Bill....and it will only get better! We are far ahead of schedule. **2/11/2018 19:15**

Rep. Lou Barletta a Great Republican from Pennsylvania who was one of my very earliest supporters will make a FANTASTIC Senator. He is strong & smart loves Pennsylvania & loves our Country! Voted for Tax Cuts unlike Bob Casey who listened to Tax Hikers Pelosi and Schumer! **2/11/2018 20:26**

This will be a big week for Infrastructure. After so stupidly spending $7 trillion in the Middle East it is now time to start investing in OUR Country! **2/12/2018 12:46**

Thank you to Sue Kruczek who lost her wonderful and talented son Nick to the Opioid scourge for your kind words while on @foxandfriends. We are fighting this terrible epidemic hard - Nick will not have died in vain! **2/12/2018 12:54**

Our infrastructure plan has been put forward and has received great reviews by everyone except of course the Democrats. After many years we have taken care of our Military now we have to fix our roads bridges tunnels airports and more. Bipartisan make deal Dems? **2/13/2018 10:43**

Negotiations on DACA have begun. Republicans want to make a deal and Democrats say they want to make a deal. Wouldn't it be great if we could finally after so many years solve the DACA puzzle. This will be our last chance there will never be another opportunity! March 5th. **2/13/2018 10:52**

My prayers and condolences to the families of the victims of the terrible Florida shooting. No child teacher or anyone else should ever feel unsafe in an American school.

2/14/2018 20:50

Just spoke to Governor Rick Scott. We are working closely with law enforcement on the terrible Florida school shooting. **2/14/2018 20:55**

So many signs that the Florida shooter was mentally disturbed even expelled from school for bad and erratic behavior. Neighbors and classmates knew he was a big problem. Must always report such instances to authorities again and again! **2/15/2018 12:12**

While the Republicans and Democrats in Congress are working hard to come up with a solution to DACA they should be strongly considering a system of Merit Based Immigration so that we will have the people ready willing and able to help all of those companies moving into the USA! **2/15/2018 14:57**

In times of tragedy the bonds that sustain us are those of family faith community and country. These bonds are stronger than the forces of hatred and evil - and these bonds grow even stronger in the hours of our greatest need. https://t.co/bu14Onscez https://t.co/OoTXMCSexB **2/15/2018 17:33**

I will be leaving for Florida today to meet with some of the bravest people on earth - but people whose lives have been totally shattered. Am also working with Congress on many fronts. **2/16/2018 14:37**

Cannot believe how BADLY DACA recipients have been treated by the Democrats...totally abandoned! Republicans are still working hard. **2/16/2018 14:49**

Russia started their anti-US campaign in 2014 long before I announced that I would run for President. The results of the election were not impacted. The Trump campaign did nothing wrong - no collusion! **2/16/2018 20:18**

Our entire Nation w/one heavy heart continues to pray for the victims & their families in Parkland FL. To teachers law enforcement first responders & medical professionals who responded so bravely in the face of danger: We THANK YOU for your courage! https://t.co/3yJsrebZMG https://t.co/ti791dENTy **2/17/2018 4:53**

Melania and I met such incredible people last night in Broward County Florida. Will never forget them or the evening! **2/17/2018 19:04**

Deputy A.G. Rod Rosenstein stated at the News Conference: "There is no allegation in the indictment that any American was a knowing participant in this illegal activity. There is no allegation in the indictment that the charged conduct altered the outcome of the 2016 election. **2/17/2018 19:36**

Funny how the Fake News Media doesn't want to say that the Russian group was formed in 2014 long before my run for President. Maybe they knew I was going to run even though I didn't know! **2/17/2018 19:46**

Just like they don't want to solve the DACA problem why didn't the Democrats pass gun control legislation when they had both the House & Senate during the Obama Administration. Because they didn't want to and now they just talk! **2/17/2018 23:45**

Very sad that the FBI missed all of the many signals sent out by the Florida school shooter. This is not acceptable. They are spending too much time trying to prove Russian collusion with the Trump campaign - there is no collusion. Get back to the basics and make us all proud! **2/18/2018 4:08**

General McMaster forgot to say that the results of the 2016 election were not impacted or changed by the

Russians and that the only Collusion was between Russia and Crooked H the DNC and the Dems. Remember the Dirty Dossier Uranium Speeches Emails and the Podesta Company! **2/18/2018 4:22**

Never gotten over the fact that Obama was able to send $1.7 Billion Dollars in CASH to Iran and nobody in Congress the FBI or Justice called for an investigation! **2/18/2018 12:02**

Finally Liddle' Adam Schiff the leakin' monster of no control is now blaming the Obama Administration for Russian meddling in the 2016 Election. He is finally right about something. Obama was President knew of the threat and did nothing. Thank you Adam! **2/18/2018 12:22**

I never said Russia did not meddle in the election I said "it may be Russia or China or another country or group or it may be a 400 pound genius sitting in bed and playing with his computer." The Russian "hoax" was that the Trump campaign colluded with Russia - it never did! **2/18/2018 12:33**

Now that Adam Schiff is starting to blame President Obama for Russian meddling in the election he is probably doing so as yet another excuse that the Democrats lead by their fearless leader Crooked Hillary Clinton lost the 2016 election. But wasn't I a great candidate? **2/18/2018 12:43**

If it was the GOAL of Russia to create discord disruption and chaos within the U.S. then with all of the Committee Hearings Investigations and Party hatred they have succeeded beyond their wildest dreams. They are laughing their asses off in Moscow. Get smart America! **2/18/2018 13:11**

Great Pollster John McLaughlin now has the GOP up in the Generic Congressional Ballot. Big gain over last 4 weeks. I guess people are loving the big Tax Cuts given them by the Republicans the Cuts the Dems want to take away. We need more Republicans! **2/18/2018 13:55**

My great friends from NASCAR are having their big race today The Daytona 500. Brian France and the France family are special people. Enjoy the race! **2/18/2018 19:13**

Just watched a very insecure Oprah Winfrey who at one point I knew very well interview a panel of people on 60 Minutes. The questions were biased and slanted the facts incorrect. Hope Oprah runs so she can be exposed and defeated just like all of the others! **2/19/2018 4:28**

Have a great but very reflective President's Day! **2/19/2018 13:42**

Obama was President up to and beyond the 2016 Election. So why didn't he do something about Russian meddling? **2/19/2018 19:55**

The U.S. economy is looking very good in my opinion even better than anticipated. Companies are pouring back into our country reversing the long term trend of leaving. The unemployment numbers are looking great and Regulations & Taxes have been massively Cut! JOBS JOBS JOBS **2/20/2018 2:29**

....The President Obama quote just before election. That's because he thought Crooked Hillary was going to win and he didn't want to "rock the boat." When I easily won the Electoral College the whole game changed and the Russian excuse became the narrative of the Dems. **2/20/2018 12:46**

A woman I don't know and to the best of my knowledge never met is on the FRONT PAGE of the Fake News Washington Post saying I kissed her (for two minutes yet) in the lobby of Trump Tower 12 years ago. Never happened! Who would do this in a public space with live security...... **2/20/2018 15:16**

Bad ratings @CNN & @MSNBC got scammed when they covered the anti-Trump Russia rally wall-to-wall. They probably knew it was Fake News but because it was a rally against me they pushed it hard anyway. Two really dishonest newscasters but the public is wise! **2/21/2018 1:08**

So true thank you! https://t.co/9TTXlfokYz **2/21/2018 1:14**

The GREAT Billy Graham is dead. There was nobody like him! He will be missed by Christians and all religions. A very special man. **2/21/2018 14:22**

Question: If all of the Russian meddling took place during the Obama Administration right up to January 20th why aren't they the subject of the investigation? Why didn't Obama do something about the meddling? Why aren't Dem crimes under investigation? Ask Jeff Sessions! **2/21/2018 14:40**

.@FLOTUS Melania and I join millions of people around the world in mourning the passing of Billy Graham. Our prayers are with his children grandchildren great-grandchildren and all who worked closely with Reverend Graham in his lifelong ministry. https://t.co/e1697tcyal **2/21/2018 21:12**

I will always remember the time I spent today with courageous students teachers and families. So much love in the midst of so much pain. We must not let them down. We must keep our children safe!!Full Listening Session: https://t.co/x5VenyQX5p https://t.co/CAPfX5odlp **2/22/2018 1:40**

I never said "give teachers guns" like was stated on Fake News @CNN & @NBC. What I said was to look at the possibility of giving "concealed guns to gun adept teachers with military or special training experience - only the best. 20% of teachers a lot would now be able to **2/22/2018 12:26**

....immediately fire back if a savage sicko came to a school with bad intentions. Highly trained teachers would also serve as a deterrent to the cowards that do this. Far more assets at much less cost than guards. A "gun free" school is a magnet for bad people. ATTACKS WOULD END! **2/22/2018 12:40**

....History shows that a school shooting lasts on average 3 minutes. It takes police & first responders approximately 5 to 8 minutes to get to site of crime. Highly trained gun adept teachers/coaches would solve the problem instantly before police arrive. GREAT DETERRENT! **2/22/2018 12:54**

....If a potential "sicko shooter" knows that a school has a large number of very weapons talented teachers (and others) who will be instantly shooting the sicko will NEVER attack that school. Cowards won't go there... problem solved. Must be offensive defense alone won't work! **2/22/2018 13:05**

I will be strongly pushing Comprehensive Background Checks with an emphasis on Mental Health. Raise age to 21 and end sale of Bump Stocks! Congress is in a mood to finally do something on this issue - I hope!

2/22/2018 13:13

What many people don't understand or don't want to understand is that Wayne Chris and the folks who work so hard at the @NRA are Great People and Great American Patriots. They love our Country and will do the right thing. MAKE AMERICA GREAT AGAIN! **2/22/2018 14:31**

Will be meeting with Lawmakers today at 11:30 A.M. to discuss School Safety. Next week it will be with our Nation's Governors. It's been many years of all talk no action. We'll get it done! **2/22/2018 14:53**

On behalf of an entire Nation CONGRATULATIONS to the U.S. Women's Hockey Team on winning the GOLD! #GoTeamUSA #Olympics https://t.co/3cUZwLVGua

2/22/2018 16:29

Today it was my great honor to host a School Safety Roundtable at the @WhiteHouse with State and local leaders law enforcement officers and education officials. There is nothing more important than protecting our children. They deserve to be safe and we will deliver! https://t.co/WhC2AxgWXO **2/22/2018 20:07**

"School shooting survivor says he quit @CNN Town Hall after refusing scripted question." @TuckerCarlson. Just like so much of CNN Fake News. That's why their ratings are so bad! MSNBC may be worse. **2/23/2018 1:26**

MS-13 gang members are being removed by our Great ICE and Border Patrol Agents by the thousands but these killers come back in from El Salvador and through Mexico like water. El Salvador just takes our money and Mexico must help MORE with this problem. We need The Wall! **2/23/2018 11:28**

My daughter Ivanka just arrived in South Korea. We cannot have a better or smarter person representing our country. **2/23/2018 13:07**

For those of you who are still interested the Democrats have totally forgotten about DACA. Not a lot of interest on this subject from them! **2/23/2018 13:09**

Our nation's motto is IN GOD WE TRUST. This week our nation lost an incredible leader who devoted his life to helping us understand what those words really mean. We will never forget the historic crowds the voice the energy and the profound faith of Billy Graham! #CPAC2018 https://t.co/5GDh7Jonkv **2/23/2018 17:12**

Thank you to the great men and women of the United States @SecretService for a job well done! **2/23/2018 22:46**

Armed Educators (and trusted people who work within a school) love our students and will protect them. Very smart people. Must be firearms adept & have annual training. Should get yearly bonus. Shootings will not happen again - a big & very inexpensive deterrent. Up to States. **2/24/2018 18:54**

Dems are no longer talking DACA! "Out of sight out of mind" they say. DACA beneficiaries should not be happy. Nancy Pelosi truly doesn't care about them. Republicans stand ready to make a deal! **2/24/2018 21:18**

BIG CPAC STRAW POLL RESULTS: 93% APPROVE OF THE JOB PRESIDENT TRUMP IS DOING (Thank you!). 50% say President Trump should Tweet MORE or SAME (funny!). 79% say Republicans in Congress should do a better job of working with President Trump (starting to happen). **2/24/2018 22:26**

The Democrat memo response on government surveillance abuses is a total political and legal BUST. Just confirms all of the terrible things that were done. SO ILLEGAL! **2/24/2018 23:16**

"We've seen NO EVIDENCE OF COLLUSION....I have seen nothing the firing of James Comey and all of the aftermath that suggests that the President has obstructed justice because he's exercising his power as the President of the U.S. I just don't see it." Judge Ken Starr **2/27/2018 12:45**

WITCH HUNT! **2/27/2018 12:49**

I want to encourage all of my many Texas friends to vote in the primary for Governor Greg Abbott Senator Ted Cruz Lt. Gov. Dan Patrick and Attorney General Ken Paxton. They are helping me to Make America Great Again! Vote early or on March 6th. **2/27/2018 18:11**

Big legal win today. U.S. judge sided with the Trump Administration and rejected the attempt to stop the government from building a great Border Wall on the Southern Border. Now this important project can go forward! **2/28/2018 4:28**

The Heritage Foundation has just stated that 64% of the Trump Agenda is already done faster than even Ronald Reagan. "We're blown away" said Thomas Binion of Heritage President Trump "is very active very conservative and very effective. Huge volume & spectrum of issues." **2/28/2018 12:02**

I have decided that sections of the Wall that California wants built NOW will not be built until the whole Wall is approved. Big victory yesterday with ruling from the courts that allows us to proceed. OUR COUNTRY MUST HAVE BORDER SECURITY! **2/28/2018 12:29**

45 year low on illegal border crossings this year. Ice and Border Patrol Agents are doing a great job for our Country. MS-13 thugs being hit hard. **2/28/2018 14:08**

Why is A.G. Jeff Sessions asking the Inspector General to investigate potentially massive FISA abuse. Will take forever has no prosecutorial power and already late with reports on Comey etc. Isn't the I.G. an Obama guy? Why not use Justice Department lawyers? DISGRACEFUL! **2/28/2018 14:34**

Our Steel and Aluminum industries (and many others) have been decimated by decades of unfair trade and bad policy with countries from around the world. We must not let our country companies and workers be taken advantage of any longer. We want free fair and SMART TRADE! **3/1/2018 12:12**

Good (Great) meeting in the Oval Office tonight with the NRA! **3/2/2018 3:04**

When a country (USA) is losing many billions of dollars on trade with virtually every country it does business with trade wars are good and easy to win. Example when we are down $100 billion with a certain country and they get cute don't trade anymore-we win big. It's easy! **3/2/2018 10:50**

Alec Baldwin whose dying mediocre career was saved by his terrible impersonation of me on SNL now says playing me was agony. Alec it was agony for those who were forced to watch. Bring back Darrell Hammond funnier and a far greater talent! **3/2/2018 11:07**

We must protect our country and our workers. Our steel industry is in bad shape. IF YOU DON'T HAVE STEEL YOU DON'T HAVE A COUNTRY! **3/2/2018 13:01**

When a country Taxes our products coming in at say 50% and we Tax the same product coming into our country at ZERO not fair or smart. We will soon be starting RECIPROCAL TAXES so that we will charge the same thing as they charge us. $800 Billion Trade Deficit-have no choice! **3/2/2018 13:57**

REST IN PEACE BILLY GRAHAM! https://t.co/2qMoUccVC2 **3/2/2018 19:48**

Happy National Anthem Day! https://t.co/cf1eugMbKU **3/3/2018 14:15**

The United States has an $800 Billion Dollar Yearly Trade Deficit because of our "very stupid" trade deals and policies. Our jobs and wealth are being given to other countries that have taken advantage of us for years. They laugh at what fools our leaders have been. No more! **3/3/2018 17:43**

If the E.U. wants to further increase their already massive tariffs and barriers on U.S. companies doing business there we will simply apply a Tax on their Cars which freely pour into the U.S. They make it impossible for our cars (and more) to sell there. Big trade imbalance! **3/3/2018 17:53**

The Gridiron Dinner last night was great fun. I am accomplishing a lot in Washington and have never had a better time doing something and especially since this is for the American People! **3/4/2018 17:42**

We are on the losing side of almost all trade deals. Our friends and enemies have taken advantage of the U.S. for many years. Our Steel and Aluminum industries are dead. Sorry it's time for a change! MAKE AMERICA GREAT AGAIN! **3/5/2018 0:10**

...treat our farmers much better. Highly restrictive. Mexico must do much more on stopping drugs from pouring into the U.S. They have not done what needs to be done. Millions of people addicted and dying. **3/5/2018 11:53**

To protect our Country we must protect American Steel! #AMERICA FIRST **3/5/2018 12:57**

Why did the Obama Administration start an investigation into the Trump Campaign (with zero proof of wrongdoing) long before the Election in November? Wanted to discredit so Crooked H would win. Unprecedented. Bigger than Watergate! Plus Obama did NOTHING about Russian meddling. **3/5/2018 13:22**

It's March 5th and the Democrats are nowhere to be found on DACA. Gave them 6 months they just don't care. Where are they? We are ready to make a deal! **3/5/2018 20:37**

The new Fake News narrative is that there is CHAOS in the White House. Wrong! People will always come & go and I want strong dialogue before making a final decision. I still have some people that I want to change (always seeking perfection). There is no Chaos only great Energy! **3/6/2018 12:55**

Lowest rated Oscars in HISTORY. Problem is we don't have Stars anymore - except your President (just kidding of course)! **3/6/2018 13:25**

Federal Judge in Maryland has just ruled that "President Trump has the right to end DACA." President Obama had 8 years to fix this problem and didn't. I am waiting for the Dems they are running for the hills! **3/6/2018 13:46**

Possible progress being made in talks with North Korea. For the first time in many years a serious effort is being made by all parties concerned. The World is watching and waiting! May be false hope but the U.S. is ready to go hard in either direction! **3/6/2018 14:11**

Will be making a decision soon on the appointment of new Chief Economic Advisor. Many people wanting the job - will choose wisely! **3/7/2018 0:49**

From Bush 1 to present our Country has lost more than 55000 factories 6000000 manufacturing jobs and accumulated Trade Deficits of more than 12 Trillion Dollars. Last year we had a Trade Deficit of almost 800 Billion Dollars. Bad Policies & Leadership. Must WIN again! #MAGA **3/7/2018 11:40**

China has been asked to develop a plan for the year of a One Billion Dollar reduction in their massive Trade Deficit with the United States. Our relationship with China has been a very good one and we look forward to seeing what ideas they come back with. We must act soon! **3/7/2018 15:10**

The U.S. is acting swiftly on Intellectual Property theft. We cannot allow this to happen as it has for many years!
3/7/2018 15:38

Looking forward to 3:30 P.M. meeting today at the White House. We have to protect & build our Steel and Aluminum Industries while at the same time showing great flexibility and cooperation toward those that are real friends and treat us fairly on both trade and the military. **3/8/2018 12:38**

Kim Jong Un talked about denuclearization with the South Korean Representatives not just a freeze. Also no missile testing by North Korea during this period of time. Great progress being made but sanctions will remain until an agreement is reached. Meeting being planned!
3/9/2018 1:08

The deal with North Korea is very much in the making and will be if completed a very good one for the World. Time and place to be determined. **3/10/2018 0:42**

Congratulations to Kristian Saucier a man who has served proudly in the Navy on your newly found Freedom. Now you can go out and have the life you deserve! **3/10/2018 15:52**

Chinese President XI JINPING and I spoke at length about the meeting with KIM JONG UN of North Korea. President XI told me he appreciates that the U.S. is working to solve the problem diplomatically rather than going with the ominous alternative. China continues to be helpful!
3/10/2018 16:15

North Korea has not conducted a Missile Test since November 28 2017 and has promised not to do so through our meetings. I believe they will honor that commitment!

3/10/2018 18:38

In the first hours after hearing that North Korea's leader wanted to meet with me to talk denuclearization and that missile launches will end the press was startled & amazed. They couldn't believe it. But by the following morning the news became FAKE.They said so what who cares!

3/10/2018 20:02

The European Union wonderful countries who treat the U.S. very badly on trade are complaining about the tariffs on Steel & Aluminum. If they drop their horrific barriers & tariffs on U.S. products going in we will likewise drop ours. Big Deficit. If not we Tax Cars etc. FAIR! **3/10/2018 21:29**

The Failing New York Times purposely wrote a false story stating that I am unhappy with my legal team on the Russia case and am going to add another lawyer to help out. Wrong. I am VERY happy with my lawyers John Dowd Ty Cobb and Jay Sekulow. They are doing a great job and.....

3/11/2018 13:41

...have shown conclusively that there was no Collusion with Russia..just excuse for losing. The only Collusion was that done by the DNC the Democrats and Crooked Hillary. The writer of the story Maggie Haberman a Hillary flunky knows nothing about me and is not given access. **3/11/2018 13:50**

The Democrats continue to Obstruct the confirmation of hundreds of good and talented people who are needed to run our government...A record in U.S. history. State Department Ambassadors and many others are being slow walked. Senate must approve NOW! **3/11/2018 14:49**

Rasmussen and others have my approval ratings at around 50% which is higher than Obama and yet the political pundits love saying my approval ratings are "somewhat low." They know they are lying when they say it. Turn off the show - FAKE NEWS! **3/11/2018 15:16**

THE HOUSE INTELLIGENCE COMMITTEE HAS AFTER A 14 MONTH LONG IN-DEPTH INVESTIGATION FOUND NO EVIDENCE OF COLLUSION OR COORDINATION BETWEEN THE TRUMP CAMPAIGN AND RUSSIA TO INFLUENCE THE 2016 PRESIDENTIAL ELECTION.
3/13/2018 0:49

Mike Pompeo Director of the CIA will become our new Secretary of State. He will do a fantastic job! Thank you to Rex Tillerson for his service! Gina Haspel will become the new Director of the CIA and the first woman so chosen. Congratulations to all! **3/13/2018 12:44**

Heading to see the BORDER WALL prototypes in California! https://t.co/fU6Ukc271l **3/13/2018 14:37**

California's sanctuary policies are illegal and unconstitutional and put the safety and security of our entire nation at risk. Thousands of dangerous & violent criminal aliens are released as a result of sanctuary policies set free to prey on innocent Americans. THIS MUST STOP!
3/13/2018 15:27

If we don't have a wall system we're not going to have a country. Congress must fund the BORDER WALL & prohibit grants to sanctuary jurisdictions that threaten the security of our country & the people of our country. We must enforce our laws & protect our people! #BuildTheWall https://t.co/NGqNueukvj **3/13/2018 22:23**

All across this nation we pray for our country and we THANK GOD for our United States Marines! Thank you. God Bless You. And God Bless America!
https://t.co/vKXBd0CGH1 **3/14/2018 0:34**

Hundreds of good people including very important Ambassadors and Judges are being blocked and/or slow walked by the Democrats in the Senate. Many important positions in Government are unfilled because of this obstruction. Worst in U.S. history! **3/14/2018 13:02**

We cannot keep a blind eye to the rampant unfair trade practices against our Country! **3/14/2018 14:37**

Today the House took major steps toward securing our schools by passing the STOP School Violence Act. We must put the safety of America's children FIRST by improving training and by giving schools and law enforcement better tools. A tragedy like Parkland can't happen ever again!
3/14/2018 21:25

Continuing to monitor the heartbreaking bridge collapse at FIU - so tragic. Many brave First Responders rushed in to save lives. Thank you for your courage. Praying this evening for all who are affected. **3/15/2018 23:10**

Our thoughts and prayers go out to the families and loved ones of the brave troops lost in the helicopter crash on the Iraq-Syria border yesterday. Their sacrifice in service to our country will never be forgotten. **3/16/2018 14:40**

Andrew McCabe FIRED a great day for the hard working men and women of the FBI - A great day for Democracy. Sanctimonious James Comey was his boss and made McCabe look like a choirboy. He knew all about the lies and corruption going on at the highest levels of the FBI!

3/17/2018 4:08

Happy #StPatricksDay https://t.co/4vVsW2smhB
3/17/2018 15:00

As the House Intelligence Committee has concluded there was no collusion between Russia and the Trump Campaign. As many are now finding out however there was tremendous leaking lying and corruption at the highest levels of the FBI Justice & State. #DrainTheSwamp

3/17/2018 17:11

The Fake News is beside themselves that McCabe was caught called out and fired. How many hundreds of thousands of dollars was given to wife's campaign by Crooked H friend Terry M who was also under investigation? How many lies? How many leaks? Comey knew it all and much more! **3/17/2018 17:34**

The Mueller probe should never have been started in that there was no collusion and there was no crime. It was based on fraudulent activities and a Fake Dossier paid for by Crooked Hillary and the DNC and improperly used in FISA COURT for surveillance of my campaign. WITCH HUNT!

3/18/2018 0:12

Wow watch Comey lie under oath to Senator G when asked "have you ever been an anonymous source...or known someone else to be an anonymous source...?" He said strongly "never no." He lied as shown clearly on @ foxandfriends. **3/18/2018 12:02**

Spent very little time with Andrew McCabe but he never took notes when he was with me. I don't believe he made memos except to help his own agenda probably at a later date. Same with lying James Comey. Can we call them Fake Memos? **3/18/2018 12:22**

Why does the Mueller team have 13 hardened Democrats some big Crooked Hillary supporters and Zero Republicans? Another Dem recently added...does anyone think this is fair? And yet there is NO COLLUSION! **3/18/2018 12:35**

A total WITCH HUNT with massive conflicts of interest!

3/19/2018 13:07

The Democrats do not want to help DACA. Would be so easy to make a deal! **3/20/2018 0:28**

Our Nation was founded by farmers. Our independence was won by farmers. And our continent was tamed by farmers. Our farmers always lead the way -- we are PROUD of them and we are DELIVERING for them! #NationalAgricultureDay **3/20/2018 15:36**

AUSTIN BOMBING SUSPECT IS DEAD. Great job by law enforcement and all concerned! **3/21/2018 10:28**

...there was no probable cause for believing that there was any crime collusion or otherwise or obstruction of justice!" So stated by Harvard Law Professor Alan Dershowitz. **3/21/2018 11:11**

I called President Putin of Russia to congratulate him on his election victory (in past Obama called him also). The Fake News Media is crazed because they wanted me to excoriate him. They are wrong! Getting along with Russia (and others) is a good thing not a bad thing....... (1/2) **3/21/2018 18:56**

.....They can help solve problems with North Korea Syria Ukraine ISIS Iran and even the coming Arms Race. Bush tried to get along but didn't have the "smarts." Obama and Clinton tried but didn't have the energy or chemistry (remember RESET). PEACE THROUGH STRENGTH! (2/2) **3/21/2018 19:05**

Got $1.6 Billion to start Wall on Southern Border rest will be forthcoming. Most importantly got $700 Billion to rebuild our Military $716 Billion next year...most ever. Had to waste money on Dem giveaways in order to take care of military pay increase and new equipment. **3/22/2018 3:00**

Democrats refused to take care of DACA. Would have been so easy but they just didn't care. I had to fight for Military and start of Wall. **3/22/2018 3:04**

Crazy Joe Biden is trying to act like a tough guy. Actually he is weak both mentally and physically and yet he threatens me for the second time with physical assault. He doesn't know me but he would go down fast and hard crying all the way. Don't threaten people Joe!
3/22/2018 10:19

Remember when they were saying during the campaign that Donald Trump is giving great speeches and drawing big crowds but he is spending much less money and not using social media as well as Crooked Hillary's large and highly sophisticated staff. Well not saying that anymore!
3/22/2018 10:40

I am pleased to announce that effective 4/9/18 @AmbJohnBolton will be my new National Security Advisor. I am very thankful for the service of General H.R. McMaster who has done an outstanding job & will always remain my friend. There will be an official contact handover on 4/9.
3/22/2018 22:26

I am considering a VETO of the Omnibus Spending Bill based on the fact that the 800000 plus DACA recipients have been totally abandoned by the Democrats (not even mentioned in Bill) and the BORDER WALL which is desperately needed for our National Defense is not fully funded. **3/23/2018 12:55**

Our thoughts and prayers are with the victims of the horrible attack in France yesterday and we grieve the nation's loss. We also condemn the violent actions of the attacker and anyone who would provide him support. We are with you @EmmanuelMacron! **3/24/2018 16:40**

France honors a great hero. Officer died after bravely swapping places with hostage in ISIS related terror attack.

So much bravery around the world constantly fighting radical Islamic terrorism. Even stronger measures needed especially at borders! **3/25/2018 10:10**

Because of the $700 & $716 Billion Dollars gotten to rebuild our Military many jobs are created and our Military is again rich. Building a great Border Wall with drugs (poison) and enemy combatants pouring into our Country is all about National Defense. Build WALL through M! **3/25/2018 10:33**

The economy is looking really good. It has been many years that we have seen these kind of numbers. The underlying strength of companies has perhaps never been better. **3/26/2018 11:05**

So much Fake News. Never been more voluminous or more inaccurate. But through it all our country is doing great! **3/26/2018 12:38**

Trade talks going on with numerous countries that for many years have not treated the United States fairly. In the end all will be happy! **3/27/2018 0:44**

THE SECOND AMENDMENT WILL NEVER BE REPEALED! As much as Democrats would like to see this happen and despite the words yesterday of former Supreme Court Justice Stevens NO WAY. We need more Republicans in 2018 and must ALWAYS hold the Supreme Court!
3/28/2018 9:52

For years and through many administrations everyone said that peace and the denuclearization of the Korean Peninsula was not even a small possibility. Now there is a good chance that Kim Jong Un will do what is right for his people and for humanity. Look forward to our meeting! **3/28/2018 10:05**

Received message last night from XI JINPING of China that his meeting with KIM JONG UN went very well and that KIM looks forward to his meeting with me. In the meantime and unfortunately maximum sanctions and pressure must be maintained at all cost! **3/28/2018 10:16**

My Administration stands in solidarity with the brave citizens in Orange County defending their rights against California's illegal and unconstitutional Sanctuary policies. California's Sanctuary laws.... **3/28/2018 16:18**

Great briefing this afternoon on the start of our Southern Border WALL! https://t.co/pmCNoxxlkH **3/28/2018 19:47**

I have stated my concerns with Amazon long before the Election. Unlike others they pay little or no taxes to state & local governments use our Postal System as their Delivery Boy (causing tremendous loss to the U.S.) and are putting many thousands of retailers out of business! **3/29/2018 11:57**

Washington spent trillions building up foreign countries while allowing OUR OWN infrastructure to fall into a state of total disrepair. No more! It's time to REBUILD and we will do it with American WORKERS American GRIT and American PRIDE! https://t.co/Q9rPZi2D2s **3/29/2018 20:06**

...does not include the Fake Washington Post which is used as a "lobbyist" and should so REGISTER. If the P.O. "increased its parcel rates Amazon's shipping costs would rise by $2.6 Billion." This Post Office scam must stop. Amazon must pay real costs (and taxes) now! **3/31/2018 12:52**

Governor Jerry "Moonbeam" Brown pardoned 5 criminal illegal aliens whose crimes include (1) Kidnapping and Robbery (2) Badly beating wife and threatening a crime with intent to terrorize (3) Dealing drugs. Is this really what the great people of California want? @FoxNews **3/31/2018 12:53**

APRIL 2018 - JUNE 2018

★★★★★★★★★★★★★★★★★★★★★★★★★★★

North Korea agrees to suspend all nuclear tests, substantially diminishing the threat of war on the peninsula. Kanye West comes out in support of President Trump, bolstering Trump's status with African-Americans. While the Mueller investigation intensifies, so does the backlash against it, as the DOJ begins to investigate whether or not the FBI illegally surveilled the Trump campaign in 2016. Intensifying the conflict, Trump repeatedly tweets that the investigation is a "witch hunt" stoked by FBI lovers Peter Strzok and Lisa Page. With caravans of Central Americans heading to the USA dominating the news, the Supreme Court upholds Trump's travel ban.

HAPPY EASTER!

4/1/2018 12:27

Border Patrol Agents are not allowed to properly do their job at the Border because of ridiculous liberal (Democrat) laws like Catch & Release. Getting more dangerous. "Caravans" coming. Republicans must go to Nuclear Option to pass tough laws NOW. NO MORE DACA DEAL!

4/1/2018 13:56

Mexico is doing very little if not NOTHING at stopping people from flowing into Mexico through their Southern Border and then into the U.S. They laugh at our dumb immigration laws. They must stop the big drug and people flows or I will stop their cash cow NAFTA. NEED WALL!

4/1/2018 14:25

These big flows of people are all trying to take advantage of DACA. They want in on the act! **4/1/2018 14:28**

...Congress must immediately pass Border Legislation use Nuclear Option if necessary to stop the massive inflow of Drugs and People. Border Patrol Agents (and ICE) are GREAT but the weak Dem laws don't allow them to do their job. Act now Congress our country is being stolen!

4/2/2018 11:10

DACA is dead because the Democrats didn't care or act and now everyone wants to get onto the DACA bandwagon... No longer works. Must build Wall and secure our borders with proper Border legislation. Democrats want No Borders hence drugs and crime! **4/2/2018 11:17**

As ridiculous as it sounds the laws of our country do not easily allow us to send those crossing our Southern Border back where they came from. A whole big wasted procedure must take place. Mexico & Canada have tough immigration laws whereas ours are an Obama joke. ACT CONGRESS

4/3/2018 0:00

39% of my nominations including Diplomats to foreign lands have not been confirmed due to Democrat obstruction and delay. At this rate it would take more than 7 years before I am allowed to have these great people start working. Never happened before. Disgraceful! **4/3/2018 0:24**

The Fake News Networks those that knowingly have a sick and biased AGENDA are worried about the competition and quality of Sinclair Broadcast. The "Fakers" at CNN NBC ABC & CBS have done so much dishonest reporting that they should only be allowed to get awards for fiction! **4/3/2018 10:34**

The big Caravan of People from Honduras now coming across Mexico and heading to our "Weak Laws" Border had better be stopped before it gets there. Cash cow NAFTA is in play as is foreign aid to Honduras and the countries that allow this to happen. Congress MUST ACT NOW! **4/3/2018 10:49**

Thank you to Rasmussen for the honest polling. Just hit 50% which is higher than Cheatin' Obama at the same time in his Administration. **4/3/2018 11:08**

I am right about Amazon costing the United States Post Office massive amounts of money for being their Delivery Boy. Amazon should pay these costs (plus) and not have them bourne by the American Taxpayer. Many billions of dollars. P.O. leaders don't have a clue (or do they?)! **4/3/2018 13:55**

WE WILL PROTECT OUR SOUTHERN BORDER! https://t.co/Z7fqQKcnez **4/3/2018 19:59**

Was just briefed on the shooting at YouTube's HQ in San Bruno California. Our thoughts and prayers are with everybody involved. Thank you to our phenomenal Law Enforcement Officers and First Responders that are currently on the scene. **4/3/2018 21:49**

Our Border Laws are very weak while those of Mexico & Canada are very strong. Congress must change these

Obama era and other laws NOW! The Democrats stand in our way - they want people to pour into our country unchecked....CRIME! We will be taking strong action today.
4/4/2018 11:19

We are not in a trade war with China that war was lost many years ago by the foolish or incompetent people who represented the U.S. Now we have a Trade Deficit of $500 Billion a year with Intellectual Property Theft of another $300 Billion. We cannot let this continue! **4/4/2018 11:22**

When you're already $500 Billion DOWN you can't lose!
4/4/2018 13:20

Our thoughts and prayers are with the four U.S. Marines from the 3rd Marine Aircraft Wing who lost their lives in yesterday's Southern California helicopter crash. We pray for their families and our great @USMC. **4/4/2018 14:50**

"Still Rising: Rasmussen Poll Shows Donald Trump Approval Ratings Now at 51 Percent" https://t.co/q80PaE0gQo
4/4/2018 23:08

The Caravan is largely broken up thanks to the strong immigration laws of Mexico and their willingness to use them so as not to cause a giant scene at our Border. Because of the Trump Administrations actions Border crossings are at a still UNACCEPTABLE 46 year low. Stop drugs! **4/5/2018 11:40**

The Fake News Washington Post Amazon's "chief lobbyist" has another (of many) phony headlines "Trump Defiant As China Adds Trade Penalties." WRONG! Should read "Trump Defiant as U.S. Adds Trade Penalties Will End Barriers And Massive I.P. Theft." Typically bad reporting! **4/5/2018 13:10**

China which is a great economic power is considered a Developing Nation within the World Trade Organization. They therefore get tremendous perks and advantages especially over the U.S. Does anybody think this is fair. We were badly represented. The WTO is unfair to U.S.
4/6/2018 14:32

Do you believe that the Fake News Media is pushing hard on a story that I am going to replace A.G. Jeff Sessions with EPA Chief Scott Pruitt who is doing a great job but is TOTALLY under siege? Do people really believe this stuff? So much of the media is dishonest and corrupt! **4/6/2018 14:46**

"BET founder: Trump's economy is bringing black workers back into the labor force" https://t.co/TtMDfi4bvO **4/6/2018 20:23**

Just spoke to @JustinTrudeau to pay my highest respect and condolences to the families of the terrible Humboldt Team tragedy. May God be with them all! **4/7/2018 17:35**

The United States hasn't had a Trade Surplus with China in 40 years. They must end unfair trade take down barriers and charge only Reciprocal Tariffs. The U.S. is losing $500 Billion a year and has been losing Billions of Dollars for decades. Cannot continue! **4/7/2018 18:03**

We are sealing up our Southern Border. The people of our great country want Safety and Security. The Dems have been a disaster on this very important issue! **4/7/2018 18:11**

What does the Department of Justice and FBI have to hide? Why aren't they giving the strongly requested documents (unredacted) to the HOUSE JUDICIARY COMMITTEE? Stalling but for what reason? Not looking good! **4/7/2018 21:00**

Fire at Trump Tower is out. Very confined (well built building). Firemen (and women) did a great job. THANK YOU! **4/7/2018 22:42**

President Xi and I will always be friends no matter what happens with our dispute on trade. China will take down its Trade Barriers because it is the right thing to do. Taxes will become Reciprocal & a deal will be made on Intellectual Property. Great future for both countries! **4/8/2018 12:12**

Many dead including women and children in mindless CHEMICAL attack in Syria. Area of atrocity is in lockdown and encircled by Syrian Army making it completely

inaccessible to outside world. President Putin Russia and Iran are responsible for backing Animal Assad. Big price...
4/8/2018 13:00

If President Obama had crossed his stated Red Line In The Sand the Syrian disaster would have ended long ago! Animal Assad would have been history! **4/8/2018 13:12**

Congratulations to Patrick Reed on his great and courageous MASTERS win! When Patrick had his amazing win at Doral 5 years ago people saw his great talent and a bright future ahead. Now he is the Masters Champion!
4/9/2018 0:43

When a car is sent to the United States from China there is a Tariff to be paid of 2 1/2%. When a car is sent to China from the United States there is a Tariff to be paid of 25%. Does that sound like free or fair trade. No it sounds like STUPID TRADE - going on for years!
4/9/2018 10:03

The Democrats are not doing what's right for our country. I will not rest until we have secured our borders and restored the rule of law! https://t.co/zKGgPlaadS **4/9/2018 19:17**

Attorney–client privilege is dead! **4/10/2018 11:07**

A TOTAL WITCH HUNT!!! **4/10/2018 11:08**

Last night it was my great honor to host America's senior defense and military leaders for dinner at the White House. America's military is the GREATEST fighting force in the history of the world. They all have my pledge of unwavering commitment to our men and women in uniform! https://t.co/BjWKcMX0iL **4/10/2018 13:30**

Very thankful for President Xi of China's kind words on tariffs and automobile barriers...also his enlightenment on intellectual property and technology transfers. We will make great progress together! **4/10/2018 18:30**

Russia vows to shoot down any and all missiles fired at Syria. Get ready Russia because they will be coming nice and new and "smart!" You shouldn't be partners with a Gas Killing Animal who kills his people and enjoys it!

4/11/2018 10:57

Our relationship with Russia is worse now than it has ever been and that includes the Cold War. There is no reason for this. Russia needs us to help with their economy something that would be very easy to do and we need all nations to work together. Stop the arms race? **4/11/2018 11:37**

Much of the bad blood with Russia is caused by the Fake & Corrupt Russia Investigation headed up by the all Democrat loyalists or people that worked for Obama. Mueller is most conflicted of all (except Rosenstein who signed FISA & Comey letter). No Collusion so they go crazy! **4/11/2018 13:00**

If I wanted to fire Robert Mueller in December as reported by the Failing New York Times I would have fired him. Just more Fake News from a biased newspaper! **4/12/2018 10:03**

California Governor Jerry Brown is doing the right thing and sending the National Guard to the Border. Thank you Jerry good move for the safety of our Country! **4/12/2018 10:08**

Never said when an attack on Syria would take place. Could be very soon or not so soon at all! In any event the United States under my Administration has done a great job of ridding the region of ISIS. Where is our "Thank you America?" **4/12/2018 10:15**

I have agreed with the historically cooperative disciplined approach that we have engaged in with Robert Mueller (Unlike the Clintons!). I have full confidence in Ty Cobb my Special Counsel and have been fully advised throughout each phase of this process. **4/12/2018 16:46**

Tremendous pressure is building like never before for the Border Wall and an end to crime cradling Sanctuary Cities. Started the Wall in San Diego where the people were pushing really hard to get it. They will soon be protected! **4/13/2018 11:44**

James Comey is a proven LEAKER & LIAR. Virtually everyone in Washington thought he should be fired for the terrible job he did-until he was in fact fired. He leaked CLASSIFIED information for which he should be prosecuted. He lied to Congress under OATH. He is a weak and..... (1/2) **4/13/2018 12:01**

....untruthful slime ball who was as time has proven a terrible Director of the FBI. His handling of the Crooked Hillary Clinton case and the events surrounding it will go down as one of the worst "botch jobs" of history. It was my great honor to fire James Comey! (2/2) **4/13/2018 12:17**

We are bringing back our factories we are bringing back our jobs and we are bringing back those four beautiful words: MADE IN THE USA! https://t.co/grABSrYUBX **4/13/2018 16:21**

DOJ just issued the McCabe report - which is a total disaster. He LIED! LIED! LIED! McCabe was totally controlled by Comey - McCabe is Comey!! No collusion all made up by this den of thieves and lowlifes! **4/13/2018 19:36**

A perfectly executed strike last night. Thank you to France and the United Kingdom for their wisdom and the power of their fine Military. Could not have had a better result. Mission Accomplished! **4/14/2018 12:21**

So proud of our great Military which will soon be after the spending of billions of fully approved dollars the finest that our Country has ever had. There won't be anything or anyone even close!
4/14/2018 12:29

Unbelievably James Comey states that Polls where Crooked Hillary was leading were a factor in the handling (stupidly) of the Clinton Email probe. In other words he was making decisions based on the fact that he thought she was going to win and he wanted a job. Slimeball! **4/15/2018 11:42**

The big questions in Comey's badly reviewed book aren't answered like how come he gave up Classified Information (jail) why did he lie to Congress (jail) why did the DNC refuse to give Server to the FBI (why didn't they TAKE it) why the phony memos McCabe's $700000 & more?
4/15/2018 11:57

Comey throws AG Lynch "under the bus!" Why can't we all find out what happened on the tarmac in the back of the plane with Wild Bill and Lynch? Was she promised a Supreme Court seat or AG in order to lay off Hillary. No golf and grandkids talk (give us all a break)! **4/15/2018 12:08**

The Syrian raid was so perfectly carried out with such precision that the only way the Fake News Media could demean was by my use of the term "Mission Accomplished." I knew they would seize on this but felt it is such a great Military term it should be brought back. Use often!
4/15/2018 12:19

I never asked Comey for Personal Loyalty. I hardly even knew this guy. Just another of his many lies. His "memos" are self serving and FAKE! **4/15/2018 12:32**

Attorney Client privilege is now a thing of the past. I have many (too many!) lawyers and they are probably

wondering when their offices and even homes are going to be raided with everything including their phones and computers taken. All lawyers are deflated and concerned!
4/15/2018 12:56

Slippery James Comey a man who always ends up badly and out of whack (he is not smart!) will go down as the WORST FBI Director in history by far! **4/15/2018 13:07**

Just hit 50% in the Rasmussen Poll much higher than President Obama at same point. With all of the phony stories and Fake News it's hard to believe! Thank you America we are doing Great Things. **4/15/2018 14:44**

Comey drafted the Crooked Hillary exoneration long before he talked to her (lied in Congress to Senator G) then based his decisions on her poll numbers. Disgruntled he McCabe and the others committed many crimes! **4/16/2018 12:25**

Russia and China are playing the Currency Devaluation game as the U.S. keeps raising interest rates. Not acceptable! **4/16/2018 12:31**

Employment is up Taxes are DOWN. Enjoy! **4/17/2018 12:24**

So many people are seeing the benefits of the Tax Cut Bill. Everyone is talking really nice to see! **4/17/2018 12:24**

Pastor Andrew Brunson a fine gentleman and Christian leader in the United States is on trial and being persecuted in Turkey for no reason. They call him a Spy but I am more a Spy than he is. Hopefully he will be allowed to come home to his beautiful family where he belongs! **4/18/2018 2:32**

There is a Revolution going on in California. Soooo many Sanctuary areas want OUT of this ridiculous crime infested & breeding concept. Jerry Brown is trying to back out of the National Guard at the Border but the people of the State are not happy. Want Security & Safety NOW!
4/18/2018 9:59

Mike Pompeo met with Kim Jong Un in North Korea last week. Meeting went very smoothly and a good relationship was formed. Details of Summit are being worked out now. Denuclearization will be a great thing for World but also for North Korea! **4/18/2018 10:42**

Slippery James Comey the worst FBI Director in history was not fired because of the phony Russia investigation where by the way there was NO COLLUSION (except by the Dems)! **4/18/2018 12:05**

Best wishes to Prime Minister @Netanyahu and all of the people of Israel on the 70th Anniversary of your Great Independence. We have no better friends anywhere. Looking forward to moving our Embassy to Jerusalem next month! **4/18/2018 16:30**

Thank you San Diego County for defending the rule of law and supporting our lawsuit against California's illegal and unconstitutional 'Sanctuary' policies. California's dangerous policies release violent criminals back into our communities putting all Americans at risk. **4/19/2018 15:23**

Governor Jerry Brown announced he will deploy "up to 400 National Guard Troops" to do nothing. The crime rate in California is high enough and the Federal Government will not be paying for Governor Brown's charade. We need border security and action not words! **4/19/2018 15:48**

Democrats are obstructing good (hopefully great) people wanting to give up a big portion of their life to work for our Government hence the American People. They are "slow walking" all of my nominations - hundreds of people. At this rate it would take 9 years for all approvals! **4/19/2018 20:21**

Mike Pompeo is outstanding. First in his class at West Point. A top student at Harvard Law School. A success at whatever he has done. We need the Senate to approve Mike ASAP. He will be a great Secretary of State! **4/19/2018 20:31**

James Comey just threw Andrew McCabe "under the bus." Inspector General's Report on McCabe is a disaster for both of them! Getting a little (lot) of their own medicine?
4/19/2018 22:46

James Comey Memos just out and show clearly that there was NO COLLUSION and NO OBSTRUCTION. Also he leaked classified information. WOW! Will the Witch Hunt continue? **4/20/2018 3:37**

So General Michael Flynn's life can be totally destroyed while Shadey James Comey can Leak and Lie and make lots of money from a third rate book (that should never have been written). Is that really the way life in America is supposed to work? I don't think so! **4/20/2018 10:34**

So exciting! I have agreed to be the Commencement Speaker at our GREAT Naval Academy on May 25th in Annapolis Maryland. Looking forward to being there.
4/20/2018 10:43

Nancy Pelosi is going absolutely crazy about the big Tax Cuts given to the American People by the Republicans...got not one Democrat Vote! Here's a choice. They want to end them and raise your taxes substantially. Republicans are working on making them permanent and more cuts!
4/20/2018 10:50

Looks like OPEC is at it again. With record amounts of Oil all over the place including the fully loaded ships at sea Oil prices are artificially Very High! No good and will not be accepted! **4/20/2018 10:57**

Can you believe that despite 93% bad stories from the Fake News Media (should be getting good stories) today we had just about our highest Poll Numbers including those on Election Day? The American public is wise to the phony an dishonest press. Make America Great Again! **4/20/2018 20:25**

North Korea has agreed to suspend all Nuclear Tests and close up a major test site. This is very good news for North Korea and the World - big progress! Look forward to our Summit.

4/20/2018 22:50

Just heard the Campaign was sued by the Obstructionist Democrats. This can be good news in that we will now counter for the DNC Server that they refused to give to the FBI the Debbie Wasserman Schultz Servers and Documents held by the Pakistani mystery man and Clinton Emails.

4/20/2018 23:19

James Comey illegally leaked classified documents to the press in order to generate a Special Council? Therefore the Special Council was established based on an illegal act? Really does everybody know what that means? **4/21/2018 3:13**

A message from Kim Jong Un: "North Korea will stop nuclear tests and launches of intercontinental ballistic missiles."Also will "Shut down a nuclear test site in the country's Northern Side to prove the vow to suspend nuclear tests." Progress being made for all! **4/21/2018 3:22**

So funny the Democrats have sued the Republicans for Winning. Now he R's counter and force them to turn over a treasure trove of material including Servers and Emails!

4/21/2018 18:52

Sylvester Stallone called me with the story of heavyweight boxing champion Jack Johnson. His trials and tribulations were great his life complex and controversial. Others have looked at this over the years most thought it would be done but yes I am considering a Full Pardon! **4/21/2018 19:02**

"At least two Memos Comey shared with a friend contained Classified Information." Wall Street Journal **4/21/2018 22:30**

"GOP Lawmakers asking Sessions to Investigate Comey and Hillary Clinton." @FoxNews Good luck with that request!
4/22/2018 12:22

Sleepy Eyes Chuck Todd of Fake News NBC just stated that we have given up so much in our negotiations with North Korea and they have given up nothing. Wow we haven't given up anything & they have agreed to denuclearization (so great for World) site closure & no more testing!
4/22/2018 12:50

....We are a long way from conclusion on North Korea maybe things will work out and maybe they won't - only time will tell....But the work I am doing now should have been done a long time ago! **4/22/2018 13:02**

"I can die happy now with Trump Job performance" stated Mary Matalin. "A great overall President stunning!" Thank you Mary. **4/22/2018 14:06**

A complete Witch Hunt! **4/22/2018 17:23**

Funny how all of the Pundits that couldn't come close to making a deal on North Korea are now all over the place telling me how to make a deal! **4/22/2018 18:43**

Kim Strassel of the WSJ just said after reviewing the dumb Comey Memos "you got to ask what was the purpose of the Special Counsel? There's no there there." Dan Henninger of the WSJ said Memos would show that this would be one of the weakest obstruction cases ever brought! **4/22/2018 20:04**

Thank you to the incredible Law Enforcement Officers from the Palm Beach County Sheriff's Office. They keep us safe and are very cool about it! https://t.co/NlhxpPwmzT
4/22/2018 20:12

Hard to believe Obstructionists May vote against Mike Pompeo for Secretary of State. The Dems will not approve hundreds of good people including the Ambassador to Germany. They are maxing out the time on approval process for all never happened before. Need more Republicans! **4/23/2018 13:15**

Despite the Democrat inspired laws on Sanctuary Cities and the Border being so bad and one sided I have instructed the Secretary of Homeland Security not to let these large Caravans of people into our Country. It is a disgrace. We are the only Country in the World so naive! WALL **4/23/2018 13:44**

Mexico whose laws on immigration are very tough must stop people from going through Mexico and into the U.S. We may make this a condition of the new NAFTA Agreement. Our Country cannot accept what is happening! Also we must get Wall funding fast. **4/23/2018 13:51**

Here's a great stat - since January 2017 the number of people forced to use food stamps is down 1.9 million. The American people are finally back to work! **4/23/2018 20:08**

Our two great republics are linked together by the timeless bonds of history culture and destiny. We are people who cherish our values protect our civilization and recognize the image of God in every human soul. https://t.co/01c8iSGDB3 **4/24/2018 20:18**

Congratulations to Republican Debbie Lesko on her big win in the Special Election for Arizona House seat. Debbie will do a Great Job! Press is so silent. **4/25/2018 11:53**

.@FLOTUS did a spectacular job hosting the President of France @EmmanuelMacron and his wife Brigitte. Every detail was done to perfection. The State Dining Room never looked more beautiful and Washington is abuzz over what an incredible job Melania did. **4/25/2018 14:10**

Looking forward to my meeting with Tim Cook of Apple. We will be talking about many things including how the U.S. has been treated unfairly for many years by many countries on trade. **4/25/2018 14:11**

Thank you Kanye very cool! https://t.co/vRIC87M21X

4/25/2018 19:33

MAGA! https://t.co/jFf5ONASlv **4/25/2018 21:18**

The U.S. has put together a STRONG bid w/ Canada & Mexico for the 2026 World Cup. It would be a shame if countries that we always support were to lobby against the U.S. bid. Why should we be supporting these countries when they don't support us (including at the United Nations)? **4/26/2018 23:39**

Is everybody believing what is going on. James Comey can't define what a leak is. He illegally leaked CLASSIFIED INFORMATION but doesn't understand what he did or how serious it is. He lied all over the place to cover it up. He's either very sick or very dumb. Remember sailor!

4/27/2018 10:26

After a furious year of missile launches and Nuclear testing a historic meeting between North and South Korea is now taking place. Good things are happening but only time will tell! **4/27/2018 10:41**

KOREAN WAR TO END! The United States and all of its GREAT people should be very proud of what is now taking place in Korea! **4/27/2018 10:55**

Please do not forget the great help that my good friend President Xi of China has given to the United States particularly at the Border of North Korea. Without him it would have been a much longer tougher process!

4/27/2018 11:50

Kanye West has performed a great service to the Black Community - Big things are happening and eyes are being opened for the first time in Decades - Legacy Stuff! Thank you also to Chance and Dr. Darrell Scott they really get it

(lowest Black & Hispanic unemployment in history).
4/27/2018 13:11

Just Out: House Intelligence Committee Report released. "No evidence" that the Trump Campaign "colluded coordinated or conspired with Russia." Clinton Campaign paid for Opposition Research obtained from Russia- Wow! A total Witch Hunt! MUST END NOW! **4/27/2018 14:14**

House Intelligence Committee rules that there was NO COLLUSION between the Trump Campaign and Russia. As I have been saying all along it is all a big Hoax by the Democrats based on payments and lies. There should never have been a Special Counsel appointed. Witch Hunt!
4/28/2018 2:04

Allegations made by Senator Jon Tester against Admiral/ Doctor Ron Jackson are proving false. The Secret Service is unable to confirm (in fact they deny) any of the phony Democrat charges which have absolutely devastated the wonderful Jackson family. Tester should resign. The..... (1/2)
4/28/2018 12:07

....great people of Montana will not stand for this kind of slander when talking of a great human being. Admiral Jackson is the kind of man that those in Montana would most respect and admire and now for no reason whatsoever his reputation has been shattered. Not fair Tester! (2/2)
4/28/2018 12:15

Just had a long and very good talk with President Moon of South Korea. Things are going very well time and location of meeting with North Korea is being set. Also spoke to Prime Minister Abe of Japan to inform him of the ongoing negotiations. **4/28/2018 13:45**

Look forward to being in the Great State of Michigan tonight. Major business expansion and jobs pouring into your State. Auto companies expanding at record pace. Big crowd tonight will be live on T.V. **4/28/2018 13:54**

Secret Service has just informed me that Senator Jon Tester's statements on Admiral Jackson are not true. There were no such findings. A horrible thing that we in D.C. must live with just like phony Russian Collusion. Tester should lose race in Montana. Very dishonest and sick! **4/28/2018 19:11**

Great evening last night in Washington Michigan. The enthusiasm knowledge and love in that room was unreal. To the many thousands of people who couldn't get in I cherish you....and will be back! **4/29/2018 11:21**

While Washington Michigan was a big success Washington D.C. just didn't work. Everyone is talking about the fact that the White House Correspondents Dinner was a very big boring bust...the so-called comedian really "bombed." @ greggutfeld should host next year! @PeteHegseth **4/29/2018 11:45**

Just got recent Poll - much higher than President O at same time....Well much more has been accomplished! **4/29/2018 11:54**

The White House Correspondents' Dinner was a failure last year but this year was an embarrassment to everyone associated with it. The filthy "comedian" totally bombed (couldn't even deliver her lines-much like the Seth Meyers weak performance). Put Dinner to rest or start over! **4/30/2018 2:38**

Headline: "Kim Prepared to Cede Nuclear Weapons if U.S. Pledges Not to Invade" - from the Failing New York Times. Also will shut down Nuclear Test Site in May. **4/30/2018 2:59**

The White House Correspondents' Dinner is DEAD as we know it. This was a total disaster and an embarrassment to our great Country and all that it stands for. FAKE NEWS is alive and well and beautifully represented on Saturday night! **4/30/2018 12:10**

Numerous countries are being considered for the MEETING but would Peace House/Freedom House on the Border of North & South Korea be a more Representative Important

and Lasting site than a third party country? Just asking!
4/30/2018 12:19

I recently had a terrific meeting with a bipartisan group of freshman lawmakers who feel very strongly in favor of Congressional term limits. I gave them my full support and endorsement for their efforts. #DrainTheSwamp
4/30/2018 18:54

The migrant 'caravan' that is openly defying our border shows how weak & ineffective U.S. immigration laws are. Yet Democrats like Jon Tester continue to support the open borders agenda – Tester even voted to protect Sanctuary Cities. We need lawmakers who will put America First.
4/30/2018 22:38

During Small Business Week we celebrate the great hard-working entrepreneurs across our country who have started and operate a small business! **4/30/2018 22:39**

The Fake News is going crazy making up false stories and using only unnamed sources (who don't exist). They are totally unhinged and the great success of this Administration is making them do and say things that even they can't believe they are saying. Truly bad people!
4/30/2018 22:49

The White House is running very smoothly despite phony Witch Hunts etc. There is great Energy and unending Stamina both necessary to get things done. We are accomplishing the unthinkable and setting positive records while doing so! Fake News is going "bonkers!" **4/30/2018 23:02**

So disgraceful that the questions concerning the Russian Witch Hunt were "leaked" to the media. No questions on Collusion. Oh I see...you have a made up phony crime Collusion that never existed and an investigation begun with illegally leaked classified information. Nice! **5/1/2018 10:47**

Delegation heading to China to begin talks on the Massive Trade Deficit that has been created with our Country. Very much like North Korea this should have been fixed years ago not now. Same with other countries and NAFTA...but it will all get done. Great Potential for USA! **5/1/2018 11:00**

It would seem very hard to obstruct justice for a crime that never happened! Witch Hunt! **5/1/2018 11:34**

Today it was my great honor to thank and welcome heroic crew members and passengers of Southwest Airlines Flight 1380 at the @WhiteHouse! https://t.co/fYYgWToddi **5/1/2018 19:42**

There was no Collusion (it is a Hoax) and there is no Obstruction of Justice (that is a setup & trap). What there is is Negotiations going on with North Korea over Nuclear War Negotiations going on with China over Trade Deficits Negotiations on NAFTA and much more. Witch Hunt! **5/2/2018 11:45**

NEW BOOK - A MUST READ! "The Russia Hoax - The Illicit Scheme to Clear Hillary Clinton and Frame Donald Trump" by the brilliant Fox News Legal Analyst Gregg Jarrett. A sad chapter for law enforcement. A rigged system! **5/2/2018 13:33**

A Rigged System - They don't want to turn over Documents to Congress. What are they afraid of? Why so much redacting? Why such unequal "justice?" At some point I will have no choice but to use the powers granted to the Presidency and get involved! **5/2/2018 14:45**

I have been briefed on the U.S. C-130 "Hercules" cargo plane from the Puerto Rico National Guard that crashed near Savannah Hilton Head International Airport. Please join me in thoughts and prayers for the victims their families and the great men and women of the National Guard. **5/2/2018 20:27**

"This isn't some game. You are screwing with the work of the president of the United States." John Dowd March 2018. With North Korea China the Middle East and so much more there is not much time to be thinking about this especially since there was no Russian "Collusion." **5/2/2018 22:40**

As everybody is aware the past Administration has long been asking for three hostages to be released from a North Korean Labor camp but to no avail. Stay tuned! **5/3/2018 0:53**

Ainsley Earnhardt a truly great person just wrote a wonderful book "The Light Within Me" which is doing really well. She is very special and so is her new book...bring it to number one! **5/3/2018 3:37**

...despite already having signed a detailed letter admitting that there was no affair. Prior to its violation by Ms. Clifford and her attorney this was a private agreement. Money from the campaign or campaign contributions played no roll in this transaction. **5/3/2018 11:00**

Because Jobs in the U.S. are doing so well Americans receiving unemployment aid is the lowest since 1973. Great! **5/4/2018 10:28**

NBC NEWS is wrong again! They cite "sources" which are constantly wrong. Problem is like so many others the sources probably don't exist they are fabricated fiction! NBC my former home with the Apprentice is now as bad as Fake News CNN. Sad! **5/4/2018 10:45**

Going to Dallas (the GREAT State of Texas) today. Leaving soon! **5/4/2018 10:57**

JUST OUT: 3.9% Unemployment. 4% is Broken! In the meantime WITCH HUNT! **5/4/2018 13:27**

Democrats and liberals in Congress want to disarm law-abiding Americans at the same time they are releasing dangerous criminal aliens and savage gang members onto our streets. Politicians who put criminal aliens before American Citizens should be voted out of office! **5/4/2018 21:58**

We are going to demand Congress secure the border in the upcoming CR. Illegal immigration must end! **5/4/2018 21:59**

Just returned home to the beautiful White House from Dallas where the Arena was packed to the rafters with the great fans and supporters of the @NRA. It was so wonderful to be there! **5/5/2018 0:17**

My highly respected nominee for CIA Director Gina Haspel has come under fire because she was too tough on Terrorists. Think of that in these very dangerous times we have the most qualified person a woman who Democrats want OUT because she is too tough on terror. Win Gina! **5/7/2018 11:04**

The Russia Witch Hunt is rapidly losing credibility. House Intelligence Committee found No Collusion Coordination or anything else with Russia. So now the Probe says OK what else is there? How about Obstruction for a made up phony crime.There is no O it's called Fighting Back **5/7/2018 11:27**

The 13 Angry Democrats in charge of the Russian Witch Hunt are starting to find out that there is a Court System in place that actually protects people from injustice...and just wait 'till the Courts get to see your unrevealed Conflicts of Interest! **5/7/2018 11:39**

Lisa Page who may hold the record for the most Emails in the shortest period of time (to her Lover Peter S) and attorney Baker are out at the FBI as part of the Probers getting caught? Why is Peter S still there? What a total mess. Our Country has to get back to Business! **5/7/2018 13:29**

Is this Phony Witch Hunt going to go on even longer so it wrongfully impacts the Mid-Term Elections which is what the Democrats always intended? Republicans better get tough and smart before it is too late! **5/7/2018 13:35**

The United States does not need John Kerry's possibly illegal Shadow Diplomacy on the very badly negotiated Iran Deal. He was the one that created this MESS in the first place! **5/7/2018 14:08**

I will be announcing my decision on the Iran Deal tomorrow from the White House at 2:00pm. **5/7/2018 18:44**

Gina Haspel my highly respected nominee to lead the CIA is being praised for the fact that she has been and alway will be TOUGH ON TERROR! This is a woman who has been a leader wherever she has gone. The CIA wants her to lead them into America's bright and glorious future! **5/8/2018 11:09**

I will be speaking to my friend President Xi of China this morning at 8:30. The primary topics will be Trade where good things will happen and North Korea where relationships and trust are building. **5/8/2018 11:22**

John Kerry can't get over the fact that he had his chance and blew it! Stay away from negotiations John you are hurting your country! **5/8/2018 11:30**

The Iran Deal is defective at its core. If we do nothing we know what will happen. In just a short time the world's leading state sponsor of terror will be on the cusp of acquiring the world's most dangerous weapons.... https://t.co/58qwBLzxIH **5/8/2018 22:11**

The Republican Party had a great night. Tremendous voter energy and excitement and all candidates are those who have a great chance of winning in November. The Economy is sooo strong and with Nancy Pelosi wanting to end the big Tax Cuts and Raise Taxes why wouldn't we win? **5/9/2018 11:24**

The Fake News is working overtime. Just reported that despite the tremendous success we are having with the economy & all things else 91% of the Network News about me is negative (Fake). Why do we work so hard in working with the media when it is corrupt? Take away credentials? **5/9/2018 11:38**

Candace Owens of Turning Point USA is having a big impact on politics in our Country. She represents an ever expanding group of very smart "thinkers" and it is wonderful to watch and hear the dialogue going on...so good for our Country! **5/9/2018 11:48**

I am pleased to inform you that Secretary of State Mike Pompeo is in the air and on his way back from North Korea with the 3 wonderful gentlemen that everyone is looking so forward to meeting. They seem to be in good health. Also good meeting with Kim Jong Un. Date & Place set.

5/9/2018 12:30

Secretary Pompeo and his "guests" will be landing at Andrews Air Force Base at 2:00 A.M. in the morning. I will be there to greet them. Very exciting! **5/9/2018 12:35**

The Failing New York Times criticized Secretary of State Pompeo for being AWOL (missing) when in fact he was flying to North Korea. Fake News so bad! **5/9/2018 22:38**

Looking forward to greeting the Hostages (no longer) at 2:00 A.M. **5/9/2018 22:41**

Gina Haspel did a spectacular job today. There is nobody even close to run the CIA! **5/10/2018 2:19**

Senator Cryin' Chuck Schumer fought hard against the Bad Iran Deal even going at it with President Obama & then Voted AGAINST it! Now he says I should not have terminated the deal - but he doesn't really believe that! Same with Comey. Thought he was terrible until I fired him! **5/10/2018 14:30**

Five Most Wanted leaders of ISIS just captured! **5/10/2018 14:33**

The highly anticipated meeting between Kim Jong Un and myself will take place in Singapore on June 12th. We will both try to make it a very special moment for World Peace! **5/10/2018 14:37**

Thank you Indiana! #MAGA https://t.co/fCv76VyUax
5/11/2018 0:49

Today my Administration is launching the most sweeping action in history to lower the price of prescription drugs for the American People. We will have tougher negotiation more competition and much lower prices at the pharmacy counter! https://t.co/xdakX43a4d **5/11/2018 19:30**

The American people deserve a healthcare system that takes care of them - not one that takes advantage of them. We will work every day to ensure all Americans have access to the quality affordable medication they need and deserve. We will not rest until the job is done!
https://t.co/9BzevAniNx **5/11/2018 20:56**

Big week next week when the American Embassy in Israel will be moved to Jerusalem. Congratulations to all!
5/11/2018 23:39

Why doesn't the Fake News Media state that the Trump Administration's Anti-Trust Division has been and is opposed to the AT&T purchase of Time Warner in a currently ongoing Trial. Such a disgrace in reporting!
5/11/2018 23:49

North Korea has announced that they will dismantle Nuclear Test Site this month ahead of the big Summit Meeting on June 12th. Thank you a very smart and gracious gesture!

5/12/2018 21:08

Iran's Military Budget is up more than 40% since the Obama negotiated Nuclear Deal was reached...just another indicator that it was all a big lie. But not anymore! **5/12/2018 22:02**

The Senate should get funding done before the August break or NOT GO HOME. Wall and Border Security should be included. Also waiting for approval of almost 300 nominations worst in history. Democrats are doing everything possible to obstruct all they know how to do. STAY! **5/12/2018 22:20**

Happy Mother's Day!!! https://t.co/zw71dnT7TJ **5/13/2018 12:29**

President Xi of China and I are working together to give massive Chinese phone company ZTE a way to get back into business fast. Too many jobs in China lost. Commerce Department has been instructed to get it done! **5/13/2018 15:01**

China and the United States are working well together on trade but past negotiations have been so one sided in favor of China for so many years that it is hard for them to make a deal that benefits both countries. But be cool it will all work out! **5/13/2018 19:22**

Remember how badly Iran was behaving with the Iran Deal in place. They were trying to take over the Middle East by whatever means necessary. Now that will not happen! **5/13/2018 20:11**

So sad to see the Terror Attack in Paris. At some point countries will have to open their eyes & see what is really going on. This kind of sickness & hatred is not compatible with a loving peaceful & successful country! Changes to our thought process on terror must be made. **5/14/2018 0:03**

U.S. Embassy opening in Jerusalem will be covered live on @FoxNews & @FoxBusiness. Lead up to 9:00 A.M. (eastern) event has already begun. A great day for Israel! **5/14/2018 10:54**

Big day for Israel. Congratulations!
5/14/2018 13:36

The so-called leaks coming out of the White House are a massive over exaggeration put out by the Fake News Media in order to make us look as bad as possible. With that being said leakers are traitors and cowards and we will find out who they are! **5/14/2018 20:46**

Heading over to Walter Reed Medical Center to see our great First Lady Melania. Successful procedure she is in good spirits. Thank you to all of the well-wishers! **5/14/2018 21:09**

Our great First Lady is doing really well. Will be leaving hospital in 2 or 3 days. Thank you for so much love and support! **5/15/2018 12:26**

Can you believe that with all of the made up unsourced stories I get from the Fake News Media together with the $10000000 Russian Witch Hunt (there is no Collusion) I now have my best Poll Numbers in a year. Much of the Media may be corrupt but the People truly get it! **5/15/2018 14:08**

Today is one of the most important and solemn occasions of the year – the day we pay tribute to the Law Enforcement Heroes who gave their lives in the line of duty. They made the ultimate sacrifice so that we could live in safety and peace. We stand with our police (HEROES) 100%! https://t.co/XDtYRUeOk1 **5/15/2018 18:39**

Congratulations to Lou Barletta of Pennsylvania. He will be a great Senator and will represent his people well - like they haven't been represented in many years. Lou is a friend of mine and a special guy he will very much help MAKE AMERICA GREAT AGAIN! **5/16/2018 12:07**

Congratulations America we are now into the second year of the greatest Witch Hunt in American History...and there is still No Collusion and No Obstruction. The only Collusion was that done by Democrats who were unable to win an Election despite the spending of far more money! **5/17/2018 11:28**

Wow word seems to be coming out that the Obama FBI "SPIED ON THE TRUMP CAMPAIGN WITH AN EMBEDDED INFORMANT." Andrew McCarthy says "There's probably no doubt that they had at least one confidential informant in the campaign." If so this is bigger than Watergate! **5/17/2018 12:45**

Despite the disgusting illegal and unwarranted Witch Hunt we have had the most successful first 17 month Administration in U.S. history - by far! Sorry to the Fake News Media and "Haters" but that's the way it is! **5/17/2018 13:52**

Congratulations to our new CIA Director Gina Haspel! https://t.co/n1xj9LSV9D **5/17/2018 21:00**

Great talk with my friend President Mauricio Macri of Argentina this week. He is doing such a good job for Argentina. I support his vision for transforming his country's economy and unleashing its potential! **5/17/2018 21:53**

Fake News Media had me calling Immigrants or Illegal Immigrants "Animals." Wrong! They were begrudgingly forced to withdraw their stories. I referred to MS 13 Gang Members as "Animals" a big difference - and so true. Fake News got it purposely wrong as usual!

5/18/2018 10:51

Why isn't disgraced FBI official Andrew McCabe being investigated for the $700000 Crooked Hillary Democrats in Virginia led by Clinton best friend Terry M (under FBI investigation that they killed) gave to McCabe's wife in her run for office? Then dropped case on Clinton! **5/18/2018 13:38**

Reports are there was indeed at least one FBI representative implanted for political purposes into my campaign for president. It took place very early on and long before the phony Russia Hoax became a "hot" Fake News story. If true - all time biggest political scandal! **5/18/2018 13:50**

School shooting in Texas. Early reports not looking good. God bless all! **5/18/2018 15:05**

California finally deserves a great Governor one who understands borders crime and lowering taxes. John Cox is the man - he'll be the best Governor you've ever had. I fully endorse John Cox for Governor and look forward to working with him to Make California Great Again! **5/18/2018 22:00**

America is blessed with extraordinary energy abundance including more than 250 years worth of beautiful clean coal. We have ended the war on coal and will continue to work to promote American energy dominance! **5/18/2018 22:57**

Great to have our incredible First Lady back home in the White House. Melania is feeling and doing really well. Thank you for all of your prayers and best wishes! **5/19/2018 18:37**

If the FBI or DOJ was infiltrating a campaign for the benefit of another campaign that is a really big deal. Only the release or review of documents that the House Intelligence Committee (also Senate Judiciary) is asking for can give the conclusive answers. Drain the Swamp! **5/19/2018 21:27**

Things are really getting ridiculous. The Failing and Crooked (but not as Crooked as Hillary Clinton) @nytimes has done a long & boring story indicating that the World's most expensive Witch Hunt has found nothing on Russia & me so now they are looking at the rest of the World! (1/3) **5/20/2018 13:04**

....At what point does this soon to be $20000000 Witch Hunt composed of 13 Angry and Heavily Conflicted Democrats and two people who have worked for Obama for 8 years STOP! They have found no Collussion with Russia No Obstruction but they aren't looking at the corruption... (2/3) **5/20/2018 13:11**

...in the Hillary Clinton Campaign where she deleted 33000 Emails got $145000000 while Secretary of State paid McCabes wife $700000 (and got off the FBI hook along with Terry M) and so much more. Republicans and real Americans should start getting tough on this Scam. (3/3)

5/20/2018 13:19

Now that the Witch Hunt has given up on Russia and is looking at the rest of the World they should easily be able to take it into the Mid-Term Elections where they can put some hurt on the Republican Party. Don't worry about Dems FISA Abuse missing Emails or Fraudulent Dossier!

5/20/2018 13:29

What ever happened to the Server at the center of so much Corruption that the Democratic National Committee REFUSED to hand over to the hard charging (except in the case of Democrats) FBI? They broke into homes & offices early in the morning but were afraid to take the Server? (1/2)

5/20/2018 13:37

....and why hasn't the Podesta brother been charged and arrested like others after being forced to close down his very large and successful firm? Is it because he is a VERY well connected Democrat working in the Swamp of Washington D.C.? (2/2)

5/20/2018 14:04

The Witch Hunt finds no Collusion with Russia - so now they're looking at the rest of the World. Oh' great!

5/20/2018 17:13

I hereby demand and will do so officially tomorrow that the Department of Justice look into whether or not the FBI/DOJ infiltrated or surveilled the Trump Campaign for Political Purposes - and if any such demands or requests were made by people within the Obama Administration!

5/20/2018 17:37

"John Brennan is panicking. He has disgraced himself he has disgraced the Country he has disgraced the entire Intelligence Community. He is the one man who is largely responsible for the destruction of American's faith in the Intelligence Community and in some people at the.... **5/21/2018 11:53**

...they then used to start an investigation about Trump. It is that simple. This guy is the genesis of this whole Debacle. This was a Political hit job this was not an Intelligence Investigation. Brennan has disgraced himself he's worried about staying out of Jail." Dan Bongino **5/21/2018 12:12**

The Wall Street Journal asks "WHERE IN THE WORLD WAS BARACK OBAMA?" A very good question! **5/21/2018 12:51**

Under our potential deal with China they will purchase from our Great American Farmers practically as much as our Farmers can produce. **5/21/2018 13:16**

For the first time since Roe v. Wade America has a Pro-Life President a Pro-Life Vice President a Pro-Life House of Representatives and 25 Pro-Life Republican State Capitals! https://t.co/EfF54tmetT **5/23/2018 0:40**

If the person placed very early into my campaign wasn't a SPY put there by the previous Administration for political purposes how come such a seemingly massive amount of money was paid for services rendered - many times higher than normal... **5/23/2018 1:13**

...Follow the money! The spy was there early in the campaign and yet never reported Collusion with Russia because there was no Collusion. He was only there to spy for political reasons and to help Crooked Hillary win - just like they did to Bernie Sanders who got duped! **5/23/2018 1:13**

Look how things have turned around on the Criminal Deep State. They go after Phony Collusion with Russia a made up Scam and end up getting caught in a major SPY scandal the likes of which this country may never have seen before! What goes around comes around! **5/23/2018 10:54**

SPYGATE could be one of the biggest political scandals in history! **5/23/2018 11:12**

Everybody is with Tomi Lahren a truly outstanding and respected young woman! @foxandfriends **5/23/2018 11:22**

"Trump should be happy that the FBI was SPYING on his campaign" No James Clapper I am not happy. Spying on a campaign would be illegal and a scandal to boot! **5/23/2018 11:33**

There will be big news coming soon for our great American Autoworkers. After many decades of losing your jobs to other countries you have waited long enough! **5/23/2018 13:18**

WITCH HUNT! **5/23/2018 13:34**

Clapper has now admitted that there was Spying in my campaign. Large dollars were paid to the Spy far beyond normal. Starting to look like one of the biggest political scandals in U.S. history. SPYGATE - a terrible thing! **5/24/2018 12:21**

Not surprisingly the GREAT Men & Women of the FBI are starting to speak out against Comey McCabe and all of the political corruption and poor leadership found within the top ranks of the FBI. Comey was a terrible and corrupt leader who inflicted great pain on the FBI! #SPYGATE **5/24/2018 12:34**

Can anyone even imagine having Spies placed in a competing campaign by the people and party in absolute power for the sole purpose of political advantage and gain? And to think that the party in question even with the expenditure of far more money LOST! **5/25/2018 12:04**

Democrats are so obviously rooting against us in our negotiations with North Korea. Just like they are coming to the defense of MS 13 thugs saying that they are individuals & must be nurtured or asking to end your big Tax Cuts & raise your taxes instead. Dems have lost touch! **5/25/2018 12:04**

Very good news to receive the warm and productive statement from North Korea. We will soon see where it will lead hopefully to long and enduring prosperity and peace. Only time (and talent) will tell! **5/25/2018 12:14**

Chicago Police have every right to legally protest against the mayor and an administration that just won't let them do their job. The killings are at a record pace and tough police work which Chicago will not allow would bring things back to order fast...the killings must stop! **5/25/2018 22:14**

Funny to watch the Democrats criticize Trade Deals being negotiated by me when they don't even know what the deals are and when for 8 years the Obama Administration did NOTHING on trade except let other countries rip off the United States. Lost almost $800 Billion/year under "O"
5/25/2018 22:45

Senator Schumer and Obama Administration let phone company ZTE flourish with no security checks. I closed it down then let it reopen with high level security guarantees change of management and board must purchase U.S. parts and pay a $1.3 Billion fine. Dems do nothing.... **5/25/2018 23:07**

We are having very productive talks with North Korea about reinstating the Summit which if it does happen will likely remain in Singapore on the same date June 12th. and if necessary will be extended beyond that date. **5/26/2018 0:37**

Good news about the release of the American hostage from Venezuela. Should be landing in D.C. this evening and be in the White House with his family at about 7:00 P.M. The great people of Utah will be very happy! **5/26/2018 13:22**

Put pressure on the Democrats to end the horrible law that separates children from there parents once they cross the Border into the U.S. Catch and Release Lottery and Chain must also go with it and we MUST continue building the WALL! DEMOCRATS ARE PROTECTING MS-13 THUGS.
5/26/2018 13:59

Thanks to very brave Teacher & Hero Jason Seaman of Noblesville Indiana for his heroic act in saving so many precious young lives. His quick and automatic action is being talked about all over the world! **5/26/2018 14:47**

The Failing @nytimes quotes "a senior White House official" who doesn't exist as saying "even if the meeting were reinstated holding it on June 12 would be impossible given the lack of time and the amount of planning needed." WRONG AGAIN! Use real people not phony sources. **5/26/2018 15:21**

This whole Russia Probe is Rigged. Just an excuse as to why the Dems and Crooked Hillary lost the Election and States that haven't been lost in decades. 13 Angry Democrats and all Dems if you include the people who worked for Obama for 8 years. #SPYGATE & CONFLICTS OF INTEREST! **5/26/2018 19:41**

When will the 13 Angry Democrats (& those who worked for President O) reveal their disqualifying Conflicts of Interest? It's been a long time now! Will they be indelibly written into the Report along with the fact that the only Collusion is with the Dems Justice FBI & Russia? **5/26/2018 19:56**

Who's going to give back the young and beautiful lives (and others) that have been devastated and destroyed by the phony Russia Collusion Witch Hunt? They journeyed down to Washington D.C. with stars in their eyes and wanting to help our nation...They went back home in tatters! **5/27/2018 12:41**

Fantastic to have 400000 GREAT MEN & WOMEN of Rolling Thunder in D.C. showing their patriotism. They love our Country they love our Flag they stand for our National Anthem! Thanks to Executive Director Artie Muller. **5/27/2018 13:14**

Why didn't the 13 Angry Democrats investigate the campaign of Crooked Hillary Clinton many crimes much Collusion with Russia? Why didn't the FBI take the Server from the DNC? Rigged Investigation! **5/27/2018 14:13**

Our United States team has arrived in North Korea to make arrangements for the Summit between Kim Jong Un and myself. I truly believe North Korea has brilliant potential and will be a great economic and financial Nation one day. Kim Jong Un agrees with me on this. It will happen! **5/27/2018 20:09**

Why didn't President Obama do something about the so-called Russian Meddling when he was told about it by the FBI before the Election? Because he thought Crooked Hillary was going to win and he didn't want to upset the apple cart! He was in charge not me and did nothing.
5/27/2018 20:32

Happy Memorial Day! Those who died for our great country would be very happy and proud at how well our country is doing today. Best economy in decades lowest unemployment numbers for Blacks and Hispanics EVER (& women in 18years) rebuilding our Military and so much more. Nice! **5/28/2018 12:58**

A Democratic lawmaker just introduced a bill to Repeal the GOP Tax Cuts (no chance). This is too good to be true for Republicans...Remember the Nancy Pelosi Dems are also weak on Crime the Border and want to be gentle and kind to MS-13 gang members...not good! **5/28/2018 21:22**

California has a rare opportunity to turn things around and solve its high crime high tax problems - along with so many others. On June 5th. vote for GOP Gubernatorial Candidate JOHN COX a really good and highly competent man. He'll Make California Great Again! **5/28/2018 21:53**

Democrats mistakenly tweet 2014 pictures from Obama's term showing children from the Border in steel cages. They thought it was recent pictures in order to make us look bad but backfires. Dems must agree to Wall and new Border Protection for good of country...Bipartisan Bill! **5/29/2018 10:07**

The 13 Angry Democrats (plus people who worked 8 years for Obama) working on the rigged Russia Witch Hunt will be MEDDLING with the mid-term elections especially now that Republicans (stay tough!) are taking the lead in Polls.

There was no Collusion except by the Democrats!
5/29/2018 11:00

Sorry I've got to start focusing my energy on North Korea Nuclear bad Trade Deals VA Choice the Economy rebuilding the Military and so much more and not on the Rigged Russia Witch Hunt that should be investigating Clinton/Russia/FBI/Justice/Obama/Comey/Lynch etc.
5/29/2018 11:27

The Fake Mainstream Media has from the time I announced I was running for President run the most highly sophisticated & dishonest Disinformation Campaign in the history of politics. No matter how well WE do they find fault. But the forgotten men & women WON I'm President! **5/29/2018 13:30**

The Failing and Corrupt @nytimes estimated the crowd last night at "1000 people" when in fact it was many times that number - and the arena was rockin'. This is the way they demean and disparage. They are very dishonest people who don't "get" me and never did! **5/30/2018 14:35**

Bob Iger of ABC called Valerie Jarrett to let her know that "ABC does not tolerate comments like those" made by Roseanne Barr. Gee he never called President Donald J. Trump to apologize for the HORRIBLE statements made and said about me on ABC. Maybe I just didn't get the call?

5/30/2018 15:31

Great meeting with @KimKardashian today talked about prison reform and sentencing. https://t.co/uOy4UJ41JF
5/30/2018 22:59

The soon to be released book "The Russia Hoax The Illicit Scheme To Clear Hillary Clinton And Frame Donald Trump" written by Gregg Jarrett looks like a real deal big hit. The

Phony Witch Hunt will be opened up for the world to see! Out in 5 weeks. **5/31/2018 3:06**

RUSH LIMBAUGH "If the FBI was so concerned and if they weren't targeting Trump they should have told Trump. If they were really concerned about the Russians infiltrating a campaign (hoax) then why not try to stop it? Why not tell Trump? Because they were pushing this scam." **5/31/2018 10:55**

Iger where is my call of apology? You and ABC have offended millions of people and they demand a response. How is Brian Ross doing? He tanked the market with an ABC lie yet no apology. Double Standard! **5/31/2018 11:53**

The corrupt Mainstream Media is working overtime not to mention the infiltration of people Spies (Informants) into my campaign! Surveillance much? **5/31/2018 12:05**

Very good meetings with North Korea. **5/31/2018 13:15**

Will be giving a Full Pardon to Dinesh D'Souza today. He was treated very unfairly by our government! **5/31/2018 13:18**

FAIR TRADE! **5/31/2018 21:19**

A.P. has just reported that the Russian Hoax Investigation has now cost our government over $17 million and going up fast. No Collusion except by the Democrats! **6/1/2018 11:05**

Why aren't they firing no talent Samantha Bee for the horrible language used on her low ratings show? A total double standard but that's O.K. we are Winning and will be doing so for a long time to come! **6/1/2018 11:15**

Today it was my great honor to be with the brave men and women of the United States Coast Guard! https://t.co/RAyPbOGXuZ **6/1/2018 21:40**

"John Brennan no single figure in American history has done more to discredit the intelligence community than this liar. Not only is he a liar he's a liar about being a liar." Dan Bongino on @foxandfriends **6/2/2018 12:06**

The United States must at long last be treated fairly on Trade. If we charge a country ZERO to sell their goods and they charge us 25 50 or even 100 percent to sell ours it is UNFAIR and can no longer be tolerated. That is not Free or Fair Trade it is Stupid Trade! **6/2/2018 17:51**

When you're almost 800 Billion Dollars a year down on Trade you can't lose a Trade War! The U.S. has been ripped off by other countries for years on Trade time to get smart! **6/2/2018 21:23**

Jesse Watters "The only thing Trump obstructed was Hillary getting to the White House." So true! **6/3/2018 12:59**

As only one of two people left who could become President why wouldn't the FBI or Department of "Justice" have told me that they were secretly investigating Paul Manafort (on charges that were 10 years old and had been previously dropped) during my campaign? Should have told me! **6/3/2018 13:25**

....Paul Manafort came into the campaign very late and was with us for a short period of time (he represented Ronald Reagan Bob Dole & many others over the years) but we should have been told that Comey and the boys were doing a number on him and he wouldn't have been hired! **6/3/2018 13:34**

Mark Penn "Why are there people from the Clinton Foundation on the Mueller Staff? Why is there an Independent Counsel? To go after people and their families for unrelated offenses...Constitution was set up to prevent this...Stormtrooper tactics almost." A disgrace! **6/3/2018 17:34**

This is my 500th. Day in Office and we have accomplished a lot - many believe more than any President in his first 500 days. Massive Tax & Regulation Cuts Military & Vets Lower Crime & Illegal Immigration Stronger Borders Judgeships Best Economy & Jobs EVER and much more... **6/4/2018 11:35**

As has been stated by numerous legal scholars I have the absolute right to PARDON myself but why would I do that when I have done nothing wrong? In the meantime the never ending Witch Hunt led by 13 very Angry and Conflicted Democrats (& others) continues into the mid-terms! **6/4/2018 12:35**

The Fake News Media is desperate to distract from the economy and record setting economic numbers and so they keep talking about the phony Russian Witch Hunt. **6/4/2018 20:41**

In many ways this is the greatest economy in the HISTORY of America and the best time EVER to look for a job! **6/4/2018 20:42**

The Philadelphia Eagles Football Team was invited to the White House. Unfortunately only a small number of players decided to come and we canceled the event. Staying in the Locker Room for the playing of our National Anthem is as disrespectful to our country as kneeling. Sorry! **6/5/2018 2:55**

What is taking so long with the Inspector General's Report on Crooked Hillary and Slippery James Comey. Numerous delays. Hope Report is not being changed and made weaker! There are so many horrible things to tell the public has the right to know. Transparency! **6/5/2018 10:38**

Imagine how much wasteful spending we'd save if we didn't have Chuck and Nancy standing in our way! For years Democrats in Congress have depleted our military and busted our budgets on needless spending and to what end? No more. **6/5/2018 20:07**

Wow Strzok-Page the incompetent & corrupt FBI lovers have texts referring to a counter-intelligence operation into the Trump Campaign dating way back to December 2015. SPYGATE is in full force! Is the Mainstream Media interested yet? Big stuff! **6/6/2018 0:37**

...This is a level of criminality beyond the pale. This is such a grave abuse of power and authority it's like nothing else we've seen in our history. This makes the Nixon Watergate burglary look like keystone cop stuff **6/6/2018 1:27**

Mitch McConnell announced he will cancel the Senate's August Recess. Great maybe the Democrats will finally get something done other than their acceptance of High Crime and High Taxes. We need Border Security! **6/6/2018 4:02**

Great night for Republicans! Congratulations to John Cox on a really big number in California. He can win. Even Fake News CNN said the Trump impact was really big much bigger than they ever thought possible. So much for the big Blue Wave it may be a big Red Wave. Working hard! **6/6/2018 13:16**

The Fake News Media has been so unfair and vicious to my wife and our great First Lady Melania. During her recovery from surgery they reported everything from near death to facelift to left the W.H. (and me) for N.Y. or Virginia to abuse. All Fake she is doing really well! **6/6/2018 13:48**

...Four reporters spotted Melania in the White House last week walking merrily along to a meeting. They never reported the sighting because it would hurt the sick narrative that she was living in a different part of the world was really ill or whatever. Fake News is really bad! **6/6/2018 13:54**

Isn't it Ironic? Getting ready to go to the G-7 in Canada to fight for our country on Trade (we have the worst trade deals ever made) then off to Singapore to meet with North Korea & the Nuclear Problem...But back home we still have the 13 Angry Democrats pushing the Witch Hunt! **6/7/2018 11:57**

Good luck to Alice Johnson. Have a wonderful life! **6/7/2018 12:07**

Our Justice Department must not let Awan & Debbie Wasserman Schultz off the hook. The Democrat I.T. scandal is a key to much of the corruption we see today. They want to make a "plea deal" to hide what is on their Server. Where is Server? Really bad! **6/7/2018 14:07**

When will people start saying "thank you Mr. President for firing James Comey?" **6/7/2018 15:10**

The Obama Administration is now accused of trying to give Iran secret access to the financial system of the United States. This is totally illegal. Perhaps we could get the 13 Angry Democrats to divert some of their energy to this "matter" (as Comey would call it). Investigate! **6/7/2018 15:15**

MAKING AMERICA GREAT AGAIN! https://t.co/KppRUU5OZ3 **6/7/2018 15:42**

Please tell Prime Minister Trudeau and President Macron that they are charging the U.S. massive tariffs and create non-monetary barriers. The EU trade surplus with the U.S. is $151 Billion and Canada keeps our farmers and others out. Look forward to seeing them tomorrow. **6/7/2018 22:04**

Prime Minister Trudeau is being so indignant bringing up the relationship that the U.S. and Canada had over the many years and all sorts of other things...but he doesn't bring up the fact that they charge us up to 300% on dairy — hurting our Farmers killing our Agriculture! **6/7/2018 23:44**

Why isn't the European Union and Canada informing the public that for years they have used massive Trade Tariffs and non-monetary Trade Barriers against the U.S. Totally unfair to our farmers workers & companies. Take down your tariffs & barriers or we will more than match you! **6/8/2018 2:15**

Obama Schumer and Pelosi did NOTHING about North Korea and now weak on Crime High Tax Schumer is telling me what to do at the Summit the Dems could never set up. Schumer failed with North Korea and Iran we don't need his advice! **6/8/2018 10:06**

Canada charges the U.S. a 270% tariff on Dairy Products! They didn't tell you that did they? Not fair to our farmers! **6/8/2018 10:16**

Congratulations to the Washington Capitals on their GREAT play and winning the Stanley Cup Championship. Alex Ovechkin the team captain was spectacular - a true Superstar! D.C. is popping in many ways. What a time! **6/8/2018 11:12**

I am heading for Canada and the G-7 for talks that will mostly center on the long time unfair trade practiced against the United States. From there I go to Singapore and talks with North Korea on Denuclearization. Won't be talking about the Russian Witch Hunt Hoax for a while!
6/8/2018 11:22

My thoughts and prayers are with the families of our serviceman who was killed and his fellow servicemen who were wounded in Somalia. They are truly all HEROES.
6/9/2018 4:22

Just met the new Prime Minister of Italy @GiuseppeContelT a really great guy. He will be honored in Washington at the @WhiteHouse shortly. He will do a great job - the people of Italy got it right! **6/9/2018 20:43**

The United States will not allow other countries to impose massive Tariffs and Trade Barriers on its farmers workers and companies. While sending their product into our country tax free. We have put up with Trade Abuse for many decades — and that is long enough. **6/9/2018 20:57**

I am on my way to Singapore where we have a chance to achieve a truly wonderful result for North Korea and the World. It will certainly be an exciting day and I know that Kim Jong-un will work very hard to do something that has rarely been done before... **6/9/2018 20:58**

Based on Justin's false statements at his news conference and the fact that Canada is charging massive Tariffs to our U.S. farmers workers and companies I have instructed our U.S. Reps not to endorse the Communique as we look at Tariffs on automobiles flooding the U.S. Market! **6/9/2018 23:03**

PM Justin Trudeau of Canada acted so meek and mild during our @G7 meetings only to give a news conference after I left saying that "US Tariffs were kind of insulting" and he "will not be pushed around." Very dishonest & weak. Our Tariffs are in response to his of 270% on dairy! **6/9/2018 23:04**

Fair Trade is now to be called Fool Trade if it is not Reciprocal. According to a Canada release they make almost 100 Billion Dollars in Trade with U.S. (guess they were bragging and got caught!). Minimum is 17B. Tax Dairy from us at 270%. Then Justin acts hurt when called out!
6/11/2018 1:05

Why should I as President of the United States allow countries to continue to make Massive Trade Surpluses as they have for decades while our Farmers Workers & Taxpayers have such a big and unfair price to pay? Not fair to the PEOPLE of America! $800 Billion Trade Deficit... (1/3)
6/11/2018 1:17

....And add to that the fact that the U.S. pays close to the entire cost of NATO-protecting many of these same countries that rip us off on Trade (they pay only a fraction of the cost-and laugh!). The European Union had a $151 Billion Surplus-should pay much more for Military! (2/3)
6/11/2018 1:29

....Germany pays 1% (slowly) of GDP towards NATO while we pay 4% of a MUCH larger GDP. Does anybody believe that makes sense? We protect Europe (which is good) at great financial loss and then get unfairly clobbered on Trade. Change is coming! (3/3) **6/11/2018 1:42**

Great to be in Singapore excitement in the air! **6/11/2018 1:45**

Sorry we cannot let our friends or enemies take advantage of us on Trade anymore. We must put the American worker first! **6/11/2018 2:41**

Thank you Prime Minister Lee Hsien Loong! https://t.co/8MMYGuOj8Q **6/11/2018 7:51**

Meetings between staffs and representatives are going well and quickly....but in the end that doesn't matter. We will all know soon whether or not a real deal unlike those of the past can happen! **6/11/2018 21:27**

Stock Market up almost 40% since the Election with 7 Trillion Dollars of U.S. value built throughout the economy. Lowest unemployment rate in many decades with Black & Hispanic unemployment lowest in History and Female unemployment lowest in 21 years. Highest confidence ever!
6/11/2018 21:52

The fact that I am having a meeting is a major loss for the U.S. say the haters & losers. We have our hostages testing research and all missle launches have stoped and these pundits who have called me wrong from the beginning have nothing else they can say! We will be fine! **6/11/2018 22:04**

Just won big Supreme Court decision on Voting! Great News! **6/12/2018 0:03**

Our Great Larry Kudlow who has been working so hard on trade and the economy has just suffered a heart attack. He is now in Walter Reed Medical Center. **6/12/2018 0:35**

Heading back home from Singapore after a truly amazing visit. Great progress was made on the denuclearization of North Korea. Hostages are back home will be getting the remains of our great heroes back to their families no missiles shot no research happening sites closing...
6/12/2018 20:40

...Got along great with Kim Jong-un who wants to see wonderful things for his country. As I said earlier today: Anyone can make war but only the most courageous can make peace! #SingaporeSummit **6/12/2018 20:40**

Robert De Niro a very Low IQ individual has received to many shots to the head by real boxers in movies. I watched him last night and truly believe he may be "punch-drunk." I guess he doesn't... (1/2) **6/12/2018 20:53**

...realize the economy is the best it's ever been with employment being at an all time high and many companies pouring back into our country. Wake up Punchy! (2/2)
6/12/2018 20:53

There is no limit to what NoKo can achieve when it gives up its nuclear weapons and embraces commerce & engagement w/ the world. Chairman Kim has before him the opportunity to be remembered as the leader who ushered in a glorious new era of security & prosperity for his citizens! https://t.co/Xbup4Zyz33 **6/13/2018 0:02**

I want to thank Chairman Kim for taking the first bold step toward a bright new future for his people. Our unprecedented meeting - the first between an American President and a leader of North Korea - proves that real change is possible! https://t.co/yF3iwD23YQ **6/13/2018 0:11**

The World has taken a big step back from potential Nuclear catastrophe! No more rocket launches nuclear testing or research! The hostages are back home with their families. Thank you to Chairman Kim our day together was historic!
6/13/2018 0:27

A year ago the pundits & talking heads people that couldn't do the job before were begging for conciliation and peace - "please meet don't go to war." Now that we meet and have a great relationship with Kim Jong Un the same haters shout out "you shouldn't meet do not meet!" **6/13/2018 1:14**

Robert De Niro a very Low IQ individual has received too many shots to the head by real boxers in movies. I watched him last night and truly believe he may be "punch-drunk." I guess he doesn't... **6/13/2018 9:40**

Just landed - a long trip but everybody can now feel much safer than the day I took office. There is no longer a Nuclear Threat from North Korea. Meeting with Kim Jong Un was an interesting and very positive experience. North Korea has great potential for the future! **6/13/2018 9:56**

Before taking office people were assuming that we were going to War with North Korea. President Obama said that North Korea was our biggest and most dangerous problem. No longer - sleep well tonight! **6/13/2018 10:01**

We save a fortune by not doing war games as long as we are negotiating in good faith - which both sides are!
6/13/2018 11:10

The U.S. together with Mexico and Canada just got the World Cup. Congratulations - a great deal of hard work!
6/13/2018 11:49

Oil prices are too high OPEC is at it again. Not good!
6/13/2018 11:52

So funny to watch the Fake News especially NBC and CNN. They are fighting hard to downplay the deal with North Korea. 500 days ago they would have "begged" for this deal-looked like war would break out. Our Country's biggest enemy is the Fake News so easily promulgated by fools!
6/13/2018 13:30

Senator Claire McCaskill of the GREAT State of Missouri flew around in a luxurious private jet during her RV tour of the state. RV's are not for her. People are really upset so phony! Josh Hawley should win big and has my full endorsement.
6/13/2018 20:11

Congratulations to Danny Tarkanian on his big GOP primary win in Nevada. Danny worked hard an got a great result. Looking good in November!
6/13/2018 20:17

The Republican Party is starting to show very big numbers. People are starting to see what is being done. Results are speaking loudly. North Korea and our greatest ever economy are leading the way!
6/14/2018 12:34

So the Democrats make up a phony crime Collusion with the Russians pay a fortune to make the crime sound real illegally leak (Comey) classified information so that a

Special Councel will be appointed and then Collude to make this pile of garbage take on life in Fake News! **6/14/2018 15:08**

The sleazy New York Democrats and their now disgraced (and run out of town) A.G. Eric Schneiderman are doing everything they can to sue me on a foundation that took in $18800000 and gave out to charity more money than it took in $19200000. I won't settle this case!... **6/14/2018 15:09**

Happy #FlagDay https://t.co/KEUMfnoHlv **6/14/2018 17:34**

FBI Agent Peter Strzok who headed the Clinton & Russia investigations texted to his lover Lisa Page in the IG Report that "we'll stop" candidate Trump from becoming President. Doesn't get any lower than that! **6/15/2018 10:35**

The IG Report is a total disaster for Comey his minions and sadly the FBI. Comey will now officially go down as the worst leader by far in the history of the FBI. I did a great service to the people in firing him. Good Instincts. Christopher Wray will bring it proudly back! **6/15/2018 10:55**

U.S.A. Jobs numbers are the BEST in 44 years. If my opponent (the Democrats) had won the election they would have raised taxes substantially and increased regulations - the economy and jobs would have been a disaster! **6/15/2018 11:45**

Wow the highest rated (by far) morning show @ foxandfriends is on the Front Lawn of the White House. Maybe I'll have to take an unannounced trip down to see them? **6/15/2018 11:50**

The Democrats are forcing the breakup of families at the Border with their horrible and cruel legislative agenda. Any Immigration Bill MUST HAVE full funding for the Wall end Catch & Release Visa Lottery and Chain and go to Merit Based Immigration. Go for it! WIN! **6/15/2018 17:08**

Wow what a tough sentence for Paul Manafort who has represented Ronald Reagan Bob Dole and many other top political people and campaigns. Didn't know Manafort was the head of the Mob. What about Comey and Crooked Hillary and all of the others? Very unfair! **6/15/2018 17:41**

I've had to beat 17 very talented people including the Bush Dynasty then I had to beat the Clinton Dynasty and now I have to beat a phony Witch Hunt and all of the dishonest people covered in the IG Report...and never forget the Fake News Media. It never ends! **6/15/2018 17:49**

Democrats can fix their forced family breakup at the Border by working with Republicans on new legislation for a change! This is why we need more Republicans elected in November. Democrats are good at only three things High Taxes High Crime and Obstruction. Sad! **6/16/2018 13:03**

My supporters are the smartest strongest most hard working and most loyal that we have seen in our countries history. It is a beautiful thing to watch as we win elections and gather support from all over the country. As we get stronger so does our country. Best numbers ever!

6/16/2018 13:12

The IG Report totally destroys James Comey and all of his minions including the great lovers Peter Strzok and Lisa Page who started the disgraceful Witch Hunt against so many innocent people. It will go down as a dark and dangerous period in American History! **6/16/2018 14:01**

Chuck Schumer said "the Summit was what the Texans call all cattle and no hat." Thank you Chuck but are you sure you got that right? No more nuclear testing or rockets flying all over the place blew up launch sites. Hostages already back hero remains coming home & much more!

6/17/2018 11:52

Our economy is perhaps BETTER than it has ever been. Companies doing really well and moving back to America and jobs numbers are the best in 44 years. **6/17/2018 13:08**

WITCH HUNT! There was no Russian Collusion. Oh I see there was no Russian Collusion so now they look for obstruction on the no Russian Collusion. The phony Russian Collusion was a made up Hoax. Too bad they didn't look at Crooked Hillary like this. Double Standard! **6/17/2018 14:54**

Why was the FBI giving so much information to the Fake News Media. They are not supposed to be doing that and knowing the enemy of the people Fake News they put their own spin on it - truth doesn't matter to them! **6/18/2018 0:25**

Why was the FBI's sick loser Peter Strzok working on the totally discredited Mueller team of 13 Angry & Conflicted Democrats when Strzok was giving Crooked Hillary a free pass yet telling his lover lawyer Lisa Page that "we'll stop" Trump from becoming President? Witch Hunt! **6/18/2018 0:42**

The Democrats should get together with their Republican counterparts and work something out on Border Security & Safety. Don't wait until after the election because you are going to lose! **6/18/2018 0:49**

"The highest level of bias I've ever witnessed in any law enforcement officer." Trey Gowdy on the FBI's own Peter Strzok. Also remember that they all worked for Slippery James Comey and that Comey is best friends with Robert Mueller. A really sick deal isn't it? **6/18/2018 1:03**

Why don't the Democrats give us the votes to fix the world's worst immigration laws? Where is the outcry for the killings and crime being caused by gangs and thugs including MS-13 coming into our country illegally? **6/18/2018 12:46**

The people of Germany are turning against their leadership as migration is rocking the already tenuous Berlin coalition. Crime in Germany is way up. Big mistake made all over

Europe in allowing millions of people in who have so strongly and violently changed their culture! **6/18/2018 13:02**

We don't want what is happening with immigration in Europe to happen with us! **6/18/2018 13:04**

Children are being used by some of the worst criminals on earth as a means to enter our country. Has anyone been looking at the Crime taking place south of the border. It is historic with some countries the most dangerous places in the world. Not going to happen in the U.S. **6/18/2018 13:50**

CHANGE THE LAWS! **6/18/2018 13:50**

It is the Democrats fault for being weak and ineffective with Boarder Security and Crime. Tell them to start thinking about the people devastated by Crime coming from illegal immigration. Change the laws! **6/18/2018 13:53**

If President Obama (who got nowhere with North Korea and would have had to go to war with many millions of people being killed) had gotten along with North Korea and made the initial steps toward a deal that I have the Fake News would have named him a national hero! **6/18/2018 14:57**

Comey gave Strozk his marching orders. Mueller is Comey's best friend. Witch Hunt! **6/18/2018 15:27**

I can't think of something more concerning than a law enforcement officer suggesting that their going to use their powers to affect an election!" Inspector General Horowitz on what was going on with numerous people regarding my election. A Rigged Witch Hunt!p **6/19/2018 13:52**

If you don't have Borders you don't have a Country!

6/19/2018 13:52

Democrats are the problem. They don't care about crime and want illegal immigrants no matter how bad they may be to pour into and infest our Country like MS-13. They can't win on their terrible policies so they view them as potential voters! **6/19/2018 13:52**

We must always arrest people coming into our Country illegally. Of the 12000 children 10000 are being sent by their parents on a very dangerous trip and only 2000 are with their parents many of whom have tried to enter our Country illegally on numerous occasions. **6/19/2018 14:07**

I want to take a moment to address the current illegal immigration crisis on the Southern Border...it has been going on for many many decades... https://t.co/1F7EK9Ef88 **6/19/2018 18:04**

Homeland Security @SecNielsen did a fabulous job yesterday at the press conference explaining security at the border and for our country while at the same time recommending changes to obsolete & nasty laws which force family separation. We want "heart" and security in America! **6/20/2018 1:06**

The Fake News is not mentioning the safety and security of our Country when talking about illegal immigration. Our immigration laws are the weakest and worst anywhere in the world and the Dems will do anything not to change them & to obstruct-want open borders which means crime! **6/20/2018 12:25**

It's the Democrats fault they won't give us the votes needed to pass good immigration legislation. They want open borders which breeds horrible crime. Republicans want security. But I am working on something - it never ends! **6/20/2018 13:41**

"FBI texts have revealed anti-Trump Bias." @FoxNews Big News but the Fake News doesn't want to cover. Total corruption - the Witch Hunt has turned out to be a scam! At some point soon the Mainstream Media will have to cover correctly too big a story! **6/20/2018 14:00**

Don't worry the Republicans and your President will fix it! https://t.co/xsbuPzXbHj

6/20/2018 20:39

So sorry people wanting to get into the already packed arena - I LOVE YOU ALL! https://t.co/PFvXrsvgkA

6/20/2018 23:30

Just returning from the Great State of Minnesota where we had an incredible rally with 9000 people and at least 10000 who could not get in - I will return! Congratulations to @ PeteStauber who is loved and respected in Minnesota!

6/21/2018 3:24

We shouldn't be hiring judges by the thousands as our ridiculous immigration laws demand we should be changing our laws building the Wall hire Border Agents and Ice and not let people come into our country based on the legal phrase they are told to say as their password. **6/21/2018 12:12**

Democrats want open Borders where anyone can come into our Country and stay. This is Nancy Pelosi's dream. It won't happen! **6/21/2018 14:38**

"I REALLY DON'T CARE DO U?" written on the back of Melania's jacket refers to the Fake News Media. Melania has learned how dishonest they are and she truly no longer cares! **6/21/2018 21:51**

We have to maintain strong borders or we will no longer have a country that we can be proud of - and if we show any weakness millions of people will journey into our country. **6/21/2018 22:40**

You cannot pass legislation on immigration whether it be for safety and security or any other reason including "heart" without getting Dem votes. Problem is they don't care about security and R's do. Zero Dems voted to support the Goodlatte Bill. They won't vote for anything! **6/21/2018 23:07**

Our great Judge Jeanine Pirro is out with a new book "Liars Leakers and Liberals the Case Against the Anti-Trump Conspiracy" which is fantastic. Go get it! **6/22/2018 10:41**

Elect more Republicans in November and we will pass the finest fairest and most comprehensive Immigration Bills anywhere in the world. Right now we have the dumbest and the worst. Dems are doing nothing but Obstructing. Remember their motto RESIST! Ours is PRODUCE!

6/22/2018 11:00

Republicans should stop wasting their time on Immigration until after we elect more Senators and Congressmen/women in November. Dems are just playing games have no intention of doing anything to solves this decades old problem. We can pass great legislation after the Red Wave!

6/22/2018 11:06

Congressman Ron DeSantis a top student at Yale and Harvard Law School is running for Governor of the Great State of Florida. Ron is strong on Borders tough on Crime & big on Cutting Taxes - Loves our Military & our Vets. He will be a Great Governor & has my full Endorsement! **6/22/2018 11:58**

80% of Mexico's Exports come to the United States. They totally rely on us which is fine with me. They do have though very strong Immigration Laws. The U.S. has pathetically weak and ineffective Immigration Laws that the Democrats refuse to help us fix. Will speak to Mexico!

6/22/2018 13:30

We must maintain a Strong Southern Border. We cannot allow our Country to be overrun by illegal immigrants as the Democrats tell their phony stories of sadness and grief hoping it will help them in the elections. Obama and others had the same pictures and did nothing about it! **6/22/2018 13:43**

We are gathered today to hear directly from the AMERICAN VICTIMS of ILLEGAL IMMIGRATION. These are the American Citizens permanently separated from their loved ones b/c they were killed by criminal illegal aliens. These are the families the media ignores... https://t.co/ZjXESYAcjY **6/22/2018 19:40**

Our first duty and our highest loyalty is to the citizens of the United States. We will not rest until our border is secure our citizens are safe and we finally end the immigration crisis once and for all. https://t.co/7YfZ9kjB23 **6/22/2018 20:23**

Based on the Tariffs and Trade Barriers long placed on the U.S. & its great companies and workers by the European Union if these Tariffs and Barriers are not soon broken down and removed we will be placing a 20% Tariff on all of their cars coming into the U.S. Build them here! **6/23/2018 0:34**

.@FoxNews Poll numbers plummet on the Democrat inspired and paid for Russian Witch Hunt. With all of the bias lying and hate by the investigators people want the investigators investigated. Much more will come out. A total scam and excuse for the Dems losing the Election!

6/23/2018 11:33

The Russian Witch Hunt is Rigged! **6/23/2018 11:36**

Drudge Report "OBAMA KEPT THEM IN CAGES WRAPPED THEM IN FOIL" We do a much better job while at the same time maintaining a MUCH stronger Border! Mainstream Fake Media hates this story. **6/23/2018 12:52**

It's very sad that Nancy Pelosi and her sidekick Cryin' Chuck Schumer want to protect illegal immigrants far more than the citizens of our country. The United States cannot stand for this. We wants safety and security at our borders!

6/23/2018 17:05

Happy Birthday to Supreme Court Justice Clarence Thomas a friend and great man! https://t.co/hlXYYkTjcv **6/23/2018 17:12**

Democrats fix the laws. Don't RESIST. We are doing a far better job than Bush and Obama but we need strength and security at the Border! Cannot accept all of the people

trying to break into our Country. Strong Borders No Crime!
6/24/2018 13:12

We cannot allow all of these people to invade our Country. When somebody comes in we must immediately with no Judges or Court Cases bring them back from where they came. Our system is a mockery to good immigration policy and Law and Order. Most children come without parents... (1/2) **6/24/2018 15:02**

....Our Immigration policy laughed at all over the world is very unfair to all of those people who have gone through the system legally and are waiting on line for years! Immigration must be based on merit - we need people who will help to Make America Great Again! (2/2) **6/24/2018 15:08**

The United States is insisting that all countries that have placed artificial Trade Barriers and Tariffs on goods going into their country remove those Barriers & Tariffs or be met with more than Reciprocity by the U.S.A. Trade must be fair and no longer a one way street! **6/24/2018 20:12**

.@jimmyfallon is now whimpering to all that he did the famous "hair show" with me (where he seriously messed up my hair) & that he would have now done it differently because it is said to have "humanized" me-he is taking heat. He called & said "monster ratings." Be a man Jimmy!
6/25/2018 0:01

House Republicans could easily pass a Bill on Strong Border Security but remember it still has to pass in the Senate and for that we need 10 Democrat votes and all they do is RESIST. They want Open Borders and don't care about Crime! Need more Republicans to WIN in November!
6/25/2018 0:08

The Red Hen Restaurant should focus more on cleaning its filthy canopies doors and windows (badly needs a paint job) rather than refusing to serve a fine person like Sarah Huckabee Sanders. I always had a rule if a restaurant is dirty on the outside it is dirty on the inside! **6/25/2018 11:41**

I have tried to stay uninvolved with the Department of Justice and FBI (although I do not legally have to) because of the now totally discredited and very expensive Witch Hunt currently going on. But you do have to ask why the DOJ & FBI aren't giving over requested documents?
6/25/2018 12:02

Such a difference in the media coverage of the same immigration policies between the Obama Administration and ours. Actually we have done a far better job in that our facilities are cleaner and better run than were the facilities under Obama. Fake News is working overtime! **6/25/2018 12:36**

Hiring manythousands of judges and going through a long and complicated legal process is not the way to go - will always be disfunctional. People must simply be stopped at the Border and told they cannot come into the U.S. illegally. Children brought back to their country...... (1/2) **6/25/2018 12:43**

....If this is done illegal immigration will be stopped in it's tracks - and at very little by comparison cost. This is the only real answer - and we must continue to BUILD THE WALL! (2/2) **6/25/2018 12:54**

Congresswoman Maxine Waters an extraordinarily low IQ person has become together with Nancy Pelosi the Face of the Democrat Party. She has just called for harm to supporters of which there are many of the Make America Great Again movement. Be careful what you wish for Max!
6/25/2018 17:11

Why is Senator Mark Warner (D-VA) perhaps in a near drunken state claiming he has information that only he and Bob Mueller the leader of the 13 Angry Democrats on a Witch Hunt knows? Isn't this highly illegal. Is it being investigated? **6/25/2018 23:22**

The hearing of Peter Strzok and the other hating frauds at the FBI & DOJ should be shown to the public on live television not a closed door hearing that nobody will see. We should expose these people for what they are - there should be total transparency! **6/25/2018 23:30**

A Harley-Davidson should never be built in another country-never! Their employees and customers are already very angry at them. If they move watch it will be the beginning of the end - they surrendered they quit! The Aura will be gone and they will be taxed like never before! **6/26/2018 12:17**

The face of the Democrats is now Maxine Waters who together with Nancy Pelosi have established a fine leadership team. They should always stay together and lead the Democrats who want Open Borders and Unlimited Crime well into the future....and pick Crooked Hillary for Pres. **6/26/2018 12:36**

"The most profound question of our era: Was there a conspiracy in the Obama Department of Justice and the FBI to prevent Donald Trump from becoming President of the U.S. and was Strzok at the core of the conspiracy?" Judge Andrew Napolitano **6/26/2018 13:30**

SUPREME COURT UPHOLDS TRUMP TRAVEL BAN. Wow!

6/26/2018 14:40

Wow! Big Trump Hater Congressman Joe Crowley who many expected was going to take Nancy Pelosi's place just LOST his primary election. In other words he's out! That is a big one that nobody saw happening. Perhaps he should have been nicer and more respectful to his President! **6/27/2018 2:18**

Congratulations to Maxine Waters whose crazy rants have made her together with Nancy Pelosi the unhinged FACE of the Democrat Party. Together they will Make America Weak Again! But have no fear America is now stronger than ever before and I'm not going anywhere! **6/27/2018 11:18**

HOUSE REPUBLICANS SHOULD PASS THE STRONG BUT FAIR IMMIGRATION BILL KNOWN AS GOODLATTE II IN THEIR AFTERNOON VOTE TODAY EVEN THOUGH THE DEMS WON'T LET IT PASS IN THE SENATE. PASSAGE

WILL SHOW THAT WE WANT STRONG BORDERS & SECURITY WHILE THE DEMS WANT OPEN BORDERS = CRIME. WIN! **6/27/2018 12:39**

Supreme Court rules in favor of non-union workers who are now as an example able to support a candidate of his or her choice without having those who control the Union deciding for them. Big loss for the coffers of the Democrats! **6/27/2018 14:11**

Harley-Davidson should stay 100% in America with the people that got you your success. I've done so much for you and then this. Other companies are coming back where they belong! We won't forget and neither will your customers or your now very HAPPY competitors! **6/27/2018 15:26**

Russia continues to say they had nothing to do with Meddling in our Election! Where is the DNC Server and why didn't Shady James Comey and the now disgraced FBI agents take and closely examine it? Why isn't Hillary/Russia being looked at? So many questions so much corruption! **6/28/2018 11:25**

I am in Milwaukee Wisconsin for meetings. Soon to leave for a big groundbreaking for Foxconn which is building a great new electronics plant in Wisconsin. 15000 Jobs so great! **6/28/2018 13:06**

Today we broke ground on a plant that will provide jobs for up to 15000 Wisconsin Workers! As Foxconn has discovered there is no better place to build hire and grow than right here in the United States! https://t.co/tOFFodZYvK **6/28/2018 18:57**

Prior to departing Wisconsin I was briefed on the shooting at Capital Gazette in Annapolis Maryland. My thoughts and prayers are with the victims and their families. Thank you to all of the First Responders who are currently on the scene. **6/28/2018 20:49**

Six months after our TAX CUTS more than 6 MILLION workers have received bonuses pay raises and retirement account contributions.#TaxCutsandJobsAct https://t.co/MevjwlINGU **6/29/2018 18:06**

The Democrats are making a strong push to abolish ICE one of the smartest toughest and most spirited law enforcement groups of men and women that I have ever seen. I have watched ICE liberate towns from the grasp of MS-13 & clean out the toughest of situations. They are great! **6/30/2018 11:07**

To the great and brave men and women of ICE do not worry or lose your spirit. You are doing a fantastic job of keeping us safe by eradicating the worst criminal elements. So brave! The radical left Dems want you out. Next it will be all police. Zero chance It will never happen! **6/30/2018 11:22**

Just spoke to King Salman of Saudi Arabia and explained to him that because of the turmoil & disfunction in Iran and Venezuela I am asking that Saudi Arabia increase oil production maybe up to 2000000 barrels to make up the difference...Prices to high! He has agreed! **6/30/2018 11:37**

I will be making my choice for Justice of the United States Supreme Court on the first Monday after the July 4th Holiday July 9th! **6/30/2018 12:33**

Either we need to elect more Republicans in November or Republicans must end the ridiculous 60 vote or Filibuster rule - or better yet do both. Cryin' Chuck would do it on day one but we'll never give him the chance. Some great legislation awaits - be smart! **6/30/2018 19:26**

When people come into our Country illegally we must IMMEDIATELY escort them back out without going through years of legal maneuvering. Our laws are the dumbest anywhere in the world. Republicans want Strong Borders and no Crime. Dems want Open Borders and are weak on Crime! **6/30/2018 19:44**

JULY 2018 - SEPTEMBER 2018

★ ★

With the Caliphate atrophying and terrorism from ISIS diminishing, Iranian President Rouhani's pugilistic threats toward the U.S. become the most significant threat to peace in the Middle East. Domestically, the immigration crisis escalates as Democrats oppose Trump building the wall, supporting ICE, and providing assistance for those who have crossed illegally. Conflict between Trump and his Attorney General, Jeff Sessions, intensifies. Meanwhile, the Mueller investigation relentlessly continues. Senator John McCain (R-AZ) dies. With the retirement of Justice Kennedy, Trump appoints Judge Brett Kavanaugh to replace him. The opposition to this nomination is so fierce that it dominates the news. The story replaces Russian collusion in importance for more than a month, as Christine Blasey Ford becomes a well-known figure throughout America.

The Liberal Left also known as the Democrats want to get rid of ICE who do a fantastic job and want Open Borders. Crime would be rampant and uncontrollable! Make America Great Again **7/1/2018 12:11**

A big week especially with our numerous victories in the Supreme Court. Heading back to the White House now. Focus will be on the selection of a new Supreme Court Justice. Exciting times for our country. Economy may be stronger than it has ever been! **7/1/2018 19:39**

Congratulations to Andres Manuel Lopez Obrador on becoming the next President of Mexico. I look very much forward to working with him. There is much to be done that will benefit both the United States and Mexico!

7/2/2018 3:01

Many Democrats are deeply concerned about the fact that their "leadership" wants to denounce and abandon the great men and women of ICE thereby declaring war on Law & Order. These people will be voting for Republicans in November and in many cases joining the Republican Party! **7/3/2018 2:43**

Crazy Maxine Waters said by some to be one of the most corrupt people in politics is rapidly becoming together with Nancy Pelosi the FACE of the Democrat Party. Her ranting and raving even referring to herself as a wounded animal will make people flee the Democrats! **7/3/2018 10:16**

When we have an "infestation" of MS-13 GANGS in certain parts of our country who do we send to get them out? ICE! They are tougher and smarter than these rough criminal elelments that bad immigration laws allow into our country. Dems do not appreciate the great job they do! Nov. **7/3/2018 10:49**

How can the Democrats who are weak on the Border and weak on Crime do well in November. The people of our Country want and demand Safety and Security while the Democrats are more interested in ripping apart and demeaning (and not properly funding) our great Law Enforcement! **7/3/2018 10:57**

Many good conversations with North Korea-it is going well! In the meantime no Rocket Launches or Nuclear Testing in 8 months. All of Asia is thrilled. Only the Opposition Party which includes the Fake News is complaining. If not for me we would now be at War with North Korea! **7/3/2018 11:16**

Just out that the Obama Administration granted citizenship during the terrible Iran Deal negotiation to 2500 Iranians - including to government officials. How big (and bad) is that? **7/3/2018 12:03**

Now that Harley-Davidson is moving part of its operation out of the U.S. my Administration is working with other Motor Cycle companies who want to move into the U.S. Harley customers are not happy with their move - sales are down 7% in 2017. The U.S. is where the Action is! **7/3/2018 14:00**

Wow! The NSA has deleted 685 million phone calls and text messages. Privacy violations? They blame technical irregularities. Such a disgrace. The Witch Hunt continues! **7/3/2018 14:18**

The Washington Post is constantly quoting "anonymous sources" that do not exist. Rarely do they use the name of anyone because there is no one to give them the kind of negative quote that they are looking for. They are a disgrace to journalism but then again so are many others! **7/3/2018 21:35**

After having written many best selling books and somewhat priding myself on my ability to write it should be noted that the Fake News constantly likes to pore over my tweets looking for a mistake. I capitalize certain words only for emphasis not b/c they should be capitalized! **7/3/2018 23:13**

Tonight we gathered to celebrate the courageous men and women who make freedom possible: our brave service members and our wonderful Veterans. For 242 years American Independence... **7/3/2018 23:52**

Tomorrow families across our Nation will gather to celebrate the Fourth of July. As we do we will think of the men & women serving overseas at this very moment far away from their families protecting America - & we will thank GOD for blessing us with these incredible HEROES! https://t.co/FQ1D7oEta2 **7/4/2018 0:36**

Happy Fourth of July....Our Country is doing GREAT!

7/4/2018 14:42

The OPEC Monopoly must remember that gas prices are up & they are doing little to help. If anything they are driving prices higher as the United States defends many of their members for very little $'s. This must be a two way street. REDUCE PRICING NOW! **7/4/2018 20:46**

Happy Birthday America! https://t.co/Sli6xXsfof **7/5/2018 2:47**

Congress must pass smart fast and reasonable Immigration Laws now. Law Enforcement at the Border is doing a great job but the laws they are forced to work with are insane. When people with or without children enter our Country they must be told to leave without our........ (1/2) **7/5/2018 14:08**

.....Country being forced to endure a long and costly trial. Tell the people "OUT" and they must leave just as they would if they were standing on your front lawn. Hiring thousands of "judges" does not work and is not acceptable - only Country in the World that does this! (2/2) **7/5/2018 14:16**

Congress - FIX OUR INSANE IMMIGRATION LAWS NOW! **7/5/2018 14:17**

A vote for Democrats in November is a vote to let MS-13 run wild in our communities to let drugs pour into our cities and to take jobs and benefits away from hardworking Americans. Democrats want anarchy amnesty and chaos - Republicans want LAW ORDER and JUSTICE! **7/6/2018 0:44**

Every day the brave men and women of ICE are liberating communities from savage gangs like MS-13. We will NOT stand for these vile Democrat smears in law enforcement. We will always stand proudly with the BRAVE HEROES of ICE and BORDER PATROL! **7/6/2018 0:58**

Thanks to REPUBLICAN LEADERSHIP America is WINNING AGAIN - and America is being RESPECTED again all over the world. Because we are finally putting AMERICA FIRST! **7/6/2018 1:06**

JOBS JOBS JOBS! https://t.co/Tz2PQ2xetT **7/6/2018 16:12**

Just won lawsuit filed by the DNC and a bunch of Democrat crazies trying to claim the Trump Campaign (and others) colluded with Russia. They haven't figured out that this was an excuse for them losing the election! **7/6/2018 16:57**

Twitter is getting rid of fake accounts at a record pace. Will that include the Failing New York Times and propaganda machine for Amazon the Washington Post who constantly quote anonymous sources that in my opinion don't exist - They will both be out of business in 7 years! **7/7/2018 13:21**

Big decision will soon be made on our next Justice of the Supreme Court! **7/7/2018 13:24**

Public opinion has turned strongly against the Rigged Witch Hunt and the "Special" Counsel because the public understands that there was no Collusion with Russia (so ridiculous) that the two FBI lovers were a fraud against our Nation & that the only Collusion was with the Dems! **7/7/2018 20:42**

The Rigged Witch Hunt originally headed by FBI lover boy Peter S (for one year) & now 13 Angry Democrats should look into the missing DNC Server Crooked Hillary's illegally deleted Emails the Pakistani Fraudster Uranium One Podesta & so much more. It's a Democrat Con Job!
7/7/2018 22:24

The U.S. is working very closely with the Government of Thailand to help get all of the children out of the cave and to safety. Very brave and talented people! **7/8/2018 13:14**

Looking forward to announcing my final decision on the United States Supreme Court Justice at 9:00pmE tomorrow night at the @WhiteHouse. An exceptional person will be chosen! **7/8/2018 21:27**

They just didn't get it but they do now! https://t.co/9T5ONupkDy
7/8/2018 21:58

I have long heard that the most important decision a U.S. President can make is the selection of a Supreme Court Justice - Will be announced tonight at 9:00 P.M. **7/9/2018 12:14**

I have confidence that Kim Jong Un will honor the contract we signed & even more importantly our handshake. We agreed to the denuclearization of North Korea. China on the other hand may be exerting negative pressure on a deal because of our posture on Chinese Trade-Hope Not!
7/9/2018 14:25

The failing NY Times Fake News story today about breast feeding must be called out. The U.S. strongly supports breast feeding but we don't believe women should be denied access to formula. Many women need this option because of malnutrition and poverty. **7/9/2018 17:04**

Pfizer & others should be ashamed that they have raised drug prices for no reason. They are merely taking advantage of the poor & others unable to defend themselves while at the same time giving bargain basement prices to other countries in Europe & elsewhere. We will respond! **7/9/2018 17:08**

Thank you to all of my great supporters really big progress being made. Other countries wanting to fix crazy trade deals. Economy is ROARING. Supreme Court pick getting GREAT REVIEWS. New Poll says Trump at over 90% is the most popular Republican in history of the Party. Wow!
7/10/2018 10:59

On behalf of the United States congratulations to the Thai Navy SEALs and all on the successful rescue of the 12 boys and their coach from the treacherous cave in Thailand. Such a beautiful moment - all freed great job!
7/10/2018 12:39

I am on Air Force One flying to NATO and hear reports that the FBI lovers Peter Strzok and Lisa Page are getting cold feet on testifying about the Rigged Witch Hunt headed by 13 Angry Democrats and people that worked for Obama for 8 years. Total disgrace! **7/10/2018 14:40**

A recent Emerson College ePoll said that most Americans especially Hispanics feel that they are better off under President Trump than they were under President Obama.
7/10/2018 18:42

The European Union makes it impossible for our farmers and workers and companies to do business in Europe (U.S. has a $151 Billion trade deficit) and then they want us to happily defend them through NATO and nicely pay for it. Just doesn't work! **7/10/2018 18:52**

Just talked with Pfizer CEO and @SecAzar on our drug pricing blueprint. Pfizer is rolling back price hikes so American patients don't pay more. We applaud Pfizer for this decision and hope other companies do the same. Great news for the American people! **7/10/2018 22:37**

Democrats in Congress must no longer Obstruct - vote to fix our terrible Immigration Laws now. I am watching what is going on from Europe - it would be soooo simple to fix. Judges run the system and illegals and traffickers know how it works. They are just using children! **7/11/2018 16:41**

What good is NATO if Germany is paying Russia billions of dollars for gas and energy? Why are there only 5 out of 29 countries that have met their commitment? The U.S. is paying for Europe's protection then loses billions on Trade. Must pay 2% of GDP IMMEDIATELY not by 2025.**7/11/2018 17:07**

If the Democrats want to win Supreme Court and other Court picks don't Obstruct and Resist but rather do it the good ol' fashioned way WIN ELECTIONS! **7/11/2018 21:09**

Ex-FBI LAYER Lisa Page today defied a House of Representatives issued Subpoena to testify before Congress! Wow but is anybody really surprised! Together with her lover FBI Agent Peter Strzok she worked on the Rigged Witch Hunt perhaps the most tainted and corrupt case EVER! **7/11/2018 21:53**

How can the Rigged Witch Hunt proceed when it was started influenced and worked on for an extended period of time by former FBI Agent/Lover Peter Strzok? Read his hate filled and totally biased Emails and the answer is clear! **7/11/2018 22:47**

....On top of it all Germany just started paying Russia the country they want protection from Billions of Dollars for their Energy needs coming out of a new pipeline from Russia. Not acceptable! All NATO Nations must meet their 2% commitment and that must ultimately go to 4%! **7/12/2018 6:12**

A very nice note from Chairman Kim of North Korea. Great progress being made! https://t.co/6NI6AqL0xt **7/12/2018 16:32**

Great success today at NATO! Billions of additional dollars paid by members since my election. Great spirit! **7/12/2018 17:52**

Congressman Matt Gaetz of Florida is one of the finest and most talented people in Congress. Strong on Crime the Border Illegal Immigration the 2nd Amendment our great Military & Vets Matt worked tirelessly on helping to get our Massive Tax Cuts. He has my Full Endorsement! **7/13/2018 6:02**

I have arrived in Scotland and will be at Trump Turnberry for two days of meetings calls and hopefully some golf - my primary form of exercise! The weather is beautiful and this place is incredible! Tomorrow I go to Helsinki for a Monday meeting with Vladimir Putin. **7/14/2018 9:43**

The Stock Market hit 25000 yesterday. Jobs are at an all time record - and that is before we fix some of the worst trade deals and conditions ever seen by any government. It is all happening! **7/14/2018 9:46**

....Where is the DNC Server and why didn't the FBI take possession of it? Deep State? **7/14/2018 9:57**

The stories you heard about the 12 Russians yesterday took place during the Obama Administration not the Trump Administration. Why didn't they do something about it especially when it was reported that President Obama was informed by the FBI in September before the Election?
7/14/2018 10:08

So funny! I just checked out Fake News CNN for the first time in a long time (they are dying in the ratings) to see if they covered my takedown yesterday of Jim Acosta (actually a nice guy). They didn't! But they did say I already lost in my meeting with Putin. Fake News...... (1/2)
7/14/2018 11:24

....Remember it was Little Jeff Z and his people who are told exactly what to say who said I could not win the election in that "there was no way to 270" (over & over again) in the

Electoral College. I got 306! They were sooooo wrong in their election coverage. Still hurting! (2/2) **7/14/2018 11:34**

These Russian individuals did their work during the Obama years. Why didn't Obama do something about it? Because he thought Crooked Hillary Clinton would win that's why. Had nothing to do with the Trump Administration but Fake News doesn't want to report the truth as usual! **7/14/2018 18:17**

There hasn't been a missile or rocket fired in 9 months in North Korea there have been no nuclear tests and we got back our hostages. Who knows how it will all turn out in the end but why isn't the Fake News talking about these wonderful facts? Because it is FAKE NEWS! **7/15/2018 16:11**

Congratulations to France who played extraordinary soccer on winning the 2018 World Cup. Additionally congratulations to President Putin and Russia for putting on a truly great World Cup Tournament -- one of the best ever! **7/15/2018 17:03**

Received many calls from leaders of NATO countries thanking me for helping to bring them together and to get them focused on financial obligations both present & future. We had a truly great Summit that was inaccurately covered by much of the media. NATO is now strong & rich! **7/16/2018 5:23**

President Obama thought that Crooked Hillary was going to win the election so when he was informed by the FBI about Russian Meddling he said it couldn't happen was no big deal & did NOTHING about it. When I won it became a big deal and the Rigged Witch Hunt headed by Strzok! **7/16/2018 5:37**

Our relationship with Russia has NEVER been worse thanks to many years of U.S. foolishness and stupidity and now the Rigged Witch Hunt! **7/16/2018 6:05**

As I said today and many times before "I have GREAT confidence in MY intelligence people." However I also recognize that in order to build a brighter future we cannot

exclusively focus on the past - as the world's two largest nuclear powers we must get along! #HELSINKI2018
7/16/2018 19:40

I would rather take a political risk in pursuit of peace than to risk peace in pursuit of politics. #HELSINKI2018 https://t.co/XdlrJWLPIh **7/16/2018 20:29**

A productive dialogue is not only good for the United States and good for Russia but it is good for the world. #HELSINKI2018 https://t.co/Q2Y1PhM9au **7/16/2018 20:34**

I had a great meeting with NATO. They have paid $33 Billion more and will pay hundreds of Billions of Dollars more in the future only because of me. NATO was weak but now it is strong again (bad for Russia). The media only says I was rude to leaders never mentions the money!
7/17/2018 13:53

While I had a great meeting with NATO raising vast amounts of money I had an even better meeting with Vladimir Putin of Russia. Sadly it is not being reported that way - the Fake News is going Crazy! **7/17/2018 14:22**

Thank you @RandPaul. "The President has gone through a year and a half of totally partisan investigations - what's he supposed to think?" **7/17/2018 14:33**

The economy of the United States is stronger than ever before! **7/17/2018 14:39**

The meeting between President Putin and myself was a great success except in the Fake News Media! **7/18/2018 0:21**

The Democrats want to abolish ICE which will mean more crime in our country. I want to give ICE a big cheer! Vote Republican in November. **7/18/2018 0:27**

"Prosperity is returning. Donald Trump is doing exactly what he said he would do as a candidate now as the most effective president the most successful president in modern

American history." Thank you to the great Lou Dobbs!
7/18/2018 4:10

So many people at the higher ends of intelligence loved my press conference performance in Helsinki. Putin and I discussed many important subjects at our earlier meeting. We got along well which truly bothered many haters who wanted to see a boxing match. Big results will come!
7/18/2018 9:53

Some people HATE the fact that I got along well with President Putin of Russia. They would rather go to war than see this. It's called Trump Derangement Syndrome!
7/18/2018 11:27

3.4 million jobs created since our great Election Victory - far greater than ever anticipated and only getting better as new and greatly improved Trade Deals start coming to fruition! **7/18/2018 11:33**

Brian Kemp is running for Governor of the great state of Georgia. The Primary is on Tuesday. Brian is tough on crime strong on the border and illegal immigration. He loves our Military and our Vets and protects our Second Amendment. I give him my full and total endorsement. **7/18/2018 19:25**

The two biggest opponents of ICE in America today are the Democratic Party and MS-13! **7/18/2018 21:30**

A total disgrace that Turkey will not release a respected U.S. Pastor Andrew Brunson from prison. He has been held hostage far too long. @RT_Erdogan should do something to free this wonderful Christian husband & father. He has done nothing wrong and his family needs him! **7/19/2018 1:35**

The Fake News Media is going Crazy! They make up stories without any backup sources or proof. Many of the stories written about me and the good people surrounding me are total fiction. Problem is when you complain you just give them more publicity. But I'll complain anyway! **7/19/2018 10:37**

The Fake News Media wants so badly to see a major confrontation with Russia even a confrontation that could lead to war. They are pushing so recklessly hard and hate the fact that I'll probably have a good relationship with Putin. We are doing MUCH better than any other country!
7/19/2018 10:59

I told you so! The European Union just slapped a Five Billion Dollar fine on one of our great companies Google. They truly have taken advantage of the U.S. but not for long!
7/19/2018 13:11

The Summit with Russia was a great success except with the real enemy of the people the Fake News Media. I look forward to our second meeting so that we can start implementing some of the many things discussed including stopping terrorism security for Israel nuclear........ **7/19/2018 13:24**

Will the Dems and Fake News ever learn? This is classic! https://t.co/kSX3ROI4QG **7/19/2018 18:14**

My deepest sympathies to the families and friends of those involved in the terrible boat accident which just took place in Missouri. Such a tragedy such a great loss. May God be with you all! **7/20/2018 12:31**

....The United States should not be penalized because we are doing so well. Tightening now hurts all that we have done. The U.S. should be allowed to recapture what was lost due to illegal currency manipulation and BAD Trade Deals. Debt coming due & we are raising rates - Really? **7/20/2018 12:51**

I got severely criticized by the Fake News Media for being too nice to President Putin. In the Old Days they would call it Diplomacy. If I was loud & vicious I would have been criticized for being too tough. Remember when they said I was too tough with Chairman Kim? Hypocrites! **7/20/2018 21:50**

The NFL National Anthem Debate is alive and well again - can't believe it! Isn't it in contract that players must stand at attention hand on heart? The $40000000 Commissioner must now make a stand. First time kneeling out for game. Second time kneeling out for season/no pay! **7/20/2018 22:17**

Inconceivable that the government would break into a lawyer's office (early in the morning) - almost unheard of. Even more inconceivable that a lawyer would tape a client - totally unheard of & perhaps illegal. The good news is that your favorite President did nothing wrong!

7/21/2018 12:10

The Rigged Witch Hunt headed by the 13 Angry Democrats (and now 4 more have been added one who worked directly for Obama W.H.) seems intent on damaging the Republican Party's chances in the November Election. This Democrat excuse for losing the '16 Election never ends!

7/21/2018 22:40

No Collusion No Obstruction - but that doesn't matter because the 13 Angry Democrats who are only after Republicans and totally protecting Democrats want this Witch Hunt to drag out to the November Election. Republicans better get smart fast and expose what they are doing! **7/21/2018 22:50**

Troy Balderson of Ohio is running for Congress against a Nancy Pelosi Liberal who is WEAK on Crime & Borders. Troy is the total opposite and loves our Military Vets & 2nd Amendment. EARLY VOTING just started with Election Day on August 7th. Troy has my Full & Total Endorsement!

7/21/2018 23:23

Congratulations to @JudicialWatch and @TomFitton on being successful in getting the Carter Page FISA documents. As usual they are ridiculously heavily redacted but confirm with little doubt that the Department of "Justice" and FBI misled the courts. Witch Hunt Rigged a Scam! **7/22/2018 10:28**

Looking more & more like the Trump Campaign for President was illegally being spied upon (surveillance) for the political gain of Crooked Hillary Clinton and the DNC. Ask her how that worked out - she did better with Crazy Bernie. Republicans must get tough now. An illegal Scam!
7/22/2018 10:49

Andrew McCarthy - "I said this could never happen. This is so bad that they should be looking at the judges who signed off on this stuff not just the people who gave it. It is so bad it screams out at you." On the whole FISA scam which led to the rigged Mueller Witch Hunt! **7/22/2018 12:22**

I had a GREAT meeting with Putin and the Fake News used every bit of their energy to try and disparage it. So bad for our country! **7/22/2018 13:15**

So President Obama knew about Russia before the Election. Why didn't he do something about it? Why didn't he tell our campaign? Because it is all a big hoax that's why and he thought Crooked Hillary was going to win!!! **7/22/2018 22:23**

To Iranian President Rouhani: NEVER EVER THREATEN THE UNITED STATES AGAIN OR YOU WILL SUFFER CONSEQUENCES THE LIKES OF WHICH FEW THROUGHOUT HISTORY HAVE EVER SUFFERED BEFORE. WE ARE NO LONGER A COUNTRY THAT WILL STAND FOR YOUR DEMENTED WORDS OF VIOLENCE & DEATH. BE CAUTIOUS!
7/23/2018 3:24

So we now find out that it was indeed the unverified and Fake Dirty Dossier that was paid for by Crooked Hillary Clinton and the DNC that was knowingly & falsely submitted to FISA and which was responsible for starting the totally conflicted and discredited Mueller Witch Hunt! **7/23/2018 10:30**

"It was classified to cover up misconduct by the FBI and the Justice Department in misleading the Court by using this Dossier in a dishonest way to gain a warrant to target the Trump Team. This is a Clinton Campaign document. It was a fraud and a hoax designed to target Trump.... **7/23/2018 10:52**

When you hear the Fake News talking negatively about my meeting with President Putin and all that I gave up remember I gave up NOTHING we merely talked about future benefits for both countries. Also we got along very well which is a good thing except for the Corrupt Media!

7/23/2018 12:25

A Rocket has not been launched by North Korea in 9 months. Likewise no Nuclear Tests. Japan is happy all of Asia is happy. But the Fake News is saying without ever asking me (always anonymous sources) that I am angry because it is not going fast enough. Wrong very happy!

7/23/2018 13:06

The Amazon Washington Post has gone crazy against me ever since they lost the Internet Tax Case in the U.S. Supreme Court two months ago. Next up is the U.S. Post Office which they use at a fraction of real cost as their "delivery boy" for a BIG percentage of their packages.... (1/2)

7/23/2018 13:21

....In my opinion the Washington Post is nothing more than an expensive (the paper loses a fortune) lobbyist for Amazon. Is it used as protection against antitrust claims which many feel should be brought? (2/2) **7/23/2018 13:35**

Countries that have treated us unfairly on trade for years are all coming to Washington to negotiate. This should have taken place many years ago butas the saying goes better late than never! **7/24/2018 11:09**

Tariffs are the greatest! Either a country which has treated the United States unfairly on Trade negotiates a fair deal or it gets hit with Tariffs. It's as simple as that - and everybody's talking! Remember we are the "piggy bank" that's being robbed. All will be Great! **7/24/2018 11:29**

Our Country is doing GREAT. Best financial numbers on the Planet. Great to have USA WINNING AGAIN! **7/24/2018 13:46**

MAKE AMERICA GREAT AGAIN! **7/24/2018 13:54**

I'm very concerned that Russia will be fighting very hard to have an impact on the upcoming Election. Based on the fact that no President has been tougher on Russia than me they will be pushing very hard for the Democrats. They definitely don't want Trump! **7/24/2018 15:50**

The European Union is coming to Washington tomorrow to negotiate a deal on Trade. I have an idea for them. Both the U.S. and the E.U. drop all Tariffs Barriers and Subsidies! That would finally be called Free Market and Fair Trade! Hope they do it we are ready - but they won't! **7/25/2018 0:08**

So sad and unfair that the FCC wouldn't approve the Sinclair Broadcast merger with Tribune. This would have been a great and much needed Conservative voice for and of the People. Liberal Fake News NBC and Comcast gets approved much bigger but not Sinclair. Disgraceful!
7/25/2018 0:39

"The Russia Hoax The Illicit Scheme To Clear Hillary Clinton & Frame Donald Trump" is a Hot Seller already Number One! More importantly it is a great book that everyone is talking about. It covers the Rigged Witch Hunt brilliantly. Congratulations to Gregg Jarrett! **7/25/2018 1:05**

Every time I see a weak politician asking to stop Trade talks or the use of Tariffs to counter unfair Tariffs I wonder what can they be thinking? Are we just going to continue and let our farmers and country get ripped off? Lost $817 Billion on Trade last year. No weakness! **7/25/2018 11:01**

When you have people snipping at your heels during a negotiation it will only take longer to make a deal and the deal will never be as good as it could have been with unity. Negotiations are going really well be cool. The end result will be worth it! **7/25/2018 11:08**

China is targeting our farmers who they know I love & respect as a way of getting me to continue allowing them to take advantage of the U.S. They are being vicious in what will be their failed attempt. We were being nice - until now! China made $517 Billion on us last year. **7/25/2018 11:20**

What kind of a lawyer would tape a client? So sad! Is this a first never heard of it before? Why was the tape so abruptly terminated (cut) while I was presumably saying positive things? I hear there are other clients and many reporters that are taped - can this be so? Too bad! **7/25/2018 12:34**

Congratulations to Brian Kemp on your very big win in Georgia last night. Wow 69-30 those are big numbers. Now go win against the open border crime loving opponent that the Democrats have given you. She is weak on Vets the Military and the 2nd Amendment. Win! **7/25/2018 12:41**

Great to be back on track with the European Union. This was a big day for free and fair trade! **7/26/2018 1:01**

European Union representatives told me that they would start buying soybeans from our great farmers immediately. Also they will be buying vast amounts of LNG! **7/26/2018 1:07**

Twitter "SHADOW BANNING" prominent Republicans. Not good. We will look into this discriminatory and illegal practice at once! Many complaints. **7/26/2018 11:46**

The United States will impose large sanctions on Turkey for their long time detainment of Pastor Andrew Brunson a great Christian family man and wonderful human being. He is suffering greatly. This innocent man of faith should be released immediately! **7/26/2018 15:22**

America is OPEN FOR BUSINESS and U.S. Steel is back! https://t.co/lJTcr6JHBW **7/27/2018 2:37**

The Remains of American Servicemen will soon be leaving North Korea and heading to the United States! After so many years this will be a great moment for so many families. Thank you to Kim Jong Un. **7/27/2018 3:50**

....the only Collusion with Russia was with the Democrats so now they are looking at my Tweets (along with 53 million other people) - the rigged Witch Hunt continues! How stupid and unfair to our Country....And so the Fake News doesn't waste my time with dumb questions NO.... (1/2) **7/27/2018 11:38**

.....I did NOT know of the meeting with my son Don jr. Sounds to me like someone is trying to make up stories in order to get himself out of an unrelated jam (Taxi cabs maybe?). He even retained Bill and Crooked Hillary's lawyer. Gee I wonder if they helped him make the choice! (2/2) **7/27/2018 11:56**

I am thrilled to announce that in the second quarter of this year the U.S. Economy grew at the amazing rate of 4.1%! https://t.co/xeAPwAAOXN **7/27/2018 16:12**

Democrats who want Open Borders and care little about Crime are incompetent but they have the Fake News Media almost totally on their side! **7/27/2018 22:45**

The only things the Democrats do well is "Resist" which is their campaign slogan and "Obstruct." Cryin' Chuck Schumer has almost 400 great American people that are waiting "forever" to serve our Country! A total disgrace. Mitch M should not let them go home until all approved! **7/28/2018 0:47**

Tom Homan fmr ICE Director: "There is nobody that has done more for border security & public safety than President Trump. I've worked for six presidents and I respect them all but nobody has done more than this Administration & President Trump that's just a stone cold fact!" **7/29/2018 11:31**

Wow highest Poll Numbers in the history of the Republican Party. That includes Honest Abe Lincoln and Ronald Reagan. There must be something wrong please recheck that poll! **7/29/2018 11:44**

Please understand there are consequences when people cross our Border illegally whether they have children or not - and many are just using children for their own sinister purposes. Congress must act on fixing the DUMBEST & WORST immigration laws anywhere in the world! Vote "R"
7/29/2018 11:58

The biggest and best results coming out of the good GDP report was that the quarterly Trade Deficit has been reduced by $52 Billion and of course the historically low unemployment numbers especially for African Americans Hispanics Asians and Women. **7/29/2018 12:42**

I would be willing to "shut down" government if the Democrats do not give us the votes for Border Security which includes the Wall! Must get rid of Lottery Catch & Release etc. and finally go to system of Immigration based on MERIT! We need great people coming into our Country!
7/29/2018 13:13

When the media - driven insane by their Trump Derangement Syndrome - reveals internal deliberations of our government it truly puts the lives of many not just journalists at risk! Very unpatriotic! Freedom of the press also comes with a responsibility to report the news...
7/29/2018 19:09

There is No Collusion! The Robert Mueller Rigged Witch Hunt headed now by 17 (increased from 13 including an Obama White House lawyer) Angry Democrats was started by a fraudulent Dossier paid for by Crooked Hillary and the DNC. Therefore the Witch Hunt is an illegal Scam!
7/29/2018 19:35

Is Robert Mueller ever going to release his conflicts of interest with respect to President Trump including the fact that we had a very nasty & contentious business relationship I turned him down to head the FBI (one day before appointment as S.C.) & Comey is his close friend.. (1/2) **7/29/2018 20:12**

....Also why is Mueller only appointing Angry Dems some of whom have worked for Crooked Hillary others including himself have worked for Obama....And why isn't Mueller looking at all of the criminal activity & real Russian Collusion on the Democrats side-Podesta Dossier? (2/2) **7/29/2018 20:20**

We must have Border Security get rid of Chain Lottery Catch & Release Sanctuary Cities - go to Merit based Immigration. Protect ICE and Law Enforcement and of course keep building but much faster THE WALL! **7/30/2018 11:57**

Congratulations to Judge Jeanine on the tremendous success of her new #1 best-selling book "Liars Leakers and Liberals – The Case Against the Anti-Trump Conspiracy!" **7/30/2018 22:31**

A highly respected Federal judge today stated that the "Trump Administration gets great credit" for reuniting illegal families. Thank you and please look at the previous administrations record - not good! **7/31/2018 0:56**

MAKING AMERICA GREAT AGAIN! https://t.co/OnMGXvldVT **7/31/2018 2:01**

The globalist Koch Brothers who have become a total joke in real Republican circles are against Strong Borders and Powerful Trade. I never sought their support because I don't need their money or bad ideas. They love my Tax & Regulation Cuts Judicial picks & more. I made..... **7/31/2018 10:14**

One of the reasons we need Great Border Security is that Mexico's murder rate in 2017 increased by 27% to 31174 people killed a record! The Democrats want Open Borders. I want Maximum Border Security and respect for ICE and our

great Law Enforcement Professionals! @FoxNews
7/31/2018 11:00

Collusion is not a crime but that doesn't matter because there was No Collusion (except by Crooked Hillary and the Democrats)! **7/31/2018 11:58**

The Fake News Media is going CRAZY! They are totally unhinged and in many ways after witnessing first hand the damage they do to so many innocent and decent people I enjoy watching. In 7 years when I am no longer in office their ratings will dry up and they will be gone! **7/31/2018 13:34**

I don't care what the political ramifications are our immigration laws and border security have been a complete and total disaster for decades and there is no way that the Democrats will allow it to be fixed without a Government Shutdown... **7/31/2018 17:33**

..This is a terrible situation and Attorney General Jeff Sessions should stop this Rigged Witch Hunt right now before it continues to stain our country any further. Bob Mueller is totally conflicted and his 17 Angry Democrats that are doing his dirty work are a disgrace to USA! **8/1/2018 13:24**

Paul Manafort worked for Ronald Reagan Bob Dole and many other highly prominent and respected political leaders. He worked for me for a very short time. Why didn't government tell me that he was under investigation. These old charges have nothing to do with Collusion - a Hoax!
8/1/2018 13:34

Russian Collusion with the Trump Campaign one of the most successful in history is a TOTAL HOAX. The Democrats paid for the phony and discredited Dossier which was along with Comey McCabe Strzok and his lover the lovely Lisa Page used to begin the Witch Hunt. Disgraceful! **8/1/2018 14:01**

Incredibly beautiful ceremony as U.S. Korean War remains are returned to American soil. Thank you to Honolulu and all of our great Military participants on a job well done. A special thanks to Vice President Mike Pence on delivering a truly magnificent tribute! **8/2/2018 3:32**

Thank you to Chairman Kim Jong Un for keeping your word & starting the process of sending home the remains of our great and beloved missing fallen! I am not at all surprised that you took this kind action. Also thank you for your nice letter - I look forward to seeing you soon! **8/2/2018 4:47**

Charles Koch of Koch Brothers who claims to be giving away millions of dollars to politicians even though I know very few who have seen this (?) now makes the ridiculous statement that what President Trump is doing is unfair to "foreign workers." He is correct AMERICA FIRST! **8/2/2018 10:38**

Wow @foxandfriends is blowing away the competition in the morning ratings. Morning Joe is a dead show with very few people watching and sadly Fake News CNN is also doing poorly. Too much hate and inaccurately reported stories - too predictable! **8/2/2018 11:04**

They asked my daughter Ivanka whether or not the media is the enemy of the people. She correctly said no. It is the FAKE NEWS which is a large percentage of the media that is the enemy of the people! **8/2/2018 20:24**

Almost 500000 Manufacturing Jobs created since I won the Election. Remember when my opponents were saying that we couldn't create this type of job anymore. Wrong in fact these are among our best and most important jobs! **8/3/2018 22:59**

Lebron James was just interviewed by the dumbest man on television Don Lemon. He made Lebron look smart which isn't easy to do. I like Mike!
8/4/2018 3:37

Tariffs are working far better than anyone ever anticipated. China market has dropped 27% in last 4months and they are talking to us. Our market is stronger than ever and will go up dramatically when these horrible Trade Deals are successfully renegotiated. America First....... **8/4/2018 19:47**

Iran and it's economy is going very bad and fast! I will meet or not meet it doesn't matter - it is up to them! **8/4/2018 20:53**

The Fake News hates me saying that they are the Enemy of the People only because they know it's TRUE. I am providing a great service by explaining this to the American People. They purposely cause great division & distrust. They can also cause War! They are very dangerous & sick!
8/5/2018 11:38

Fake News reporting a complete fabrication that I am concerned about the meeting my wonderful son Donald had in Trump Tower. This was a meeting to get information on an opponent totally legal and done all the time in politics - and it went nowhere. I did not know about it! **8/5/2018 12:35**

...Why aren't Mueller and the 17 Angry Democrats looking at the meetings concerning the Fake Dossier and all of the lying that went on in the FBI and DOJ? This is the most one sided Witch Hunt in the history of our country. Fortunately the facts are all coming out and fast! **8/5/2018 12:45**

Too bad a large portion of the Media refuses to report the lies and corruption having to do with the Rigged Witch Hunt - but that is why we call them FAKE NEWS!**8/5/2018 12:49**

Presidential Approval numbers are very good - strong economy military and just about everything else. Better numbers than Obama at this point by far. We are winning on just about every front and for that reason there will not be a Blue Wave but there might be a Red Wave! **8/5/2018 20:01**

California wildfires are being magnified & made so much worse by the bad environmental laws which aren't allowing massive amount of readily available water to be properly utilized. It is being diverted into the Pacific Ocean. Must also tree clear to stop fire spreading! **8/5/2018 22:06**

"Collusion with Russia was very real. Hillary Clinton and her team 100% colluded with the Russians and so did Adam Schiff who is on tape trying to collude with what he thought was Russians to obtain compromising material on DJT. We also know that Hillary Clinton paid through.... **8/6/2018 14:13**

Democrats want Open Borders and they want to abolish ICE the brave men and women that are protecting our Country from some of the most vicious and dangerous people on earth! Sorry we can't let that happen! Also change the rules in the Senate and approve STRONG Border Security!

8/6/2018 21:46

The Iran sanctions have officially been cast. These are the most biting sanctions ever imposed and in November they ratchet up to yet another level. Anyone doing business with Iran will NOT be doing business with the United States. I am asking for WORLD PEACE nothing less! **8/7/2018 9:31**

Ohio vote today for Troy Balderson for Congress. His opponent controlled by Nancy Pelosi is weak on Crime the Border Military Vets your 2nd Amendment - and will end your Tax Cuts. Troy will be a great Congressman. #MAGA

8/7/2018 10:46

When I decided to go to Ohio for Troy Balderson he was down in early voting 64 to 36. That was not good. After my speech on Saturday night there was a big turn for the better. Now Troy wins a great victory during a very tough time of the year for voting. He will win BIG in Nov. **8/8/2018 2:59**

.....Congratulations to Troy Balderson on a great win in Ohio. A very special and important race! **8/8/2018 3:18**

Congratulations to a future STAR of the Republican Party future Senator John James. A big and bold victory tonight in the Great State of Michigan - the first of many. November can't come fast enough! **8/8/2018 3:23**

5 for 5! **8/8/2018 14:31**

The Republicans have now won 8 out of 9 House Seats yet if you listen to the Fake News Media you would think we are being clobbered. Why can't they play it straight so unfair to the Republican Party and in particular your favorite President! **8/8/2018 15:14**

As long as I campaign and/or support Senate and House candidates (within reason) they will win! I LOVE the people & they certainly seem to like the job I'm doing. If I find the time in between China Iran the Economy and much more which I must we will have a giant Red Wave! **8/8/2018 15:25**

RED WAVE! **8/8/2018 18:51**

"There has been no evidence whatsoever that Donald Trump or the campaign was involved in any kind of collusion to fix the 2016 election. In fact the evidence is the opposite that Hillary Clinton & the Democrats colluded with the Russians to fix the 2016 election." @GrahamLedger **8/9/2018 13:22**

This is an illegally brought Rigged Witch Hunt run by people who are totally corrupt and/or conflicted. It was started and paid for by Crooked Hillary and the Democrats. Phony Dossier FISA disgrace and so many lying and dishonest people already fired. 17 Angry Dems? Stay tuned! **8/9/2018 16:02**

Space Force all the way! **8/9/2018 16:03**

Jenna Ellis "FBI thought they wouldn't get caught because they thought that Hillary was going to win. There is overt bias and that depends on whether you are Democrat or Republican - a double standard that needs to stop." **8/9/2018 22:50**

The NFL players are at it again - taking a knee when they should be standing proudly for the National Anthem. Numerous players from different teams wanted to show their "outrage" at something that most of them are unable to define. They make a fortune doing what they love...... (1/2) **8/10/2018 12:18**

.....Be happy be cool! A football game that fans are paying soooo much money to watch and enjoy is no place to protest. Most of that money goes to the players anyway. Find another way to protest. Stand proudly for your National Anthem or be Suspended Without Pay! (2/2)
8/10/2018 12:32

I have just authorized a doubling of Tariffs on Steel and Aluminum with respect to Turkey as their currency the Turkish Lira slides rapidly downward against our very strong Dollar! Aluminum will now be 20% and Steel 50%. Our relations with Turkey are not good at this time! **8/10/2018 12:47**

Democrats please do not distance yourselves from Nancy Pelosi. She is a wonderful person whose ideas & policies may be bad but who should definitely be given a 4th chance. She is trying very hard & has every right to take down the Democrat Party if she has veered too far left!
8/10/2018 21:30

Thank you to Kanye West and the fact that he is willing to tell the TRUTH. One new and great FACT - African American unemployment is the lowest ever recorded in the history of our Country. So honored by this. Thank you Kanye for your support. It is making a big difference!
8/10/2018 22:58

Deal with Mexico is coming along nicely. Autoworkers and farmers must be taken care of or there will be no deal. New President of Mexico has been an absolute gentleman. Canada must wait. Their Tariffs and Trade Barriers are far too high. Will tax cars if we can't make a deal! **8/10/2018 23:12**

.....Will the FBI ever recover it's once stellar reputation so badly damaged by Comey McCabe Peter S and his lover the lovely Lisa Page and other top officials now dismissed or fired? So many of the great men and women of the FBI have been hurt by these clowns and losers! **8/11/2018 13:18**

The riots in Charlottesville a year ago resulted in senseless death and division. We must come together as a nation. I condemn all types of racism and acts of violence. Peace to ALL Americans! **8/11/2018 13:26**

I am proud to have fought for and secured the LOWEST African American and Hispanic unemployment rates in history. Now I'm pushing for prison reform to give people who have paid their debt to society a second chance. I will never stop fighting for ALL Americans! **8/11/2018 13:41**

The big story that the Fake News Media refuses to report is lowlife Christopher Steele's many meetings with Deputy A.G. Bruce Ohr and his beautiful wife Nelly. It was Fusion GPS that hired Steele to write the phony & discredited Dossier paid for by Crooked Hillary & the DNC.... (1/2)
8/11/2018 18:28

....Do you believe Nelly worked for Fusion and her husband STILL WORKS FOR THE DEPARTMENT OF "JUSTICE." I have never seen anything so Rigged in my life. Our A.G. is scared stiff and Missing in Action. It is all starting to be revealed - not pretty. IG Report soon? Witch Hunt! (2/2)
8/11/2018 18:54

Hundreds of Bikers for Trump just joined me at Bedminster. Quite a scene - great people who truly love our Country!
8/11/2018 18:59

.@JudgeJeanine "Bob Mueller isn't your whole investigation premised on a Fake Dossier paid for by Hillary created by a man who hates Donald Trump & used to con a FISA Court Judge. Bob I really think it's time for you to give up your phony investigation." No Collusion! **8/12/2018 12:24**

.@GovMikeHuckabee "Your paycheck is bigger your pension is stronger." @foxandfriends Unemployment numbers are better than they have been in 50 years & perhaps ever. Our

country is booming like never before - and it will get even better! Many companies moving back to the U.S.A.
8/12/2018 12:34

Many @harleydavidson owners plan to boycott the company if manufacturing moves overseas. Great! Most other companies are coming in our direction including Harley competitors. A really bad move! U.S. will soon have a level playing field or better. **8/12/2018 12:57**

"Seems like the Department of Justice (and FBI) had a program to keep Donald Trump from becoming President". @DarrellIssa @foxandfriends If this had happened to the other side everybody involved would be in jail. This is a Media coverup of the biggest story of our time. **8/12/2018 13:25**

Wacky Omarosa who got fired 3 times on the Apprentice now got fired for the last time. She never made it never will. She begged me for a job tears in her eyes I said Ok. People in the White House hated her. She was vicious but not smart. I would rarely see her but heard.... **8/13/2018 13:27**

While I know it's "not presidential" to take on a lowlife like Omarosa and while I would rather not be doing so this is a modern day form of communication and I know the Fake News Media will be working overtime to make even Wacky Omarosa look legitimate as possible. Sorry! **8/13/2018 14:21**

Agent Peter Strzok was just fired from the FBI - finally. The list of bad players in the FBI & DOJ gets longer & longer. Based on the fact that Strzok was in charge of the Witch Hunt will it be dropped? It is a total Hoax. No Collusion No Obstruction - I just fight back! **8/13/2018 16:04**

Just fired Agent Strzok formerly of the FBI was in charge of the Crooked Hillary Clinton sham investigation. It was a total fraud on the American public and should be properly redone! **8/13/2018 16:09**

When you give a crazed crying lowlife a break and give her a job at the White House I guess it just didn't work out.

Good work by General Kelly for quickly firing that dog!
8/14/2018 11:31

Another terrorist attack in London...These animals are crazy and must be dealt with through toughness and strength!
8/14/2018 11:42

Fired FBI Agent Peter Strzok is a fraud as is the rigged investigation he started. There was no Collusion or Obstruction with Russia and everybody including the Democrats know it. The only Collusion and Obstruction was by Crooked Hillary the Democrats and the DNC! **8/14/2018 13:01**

Strzok started the illegal Rigged Witch Hunt - why isn't this so-called "probe" ended immediately? Why aren't these angry and conflicted Democrats instead looking at Crooked Hillary? **8/14/2018 13:10**

Great Republican election results last night. So far we have the team we want. 8 for 9 in Special Elections. Red Wave!
8/15/2018 12:30

"People who enter the United States without our permission are illegal aliens and illegal aliens should not be treated the same as people who entered the U.S. legally." Chuck Schumer in 2009 before he went left and haywire! @ foxandfriends **8/15/2018 13:18**

Happy Birthday to the leader of the Democrat Party Maxine Waters! **8/15/2018 14:57**

Chuck Schumer I agree! https://t.co/KfoLkQU5Hv
8/15/2018 18:34

"John Brennan is a stain on the Country we deserve better than this." Former Secret Service Agent and author of new book "Spygate the Attempted Sabotage of Donald J. Trump" Dan Bongino. Thank you Dan and good luck with the book! **8/16/2018 1:00**

"Hillary Clinton clearly got a pass by the FBI. We have the unfortunate situation where they then decided they were

going to frame Donald Trump" concerning the Rigged Witch Hunt. JOE DIGENOVA former U.S. Attorney.
8/16/2018 1:14

"WE'RE NOT GOING TO MAKE AMERICA GREAT AGAIN IT WAS NEVER THAT GREAT." Can you believe this is the Governor of the Highest Taxed State in the U.S. Andrew Cuomo having a total meltdown! **8/16/2018 2:02**

Mark Levin "When they had power they didn't stop the Russians the Chinese the North Koreans they funded the Iranians & are responsible for the greatest scandal in American history by interfering with our election & trying to undermine the Trump Campaign and Trump Presidency."
8/16/2018 2:31

"I'd strip the whole bunch of them. They're all corrupt. They've all abused their power. They've all betrayed the American people with a political agenda. They tried to steal and influence an election in the United States." @ seanhannity **8/16/2018 2:40**

Our Economy is doing better than ever. Money is pouring into our cherished DOLLAR like rarely before companies earnings are higher than ever inflation is low & business optimism is higher than it has ever been. For the first time in many decades we are protecting our workers! **8/16/2018 12:43**

THE FAKE NEWS MEDIA IS THE OPPOSITION PARTY. It is very bad for our Great Country....BUT WE ARE WINNING!
8/16/2018 12:50

There is nothing that I would want more for our Country than true FREEDOM OF THE PRESS. The fact is that the Press is FREE to write and say anything it wants but much of what it says is FAKE NEWS pushing a political agenda or just plain trying to hurt people. HONESTY WINS!
8/16/2018 14:10

The Queen of Soul Aretha Franklin is dead. She was a great woman with a wonderful gift from God her voice. She will be missed! **8/16/2018 15:36**

Thank you for the kind words Omarosa! https://t.co/PMmNG6iIsi **8/16/2018 18:55**

Turkey has taken advantage of the United States for many years. They are now holding our wonderful Christian Pastor who I must now ask to represent our Country as a great patriot hostage. We will pay nothing for the release of an innocent man but we are cutting back on Turkey! **8/16/2018 23:30**

How can "Senator" Richard Blumenthal who went around for twenty years as a Connecticut politician bragging that he was a great Marine war hero in Vietnam (then got caught and sobbingly admitted he was neither a Marine nor ever in Vietnam) pass judgement on anyone? Loser! **8/17/2018 0:56**

"....An incredibly corrupt FBI & DOJ trying to steer the outcome of a Presidential Election. Brennan has gone off the deep end he's disgraced and discredited himself. His conduct has been outrageous." Chris Farrell Judicial Watch. **8/17/2018 1:49**

The local politicians who run Washington D.C. (poorly) know a windfall when they see it. When asked to give us a price for holding a great celebratory military parade they wanted a number so ridiculously high that I cancelled it. Never let someone hold you up! I will instead... **8/17/2018 11:57**

Just announced youth unemployment is at a 50 year low! @foxandfriends **8/17/2018 12:29**

The U.S. has more than double the growth rate than it had 18 months ago. **8/17/2018 12:38**

Wow! Big pushback on Governor Andrew Cuomo of New York for his really dumb statement about America's lack of greatness. I have already MADE America Great Again just look at the markets jobs military- setting records and we will do even better. Andrew "choked" badly mistake!

8/17/2018 14:10

When a politician admits that "We're not going to make America great again" there doesn't seem to be much reason to ever vote for him. This could be a career threatening statement by Andrew Cuomo with many wanting him to resign-he will get higher ratings than his brother Chris!

8/17/2018 14:17

"Fox News has learned that Bruce Ohr wrote Christopher Steele following the firing of James Comey saying that he was afraid the anti-Trump Russia probe will be exposed." Charles Payne @FoxBusiness How much more does Mueller have to see? They have blinders on - RIGGED!

8/17/2018 22:29

Social Media is totally discriminating against Republican/ Conservative voices. Speaking loudly and clearly for the Trump Administration we won't let that happen. They are closing down the opinions of many people on the RIGHT while at the same time doing nothing to others....... (1/3)

8/18/2018 11:23

.....Censorship is a very dangerous thing & absolutely impossible to police. If you are weeding out Fake News there is nothing so Fake as CNN & MSNBC & yet I do not ask that their sick behavior be removed. I get used to it and watch with a grain of salt or don't watch at all.. (2/3)

8/18/2018 11:32

....Too many voices are being destroyed some good & some bad and that cannot be allowed to happen. Who is making the choices because I can already tell you that too many mistakes are being made. Let everybody participate good & bad and we will all just have to figure it out! (3/3)

8/18/2018 11:40

All of the fools that are so focused on looking only at Russia should start also looking in another direction China. But in the end if we are smart tough and well prepared we will get along with everyone! **8/18/2018 11:46**

Has anyone looked at the mistakes that John Brennan made while serving as CIA Director? He will go down as easily the WORST in history & since getting out he has become nothing less than a loudmouth partisan political hack who cannot be trusted with the secrets to our country! **8/18/2018 13:12**

The Economy is stronger and better than ever before. Importantly there remains tremendous potential - it will only get better with time! **8/18/2018 13:39**

The United States has ended the ridiculous 230 Million Dollar yearly development payment to Syria. Saudi Arabia and other rich countries in the Middle East will start making payments instead of the U.S. I want to develop the U.S. our military and countries that help us! **8/18/2018 21:51**

I allowed White House Counsel Don McGahn and all other requested members of the White House Staff to fully cooperate with the Special Counsel. In addition we readily gave over one million pages of documents. Most transparent in history. No Collusion No Obstruction. Witch Hunt! **8/18/2018 22:12**

No Collusion and No Obstruction except by Crooked Hillary and the Democrats. All of the resignations and corruption yet heavily conflicted Bob Mueller refuses to even look in that direction. What about the Brennan Comey McCabe Strzok lies to Congress or Crooked's Emails! **8/19/2018 11:30**

The Failing New York Times wrote a story that made it seem like the White House Councel had TURNED on the President when in fact it is just the opposite - & the two Fake reporters knew this. This is why the Fake News Media has become the Enemy of the People. So bad for America! **8/19/2018 12:06**

Some members of the media are very Angry at the Fake Story in the New York Times. They actually called to complain and apologize - a big step forward. From the day I announced the Times has been Fake News and with their disgusting new Board Member it will only get worse!

8/19/2018 12:14

Study the late Joseph McCarthy because we are now in period with Mueller and his gang that make Joseph McCarthy look like a baby! Rigged Witch Hunt! **8/19/2018 12:24**

....looking for trouble. They are enjoying ruining people's lives and REFUSE to look at the real corruption on the Democrat side - the lies the firings the deleted Emails and soooo much more! Mueller's Angry Dems are looking to impact the election. They are a National Disgrace!

8/20/2018 11:38

Where's the Collusion? They made up a phony crime called Collusion and when there was no Collusion they say there was Obstruction (of a phony crime that never existed). If you FIGHT BACK or say anything bad about the Rigged Witch Hunt they scream Obstruction! **8/20/2018 11:48**

I hope John Brennan the worst CIA Director in our country's history brings a lawsuit. It will then be very easy to get all of his records texts emails and documents to show not only the poor job he did but how he was involved with the Mueller Rigged Witch Hunt. He won't sue! **8/20/2018 14:13**

Everybody wants to keep their Security Clearance it's worth great prestige and big dollars even board seats and that is why certain people are coming forward to protect Brennan. It certainly isn't because of the good job he did! He is a political "hack." **8/20/2018 14:23**

It is outrageous that Poisonous Synthetic Heroin Fentanyl comes pouring into the U.S. Postal System from China. We can and must END THIS NOW! The Senate should pass the STOP ACT – and firmly STOP this poison from killing our children and destroying our country. No more delay!

8/20/2018 17:14

I am hearing so many great things about the Republican Party's California Gubernatorial Candidate John Cox. He is a very successful businessman who is tired of high Taxes & Crime. He will Make California Great Again & make you proud of your Great State again. Total Endorsement!
8/21/2018 3:53

A Blue Wave means Crime and Open Borders. A Red Wave means Safety and Strength! **8/21/2018 10:38**

I am sorry to have to reiterate that there are serious and unpleasant consequences to crossing the Border into the United States ILLEGALLY! If there were no serious consequences our country would be overrun with people trying to get in and our system could not handle it!
8/21/2018 11:41

If anyone is looking for a good lawyer I would strongly suggest that you don't retain the services of Michael Cohen!
8/22/2018 12:44

I feel very badly for Paul Manafort and his wonderful family. "Justice" took a 12 year old tax case among other things applied tremendous pressure on him and unlike Michael Cohen he refused to "break" - make up stories in order to get a "deal." Such respect for a brave man! **8/22/2018 13:21**

Michael Cohen plead guilty to two counts of campaign finance violations that are not a crime. President Obama had a big campaign finance violation and it was easily settled! **8/22/2018 13:37**

Longest bull run in the history of the stock market congratulations America! **8/22/2018 20:07**

The only thing that I have done wrong is to win an election that was expected to be won by Crooked Hillary Clinton and the Democrats. The problem is they forgot to campaign in numerous states! **8/23/2018 0:56**

I have asked Secretary of State @SecPompeo to closely study the South Africa land and farm seizures and expropriations and the large scale killing of farmers. "South African Government is now seizing land from white farmers." @TuckerCarlson @FoxNews **8/23/2018 2:28**

NO COLLUSION - RIGGED WITCH HUNT! **8/23/2018 5:10**

Our Economy is setting records on virtually every front - Probably the best our country has ever done. Tremendous value created since the Election. The World is respecting us again! Companies are moving back to the U.S.A. **8/24/2018 10:04**

"Department of Justice will not be improperly influenced by political considerations." Jeff this is GREAT what everyone wants so look into all of the corruption on the "other side" including deleted Emails Comey lies & leaks Mueller conflicts McCabe Strzok Page Ohr...... (1/2) **8/24/2018 10:17**

....FISA abuse Christopher Steele & his phony and corrupt Dossier the Clinton Foundation illegal surveillance of Trump Campaign Russian collusion by Dems - and so much more. Open up the papers & documents without redaction? Come on Jeff you can do it the country is waiting! (2/2) **8/24/2018 10:28**

Ex-NSA contractor to spend 63 months in jail over "classified" information. Gee this is "small potatoes" compared to what Hillary Clinton did! So unfair Jeff Double Standard. **8/24/2018 11:10**

Social Media Giants are silencing millions of people. Can't do this even if it means we must continue to hear Fake News like CNN whose ratings have suffered gravely. People have to figure out what is real and what is not without censorship!
8/24/2018 11:34

Jeff Sessions said he wouldn't allow politics to influence him only because he doesn't understand what is happening underneath his command position. Highly conflicted Bob Mueller and his gang of 17 Angry Dems are having a field day as real corruption goes untouched. No Collusion!
8/25/2018 12:36

Big story out that the FBI ignored tens of thousands of Crooked Hillary Emails many of which are REALLY BAD. Also gave false election info. I feel sure that we will soon be getting to the bottom of all of this corruption. At some point I may have to get involved! **8/25/2018 13:05**

"The FBI only looked at 3000 of 675000 Crooked Hillary Clinton Emails." They purposely didn't look at the disasters. This news is just out. @FoxNews **8/25/2018 13:11**

"The FBI looked at less than 1%" of Crooked's Emails!
8/25/2018 13:14

Our relationship with Mexico is getting closer by the hour. Some really good people within both the new and old government and all working closely together....A big Trade Agreement with Mexico could be happening soon!
8/25/2018 13:22

Stock Market hit all time high on Friday. Congratulations U.S.A.! **8/25/2018 23:45**

My deepest sympathies and respect go out to the family of Senator John McCain. Our hearts and prayers are with you!
8/26/2018 0:44

Fantastic numbers on consumer spending released on Friday. Stock Market hits all time high! **8/26/2018 14:31**

"Mainstream Media tries to rewrite history to credit Obama for Trump accomplishments. Since President Trump took office the economy is booming. The stronger the economy

gets the more desperate his critics are. O had weakest recovery since Great Depression." @WashTimes
8/26/2018 22:01

Over 90% approval rating for your all time favorite (I hope) President within the Republican Party and 52% overall. This despite all of the made up stories by the Fake News Media trying endlessly to make me look as bad and evil as possible. Look at the real villains please!
8/27/2018 0:39

Thank you to the great @JimBrownNFL32 perhaps the greatest running back of all time for your wonderful words and support. Since our meeting in New York African-American UNEMPLOYMENT has reached the LOWEST LEVEL IN HISTORY. You get it! **8/27/2018 12:57**

The Fake News Media worked hard to get Tiger Woods to say something that he didn't want to say. Tiger wouldn't play the game - he is very smart. More importantly he is playing great golf again! **8/27/2018 13:37**

A big deal looking good with Mexico! **8/27/2018 13:39**

NASDAQ has just gone above 8000 for the first time in history! **8/28/2018 9:57**

I smile at Senators and others talking about how good free trade is for the U.S. What they don't say is that we lose Jobs and over 800 Billion Dollars a year on really dumb Trade Deals....and these same countries Tariff us to death. These lawmakers are just fine with this! **8/28/2018 14:21**

Google search results for "Trump News" shows only the viewing/reporting of Fake News Media. In other words they have it RIGGED for me & others so that almost all stories & news is BAD. Fake CNN is prominent. Republican/

Conservative & Fair Media is shut out. Illegal? 96% of....
8/28/2018 15:02

Report just out: "China hacked Hillary Clinton's private Email Server." Are they sure it wasn't Russia (just kidding!)? What are the odds that the FBI and DOJ are right on top of this? Actually a very big story. Much classified information!
8/29/2018 1:16

Add the 2026 World Cup to our long list of accomplishments! **8/29/2018 1:21**

New Poll - A majority of Americans think that John Brennan and James Comey should have their Security Clearances Revoked. Not surprised! @FoxNews **8/29/2018 2:26**

Hillary Clinton's Emails many of which are Classified Information got hacked by China. Next move better be by the FBI & DOJ or after all of their other missteps (Comey McCabe Strzok Page Ohr FISA Dirty Dossier etc.) their credibility will be forever gone! **8/29/2018 4:11**

"The Obama people did something that's never been done... They spied on a rival presidential campaign. Would it be OK if Trump did it next? I am losing faith that our system is on the level. I'm beginning to think it is rotten & corrupt. Scary stuff Obama did." @TuckerCarlson DOJ **8/29/2018 12:12**

"Anonymous Sources are really starting to BURN the media." @FoxNews The fact is that many anonymous sources don't even exist. They are fiction made up by the Fake News reporters. Look at the lie that Fake CNN is now in. They got caught red handed! Enemy of the People! **8/29/2018 12:40**

When you see "anonymous source" stop reading the story it is fiction! **8/29/2018 12:41**

How the hell is Bruce Ohr still employed at the Justice Department? Disgraceful! Witch Hunt! **8/29/2018 15:12**

#StopTheBias https://t.co/xqz599iQZw **8/29/2018 20:55**

CNN is being torn apart from within based on their being caught in a major lie and refusing to admit the mistake. Sloppy @carlbernstein a man who lives in the past and thinks like a degenerate fool making up story after story is being laughed at all over the country! Fake News

8/29/2018 22:43

"Lanny Davis admits being anonymous source in CNN Report." @BretBaier Oh well so much for CNN saying it wasn't Lanny. No wonder their ratings are so low it's FAKE NEWS! **8/30/2018 0:44**

The hatred and extreme bias of me by @CNN has clouded their thinking and made them unable to function. But actually as I have always said this has been going on for a long time. Little Jeff Z has done a terrible job his ratings suck & AT&T should fire him to save credibility! **8/30/2018 10:50**

I just cannot state strongly enough how totally dishonest much of the Media is. Truth doesn't matter to them they only have their hatred & agenda. This includes fake books which come out about me all the time always anonymous sources and are pure fiction. Enemy of the People!

8/30/2018 11:11

Wow Nellie Ohr Bruce Ohr's wife is a Russia expert who is fluent in Russian. She worked for Fusion GPS where she was paid a lot. Collusion! Bruce was a boss at the Department of Justice and is unbelievably still there! **8/30/2018 12:54**

CNN is working frantically to find their "source." Look hard because it doesn't exist. Whatever was left of CNN's credibility is now gone! **8/30/2018 16:54**

I will be doing a major rally for Senator Ted Cruz in October. I'm picking the biggest stadium in Texas we can find. As you know Ted has my complete and total Endorsement. His opponent is a disaster for Texas - weak on Second Amendment Crime Borders Military and Vets! **8/31/2018 17:09**

Wow I made OFF THE RECORD COMMENTS to Bloomberg concerning Canada and this powerful understanding was

BLATANTLY VIOLATED. Oh well just more dishonest reporting. I am used to it. At least Canada knows where I stand! **8/31/2018 18:37**

.@Rasmussen_Poll just came out at 48% approval rate despite the constant and intense Fake News. Higher than Election Day and higher than President Obama. Rasmussen was one of the most accurate Election Day polls! **9/1/2018 2:25**

I love Canada but they've taken advantage of our Country for many years! **9/1/2018 11:21**

"You have a Fake Dossier gathered by Steele paid by the Clinton team to get information on Trump. The Dossier is Fake nothing in it has been verified. It then filters into our American court system in order to spy on Barrack Obama and Hillary Clinton's political opponent...... (1/2) **9/1/2018 13:19**

....Donald Trump and now we find out that there wasn't even a hearing - that Donald Trump's 4th Amendment right to privacy was signed away...and someone in there is swearing that this stuff is true when it wasn't? This is the scandal here - a police state." Dan Bongino (2/2) **9/1/2018 13:27**

There is no political necessity to keep Canada in the new NAFTA deal. If we don't make a fair deal for the U.S. after decades of abuse Canada will be out. Congress should not interfere w/ these negotiations or I will simply terminate NAFTA entirely & we will be far better off... **9/1/2018 15:03**

MAKE AMERICA GREAT AGAIN!
9/1/2018 22:53

We shouldn't have to buy our friends with bad Trade Deals and Free Military Protection! **9/1/2018 22:55**

"There's no fairness here if you're a Democrat or a friend of Hillary you get immunity or off scott free. If you're connected to Donald Trump you get people like Robert Mueller & Andrew Weissman and his team of partisans

coming after you with a vengeance and abusing their....
9/2/2018 0:46

"There is no possible way the Trump Tower meeting between Don Trump jr and a couple of Russians who have very deep connections to both the Clintons & Fusion GPS & where no information on the Clintons was exchanged is a crime. Dems are blinded by their hatred of Trump." Bongino
9/2/2018 1:21

Tiger Woods showed great class in the way he answered the question about the Office of the Presidency and me. Now they say the so-called "left" is angry at him. So sad but the "center & right" loves Tiger Kanye George Foreman Jim Brown & so many other greats even more....... (1/2)
9/2/2018 13:28

....The fact is that African/American unemployment is now the lowest in the history of our country. Same with Asian Hispanic and almost every other group. The Democrats have been all talk and no action. My Administration has already produced like no other and everyone sees it! (2/2)
9/2/2018 13:37

Happy Labor Day! Our country is doing better than ever before with unemployment setting record lows. The U.S. has tremendous upside potential as we go about fixing some of the worst Trade Deals ever made by any country in the world. Big progress being made! **9/3/2018 11:28**

The Worker in America is doing better than ever before. Celebrate Labor Day! **9/3/2018 12:23**

....The Democrats none of whom voted for Jeff Sessions must love him now. Same thing with Lyin' James Comey. The Dems all hated him wanted him out thought he was disgusting - UNTIL I FIRED HIM! Immediately he became a wonderful man a saint like figure in fact. Really sick!
9/3/2018 18:39

I see that John Kerry the father of the now terminated Iran deal is thinking of running for President. I should only be so lucky - although the field that is currently assembling looks really good - FOR ME! **9/3/2018 18:55**

President Bashar al-Assad of Syria must not recklessly attack Idlib Province. The Russians and Iranians would be making a grave humanitarian mistake to take part in this potential human tragedy. Hundreds of thousands of people could be killed. Don't let that happen! **9/3/2018 22:20**

NBC FAKE NEWS which is under intense scrutiny over their killing the Harvey Weinstein story is now fumbling around making excuses for their probably highly unethical conduct. I have long criticized NBC and their journalistic standards-worse than even CNN. Look at their license? **9/4/2018 14:58**

The Brett Kavanaugh hearings for the future Justice of the Supreme Court are truly a display of how mean angry and despicable the other side is. They will say anything and are only.... **9/4/2018 20:41**

The Woodward book has already been refuted and discredited by General (Secretary of Defense) James Mattis and General (Chief of Staff) John Kelly. Their quotes were made up frauds a con on the public. Likewise other stories and quotes. Woodward is a Dem operative? Notice timing? **9/4/2018 23:18**

Sleepy Eyes Chuck Todd of Fake NBC News said it's time for the Press to stop complaining and to start fighting back. Actually Chuck they've been doing that from the day I announced for President. They've gone all out and I WON and now they're going CRAZY! **9/5/2018 2:50**

The already discredited Woodward book so many lies and phony sources has me calling Jeff Sessions "mentally retarded" and "a dumb southerner." I said NEITHER never used those terms on anyone including Jeff and being a southerner is a GREAT thing. He made this up to divide! **9/5/2018 3:01**

Isn't it a shame that someone can write an article or book totally make up stories and form a picture of a person that is literally the exact opposite of the fact and get away with it without retribution or cost. Don't know why Washington politicians don't change libel laws? **9/5/2018 11:33**

Almost everyone agrees that my Administration has done more in less than two years than any other Administration in the history of our Country. I'm tough as hell on people & if I weren't nothing would get done. Also I question everybody & everything-which is why I got elected! **9/5/2018 13:20**

Just like the NFL whose ratings have gone WAY DOWN Nike is getting absolutely killed with anger and boycotts. I wonder if they had any idea that it would be this way? As far as the NFL is concerned I just find it hard to watch and always will until they stand for the FLAG! **9/5/2018 13:39**

The Failing New York Times! https://t.co/SHsXvYKpBf **9/5/2018 21:45**

TREASON? **9/5/2018 22:15**

Does the so-called "Senior Administration Official" really exist or is it just the Failing New York Times with another phony source? If the GUTLESS anonymous person does indeed exist the Times must for National Security purposes turn him/her over to government at once! **9/5/2018 23:40**

I'm draining the Swamp and the Swamp is trying to fight back. Don't worry we will win! **9/6/2018 3:22**

Kim Jong Un of North Korea proclaims "unwavering faith in President Trump." Thank you to Chairman Kim. We will get it done together! **9/6/2018 10:58**

The Deep State and the Left and their vehicle the Fake News Media are going Crazy - & they don't know what to do. The Economy is booming like never before Jobs are at Historic Highs soon TWO Supreme Court Justices & maybe Declassification to find Additional Corruption. Wow! **9/6/2018 11:19**

"The record is quite remarkable. The President has faithfully followed the agenda he campaigned on in 2016. People should focus on the results and they're extraordinary!" James Freeman - Wall Street Journal **9/6/2018 14:09**

Are the investigative "journalists" of the New York Times going to investigate themselves - who is the anonymous letter writer? **9/6/2018 23:12**

What was Nike thinking? **9/7/2018 10:56**

The Woodward book is a scam. I don't talk the way I am quoted. If I did I would not have been elected President. These quotes were made up. The author uses every trick in the book to demean and belittle. I wish the people could see the real facts - and our country is doing GREAT! **9/7/2018 11:32**

Under our horrible immigration laws the Government is frequently blocked from deporting criminal aliens with violent felony convictions. House GOP just passed a bill to increase our ability to deport violent felons (Crazy Dems opposed). Need to get this bill to my desk fast! **9/7/2018 16:35**

14 days for $28 MILLION - $2 MILLION a day No Collusion. A great day for America! **9/7/2018 21:39**

We are breaking all Jobs and Economic Records but importantly our Country has TREMENDOUS FUTURE POTENTIAL. We have just begun! **9/8/2018 14:51**

Apple prices may increase because of the massive Tariffs we may be imposing on China - but there is an easy solution where there would be ZERO tax and indeed a tax incentive. Make your products in the United States instead of China. Start building new plants now. Exciting! #MAGA **9/8/2018 15:45**

Our Social Media (and beyond) Stars @DiamondandSilk are terrific people who are doing really well. We are all very proud of them and their great success! **9/9/2018 0:07**

Republicans are doing really well with the Senate Midterms. Races that we were not even thinking about winning are now very close or even leading. Election night will be very interesting indeed! **9/9/2018 1:38**

The Dems have tried every trick in the playbook-call me everything under the sun. But if I'm all of those terrible things how come I beat them so badly 306-223? Maybe they're just not very good! The fact is they are going CRAZY only because they know they can't beat me in 2020! **9/9/2018 1:47**

"Barack Obama talked a lot about hope but Donald Trump delivered the American Dream. All the economic indicators what's happening overseas Donald Trump has proven to be far more successful than Barack Obama. President Trump is delivering the American Dream." Jason Chaffetz **9/9/2018 13:32**

"Ford has abruptly killed a plan to sell a Chinese-made small vehicle in the U.S. because of the prospect of higher U.S. Tariffs." CNBC. This is just the beginning. This car can now be BUILT IN THE U.S.A. and Ford will pay no tariffs! **9/9/2018 13:49**

If the U.S. sells a car into China there is a tax of 25%. If China sells a car into the U.S. there is a tax of 2%. Does anybody think that is FAIR? The days of the U.S. being ripped-off by other nations is OVER! **9/9/2018 14:01**

Wow NFL first game ratings are way down over an already really bad last year comparison. Viewership declined 13% the lowest in over a decade. If the players stood proudly for our Flag and Anthem and it is all shown on broadcast maybe ratings could come back? Otherwise worse! **9/9/2018 14:42**

North Korea has just staged their parade celebrating 70th anniversary of founding without the customary display of nuclear missiles. Theme was peace and economic development. "Experts believe that North Korea cut out the nuclear missiles to show President Trump...... **9/9/2018 15:21**

The GDP Rate (4.2%) is higher than the Unemployment Rate (3.9%) for the first time in over 100 years! **9/10/2018 11:03**

The Economy is soooo good perhaps the best in our country's history (remember it's the economy stupid!) that the Democrats are flailing & lying like CRAZY! Phony books articles and T.V. "hits" like no other pol has had to endure-and they are losing big. Very dishonest people! **9/10/2018 13:57**

"President Trump would need a magic wand to get to 4% GDP" stated President Obama. I guess I have a magic wand 4.2% and we will do MUCH better than this! We have just begun. **9/10/2018 14:42**

To the incredible citizens of North Carolina South Carolina and the entire East Coast - the storm looks very bad! Please take all necessary precautions. We have already began mobilizing our assets to respond accordingly and we are here for you! https://t.co/g74cyD6b6K **9/10/2018 19:41**

Chuck Schumer is holding up 320 appointments (Ambassadors Executives etc.) of great people who have left jobs and given up so much in order to come into Government. Schumer and the Democrats continue to OBSTRUCT! **9/10/2018 21:18**

My people just informed me that this is one of the worst storms to hit the East Coast in many years. Also looking like a direct hit on North Carolina South Carolina and Virginia. Please be prepared be careful and be SAFE! **9/10/2018 23:17**

New Strzok-Page texts reveal "Media Leak Strategy." @ FoxNews So terrible and NOTHING is being done at DOJ or FBI - but the world is watching and they get it completely. **9/11/2018 11:19**

Rudy Giuliani did a GREAT job as Mayor of NYC during the period of September 11th. His leadership bravery and skill must never be forgotten. Rudy is a TRUE WARRIOR! **9/11/2018 11:59**

17 years since September 11th! **9/11/2018 12:58**

Crazy Maxine Waters: "After we impeach Trump we'll go after Mike Pence. We'll get him." @FoxNews Where are the Democrats coming from? The best Economy in the history of our country would totally collapse if they ever took control! **9/12/2018 1:55**

.....This was done by the Democrats in order to make me look as bad as possible when I was successfully raising Billions of Dollars to help rebuild Puerto Rico. If a person died for any reason like old age just add them onto the list. Bad politics. I love Puerto Rico! **9/13/2018 12:49**

The Wall Street Journal has it wrong we are under no pressure to make a deal with China they are under pressure to make a deal with us. Our markets are surging theirs are collapsing. We will soon be taking in Billions in Tariffs & making products at home. If we meet we meet? **9/13/2018 14:15**

John Kerry had illegal meetings with the very hostile Iranian Regime which can only serve to undercut our great work to the detriment of the American people. He told them to wait out the Trump Administration! Was he registered under the Foreign Agents Registration Act? BAD! **9/14/2018 1:10**

Incredible job being done by FEMA First Responders Law Enforcement and all. Thank you! **9/14/2018 12:19**

When President Obama said that he has been to "57 States" very little mention in Fake News Media. Can you imagine if I said that...story of the year! @IngrahamAngle **9/15/2018 3:08**

While my (our) poll numbers are good with the Economy being the best ever if it weren't for the Rigged Russian Witch Hunt they would be 25 points higher! Highly conflicted Bob Mueller & the 17 Angry Democrats are using this Phony issue to hurt us in the Midterms. No Collusion! **9/15/2018 22:08**

When will Republican leadership learn that they are being played like a fiddle by the Democrats on Border Security and Building the Wall? Without Borders we don't have a country. With Open Borders which the Democrats want we have nothing but crime! Finish the Wall! **9/15/2018 22:38**

The illegal Mueller Witch Hunt continues in search of a crime. There was never Collusion with Russia except by the Clinton campaign so the 17 Angry Democrats are looking at anything they can find. Very unfair and BAD for the country. ALSO not allowed under the LAW! **9/16/2018 14:20**

Congratulations to all of our Mexican friends on National Independence Day. We will be doing great things together! **9/16/2018 21:28**

Best economic numbers in decades. If the Democrats take control kiss your newfound wealth goodbye! **9/16/2018 22:18**

Immediately after Comey's firing Peter Strzok texted to his lover Lisa Page "We need to Open the case we've been waiting on now while Andy (McCabe also fired) is acting. Page answered "We need to lock in (redacted). In a formal chargeable way. Soon." Wow a conspiracy caught? **9/17/2018 14:36**

Americans deserve to know the lowest drug price at their pharmacy but "gag clauses" prevent your pharmacist from telling you! I support legislation that will remove gag clauses and urge the Senate to act. #AmericanPatientsFirst **9/17/2018 18:10**

China has openly stated that they are actively trying to impact and change our election by attacking our farmers ranchers and industrial workers because of their loyalty to me. What China does not understand is that these people are great patriots and fully understand that..... **9/18/2018 12:50**

The Supreme Court is one of the main reasons I got elected President. I hope Republican Voters and others are watching and studying the Democrats Playbook. **9/19/2018 3:45**

Kim Jong Un has agreed to allow Nuclear inspections subject to final negotiations and to permanently dismantle a test site and launch pad in the presence of international experts. In the meantime there will be no Rocket or Nuclear testing. Hero remains to continue being........ **9/19/2018 4:04**

"North Korea recommits to denuclearization - we've come a long way." @FoxNews **9/19/2018 11:43**

Just returned to the White House from the Great States of North Carolina and South Carolina where incredible work is being done on the ongoing fight against hurricane Florence. Tremendous talent and spirit! **9/19/2018 23:37**

I want to know where is the money for Border Security and the WALL in this ridiculous Spending Bill and where will it come from after the Midterms? Dems are obstructing Law Enforcement and Border Security. REPUBLICANS MUST FINALLY GET TOUGH! **9/20/2018 11:43**

S&P 500 HITS ALL-TIME HIGH Congratulations USA! **9/20/2018 13:34**

Judge Brett Kavanaugh is a fine man with an impeccable reputation who is under assault by radical left wing politicians who don't want to know the answers they just want to destroy and delay. Facts don't matter. I go through this with them every single day in D.C. **9/21/2018 12:56**

I have no doubt that if the attack on Dr. Ford was as bad as she says charges would have been immediately filed with local Law Enforcement Authorities by either her or her loving parents. I ask that she bring those filings forward so that we can learn date time and place! **9/21/2018 13:14**

Senator Feinstein and the Democrats held the letter for months only to release it with a bang after the hearings were OVER - done very purposefully to Obstruct & Resist & Delay. Let her testify or not and TAKE THE VOTE! **9/21/2018 15:29**

GOD BLESS THE U.S.A.! https://t.co/n9OkDlqz11 **9/22/2018 3:20**

New Economic Records being set on a daily basis - and it is not by accident! **9/22/2018 14:01**

Tiger is playing great. Looks like a big win could happen. Very exciting! @TigerWoods **9/23/2018 20:43**

Going to New York. Will be with Prime Minister Abe of Japan tonight talking Military and Trade. We have done much to help Japan would like to see more of a reciprocal relationship. It will all work out! **9/23/2018 20:52**

Prime Minster @AbeShinzo is coming up to Trump Tower for dinner but most importantly he just had a great landslide victory in Japan. I will congratulate him on behalf of the American people! **9/23/2018 22:48**

Brett Kavanaugh and his wife Ashley will be interviewed tonight at 7pmE on @marthamaccallum @FoxNews. This is an outstanding family who must be treated fairly! **9/24/2018 21:33**

REMEMBER THE MIDTERMS! **9/25/2018 2:38**

The Democrats are working hard to destroy a wonderful man and a man who has the potential to be one of our greatest Supreme Court Justices ever with an array of False Accusations the likes of which have never been seen before! **9/25/2018 2:50**

Will be speaking at the United Nations this morning. Our country is much stronger and much richer than it was when I took office less than two years ago. We are also MUCH safer! **9/25/2018 13:14**

Rush Limbaugh to Republicans: "You can kiss the MIDTERMS goodbye if you don't get highly qualified Kavanaugh approved." **9/25/2018 16:45**

The Democrats are playing a high level CON GAME in their vicious effort to destroy a fine person. It is called the politics of destruction. Behind the scene the Dems are laughing. Pray for Brett Kavanaugh and his family! **9/26/2018 2:55**

Consumer confidence hits an 18 year high close to breaking the all-time record. A big jump from last 8 years. People are excited about the USA again! We are getting Bigger and Richer and Stronger. WAY MORE TO GO! **9/26/2018 10:54**

Jobless Claims fell to their lowest level in 49 years! **9/26/2018 10:57**

Avenatti is a third rate lawyer who is good at making false accusations like he did on me and like he is now doing on Judge Brett Kavanaugh. He is just looking for attention and doesn't want people to look at his past record and relationships - a total low-life! **9/26/2018 16:47**

Judge Kavanaugh showed America exactly why I nominated him. His testimony was powerful honest and riveting. Democrats' search and destroy strategy is disgraceful and this process has been a total sham and effort to delay obstruct and resist. The Senate must vote!

9/27/2018 22:46

Just started tonight our 7th FBI investigation of Judge Brett Kavanaugh. He will someday be recognized as a truly great Justice of The United States Supreme Court! **9/29/2018 0:27**

Senator Richard Blumenthal must talk about his fraudulent service in Vietnam where for 12 years he told the people of Connecticut as their Attorney General that he was a great Marine War Hero. Talked about his many battles of near death but was never in Vietnam. Total Phony! **9/29/2018 20:33**

NBC News incorrectly reported (as usual) that I was limiting the FBI investigation of Judge Kavanaugh and witnesses only to certain people. Actually I want them to interview whoever they deem appropriate at their discretion. Please correct your reporting! **9/30/2018 2:49**

Like many I don't watch Saturday Night Live (even though I past hosted it) - no longer funny no talent or charm. It is just a political ad for the Dems. Word is that Kanye West who put on a MAGA hat after the show (despite being told "no") was great. He's leading the charge!

9/30/2018 16:57

So if African-American unemployment is now at the lowest number in history median income the highest and you then add all of the other things I have done how do Democrats who have done NOTHING for African-Americans but TALK win the Black Vote? And it will only get better! **9/30/2018 17:47**

Wow! Just starting to hear the Democrats who are only thinking Obstruct and Delay are starting to put out the word that the "time" and "scope" of FBI looking into Judge Kavanaugh and witnesses is not enough. Hello! For them it will never be enough - stay tuned and watch! **9/30/2018 18:56**

OCTOBER 2018 - DECEMBER 2018

★★★★★★★★★★★★★★★★★★★★★★★★★★

Ending the most contentious and partisan confirmation battle in U.S. history, the Senate narrowly confirms Judge Kavanaugh to the Supreme Court. Dubbing Senator Elizabeth Warren as "Pocahontas," Trump challenges her heritage and her presidential qualifications to run in 2020. With immigration being a major campaign issue in the midterm elections, the Republicans maintain the Senate but lose control of the House of Representatives to the Democrats. Immediately following the election, Trump fires Attorney General Jeff Sessions. As caravans of Central Americans continue to head to the southern U.S. border, former President George H.W. Bush dies. Nevertheless, the major story continues to be the Mueller investigation, which is finally winding down.

Late last night our deadline we reached a wonderful new Trade Deal with Canada to be added into the deal already reached with Mexico. The new name will be The United States Mexico Canada Agreement or USMCA. It is a great deal for all three countries solves the many...... **10/1/2018 10:30**

Congratulations to Mexico and Canada! **10/1/2018 10:56**

Happy 7th birthday to Tristan a very special member of the Trump family! **10/2/2018 14:52**

THE ONLY REASON TO VOTE FOR A DEMOCRAT IS IF YOU'RE TIRED OF WINNING!

10/2/2018 16:08

GOD BLESS THE U.S.A.! #MAGA https://t.co/pquqyy5S3G **10/3/2018 1:25**

The Stock Market just reached an All-Time High during my Administration for the 102nd Time a presidential record by far for less than two years. So much potential as Trade and Military Deals are completed. **10/3/2018 13:04**

I see it each time I go out to Rallies in order to help some of our great Republican candidates. VOTERS ARE REALLY ANGRY AT THE VICIOUS AND DESPICABLE WAY DEMOCRATS ARE TREATING BRETT KAVANAUGH! He and his wonderful family deserve much better. **10/3/2018 14:29**

My thoughts and prayers are with the Florence County Sheriff's Office and the Florence Police Department tonight in South Carolina. We are forever grateful for what our Law Enforcement Officers do 24/7/365. https://t.co/ZwDmDthItD **10/4/2018 0:01**

Wow such enthusiasm and energy for Judge Brett Kavanaugh. Look at the Energy look at the Polls. Something very big is happening. He is a fine man and great intellect. The country is with him all the way! **10/4/2018 2:23**

The harsh and unfair treatment of Judge Brett Kavanaugh is having an incredible upward impact on voters. The PEOPLE get it far better than the politicians. Most importantly this great life cannot be ruined by mean & despicable Democrats and totally uncorroborated allegations!
10/4/2018 12:16

Our country's great First Lady Melania is doing really well in Africa. The people love her and she loves them! It is a beautiful thing to see. **10/4/2018 13:34**

This is a very important time in our country. Due Process Fairness and Common Sense are now on trial! **10/4/2018 13:54**

This is now the 7th. time the FBI has investigated Judge Kavanaugh. If we made it 100 it would still not be good enough for the Obstructionist Democrats. **10/4/2018 14:17**

The very rude elevator screamers are paid professionals only looking to make Senators look bad. Don't fall for it! Also look at all of the professionally made identical signs. Paid for by Soros and others. These are not signs made in the basement from love! #Troublemakers **10/5/2018 13:03**

Just out: 3.7% Unemployment is the lowest number since 1969! **10/5/2018 13:06**

Very proud of the U.S. Senate for voting "YES" to advance the nomination of Judge Brett Kavanaugh!
10/5/2018 14:59

Women for Kavanaugh and many others who support this very good man are gathering all over Capitol Hill in preparation for a 3-5 P.M. VOTE. It is a beautiful thing to see - and they are not paid professional protesters who are handed expensive signs. Big day for America! **10/6/2018 16:08**

I have asked Steve Daines our great Republican Senator from Montana to attend his daughter Annie's wedding

rather than coming to today's vote. Steve was ready to do whatever he had to but we had the necessary number. To the Daines Family congratulations-have a wonderful day!
10/6/2018 20:06

I applaud and congratulate the U.S. Senate for confirming our GREAT NOMINEE Judge Brett Kavanaugh to the United States Supreme Court. Later today I will sign his Commission of Appointment and he will be officially sworn in. Very exciting! **10/6/2018 20:15**

The crowd in front of the U.S. Supreme Court is tiny looks like about 200 people (& most are onlookers) - that wouldn't even fill the first couple of rows of our Kansas Rally or any of our Rallies for that matter! The Fake News Media tries to make it look sooo big & it's not!
10/6/2018 21:57

You don't hand matches to an arsonist and you don't give power to an angry left-wing mob. Democrats have become too EXTREME and TOO DANGEROUS to govern. Republicans believe in the rule of law - not the rule of the mob. VOTE REPUBLICAN! **10/7/2018 1:21**

.@SecPompeo had a good meeting with Chairman Kim today in Pyongyang. Progress made on Singapore Summit Agreements! I look forward to seeing Chairman Kim again in the near future. https://t.co/bUa2pkq80s **10/7/2018 14:42**

The paid D.C. protesters are now ready to REALLY protest because they haven't gotten their checks - in other words they weren't paid! Screamers in Congress and outside were far too obvious - less professional than anticipated by those paying (or not paying) the bills! **10/9/2018 12:32**

Great evening last night at the White House honoring Justice Kavanaugh and family. Our country is very proud of them! **10/9/2018 12:37**

Despite so many positive events and victories Media Reseach Center reports that 92% of stories on Donald Trump are negative on ABC CBS and ABC. It is FAKE NEWS! Don't worry the Failing New York Times didn't even put the Brett Kavanaugh victory on the Front Page yesterday-A17! **10/10/2018 13:01**

Massive overflow crowd tonight in Erie Pennsylvania. THANK YOU to everyone who came out and joined us. Together we are MAKING AMERICA GREAT AGAIN! https://t.co/FkPNNVpccX **10/11/2018 1:00**

Florida Highway Patrol Troopers are all en route to the Panhandle from all across the state of Florida - to help those affected by #HurricaneMichael. If you see them be sure to shake their hands and say THANK YOU! #LESM https://t.co/rB7uNBudY5 **10/11/2018 3:44**

PASTOR BRUNSON JUST RELEASED. WILL BE HOME SOON! **10/12/2018 14:26**

People have no idea how hard Hurricane Michael has hit the great state of Georgia. I will be visiting both Florida and Georgia early next week. We are working very hard on every area and every state that was hit - we are with you! **10/12/2018 18:09**

The GREAT football (and lacrosse) player Jim Brown outside the West Wing of the @WhiteHouse. He is also a tremendous man and mentor to many young people! https://t.co/yo7MxoGL6C **10/12/2018 22:14**

There was NO DEAL made with Turkey for the release and return of Pastor Andrew Brunson. I don't make deals for hostages. There was however great appreciation on behalf of the United States which will lead to good perhaps great relations between the United States & Turkey! **10/13/2018 14:17**

Highly respected Congressman Keith Rothfus (R) of Pennsylvania is in the fight of his life because the Dems changed the District Map. He must win. Strong on crime borders big tax & reg cuts Military & Vets. Opponent Lamb a Pelosi puppet-weak on crime. BIG ENDORSEMENT FOR KEITH **10/13/2018 17:43**

WELCOME HOME PASTOR ANDREW BRUNSON! https://t.co/HijeAGU1gy **10/13/2018 20:48**

Big day! Pastor Andrew Brunson who could have spent 35 years in a Turkish prison was returned safely home to his family today. Met in Oval Office great people! Then off to Kentucky for a Rally for Congressman Andy Barr. Tremendous crowd & spirit! Just returned to White House. **10/14/2018 3:42**

Congratulations to Tucker Carlson on the great success of his book "Ship of Fools." It just went to NUMBER ONE! **10/14/2018 3:53**

NBC News has totally and purposely changed the point and meaning of my story about General Robert E Lee and General Ulysses Grant. Was actually a shoutout to warrior Grant and the great state in which he was born. As usual dishonest reporting. Even mainstream media embarrassed! **10/14/2018 13:56**

"The only way to shut down the Democrats new Mob Rule strategy is to stop them cold at the Ballot Box. The fight for America's future is never over!" Ben Shapiro **10/15/2018 11:46**

The crowds at my Rallies are far bigger than they have ever been before including the 2016 election. Never an empty seat in these large venues many thousands of people watching screens outside. Enthusiasm & Spirit is through the roof. SOMETHING BIG IS HAPPENING - WATCH! **10/15/2018 12:11**

Just spoke to the King of Saudi Arabia who denies any knowledge of whatever may have happened "to our Saudi Arabian citizen." He said that they are working closely with Turkey to find answer. I am immediately sending our Secretary of State to meet with King! **10/15/2018 12:37**

TOGETHER WE WILL PREVAIL! https://t.co/C1TLMVkDmt **10/16/2018 0:26**

Pocahontas (the bad version) sometimes referred to as Elizabeth Warren is getting slammed. She took a bogus DNA test and it showed that she may be 1/1024 far less than the average American. Now Cherokee Nation denies her "DNA test is useless." Even they don't want her. Phony! **10/16/2018 12:06**

Now that her claims of being of Indian heritage have turned out to be a scam and a lie Elizabeth Warren should apologize for perpetrating this fraud against the American Public. Harvard called her "a person of color" (amazing con) and would not have taken her otherwise! **10/16/2018 12:16**

Thank you to the Cherokee Nation for revealing that Elizabeth Warren sometimes referred to as Pocahontas is a complete and total Fraud! **10/16/2018 12:24**

The United States has strongly informed the President of Honduras that if the large Caravan of people heading to the U.S. is not stopped and brought back to Honduras no more money or aid will be given to Honduras effective immediately! **10/16/2018 13:05**

Incredible number just out 7036000 job openings. Astonishing - it's all working! Stock Market up big on tremendous potential of USA. Also Strong Profits. We are Number One in World by far! **10/16/2018 14:12**

"Federal Judge throws out Stormy Danials lawsuit versus Trump. Trump is entitled to full legal fees." @FoxNews Great now I can go after Horseface and her 3rd rate lawyer in the Great State of Texas. She will confirm the letter she signed! She knows nothing about me a total con! **10/16/2018 15:04**

Is it really possible that Bruce Ohr whose wife Nellie was paid by Simpson and GPS Fusion for work done on the

Fake Dossier and who was used as a Pawn in this whole SCAM (WITCH HUNT) is still working for the Department of Justice????? Can this really be so????? **10/16/2018 15:26**

WOW John James is making headway in Michigan. We are bringing jobs back to the State and the People of Michigan appreciate it. Debbie Stabenow has been no help if anything a major hindrance. John James is a star I hope the voters see it. Polls are tightening! **10/16/2018 18:50**

We have today informed the countries of Honduras Guatemala and El Salvador that if they allow their citizens or others to journey through their borders and up to the United States with the intention of entering our country illegally all payments made to them will STOP (END)! **10/17/2018 1:19**

Anybody entering the United States illegally will be arrested and detained prior to being sent back to their country! **10/17/2018 1:24**

Elizabeth Warren is being hammered even by the Left. Her false claim of Indian heritage is only selling to VERY LOW I.Q. individuals! **10/17/2018 2:36**

"Trump could be the most honest president in modern history. When you look at the real barometer of presidential truthfulness which is promise keeping he is probably the most honest president in American history. He's done exactly what he said he would do." Marc Thiessen WPost **10/17/2018 11:30**

Hard to believe that with thousands of people from South of the Border walking unimpeded toward our country in the form of large Caravans that the Democrats won't approve legislation that will allow laws for the protection of our country. Great Midterm issue for Republicans! **10/17/2018 13:45**

College educated women want safety security and healthcare protections - very much along with financial and economic health for themselves and our Country. I supply all of this far better than any Democrat (for decades actually). That's why they will be voting for me! **10/17/2018 19:24**

Ever since his vicious and totally false statements about Admiral Ron Jackson the highly respected White House Doctor for Obama Bush & me Senator John Tester looks to be in big trouble in the Great State of Montana! He behaved worse than the Democrat Mob did with Justice K!

10/18/2018 2:03

I am watching the Democrat Party led (because they want Open Borders and existing weak laws) assault on our country by Guatemala Honduras and El Salvador whose leaders are doing little to stop this large flow of people INCLUDING MANY CRIMINALS from entering Mexico to U.S..... (1/3) **10/18/2018 11:25**

....In addition to stopping all payments to these countries which seem to have almost no control over their population I must in the strongest of terms ask Mexico to stop this onslaught - and if unable to do so I will call up the U.S. Military and CLOSE OUR SOUTHERN BORDER!.. (2/3)

10/18/2018 11:35

....The assault on our country at our Southern Border including the Criminal elements and DRUGS pouring in is far more important to me as President than Trade or the USMCA. Hopefully Mexico will stop this onslaught at their Northern Border. All Democrats fault for weak laws! (3/3)

10/18/2018 11:45

All Republicans support people with pre-existing conditions and if they don't they will after I speak to them. I am in total support. Also Democrats will destroy your Medicare and I will keep it healthy and well! **10/18/2018 19:43**

#JobsNotMobs! **10/19/2018 3:23**

When referring to the USA I will always capitalize the word Country! **10/19/2018 14:04**

Beto O'Rourke is a total lightweight compared to Ted Cruz and he comes nowhere near representing the values and desires of the people of the Great State of Texas. He will never be allowed to turn Texas into Venezuela! **10/19/2018 17:34**

This is what it is all about for the Republican Party! #JobsNotMobs https://t.co/8OabccPec5 **10/19/2018 23:47**

If the Democrats would stop being obstructionists and come together we could write up and agree to new immigration laws in less than one hour. Look at the needless pain and suffering that they are causing. Look at the horrors taking place on the Border. Chuck & Nancy call me! **10/20/2018 14:35**

All levels of government and Law Enforcement are watching carefully for VOTER FRAUD including during EARLY VOTING. Cheat at your own peril. Violators will be subject to maximum penalties both civil and criminal! **10/21/2018 0:36**

Watched North Dakota's Rep. Kevin Cramer easily win debate with Senator Heidi Heitkamp. Great job Kevin you will be a great Senator! **10/21/2018 2:45**

Full efforts are being made to stop the onslaught of illegal aliens from crossing our Souther Border. People have to apply for asylum in Mexico first and if they fail to do that the U.S. will turn them away. The courts are asking the U.S. to do things that are not doable! **10/21/2018 19:11**

The Caravans are a disgrace to the Democrat Party. Change the immigration laws NOW! **10/21/2018 19:14**

Best Jobs Numbers in the history of our great Country! Many other things likewise. So why wouldn't we win the Midterms? Dems can never do even nearly as well! Think of what will happen to your now beautiful 401-k's! **10/21/2018 19:26**

Facebook has just stated that they are setting up a system to "purge" themselves of Fake News. Does that mean CNN will finally be put out of business?

10/21/2018 22:48

Sadly it looks like Mexico's Police and Military are unable to stop the Caravan heading to the Southern Border of the United States. Criminals and unknown Middle Easterners are mixed in. I have alerted Border Patrol and Military that this is a National Emergy. Must change laws! **10/22/2018 12:37**

Every time you see a Caravan or people illegally coming or attempting to come into our Country illegally think of and blame the Democrats for not giving us the votes to change our pathetic Immigration Laws! Remember the Midterms! So unfair to those who come in legally. **10/22/2018 12:49**

Guatemala Honduras and El Salvador were not able to do the job of stopping people from leaving their country and coming illegally to the U.S. We will now begin cutting off or substantially reducing the massive foreign aid routinely given to them. **10/22/2018 12:57**

The people of Puerto Rico are wonderful but the inept politicians are trying to use the massive and ridiculously high amounts of hurricane/disaster funding to pay off other obligations. The U.S. will NOT bail out long outstanding & unpaid obligations with hurricane relief money! **10/23/2018 15:24**

Billions of dollars are and will be coming into United States coffers because of Tariffs. Great also for negotiations - if a country won't give us a fair Trade Deal we will institute Tariffs on them. Used or not jobs and businesses will be created. U.S. respected again! **10/23/2018 16:43**

I agree with President Obama 100%! https://t.co/PI3aW1Zh5Q

10/23/2018 23:18

For those who want and advocate for illegal immigration just take a good look at what has happened to Europe over the last 5 years. A total mess! They only wish they had that decision to make over again. **10/24/2018 11:52**

We are a great Sovereign Nation. We have Strong Borders and will never accept people coming into our Country illegally! **10/24/2018 11:56**

Republicans will totally protect people with Pre-Existing Conditions Democrats will not! Vote Republican.

10/24/2018 12:45

The safety of the American People is my highest priority. I have just concluded a briefing with the FBI Department of Justice Department of Homeland Security and the U.S. Secret Service... https://t.co/nEUBcq4NOh **10/24/2018 18:55**

Brandon Judd of the National Border Patrol Council is right when he says on @foxandfriends that the Democrat inspired laws make it tough for us to stop people at the Border. MUST BE CHANDED but I am bringing out the military for this National Emergency. They will be stopped!

10/25/2018 11:05

A very big part of the Anger we see today in our society is caused by the purposely false and inaccurate reporting of the Mainstream Media that I refer to as Fake News. It has gotten so bad and hateful that it is beyond description. Mainstream Media must clean up its act FAST! **10/25/2018 11:18**

The New York Times has a new Fake Story that now the Russians and Chinese (glad they finally added China) are listening to all of my calls on cellphones. Except that I rarely use a cellphone & when I do it's government authorized. I like Hard Lines. Just more made up Fake News! **10/25/2018 13:57**

To those in the Caravan turnaround we are not letting people into the United States illegally. Go back to your Country and if you want apply for citizenship like millions of others are doing! **10/25/2018 18:31**

Funny how lowly rated CNN and others can criticize me at will even blaming me for the current spate of Bombs and ridiculously comparing this to September 11th and the Oklahoma City bombing yet when I criticize them they go wild and scream "it's just not Presidential!" **10/26/2018 7:14**

The United States has been spending Billions of Dollars a year on Illegal Immigration. This will not continue. Democrats must give us the votes to pass strong (but fair) laws. If not we will be forced to play a much tougher hand. **10/26/2018 13:55**

Twitter has removed many people from my account and more importantly they have seemingly done something that makes it much harder to join - they have stifled growth to a point where it is obvious to all. A few weeks ago it was a Rocket Ship now it is a Blimp! Total Bias? **10/26/2018 14:05**

Republicans are doing so well in early voting and at the polls and now this "Bomb" stuff happens and the momentum greatly slows - news not talking politics. Very unfortunate what is going on. Republicans go out and vote! **10/26/2018 14:19**

I want to applaud the FBI Secret Service Department of Justice the U.S. Attorneys' Office for the Southern District of New York the NYPD and all Law Enforcement partners across the Country for their incredible work skill and determination! **10/26/2018 17:59**

Whether you are African-American Hispanic-American or ANY AMERICAN at all – you have the right to live in a Country that puts YOUR NEEDS FIRST! https://t.co/hwDICbpOT7 **10/26/2018 18:48**

If you meet every day with optimism - if you confront every obstacle with determination - if you refuse to give up if you never quit if you face every challenge with confidence and pride - then there is no goal you cannot achieve and no dream beyond your reach! #YBLS2018 https://t.co/Uqmw5fLmxW **10/26/2018 21:47**

#Walkaway Walkaway from the Democrat Party movement marches today in D.C. Congratulations to Brandon Straka for starting something very special. @foxandfriends **10/27/2018 14:02**

Watching the events unfolding in Pittsburgh Pennsylvania. Law enforcement on the scene. People in Squirrel Hill area should remain sheltered. Looks like multiple fatalities. Beware of active shooter. God Bless All! **10/27/2018 15:08**

Events in Pittsburgh are far more devastating than originally thought. Spoke with Mayor and Governor to inform them that the Federal Government has been and will be with them all the way. I will speak to the media shortly and make further statement at Future Farmers of America. **10/27/2018 16:26**

All of America is in mourning over the mass murder of Jewish Americans at the Tree of Life Synagogue in Pittsburgh. We pray for those who perished and their loved ones and our hearts go out to the brave police officers who sustained serious injuries... (1/2) **10/27/2018 21:41**

...This evil Anti-Semitic attack is an assault on humanity. It will take all of us working together to extract the poison of Anti-Semitism from our world. We must unite to conquer hate. (2/2) **10/27/2018 21:41**

Watching the Dodgers/Red Sox final innings. It is amazing how a manager takes out a pitcher who is loose & dominating through almost 7 innings Rich Hill of Dodgers and brings in nervous reliever(s) who get shellacked. 4 run lead gone. Managers do it all the time big mistake! **10/28/2018 3:46**

Just watched Wacky Tom Steyer who I have not seen in action before be interviewed by @jaketapper. He comes off as a crazed & stumbling lunatic who should be running out of money pretty soon. As bad as their field is if he is running for President the Dems will eat him alive! **10/28/2018 17:03**

The Fake News is doing everything in their power to blame Republicans Conservatives and me for the division and hatred that has been going on for so long in our Country. Actually it is their Fake & Dishonest reporting which is causing problems far greater than they understand!

10/29/2018 0:12

There is great anger in our Country caused in part by inaccurate and even fraudulent reporting of the news. The Fake News Media the true Enemy of the People must stop the open & obvious hostility & report the news accurately & fairly. That will do much to put out the flame... **10/29/2018 12:03**

Had a very good conversation with the newly elected President of Brazil Jair Bolsonaro who won his race by a substantial margin. We agreed that Brazil and the United States will work closely together on Trade Military and everything else! Excellent call wished him congrats! **10/29/2018 12:28**

Many Gang Members and some very bad people are mixed into the Caravan heading to our Southern Border. Please go back you will not be admitted into the United States unless you go through the legal process. This is an invasion of our Country and our Military is waiting for you! **10/29/2018 14:41**

In Florida there is a choice between a Harvard/Yale educated man named @RonDeSantisFL who has been a great Congressman and will be a great Governor - and a Dem who is a thief and who is Mayor of poorly run

Tallahassee said to be one of the most corrupt cities in the Country! **10/29/2018 14:54**

CNN and others in the Fake News Business keep purposely and inaccurately reporting that I said the "Media is the Enemy of the People." Wrong! I said that the "Fake News (Media) is the Enemy of the People" a very big difference. When you give out false information - not good! **10/30/2018 0:00**

Check out tweets from last two days. I refer to Fake News Media when mentioning Enemy of the People - but dishonest reporters use only the word "Media." The people of our Great Country are angry and disillusioned at receiving so much Fake News. They get it and fully understand! **10/30/2018 0:14**

The Stock Market is up massively since the Election but is now taking a little pause - people want to see what happens with the Midterms. If you want your Stocks to go down I strongly suggest voting Democrat. They like the Venezuela financial model High Taxes & Open Borders! **10/30/2018 12:33**

Just out: Consumer Confidence hits highest level since 2000. **10/30/2018 15:10**

Our military is being mobilized at the Southern Border. Many more troops coming. We will NOT let these Caravans which are also made up of some very bad thugs and gang members into the U.S. Our Border is sacred must come in legally. TURN AROUND! **10/31/2018 12:45**

So-called Birthright Citizenship which costs our Country billions of dollars and is very unfair to our citizens will be ended one way or the other. It is not covered by the 14th Amendment because of the words "subject to the jurisdiction thereof." Many legal scholars agree..... **10/31/2018 13:25**

Paul Ryan should be focusing on holding the Majority rather than giving his opinions on Birthright Citizenship something he knows nothing about! Our new Republican Majority will work on this Closing the Immigration Loopholes and Securing our Border! **10/31/2018 16:43**

It is outrageous what the Democrats are doing to our Country. Vote Republican now! https://t.co/0pWiwCHGbh https://t.co/2crea9HF7G **10/31/2018 20:18**

Just had a long and very good conversation with President Xi Jinping of China. We talked about many subjects with a heavy emphasis on Trade. Those discussions are moving along nicely with meetings being scheduled at the G-20 in Argentina. Also had good discussion on North Korea! **11/1/2018 14:09**

Illegal immigration affects the lives of all Americans. Illegal Immigration hurts American workers burdens American taxpayers undermines public safety and places enormous strain on local schools hospitals and communities... https://t.co/eN1IqPNBJY **11/1/2018 20:54**

Together we are Making America Safe and Great Again! https://t.co/0pWiwCHGbh https://t.co/rWI5aSpY3O **11/1/2018 22:46**

Wow! The U.S. added 250000 Jobs in October - and this was despite the hurricanes. Unemployment at 3.7%. Wages UP! These are incredible numbers. Keep it going Vote Republican! **11/2/2018 13:46**

Will be going to West Virginia and Indiana today TWO RALLIES! Don't tell anyone (big secret) but I will be bringing Coach Bobby Knight to Indiana. He's been a supporter right from the beginning of the Greatest Political Movement in American History! **11/2/2018 13:54**

Congresswoman Maxine Waters was called the most Corrupt Member of Congress! @FoxNews If Dems win she would be put in charge of our Country's finances. The beginning of the end! **11/3/2018 10:54**

A vicious accuser of Justice Kavanaugh has just admitted that she was lying her story was totally made up or FAKE!

Can you imagine if he didn't become a Justice of the Supreme Court because of her disgusting False Statements. What about the others? Where are the Dems on this?
11/3/2018 13:38

Rumor has it that Senator Joe Donnelly of Indiana is paying for Facebook ads for his so-called opponent on the libertarian ticket. Donnelly is trying to steal the election? Isn't that what Russia did!? **11/3/2018 21:05**

New Fox Poll shows a "40% Approval Rating by African Americans for President Trump a record for Republicans." Thank you a great honor! **11/4/2018 15:15**

Thank you for joining us tonight in Tennessee @TheLeeGreenwood. GOD BLESS THE U.S.A.! https://t.co/hfxi4Ct6Pv **11/5/2018 1:36**

So funny to see the CNN Fake Suppression Polls and false rhetoric. Watch for real results Tuesday. We are lucky CNN's ratings are so low. Don't fall for the Suppression Game. Go out & VOTE. Remember we now have perhaps the greatest Economy (JOBS) in the history of our Country!
11/5/2018 15:18

Law Enforcement has been strongly notified to watch closely for any ILLEGAL VOTING which may take place in Tuesday's Election (or Early Voting). Anyone caught will be subject to the Maximum Criminal Penalties allowed by law. Thank you! **11/5/2018 15:41**

There is a rumor put out by the Democrats that Josh Hawley of Missouri left the Arena last night early. It is Fake News. He met me at the plane when I arrived spoke at the great Rally & stayed to the very end. In fact I said goodbye to him and left before he did. Deception! **11/6/2018 15:20**

Tremendous success tonight. Thank you to all!

11/7/2018 4:14

"There's only been 5 times in the last 105 years that an incumbent President has won seats in the Senate in the off year election. Mr. Trump has magic about him. This guy has magic coming out of his ears. He is an astonishing vote getter & campaigner. The Republicans are......... (1/2)

11/7/2018 6:27

....unbelievably lucky to have him and I'm just awed at how well they've done. It's all the Trump magic - Trump is the magic man. Incredible he's got the entire media against him attacking him every day and he pulls out these enormous wins." Ben Stein "The Capitalist Code" (2/2) **11/7/2018 6:37**

Received so many Congratulations from so many on our Big Victory last night including from foreign nations (friends) that were waiting me out and hoping on Trade Deals. Now we can all get back to work and get things done! **11/7/2018 11:21**

Ron DeSantis showed great courage in his hard fought campaign to become the Governor of Florida. Congratulations to Ron and family! **11/7/2018 11:55**

Those that worked with me in this incredible Midterm Election embracing certain policies and principles did very well. Those that did not say goodbye! Yesterday was such a very Big Win and all under the pressure of a Nasty and Hostile Media! **11/7/2018 12:07**

To any of the pundits or talking heads that do not give us proper credit for this great Midterm Election just remember two words - FAKE NEWS! **11/7/2018 12:52**

If the Democrats think they are going to waste Taxpayer Money investigating us at the House level then we will likewise be forced to consider investigating them for all of the leaks of Classified Information and much else at the Senate level. Two can play that game! **11/7/2018 13:04**

In all fairness Nancy Pelosi deserves to be chosen Speaker of the House by the Democrats. If they give her a hard time perhaps we will add some Republican votes. She has earned this great honor! **11/7/2018 13:31**

According to NBC News Voters Nationwide Disapprove of the so-called Mueller Investigation (46%) more than they Approve (41%). You mean they are finally beginning to understand what a disgusting Witch Hunt led by 17 Angry Democrats is all about! **11/7/2018 15:39**

We are pleased to announce that Matthew G. Whitaker Chief of Staff to Attorney General Jeff Sessions at the Department of Justice will become our new Acting Attorney General of the United States. He will serve our Country well.... (1/2)

11/7/2018 19:44

....We thank Attorney General Jeff Sessions for his service and wish him well! A permanent replacement will be nominated at a later date. (2/2) **11/7/2018 19:44**

I have been fully briefed on the terrible shooting in California. Law Enforcement and First Responders together with the FBI are on scene. 13 people at this time have been reported dead. Likewise the shooter is dead along with the first police officer to enter the bar.... (1/2) **11/8/2018 12:38**

....Great bravery shown by police. California Highway Patrol was on scene within 3 minutes with first officer to enter shot numerous times. That Sheriff's Sergeant died in the hospital. God bless all of the victims and families of the victims. Thank you to Law Enforcement. (2/2) **11/8/2018 12:51**

Law Enforcement is looking into another big corruption scandal having to do with Election Fraud in #Broward and Palm Beach. Florida voted for Rick Scott! **11/9/2018 2:38**

.@BrianKempGA ran a great race in Georgia – he won. It is time to move on! **11/9/2018 15:55**

You mean they are just now finding votes in Florida and Georgia – but the Election was on Tuesday? Let's blame the

Russians and demand an immediate apology from President Putin! **11/9/2018 15:58**

As soon as Democrats sent their best Election stealing lawyer Marc Elias to Broward County they miraculously started finding Democrat votes. Don't worry Florida - I am sending much better lawyers to expose the FRAUD!

11/9/2018 16:52

Jeff Flake(y) doesn't want to protect the Non-Senate confirmed Special Counsel he wants to protect his future after being unelectable in Arizona for the "crime" of doing a terrible job! A weak and ineffective guy! **11/9/2018 17:10**

Rick Scott was up by 50000+ votes on Election Day now they "found" many votes and he is only up 15000 votes. "The Broward Effect." How come they never find Republican votes? **11/9/2018 17:36**

Mayor Gillum conceded on Election Day and now Broward County has put him "back into play." Bill Nelson conceded Election - now he's back in play!? This is an embarrassment to our Country and to Democracy! **11/9/2018 18:14**

In the 2016 Election I was winning by so much in Florida that Broward County which was very late with vote tabulation and probably getting ready to do a "number" couldn't do it because not enough people live in Broward for them to falsify a victory! **11/9/2018 18:20**

Thank you @marcorubio for helping to expose the potential corruption going on with respect to Election Theft in Broward and Palm Beach Counties. The WORLD is now watching closely! **11/9/2018 18:39**

Just out — in Arizona SIGNATURES DON'T MATCH. Electoral corruption - Call for a new Election? We must protect our Democracy!

11/9/2018 20:33

President Macron of France has just suggested that Europe build its own military in order to protect itself from the U.S. China and Russia. Very insulting but perhaps Europe should first pay its fair share of NATO which the U.S. subsidizes greatly! **11/9/2018 21:10**

There is no reason for these massive deadly and costly forest fires in California except that forest management is so poor. Billions of dollars are given each year with so many lives lost all because of gross mismanagement of the forests. Remedy now or no more Fed payments! **11/10/2018 8:08**

I am in Paris getting ready to celebrate the end of World War One. Is there anything better to celebrate than the end of a war in particular that one which was one of the bloodiest and worst of all time? **11/10/2018 8:17**

Happy 243rd Birthday to our GREAT U.S. Marine Corps https://t.co/1cPtoMfmxP **11/10/2018 14:09**

Had very productive meetings and calls for our Country today. Meeting tonight with World Leaders! **11/10/2018 19:06**

Trying to STEAL two big elections in Florida! We are watching closely! **11/10/2018 19:09**

More than 4000 are fighting the Camp and Woolsey Fires in California that have burned over 170000 acres. Our hearts are with those fighting the fires the 52000 who have evacuated and the families of the 11 who have died. The destruction is catastrophic. God Bless them all. **11/10/2018 22:19**

These California fires are expanding very very quickly (in some cases 80-100 acres a minute). If people don't evacuate quickly they risk being overtaken by the fire. Please listen to evacuation orders from State and local officials! **11/10/2018 22:20**

With proper Forest Management we can stop the devastation constantly going on in California. Get Smart! **11/11/2018 9:40**

Beautiful ceremony today in Paris commemorating the end of World War One. Many World leaders in attendance. Thank you to @EmmanuelMacron President of France! Now off to Suresnes American Cemetery to make speech in honor of our great heroes! Then back to the U.S.A.

11/11/2018 14:52

Poland a great country - Congratulations on the 100th Anniversary of your Independence. I will never forget my time there! https://t.co/gEme6McF1x **11/11/2018 16:03**

Exactly 100 years ago today on November 11th 1918 World War I came to an end. We are gathered together at this hallowed resting place to pay tribute to the brave Americans who gave their last breath in that mighty struggle.... https://t.co/JPUkOr4rW1 **11/12/2018 4:38**

Just returned from France where much was accomplished in my meetings with World Leaders. Never easy bringing up the fact that the U.S. must be treated fairly which it hasn't on both Military and Trade. We pay for LARGE portions of other countries military protection........ (1/2) **11/12/2018 12:03**

.....of money spent on protecting other countries and we get nothing but Trade Deficits and Losses. It is time that these very rich countries either pay the United States for its great military protection or protect themselves...and Trade must be made FREE and FAIR! (2/2) **11/12/2018 12:21**

The Florida Election should be called in favor of Rick Scott and Ron DeSantis in that large numbers of new ballots showed up out of nowhere and many ballots are missing or forged. An honest vote count is no longer possible-ballots massively infected. Must go with Election Night! **11/12/2018 12:44**

The prospect of Presidential Harassment by the Dems is causing the Stock Market big headaches! **11/12/2018 15:34**

The California Fire Fighters FEMA and First Responders are amazing and very brave. Thank you and God Bless you all!

11/12/2018 16:31

I just approved an expedited request for a Major Disaster Declaration for the State of California. Wanted to respond quickly in order to alleviate some of the incredible suffering going on. I am with you all the way. God Bless all of the victims and families affected. **11/13/2018 1:19**

Emmanuel Macron suggests building its own army to protect Europe against the U.S. China and Russia. But it was Germany in World Wars One & Two - How did that work out for France? They were starting to learn German in Paris before the U.S. came along. Pay for NATO or not!
11/13/2018 11:50

On Trade France makes excellent wine but so does the U.S. The problem is that France makes it very hard for the U.S. to sell its wines into France and charges big Tariffs whereas the U.S. makes it easy for French wines and charges very small Tariffs. Not fair must change! **11/13/2018 13:07**

The problem is that Emmanuel suffers from a very low Approval Rating in France 26% and an unemployment rate of almost 10%. He was just trying to get onto another subject. By the way there is no country more Nationalist than France very proud people-and rightfully so!........ (1/2)
11/13/2018 13:17

......MAKE FRANCE GREAT AGAIN! (2/2) **11/13/2018 13:18**

By the way when the helicopter couldn't fly to the first cemetery in France because of almost zero visibility I suggested driving. Secret Service said NO too far from airport & big Paris shutdown. Speech next day at American Cemetery in pouring rain! Little reported-Fake News!
11/13/2018 15:49

When will Bill Nelson concede in Florida? The characters running Broward and Palm Beach voting will not be able to "find" enough votes too much spotlight on them now!
11/13/2018 16:32

The story in the New York Times concerning North Korea developing missile bases is inaccurate. We fully know about the sites being discussed nothing new - and nothing happening out of the normal. Just more Fake News. I will be the first to let you know if things go bad! **11/13/2018 17:07**

"Boom: Record high business optimism need for employees at 45-year high" https://t.co/jBFjEwAcfd **11/13/2018 21:35**

Not seen in many years America's steelworkers get a hard-earned raise because of my Administration's policies to help bring back the U.S. steel industry which is critical to our National Security. I will always protect America and its workers! **11/14/2018 19:28**

Just spoke to Governor Jerry Brown to let him know that we are with him and the people of California all the way! **11/14/2018 19:58**

The White House is running very smoothly and the results for our Nation are obviously very good. We are the envy of the world. But anytime I even think about making changes the FAKE NEWS MEDIA goes crazy always seeking to make us look as bad as possible! Very dishonest! **11/15/2018 11:59**

The inner workings of the Mueller investigation are a total mess. They have found no collusion and have gone absolutely nuts. They are screaming and shouting at people horribly threatening them to come up with the answers they want. They are a disgrace to our Nation and don't... (1/2) **11/15/2018 12:14**

....care how many lives the ruin. These are Angry People including the highly conflicted Bob Mueller who worked for Obama for 8 years. They won't even look at all of the bad acts and crimes on the other side. A TOTAL WITCH HUNT LIKE NO OTHER IN AMERICAN HISTORY! (2/2) **11/15/2018 12:32**

Universities will someday study what highly conflicted (and NOT Senate approved) Bob Mueller and his gang of Democrat thugs have done to destroy people. Why is he protecting Crooked Hillary Comey McCabe Lisa Page & her lover Peter S and all of his friends on the other side? **11/15/2018 14:49**

The only "Collusion" is that of the Democrats with Russia and many others. Why didn't the FBI take the Server from the DNC? They still don't have it. Check out how biased Facebook Google and Twitter are in favor of the Democrats. That's the real Collusion! **11/15/2018 14:59**

People are not being told that the Republican Party is on track to pick up two seats in the U.S. Senate and epic victory: 53 to 47. The Fake News Media only wants to speak of the House where the Midterm results were better than other sitting Presidents. **11/16/2018 19:41**

Congratulations to Ron DeSantis on becoming the new Governor of Florida. Against all odds he fought & fought & fought the result being a historic victory. He never gave up and never will. He will be a great Governor! **11/17/2018 0:36**

Congratulations to Brian Kemp on becoming the new Governor of Georgia. Stacey Abrams fought brilliantly and hard - she will have a terrific political future! Brian was unrelenting and will become a great Governor for the truly Wonderful People of Georgia! **11/17/2018 0:37**

Isn't it ironic that large Caravans of people are marching to our border wanting U.S.A. asylum because they are fearful of being in their country - yet they are proudly waving.... (1/2) **11/17/2018 0:43**

....their country's flag. Can this be possible? Yes because it is all a BIG CON and the American taxpayer is paying for it! (2/2) **11/17/2018 0:43**

....I can't imagine any President having a better or closer relationship with their Vice President then the two of us. Just more FAKE NEWS the Enemy of the People! **11/17/2018 16:42**

Incredible to be with our GREAT HEROES today in California. We will always be with you! https://t.co/B1MCTF83Zf **11/18/2018 2:48**

So funny to see little Adam Schitt (D-CA) talking about the fact that Acting Attorney General Matt Whitaker was not approved by the Senate but not mentioning the fact that Bob Mueller (who is highly conflicted) was not approved by the Senate! **11/18/2018 18:01**

The Mayor of Tijuana Mexico just stated that "the City is ill-prepared to handle this many migrants the backlog could last 6 months." Likewise the U.S. is ill-prepared for this invasion and will not stand for it. They are causing crime and big problems in Mexico. Go home! **11/18/2018 18:42**

Catch and Release is an obsolete term. It is now Catch and Detain. Illegal Immigrants trying to come into the U.S.A. often proudly flying the flag of their nation as they ask for U.S. Asylum will be detained or turned away. Dems must approve Border Security & Wall NOW! **11/18/2018 19:55**

From day one Rick Scott never wavered. He was a great Governor and will be even a greater Senator in representing the People of Florida. Congratulations to Rick on having waged such a courageous and successful campaign!

11/18/2018 19:59

Of course we should have captured Osama Bin Laden long before we did. I pointed him out in my book just BEFORE the attack on the World Trade Center. President Clinton famously missed his shot. We paid Pakistan Billions of Dollars & they never told us he was living there. Fools!.. (1/2)

11/19/2018 15:26

....We no longer pay Pakistan the $Billions because they would take our money and do nothing for us Bin Laden being a prime example Afghanistan being another. They were just one of many countries that take from the United

States without giving anything in return. That's ENDING! (2/2) **11/19/2018 15:41**

The Fake News is showing old footage of people climbing over our Ocean Area Fence. This is what it really looks like - no climbers anymore under our Administration! https://t.co/CD4ltRePML **11/19/2018 19:10**

I hope the discovery and eventual recovery of the Argentine submarine San Juan brings needed closure to the wonderful families of those brave missing sailors. I look forward to hearing more from my friend President @ MauricioMacri in Argentina later this month. **11/20/2018 4:19**

So-called comedian Michelle Wolf bombed so badly last year at the White House Correspondents' Dinner that this year for the first time in decades they will have an author instead of a comedian. Good first step in comeback of a dying evening and tradition! Maybe I will go? **11/21/2018 3:43**

AMERICA FIRST!

11/21/2018 4:40

Oil prices getting lower. Great! Like a big Tax Cut for America and the World. Enjoy! $54 was just $82. Thank you to Saudi Arabia but let's go lower! **11/21/2018 12:49**

MAKE AMERICA GREAT AGAIN! **11/21/2018 12:50**

Sorry Chief Justice John Roberts but you do indeed have "Obama judges" and they have a much different point of view than the people who are charged with the safety of our country. It would be great if the 9th Circuit was indeed an "independent judiciary" but if it is why...... (1/2) **11/21/2018 20:51**

.....are so many opposing view (on Border and Safety) cases filed there and why are a vast number of those cases overturned. Please study the numbers they are shocking. We need protection and security - these rulings are making our country unsafe! Very dangerous and unwise! (2/2)

11/21/2018 21:09

There are a lot of CRIMINALS in the Caravan. We will stop them. Catch and Detain! Judicial Activism by people who know nothing about security and the safety of our citizens is putting our country in great danger. Not good!

11/21/2018 21:42

Brutal and Extended Cold Blast could shatter ALL RECORDS - Whatever happened to Global Warming?

11/22/2018 0:23

You just can't win with the Fake News Media. A big story today is that because I have pushed so hard and gotten Gasoline Prices so low more people are driving and I have caused traffic jams throughout our Great Nation. Sorry everyone!

11/22/2018 0:36

HAPPY THANKSGIVING TO ALL! **11/22/2018 12:01**

Justice Roberts can say what he wants but the 9th Circuit is a complete & total disaster. It is out of control has a horrible reputation is overturned more than any Circuit in the Country 79% & is used to get an almost guaranteed result. Judges must not Legislate Security... (1/2) **11/22/2018 12:21**

....and Safety at the Border or anywhere else. They know nothing about it and are making our Country unsafe. Our great Law Enforcement professionals MUST BE ALLOWED TO DO THEIR JOB! If not there will be only bedlam chaos injury and death. We want the Constitution as written! (2/2)

11/22/2018 12:30

Will be speaking with our great military in different parts of the world through teleconference at 9:00 A.M. Eastern. Then it will be off to see our Coast Guard patriots & to thank them for the great job they have been doing especially with the hurricanes. Happy Thanksgiving! **11/22/2018 13:42**

This is the coldest weather in the history of the Thanksgiving Day Parade in NYC and one of the coldest Thanksgivings on record! **11/22/2018 21:26**

Our highly trained security professionals are not allowed to do their job on the Border because of the Judicial Activism and Interference by the 9th Circuit. Nevertheless they are working hard to make America a safer place though hard to do when anybody filing a lawsuit wins! **11/22/2018 23:07**

Republicans and Democrats MUST come together finally with a major Border Security package which will include funding for the Wall. After 40 years of talk it is finally time for action. Fix the Border for once and for all NOW!

11/23/2018 12:41

I am extremely happy and proud of the job being done by @USTreasury Secretary @StevenMnuchin1. The FAKE NEWS likes to write stories to the contrary quoting phony sources or jealous people but they aren't true. They never like to ask me for a quote b/c it would kill their story.

11/23/2018 23:48

Migrants at the Southern Border will not be allowed into the United States until their claims are individually approved in court. We only will allow those who come into our Country legally. Other than that our very strong policy is Catch and Detain. No "Releasing" into the U.S... (1/2)

11/24/2018 23:49

....All will stay in Mexico. If for any reason it becomes necessary we will CLOSE our Southern Border. There is no way that the United States will after decades of abuse put

up with this costly and dangerous situation anymore! (2/2)
11/24/2018 23:56

Would be very SMART if Mexico would stop the Caravans long before they get to our Southern Border or if originating countries would not let them form (it is a way they get certain people out of their country and dump in U.S. No longer). Dems created this problem. No crossings!
11/25/2018 13:28

So great that oil prices are falling (thank you President T). Add that which is like a big Tax Cut to our other good Economic news. Inflation down (are you listening Fed)!
11/25/2018 13:46

General Anthony Tata: "President Trump is a man of his word & he said he was going to be tough on the Border and he is tough on the Border. He has rightfully strengthened the Border in the face of an unprecedented threat. It's the right move by President Trump." Thanks General!
11/25/2018 20:20

Europe has to pay their fair share for Military Protection. The European Union for many years has taken advantage of us on Trade and then they don't live up to their Military commitment through NATO. Things must change fast!
11/25/2018 20:27

Clinton Foundation donations drop 42% - which shows that they illegally played the power game. They monetized their political influence through the Foundation. "During her tenure the State Department was put in the service of the Clinton Foundation." Andrew McCarthy **11/25/2018 20:39**

.@60Minutes did a phony story about child separation when they know we had the exact same policy as the Obama Administration. In fact a picture of children in jails was used by other Fake Media to show how bad (cruel) we are but it was in 2014 during O years. Obama separated.... (1/2)
11/26/2018 1:59

....children from parents as did Bush etc. because that is the policy and law. I tried to keep them together but the problem is when you do that vast numbers of additional people storm the Border. So with Obama seperation is fine but with Trump it's not. Fake 60 Minutes! (2/2) **11/26/2018 2:07**

Mexico should move the flag waving Migrants many of whom are stone cold criminals back to their countries. Do it by plane do it by bus do it anyway you want but they are NOT coming into the U.S.A. We will close the Border permanently if need be. Congress fund the WALL!
11/26/2018 11:19

When Mueller does his final report will he be covering all of his conflicts of interest in a preamble will he be recommending action on all of the crimes of many kinds from those "on the other side"(whatever happened to Podesta?) and will he be putting in statements from..... (1/2)
11/26/2018 14:33

....hundreds of people closely involved with my campaign who never met saw or spoke to a Russian during this period? So many campaign workers people inside from the beginning ask me why they have not been called (they want to be). There was NO Collusion & Mueller knows it! (2/2)
11/26/2018 14:44

On the ten-year anniversary of the Mumbai terror attack the U.S. stands with the people of India in their quest for justice. The attack killed 166 innocents including six Americans. We will never let terrorists win or even come close to winning!
11/26/2018 19:45

While CNN doesn't do great in the United States based on ratings outside of the U.S. they have very little competition. Throughout the world CNN has a powerful voice portraying the United States in an unfair.... (1/2) **11/26/2018 19:47**

....and false way. Something has to be done including the possibility of the United States starting our own Worldwide Network to show the World the way we really are GREAT! (2/2) **11/26/2018 19:47**

The Phony Witch Hunt continues but Mueller and his gang of Angry Dems are only looking at one side not the other. Wait until it comes out how horribly & viciously they are treating people ruining lives for them refusing to lie. Mueller is a conflicted prosecutor gone rogue.... (1/3) **11/27/2018 12:30**

....The Fake News Media builds Bob Mueller up as a Saint when in actuality he is the exact opposite. He is doing TREMENDOUS damage to our Criminal Justice System where he is only looking at one side and not the other. Heroes will come of this and it won't be Mueller and his... (2/3) **11/27/2018 12:42**

....terrible Gang of Angry Democrats. Look at their past and look where they come from. The now $30000000 Witch Hunt continues and they've got nothing but ruined lives. Where is the Server? Let these terrible people go back to the Clinton Foundation and "Justice" Department! (3/3) **11/27/2018 13:07**

Very disappointed with General Motors and their CEO Mary Barra for closing plants in Ohio Michigan and Maryland. Nothing being closed in Mexico & China. The U.S. saved General Motors and this is the THANKS we get! We are now looking at cutting all @GM subsidies including.... (1/2) **11/27/2018 19:05**

....for electric cars. General Motors made a big China bet years ago when they built plants there (and in Mexico) - don't think that bet is going to pay off. I am here to protect America's Workers! (2/2) **11/27/2018 19:05**

The Mueller Witch Hunt is a total disgrace. They are looking at supposedly stolen Crooked Hillary Clinton Emails (even though they don't want to look at the DNC Server) but have no interest in the Emails that Hillary DELETED & acid washed AFTER getting a Congressional Subpoena! **11/28/2018 0:31**

Brenda Snipes in charge of voting in Broward County Florida was just spotted wearing a beautiful dress with 300 I VOTED signs on it. Just kidding she is a fine very honorable and highly respected voting tactician! **11/28/2018 3:38**

Congratulations to Senator Cindy Hyde-Smith on your big WIN in the Great State of Mississippi. We are all very proud of you! **11/28/2018 3:42**

While the disgusting Fake News is doing everything within their power not to report it that way at least 3 major players are intimating that the Angry Mueller Gang of Dems is viciously telling witnesses to lie about facts & they will get relief. This is our Joseph McCarthy Era! **11/28/2018 13:39**

Steel Dynamics announced that it will build a brand new 3 million ton steel mill in the Southwest that will create 600 good-paying U.S. JOBS. Steel JOBS are coming back to America just like I predicted. Congratulations to Steel Dynamics! **11/28/2018 16:09**

On behalf of @FLOTUS Melania and the entire Trump family I want to wish you all a very MERRY CHRISTMAS! May this Christmas Season bring peace to your hearts warmth to your homes cheer to your spirits and JOY TO THE WORLD! #NCTL2018 https://t.co/XNMJQ5JDSU **11/28/2018 23:32**

So much happening with the now discredited Witch Hunt. This total Hoax will be studied for years! **11/29/2018 4:39**

General Motors is very counter to what other auto and other companies are doing. Big Steel is opening and renovating plants all over the country. Auto companies are pouring into the U.S. including BMW which just announced a major new plant. The U.S.A. is booming! **11/29/2018 11:37**

Did you ever see an investigation more in search of a crime? At the same time Mueller and the Angry Democrats aren't even looking at the atrocious and perhaps subversive crimes that were committed by Crooked Hillary Clinton and the Democrats. A total disgrace! **11/29/2018 11:54**

When will this illegal Joseph McCarthy style Witch Hunt one that has shattered so many innocent lives ever end-or will it just go on forever? After wasting more than $40000000 (is that possible?) it has proven only one thing-there was NO Collusion with Russia. So Ridiculous! **11/29/2018 12:16**

Billions of Dollars are pouring into the coffers of the U.S.A. because of the Tariffs being charged to China and there is a long way to go. If companies don't want to pay Tariffs build in the U.S.A. Otherwise lets just make our Country richer than ever before! **11/29/2018 12:32**

Alan Dershowitz: "These are not crimes. He (Mueller) has no authority to be a roving Commissioner. I don't see any evidence of crimes." This is an illegal Hoax that should be ended immediately. Mueller refuses to look at the real crimes on the other side. Where is the IG REPORT? **11/30/2018 3:04**

Arrived in Argentina with a very busy two days planned. Important meetings scheduled throughout. Our great Country is extremely well represented. Will be very productive! **11/30/2018 3:31**

Oh I get it! I am a very good developer happily living my life when I see our Country going in the wrong direction (to put it mildly). Against all odds I decide to run for President & continue to run my business-very legal & very cool talked about it on the campaign trail... (1/2) **11/30/2018 9:52**

....Lightly looked at doing a building somewhere in Russia. Put up zero money zero guarantees and didn't do the project. Witch Hunt! (2/2) **11/30/2018 9:59**

Just signed one of the most important and largest Trade Deals in U.S. and World History. The United States Mexico and Canada worked so well together in crafting this great document. The terrible NAFTA will soon be gone. The USMCA will be fantastic for all! **11/30/2018 14:45**

To the Great people of Alaska. You have been hit hard by a "big one." Please follow the directions of the highly trained professionals who are there to help you. Your Federal Government will spare no expense. God Bless you ALL!

11/30/2018 20:19

President George H.W. Bush led a long successful and beautiful life. Whenever I was with him I saw his absolute joy for life and true pride in his family. His accomplishments were great from beginning to end. He was a truly wonderful man and will be missed by all!

12/1/2018 11:16

I was very much looking forward to having a press conference just prior to leaving Argentina because we have had such great success in our dealing with various countries and their leaders at the G20.... (1/2) **12/1/2018 15:21**

....However out of respect for the Bush Family and former President George H.W. Bush we will wait until after the funeral to have a press conference. (2/2) **12/1/2018 15:21**

China has agreed to reduce and remove tariffs on cars coming into China from the U.S. Currently the tariff is 40%.

12/3/2018 4:00

Farmers will be a a very BIG and FAST beneficiary of our deal with China. They intend to start purchasing agricultural product immediately. We make the finest and cleanest product in the World and that is what China wants. Farmers I LOVE YOU! **12/3/2018 13:01**

I am certain that at some time in the future President Xi and I together with President Putin of Russia will start talking about a meaningful halt to what has become a major and uncontrollable Arms Race. The U.S. spent 716 Billion Dollars this year. Crazy! **12/3/2018 13:30**

We would save Billions of Dollars if the Democrats would give us the votes to build the Wall. Either way people will NOT be allowed into our Country illegally! We will close the entire Southern Border if necessary. Also STOP THE DRUGS! **12/3/2018 13:45**

"I will never testify against Trump." This statement was recently made by Roger Stone essentially stating that he will not be forced by a rogue and out of control prosecutor to make up lies and stories about "President Trump." Nice to know that some people still have "guts!" **12/3/2018 15:48**

Bob Mueller (who is a much different man than people think) and his out of control band of Angry Democrats don't want the truth they only want lies. The truth is very bad for their mission! **12/3/2018 15:56**

Looking forward to being with the Bush Family to pay my respects to President George H.W. Bush. **12/3/2018 16:37**

Congratulations to newly inaugurated Mexican President @ lopezobrador_. He had a tremendous political victory with the great support of the Mexican People. We will work well together for many years to come! **12/3/2018 19:42**

....I am a Tariff Man. When people or countries come in to raid the great wealth of our Nation I want them to pay for the privilege of doing so. It will always be the best way to max out our economic power. We are right now taking in $billions in Tariffs. MAKE AMERICA RICH AGAIN**12/4/2018 15:03**

Could somebody please explain to the Democrats (we need their votes) that our Country losses 250 Billion Dollars a year on illegal immigration not including the terrible drug flow. Top Border Security including a Wall is $25 Billion. Pays for itself in two months. Get it done! **12/4/2018 16:22**

I am glad that my friend @EmmanuelMacron and the protestors in Paris have agreed with the conclusion I reached two years ago. The Paris Agreement is fatally flawed because it raises the price of energy for responsible countries while whitewashing some of the worst polluters.... (1/2) **12/4/2018 22:56**

....in the world. I want clean air and clean water and have been making great strides in improving America's environment. But American taxpayers - and American workers - shouldn't pay to clean up others countries' pollution. (2/2) **12/4/2018 22:56**

We are either going to have a REAL DEAL with China or no deal at all - at which point we will be charging major Tariffs against Chinese product being shipped into the United States. Ultimately I believe we will be making a deal - either now or into the future.... **12/5/2018 0:20**

Very strong signals being sent by China once they returned home from their long trip including stops from Argentina. Not to sound naive or anything but I believe President Xi meant every word of what he said at our long and hopefully historic meeting. ALL subjects discussed! **12/5/2018 13:19**

Looking forward to being with the Bush family. This is not a funeral this is a day of celebration for a great man who has led a long and distinguished life. He will be missed! **12/5/2018 13:56**

Hopefully OPEC will be keeping oil flows as is not restricted. The World does not want to see or need higher oil prices! **12/5/2018 14:44**

Without the phony Russia Witch Hunt and with all that we have accomplished in the last almost two years (Tax & Regulation Cuts Judge's Military Vets etc.) my approval rating would be at 75% rather than the 50% just reported by Rasmussen. It's called Presidential Harassment! **12/6/2018 15:17**

Does the Fake News Media ever mention the fact that Republicans with the very important help of my campaign Rallies WON THE UNITED STATES SENATE 53 to 47? All I hear is that the Open Border Dems won the House. Senate alone approves judges & others. Big Republican Win! **12/7/2018 0:27**

FAKE NEWS - THE ENEMY OF THE PEOPLE! **12/7/2018 3:08**

Arizona together with our Military and Border Patrol is bracing for a massive surge at a NON-WALLED area. WE WILL NOT LET THEM THROUGH. Big danger. Nancy and Chuck must approve Boarder Security and the Wall!
12/7/2018 3:15

Robert Mueller and Leakin' Lyin' James Comey are Best Friends just one of many Mueller Conflicts of Interest. And bye the way wasn't the woman in charge of prosecuting Jerome Corsi (who I do not know) in charge of "legal" at the corrupt Clinton Foundation? A total Witch Hunt... (1/2)
12/7/2018 11:18

...the lying and leaking by the people doing the Report & also Bruce Ohr (and his lovely wife Molly) Comey Brennan Clapper & all of the many fired people of the FBI be listed in the Report? Will the corruption within the DNC & Clinton Campaign be exposed?..And so much more! (2/2)
12/7/2018 12:15

China talks are going very well! **12/7/2018 13:13**

We will be doing a major Counter Report to the Mueller Report. This should never again be allowed to happen to a future President of the United States! **12/7/2018 14:56**

Mike Pompeo is doing a great job I am very proud of him. His predecessor Rex Tillerson didn't have the mental capacity needed. He was dumb as a rock and I couldn't get rid of him fast enough. He was lazy as hell. Now it is a whole new ballgame great spirit at State! **12/7/2018 20:02**

It is being reported that Leakin' James Comey was told by Department of Justice attorneys not to answer the most important questions. Total bias and corruption at the highest levels of previous Administration. Force him to answer the questions under oath! **12/7/2018 21:49**

Totally clears the President. Thank you! **12/7/2018 23:00**

The Paris Agreement isn't working out so well for Paris. Protests and riots all over France. People do not want to pay large sums of money much to third world countries (that are questionably run) in order to maybe protect the environment. Chanting "We Want Trump!" Love France.
12/8/2018 12:34

The idea of a European Military didn't work out too well in W.W. I or 2. But the U.S. was there for you and always will be. All we ask is that you pay your fair share of NATO. Germany is paying 1% while the U.S. pays 4.3% of a much larger GDP - to protect Europe. Fairness! **12/8/2018 12:52**

AFTER TWO YEARS AND MILLIONS OF PAGES OF DOCUMENTS (and a cost of over $30000000) NO COLLUSION! **12/8/2018 13:01**

"This is collusion illusion there is no smoking gun here. At this late date after all that we have gone through after millions have been spent we have no Russian Collusion. There is nothing impeachable here." @GeraldoRivera Time for the Witch Hunt to END! **12/8/2018 16:01**

Very sad day & night in Paris. Maybe it's time to end the ridiculous and extremely expensive Paris Agreement and return money back to the people in the form of lower taxes? The U.S. was way ahead of the curve on that and the only major country where emissions went down last year!
12/8/2018 17:22

It was my honor to attend today's #ArmyNavyGame in Philadelphia. A GREAT game played all around by our HEROES. Congratulations @ArmyWP_Football on the win! https://t.co/WDLkM6VE2T **12/8/2018 23:31**

On 245 occasions former FBI Director James Comey told House investigators he didn't know didn't recall or couldn't remember things when asked. Opened investigations on 4 Americans (not 2) - didn't know who signed off and didn't know Christopher Steele. All lies! **12/9/2018 13:38**

Leakin' James Comey must have set a record for who lied the most to Congress in one day. His Friday testimony was so untruthful! This whole deal is a Rigged Fraud headed up by dishonest people who would do anything so that I could not become President. They are now exposed! **12/9/2018 13:53**

The Trump Administration has accomplished more than any other U.S. Administration in its first two (not even) years of existence & we are having a great time doing it! All of this despite the Fake News Media which has gone totally out of its mind-truly the Enemy of the People! **12/9/2018 22:43**

I am in the process of interviewing some really great people for the position of White House Chief of Staff. Fake News has been saying with certainty it was Nick Ayers a spectacular person who will always be with our #MAGA agenda. I will be making a decision soon! **12/10/2018 1:27**

"Democrats can't find a Smocking Gun tying the Trump campaign to Russia after James Comey's testimony. No Smocking Gun...No Collusion." @FoxNews That's because there was NO COLLUSION. So now the Dems go to a simple private transaction wrongly call it a campaign contribution... (1/2) **12/10/2018 11:46**

....which it was not (but even if it was it is only a CIVIL CASE like Obama's - but it was done correctly by a lawyer and there would not even be a fine. Lawyer's liability if he made a mistake not me). Cohen just trying to get his sentence reduced. WITCH HUNT! (2/2) **12/10/2018 12:00**

James Comey's behind closed doors testimony reveals that "there was not evidence of Campaign Collusion" with Russia when he left the FBI. In other words the Witch Hunt is illegal and should never have been started! **12/11/2018 2:11**

Despite the large Caravans that WERE forming and heading to our Country people have not been able to get through our newly built Walls makeshift Walls & Fences or Border Patrol Officers & Military. They are now staying in Mexico or going back to their original countries....... (1/3) **12/11/2018 11:52**

....however for strictly political reasons and because they have been pulled so far left do NOT want Border Security. They want Open Borders for anyone to come in. This brings large scale crime and disease. Our Southern Border is now Secure and will remain that way....... (2/3) **12/11/2018 12:12**

....People do not yet realize how much of the Wall including really effective renovation has already been built. If the Democrats do not give us the votes to secure our Country the Military will build the remaining sections of the Wall. They know how important it is! (3/3) **12/11/2018 12:42**

Fake News has it purposely wrong. Many over ten are vying for and wanting the White House Chief of Staff position. Why wouldn't someone want one of the truly great and meaningful jobs in Washington. Please report news correctly. Thank you! **12/11/2018 13:30**

James Comey just totally exposed his partisan stance by urging his fellow Democrats to take back the White House in 2020. In other words he is and has been a Democrat. Comey had no right heading the FBI at any time but especially after his mind exploded! **12/11/2018 18:50**

"I don't care what you think of the President...it cannot bleed over to the FBI...Comey is confirming there is bias in the FBI..." -Chris Swecker **12/11/2018 18:55**

Thanks to Leader McConnell for agreeing to bring a Senate vote on Criminal Justice this week! These historic changes will make communities SAFER and SAVE tremendous taxpayers dollars. It brings much needed hope to many families during the Holiday Season. **12/11/2018 22:09**

Another very bad terror attack in France. We are going to strengthen our borders even more. Chuck and Nancy must give us the votes to get additional Border Security!

12/12/2018 12:34

The Democrats and President Obama gave Iran 150 Billion Dollars and got nothing but they can't give 5 Billion Dollars for National Security and a Wall? **12/12/2018 12:50**

I often stated "One way or the other Mexico is going to pay for the Wall." This has never changed. Our new deal with Mexico (and Canada) the USMCA is so much better than the old very costly & anti-USA NAFTA deal that just by the money we save MEXICO IS PAYING FOR THE WALL! **12/13/2018 12:38**

They gave General Flynn a great deal because they were embarrassed by the way he was treated - the FBI said he didn't lie and they overrode the FBI. They want to scare everybody into making up stories that are not true by catching them in the smallest of misstatements. Sad!...... **12/13/2018 16:07**

WITCH HUNT! **12/13/2018 16:08**

Let's not do a shutdown Democrats - do what's right for the American People! https://t.co/bZg07ZKQqo **12/13/2018 21:21**

China just announced that their economy is growing much slower than anticipated because of our Trade War with them. They have just suspended U.S. Tariff Hikes. U.S. is doing very well. China wants to make a big and very comprehensive deal. It could happen and rather soon! **12/14/2018 16:35**

As I predicted all along Obamacare has been struck down as an UNCONSTITUTIONAL disaster! Now Congress must pass a STRONG law that provides GREAT healthcare and protects pre-existing conditions. Mitch and Nancy get it done! **12/15/2018 2:07**

Wow but not surprisingly ObamaCare was just ruled UNCONSTITUTIONAL by a highly respected judge in Texas. Great news for America! **12/15/2018 2:16**

Never in the history of our Country has the "press" been more dishonest than it is today. Stories that should be good are bad. Stories that should be bad are horrible. Many stories like with the REAL story on Russia Clinton & the DNC seldom get reported. Too bad! **12/15/2018 15:37**

The pathetic and dishonest Weekly Standard run by failed prognosticator Bill Kristol (who like many others never had a clue) is flat broke and out of business. Too bad. May it rest in peace! **12/15/2018 16:15**

Wow 19000 Texts between Lisa Page and her lover Peter S of the FBI in charge of the Russia Hoax were just reported as being wiped clean and gone. Such a big story that will never be covered by the Fake News. Witch Hunt! **12/15/2018 16:45**

A REAL scandal is the one sided coverage hour by hour of networks like NBC & Democrat spin machines like Saturday Night Live. It is all nothing less than unfair news coverage and Dem commercials. Should be tested in courts can't be legal? Only defame & belittle! Collusion? **12/16/2018 13:58**

So where are all the missing Text messages between fired FBI agents Peter S and the lovely Lisa Page his lover. Just reported that they have been erased and wiped clean. What an outrage as the totally compromised and conflicted Witch Hunt moves ever so slowly forward. Want them! **12/16/2018 14:11**

Remember Michael Cohen only became a "Rat" after the FBI did something which was absolutely unthinkable & unheard of until the Witch Hunt was illegally started. They BROKE INTO AN ATTORNEY'S OFFICE! Why didn't they break into the DNC to get the Server or Crooked's office? **12/16/2018 14:39**

At the request of many I will be reviewing the case of a "U.S. Military hero" Major Matt Golsteyn who is charged with murder. He could face the death penalty from our own government after he admitted to killing a Terrorist bomb maker while overseas. @PeteHegseth @FoxNews **12/16/2018 15:03**

Judge Ken Starr former Solicitor Generel & Independent Counsel just stated that after two years "there is no evidence or proof of collusion" & further that "there is no evidence that there was a campaign financing violation involving the President." Thank you Judge. @FoxNews
12/16/2018 15:20

The Democrats policy of Child Seperation on the Border during the Obama Administration was far worse than the way we handle it now. Remember the 2014 picture of children in cages - the Obama years. However if you don't separate FAR more people will come. Smugglers use the kids! **12/16/2018 16:25**

....a persecution of the President." Daniel Henninger The Wall Street Journal. Thank you people are starting to see and understand what this Witch Hunt is all about. Jeff Sessions should be ashamed of himself for allowing this total HOAX to get started in the first place! **12/16/2018 20:37**

....The Russian Witch Hunt Hoax started as the "insurance policy" long before I even got elected is very bad for our Country. They are Entrapping people for misstatements lies or unrelated things that took place many years ago. Nothing to do with Collusion. A Democrat Scam!
12/16/2018 20:56

The DEDUCTIBLE which comes with ObamaCare is so high that it is practically not even useable! Hurts families badly. We have a chance working with the Democrats to deliver great HealthCare! A confirming Supreme Court Decision will lead to GREAT HealthCare results for Americans!
12/17/2018 13:02

It is incredible that with a very strong dollar and virtually no inflation the outside world blowing up around us Paris is burning and China way down the Fed is even considering yet another interest rate hike. Take the Victory! **12/17/2018 13:27**

Anytime you hear a Democrat saying that you can have good Border Security without a Wall write them off as just another politician following the party line. Time for us to save billions of dollars a year and have at the same time far greater safety and control! **12/17/2018 16:05**

Today I am making good on my promise to defend our Farmers & Ranchers from unjustified trade retaliation by foreign nations. I have authorized Secretary Perdue to implement the 2nd round of Market Facilitation Payments. Our economy is stronger than ever–we stand with our Farmers! **12/17/2018 21:14**

Facebook Twitter and Google are so biased toward the Dems it is ridiculous! Twitter in fact has made it much more difficult for people to join @realDonaldTrump. They have removed many names & greatly slowed the level and speed of increase. They have acknowledged-done NOTHING! **12/18/2018 12:26**

Illegal immigration costs the United States more than 200 Billion Dollars a year. How was this allowed to happen? **12/18/2018 12:55**

The Democrats are saying loud and clear that they do not want to build a Concrete Wall - but we are not building a Concrete Wall we are building artistically designed steel slats so that you can easily see through it.... **12/19/2018 1:13**

America is the greatest Country in the world and my job is to fight for ALL citizens even those who have made mistakes. Congratulations to the Senate on the bi-partisan passing of a historic Criminal Justice Reform Bill.... **12/19/2018 2:07**

In our Country so much money has been poured down the drain for so many years but when it comes to Border Security and the Military the Democrats fight to the death. We won on the Military which is being completely rebuilt. One way or the other we will win on the Wall! **12/19/2018 12:35**

Mexico is paying (indirectly) for the Wall through the new USMCA the replacement for NAFTA! Far more money coming to the U.S. Because of the tremendous dangers at the Border including large scale criminal and drug inflow the United States Military will build the Wall! **12/19/2018 13:43**

We have defeated ISIS in Syria my only reason for being there during the Trump Presidency. **12/19/2018 14:29**

After historic victories against ISIS it's time to bring our great young people home! https://t.co/xoNjFzQFTp **12/19/2018 23:10**

Does the USA want to be the Policeman of the Middle East getting NOTHING but spending precious lives and trillions of dollars protecting others who in almost all cases do not appreciate what we are doing? Do we want to be there forever? Time for others to finally fight..... **12/20/2018 11:56**

The Democrats who know Steel Slats (Wall) are necessary for Border Security are putting politics over Country. What they are just beginning to realize is that I will not sign any of their legislation including infrastructure unless it has perfect Border Security. U.S.A. WINS! **12/20/2018 12:28**

With so much talk about the Wall people are losing sight of the great job being done on our Southern Border by Border Patrol ICE and our great Military. Remember the Caravans? Well they didn't get through and none are forming or on their way. Border is tight. Fake News silent! **12/20/2018 12:39**

When I begrudgingly signed the Omnibus Bill I was promised the Wall and Border Security by leadership. Would be done by end of year (NOW). It didn't happen! We foolishly fight for Border Security for other countries - but not for our beloved U.S.A. Not good! **12/20/2018 15:28**

So hard to believe that Lindsey Graham would be against saving soldier lives & billions of $$$. Why are we fighting for our enemy Syria by staying & killing ISIS for them Russia Iran & other locals? Time to focus on our Country & bring our youth back home where they belong! **12/20/2018 19:22**

Farm Bill signing in 15 minutes! #Emmys #TBT https://t.co/KtSS17xvIn **12/20/2018 20:14**

Democrats it is time to come together and put the SAFETY of the AMERICAN PEOPLE before POLITICS. Border security must become a #1 priority! https://t.co/Wck6UpQGil **12/20/2018 21:48**

General Jim Mattis will be retiring with distinction at the end of February after having served my Administration as Secretary of Defense for the past two years. During Jim's tenure tremendous progress has been made especially with respect to the purchase of new fighting.... **12/20/2018 22:21**

Thank you to our GREAT Republican Members of Congress for your VOTE to fund Border Security and the Wall. The final numbers were 217-185 and many have said that the enthusiasm was greater than they have ever seen before. So proud of you all. Now on to the Senate! **12/21/2018 3:13**

Soon to be Speaker Nancy Pelosi said last week live from the Oval Office that the Republicans didn't have the votes for Border Security. Today the House Republicans voted and won 217-185. Nancy does not have to apologize. All I want is GREAT BORDER SECURITY! **12/21/2018 3:20**

The Democrats are trying to belittle the concept of a Wall calling it old fashioned. The fact is there is nothing else's that will work and that has been true for thousands of years. It's like the wheel there is nothing better. I know tech better than anyone & technology..... **12/21/2018 11:58**

Shutdown today if Democrats do not vote for Border Security! **12/21/2018 12:31**

Even President Ronald Reagan tried for 8 years to build a Border Wall or Fence and was unable to do so. Others also have tried. We will get it done one way or the other! **12/21/2018 12:38**

Mitch use the Nuclear Option and get it done! Our Country is counting on you! **12/21/2018 13:02**

The Democrats now own the shutdown! **12/21/2018 15:07**

I've done more damage to ISIS than all recent presidents…. not even close! **12/21/2018 15:31**

A design of our Steel Slat Barrier which is totally effective while at the same time beautiful! https://t.co/sGltXh0cu9 **12/21/2018 22:14**

Some of the many Bills that I am signing in the Oval Office right now. Cancelled my trip on Air Force One to Florida while we wait to see if the Democrats will help us to protect America's Southern Border! https://t.co/ws6LYhKcKl **12/21/2018 23:23**

Wishing Supreme Court Justice Ruth Bader Ginsburg a full and speedy recovery! **12/22/2018 0:16**

OUR GREAT COUNTRY MUST HAVE BORDER SECURITY! https://t.co/ZGcYygMf3a **12/22/2018 2:49**

I am in the White House working hard. News reports concerning the Shutdown and Syria are mostly FAKE. We are negotiating with the Democrats on desperately needed Border Security (Gangs Drugs Human Trafficking & more) but it could be a long stay. On Syria we were originally… (1/2) **12/22/2018 16:18**

….going to be there for three months and that was seven years ago - we never left. When I became President ISIS was going wild. Now ISIS is largely defeated and other local countries including Turkey should be able to easily take care of whatever remains. We're coming home! (2/2) **12/22/2018 16:30**

Will be having lunch in White House residence with large group concerning Border Security. **12/22/2018 17:02**

The crisis of illegal activity at our Southern Border is real and will not stop until we build a great Steel Barrier or Wall. Let work begin! **12/22/2018 20:03**

I won an election said to be one of the greatest of all time based on getting out of endless & costly foreign wars & also based on Strong Borders which will keep our Country safe. We fight for the borders of other countries but we won't fight for the borders of our own!
12/22/2018 20:28

I will not be going to Florida because of the Shutdown - Staying in the White House! #MAGA **12/22/2018 23:58**

Brett McGurk who I do not know was appointed by President Obama in 2015. Was supposed to leave in February but he just resigned prior to leaving. Grandstander? The Fake News is making such a big deal about this nothing event! **12/23/2018 1:48**

If anybody but your favorite President Donald J. Trump announced that after decimating ISIS in Syria we were going to bring our troops back home (happy & healthy) that person would be the most popular hero in America. With me hit hard instead by the Fake News Media. Crazy!
12/23/2018 1:59

When President Obama ingloriously fired Jim Mattis I gave him a second chance. Some thought I shouldn't I thought I should. Interesting relationship-but I also gave all of the resources that he never really had. Allies are very important-but not when they take advantage of U.S.
12/23/2018 2:20

The only way to stop drugs gangs human trafficking criminal elements and much else from coming into our Country is with a Wall or Barrier. Drones and all of the rest are wonderful and lots of fun but it is only a good old fashioned Wall that works! **12/23/2018 14:17**

I am pleased to announce that our very talented Deputy Secretary of Defense Patrick Shanahan will assume the title of Acting Secretary of Defense starting January 1 2019. Patrick has a long list of accomplishments while serving as Deputy & previously Boeing. He will be great! **12/23/2018 16:46**

We signed two pieces of major legislation this week Criminal Justice Reform and the Farm Bill. These are two Big Deals but all the Fake News Media wants to talk about is "the mistake" of bringing our young people back home from the Never Ending Wars. It all began 19 years ago! **12/23/2018 19:45**

.....Bob Corker was responsible for giving us the horrible Iran Nuclear Deal which I ended yet he badmouths me for wanting to bring our young people safely back home. Bob wanted to run and asked for my endorsement. I said NO and the game was over. #MAGA I LOVE TENNESSEE! **12/23/2018 20:20**

Thanks @RandPaul "I am very proud of the President. This is exactly what he promised and I think the people agree with him. We've been at war too long and in too many places...spent several trillion dollars on these wars everywhere. He's different...that's why he got elected." **12/23/2018 21:18**

"It should not be the job of America to replace regimes around the world. This is what President Trump recognized in Iraq that it was the biggest foreign policy disaster of the last several decades and he's right...The generals still don't get the mistake." @RandPaul **12/24/2018 3:32**

Mitch McConnell just told a group of people and me that he has been in the U.S. Senate for 32 years and the last two have been by far the best & most productive of his career. Tax & Regulation Cuts VA Choice Farm Bill Criminal Justice Reform Judgeships & much more. Great! **12/24/2018 3:47**

The most important way to stop gangs drugs human trafficking and massive crime is at our Southern Border. We need Border Security and as EVERYONE knows you

can't have Border Security without a Wall. The Drones & Technology are just bells and whistles. Safety for America!
12/24/2018 4:05

President @RT_Erdogan of Turkey has very strongly informed me that he will eradicate whatever is left of ISIS in Syria....and he is a man who can do it plus Turkey is right "next door." Our troops are coming home! **12/24/2018 4:54**

Virtually every Democrat we are dealing with today strongly supported a Border Wall or Fence. It was only when I made it an important part of my campaign because people and drugs were pouring into our Country unchecked that they turned against it. Desperately needed! **12/24/2018 14:31**

To those few Senators who think I don't like or appreciate being allied with other countries they are wrong I DO. What I don't like however is when many of these same countries take advantage of their friendship with the United States both in Military Protection and Trade... (1/2) **12/24/2018 14:41**

....We are substantially subsidizing the Militaries of many VERY rich countries all over the world while at the same time these countries take total advantage of the U.S. and our TAXPAYERS on Trade. General Mattis did not see this as a problem. I DO and it is being fixed! (2/2) **12/24/2018 14:59**

For all of the sympathizers out there of Brett McGurk remember he was the Obama appointee who was responsible for loading up airplanes with 1.8 Billion Dollars in CASH & sending it to Iran as part of the horrific Iran Nuclear Deal (now terminated) approved by Little Bob Corker.
12/24/2018 15:23

AMERICA IS RESPECTED AGAIN! **12/24/2018 15:33**

The only problem our economy has is the Fed. They don't have a feel for the Market they don't understand necessary Trade Wars or Strong Dollars or even Democrat Shutdowns over Borders. The Fed is like a powerful golfer who can't score because he has no touch - he can't putt! **12/24/2018 15:55**

I never "lashed out" at the Acting Attorney General of the U.S. a man for whom I have great respect. This is a made up story one of many by the Fake News Media! **12/24/2018 16:55**

The Wall is different than the 25 Billion Dollars in Border Security. The complete Wall will be built with the Shutdown money plus funds already in hand. The reporting has been inaccurate on the point. The problem is without the Wall much of the rest of Dollars are wasted! **12/24/2018 17:10**

Saudi Arabia has now agreed to spend the necessary money needed to help rebuild Syria instead of the United States. See? Isn't it nice when immensely wealthy countries help rebuild their neighbors rather than a Great Country the U.S. that is 5000 miles away. Thanks to Saudi A!
12/24/2018 17:23

I am all alone (poor me) in the White House waiting for the Democrats to come back and make a deal on desperately needed Border Security. At some point the Democrats not wanting to make a deal will cost our Country more money than the Border Wall we are all talking about. Crazy!
12/24/2018 17:32

Christmas Eve briefing with my team working on North Korea – Progress being made. Looking forward to my next summit with Chairman Kim! https://t.co/zPTtDbrP0o
12/24/2018 21:14

I am in the Oval Office & just gave out a 115 mile long contract for another large section of the Wall in Texas. We are already building and renovating many miles of Wall some complete. Democrats must end Shutdown and finish funding. Billions of Dollars & lives will be saved!
12/24/2018 22:24

Merry Christmas! **12/25/2018 12:59**

I hope everyone even the Fake News Media is having a great Christmas! Our Country is doing very well. We are securing our Borders making great new Trade Deals and bringing our Troops Back Home. We are finally putting America First. MERRY CHRISTMAS! #MAGA **12/25/2018 23:18**

.@FLOTUS Melania and I were honored to visit our incredible troops at Al Asad Air Base in Iraq. GOD BLESS THE U.S.A.! https://t.co/rDlhITDvm1

12/26/2018 20:35

Just returned from visiting our troops in Iraq and Germany. One thing is certain we have incredible people representing our Country - people that know how to win! **12/27/2018 11:59**

Have the Democrats finally realized that we desperately need Border Security and a Wall on the Southern Border. Need to stop Drugs Human TraffickingGang Members & Criminals from coming into our Country. Do the Dems realize that most of the people not getting paid are Democrats? **12/27/2018 12:06**

The Democrats OBSTRUCTION of the desperately needed Wall where they almost all recently agreed it should be built is exceeded only by their OBSTRUCTION of 350 great people wanting & expecting to come into Government after being delayed for more than two years a U.S. record!

12/27/2018 19:41

"Border Patrol Agents want the Wall." Democrat's say they don't want the Wall (even though they know it is really needed) and they don't want ICE. They don't have much to campaign on do they? An Open Southern Border and the large scale crime that comes with such stupidity!

12/27/2018 20:39

There is right now a full scale manhunt going on in California for an illegal immigrant accused of shooting and killing a police officer during a traffic stop. Time to get tough on Border Security. Build the Wall! **12/27/2018 21:04**

Brad Blakeman: "The American people understand that we have been played by foreign actors who would rather have us fight their battles for them. The President says look this is your neighborhood you've got to stand up to protect yourselves. Don't always look to America." **12/27/2018 21:26**

This isn't about the Wall everybody knows that a Wall will work perfectly (In Israel the Wall works 99.9%). This is only about the Dems not letting Donald Trump & the Republicans have a win. They may have the 10 Senate votes but we have the issue Border Security. 2020! **12/27/2018 22:10**

CNN & others within the Fake News Universe were going wild about my signing MAGA hats for our military in Iraq and Germany. If these brave young people ask me to sign their hat I will sign. Can you imagine my saying NO? We brought or gave NO hats as the Fake News first reported! **12/27/2018 23:23**

We will be forced to close the Southern Border entirely if the Obstructionist Democrats do not give us the money to finish the Wall & also change the ridiculous immigration laws that our Country is saddled with. Hard to believe there was a Congress & President who would approve! **12/28/2018 12:16**

....The United States looses soooo much money on Trade with Mexico under NAFTA over 75 Billion Dollars a year (not including Drug Money which would be many times that amount) that I would consider closing the Southern Border a "profit making operation." We build a Wall or..... (1/3)

12/28/2018 12:42

.....close the Southern Border. Bring our car industry back into the United States where it belongs. Go back to pre-NAFTA before so many of our companies and jobs were so foolishly sent to Mexico. Either we build (finish) the Wall or we close the Border...... (2/3) **12/28/2018 12:49**

.....Honduras Guatemala and El Salvador are doing nothing for the United States but taking our money. Word is that a new Caravan is forming in Honduras and they are doing nothing about it. We will be cutting off all aid to these 3 countries - taking advantage of U.S. for years! (3/3) **12/28/2018 13:06**

Thank you to Sean Parnell for the nice comments on @ foxandfriends about the troops wonderful reaction to Melania and I in Iraq and Germany. Great things are happening! **12/28/2018 14:51**

The Mueller Angry Democrats recently deleted approximately 19000 Text messages between FBI Agent Lisa Page and her lover Agent Peter S. These Texts were asked for and INVALUABLE to the truth of the Witch Hunt Hoax. This is a total Obstruction of Justice. All Texts Demanded! **12/29/2018 15:42**

I am in the White House waiting for the Democrats to come on over and make a deal on Border Security. From what I hear they are spending so much time on Presidential Harassment that they have little time left for things like stopping crime and our military! **12/29/2018 15:52**

Just had a long and very good call with President Xi of China. Deal is moving along very well. If made it will be very comprehensive covering all subjects areas and points of dispute. Big progress being made! **12/29/2018 16:03**

Any deaths of children or others at the Border are strictly the fault of the Democrats and their pathetic immigration policies that allow people to make the long trek thinking they can enter our country illegally. They can't. If we had a Wall they wouldn't even try! The two..... (1/2) **12/29/2018 18:30**

...children in question were very sick before they were given over to Border Patrol. The father of the young girl said it was not their fault he hadn't given her water in days. Border Patrol needs the Wall and it will all end. They are working so hard & getting so little credit! (2/2) **12/29/2018 18:36**

For those that naively ask why didn't the Republicans get approval to build the Wall over the last year it is because IN THE SENATE WE NEED 10 DEMOCRAT VOTES and they will gives us "NONE" for Border Security! Now we have to do it the hard way with a Shutdown. Too bad! @FoxNews
12/29/2018 19:25

2018 is being called "THE YEAR OF THE WORKER" by Steve Moore co-author of "Trumponomics." It was indeed a great year for the American Worker with the "best job market in 50 years and the lowest unemployment rate ever for blacks and Hispanics and all workers. Big wage gains."
12/29/2018 21:06

"Absolutely nothing" (on Russian Collusion). Kimberley Strassel The Wall Street Journal. The Russian Collusion fabrication is the greatest Hoax in the history of American politics. The only Russian Collusion was with Hillary and the Democrats! **12/30/2018 3:01**

"It turns out to be true now that the Department of Justice and the FBI under President Obama rigged the investigation for Hillary and really turned the screws on Trump and now it looks like in a corrupt & illegal way. The facts are out now. Whole Hoax exposed. @JesseBWatters
12/30/2018 3:15

Veterans on President Trump's handling of Border Security - 62% Approval Rating. On being a strong leader - 59%. AP Poll. Thank you! **12/30/2018 15:28**

Great work by my Administration over the holidays to save Coast Guard pay during this #SchumerShutdown. No thanks to the Democrats who left town and are not concerned about the safety and security of Americans!

12/30/2018 16:56

President and Mrs. Obama built/has a ten foot Wall around their D.C. mansion/ compound. I agree totally necessary for their safety and security. The U.S. needs the same thing slightly larger version!

12/30/2018 21:59

An all concrete Wall was NEVER ABANDONED as has been reported by the media. Some areas will be all concrete but the experts at Border Patrol prefer a Wall that is see through (thereby making it possible to see what is happening on both sides). Makes sense to me! **12/31/2018 12:51**

...I campaigned on getting out of Syria and other places. Now when I start getting out the Fake News Media or some failed Generals who were unable to do the job before I arrived like to complain about me & my tactics which are working. Just doing what I said I was going to do!

12/31/2018 13:12

I campaigned on Border Security which you cannot have without a strong and powerful Wall. Our Southern Border has long been an "Open Wound" where drugs criminals (including human traffickers) and illegals would pour into our Country. Dems should get back here an fix now!

12/31/2018 13:29

I am the only person in America who could say that "I'm bringing our great troops back home with victory" and get BAD press. It is Fake News and Pundits who have FAILED for years that are doing the complaining. If I stayed in Endless Wars forever they would still be unhappy!

12/31/2018 14:38

I'm in the Oval Office. Democrats come back from vacation now and give us the votes necessary for Border Security including the Wall. You voted yes in 2006 and 2013. One more yes but with me in office I'll get it built and Fast!
12/31/2018 15:37

It's incredible how Democrats can all use their ridiculous sound bite and say that a Wall doesn't work. It does and properly built almost 100%! They say it's old technology - but so is the wheel. They now say it is immoral- but it is far more immoral for people to be dying! **12/31/2018 15:39**

JANUARY 2019 - MARCH 2019

★★★★★★★★★★★★★★★★★★★★★★★★★★★

As Rep. Nancy Pelosi (D-CA) becomes the Speaker of the House, the Democrats announce their intention to oppose nearly all of Trump's agenda, choosing instead to try to impeach him. As new jobs increase and unemployment decreases, funding for the wall continues to be a divisive issue. Concurrently, the immigration crisis from the caravans continues to be contentious. As daily briefings from press secretary Sanders cease, Trump begins to address the media almost daily as he leaves and returns from the White House. As Senators Elizabeth Warren and Bernie Sanders announce their candidacies for president, conflicts over funding for the wall continue. The Mueller investigation ends with Trump being exonerated by many and condemned by many others.

MEXICO IS PAYING FOR THE WALL through the many billions of dollars a year that the U.S.A. is saving through the new Trade Deal the USMCA that will replace the horrendous NAFTA Trade Deal which has so badly hurt our Country. Mexico & Canada will also thrive - good for all! **1/1/2019 0:40**

The Democrats will probably submit a Bill being cute as always which gives everything away but gives NOTHING to Border Security namely the Wall. You see without the Wall there can be no Border Security - the Tech "stuff" is just by comparison meaningless bells & whistles... (1/2) **1/1/2019 0:51**

...Remember this. Throughout the ages some things NEVER get better and NEVER change. You have Walls and you have Wheels. It was ALWAYS that way and it will ALWAYS be that way! Please explain to the Democrats that there can NEVER be a replacement for a good old fashioned WALL! (2/2) **1/1/2019 1:05**

HAPPY NEW YEAR TO EVERYONE INCLUDING THE HATERS AND THE FAKE NEWS MEDIA! 2019 WILL BE A FANTASTIC YEAR FOR THOSE NOT SUFFERING FROM TRUMP DERANGEMENT SYNDROME. JUST CALM DOWN AND ENJOY THE RIDE GREAT THINGS ARE HAPPENING FOR OUR COUNTRY!

1/1/2019 13:08

Happy New Year! **1/1/2019 14:25**

The Democrats much as I suspected have allocated no money for a new Wall. So imaginative! The problem is without a Wall there can be no real Border Security - and our Country must finally have a Strong and Secure Southern Border! **1/1/2019 14:32**

One thing has now been proven. The Democrats do not care about Open Borders and all of the crime and drugs that Open Borders bring! **1/1/2019 15:51**

Congratulations to President @JairBolsonaro who just made a great inauguration speech - the U.S.A. is with you! **1/1/2019 18:12**

Border Security and the Wall "thing" and Shutdown is not where Nancy Pelosi wanted to start her tenure as Speaker! Let's make a deal? **1/1/2019 19:02**

Gas prices are low and expected to go down this year. This would be good! **1/1/2019 22:44**

"Kim Jong Un says North Korea will not make or test nuclear weapons or give them to others - & he is ready to meet President Trump anytime." PBS News Hour. I also look forward to meeting with Chairman Kim who realizes so well that North Korea possesses great economic potential! **1/1/2019 23:11**

Do you think it's just luck that gas prices are so low and falling? Low gas prices are like another Tax Cut! **1/1/2019 23:39**

For FAR TOO LONG Senate Democrats have been Obstructing more than 350 Nominations. These great Americans left their jobs to serve our Country but can't because Dems are blocking them some for two years-historic record. Passed committees but Schumer putting them on hold. Bad! **1/2/2019 0:43**

Here we go with Mitt Romney but so fast! Question will be is he a Flake? I hope not. Would much prefer that Mitt focus on Border Security and so many other things where he can be helpful. I won big and he didn't. He should be happy for all Republicans. Be a TEAM player & WIN! **1/2/2019 12:53**

Mexico is paying for the Wall through the new USMCA Trade Deal. Much of the Wall has already been fully renovated or built. We have done a lot of work. $5.6 Billion Dollars that House has approved is very little in comparison to the benefits of National Security. Quick payback! **1/2/2019 13:35**

Important meeting today on Border Security with Republican and Democrat Leaders in Congress. Both parties must work together to pass a Funding Bill that protects this Nation and its people - this is the first and most important duty of government... (1/2) **1/3/2019 0:07**

...I remain ready and willing to work with Democrats to pass a bill that secures our borders supports the agents and officers on the ground and keeps America Safe. Let's get it done! (2/2) **1/3/2019 0:07**

Sadly there can be no REAL Border Security without the Wall! **1/3/2019 4:09**

The Shutdown is only because of the 2020 Presidential Election. The Democrats know they can't win based on all of the achievements of "Trump" so they are going all out on the desperately needed Wall and Border Security - and Presidential Harassment. For them strictly politics! **1/3/2019 14:44**

The United States Treasury has taken in MANY billions of dollars from the Tariffs we are charging China and other countries that have not treated us fairly. In the meantime we are doing well in various Trade Negotiations currently going on. At some point this had to be done! **1/3/2019 14:52**

The RNC has a great Chairwoman in Ronna McDaniel and the @GOP has never been stronger. We achieved historic wins with her help last year! #MAGA 🇺🇸 **1/3/2019 17:40**

https://t.co/jsOrDtwdEa **1/3/2019 20:25**

Michael Pillsbury interviewed by @cvpayne: "They have the motive of making the President look bad - instead

of President Trump being portrayed as a HERO. The first President to take China on it's 20 years overdue.... (1/2)
1/4/2019 1:19

....President Trump deserves a lot of credit but again you have the anti-Trump people who are not going to give him a lot of credit." (2/2) **1/4/2019 1:19**

As I have stated many times if the Democrats take over the House or Senate there will be disruption to the Financial Markets. We won the Senate they won the House. Things will settle down. They only want to impeach me because they know they can't win in 2020 too much success! **1/4/2019 13:06**

How do you impeach a president who has won perhaps the greatest election of all time done nothing wrong (no Collusion with Russia it was the Dems that Colluded) had the most successful first two years of any president and is the most popular Republican in party history 93%?

1/4/2019 13:16

GREAT JOBS NUMBERS JUST ANNOUNCED! **1/4/2019 14:39**

The story in the New York Times regarding Jim Webb being considered as the next Secretary of Defense is FAKE NEWS. I'm sure he is a fine man but I don't know Jim and never met him. Patrick Shanahan who is Acting Secretary of Defense is doing a great job! **1/4/2019 21:45**

Thank you to Kanye West for your nice words. Criminal Justice Reform is now law - passed in a very bipartisan way! **1/5/2019 12:17**

Great support coming from all sides for Border Security (including Wall) on our very dangerous Southern Border.

Teams negotiating this weekend! Washington Post and NBC reporting of events including Fake sources has been very inaccurate (to put it mildly)! **1/5/2019 12:31**

The Democrats could solve the Shutdown problem in a very short period of time. All they have to do is approve REAL Border Security (including a Wall) something which everyone other than drug dealers human traffickers and criminals want very badly! This would be so easy to do! **1/5/2019 12:57**

Many people currently a part of my opposition including President Obama & the Dems have had campaign violations in some cases for very large sums of money. These are civil cases. They paid a fine & settled. While no big deal I did not commit a campaign violation! **1/5/2019 13:55**

I don't care that most of the workers not getting paid are Democrats I want to stop the Shutdown as soon as we are in agreement on Strong Border Security! I am in the White House ready to go where are the Dems? **1/5/2019 14:48**

We are working hard at the Border but we need a WALL! In 2018 1.7 million pounds of narcotics seized 17000 adults arrested with criminal records and 6000 gang members including MS-13 apprehended. A big Human Trafficking problem. **1/5/2019 15:16**

The Democrats want Billions of Dollars for Foreign Aid but they don't want to spend a small fraction of that number on properly securing our Border. Figure that one out! **1/5/2019 15:54**

"Former @NYTimes editor Jill Abramson rips paper's 'unmistakably anti-Trump' bias."Ms. Abramson is 100% correct. Horrible and totally dishonest reporting on almost everything they write. Hence the term Fake News Enemy of the People and Opposition Party! **1/5/2019 17:27**

Drug makers and companies are not living up to their commitments on pricing. Not being fair to the consumer or to our Country! **1/5/2019 20:49**

V.P. Mike Pence and team just left the White House. Briefed me on their meeting with the Schumer/Pelosi representatives. Not much headway made today. Second meeting set for tomorrow. After so many decades must finally and permanently fix the problems on the Southern Border! **1/5/2019 21:05**

"Jobs up big plus 312000. Record number working. Manufacturing best in 20 years (Previous administration said this could not happen). Hispanic unemployment lowest ever. Dow plus 747 (for day)." @DRUDGE_REPORT **1/6/2019 1:00**

AP-NORC POLL: "Immigration among the top concerns in 2019." People want to stop drugs and criminals at the Border. Want Border Security! Tell the Dems to do the inevitable now rather than later. The wait is costly and dangerous! **1/6/2019 1:47**

Will be going to Camp David tomorrow morning for meetings on Border Security and many other topics with @WhiteHouse senior staff. **1/6/2019 2:06**

"We simply cannot allow people to pour into the United States undetected undocumented unchecked..." Barrack Obama 2005. I voted when I was a Senator to build a barrier to try to prevent illegal immigrants from coming in..." Hillary Clinton 2015. **1/6/2019 12:01**

....The only reason they do not want to build a Wall is that Walls Work! 99% of our illegal Border crossings will end crime in our Country will go way down and we will save billions of dollars a year! A properly planned and constructed Wall will pay for itself many times a year! **1/6/2019 12:33**

Excited to see our friends in Egypt opening the biggest Cathedral in the Middle East. President El-Sisi is moving his country to a more inclusive future! **1/6/2019 14:59**

Our GREAT MILITARY has delivered justice for the heroes lost and wounded in the cowardly attack on the USS Cole. We have just killed the leader of that attack Jamal al-Badawi. Our work against al Qaeda continues. We will never stop in our fight against Radical Islamic Terrorism!

1/6/2019 15:27

V.P. Mike Pence and group had a productive meeting with the Schumer/Pelosi representatives today. Many details of Border Security were discussed. We are now planning a Steel Barrier rather than concrete. It is both stronger & less obtrusive. Good solution and made in the U.S.A. **1/6/2019 21:53**

With all of the success that our Country is having including the just released jobs numbers which are off the charts the Fake News & totally dishonest Media concerning me and my presidency has never been worse. Many have become crazed lunatics who have given up on the TRUTH!... (1/2)

1/7/2019 12:56

...The Fake News will knowingly lie and demean in order make the tremendous success of the Trump Administration and me look as bad as possible. They use non-existent sources & write stories that are total fiction. Our Country is doing so well yet this is a sad day in America! (2/2)

1/7/2019 13:09

....The Fake News Media in our Country is the real Opposition Party. It is truly the Enemy of the People! We must bring honesty back to journalism and reporting!

1/7/2019 13:31

Congressman Adam Smith the new Chairman of the House Armed Services Committee just stated "Yes there is a provision in law that says a president can declare an emergency. It's been done a number of times." No doubt but let's get our deal done in Congress! **1/7/2019 13:38**

The Failing New York Times has knowingly written a very inaccurate story on my intentions on Syria. No different from my original statements we will be leaving at a proper pace while at the same time continuing to fight ISIS and doing all else that is prudent and necessary!..... **1/7/2019 14:55**

I am pleased to inform you that I will Address the Nation on the Humanitarian and National Security crisis on our Southern Border. Tuesday night at 9:00 P.M. Eastern.

1/7/2019 18:44

Endless Wars especially those which are fought out of judgement mistakes that were made many years ago & those where we are getting little financial or military help from the rich countries that so greatly benefit from what we are doing will eventually come to a glorious end! **1/8/2019 3:50**

Economic numbers looking REALLY good. Can you imagine if I had long term ZERO interest rates to play with like the past administration rather than the rapidly raised normalized rates we have today. That would have been SO EASY! Still markets up BIG since 2016 Election! **1/8/2019 13:01**

"The President is the biggest and best supporter of the Steel Industry in many years. We are now doing really well. The Tariffs let us compete. Was unfair that the Steel Industry lost its jobs to unfair trade laws. Very positive outcome." Mark Glyptis United Steelworkers **1/8/2019 13:13**

Talks with China are going very well! **1/8/2019 13:16**

Congratulations to a truly great football team the Clemson Tigers on an incredible win last night against a powerful Alabama team. A big win also for the Great State of South

Carolina. Look forward to seeing the team and their brilliant coach for the second time at the W.H. **1/8/2019 14:42**

Thank you for soooo many nice comments regarding my Oval Office speech. A very interesting experience!
1/9/2019 4:33

Our Country is doing so well in so many ways. Great jobs numbers with a record setting December. We are rebuilding our military. Vets finally have Choice & Accountability. Economy & GDP are strong. Tax & Reg cuts historic. Trade deals great. But we MUST fix our Southern Border!
1/9/2019 14:06

Billions of dollars are sent to the State of California for Forest fires that with proper Forest Management would never happen. Unless they get their act together which is unlikely I have ordered FEMA to send no more money. It is a disgraceful situation in lives & money! **1/9/2019 15:25**

Thank you to all of America's brave police deputies sheriffs and federal law enforcement on National Law Enforcement Appreciation Day! We love you and will always support you. https://t.co/kGL6kPmpDY **1/9/2019 19:31**

Just left a meeting with Chuck and Nancy a total waste of time. I asked what is going to happen in 30 days if I quickly open things up are you going to approve Border Security which includes a Wall or Steel Barrier? Nancy said NO. I said bye-bye nothing else works! **1/9/2019 20:34**

The Mainstream Media has NEVER been more dishonest than it is now. NBC and MSNBC are going Crazy. They report stories purposely the exact opposite of the facts. They are truly the Opposition Party working with the Dems. May even be worse than Fake News CNN if that is possible!
1/10/2019 3:43

Gave an OFF THE RECORD luncheon somewhat of a White House tradition or custom to network anchors yesterday - and they quickly leaked the contents of the meeting. Who would believe how bad it has gotten with the mainstream media which has gone totally bonkers! **1/10/2019 3:53**

Cryin Chuck told his favorite lie when he used his standard sound bite that I "slammed the table & walked out of the room. He had a temper tantrum." Because I knew he would say that and after Nancy said no to proper Border Security I politely said bye-bye and left no slamming! **1/10/2019 13:24**

There is GREAT unity with the Republicans in the House and Senate despite the Fake News Media working in overdrive to make the story look otherwise. The Opposition Party & the Dems know we must have Strong Border Security but don't want to give "Trump" another one of many wins!
1/10/2019 13:34

"Great support for Border Security and the Wall." @ foxandfriends Even greater than anyone would know! "Presidents supporters do not want him to cave." @ SteveDoocy I won't! **1/10/2019 13:41**

Getting ready to leave for the Great State of Texas! #MAGA
1/10/2019 13:43

MAKE AMERICA GREAT AGAIN! **1/10/2019 13:43**

President Obama thank you for your great support - I have been saying this all along! https://t.co/L506g9Aq4z
1/10/2019 16:47

Because of the Democrats intransigence on Border Security and the great importance of Safety for our Nation I am respectfully cancelling my very important trip to Davos Switzerland for the World Economic Forum. My warmest regards and apologies to the @WEF! **1/10/2019 18:14**

We lose 300 Americans a week 90% of which comes through the Southern Border. These numbers will be DRASTICALLY REDUCED if we have a Wall! **1/11/2019 2:42**

I often said during rallies with little variation that "Mexico will pay for the Wall." We have just signed a great new Trade Deal with Mexico. It is Billions of Dollars a year better than the very bad NAFTA deal which it replaces. The difference pays for Wall many times over! **1/11/2019 12:05**

H1-B holders in the United States can rest assured that changes are soon coming which will bring both simplicity and certainty to your stay including a potential path to citizenship. We want to encourage talented and highly skilled people to pursue career options in the U.S.

1/11/2019 12:40

Humanitarian Crisis at our Southern Border. I just got back and it is a far worse situation than almost anyone would understand an invasion! I have been there numerous times - The Democrats Cryin' Chuck and Nancy don't know how bad and dangerous it is for our ENTIRE COUNTRY.... (1/2)

1/11/2019 16:04

...The Steel Barrier or Wall should have been built by previous administrations long ago. They never got it done - I will. Without it our Country cannot be safe. Criminals Gangs Human Traffickers Drugs & so much other big trouble can easily pour in. It can be stopped cold! (2/2)

1/11/2019 16:16

The Fake News Media keeps saying we haven't built any NEW WALL. Below is a section just completed on the Border. Anti-climbing feature included. Very high strong and beautiful! Also many miles already renovated and in service! https://t.co/UAAGXI5Byr **1/11/2019 17:50**

I look forward to hosting right out of the great State of South Carolina the 2019 NCAA Football Champion Clemson Tigers at the White House on Monday January 14th. What a game what a coach what a team! **1/11/2019 23:00**

Drug prices declined in 2018 the first time in nearly half a century. During the first 19 months of my Administration Americans saved $26 Billion on prescription drugs. Our policies to get cheaper generic drugs to market are working! **1/11/2019 23:21**

.@CNN called a San Diego news station (@KUSINews) for negative reports on the Wall. When the station said that Walls work CNN no longer had interest. #FakeNews https://t.co/IDyXqmDsPq **1/11/2019 23:29**

Wow just learned in the Failing New York Times that the corrupt former leaders of the FBI almost all fired or forced to leave the agency for some very bad reasons opened up an investigation on me for no reason & with no proof after I fired Lyin' James Comey a total sleaze! **1/12/2019 12:05**

...Funny thing about James Comey. Everybody wanted him fired Republican and Democrat alike. After the rigged & botched Crooked Hillary investigation where she was interviewed on July 4th Weekend not recorded or sworn in and where she said she didn't know anything (a lie).... (1/3)
1/12/2019 12:18

....the FBI was in complete turmoil (see N.Y. Post) because of Comey's poor leadership and the way he handled the Clinton mess (not to mention his usurpation of powers from the Justice Department). My firing of James Comey was a great day for America. He was a Crooked Cop...... (2/3)
1/12/2019 12:33

.....who is being totally protected by his best friend Bob Mueller & the 13 Angry Democrats - leaking machines who have NO interest in going after the Real Collusion (and much more) by Crooked Hillary Clinton her Campaign and the Democratic National Committee. Just Watch! (3/3)
1/12/2019 12:53

I have been FAR tougher on Russia than Obama Bush or Clinton. Maybe tougher than any other President. At the same time & as I have often said getting along with Russia is a good thing not a bad thing. I fully expect that someday we will have good relations with Russia again! **1/12/2019 13:09**

Lyin' James Comey Andrew McCabe Peter S and his lover agent Lisa Page & more all disgraced and/or fired and caught in the act. These are just some of the losers that tried to do a number on your President. Part of the Witch Hunt. Remember the "insurance policy?" This is it! **1/12/2019 14:20**

Democrats should come back to Washington and work to end the Shutdown while at the same time ending the horrible humanitarian crisis at our Southern Border. I am in the White House waiting for you! **1/12/2019 14:28**

23% of Federal inmates are illegal immigrants. Border arrests are up 240%. In the Great State of Texas between 2011 & 2018 there were a total of 292000 crimes by illegal aliens 539 murders 32000 assaults 3426 sexual assaults and 3000 weapons charges. Democrats come back! **1/12/2019 14:42**

Democrats could solve the Shutdown in 15 minutes! Call your Dem Senator or Congresswoman/man. Tell them to get it done! Humanitarian Crisis. **1/12/2019 14:47**

I just watched a Fake reporter from the Amazon Washington Post say the White House is "chaotic there does not seem to be a strategy for this Shutdown. There is no plan." The Fakes always like talking Chaos there is NONE. In fact there's almost nobody in the W.H. but me and... (1/2) **1/12/2019 15:57**

....I do have a plan on the Shutdown. But to understand that plan you would have to understand the fact that I won the election and I promised safety and security for the American people. Part of that promise was a Wall at the Southern Border. Elections have consequences! (2/2) **1/12/2019 16:07**

We have a massive Humanitarian Crisis at our Southern Border. We will be out for a long time unless the Democrats come back from their "vacations" and get back to work. I am in the White House ready to sign! **1/12/2019 16:14**

I will be interviewed by Jeanine Pirro at 9:00 P.M. on @FoxNews. Watch @JesseBWatters before and @ greggutfeld after. All terrific people. I am in the White House waiting for Cryin' Chuck and Nancy to call so we can start helping our Country both at the Border and from within! **1/13/2019 1:37**

Democrats are saying that DACA is not worth it and don't want to include in talks. Many Hispanics will be coming over to the Republican side watch! **1/13/2019 14:58**

The building of the Wall on the Southern Border will bring down the crime rate throughout the entire Country! **1/13/2019 15:00**

I'm in the White House waiting. The Democrats are everywhere but Washington as people await their pay. They are having fun and not even talking! **1/13/2019 15:05**

The damage done to our Country from a badly broken Border - Drugs Crime and so much that is bad - is far greater than a Shutdown which the Dems can easily fix as soon as they come back to Washington! **1/13/2019 15:36**

Thousands of illegal aliens who have committed sexual crimes against children are right now in Texas prisons. Most came through our Southern Border. We can end this easily - We need a Steel Barrier or Wall. Walls Work! John Jones Texas Department of Public Safety. @FoxNews **1/13/2019 15:45**

Wish I could share with everyone the beauty and majesty of being in the White House and looking outside at the snow filled lawns and Rose Garden. Really is something - SPECIAL COUNTRY SPECIAL PLACE! **1/13/2019 22:01**

Starting the long overdue pullout from Syria while hitting the little remaining ISIS territorial caliphate hard and from many directions. Will attack again from existing nearby base if it reforms. Will devastate Turkey economically if they hit Kurds. Create 20 mile safe zone.... (1/2) **1/13/2019 22:53**

....Likewise do not want the Kurds to provoke Turkey. Russia Iran and Syria have been the biggest beneficiaries of the long term U.S. policy of destroying ISIS in Syria - natural enemies. We also benefit but it is now time to bring our troops back home. Stop the ENDLESS WARS! (2/2)
1/13/2019 23:02

So sorry to hear the news about Jeff Bozo being taken down by a competitor whose reporting I understand is far more accurate than the reporting in his lobbyist newspaper the Amazon Washington Post. Hopefully the paper will soon be placed in better & more responsible hands!
1/14/2019 1:45

If Elizabeth Warren often referred to by me as Pocahontas did this commercial from Bighorn or Wounded Knee instead of her kitchen with her husband dressed in full Indian garb it would have been a smash! https://t.co/D5KWr8EPan
1/14/2019 2:52

Best line in the Elizabeth Warren beer catastrophe is to her husband "Thank you for being here. I'm glad you're here" It's their house he's supposed to be there! **1/14/2019 3:03**

....Border is eventually going to be militarized and defended or the United States as we have known it is going to cease to exist...And Americans will not go gentle into that good night. Patrick Buchanan. The great people of our Country demand proper Border Security NOW! **1/14/2019 3:18**

"Gas prices drop across the United States because President Trump has deregulated Energy and we are now producing a great deal more oil than ever before." @foxandfriends But this is bad news for Russia why would President Trump do such a thing? Thought he worked for Kremlin? **1/14/2019 12:14**

I've been waiting all weekend. Democrats must get to work now. Border must be secured! **1/14/2019 12:23**

Nancy and Cryin' Chuck can end the Shutdown in 15 minutes. At this point it has become their and the Democrats fault! **1/14/2019 12:26**

The Fake News gets crazier and more dishonest every single day. Amazing to watch as certain people covering me and the tremendous success of this administration have truly gone MAD! Their Fake reporting creates anger and disunity. Take two weeks off and come back rested. Chill! **1/14/2019 13:44**

Spoke w/ President Erdogan of Turkey to advise where we stand on all matters including our last two weeks of success in fighting the remnants of ISIS and 20 mile safe zone. Also spoke about economic development between the U.S. & Turkey - great potential to substantially expand! **1/14/2019 22:12**

For decades politicians promised to secure the border fix our trade deals bring back our factories get tough on China move the Embassy to Jerusalem make NATO pay their fair share and so much else - only to do NOTHING (or worse).... (1/2) **1/14/2019 22:19**

....I am doing exactly what I pledged to do and what I was elected to do by the citizens of our great Country. Just as I promised I am fighting for YOU! (2/2)
1/14/2019 22:19

The rank and file of the FBI are great people who are disgusted with what they are learning about Lyin' James Comey and the so-called "leaders" of the FBI. Twelve have been fired or forced to leave. They got caught spying on my campaign and then called it an investigation. Bad! **1/15/2019 11:58**

Just announced that Veterans unemployment has reached an 18 year low really good news for our Vets and their families. Will soon be an all time low! Do you think the media will report on this and all of the other great economic news? **1/15/2019 12:16**

Volkswagen will be spending 800 million dollars in Chattanooga Tennessee. They will be making Electric Cars. Congratulations to Chattanooga and Tennessee on a job well done. A big win! **1/15/2019 12:25**

A big new Caravan is heading up to our Southern Border from Honduras. Tell Nancy and Chuck that a drone flying around will not stop them. Only a Wall will work. Only a Wall or Steel Barrier will keep our Country safe! Stop playing political games and end the Shutdown! **1/15/2019 12:37**

Polls are now showing that people are beginning to understand the Humanitarian Crisis and Crime at the Border. Numbers are going up fast over 50%. Democrats will soon be known as the Party of Crime. Ridiculous that they don't want Border Security! **1/15/2019 12:49**

Why is Nancy Pelosi getting paid when people who are working are not?

1/15/2019 13:25

Congratulations @ClemsonFB! https://t.co/w8viaxOOWY
1/15/2019 15:18

Great being with the National Champion Clemson Tigers last night at the White House. Because of the Shutdown I served them massive amounts of Fast Food (I paid) over 1000 hamburgers etc. Within one hour it was all gone. Great guys and big eaters! **1/15/2019 16:11**

There are now 77 major or significant Walls built around the world with 45 countries planning or building Walls. Over 800 miles of Walls have been built in Europe since only 2015. They have all been recognized as close to 100% successful. Stop the crime at our Southern Border!
1/16/2019 12:33

It is becoming more and more obvious that the Radical Democrats are a Party of open borders and crime. They want nothing to do with the major Humanitarian Crisis on our Southern Border. #2020! **1/16/2019 12:49**

The Left has become totally unhinged. They no longer care what is Right for our Countrty!

1/17/2019 14:04

So funny to watch Schumer groveling. He called for the firing of bad cop James Comey many times - UNTIL I FIRED HIM! **1/17/2019 15:04**

Thank you to Amy Kremer Women for Trump Co-Founder for doing such a great interview with Martha MacCallum... and by the way women have the lowest unemployment numbers in many decades - at the highest pay ever. Proud of that! **1/18/2019 1:36**

"In 2018 alone 20000 illegal aliens with criminal records were apprehended trying to cross the Border and there was a 122% increase in fentanyl being smuggled between ports of entry. Last month alone more than 20000 minors were smuggled into the U.S." @seanhannity **1/18/2019 2:42**

Gregg Jarrett: "Mueller's prosecutors knew the "Dossier" was the product of bias and deception." It was a Fake just like so much news coverage in our Country. Nothing but a Witch Hunt from beginning to end! **1/18/2019 3:03**

Border rancher: "We've found prayer rugs out here. It's unreal." Washington Examiner People coming across the Southern Border from many countries some of which would be a big surprise. **1/18/2019 13:22**

Why would Nancy Pelosi leave the Country with other Democrats on a seven day excursion when 800000 great people are not getting paid. Also could somebody please explain to Nancy & her "big donors" in wine country that

people working on farms (grapes) will have easy access in!
1/18/2019 14:00

Another big Caravan heading our way. Very hard to stop without a Wall! **1/18/2019 14:13**

Kevin Corke @FoxNews "Don't forget Michael Cohen has already been convicted of perjury and fraud and as recently as this week the Wall Street Journal has suggested that he may have stolen tens of thousands of dollars...." Lying to reduce his jail time! Watch father-in-law! **1/18/2019 15:02**

Never seen the Republican Party so unified. No "Cave" on the issue of Border and National Security. A beautiful thing to see especially when you hear the new rhetoric spewing from the mouths of the Democrats who talk Open Border High Taxes and Crime. Stop Criminals & Drugs now!
1/18/2019 15:58

MAKE AMERICA GREAT AGAIN! **1/18/2019 15:59**

AMERICA FIRST! **1/18/2019 16:00**

I will be making a major announcement concerning the Humanitarian Crisis on our Southern Border and the Shutdown tomorrow afternoon at 3 P.M. live from the @WhiteHouse.
1/18/2019 22:51

Remember it was Buzzfeed that released the totally discredited "Dossier" paid for by Crooked Hillary Clinton and the Democrats (as opposition research) on which the entire Russian probe is based! A very sad day for journalism but a great day for our Country! **1/19/2019 3:02**

Fake News is truly the ENEMY OF THE PEOPLE! **1/19/2019 3:24**

Will be leaving for Dover to be with the families of 4 very special people who lost their lives in service to our Country!
1/19/2019 11:29

.@newtgingrich just stated that there has been no president since Abraham Lincoln who has been treated worse or more unfairly by the media than your favorite President me! At the same time there has been no president who has accomplished more in his first two years in office! **1/19/2019 12:11**

The Economy is one of the best in our history with unemployment at a 50 year low and the Stock Market ready to again break a record (set by us many times) - & all you heard yesterday based on a phony story was Impeachment. You want to see a Stock Market Crash Impeach Trump!
1/19/2019 12:51

Many people are saying that the Mainstream Media will have a very hard time restoring credibility because of the way they have treated me over the past 3 years (including the election lead-up) as highlighted by the disgraceful Buzzfeed story & the even more disgraceful coverage!

1/19/2019 13:50

Mexico is doing NOTHING to stop the Caravan which is now fully formed and heading to the United States. We stopped the last two - many are still in Mexico but can't get through our Wall but it takes a lot of Border Agents if there is no Wall. Not easy! **1/19/2019 14:09**

I will be live from the White House at 4:00 P.M. **1/19/2019 19:08**

Always heard that as President "it's all about the economy!" Well we have one of the best economies in the history of our Country. Big GDP lowest unemployment companies coming back to the U.S. in BIG numbers great new trade

deals happening & more. But LITTLE media mention!
1/20/2019 12:40

Be careful and try staying in your house. Large parts of the Country are suffering from tremendous amounts of snow and near record setting cold. Amazing how big this system is. Wouldn't be bad to have a little of that good old fashioned Global Warming right now! **1/20/2019 12:59**

Nancy Pelosi and some of the Democrats turned down my offer yesterday before I even got up to speak. They don't see crime & drugs they only see 2020 - which they are not going to win. Best economy! They should do the right thing for the Country & allow people to go back to work.
1/20/2019 13:11

No Amnesty is not a part of my offer. It is a 3 year extension of DACA. Amnesty will be used only on a much bigger deal whether on immigration or something else. Likewise there will be no big push to remove the 11000000 plus people who are here illegally-but be careful Nancy! **1/20/2019 13:23**

Nancy Pelosi has behaved so irrationally & has gone so far to the left that she has now officially become a Radical Democrat. She is so petrified of the "lefties" in her party that she has lost control...And by the way clean up the streets in San Francisco they are disgusting! **1/20/2019 13:35**

Nancy I am still thinking about the State of the Union speech there are so many options - including doing it as per your written offer (made during the Shutdown security is no problem) and my written acceptance. While a contract is a contract I'll get back to you soon! **1/20/2019 13:51**

Wow just heard that my poll numbers with Hispanics has gone up 19% to 50%. That is because they know the Border issue better than anyone and they want Security which can only be gotten with a Wall. **1/20/2019 14:03**

Don't forget we are building and renovating big sections of Wall right now. Moving quickly and will cost far less than previous politicians thought possible. Building after all is

what I do best even when money is not readily available!
1/20/2019 14:20

The Media is not giving us credit for the tremendous progress we have made with North Korea. Think of where we were at the end of the Obama Administration compared to now. Great meeting this week with top Reps. Looking forward to meeting with Chairman Kim at end of February!
1/20/2019 18:16

A truly great First Lady who doesn't get the credit she deserves! https://t.co/Wc9bYtoLKq
1/21/2019 0:50

To all of the great people who are working so hard for your Country and not getting paid I say THANK YOU - YOU ARE GREAT PATRIOTS! We must now work together after decades of abuse to finally fix the Humanitarian Criminal & Drug Crisis at our Border. WE WILL WIN BIG! **1/21/2019 1:25**

Congratulations to Bob Kraft Bill Belichick Tom Brady and the entire New England Patriots team on a great game and season. Will be a fantastic Super Bowl! **1/21/2019 3:43**

"No President in modern times has kept more promises than Donald Trump!" Thank you Bill Bennett @SteveHiltonx
1/21/2019 5:03

Last year was the best year for American Manufacturing job growth since 1997 or 21 years. The previous administration said manufacturing will not come back to the U.S. "you would need a magic wand." I guess I found the MAGIC WAND - and it is only getting better! **1/21/2019 15:22**

Today we celebrate Dr. Martin Luther King Jr. for standing up for the self-evident truth Americans hold so dear that no matter what the color of our skin or the place of our birth we are all created equal by God. #MLKDay https://t.co/pEaVpCB8M4 **1/21/2019 15:39**

Democrats campaigned on working within Washington and "getting things done!" How is that working out? #2020TAKEBACKTHEHOUSE **1/21/2019 15:40**

Today it was my great honor to visit the Martin Luther King Jr. Memorial with @VP Mike Pence in honor of #MLKDay https://t.co/YsDEA3kygd **1/21/2019 17:46**

China posts slowest economic numbers since 1990 due to U.S. trade tensions and new policies. Makes so much sense for China to finally do a Real Deal and stop playing around! **1/21/2019 21:57**

If Nancy Pelosi thinks that Walls are "immoral" why isn't she requesting that we take down all of the existing Walls between the U.S. and Mexico even the new ones just built in San Diego at their very strong urging. Let millions of unchecked "strangers" just flow into the U.S. **1/21/2019 22:08**

Four people in Nevada viciously robbed and killed by an illegal immigrant who should not have been in our Country. 26 people killed on the Border in a drug and gang related fight. Two large Caravans from Honduras broke into Mexico and are headed our way. We need a powerful Wall! **1/21/2019 23:37**

Democrats are kidding themselves (they don't really believe it!) if they say you can stop Crime Drugs Human Trafficking and Caravans without a Wall or Steel Barrier. Stop playing games and give America the Security it deserves. A Humanitarian Crisis!

1/21/2019 23:45

Looking like Nick Sandman & Covington Catholic students were treated unfairly with early judgements proving out to be false - smeared by media. Not good but making big comeback! "New footage shows that media was wrong about teen's encounter with Native American" @ TuckerCarlson **1/22/2019 2:46**

Nick Sandmann and the students of Covington have become symbols of Fake News and how evil it can be. They have captivated the attention of the world and I know they will use it for the good - maybe even to bring people together. It started off unpleasant but can end in a dream! **1/22/2019 12:32**

Without a Wall our Country can never have Border or National Security. With a powerful Wall or Steel Barrier Crime Rates (and Drugs) will go substantially down all over the U.S. The Dems know this but want to play political games. Must finally be done correctly. No Cave! **1/22/2019 12:48**

FBI top lawyer confirms "unusual steps." They relied on the Clinton Campaign's Fake & Unverified "Dossier" which is illegal. "That has corrupted them. That has enabled them to gather evidence by UNCONSTITUTIONAL MEANS and that's what they did to the President." Judge Napolitano **1/22/2019 13:15**

Marist/NPR/PBS Poll shows President Trump's approval rating among Latinos going to 50% an increase in one year of 19%. Thank you working hard! **1/22/2019 13:25**

Never seen @senatemajldr and Republicans so united on an issue as they are on the Humanitarian Crisis & Security on our Southern Border. If we create a Wall or Barrier which prevents Criminals and Drugs from flowing into our Country Crime will go down by record numbers! **1/22/2019 14:48**

Last time I went to Davos the Fake News said I should not go there. This year because of the Shutdown I decided not to go and the Fake News said I should be there. The fact is that the people understand the media better than the media understands them! **1/22/2019 15:00**

The United States has a great economic story to tell. Number one in the World by far! **1/22/2019 15:01**

The reason Sarah Sanders does not go to the "podium" much anymore is that the press covers her so rudely & inaccurately in particular certain members of the press. I told her not to bother the word gets out anyway! Most will never cover us fairly & hence the term Fake News!

1/22/2019 15:28

Former FBI top lawyer James Baker just admitted involvement in FISA Warrant and further admitted there were IRREGULARITIES in the way the Russia probe was handled. They relied heavily on the unverified Trump "Dossier" paid for by the DNC & Clinton Campaign & funded through a... (1/2) **1/22/2019 15:53**

...big Crooked Hillary law firm represented by her lawyer Michael Sussmann (do you believe this?) who worked Baker hard & gave him Oppo Research for "a Russia probe." This meeting now exposed is the subject of Senate inquiries and much more. An Unconstitutional Hoax. @FoxNews (2/2)

1/22/2019 16:06

Congratulations to Mariano Rivera on unanimously being elected to the National Baseball Hall of Fame! Not only a great player but a great person. I am thankful for Mariano's support of the Opioid Drug Abuse Commission and @ FitnessGov. #EnterSandman #HOF2019 💯 https://t.co/reU1gKWHSQ **1/23/2019 0:19**

Deroy Murdock National Review: "We are now exporting oil which is the first time in my lifetime - we are right now the largest producer of oil and gas. This is not good if you're Vladimir Putin where your chief export is oil. W.H. Agent - Not good for Kremlin." @TuckerCarlson **1/23/2019 2:00**

Great unity in the Republican Party. Want to once and for all put an end to stoppable crime and drugs! Border Security and Wall. No doubt! **1/23/2019 12:48**

BUILD A WALL & CRIME WILL FALL! This is the new theme for two years until the Wall is finished (under construction now) of the Republican Party. Use it and pray! **1/23/2019 12:57**

BUILD A WALL & CRIME WILL FALL!
1/23/2019 12:59

The citizens of Venezuela have suffered for too long at the hands of the illegitimate Maduro regime. Today I have officially recognized the President of the Venezuelan National Assembly Juan Guaido as the Interim President of Venezuela. https://t.co/WItWPiG9jK **1/23/2019 18:47**

Even Trump Haters like (MS)NBC acknowledge you "BUILD A WALL & CRIME WILL FALL!" https://t.co/bKIgmHUW5P **1/23/2019 19:00**

"The Historic Results of President Donald J. Trump's First Two Years in Office" https://t.co/AFnWWiLICa **1/23/2019 19:09**

As the Shutdown was going on Nancy Pelosi asked me to give the State of the Union Address. I agreed. She then changed her mind because of the Shutdown suggesting a later date. This is her prerogative - I will do the Address when the Shutdown is over. I am not looking for an.... (1/2) **1/24/2019 4:12**

....alternative venue for the SOTU Address because there is no venue that can compete with the history tradition and importance of the House Chamber. I look forward to giving a "great" State of the Union Address in the near future! (2/2) **1/24/2019 4:18**

The economy is doing great. More people working in U.S.A. today than at any time in our HISTORY. Media barely covers! @foxandfriends **1/24/2019 11:56**

So interesting that bad lawyer Michael Cohen who sadly will not be testifying before Congress is using the lawyer of Crooked Hillary Clinton to represent him - Gee how did that happen? Remember July 4th weekend when Crooked went before FBI & wasn't sworn in no tape nothing? **1/24/2019 12:48**

The Fake News Media loves saying "so little happened at my first summit with Kim Jong Un." Wrong! After 40 years of doing nothing with North Korea but being taken to the cleaners & with a major war ready to start in a short 15 months relationships built hostages & remains.... (1/2) **1/24/2019 13:21**

...back home where they belong no more Rockets or M's being fired over Japan or anywhere else and most importantly no Nuclear Testing. This is more than has ever been accomplished with North Korea and the Fake News knows it. I expect another good meeting soon much potential! (2/2) **1/24/2019 13:34**

Without a Wall there cannot be safety and security at the Border or for the U.S.A. BUILD THE WALL AND CRIME WILL FALL! **1/24/2019 13:37**

Nancy just said she "just doesn't understand why?" Very simply without a Wall it all doesn't work. Our Country has a chance to greatly reduce Crime Human Trafficking Gangs and Drugs. Should have been done for decades. We will not Cave! **1/24/2019 16:16**

Great earnings coming out of Stock Market. Too bad Media doesn't devote much time to this! **1/25/2019 3:09**

A third rate conman who interviewed me many years ago for just a short period of time has been playing his biggest con of all on Fake News CNN. Michael D'Antonio a broken

down hack who knows nothing about me goes on night after night telling made up Trump stories. Disgraceful!
1/25/2019 3:28

Greatest Witch Hunt in the History of our Country! NO COLLUSION! Border Coyotes Drug Dealers and Human Traffickers are treated better. Who alerted CNN to be there?
1/25/2019 16:16

I wish people would read or listen to my words on the Border Wall. This was in no way a concession. It was taking care of millions of people who were getting badly hurt by the Shutdown with the understanding that in 21 days if no deal is done it's off to the races! **1/26/2019 0:33**

If Roger Stone was indicted for lying to Congress what about the lying done by Comey Brennan Clapper Lisa Page & lover Baker and soooo many others? What about Hillary to FBI and her 33000 deleted Emails? What about Lisa & Peter's deleted texts & Wiener's laptop? Much more!
1/26/2019 13:42

"I like the fact that the President is making the case (Border Security & Crime) to the American people. Now we know where Nancy Pelosi Chuck Schumer & the Democrats stand which is no Border Security. Will be big 2020 issue." Matt Schlapp Chair ACU. Bigger than anyone knows! **1/26/2019 13:52**

21 days goes very quickly. Negotiations with Democrats will start immediately. Will not be easy to make a deal both parties very dug in. The case for National Security has been greatly enhanced by what has been happening at the Border & through dialogue. We will build the Wall!
1/26/2019 14:01

We have turned away at great expense two major Caravans but a big one has now formed and is coming. At least 8000 people! If we had a powerful Wall they wouldn't even try to make the long and dangerous journey. Build the Wall and Crime will Fall! **1/26/2019 14:06**

Thank you to the Republican National Committee (the RNC) who voted UNANIMOUSLY yesterday to support me in the upcoming 2020 Election. Considering that we have done more than any Administration in the first two years this should be easy. More great things now in the works! **1/26/2019 14:23**

"We absolutely need a physical barrier or Wall whatever you want to call it. The President yesterday laid all that out. We need to do it all including the Wall. I provided the same information to the previous administration & it was ignored." Mark Morgan Border Chief for "O"! **1/26/2019 14:32**

BUILD A WALL & CRIME WILL FALL! https://t.co/a0G7GWi74k **1/26/2019 16:42**

Only fools or people with a political agenda don't want a Wall or Steel Barrier to protect our Country from Crime Drugs and Human Trafficking. It will happen - it always does! **1/26/2019 20:52**

"Ax falls quickly at BuzzFeed and Huffpost!" Headline New York Post. Fake News and bad journalism have caused a big downturn. Sadly many others will follow. The people want the Truth! **1/26/2019 21:37**

CBS reports that in the Roger Stone indictment data was "released during the 2016 Election to damage Hillary Clinton." Oh really! What about the Fake and Unverified "Dossier" a total phony conjob that was paid for by Crooked Hillary to damage me and the Trump Campaign? What... (1/2) **1/27/2019 1:39**

....about all of the one sided Fake Media coverage (collusion with Crooked H?) that I had to endure during my very successful presidential campaign. What about the now revealed bias by Facebook and many others. Roger Stone

didn't even work for me anywhere near the Election! (2/2)
1/27/2019 1:49

WITCH HUNT! **1/27/2019 1:51**

58000 non-citizens voted in Texas with 95000 non-citizens registered to vote. These numbers are just the tip of the iceberg. All over the country especially in California voter fraud is rampant. Must be stopped. Strong voter ID! @ foxandfriends **1/27/2019 13:22**

We are not even into February and the cost of illegal immigration so far this year is $18959495168. Cost Friday was $603331392. There are at least 25772342 illegal aliens not the 11000000 that have been reported for years in our Country. So ridiculous! DHS **1/27/2019 13:44**

Jens Stoltenberg NATO Secretary General just stated that because of me NATO has been able to raise far more money than ever before from its members after many years of decline. It's called burden sharing. Also more united. Dems & Fake News like to portray the opposite! **1/27/2019 15:11**

BUILD A WALL & CRIME WILL FALL!
https://t.co/yDdCG5DCxn **1/27/2019 18:22**

Never thought I'd say this but I think @johnrobertsFox and @GillianHTurner @FoxNews have even less understanding of the Wall negotiations than the folks at FAKE NEWS CNN & NBC! Look to final results! Don't know how my poll numbers are so good especially up 19% with Hispanics?
1/28/2019 1:08

After all that I have done for the Military our great Veterans Judges (99) Justices (2) Tax & Regulation Cuts the Economy Energy Trade & MUCH MORE does anybody really think I won't build the WALL? Done more in first two years than any President! MAKE AMERICA GREAT AGAIN!
1/28/2019 1:09

Tariffs on the "dumping" of Steel in the United States have totally revived our Steel Industry. New and expanded plants are happening all over the U.S. We have not only saved this important industry but created many jobs. Also billions paid to our treasury. A BIG WIN FOR U.S. **1/28/2019 13:16**

Numerous states introducing Bible Literacy classes giving students the option of studying the Bible. Starting to make a turn back? Great!

1/28/2019 13:21

Howard Schultz doesn't have the "guts" to run for President! Watched him on @60Minutes last night and I agree with him that he is not the "smartest person." Besides America already has that! I only hope that Starbucks is still paying me their rent in Trump Tower! **1/28/2019 13:41**

"In the Media's effort to destroy the President they are actually destroying themselves. Given all of the tremendous headwinds this President has faced it's amazing he has accomplished so much." DEROY MURDOCK @foxandfriends I agree! **1/28/2019 13:50**

In the beautiful Midwest windchill temperatures are reaching minus 60 degrees the coldest ever recorded. In coming days expected to get even colder. People can't last outside even for minutes. What the hell is going on with Global Waming? Please come back fast we need you!

1/29/2019 2:28

How does Da Nang Dick (Blumenthal) serve on the Senate Judiciary Committee when he defrauded the American people about his so called War Hero status in Vietnam only to later admit with tears pouring down his face that he was never in Vietnam. An embarrassment to our Country!

1/29/2019 2:46

A low level staffer that I hardly knew named Cliff Sims wrote yet another boring book based on made up stories and fiction. He pretended to be an insider when in fact he was nothing more than a gofer. He signed a non-disclosure agreement. He is a mess! **1/29/2019 13:45**

"Our economy right now is the Gold Standard throughout the World." @IngrahamAngle So true and not even close! **1/30/2019 4:00**

Maduro willing to negotiate with opposition in Venezuela following U.S. sanctions and the cutting off of oil revenues. Guaido is being targeted by Venezuelan Supreme Court. Massive protest expected today. Americans should not travel to Venezuela until further notice. **1/30/2019 11:02**

When I became President ISIS was out of control in Syria & running rampant. Since then tremendous progress made especially over last 5 weeks. Caliphate will soon be destroyed unthinkable two years ago. Negotiating are proceeding well in Afghanistan after 18 years of fighting.. (1/2) **1/30/2019 11:25**

...Time will tell what will happen with North Korea but at the end of the previous administration relationship was horrendous and very bad things were about to happen. Now a whole different story. I look forward to seeing Kim Jong Un shortly. Progress being made-big difference! (2/2) **1/30/2019 11:40**

If the committee of Republicans and Democrats now meeting on Border Security is not discussing or contemplating a Wall or Physical Barrier they are Wasting their time! **1/30/2019 11:49**

The Intelligence people seem to be extremely passive and naive when it comes to the dangers of Iran. They are wrong! When I became President Iran was making trouble all over the Middle East and beyond. Since ending the terrible Iran Nuclear Deal they are MUCH different but.... (1/2) **1/30/2019 13:50**

....a source of potential danger and conflict. They are testing Rockets (last week) and more and are coming very close to the edge. There economy is now crashing which is the only thing holding them back. Be careful of Iran. Perhaps Intelligence should go back to school! (2/2) **1/30/2019 13:56**

Dow just broke 25000. Tremendous news! **1/30/2019 21:54**

Spoke today with Venezuelan Interim President Juan Guaido to congratulate him on his historic assumption of the presidency and reinforced strong United States support for Venezuela's fight to regain its democracy.... (1/2) **1/30/2019 21:58**

....Large protests all across Venezuela today against Maduro. The fight for freedom has begun! (2/2) **1/30/2019 21:58**

So great to watch & listen to all these people who write books & talk about my presidential campaign and so many others things related to winning and how I should be doing "IT." As I take it all in I then sit back look around & say "gee I'm in the White House & they're not! **1/31/2019 12:04**

Large sections of WALL have already been built with much more either under construction or ready to go. Renovation of existing WALLS is also a very big part of the plan to finally after many decades properly Secure Our Border. The Wall is getting done one way or the other! **1/31/2019 12:13**

Lets just call them WALLS from now on and stop playing political games! A WALL is a WALL! **1/31/2019 12:16**

Republicans on the Homeland Security Committee are wasting their time. Democrats despite all of the evidence proof and Caravans coming are not going to give money to build the DESPERATELY needed WALL. I've got you covered. Wall is already being built I don't expect much help! **1/31/2019 13:21**

Democrats are becoming the Party of late term abortion high taxes Open Borders and Crime! **1/31/2019 13:36**

More troops being sent to the Southern Border to stop the attempted Invasion of Illegals through large Caravans into our Country. We have stopped the previous Caravans and we will stop these also. With a Wall it would be soooo much easier and less expensive. Being Built! **1/31/2019 14:52**

Schumer and the Democrats are big fans of being weak and passive with Iran. They have no clue as to the danger they would be inflicting on our Country. Iran is in financial chaos now because of the sanctions and Iran Deal termination. Dems put us in a bad place - but now good! **1/31/2019 15:08**

Very sadly Murder cases in Mexico in 2018 rose 33% from 2017 to 33341. This is a big contributor to the Humanitarian Crisis taking place on our Southern Border and then spreading throughout our Country. Worse even than Afghanistan. Much caused by DRUGS. Wall is being built! **1/31/2019 17:43**

Just concluded a great meeting with my Intel team in the Oval Office who told me that what they said on Tuesday at the Senate Hearing was mischaracterized by the media - and we are very much in agreement on Iran ISIS North Korea etc. Their testimony was distorted press.... https://t.co/Zl5aqBmpjF **1/31/2019 21:40**

Our great U.S. Border Patrol Agents made the biggest Fentanyl bust in our Country's history. Thanks as always for a job well done! **2/1/2019 0:14**

Just out: The big deal very mysterious Don jr telephone calls after the innocent Trump Tower meeting that the media & Dems said were made to his father (me) were just conclusively found NOT to be made to me. They were made to friends & business associates of Don. Really sad! **2/1/2019 3:03**

Nellie Ohr the wife of DOJ official Bruce Ohr was long ago investigating for pay (GPS Fusion) members of my family feeding it to her husband who was then giving it to the FBI even though it was created by ousted & discredited Christopher Steele. Illegal! WITCH HUNT **2/1/2019 3:16**

This Witch Hunt must end! https://t.co/3og7H4uUw2 **2/1/2019 4:26**

I inherited a total mess in Syria and Afghanistan the "Endless Wars" of unlimited spending and death. During my campaign I said very strongly that these wars must finally end. We spend $50 Billion a year in Afghanistan and have hit them so hard that we are now talking peace... (1/2)
2/1/2019 13:23

....after 18 long years. Syria was loaded with ISIS until I came along. We will soon have destroyed 100% of the Caliphate but will be watching them closely. It is now time to start coming home and after many years spending our money wisely. Certain people must get smart! (2/2) **2/1/2019 13:35**

Best January for the DOW in over 30 years. We have by far the strongest economy in the world! **2/1/2019 14:16**

JOBS JOBS JOBS! https://t.co/29dViqkEV7 **2/1/2019 15:48**

Thank you to Senator Rob Portman and Senator Cory Gardner for the early and warm endorsement. We will ALL WIN in 2020 together! **2/1/2019 19:25**

National African American History Month is an occasion to rediscover the enduring stories of African Americans and the gifts of freedom purpose and opportunity they have bestowed on future generations...https://t.co/n9kf58NruZ
2/1/2019 20:07

Great morning at Trump National Golf Club in Jupiter Florida with @JackNicklaus and @TigerWoods! https://t.co/mdPN4yvS8e **2/2/2019 18:10**

Democrat Governor Ralph Northam of Virginia just stated "I believe that I am not either of the people in that photo." This was 24 hours after apologizing for appearing in the picture and after making the most horrible statement on "super" late term abortion. Unforgivable! **2/3/2019 0:39**

Ed Gillespie who ran for Governor of the Great State of Virginia against Ralph Northam must now be thinking Malpractice and Dereliction of Duty with regard to his

Opposition Research Staff. If they find that terrible picture before the election he wins by 20 points! **2/3/2019 1:01**

Everyone is asking how Tiger played yesterday. The answer is Great! He was long straight & putted fantastically well. He shot a 64. Tiger is back & will be winning Majors again! Not surprisingly Jack also played really well. His putting is amazing! Jack & Tiger like each other. **2/3/2019 21:14**

With Caravans marching through Mexico and toward our Country Republicans must be prepared to do whatever is necessary for STRONG Border Security. Dems do nothing. If there is no Wall there is no Security. Human Trafficking Drugs and Criminals of all dimensions - KEEP OUT! **2/3/2019 22:03**

I am pleased to announce that David Bernhardt Acting Secretary of the Interior will be nominated as Secretary of the Interior. David has done a fantastic job from the day he arrived and we look forward to having his nomination officially confirmed! **2/4/2019 20:13**

Tremendous numbers of people are coming up through Mexico in the hopes of flooding our Southern Border. We have sent additional military. We will build a Human Wall if necessary. If we had a real Wall this would be a non-event! **2/5/2019 14:10**

I see Schumer is already criticizing my State of the Union speech even though he hasn't seen it yet. He's just upset that he didn't win the Senate after spending a fortune like he thought he would. Too bad we weren't given more credit for the Senate win by the media! **2/5/2019 15:29**

Melania and I send our greetings to those celebrating the Lunar New Year. Today people across the United States and around the world mark the beginning of the Lunar New Year with spectacular fireworks displays joyful festivals and family gatherings...https://t.co/yM6qZng5m0 **2/5/2019 17:08**

Looking forward to tonight! #SOTU https://t.co/IGKkZeaxUZ **2/5/2019 21:41**

So now Congressman Adam Schiff announces after having found zero Russian Collusion that he is going to be looking at every aspect of my life both financial and personal even though there is no reason to be doing so. Never happened before! Unlimited Presidential Harassment.... (1/2) **2/7/2019 11:13**

....The Dems and their committees are going "nuts." The Republicans never did this to President Obama there would be no time left to run government. I hear other committee heads will do the same thing. Even stealing people who work at White House! A continuation of Witch Hunt! (2/2) **2/7/2019 11:26**

Democrats at the top are killing the Great State of Virginia. If the three failing pols were Republicans far stronger action would be taken. Virginia will come back HOME Republican) in 2020! **2/7/2019 12:35**

PRESIDENTIAL HARASSMENT! It should never be allowed to happen again! **2/7/2019 12:37**

Today it was my great honor to sign a Presidential Memorandum launching the Women's Global Development and Prosperity Initiative. #WGDP Read more: https://t.co/qr3jevdayp https://t.co/HyIPPm4Q7b **2/7/2019 23:43**

So nice how well my State of the Union speech was received. Thank you to all!
2/8/2019 0:02

Highly respected Senator Richard Burr Chairman of Senate Intelligence said today that after an almost two year investigation he saw no evidence of Russia collusion. "We don't have anything that would suggest there was collusion by the Trump campaign and Russia." Thank you! **2/8/2019 2:05**

Not only did Senator Burr's Committee find No Collusion by the Trump Campaign and Russia it's important because they interviewed 200 witnesses and 300000 pages of documents & the Committee has direct access to

intelligence information that's Classified. @GreggJarrett
2/8/2019 12:23

Now we find out that Adam Schiff was spending time together in Aspen with Glenn Simpson of GPS Fusion who wrote the fake and discredited Dossier even though Simpson was testifying before Schiff. John Solomon of @thehill **2/8/2019 13:41**

The mainstream media has refused to cover the fact that the head of the VERY important Senate Intelligence Committee after two years of intensive study and access to Intelligence that only they could get just stated that they have found NO COLLUSION between "Trump" & Russia.... (1/2) **2/8/2019 13:48**

...It is all a GIANT AND ILLEGAL HOAX developed long before the election itself but used as an excuse by the Democrats as to why Crooked Hillary Clinton lost the Election! Someday the Fake News Media will turn honest & report that Donald J. Trump was actually a GREAT Candidate! (2/2) **2/8/2019 13:59**

I was a big fan of Frank Robinson both as a great player and man. He was the first African American manager in baseball and was highly respected at everything he did. He will he missed! **2/8/2019 20:15**

My representatives have just left North Korea after a very productive meeting and an agreed upon time and date for the second Summit with Kim Jong Un. It will take place in Hanoi Vietnam on February 27 & 28. I look forward to seeing Chairman Kim & advancing the cause of peace!
2/9/2019 0:33

North Korea under the leadership of Kim Jong Un will become a great Economic Powerhouse. He may surprise some but he won't surprise me because I have gotten to know him & fully understand how capable he is. North Korea will become a different kind of Rocket - an Economic one! **2/9/2019 0:50**

It was great meeting some of our outstanding young military personnel who were wounded in both Syria and Afghanistan. Their wounds are deep but their spirit is sooo high. They will recoverer & be back very soon. America loves them. Walter Reed Hospital is AMAZING - Thank you all! **2/9/2019 13:56**

The Democrats in Congress yesterday were vicious and totally showed their cards for everyone to see. When the Republicans had the Majority they never acted with such hatred and scorn! The Dems are trying to win an election in 2020 that they know they cannot legitimately win! **2/9/2019 14:30**

We have a great economy DESPITE the Obama Administration and all of its job killing Regulations and Roadblocks. If that thinking prevailed in the 2016 Election the U.S. would be in a Depression right now! We were heading down and don't let the Democrats sound bites fool you! **2/9/2019 14:36**

The Democrats just don't seem to want Border Security. They are fighting Border Agents recommendations. If you believe news reports they are not offering much for the Wall. They look to be making this a campaign issue. The Wall will get built one way or the other! **2/9/2019 22:02**

Today Elizabeth Warren sometimes referred to by me as Pocahontas joined the race for President. Will she run as our first Native American presidential candidate or has she decided that after 32 years this is not playing so well anymore? See you on the campaign TRAIL Liz!

2/9/2019 22:54

I think it is very important for the Democrats to press forward with their Green New Deal. It would be great for the so-called "Carbon Footprint" to permanently eliminate all Planes Cars Cows Oil Gas & the Military - even if no other country would do the same. Brilliant! **2/9/2019 23:21**

Senator Richard Burr The Chairman of the Senate Intelligence Committee just announced that after almost two years more than two hundred interviews and thousands of documents they have found NO COLLUSION BETWEEN TRUMP AND RUSSIA! Is anybody really surprised by this? **2/10/2019 12:41**

African Americans are very angry at the double standard on full display in Virginia! **2/10/2019 14:53**

Gallup Poll: "Open Borders will potentially attract 42 million Latin Americans." This would be a disaster for the U.S. We need the Wall now! **2/10/2019 15:24**

I don't think the Dems on the Border Committee are being allowed by their leaders to make a deal. They are offering very little money for the desperately needed Border Wall & now out of the blue want a cap on convicted violent felons to be held in detention! **2/10/2019 16:17**

It was a very bad week for the Democrats with the GREAT economic numbers The Virginia disaster and the State of the Union address. Now with the terrible offers being made by them to the Border Committee I actually believe they want a Shutdown. They want a new subject! **2/10/2019 16:24**

The media was able to get my work schedule something very easy to do but it should have been reported as a positive not negative. When the term Executive Time is used I am generally working not relaxing. In fact I probably work more hours than almost any past President..... (1/2)
2/10/2019 18:27

....The fact is when I took over as President our Country was a mess. Depleted Military Endless Wars a potential War with North Korea V.A. High Taxes & too many Regulations Border Immigration & HealthCare problems & much more. I

had no choice but to work very long hours! (2/2)
2/10/2019 18:39

"President is on sound legal ground to declare a National Emergency. There have been 58 National Emergencies declared since the law was enacted in 1976 and 31 right now that are currently active so this is hardly unprecedented." Congressman @tommcclintock **2/10/2019 21:46**

The Border Committee Democrats are behaving all of a sudden irrationally. Not only are they unwilling to give dollars for the obviously needed Wall (they overrode recommendations of Border Patrol experts) but they don't even want to take muderers into custody! What's going on?
2/10/2019 21:54

Well it happened again. Amy Klobuchar announced that she is running for President talking proudly of fighting global warming while standing in a virtual blizzard of snow ice and freezing temperatures. Bad timing. By the end of her speech she looked like a Snowman(woman)! **2/10/2019 22:04**

The U.S. will soon control 100% of ISIS territory in Syria. @ CNN (do you believe this?). **2/10/2019 22:28**

"Fact checkers have become Fake News." @JesseBWatters So True! **2/11/2019 12:41**

No president ever worked harder than me (cleaning up the mess I inherited)!
2/11/2019 12:43

The Democrats do not want us to detain or send back criminal aliens! This is a brand new demand. Crazy!
2/11/2019 13:18

The Democrats are so self righteous and ANGRY! Loosen up and have some fun. The Country is doing well! **2/11/2019 14:19**

Will be heading to El Paso very soon. Big speech on Border Security and much else tonight. Tremendous crowd! See you later! **2/11/2019 16:03**

40 years of corruption. 40 years of repression. 40 years of terror. The regime in Iran has produced only #40YearsofFailure. The long-suffering Iranian people deserve a much brighter future. https://t.co/bA8YGsw9LA **2/11/2019 19:58**

Coal is an important part of our electricity generation mix and @TVAnews should give serious consideration to all factors before voting to close viable power plants like Paradise #3 in Kentucky! **2/11/2019 22:03**

We are fighting for all Americans from all backgrounds of every age race religion birthplace color & creed. Our agenda is NOT a partisan agenda - it is the mainstream common sense agenda of the American People. Thank you El Paso Texas - I love you! https://t.co/4Lz4PUwKzV **2/12/2019 3:52**

Beautiful evening in El Paso Texas last night. God Bless the USA! https://t.co/trqA75KxLN **2/12/2019 16:35**

Was just presented the concept and parameters of the Border Security Deal by hard working Senator Richard Shelby. Looking over all aspects knowing that this will be hooked up with lots of money from other sources.... (1/2) **2/12/2019 23:47**

....Will be getting almost $23 BILLION for Border Security. Regardless of Wall money it is being built as we speak! (2/2) **2/12/2019 23:47**

I want to thank all Republicans for the work you have done in dealing with the Radical Left on Border Security. Not an easy task but the Wall is being built and will be a great achievement and contributor toward life and safety within our Country! **2/13/2019 3:23**

The Senate Intelligence Committee: THERE IS NO EVIDENCE OF COLLUSION BETWEEN THE TRUMP CAMPAIGN AND RUSSIA! **2/13/2019 10:58**

The Gallup Poll just announced that 69% of our great citizens expect their finances to improve next year a 16 year high. Nice! **2/13/2019 15:01**

California has been forced to cancel the massive bullet train project after having spent and wasted many billions of dollars. They owe the Federal Government three and a half billion dollars. We want that money back now. Whole project is a "green" disaster!

2/14/2019 1:29

Disgraced FBI Acting Director Andrew McCabe pretends to be a "poor little Angel" when in fact he was a big part of the Crooked Hillary Scandal & the Russia Hoax - a puppet for Leakin' James Comey. I.G. report on McCabe was devastating. Part of "insurance policy" in case I won.... (1/2) **2/14/2019 14:39**

....Many of the top FBI brass were fired forced to leave or left. McCabe's wife received BIG DOLLARS from Clinton people for her campaign - he gave Hillary a pass. McCabe is a disgrace to the FBI and a disgrace to our Country. MAKE AMERICA GREAT AGAIN! (2/2) **2/14/2019 14:55**

Reviewing the funding bill with my team at the @ WhiteHouse! **2/14/2019 17:27**

"Trying to use the 25th Amendment to try and circumvent the Election is a despicable act of unconstitutional power grabbing...which happens in third world countries. You have to obey the law. This is an attack on our system & Constitution." Alan Dershowitz. @TuckerCarlson **2/15/2019 3:16**

Great job by law enforcement in Aurora Illinois. Heartfelt condolences to all of the victims and their families. America is with you! **2/15/2019 23:11**

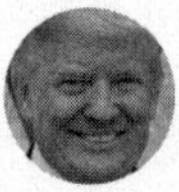

BUILDING THE WALL! **2/17/2019 0:10**

Trade negotiators have just returned from China where the meetings on Trade were very productive. Now at meetings with me at Mar-a-Lago giving the details. In the meantime Billions of Dollars are being paid to the United States by China in the form of Trade Tariffs! **2/17/2019 0:17**

The United States is asking Britain France Germany and other European allies to take back over 800 ISIS fighters that we captured in Syria and put them on trial. The Caliphate is ready to fall. The alternative is not a good one in that we will be forced to release them........ (1/2) **2/17/2019 3:51**

....The U.S. does not want to watch as these ISIS fighters permeate Europe which is where they are expected to go. We do so much and spend so much - Time for others to step up and do the job that they are so capable of doing. We are pulling back after 100% Caliphate victory! (2/2) **2/17/2019 4:01**

Democrats in the Senate are still slow walking hundreds of highly qualified people wanting to come into government. Never been such an abuse in our country's history. Mitch should not let Senate go home until all are approved. We need our Ambassadors and all others NOW! **2/17/2019 12:24**

52% Approval Rating 93% in Republican Party (a record)! Pretty amazing considering that 93% (also) of my press is REALLY BAD. The "people" are SMART! **2/17/2019 12:41**

Nothing funny about tired Saturday Night Live on Fake News NBC! Question is how do the Networks get away with these total Republican hit jobs without retribution? Likewise for many other shows? Very unfair and should be looked into. This is the real Collusion! **2/17/2019 12:52**

THE RIGGED AND CORRUPT MEDIA IS THE ENEMY OF THE PEOPLE! **2/17/2019 12:56**

"These guys the investigators ought to be in jail. What they have done working with the Obama intelligence agencies is simply unprecedented. This is one of the greatest political hoaxes ever perpetrated on the people of this Country and Mueller is a coverup." Rush Limbaugh **2/17/2019 21:32**

The Mueller investigation is totally conflicted illegal and rigged! Should never have been allowed to begin except for the Collusion and many crimes committed by the Democrats. Witch Hunt! **2/17/2019 23:45**

"After two years and interviewing more than two hundred witnesses the Senate Intelligence Committee has NOT discovered any direct evidence of a conspiracy between the Trump Campaign and Russia." Ken Dilanian @NBCNews **2/18/2019 11:56**

Wow so many lies by now disgraced acting FBI Director Andrew McCabe. He was fired for lying and now his story gets even more deranged. He and Rod Rosenstein who was hired by Jeff Sessions (another beauty) look like they were planning a very illegal act and got caught..... (1/2) **2/18/2019 12:15**

....There is a lot of explaining to do to the millions of people who had just elected a president who they really like and who has done a great job for them with the Military Vets Economy and so much more. This was the illegal and treasonous "insurance policy" in full action! (2/2) **2/18/2019 12:29**

"This was an illegal coup attempt on the President of the United States." Dan Bongino on @foxandfriends True! **2/18/2019 13:29**

Hope you are enjoying your President's Day our Country is making unprecedented progress! **2/18/2019 20:22**

We are here to proclaim that a new day is coming in Latin America. In Venezuela and across the Western Hemisphere Socialism is DYING - and liberty prosperity and democracy are being REBORN...https://t.co/hPL5W48Pmg **2/18/2019 22:26**

The people of Venezuela are standing for FREEDOM and DEMOCRACY - and the United States of America is standing right by their side! **2/18/2019 22:30**

I ask every member of the Maduro regime: End this nightmare of poverty hunger and death. LET YOUR PEOPLE GO. Set your country free! Now is the time for all Venezuelan Patriots to act together as one united people. Nothing could be better for the future of Venezuela! **2/18/2019 22:32**

Today more than 50 countries around the world now recognize the rightful government of Venezuela. The Venezuelan people have spoken and the world has heard their voice. They are turning the page on Socialism and Dictatorship; and there will be NO GOING BACK! https://t.co/C3DL5RFfiE **2/19/2019 1:17**

"The biggest abuse of power and corruption scandal in our history and it's much worse than we thought. Andrew McCabe (FBI) admitted to plotting a coup (government overthrow) when he was serving in the FBI before he was fired for lying & leaking." @seanhannity @FoxNews Treason! **2/19/2019 2:53**

Remember this Andrew McCabe didn't go to the bathroom without the approval of Leakin' James Comey! **2/19/2019 3:26**

"....(The Witch Hunt) in time likely will become recognized as the greatest scandal in American political history marking the first occasion in which the U.S. government bureaucrats sought to overturn an election (presidential)!" Victor Davis Hanson And got caught! @FoxNews **2/19/2019 12:21**

Had the opposition party (no not the Media) won the election the Stock Market would be down at least 10000 points by now. We are heading up up up! **2/19/2019 12:30**

As I predicted 16 states led mostly by Open Border Democrats and the Radical Left have filed a lawsuit in of course the 9th Circuit! California the state that has wasted billions of dollars on their out of control Fast Train with no hope of completion seems in charge! **2/19/2019 13:52**

The failed Fast Train project in California where the cost overruns are becoming world record setting is hundreds of times more expensive than the desperately needed Wall! **2/19/2019 13:53**

The Washington Post is a Fact Checker only for the Democrats. For the Republicans and for your all time favorite President it is a Fake Fact Checker! **2/19/2019 15:22**

I never said anything bad about Andrew McCabe's wife other than she (they) should not have taken large amounts of campaign money from a Crooked Hillary source when Clinton was under investigation by the FBI. I never called his wife a loser to him (another McCabe made up lie)! **2/19/2019 16:05**

Crazy Bernie has just entered the race. I wish him well!

2/20/2019 12:07

The Press has never been more dishonest than it is today. Stories are written that have absolutely no basis in fact. The writers don't even call asking for verification. They are totally out of control. Sadly I kept many of them in business. In six years they all go BUST! **2/20/2019 12:20**

"The Washington Post ignored basic journalistic standards because it wanted to advance its well-known and easily documented biased agenda against President Donald J.

Trump." Covington student suing WAPO. Go get them Nick. Fake News! **2/20/2019 12:44**

"If thinking that James Comey is not a good FBI Director is tantamount to being an agent of Russia than just list all the people that are agents of Russia - Chuck Schumer Nancy Pelosi Rod Rosenstein who wrote the memo to get rid of Comey the Inspector General...." Trey Gowdy **2/20/2019 12:54**

The New York Times reporting is false. They are a true ENEMY OF THE PEOPLE! **2/20/2019 13:49**

California now wants to scale back their already failed "fast train" project by substantially shortening the distance so that it no longer goes from L.A. to San Francisco. A different deal and record cost overruns. Send the Federal Government back the Billions of Dollars WASTED! **2/20/2019 14:13**

We have just built this powerful Wall in New Mexico. Completed on January 30 2019 - 47 days ahead of schedule! Many miles more now under construction! #FinishTheWall https://t.co/TYkj3KRdOC **2/20/2019 18:56**

I have instructed Secretary of State Mike Pompeo and he fully agrees not to allow Hoda Muthana back into the Country!
2/20/2019 21:05

I want 5G and even 6G technology in the United States as soon as possible. It is far more powerful faster and smarter than the current standard. American companies must step up their efforts or get left behind. There is no reason that we should be lagging behind on......... (1/2) **2/21/2019 13:55**

....something that is so obviously the future. I want the United States to win through competition not by blocking out currently more advanced technologies. We must always be the leader in everything we do especially when it comes to the very exciting world of technology! (2/2) **2/21/2019 13:59**

THE WALL IS UNDER CONSTRUCTION RIGHT NOW! https://t.co/exUJCiITsz **2/21/2019 14:17**

.@JussieSmollett - what about MAGA and the tens of millions of people you insulted with your racist and dangerous comments!? #MAGA

2/21/2019 16:09

Senator John Cornyn has done an outstanding job for the people of Texas. He is strong on Crime the Border the Second Amendment and loves our Military and Vets. John has my complete and total endorsement. MAKE AMERICA GREAT AGAIN! **2/21/2019 20:10**

We are here to honor the extraordinary contributions of African-Americans to every aspect of American Life History and Culture. From the earliest days of this Nation African-American Leaders Pioneers & Visionaries have uplifted & inspired our Country...https://t.co/VuFLkfd12j **2/22/2019 0:27**

Highly respected Senator Richard Burr head of Senate Intelligence said after interviewing over 200 witnesses and studying over 2 million pages of documents "WE HAVE FOUND NO COLLUSION BETWEEN THE TRUMP CAMPAIGN AND RUSSIA." The Witch Hunt so bad for our Country must end! **2/22/2019 14:11**

Fake News is so bad for our Country! https://t.co/ZwA8E0URer **2/22/2019 14:55**

I am pleased to announce that Kelly Knight Craft our current Ambassador to Canada is being nominated to be United States Ambassador to the United Nations.... (1/2) **2/22/2019 23:02**

....Kelly has done an outstanding job representing our Nation and I have no doubt that under her leadership our Country will be represented at the highest level. Congratulations to Kelly and her entire family! (2/2) **2/22/2019 23:02**

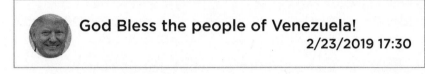

God Bless the people of Venezuela!
2/23/2019 17:30

There is far more ENERGY on the Right than there is on the Left. That's why we just won the Senate and why we will win big in 2020. The Fake News just doesn't want to report the facts. Border Security is a big factor. The under construction Wall will stop Gangs Drugs and Crime!
2/23/2019 17:52

The people of Venezuela stand at the threshold of history ready to reclaim their country - and their future.... https://t.co/ajxd1EN64c **2/23/2019 20:00**

"There's not one shred of evidence that this president's done anything Constitutionally (or anything else) wrong." Graham Ledger. Thank you Graham so true! **2/24/2019 0:01**

HOLD THE DATE! We will be having one of the biggest gatherings in the history of Washington D.C. on July 4th. It will be called "A Salute To America" and will be held at the Lincoln Memorial. Major fireworks display entertainment and an address by your favorite President me! **2/24/2019 12:43**

Very productive talks yesterday with China on Trade. Will continue today! I will be leaving for Hanoi Vietnam early tomorrow for a Summit with Kim Jong Un of North Korea where we both expect a continuation of the progress made at first Summit in Singapore. Denuclearization? **2/24/2019 12:58**

President Xi of China has been very helpful in his support of my meeting with Kim Jong Un. The last thing China wants are large scale nuclear weapons right next door. Sanctions placed on the border by China and Russia have been very helpful. Great relationship with Chairman Kim! **2/24/2019 13:05**

Poll: Suburban women are coming back into the Republican Party in droves "because of the Wall and Border Security. 70% support Border Security and the Wall." Not believing the Walls are immoral line. Beverly Hallberg Independent

Women's Forum @KatiePavlich A great USA issue!
2/24/2019 14:56

93% Approval Rating in the Republican Party. 52% Approval Rating overall! Not bad considering I get the most unfair (BAD) press in the history of presidential politics! And don't forget the Witch Hunt! **2/24/2019 15:02**

The only Collusion with the Russians was with Crooked Hillary Clinton and the Democratic National Committee... And where's the Server that the DNC refused to give to the FBI? Where are the new Texts between Agent Lisa Page and her Agent lover Peter S? We want them now!
2/24/2019 16:51

So funny to watch people who have failed for years they got NOTHING telling me how to negotiate with North Korea. But thanks anyway!
2/24/2019 17:27

I am pleased to report that the U.S. has made substantial progress in our trade talks with China on important structural issues including intellectual property protection technology transfer agriculture services currency and many other issues. As a result of these very...... (1/2) **2/24/2019 22:39**

....productive talks I will be delaying the U.S. increase in tariffs now scheduled for March 1. Assuming both sides make additional progress we will be planning a Summit for President Xi and myself at Mar-a-Lago to conclude an agreement. A very good weekend for U.S. & China! (2/2)
2/24/2019 22:50

We have a State of Emergency at our Southern Border. Border Patrol our Military and local Law Enforcement are doing a great job but without the Wall which is now under major construction you cannot have Border Security. Drugs Gangs and Human Trafficking must be stopped! **2/25/2019 11:32**

Be nice if Spike Lee could read his notes or better yet not have to use notes at all when doing his racist hit on your President who has done more for African Americans (Criminal Justice Reform Lowest Unemployment numbers in History Tax Cutsetc.) than almost any other Pres!
2/25/2019 11:50

Oil prices getting too high. OPEC please relax and take it easy. World cannot take a price hike - fragile! **2/25/2019 11:58**

Former Senator Harry Reid (he got thrown out) is working hard to put a good spin on his failed career. He led through lies and deception only to be replaced by another beauty Cryin' Chuck Schumer. Some things just never change!
2/25/2019 12:53

I hope our great Republican Senators don't get led down the path of weak and ineffective Border Security. Without strong Borders we don't have a Country - and the voters are on board with us. Be strong and smart don't fall into the Democrats "trap" of Open Borders and Crime! **2/25/2019 12:58**

"Why on earth would any Republican vote not to put up a Wall or against Border Security. Please explain that to me?" @Varneyco **2/25/2019 15:01**

Since my election as President the Dow Jones is up 43% and the NASDAQ Composite almost 50%. Great news for your 401(k)s as they continue to grow. We are bringing back America faster than anyone thought possible!
2/25/2019 15:12

It is my honor today to announce that Danny Burch a United States citizen who has been held hostage in Yemen for 18 months has been recovered and reunited with his wife and children. I appreciate the support of the United Arab Emirates in bringing Danny home... (1/3) **2/25/2019 19:08**

...Danny's recovery reflects the best of what the United States & its partners can accomplish.We work every day to bring Americans home. We maintain constant and intensive diplomatic intelligence and law enforcement cooperation

within the United States Government and with... (2/3)
2/25/2019 19:08

...our foreign partners. Recovering American hostages is a priority of my Admin and with Danny's release we have now secured freedom for 20 American captives since my election victory. We will not rest as we continue our work to bring the remaining American hostages back home! (3/3)
2/25/2019 19:08

Heading over to Vietnam for my meeting with Kim Jong Un. Looking forward to a very productive Summit! **2/25/2019 20:17**

If a deal is made with China our great American Farmers will be treated better than they have ever been treated before!
2/26/2019 0:04

Senate Democrats just voted against legislation to prevent the killing of newborn infant children. The Democrat position on abortion is now so extreme that they don't mind executing babies AFTER birth.... (1/2)
2/26/2019 1:50

....This will be remembered as one of the most shocking votes in the history of Congress. If there is one thing we should all agree on it's protecting the lives of innocent babies. (2/2) **2/26/2019 1:50**

Just arrived in Vietnam. Thank you to all of the people for the great reception in Hanoi. Tremendous crowds and so much love! **2/26/2019 15:08**

Vietnam is thriving like few places on earth. North Korea would be the same and very quickly if it would denuclearize. The potential is AWESOME a great opportunity like almost none other in history for my friend Kim Jong Un. We will know fairly soon - Very Interesting! **2/27/2019 2:31**

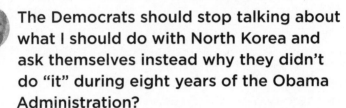

The Democrats should stop talking about what I should do with North Korea and ask themselves instead why they didn't do "it" during eight years of the Obama Administration?

2/27/2019 2:36

I have now spent more time in Vietnam than Da Nang Dick Blumenthal the third rate Senator from Connecticut (how is Connecticut doing?). His war stories of his heroism in Vietnam were a total fraud - he was never even there. We talked about it today with Vietnamese leaders! **2/27/2019 7:58**

Michael Cohen was one of many lawyers who represented me (unfortunately). He had other clients also. He was just disbarred by the State Supreme Court for lying & fraud. He did bad things unrelated to Trump. He is lying in order to reduce his prison time. Using Crooked's lawyer! **2/27/2019 9:08**

Fiat Chrysler will be adding more than 6500 JOBS in Michigan (Detroit area) doubling its hourly workforce as part of a 4.5 Billion Dollar investment. Thank you Fiat Chrysler. They are all coming back to the USA it's where the action is! **2/27/2019 9:20**

All false reporting (guessing) on my intentions with respect to North Korea. Kim Jong Un and I will try very hard to work something out on Denuclearization & then making North Korea an Economic Powerhouse. I believe that China Russia Japan & South Korea will be very helpful! **2/27/2019 9:45**

Great meetings and dinner tonight in Vietnam with Kim Jong Un of North Korea. Very good dialogue. Resuming tomorrow! **2/27/2019 15:36**

Great meeting and dinner with Kim Jong Un in Hanoi Vietnam tonight. Looking forward to continuing our discussions tomorrow! #HanoiSummit https://t.co/J3x6lUGzjS **2/27/2019 15:38**

THANK YOU to our generous hosts in Hanoi this week: President Trong Prime Minister Phuc and the wonderful people of Vietnam! https://t.co/AMqF0dfRhP **2/28/2019 10:25**

Today in Alaska it was my great honor to visit with our brave men and women of the United States Military at Joint Base Elmendorf-Richardson. We are forever grateful for their service and sacrifice. THANK YOU! https://t.co/4REVxKUsHT **3/1/2019 4:35**

Great to be back from Vietnam an amazing place. We had very substantive negotiations with Kim Jong Un - we know what they want and they know what we must have. Relationship very good let's see what happens! **3/1/2019 12:49**

Congress must demand the transcript of Michael Cohen's new book given to publishers a short time ago. Your heads will spin when you see the lies misrepresentations and contradictions against his Thursday testimony. Like a different person! He is totally discredited! **3/1/2019 13:08**

Oh' I see! Now that the 2 year Russian Collusion case has fallen apart there was no Collusion except bye Crooked Hillary and the Democrats they say "gee I have an idea let's look at Trump's finances and every deal he has ever done. Let's follow discredited Michael Cohen..... (1/2) **3/1/2019 13:19**

...and the fraudulent and dishonest statements he made on Wednesday. No way it's time to stop this corrupt and illegally brought Witch Hunt. Time to start looking at the other side where real crimes were committed. Republicans have been abused long enough. Must end now! (2/2) **3/1/2019 13:26**

Michael Cohen's book manuscript shows that he committed perjury on a scale not seen before. He must have forgotten about his book when he testified. What does Hillary Clinton's lawyer Lanny Davis say about this one. Is he being paid by Crooked Hillary. Using her lawyer? **3/1/2019 13:37**

I never like being misinterpreted but especially when it comes to Otto Warmbier and his great family. Remember

I got Otto out along with three others. The previous Administration did nothing and he was taken on their watch. Of course I hold North Korea responsible.... (1/2) **3/1/2019 21:03**

....for Otto's mistreatment and death. Most important Otto Warmbier will not have died in vain. Otto and his family have become a tremendous symbol of strong passion and strength which will last for many years into the future. I love Otto and think of him often! (2/2) **3/1/2019 21:03**

I have asked China to immediately remove all Tariffs on our agricultural products (including beef pork etc.) based on the fact that we are moving along nicely with Trade discussions.... (1/2) **3/1/2019 23:08**

....and I did not increase their second traunch of Tariffs to 25% on March 1st. This is very important for our great farmers - and me! (2/2) **3/1/2019 23:08**

Virtually everything failed lawyer Michael Cohen said in his sworn testimony last week is totally contradicted in his just released manuscript for a book about me. It's a total new love letter to "Trump" and the pols must now use it rather than his lies for sentence reduction! **3/3/2019 0:27**

We've got NASA "rocking" again. Great activity and success. Congrats to SPACEX and all!

3/3/2019 0:48

...said was a total lie but Fake Media won't show it. I am an innocent man being persecuted by some very bad conflicted & corrupt people in a Witch Hunt that is illegal & should never have been allowed to start - And only because I won the Election! Despite this great success! (2/2)
3/3/2019 15:44

After more than two years of Presidential Harassment the only things that have been proven is that Democrats and other broke the law. The hostile Cohen testimony given by

a liar to reduce his prison time proved no Collusion! His just written book manuscript showed what he..... (1/2)
3/3/2019 16:02

"Look how they're acting now and how we act when we're in the majority. What the Democrats are doing is an abuse of power. They couldn't find anything...they took a Fake Dossier & couldn't find any Collusion. Now they have a fake witness in Cohen." Congressman Mark Green (R-TN).
3/3/2019 19:23

My wonderful daughter Ivanka will be interviewed tonight by Steve Hilton on "The Next Revolution." @FoxNews 9:00 P.M. She works so hard and has achieved so much for the U.S.A.(and gets so little credit!). Then watch Mark Levin at 10:00 P.M. a great show! **3/3/2019 19:52**

The reason I do not want military drills with South Korea is to save hundreds of millions of dollars for the U.S. for which we are not reimbursed. That was my position long before I became President. Also reducing tensions with North Korea at this time is a good thing! **3/3/2019 20:18**

Presidential Harassment by "crazed" Democrats at the highest level in the history of our Country. Likewise the most vicious and corrupt Mainstream Media that any president has ever had to endure - Yet the most successful first two years for any (1/2) **3/4/2019 0:02**

....President. We are WINNING big the envy of the WORLD but just think what it could be? (2/2) **3/4/2019 0:08**

For the Democrats to interview in open hearings a convicted liar & fraudster at the same time as the very important Nuclear Summit with North Korea is perhaps a new low in American politics and may have contributed to the "walk." Never done when a president is overseas. Shame! **3/4/2019 1:01**

To the great people of Alabama and surrounding areas: Please be careful and safe. Tornadoes and storms were truly violent and more could be coming. To the families and

friends of the victims and to the injured God bless you all!
3/4/2019 3:10

The military drills or war games as I call them were never even discussed in my mtg w/ Kim Jong Un of NK—FAKE NEWS! I made that decision long ago because it costs the U.S. far too much money to have those "games" especially since we are not reimbursed for the tremendous cost!
3/4/2019 19:53

"Now that the Dems are going to try & switch from Collusion to some other reason it makes them continue to look like sore losers who didn't accept the WILL OF THE PEOPLE in the last election - they will do anything to get rid of the President." @AriFleischer It will never work! **3/4/2019 20:06**

"There is no Collusion. All of these investigations are in search of a crime. Democrats have no evidence to impeach President Trump. Ridiculous!" @DevinNunes @FoxNews
3/4/2019 20:17

"The American Media has changed forever. News organizations that seemed like a big deal are now extinct. Those that remain have now degraded themselves beyond recognition like the New Yorker - or they've been purchased by Jeff Bezos to conduct unregistered lobbying for......... **3/5/2019 2:04**

"We the people will now be subjected to the biggest display of modern day McCarthyism....which is the widest fishing net expedition....every aspect of the presidents life....all in order to get power back so they can institute Socialism." @ seanhannity **3/5/2019 3:50**

Representative Ilhan Omar is again under fire for her terrible comments concerning Israel. Jewish groups have just sent a petition to Speaker Pelosi asking her to remove Omar from Foreign Relations Committee. A dark day for Israel!
3/5/2019 4:33

Now that they realize the only Collusion with Russia was done by Crooked Hillary Clinton & the Democrats Nadler

Schiff and the Dem heads of the Committees have gone stone cold CRAZY. 81 letter sent to innocent people to harass them. They won't get ANYTHING done for our Country! **3/5/2019 13:14**

"HIV Is Cured In 2nd Patient Doctors Report." @nytimes Such great news for so many. Tremendous progress being made! **3/5/2019 13:22**

The greatest overreach in the history of our Country. The Dems are obstructing justice and will not get anything done. A big fat fishing expedition desperately in search of a crime when in fact the real crime is what the Dems are doing and have done! **3/5/2019 14:11**

PRESIDENTIAL HARASSMENT! **3/5/2019 14:12**

Republican Approval Rating just hit 93%. Sorry Haters! MAKE AMERICA GREAT AGAIN! **3/5/2019 14:15**

Just a few moments ago I signed an EO addressing one of our nation's most heartbreaking tragedies: VETERANS SUICIDE. To every Veteran—I want you to know that you have an entire nation of more than 300 million people behind you. You will NEVER be forgotten.https://t.co/DKxiV5Ku3B **3/5/2019 19:49**

"(Crooked) Hillary Clinton confirms she will not run in 2020 rules out a third bid for White House." Aw-shucks does that mean I won't get to run against her again? She will be sorely missed!
3/5/2019 22:18

Hans Von Spakovsky "I haven't seen any evidence of actual violations of the law which is usually a basis before you start an investigation. Adam Schiff seems to be copying Joseph McCarthy in wanting to open up investigations when they don't have any evidence of wrongdoing." **3/6/2019 4:27**

Senate Republicans are not voting on constitutionality or precedent they are voting on desperately needed Border Security & the Wall. Our Country is being invaded with Drugs Human Traffickers & Criminals of all shapes and sizes. That's what this vote is all about. STAY UNITED! **3/6/2019 17:54**

It is shameful that House Democrats won't take a stronger stand against Anti-Semitism in their conference. Anti-Semitism has fueled atrocities throughout history and it's inconceivable they will not act to condemn it! **3/6/2019 19:50**

Congressman Chris Stewart: "No one is accusing the President of a crime and yet they (the Democrats) are issuing hundreds of subpoenas. This is unprecedented." They are desperately trying to find anything they can even a punctuation mistake in a document! **3/6/2019 23:56**

Wall Street Journal: "More migrant families crossing into the U.S. illegally have been arrested in the first five months of the federal fiscal year than in any prior full year." We are doing a great job at the border but this is a National Emergency! **3/7/2019 0:02**

Democrats just blocked @FoxNews from holding a debate. Good then I think I'll do the same thing with the Fake News Networks and the Radical Left Democrats in the General Election debates!
3/7/2019 0:05

It was not a campaign contribution and there were no violations of the campaign finance laws by me. Fake News!
3/7/2019 14:24

We are on track to APPREHEND more than one million people coming across the Southern Border this year. Great job by Border Patrol (and others) who are working in a Broken System. Can be fixed by Congress so easily and

quickly if only the Democrats would get on board!
3/7/2019 14:38

The Wall is being built and is well under construction. Big impact will be made. Many additional contracts are close to being signed. Far ahead of schedule despite all of the Democrat Obstruction and Fake News! **3/8/2019 12:24**

I cannot believe the level of dishonesty in the media. It is totally out of control but we are winning! **3/8/2019 12:32**

PRESIDENTIAL HARASSMENT! **3/8/2019 12:34**

Unimaginable loss - Such great people! https://t.co/AV9oi8XuaE **3/8/2019 23:00**

Border Patrol and Law Enforcement has apprehended (captured) large numbers of illegal immigrants at the Border. They won't be coming into the U.S. The Wall is being built and will greatly help us in the future and now!
3/9/2019 14:07

I hope the grandstanding Governor of California is able to spend his very highly taxed citizens money on asylum holds more efficiently than money has been spent on the so-called Fast Train which is $Billions over budget & in total disarray. Time to reduce taxes in California! **3/9/2019 21:50**

Wacky Nut Job @AnnCoulter who still hasn't figured out that despite all odds and an entire Democrat Party of Far Left Radicals against me (not to mention certain Republicans who are sadly unwilling to fight) I am winning on the Border. Major sections of Wall are being built... (1/2)
3/9/2019 22:04

....and renovated with MUCH MORE to follow shortly. Tens of thousands of illegals are being apprehended (captured) at the Border and NOT allowed into our Country. With another President millions would be pouring in. I am stopping an invasion as the Wall gets built. #MAGA (2/2) **3/9/2019 22:13**

"Donald Trump's Approval Rating is at or near his highest level ever. The media is not being honest about what is happening in this Country." Jesse Watters **3/10/2019 4:32**

Despite the most hostile and corrupt media in the history of American politics the Trump Administration has accomplished more in its first two years than any other Administration. Judges biggest Tax & Regulation Cuts V.A. Choice Best Economy Lowest Unemployment & much more! **3/10/2019 12:02**

More people are working today in the United States 158000000 than at any time in our Country's history. That is a Big Deal! **3/10/2019 12:05**

"There's not one shred of evidence that President Trump has done anything wrong." @GrahamLedger One America News. So true a total Witch Hunt - All started illegally by Crooked Hillary Clinton the DNC and others! **3/10/2019 23:42**

At a recent round table meeting of business executives & long after formally introducing Tim Cook of Apple I quickly referred to Tim + Apple as Tim/Apple as an easy way to save time & words. The Fake News was disparagingly all over this & it became yet another bad Trump story! **3/11/2019 14:12**

Making Daylight Saving Time permanent is O.K. with me!

3/11/2019 14:17

Republican Senators have a very easy vote this week. It is about Border Security and the Wall (stopping Crime Drugs etc.) not Constitutionality and Precedent. It is an 80% positive issue. The Dems are 100% United as usual on a 20% issue Open Borders and Crime. Get tough R's! **3/11/2019 15:27**

"Jewish people are leaving the Democratic Party. We saw a lot of anti Israel policies start under the Obama Administration and it got worsts & worse. There is

anti-Semitism in the Democratic Party. They don't care about Israel or the Jewish people." Elizabeth Pipko Jexodus.
3/12/2019 12:12

Patrick Moore co-founder of Greenpeace: "The whole climate crisis is not only Fake News it's Fake Science. There is no climate crisis there's weather and climate all around the world and in fact carbon dioxide is the main building block of all life." @foxandfriends Wow! **3/12/2019 12:29**

Airplanes are becoming far too complex to fly. Pilots are no longer needed but rather computer scientists from MIT. I see it all the time in many products. Always seeking to go one unnecessary step further when often old and simpler is far better. Split second decisions are.... **3/12/2019 14:00**

New York State and its Governor Andrew Cuomo are now proud members of the group of PRESIDENTIAL HARASSERS. No wonder people are fleeing the State in record numbers. The Witch Hunt continues! **3/12/2019 22:17**

So many records being set with respect to our Economy. Unemployment numbers among BEST EVER. A beautiful thing to watch! **3/13/2019 4:27**

I greatly appreciate Nancy Pelosi's statement against impeachment but everyone must remember the minor fact that I never did anything wrong the Economy and Unemployment are the best ever Military and Vets are great - and many other successes! How do you impeach.... (1/2)
3/13/2019 10:50

....a man who is considered by many to be the President with the most successful first two years in history especially when he has done nothing wrong and impeachment is for "high crimes and misdemeanors"? (2/2) **3/13/2019 10:50**

"Jay Leno points out that comedy (on the very boring late night shows) is totally one-sided. It's tough when there's only one topic." @foxandfriends Actually the one-sided hatred on these shows is incredible and for me unwatchable. But remember WE are number one - President! **3/13/2019 11:15**

MAKE AMERICA GREAT AGAIN! **3/13/2019 11:17**

KEEP AMERICA GREAT! **3/13/2019 11:17**

The just revealed FBI Agent Lisa Page transcripts make the Obama Justice Department look exactly like it was a broken and corrupt machine. Hopefully justice will finally be served. Much more to come! **3/13/2019 12:21**

The Fake News photoshopped pictures of Melania then propelled conspiracy theories that it's actually not her by my side in Alabama and other places. They are only getting more deranged with time! **3/13/2019 13:44**

Republican Senators are overthinking tomorrow's vote on National Emergency. It is very simply Border Security/No Crime - Should not be thought of any other way. We have a MAJOR NATIONAL EMERGENCY at our Border and the People of our Country know it very well! **3/13/2019 16:48**

"Double Standard - Former FBI lawyer (Lisa Page) admits being told to go easy on Clinton." Very unfair! @FoxNews **3/13/2019 22:35**

I agree with Rand Paul. This is a total disgrace and should NEVER happen to another President! https://t.co/czcUbee9x7 **3/13/2019 22:52**

"Democrats are frantic to throw something else at the President. That's why you saw those 81 subpoenas. It's ridiculous. Just because your still upset over an election that happened 2 1/2 years ago you should not be allowed to ruin people's lives like this." Lara Trump @FoxNews **3/14/2019 10:28**

A big National Emergency vote today by The United States Senate on Border Security & the Wall (which is already under major construction). I am prepared to veto if necessary. The Southern Border is a National Security and Humanitarian Nightmare but it can be easily fixed! **3/14/2019 10:44**

My Administration looks forward to negotiating a large scale Trade Deal with the United Kingdom. The potential is unlimited! **3/14/2019 11:22**

The Democrats are "Border Deniers." They refuse to see or acknowledge the Death Crime Drugs and Human Trafficking at our Southern Border! **3/14/2019 11:54**

Prominent legal scholars agree that our actions to address the National Emergency at the Southern Border and to protect the American people are both CONSTITUTIONAL and EXPRESSLY authorized by Congress.... **3/14/2019 14:13**

....If at a later date Congress wants to update the law I will support those efforts but today's issue is BORDER SECURITY and Crime!!! Don't vote with Pelosi! **3/14/2019 14:13**

A vote for today's resolution by Republican Senators is a vote for Nancy Pelosi Crime and the Open Border Democrats! **3/14/2019 14:46**

VETO! **3/14/2019 19:16**

I look forward to VETOING the just passed Democrat inspired Resolution which would OPEN BORDERS while increasing Crime Drugs and Trafficking in our Country. I thank all of the Strong Republicans who voted to support Border Security and our desperately needed WALL!

3/14/2019 19:43

My warmest sympathy and best wishes goes out to the people of New Zealand after the horrible massacre in the Mosques. 49 innocent people have so senselessly died with so many more seriously injured. The U.S. stands by New Zealand for anything we can do. God bless all! **3/15/2019 11:41**

"New evidence that the Obama era team of the FBI DOJ & CIA were working together to Spy on (and take out) President Trump all the way back in 2015." A transcript of Peter Strzok's testimony is devastating. Hopefully the Mueller Report will be covering this. @OANN @ foxandfriends **3/15/2019 12:15**

So if there was knowingly & acknowledged to be "zero" crime when the Special Counsel was appointed and if the appointment was made based on the Fake Dossier (paid for by Crooked Hillary) and now disgraced Andrew McCabe (he & all stated no crime) then the Special Counsel....... (1/3) **3/15/2019 13:47**

....should never have been appointed and there should be no Mueller Report. This was an illegal & conflicted investigation in search of a crime. Russian Collusion was nothing more than an excuse by the Democrats for losing an Election that they thought they were going to win..... (2/3) **3/15/2019 13:55**

.....THIS SHOULD NEVER HAPPEN TO A PRESIDENT AGAIN! (3/3) **3/15/2019 13:56**

I'd like to thank all of the Great Republican Senators who bravely voted for Strong Border Security and the WALL. This will help stop Crime Human Trafficking and Drugs entering our Country. Watch when you get back to your State they will LOVE you more than ever before! **3/15/2019 17:42**

....that we stand in solidarity with New Zealand - and that any assistance the U.S.A. can give we stand by ready to help. We love you New Zealand! **3/15/2019 19:14**

Just spoke with Jacinda Ardern the Prime Minister of New Zealand regarding the horrific events that have taken place over the past 24 hours. I informed the Prime Minister.... **3/15/2019 19:14**

Spreading the fake and totally discredited Dossier "is unfortunately a very dark stain against John McCain." Ken Starr Former Independent Counsel. He had far worse "stains" than this including thumbs down on repeal and replace after years of campaigning to repeal and replace! **3/16/2019 20:46**

Google is helping China and their military but not the U.S. Terrible! The good news is that they helped Crooked Hillary Clinton and not Trump....and how did that turn out? **3/16/2019 21:07**

How is the Paris Environmental Accord working out for France? After 18 weeks of rioting by the Yellow Vest Protesters I guess not so well! In the meantime the United States has gone to the top of all lists on the Environment. **3/16/2019 21:22**

It's truly incredible that shows like Saturday Night Live not funny/no talent can spend all of their time knocking the same person (me) over & over without so much of a mention of "the other side." Like an advertisement without consequences. Same with Late Night Shows...... **3/17/2019 11:59**

So it was indeed (just proven in court papers) "last in his class" (Annapolis) John McCain that sent the Fake Dossier to the FBI and Media hoping to have it printed BEFORE the Election. He & the Dems working together failed (as usual). Even the Fake News refused this garbage! **3/17/2019 12:41**

Bring back @JudgeJeanine Pirro. The Radical Left Democrats working closely with their beloved partner the Fake News Media is using every trick in the book to SILENCE a majority of our Country. They have all out campaigns against @FoxNews hosts who are doing too well. Fox ..... (1/3) **3/17/2019 13:18**

....must stay strong and fight back with vigor. Stop working soooo hard on being politically correct which will only bring you down and continue to fight for our Country. The losers all want what you have don't give it to them. Be strong & prosper be weak & die! Stay true.... (2/3) **3/17/2019 13:33**

....to the people that got you there. Keep fighting for Tucker and fight hard for @JudgeJeanine. Your competitors are jealous - they all want what you've got - NUMBER ONE.

Don't hand it to them on a silver platter. They can't beat you you can only beat yourselves! (3/3) **3/17/2019 13:44**

Those Republican Senators who voted in favor of Strong Border Security (and the Wall) are being uniformly praised as they return to their States. They know there is a National Emergency at the Southern Border and they had the courage to ACT. Great job! **3/17/2019 20:58**

Just spoke to Mary Barra CEO of General Motors about the Lordstown Ohio plant. I am not happy that it is closed when everything else in our Country is BOOMING. I asked her to sell it or do something quickly. She blamed the UAW Union – I don't care I just want it open! **3/17/2019 22:27**

What the Democrats have done in trying to steal a Presidential Election first at the "ballot box" and then after that failed with the "Insurance Policy" is the biggest Scandal in the history of our Country! **3/17/2019 23:16**

MAKE AMERICA GREAT AGAIN! **3/18/2019 2:04**

....are all coming back to the U.S. So is everyone else. We now have the best Economy in the World the envy of all. Get that big beautiful plant in Ohio open now. Close a plant in China or Mexico where you invested so heavily pre-Trump but not in the U.S.A. Bring jobs home!
3/18/2019 11:45

93% Approval Rating in the Republican Party. Thank you!
3/18/2019 11:55

Joe Biden got tongue tied over the weekend when he was unable to properly deliver a very simple line about his decision to run for President. Get used to it another low I.Q. individual! **3/18/2019 13:14**

The Fake News Media is working overtime to blame me for the horrible attack in New Zealand. They will have to work very hard to prove that one. So Ridiculous! **3/18/2019 13:38**

Wow! A Suffolk/USA Today Poll just out states "50% of Americans AGREE that Robert Mueller's investigation is a Witch Hunt." @MSNBC Very few think it is legit! We will soon find out? **3/18/2019 15:07**

GDP growth during the four quarters of 2018 was the fastest since 2005. This Administration is the first on record to have experienced economic growth that meets or exceeds its own forecasts in each of its first two years in office. GROWTH is beating MARKET EXPECTATIONS! **3/18/2019 16:00**

While the press doesn't like writing about it nor do I need them to I donate my yearly Presidential salary of $400000.00 to different agencies throughout the year this to Homeland Security. If I didn't do it there would be hell to pay from the FAKE NEWS MEDIA! https://t.co/xqIGUOwh4x **3/18/2019 22:29**

The Fake News Media has NEVER been more Dishonest or Corrupt than it is right now. There has never been a time like this in American History. Very exciting but also very sad! Fake News is the absolute Enemy of the People and our Country itself! **3/19/2019 12:24**

Facebook Google and Twitter not to mention the Corrupt Media are sooo on the side of the Radical Left Democrats. But fear not we will win anyway just like we did before! #MAGA **3/19/2019 13:57**

Amazingly CNN just released a poll at 71% saying that the economy is in the best shape since 2001 18 years! WOW is CNN becoming a believer?

3/19/2019 21:28

Campaigning for the Popular Vote is much easier & different than campaigning for the Electoral College. It's like training for the 100 yard dash vs. a marathon. The brilliance of the Electoral College is that you must go to many States to win. With the Popular Vote you go to.... (1/2) **3/20/2019 2:05**

....just the large States - the Cities would end up running the Country. Smaller States & the entire Midwest would end up losing all power - & we can't let that happen. I used to like the idea of the Popular Vote but now realize the Electoral College is far better for the U.S.A. (2/2) **3/20/2019 2:17**

The Democrats are getting very "strange." They now want to change the voting age to 16 abolish the Electoral College and Increase significantly the number of Supreme Court Justices. Actually you've got to win it at the Ballot Box! **3/20/2019 4:04**

George Conway often referred to as Mr. Kellyanne Conway by those who know him is VERY jealous of his wife's success & angry that I with her help didn't give him the job he so desperately wanted. I barely know him but just take a look a stone cold LOSER & husband from hell! **3/20/2019 11:51**

I am thrilled to be here in Ohio with the hardworking men and women of the Lima Army Tank Plant! We are here today to celebrate a resounding victory for all of you for Northwest Ohio for our GREAT MILITARY and for our entire Country...https://t.co/ZWbjXOBe9m **3/20/2019 20:23**

Great news from @Ford! They are investing nearly $1 BILLION in Flat Rock Michigan for auto production on top of a $1 BILLION investment last month in a facility outside of Chicago. Companies are pouring back into the United States - they want to be where the action is! **3/20/2019 20:51**

Leaving the GREAT STATE of OHIO for the @WhiteHouse. A really great day! **3/21/2019 0:07**

"The reason we have the Special Counsel investigation is that James Comey (a dirty cop) leaked his memos to a friend who leaked them to the press on purpose." @ KennedyNation Totally illegal! **3/21/2019 2:04**

"John Solomon: As Russia Collusion fades Ukrainian plot to help Clinton emerges." @seanhannity @FoxNews **3/21/2019 2:40**

After 52 years it is time for the United States to fully recognize Israel's Sovereignty over the Golan Heights which is of critical strategic and security importance to the State of Israel and Regional Stability! **3/21/2019 16:50**

We are here today to take historic action to defend American Students and American Values. In a few moments I will be signing an Executive Order to protect FREE SPEECH on College Campuses.https://t.co/gFFnSl1bEF **3/21/2019 20:12**

Today we celebrate the lives and achievements of Americans with Down Syndrome. @VP and I will always stand with these wonderful families and together we will always stand for LIFE! #WorldDownSyndromeDay https://t.co/u7vrG7JnCP **3/21/2019 21:12**

3.1 GDP FOR THE YEAR BEST NUMBER IN 14 YEARS! **3/22/2019 10:52**

ISIS uses the internet better than almost anyone but for all of those susceptible to ISIS propaganda they are now being beaten badly at every level.... (1/2) **3/22/2019 16:15**

....There is nothing to admire about them they will always try to show a glimmer of vicious hope but they are losers and barely breathing. Think about that before you destroy your lives and the lives of your family! (2/2) **3/22/2019 16:15**

It is my pleasure to announce that @StephenMoore a very respected Economist will be nominated to serve on the Fed Board. I have known Steve for a long time - and have no doubt he will be an outstanding choice! **3/22/2019 16:47**

It was announced today by the U.S. Treasury that additional large scale Sanctions would be added to those already existing Sanctions on North Korea. I have today ordered the withdrawal of those additional Sanctions! **3/22/2019 17:22**

Today in Florida @FLOTUS and I were honored to welcome and meet with leaders from the Bahamas Dominican Republic Haiti Jamaica and Saint Lucia! https://t.co/tElFdkIYfC **3/22/2019 20:15**

Good Morning Have A Great Day! **3/24/2019 12:01**

MAKE AMERICA GREAT AGAIN! **3/24/2019 12:02**

No Collusion No Obstruction Complete and Total EXONERATION. KEEP AMERICA GREAT!

3/24/2019 20:42

"No matter your ideologies or your loyalties this is a good day for America. No American conspired to cooperate with Russia in its efforts to interfere with the 2016 election according to Robert Mueller and that is good." @BretBaier @FoxNews **3/25/2019 10:10**

"The Special Counsel did not find that the Trump Campaign or anyone associated with it conspired or coordinated with the Russian Government in these efforts despite multiple offers from Russian-affiliated individuals to assist the Trump Campaign." **3/25/2019 10:20**

"Breaking News: Mueller Report Finds No Trump-Russia Conspiracy." @MSNBC **3/25/2019 10:25**

Today it was my great honor to welcome Prime Minister @Netanyahu of Israel back to the @WhiteHouse where I signed a Presidential Proclamation recognizing Israel's sovereignty over the Golan Heights. Read more: https://t.co/yAAyR2Hxe4 https://t.co/gWp6nwRwsY **3/25/2019 18:10**

WSJ: Obama Admin Must Account for 'Abuse of Surveillance Powers' https://t.co/mIE0vOFZae via @BreitbartNews **3/26/2019 1:54**

The Mainstream Media is under fire and being scorned all over the World as being corrupt and FAKE. For two years they pushed the Russian Collusion Delusion when they always knew there was No Collusion. They truly are the Enemy of the People and the Real Opposition Party! **3/26/2019 10:54**

"What we're seeing on Capitol Hill right now is that the Democrats are walking back any charges of Collusion against the President." @ByronYork @BillHemmer Should never have been started a disgrace! **3/26/2019 14:49**

The Republican Party will become "The Party of Healthcare!" **3/26/2019 16:58**

Thank you to the House Republicans for sticking together and the BIG WIN today on the Border. Today's vote simply reaffirms Congressional Democrats are the party of Open Borders Drugs and Crime! **3/26/2019 21:31**

"I think this is probably the most consequential media screwup of the last 25 to 50 years. It is difficult to comprehend or overstate the damage that the media did to the Country to their own reputation or to the Constitution. An absolute catastrophe" Sean Davis @TuckerCarlson **3/27/2019 0:39**

The Fake News Media has lost tremendous credibility with its corrupt coverage of the illegal Democrat Witch Hunt of your all time favorite duly elected President me! T.V. ratings of CNN & MSNBC tanked last night after seeing the Mueller Report statement. @FoxNews up BIG! **3/27/2019 1:27**

Just met with @SundarPichai President of @Google who is obviously doing quite well. He stated strongly that he is totally committed to the U.S. Military not the Chinese Military.... **3/27/2019 19:38**

We are here today to award America's highest military honor to a fallen hero who made the supreme sacrifice for our nation – Staff Sergeant Travis Atkins...https://t.co/q3J8BhRnhA **3/27/2019 20:48**

The Fake News Media is going Crazy! They are suffering a major "breakdown" have ZERO credibility or respect & must be thinking about going legit. I have learned to live with Fake News which has never been more corrupt than it is right now. Someday I will tell you the secret! **3/28/2019 10:13**

Mexico is doing NOTHING to help stop the flow of illegal immigrants to our Country. They are all talk and no action. Likewise Honduras Guatemala and El Salvador have taken our money for years and do Nothing. The Dems don't care such BAD laws. May close the Southern Border! **3/28/2019 10:24**

FBI & DOJ to review the outrageous Jussie Smollett case in Chicago. It is an embarrassment to our Nation! **3/28/2019 10:34**

Congressman Adam Schiff who spent two years knowingly and unlawfully lying and leaking should be forced to resign from Congress!

3/28/2019 10:43

Wow ratings for "Morning Joe" which were really bad in the first place just "tanked" with the release of the Mueller Report. Likewise other shows on MSNBC and CNN have gone down by as much as 50%. Just shows Fake News never wins! **3/28/2019 11:04**

Very important that OPEC increase the flow of Oil. World Markets are fragile price of Oil getting too high. Thank you! **3/28/2019 12:30**

The Republican Party will become the Party of Great HealthCare! ObamaCare is a disaster far too expensive and deductibility ridiculously high - virtually unusable! Moving forward in Courts and Legislatively! **3/28/2019 19:41**

We have a National Emergency at our Southern Border. The Dems refuse to do what they know is necessary - amend our immigration laws. Would immediately solve the problem! Mexico with the strongest immigration laws in the World refuses to help with illegal immigration & drugs! **3/28/2019 19:51**

On my way to Grand Rapids Michigan right now. See you all very soon! #MAGA https://t.co/JjGAijXIRT **3/28/2019 21:06**

Beautiful #MAGARally tonight in Grand Rapids Michigan - thank you I love you! MAKE AMERICA GREAT AGAIN!! https://t.co/3xlMOaaTR5 **3/29/2019 1:16**

Massive overflow crowds in Grand Rapids Michigan tonight. Thank you for joining us tonight! #MAGA https://t.co/KQ5hTZAXsk **3/29/2019 2:30**

MAKE AMERICA GREAT AGAIN! https://t.co/Y6UPREMY7u https://t.co/6r7wdYDf66 **3/29/2019 2:41**

On this Vietnam War Veterans Day we celebrate the brave Vietnam Veterans and all of America's Veterans. Thank you for your service to our great Nation! **3/29/2019 12:48**

This has been an incredible couple of weeks for AMERICA! https://t.co/bqdB7DFx8P **3/29/2019 15:09**

The DEMOCRATS have given us the weakest immigration laws anywhere in the World. Mexico has the strongest & they make more than $100 Billion a year on the U.S. Therefore CONGRESS MUST CHANGE OUR WEAK IMMIGRATION LAWS NOW & Mexico must stop illegals from entering the U.S.... (1/3) **3/29/2019 15:23**

....through their country and our Southern Border. Mexico has for many years made a fortune off of the U.S. far greater than Border Costs. If Mexico doesn't immediately stop ALL illegal immigration coming into the United States throug our Southern Border I will be CLOSING..... (2/3) **3/29/2019 15:37**

....the Border or large sections of the Border next week. This would be so easy for Mexico to do but they just take our money and "talk." Besides we lose so much money with them especially when you add in drug trafficking etc.) that the Border closing would be a good thing! (3/3)

3/29/2019 15:43

Had the Fed not mistakenly raised interest rates especially since there is very little inflation and had they not done the ridiculously timed quantitative tightening the 3.0% GDP & Stock Market would have both been much higher & World Markets would be in a better place! **3/29/2019 21:41**

Robert Mueller was a Hero to the Radical Left Democrats until he ruled that there was No Collusion with Russia (so ridiculous to even say!). After more than two years since the "insurance policy" statement was made by a dirty cop I got the answers I wanted the Truth..... (1/2) **3/29/2019 22:31**

...The problem is no matter what the Radical Left Democrats get no matter what we give them it will never be enough. Just watch they will Harass & Complain & Resist (the theme of their movement). So maybe we should just take our victory and say NO we've got a Country to run! (2/2)

3/29/2019 23:15

So funny that The New York Times & The Washington Post got a Pulitzer Prize for their coverage (100% NEGATIVE and FAKE!) of Collusion with Russia - And there was No Collusion! So they were either duped or corrupt? In any event their prizes should be taken away by the Committee!

3/29/2019 23:25

In honor of his past service to our Country Navy Seal #EddieGallagher will soon be moved to less restrictive confinement while he awaits his day in court. Process should move quickly! @foxandfriends @RepRalphNorman

3/30/2019 12:14

It would be so easy to fix our weak and very stupid Democrat inspired immigration laws. In less than one hour and then a vote the problem would be solved. But the Dems don't care about the crime they don't want any victory for Trump and the Republicans even if good for USA! **3/30/2019 20:31**

Mexico must use its very strong immigration laws to stop the many thousands of people trying to get into the USA. Our detention areas are maxed out & we will take no more illegals. Next step is to close the Border! This will also help us with stopping the Drug flow from Mexico! **3/30/2019 20:36**

"The Trump Administration has succeeded in dramatically raising the costs to Iran for its sinister behavior at no cost to the U.S. or our allies. That's the definition of a foreign-policy achievement." Bret Stephens @nytimes We are getting stronger all over the world watch! **3/30/2019 22:24**

Everybody is asking how the phony and fraudulent investigation of the No Collusion No Obstruction Trump Campaign began. We need to know for future generations to understand. This Hoax should never be allowed to happen to another President or Administration again!

3/31/2019 19:21

"Outrageous it's the Adam Schiff problem. People abusing the access to classified data to then go out in public and make allegations that didn't prove to be true. You look at a decision to essentially investigate a political rival. Who made it?" James Freeman @WSJ **3/31/2019 19:39**

The Democrats are allowing a ridiculous asylum system and major loopholes to remain as a mainstay of our immigration system. Mexico is likewise doing NOTHING a very bad combination for our Country. Homeland Security is being sooo very nice but not for long! **3/31/2019 23:41**

APRIL 2019 – JUNE 2019

★★★★★★★★★★★★★★★★★★★★★★★★★★

As Trump and his opponents continue to skirmish over the interpretation of the Mueller Report, House Democrats champion open borders but Trump pushes back fiercely against illegal entry into the U.S. Sanctuary cities pop up throughout the U.S. in support of undocumented immigrants. Tiger Woods wins the Masters. As Joe Biden enters the race, stories about the role of the Steele Dossier abound. Attorney General William Barr begins to look into the potentially illegal actions of the FBI and the DOJ where spying on the Trump campaign and the Trump presidency are concerned. With conflicts over trade with China escalating, Trump levies heavy import taxes on them. Meanwhile, the Democrats in the House continue to oppose Trump at every turn. As talk of impeachment escalates, Trump threatens Mexico with tariffs if the caravans continue. Mexico blinks and turns back the caravans, ending this crisis.

Democrats working with Republicans in Congress can fix the Asylum and other loopholes quickly. We have a major National Emergency at our Border. GET IT DONE NOW!

4/1/2019 12:13

Can you believe that the Radical Left Democrats want to do our new and very important Census Report without the all important Citizenship Question. Report would be meaningless and a waste of the $Billions (ridiculous) that it costs to put together! **4/1/2019 13:03**

The cost of ObamaCare is far too high for our great citizens. The deductibles in many cases way over $7000 make it almost worthless or unusable. Good things are going to happen! @SenRickScott @senatemajldr @SenJohnBarrasso @SenBillCassidy **4/1/2019 13:41**

No matter what information is given to the crazed Democrats from the No Collusion Mueller Report it will never be good enough. Behind closed doors the Dems are laughing! **4/1/2019 14:43**

Democrats should stop fighting Sen. David Perdue's disaster relief bill. They are blocking funding and relief for our great farmers and rural America! **4/1/2019 16:47**

....are GREAT but the politicians are incompetent or corrupt. Puerto Rico got far more money than Texas & Florida combined yet their government can't do anything right the place is a mess - nothing works. FEMA & the Military worked emergency miracles but politicians like..... **4/2/2019 3:11**

Puerto Rico got 91 Billion Dollars for the hurricane more money than has ever been gotten for a hurricane before & all their local politicians do is complain & ask for more money. The pols are grossly incompetent spend the money foolishly or corruptly & only take from USA.... (1/2)

4/2/2019 11:33

....The best thing that ever happened to Puerto Rico is President Donald J. Trump. So many wonderful people but with such bad Island leadership and with so much money wasted. Cannot continue to hurt our Farmers and States with these massive payments and so little appreciation! (2/2) **4/2/2019 11:45**

Robert Mueller was a God-like figure to the Democrats until he ruled No Collusion in the long awaited $30000000 Mueller Report. Now the Dems don't even acknowledge his name have become totally unhinged and would like to go through the whole process again. It won't happen! **4/2/2019 12:46**

There is no amount of testimony or document production that can satisfy Jerry Nadler or Shifty Adam Schiff. It is now time to focus exclusively on properly running our great Country! **4/2/2019 12:54**

After many years (decades) Mexico is apprehending large numbers of people at their Southern Border mostly from Guatemala Honduras and El Salvador. They have ALL been taking U.S. money for years and doing ABSOLUTELY NOTHING for us just like the Democrats in Congress! **4/2/2019 14:41**

"I haven't seen any Democrats down here at the Border working with us or asking to speak to any of us. They have an open invitation. We are getting overrun our facilities are overcapacity. We are at an emergency crisis." Art Del Cueto National Border Patrol Council. **4/2/2019 14:52**

I was never planning a vote prior to the 2020 Election on the wonderful HealthCare package that some very talented people are now developing for me & the Republican Party. It will be on full display during the Election as a much better & less expensive alternative to ObamaCare... **4/3/2019 13:26**

Congress must get together and immediately eliminate the loopholes at the Border! If no action Border or large sections of Border will close. This is a National Emergency! **4/3/2019 13:45**

The First Step Act proves that our Country can achieve amazing breakthroughs when we put politics aside and put the interests of ALL Americans FIRST. https://t.co/dTKubkIBQn https://t.co/kILIFjXglO **4/3/2019 17:09**

THE REPUBLICAN PARTY IS THE PARTY OF THE AMERICAN DREAM! **4/4/2019 11:49**

According to polling few people seem to care about the Russian Collusion Hoax but some Democrats are fighting hard to keep the Witch Hunt alive. They should focus on legislation or even better an investigation of how the ridiculous Collusion Delusion got started - so illegal! **4/4/2019 12:22**

There is nothing we can ever give to the Democrats that will make them happy. This is the highest level of Presidential Harassment in the history of our Country! **4/4/2019 12:46**

The New York Times had no legitimate sources which would be totally illegal concerning the Mueller Report. In fact they probably had no sources at all! They are a Fake News paper who have already been forced to apologize for their incorrect and very bad reporting on me! **4/4/2019 15:04**

"Conservative support for Trump wall soars to 99 percent" https://t.co/Tblpox8Nsg **4/4/2019 23:45**

....However if for any reason Mexico stops apprehending and bringing the illegals back to where they came from the U.S. will be forced to Tariff at 25% all cars made in Mexico and shipped over the Border to us. If that doesn't work which it will I will close the Border....... **4/5/2019 13:11**

Heading to the Southern Border to show a section of the new Wall being built! Leaving now! **4/5/2019 13:22**

I've employed thousands of Electrical Workers. They will be voting for me! **4/5/2019 16:44**

The press is doing everything within their power to fight the magnificence of the phrase MAKE AMERICA GREAT AGAIN! They can't stand the fact that this Administration has done more than virtually any other Administration in its first 2yrs. They are truly the ENEMY OF THE PEOPLE!

4/5/2019 17:41

Will soon be landing in Calexico California to look at a portion of the new WALL being built on our Southern Border. Within two years we will have close to 400 miles built or under construction & keeping our Country SAFE - not easy when the Dems are always fighting to stop you!

4/5/2019 17:48

Just checked out the new Wall on the Border - GREAT! Leaving now for L.A.

4/5/2019 22:16

So let's get this straight! There was No Collusion and in fact the Phony Dossier was a Con Job that was paid for by Crooked Hillary and the DNC. So the 13 Angry Democrats were investigating an event that never happened and that was in fact a made up Fraud. I just fought back.... (1/2)

4/6/2019 15:52

.... against something I knew never existed Collusion with Russia (so ridiculous!) - No Obstruction. This Russia Hoax must never happen to another President and Law Enforcement must find out HOW DID IT START? (2/2)

4/6/2019 15:57

Why should I be defending a fraudulent Russian Witch Hunt. It's about time the perpetrators of this fraud on me and the American People start defending their dishonest and treasonous acts. How and why did this terrible event begin? Never Forget!

4/6/2019 20:19

....it's powerful common sense Immigration Laws to stop illegals from coming through Mexico into the U.S. and removing them back to their country of origin. Until Mexico cleans up this ridiculous & massive migration we will be

focusing on Border Security not Ports of Entry.... (1/2)
4/6/2019 23:36

....In the meantime the Democrats in Congress must help the Republicans (we need their votes) to end the horrible costly and foolish loopholes in our Immigration Laws. Once that happens all will be smooth. We can NEVER allow Open Borders! (2/2) **4/6/2019 23:36**

Looks like Bob Mueller's team of 13 Trump Haters & Angry Democrats are illegally leaking information to the press while the Fake News Media make up their own stories with or without sources - sources no longer matter to our corrupt & dishonest Mainstream Media they are a Joke!
4/7/2019 13:50

Pleased to report that the American tourist and tour guide that were abducted in Uganda have been released. God bless them and their families! **4/7/2019 19:50**

Secretary of Homeland Security Kirstjen Nielsen will be leaving her position and I would like to thank her for her service.... (1/2) **4/7/2019 22:02**

....I am pleased to announce that Kevin McAleenan the current U.S. Customs and Border Protection Commissioner will become Acting Secretary for @DHSgov. I have confidence that Kevin will do a great job! (2/2) **4/7/2019 22:02**

More apprehensions (captures)at the Southern Border than in many years. Border Patrol amazing! Country is FULL! System has been broken for many years. Democrats in Congress must agree to fix loopholes - No Open Borders (Crimes & Drugs). Will Close Southern Border If necessary... (1/2) **4/8/2019 0:45**

....Mexico must apprehend all illegals and not let them make the long march up to the United States or we will have no other choice than to Close the Border and/or institute Tariffs. Our Country is FULL! (2/2) **4/8/2019 1:03**

"The reason the whole process seems so politicized is that Democrats made up this complete lie about Collusion ....and none of it happened." Charles Hurt. The Russian Hoax never happened it was a fraud on the American people! **4/8/2019 11:39**

Uganda must find the kidnappers of the American Tourist and guide before people will feel safe in going there. Bring them to justice openly and quickly! **4/8/2019 12:22**

The Democrats will never be satisfied no matter what they get how much they get or how many pages they get. It will never end but that's the way life goes! **4/8/2019 16:48**

Congressman Jerry Nadler fought me for years on a very large development I built on the West Side of Manhattan. He wanted a Rail Yard built underneath the development or even better to stop the job. He didn't get either & the development became VERY successful. Nevertheless.... **4/9/2019 12:16**

The Mainstream Media has never been more inaccurate or corrupt than it is today. It only seems to get worse. So much Fake News! **4/9/2019 12:44**

Check this out - TRUTH! https://t.co/2HNVeEpKDu **4/9/2019 18:32**

MAKE AMERICA GREAT AGAIN! https://t.co/diXWQHuyGj **4/9/2019 20:43**

The Democrats must end the loopholes on immigration. So easy to solve! **4/10/2019 1:22**

Everybody is now acknowledging that right from the time I announced my run for President I was 100% correct on the Border. Remember the heat I took? Democrats should now get rid of the loopholes. The Border is being fixed. Mexico will not let people through! **4/10/2019 2:22**

Trump flags being waived at the Bibi @Netanyahu VICTORY celebration last night! https://t.co/SX8RVAALYW **4/10/2019 14:48**

Spoke to Bibi @Netanyahu to congratulate him on a great and hard-fought win. The United States is with him and the People of Israel all the way! https://t.co/OfFI6aKSOb
4/10/2019 19:17

So it has now been determined by 18 people that truly hate President Trump that there was No Collusion with Russia. In fact it was an illegal investigation that should never have been allowed to start. I fought back hard against this Phony & Treasonous Hoax! **4/10/2019 19:45**

I think what the Democrats are doing with the Border is TREASONOUS. Their Open Border mindset is putting our Country at risk. Will not let this happen! **4/11/2019 2:33**

Too bad that the European Union is being so tough on the United Kingdom and Brexit. The E.U. is likewise a brutal trading partner with the United States which will change. Sometimes in life you have to let people breathe before it all comes back to bite you! **4/11/2019 2:52**

Beautiful afternoon in the Oval Office today with a few great American HEROES! https://t.co/HYEI83NVrm
4/11/2019 21:23

House Democrats want to negotiate a $2 TRILLION spending increase but can't even pass their own plan. We can't afford it anyway and it's not happening! **4/11/2019 23:14**

JOBLESS CLAIMS AT 50 YEAR LOW! **4/12/2019 0:46**

President Obama's top White House lawyer Gregory B. Craig was indicted yesterday on very serious charges. This is a really big story but the Fake News New York Times didn't even put it on page one rather page 16. @ washingtonpost not much better "tiny" page one. Corrupt News! **4/12/2019 13:37**

Due to the fact that Democrats are unwilling to change our very dangerous immigration laws we are indeed as reported giving strong considerations to placing Illegal Immigrants in Sanctuary Cities only.... (1/2) **4/12/2019 16:38**

....The Radical Left always seems to have an Open Borders Open Arms policy - so this should make them very happy! (2/2) **4/12/2019 16:38**

WE WILL NEVER FORGET! https://t.co/VxrGFRFeJM

4/12/2019 21:35

If the Radical Left Democrats all of a sudden don't want the Illegal Migrants in their Sanctuary Cities (no more open arms) why should others be expected to take them into their communities? Go home and come into our Country legally and through a system of Merit! **4/13/2019 2:30**

Another Fake Story on @NBCNews that I offered Pardons to Homeland Securiy personnel in case they broke the law regarding illegal immigration and sanctuary cities. Of course this is not true. Mainstream Media is corrupt and getting worse if that is possible every day! **4/13/2019 3:33**

In New York State Democrats blocked a Bill expanding College Tuition for Gold Star families after approving aid for illegal immigrants. No wonder so many people are leaving N.Y. Very Sad! **4/13/2019 3:51**

I agree with Kim Jong Un of North Korea that our personal relationship remains very good perhaps the term excellent would be even more accurate and that a third Summit would be good in that we fully understand where we each stand. North Korea has tremendous potential for.......

4/13/2019 11:54

Why should Radical Left Democrats in Congress have a right to retry and examine the $35000000 (two years in the making) No Collusion Mueller Report when the crime committed was by Crooked Hillary the DNC and Dirty Cops? Attorney General Barr will make the decision!

4/13/2019 12:21

....When I won the Election in 2016 the @nytimes had to beg their fleeing subscribers for forgiveness in that they covered the Election (and me) so badly. They didn't have a clue it was pathetic. They even apologized to me. But now they are even worse really corrupt reporting! **4/13/2019 23:38**

I never offered Pardons to Homeland Security Officials never ordered anyone to close our Southern Border (although I have the absolute right to do so and may if Mexico does not apprehend the illegals coming to our Border) and am not "frustrated." It is all Fake & Corrupt News! **4/13/2019 23:51**

....So interesting to see the Mayor of Oakland and other Sanctuary Cities NOT WANT our currently "detained immigrants" after release due to the ridiculous court ordered 20 day rule. If they don't want to serve our Nation by taking care of them why should other cities & towns? **4/14/2019 0:01**

Democrats must change the Immigration Laws FAST. If not Sanctuary Cities must immediately ACT to take care of the Illegal Immigrants - and this includes Gang Members Drug Dealers Human Traffickers and Criminals of all shapes sizes and kinds. CHANGE THE LAWS NOW! **4/14/2019 0:08**

Just out: The USA has the absolute legal right to have apprehended illegal immigrants transferred to Sanctuary Cities. We hereby demand that they be taken care of at the highest level especially by the State of California which is well known or its poor management & high taxes!

4/14/2019 1:47

If the Fed had done its job properly which it has not the Stock Market would have been up 5000 to 10000 additional points and GDP would have been well over

4% instead of 3%...with almost no inflation. Quantitative tightening was a killer should have done the exact opposite!
4/14/2019 14:04

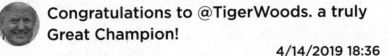

Congratulations to @TigerWoods. a truly Great Champion!
4/14/2019 18:36

Love people who are great under pressure. What a fantastic life comeback for a really great guy!
https://t.co/41MtJtYEjq **4/14/2019 19:10**

Such a "puff piece" on Nancy Pelosi by @60minutes yet her leadership has passed no meaningful Legislation. All they do is Investigate as it turns out crimes that they instigated & committed. The Mueller No Collusion decision wasn't even discussed-and she was a disaster at W.H. **4/15/2019 0:28**

What do I know about branding maybe nothing (but I did become President!) but if I were Boeing I would FIX the Boeing 737 MAX add some additional great features & REBRAND the plane with a new name.No product has suffered like this one. But again what the hell do I know?
4/15/2019 10:29

Mueller and the A.G. based on Mueller findings (and great intelligence) have already ruled No Collusion No Obstruction. These were crimes committed by Crooked Hillary the DNC Dirty Cops and others! INVESTIGATE THE INVESTIGATORS! **4/15/2019 11:15**

Congress should come back to D.C. now and FIX THE IMMIGRATION LAWS! **4/15/2019 11:28**

Before Nancy who has lost all control of Congress and is getting nothing done decides to defend her leader Rep. Omar she should look at the anti-Semitic anti-Israel and ungrateful U.S. HATE statements Omar has made. She is out of control except for her control of Nancy! **4/15/2019 13:30**

THEY SPIED ON MY CAMPAIGN (We will never forget)!
4/15/2019 13:52

I finally agree with @Cher! https://t.co/i5acSgUrCk
4/15/2019 15:33

Mark Morgan President Obama's Border Patrol Chief gave the following message to me: "President Trump stay the course." I agree and believe it or not we are making great progress with a system that has been broken for many years!
4/15/2019 15:33

Those Illegal Immigrants who can no longer be legally held (Congress must fix the laws and loopholes) will be subject to Homeland Security given to Sanctuary Cities and States!
4/15/2019 16:05

The Mueller Report which was written by 18 Angry Democrats who also happen to be Trump Haters (and Clinton Supporters) should have focused on the people who SPIED on my 2016 Campaign and others who fabricated the whole Russia Hoax. That is never forget the crime.....
4/15/2019 16:21

....Since there was no Collusion why was there an Investigation in the first place! Answer - Dirty Cops Dems and Crooked Hillary!
4/15/2019 16:24

Spoke to @TigerWoods to congratulate him on the great victory he had in yesterday's @TheMasters & to inform him that because of his incredible Success & Comeback in Sports (Golf) and more importantly LIFE I will be presenting him with the PRESIDENTIAL MEDAL OF FREEDOM!

4/15/2019 17:35

So horrible to watch the massive fire at Notre Dame Cathedral in Paris. Perhaps flying water tankers could be used to put it out. Must act quickly! **4/15/2019 17:39**

The forgotten voters of the 2016 Election are now doing great. The Steel Industry is rebuilding and expanding at a pace that it hasn't seen in decades. Our Country has one of the best Economies in many years perhaps ever. Unemployment numbers best in 51 years. Wow! **4/15/2019 21:57**

God bless the people of France!
4/15/2019 21:58

A must read Andy McCarthy's column today "Dirty dealings of dirt devils who concocted Trump-Russia probe." The greatest Scam in political history. If the Mainstream Media were honest which they are not this story would be bigger and more important than Watergate. Someday! **4/16/2019 13:02**

No Collusion - No Obstruction! **4/16/2019 13:34**

So weird to watch Crazy Bernie on @FoxNews. Not surprisingly @BretBaier and the "audience" was so smiley and nice. Very strange and now we have @donnabrazile? **4/16/2019 14:11**

Many Trump Fans & Signs were outside of the @FoxNews Studio last night in the now thriving (Thank you President Trump) Bethlehem Pennsylvania for the interview with Crazy Bernie Sanders. Big complaints about not being let in-stuffed with Bernie supporters. What's with @FoxNews? **4/17/2019 0:57**

Bernie Sanders and wife should pay the Pre-Trump Taxes on their almost $600000 in income. He is always complaining about these big TAX CUTS except when it benefits him. They made a fortune off of Trump but so did everyone else - and that's a good thing not a bad thing! **4/17/2019 1:11**

I believe it will be Crazy Bernie Sanders vs. Sleepy Joe Biden as the two finalists to run against maybe the best Economy in the history of our Country (and MANY other great things)! I look forward to facing whoever it may be. May God Rest Their Soul! **4/17/2019 1:24**

Wow! FBI made 11 payments to Fake Dossier's discredited author Trump hater Christopher Steele. @OANN @ JudicialWatch The Witch Hunt has been a total fraud on your President and the American people! It was brought to you by Dirty Cops Crooked Hillary and the DNC. **4/17/2019 11:34**

Democrats in Congress must return from their Vacations and change the Immigration Laws or the Border despite the great job being done by Border Patrol will only get worse. Big sections of Wall now being built! **4/17/2019 11:45**

Just had a wonderful conversation with @Pontifex Francis offering condolences from the People of the United States for the horrible and destructive fire at Notre Dame Cathedral. I offered the help of our great experts on renovation and construction as I did.... (1/2) **4/17/2019 16:14**

....in my conversation yesterday with President @ EmmanuelMacron of France. I also wished both Pope Francis and President Macron a very Happy Easter! (2/2)
4/17/2019 16:14

The Greatest Political Hoax of all time! Crimes were committed by Crooked Dirty Cops and DNC/The Democrats. **4/18/2019 11:54**

PRESIDENTIAL HARASSMENT! **4/18/2019 12:07**

No Collusion - No Obstruction! https://t.co/diggF8V3hl
4/18/2019 12:54

As I have been saying all along NO COLLUSION - NO OBSTRUCTION! https://t.co/BnMB5mvHAM **4/18/2019 16:59**

"Donald Trump was being framed he fought back. That is not Obstruction." @JesseBWatters I had the right to end the whole Witch Hunt if I wanted. I could have fired everyone including Mueller if I wanted. I chose not to. I had the RIGHT to use Executive Privilege. I didn't! **4/18/2019 21:31**

Anything the Russians did concerning the 2016 Election was done while Obama was President. He was told about it and did nothing! Most importantly the vote was not affected. **4/18/2019 23:28**

When there is not an underlying crime with regard to Collusion (in fact the whole thing was a made up fraud) it is difficult to say that someone is obstructing something. There was no underlying crime." @marthamaccallum @ FoxNews **4/18/2019 23:46**

"If dozens of Federal prosecutors spent two years trying to charge you with a crime and found they couldn't it would mean there wasn't any evidence you did it - and that's what happened here - that's what we just learned from the Mueller Report." @TuckerCarlson **4/19/2019 0:27**

"The Mueller Report is perhaps the single most humiliating thing that has ever happened to the White House Press in the history of this Country. They know they lied...Many reporters lied about Russia Collusion and so much more. Clapper & Brennan all lies" @TuckerCarlson **4/19/2019 0:38**

Kimberley Strassel should get the Pulitzer. She is a treasure (and I don't know her) who correctly called the Russia Hoax right from the start! Others who were soooo wrong will get the Prize. Fake News! https://t.co/TJJPY5MM6X **4/19/2019 2:34**

Statements are made about me by certain people in the Crazy Mueller Report in itself written by 18 Angry Democrat Trump Haters which are fabricated & totally untrue. Watch out for people that take so-called "notes" when the notes never existed until needed. Because I never.... **4/19/2019 11:53**

...agreed to testify it was not necessary for me to respond to statements made in the "Report" about me some of which are total bullshit & only given to make the other person look good (or me to look bad). This was an Illegally Started Hoax that never should have happened a... **4/19/2019 12:08**

....big fat waste of time energy and money - $30000000 to be exact. It is now finally time to turn the tables and bring justice to some very sick and dangerous people who have committed very serious crimes perhaps even Spying or Treason. This should never happen again!

4/19/2019 20:47

"TRUMP HAS BEEN TOTALLY VINDICATED" https://t.co/ZjmmVD1T4z **4/19/2019 22:51**

Wishing a Happy Passover to all those celebrating in America Israel and around the world! https://t.co/h3wgLZ4mxS **4/19/2019 23:10**

Despite the fact that the Mueller Report should not have been authorized in the first place & was written as nastily as possible by 13 (18) Angry Democrats who were true Trump Haters including highly conflicted Bob Mueller himself the end result is No Collusion No Obstruction! **4/20/2019 11:53**

The Fake News Media is doing everything possible to stir up and anger the pols and as many people as possible seldom mentioning the fact that the Mueller Report had as its principle conclusion the fact that there was NO COLLUSION WITH RUSSIA. The Russia Hoax is dead! **4/20/2019 12:02**

United States weekly jobless claims just hit a 50 year low. The economy is doing GREAT! **4/20/2019 12:07**

The end result of the greatest Witch Hunt in U.S. political history is No Collusion with Russia (and No Obstruction). Pretty Amazing! **4/20/2019 12:15**

If @MittRomney spent the same energy fighting Barack Obama as he does fighting Donald Trump he could have won the race (maybe)! https://t.co/p5imhMJqS1

4/20/2019 22:09

Happy Easter! I have never been happier or more content because your Country is doing so well with an Economy that is the talk of the World and may be stronger than it has ever been before. Have a great day!

4/21/2019 11:04

138 people have been killed in Sri Lanka with more that 600 badly injured in a terrorist attack on churches and hotels. The United States offers heartfelt condolences to the great people of Sri Lanka. We stand ready to help! **4/21/2019 11:20**

Do you believe this? The New York Times Op-Ed: MEDIA AND DEMOCRATS OWE TRUMP AN APOLOGY. Well they got that one right! **4/21/2019 11:40**

The Trump Haters and Angry Democrats who wrote the Mueller Report were devastated by the No Collusion finding! Nothing but a total "hit job" which should never have been allowed to start in the first place! **4/21/2019 12:37**

Despite No Collusion No Obstruction The Radical Left Democrats do not want to go on to Legislate for the good of the people but only to Investigate and waste time. This is costing our Country greatly and will cost the Dems big time in 2020! **4/21/2019 12:51**

Jobless claims in the United States have reached their lowest (BEST) level in over 50 years! **4/21/2019 13:55**

Can you believe that I had to go through the worst and most corrupt political Witch Hunt in the history of the United States (No Collusion) when it was the "other side" that illegally created the diversionary & criminal event and even spied on my campaign? Disgraceful! **4/21/2019 14:23**

How do you impeach a Republican President for a crime that was committed by the Democrats? MAKE AMERICA GREAT AGAIN! **4/21/2019 22:35**

Only high crimes and misdemeanors can lead to impeachment. There were no crimes by me (No Collusion No Obstruction) so you can't impeach. It was the Democrats that committed the crimes not your Republican President! Tables are finally turning on the Witch Hunt! **4/22/2019 13:47**

My friend Herman Cain a truly wonderful man has asked me not to nominate him for a seat on the Federal Reserve Board. I will respect his wishes. Herman is a great American who truly loves our Country! **4/22/2019 16:16**

Spoke to Prime Minister Ranil Wickremesinghe of Sri Lanka this morning to inform him that the United States stands by him and his country in the fight against terrorism. Also expressed condolences on behalf of myself and the People of the United States! **4/22/2019 18:05**

Isn't it amazing that the people who were closest to me by far and knew the Campaign better than anyone were never even called to testify before Mueller. The reason is that the 18 Angry Democrats knew they would all say 'NO COLLUSION' and only very good things! **4/22/2019 19:31**

Paul Krugman of the Fake News New York Times has lost all credibility as has the Times itself with his false and highly inaccurate writings on me. He is obsessed with hatred just as others are obsessed with how stupid he is. He said Market would crash Only Record Highs! **4/23/2019 9:59**

I wonder if the New York Times will apologize to me a second time as they did after the 2016 Election. But this one will have to be a far bigger & better apology. On this one they will have to get down on their knees & beg for

forgiveness-they are truly the Enemy of the People!
4/23/2019 10:08

I will be going to Green Bay Wisconsin for a really big Rally on Saturday Evening. Big crowd expected much to talk about. MAKE AMERICA GREAT AGAIN! **4/23/2019 10:14**

In the "old days" if you were President and you had a good economy you were basically immune from criticism. Remember "It's the economy stupid." Today I have as President perhaps the greatest economy in history...and to the Mainstream Media it means NOTHING. But it will!
4/23/2019 10:27

"The best thing ever to happen to Twitter is Donald Trump." @MariaBartiromo So true but they don't treat me well as a Republican. Very discriminatory hard for people to sign on. Constantly taking people off list. Big complaints from many people. Different names-over 100 M..... **4/23/2019 11:26**

The Wall is being rapidly built! The Economy is GREAT! Our Country is Respected again! **4/23/2019 11:46**

KEEP AMERICA GREAT!
4/23/2019 11:47

You mean the Stock Market hit an all-time record high today and they're actually talking impeachment!? Will I ever be given credit for anything by the Fake News Media or Radical Liberal Dems? NO COLLUSION! **4/23/2019 22:43**

"Former CIA analyst Larry Johnson accuses United Kingdom Intelligence of helping Obama Administration Spy on the 2016 Trump Presidential Campaign." @OANN WOW! It is now just a question of time before the truth comes out and when it does it will be a beauty! **4/24/2019 11:04**

The American people deserve to know who is in this Country. Yesterday the Supreme Court took up the Census

Citizenship question a really big deal. MAKE AMERICA GREAT AGAIN! **4/24/2019 11:18**

A very big Caravan of over 20000 people started up through Mexico. It has been reduced in size by Mexico but is still coming. Mexico must apprehend the remainder or we will be forced to close that section of the Border & call up the Military. The Coyotes & Cartels have weapons! **4/24/2019 11:25**

Mexico's Soldiers recently pulled guns on our National Guard Soldiers probably as a diversionary tactic for drug smugglers on the Border. Better not happen again! We are now sending ARMED SOLDIERS to the Border. Mexico is not doing nearly enough in apprehending & returning! **4/24/2019 12:00**

The Mueller Report despite being written by Angry Democrats and Trump Haters and with unlimited money behind it ($35000000) didn't lay a glove on me. I DID NOTHING WRONG. If the partisan Dems ever tried to Impeach I would first head to the U.S. Supreme Court. Not only...... **4/24/2019 12:10**

Can anyone comprehend what a GREAT job Border Patrol and Law Enforcement is doing on our Southern Border. So far this year they have APPREHENDED 418000 plus illegal immigrants way up from last year. Mexico is doing very little for us. DEMS IN CONGRESS MUST ACT NOW! **4/24/2019 13:34**

No Collusion No Obstruction - there has NEVER been a President who has been more transparent. Millions of pages of documents were given to the Mueller Angry Dems plus I allowed everyone to testify including W.H. counsel. I didn't have to do this but now they want more..... **4/24/2019 13:47**

....Congress has no time to legislate they only want to continue the Witch Hunt which I have already won. They should start looking at The Criminals who are already very well known to all. This was a Rigged System - WE WILL DRAIN THE SWAMP! **4/24/2019 13:52**

Rep. Alexandria Ocasio-Cortez is correct the VA is not broken it is doing great. But that is only because of the Trump Administration. We got Veterans Choice & Accountability passed. "President Trump deserves a lot of credit." Dan Caldwell Concerned Veterans of America
4/24/2019 16:54

The Great State of Tennessee is so close to passing School Choice. All of our Nation's children regardless of background deserve a shot at achieving the American Dream! Time to get this done so important! **4/24/2019 23:01**

As has been incorrectly reported by the Fake News Media I never told then White House Counsel Don McGahn to fire Robert Mueller even though I had the legal right to do so. If I wanted to fire Mueller I didn't need McGahn to do it I could have done it myself. Nevertheless.... (1/2) **4/25/2019 11:47**

....Mueller was NOT fired and was respectfully allowed to finish his work on what I and many others say was an illegal investigation (there was no crime) headed by a Trump hater who was highly conflicted and a group of 18 VERY ANGRY Democrats. DRAIN THE SWAMP! (2/2) **4/25/2019 11:57**

Welcome to the race Sleepy Joe. I only hope you have the intelligence long in doubt to wage a successful primary campaign. It will be nasty - you will be dealing with people who truly have some very sick & demented ideas. But if you make it I will see you at the Starting Gate!
4/25/2019 12:22

Our Border Control Agents have done an incredible job under very adverse conditions. I am very proud to have increased their salaries because of the great job they do. Nobody deserves it more. THANK YOU and keep up the outstanding work! https://t.co/ljy3hZOgfL **4/25/2019 18:09**

No money was paid to North Korea for Otto Warmbier not two Million Dollars not anything else. This is not the Obama Administration that paid 1.8 Billion Dollars for four hostages or gave five terroist hostages plus who soon went back to battle for traitor Sgt. Bergdahl! **4/26/2019 11:12**

"President Donald J. Trump is the greatest hostage negotiator that I know of in the history of the United States. 20 hostages many in impossible circumstances have been released in last two years. No money was paid." Cheif Hostage Negotiator USA! **4/26/2019 11:32**

Weirdo Tom Steyer who didn't have the "guts" or money to run for President is still trying to remain relevant by putting himself on ads begging for impeachment. He doesn't mention the fact that mine is perhaps the most successful first 2 year presidency in history & NO C OR O! **4/26/2019 12:39**

Just out: Real GDP for First Quarter grew 3.2% at an annual rate. This is far above expectations or projections. Importantly inflation VERY LOW. MAKE AMERICA GREAT AGAIN! **4/26/2019 14:25**

Great NRA crowd and enthusiasm in Indiana. Thank you! Leaving now for meetings in the Oval Office. **4/26/2019 17:34**

THANK YOU @NRA! #NRAAM https://t.co/SWkpe1eFhT **4/26/2019 22:57**

Congratulations to Nick Bosa on being picked number two in the NFL Draft. You will be a great player for years to come maybe one of the best. Big Talent! San Francisco will embrace you but most importantly always stay true to yourself. MAKE AMERICA GREAT AGAIN! **4/27/2019 12:06**

Thoughts and prayers to all of those affected by the shooting at the Synagogue in Poway California. God bless you all. Suspect apprehended. Law enforcement did outstanding job. Thank you! **4/27/2019 21:41**

Sincerest THANK YOU to our great Border Patrol Agent who stopped the shooter at the Synagogue in Poway

California. He may have been off duty but his talents for Law Enforcement weren't! **4/27/2019 22:47**

Beautiful #TrumpRally tonight in Green Bay Wisconsin with a massive crowd. Thank you for joining me I love you! #MAGA https://t.co/JRyhOXH7EE **4/28/2019 1:58**

Thank you to brilliant and highly respected attorney Alan Dershowitz for destroying the very dumb legal argument of "Judge" Andrew Napolitano.... (1/2) **4/28/2019 2:57**

....Ever since Andrew came to my office to ask that I appoint him to the U.S. Supreme Court and I said NO he has been very hostile! Also asked for pardon for his friend. A good "pal" of low ratings Shepard Smith. (2/2) **4/28/2019 2:57**

The Democratic National Committee sometimes referred to as the DNC is again working its magic in its quest to destroy Crazy Bernie Sanders.... (1/2) **4/28/2019 3:10**

....for the more traditional but not very bright Sleepy Joe Biden. Here we go again Bernie but this time please show a little more anger and indignation when you get screwed! (2/2) **4/28/2019 3:10**

I spoke at length yesterday to Rabbi Yisroel Goldstein Chabad of Poway where I extended my warmest condolences to him and all affected by the shooting in California. What a great guy. He had a least one finger blown off and all he wanted to do is help others. Very special! **4/29/2019 10:49**

I'll never get the support of Dues Crazy union leadership those people who rip-off their membership with ridiculously high dues medical and other expenses while being paid a fortune. But the members love Trump. They look at our record economy tax & reg cuts military etc. WIN! **4/29/2019 14:32**

The Media (Fake News) is pushing Sleepy Joe hard. Funny I'm only here because of Biden & Obama. They didn't do the job and now you have Trump who is getting it done - big time! **4/29/2019 14:42**

The Dues Sucking firefighters leadership will always support Democrats even though the membership wants me. Some things never change! **4/29/2019 14:55**

Bob Mueller was a great HERO to the Radical Left Democrats. Now that the Mueller Report is finished with a finding of NO COLLUSION & NO OBSTRUCTION (based on a review of Report by our highly respected A.G.) the Dems are going around saying "Bob who sorry don't know the man." **4/29/2019 15:06**

The New York Times has apologized for the terrible Anti-Semitic Cartoon but they haven't apologized to me for this or all of the Fake and Corrupt news they print on a daily basis. They have reached the lowest level of "journalism" and certainly a low point in @nytimes history! **4/29/2019 15:20**

The Coyotes and Drug Cartels are in total control of the Mexico side of the Southern Border. They have labs nearby where they make drugs to sell into the U.S. Mexico one of the most dangerous country's in the world must eradicate this problem now. Also stop the MARCH to U.S. **4/30/2019 1:17**

If the Democrats don't give us the votes to change our weak ineffective and dangerous Immigration Laws we must fight hard for these votes in the 2020 Election! **4/30/2019 1:23**

We have 1800 ISIS Prisoners taken hostage in our final battles to destroy 100% of the Caliphate in Syria. Decisions are now being made as to what to do with these dangerous prisoners.... **4/30/2019 16:31**

I am monitoring the situation in Venezuela very closely. The United States stands with the People of Venezuela and their Freedom!

4/30/2019 18:23

If Cuban Troops and Militia do not immediately CEASE military and other operations for the purpose of causing death and destruction to the Constitution of Venezuela a full and complete.... (1/2) **4/30/2019 21:09**

....embargo together with highest-level sanctions will be placed on the island of Cuba. Hopefully all Cuban soldiers will promptly and peacefully return to their island! (2/2) **4/30/2019 21:09**

"The Democrats can't come to grips with the fact that there was No Collusion there was No Conspiracy there was No Obstruction. What we should be focused on is what's been going on in our government at the highest levels of the FBI...." Senator Josh Hawley **5/1/2019 10:36**

I am overriding the Decommission Order of the magnificent aircraft carrier Harry S. Truman built in 1998 (fairly new) and considered one of the largest and finest in the world. It will be updated at a fraction of the cost of a new one (which also are being built)! **5/1/2019 10:50**

"No President in history has endured such vicious personal attacks by political opponents. Still the President's record is unparalleled." @LouDobbs **5/1/2019 11:11**

Why didn't President Obama do something about Russia in September (before November Election) when told by the FBI? He did NOTHING and had no intention of doing anything! **5/1/2019 12:28**

NO COLLUSION NO OBSTRUCTION. Besides how can you have Obstruction when not only was there No Collusion (by Trump) but the bad actions were done by the "other" side? The greatest con-job in the history of American Politics! **5/1/2019 13:03**

I am continuing to monitor the situation in Venezuela very closely. The United States stands with the People of Venezuela and their Freedom! https://t.co/rtGfjQjc1u **5/2/2019 2:53**

On this day of prayer we once again place our hopes in the hands of our Creator. We give thanks for this wondrous land of liberty & we pray that THIS nation - OUR home - these United States - will forever be strengthened by the Goodness and the Grace & the eternal GLORY OF GOD! https://t.co/RtSI3j1GWH **5/2/2019 20:55**

OK so after two years of hard work and each party trying their best to make the other party look as bad as possible it's time to get back to business. The Mueller Report strongly stated that there was No Collusion with Russia (of course) and in fact they were rebuffed..... (1/2) **5/3/2019 3:45**

...at every turn in attempts to gain access. But now Republicans and Democrats must come together for the good of the American people. No more costly & time consuming investigations. Lets do Immigration (Border) Infrastructure much lower drug prices & much more - and do it now! (2/2) **5/3/2019 3:45**

Finally Mainstream Media is getting involved - too "hot" to avoid. Pulitzer Prize anyone? The New York Times on front page (finally) "Details effort to spy on Trump Campaign." @ foxandfriends This is bigger than WATERGATE but the reverse! **5/3/2019 12:22**

JOBS JOBS JOBS!"Jobs surge in April unemployment rate falls to the lowest since 1969" https://t.co/4DGpumMISf **5/3/2019 13:35**

We can all agree that AMERICA is now #1. We are the ENVY of the WORLD — and the best is yet to come! https://t.co/Uc81DzHbu2 **5/3/2019 16:22**

Had a long and very good conversation with President Putin of Russia. As I have always said long before the Witch Hunt started getting along with Russia China and everyone is a good thing not a bad thing.... (1/2) **5/3/2019 17:06**

....We discussed Trade Venezuela Ukraine North Korea Nuclear Arms Control and even the "Russian Hoax." Very productive talk! (2/2) **5/3/2019 17:06**

I am continuing to monitor the censorship of AMERICAN CITIZENS on social media platforms. This is the United States of America — and we have what's known as FREEDOM OF SPEECH! We are monitoring and watching closely!!
5/3/2019 22:55

The wonderful Diamond and Silk have been treated so horribly by Facebook. They work so hard and what has been done to them is very sad - and we're looking into. It's getting worse and worse for Conservatives on social media!
5/3/2019 23:23

So surprised to see Conservative thinkers like James Woods banned from Twitter and Paul Watson banned from Facebook! https://t.co/eHX3Z5CMXb **5/3/2019 23:25**

When will the Radical Left Wing Media apologize to me for knowingly getting the Russia Collusion Delusion story so wrong? The real story is about to happen! Why is @nytimes @washingtonpost @CNN @MSNBC allowed to be on Twitter & Facebook. Much of what they do is FAKE NEWS!
5/4/2019 12:34

Anything in this very interesting world is possible but I believe that Kim Jong Un fully realizes the great economic potential of North Korea & will do nothing to interfere or end it. He also knows that I am with him & does not want to break his promise to me. Deal will happen! **5/4/2019 13:42**

Very good call yesterday with President Putin of Russia. Tremendous potential for a good/great relationship with Russia despite what you read and see in the Fake News Media. Look how they have misled you on "Russia Collusion." The World can be a better and safer place. Nice! **5/4/2019 13:49**

How can it be possible that James Woods (and many others) a strong but responsible Conservative Voice is banned from Twitter? Social Media & Fake News Media together with their partner the Democrat Party have no idea the problems they are causing for themselves. VERY UNFAIR! **5/4/2019 18:31**

I am pleased to inform all of those that believe in a strong fair and sound Immigration Policy that Mark Morgan will be joining the Trump Administration as the head of our hard working men and women of ICE. Mark is a true believer and American Patriot. He will do a great job! **5/5/2019 14:55**

For 10 months China has been paying Tariffs to the USA of 25% on 50 Billion Dollars of High Tech and 10% on 200 Billion Dollars of other goods. These payments are partially responsible for our great economic results. The 10% will go up to 25% on Friday. 325 Billions Dollars.... **5/5/2019 16:08**

After spending more than $35000000 over a two year period interviewing 500 people using 18 Trump Hating Angry Democrats & 49 FBI Agents - all culminating in a more than 400 page Report showing NO COLLUSION - why would the Democrats in Congress now need Robert Mueller....... **5/5/2019 18:03**

Once again Israel faces a barrage of deadly rocket attacks by terrorist groups Hamas and Islamic Jihad. We support Israel 100% in its defense of its citizens.... **5/6/2019 0:13**

....To the Gazan people — these terrorist acts against Israel will bring you nothing but more misery. END the violence and work towards peace - it can happen! **5/6/2019 0:13**

Despite the tremendous success that I have had as President including perhaps the greatest ECONOMY and most successful first two years of any President in history they have stolen two years of my (our) Presidency (Collusion Delusion) that we will never be able to get back..... **5/6/2019 3:05**

.....The Witch Hunt is over but we will never forget. MAKE AMERICA GREAT AGAIN! **5/6/2019 3:05**

"Democrat Texas Congressman Al Green says impeachment is the only thing that can prevent President Trump from re-election in 2020." @OANN In other words Dems can't win the election fairly. You can't impeach a president for creating the best economy in our country's history.....
5/6/2019 10:46

Also there are "No High Crimes & Misdemeanors" No Collusion No Conspiracy No Obstruction. ALL THE CRIMES ARE ON THE OTHER SIDE and that's what the Dems should be looking at but they won't. Nevertheless the tables are turning! **5/6/2019 10:46**

The United States has been losing for many years 600 to 800 Billion Dollars a year on Trade. With China we lose 500 Billion Dollars. Sorry we're not going to be doing that anymore! **5/6/2019 11:08**

Scott Walker is 100% correct when he says that the Republicans must WAKE UP to the Democrats State by State power grab. They play very dirty actually like never before. Don't allow them to get away with what they are doing! **5/6/2019 13:30**

Puerto Rico has been given more money by Congress for Hurricane Disaster Relief 91 Billion Dollars than any State in the history of the U.S. As an example Florida got $12 Billion & Texas $39 Billion for their monster hurricanes. Now the Democrats are saying NO Relief to...... (1/2) **5/6/2019 13:48**

....Alabama Iowa Nebraska Georgia South Carolina North Carolina and others unless much more money is given to Puerto Rico. The Dems don't want farmers to get any help. Puerto Rico should be very happy and the Dems should stop blocking much needed Disaster Relief! (2/2) **5/6/2019 13:48**

Just spoke to Prime Minister Abe of Japan concerning North Korea and Trade. Very good conversation! **5/6/2019 13:51**

Today it was my true honor to present the Commander-in-Chief's Trophy—for the second year in a row to the @ ArmyWP_Football Black Knights. Congratulations once again on your historic victories and keep on making us proud! https://t.co/nGOC4PQn6S **5/6/2019 20:00**

Democrats in Congress must vote to close the terrible loopholes at the Southern Border. If not harsh measures will have to be taken! **5/7/2019 14:49**

Congratulations @TigerWoods - you are truly one of a kind! https://t.co/B6YpeLZilo **5/7/2019 18:57**

He wants to impeach because they can't win election. Sad! https://t.co/oFO6wMVhYt **5/8/2019 1:15**

I am pleased to inform you that THE BIG FIREWORKS after many years of not having any are coming back to beautiful Mount Rushmore in South Dakota. Great work @ GovKristiNoem and @SecBernhardt! #MAGA **5/8/2019 1:51**

Real estate developers in the 1980's & 1990's more than 30 years ago were entitled to massive write offs and depreciation which would if one was actively building show losses and tax losses in almost all cases. Much was non monetary. Sometimes considered "tax shelter" ...... (1/2)

5/8/2019 10:56

....you would get it by building or even buying. You always wanted to show losses for tax purposes....almost all real estate developers did - and often re-negotiate with banks it was sport. Additionally the very old information put out is a highly inaccurate Fake News hit job! (2/2) **5/8/2019 10:56**

The reason for the China pullback & attempted renegotiation of the Trade Deal is the sincere HOPE that they will be able to "negotiate" with Joe Biden or one of the very weak Democrats and thereby continue to ripoff the United States (($500 Billion a year)) for years to come....

5/8/2019 12:48

Big Court win at our Southern Border! We are getting there - and Wall is being built! **5/8/2019 13:42**

GREAT NEWS FOR OHIO! Just spoke to Mary Barra CEO of General Motors who informed me that subject to a UAW agreement etc. GM will be selling their beautiful Lordstown Plant to Workhorse where they plan to build Electric Trucks. GM will also be spending $700000000 in Ohio... (1/2)
5/8/2019 15:18

....in 3 separate locations creating another 450 jobs. I have been working nicely with GM to get this done. Thank you to Mary B your GREAT Governor and Senator Rob Portman. With all the car companies coming back and much more THE USA IS BOOMING! (2/2) **5/8/2019 15:18**

Big announcement today: Drug companies have to come clean about their prices in TV ads. Historic transparency for American patients is here. If drug companies are ashamed of those prices—lower them! **5/8/2019 21:01**

MAKE AMERICA GREAT AGAIN!
https://t.co/gOXXHnHHG5 **5/9/2019 3:05**

James Comey is a disgrace to the FBI & will go down as the worst Director in its long and once proud history. He brought the FBI down almost all Republicans & Democrats thought he should be FIRED but the FBI will regain greatness because of the great men & women who work there! **5/10/2019 3:00**

Talks with China continue in a very congenial manner - there is absolutely no need to rush - as Tariffs are NOW being paid to the United States by China of 25% on 250 Billion Dollars worth of goods & products. These massive payments go directly to the Treasury of the U.S....
5/10/2019 11:43

Build your products in the United States and there are NO TARIFFS! **5/10/2019 12:08**

Your all time favorite President got tired of waiting for China to help out and start buying from our FARMERS the greatest anywhere in the World! **5/10/2019 12:55**

Looks to me like it's going to be SleepyCreepy Joe over Crazy Bernie. Everyone else is fading fast! **5/10/2019 13:20**

Over the course of the past two days the United States and China have held candid and constructive conversations on the status of the trade relationship between both countries. The relationship between President Xi and myself remains a very strong one and conversations.... **5/10/2019 19:14**

Such an easy way to avoid Tariffs? Make or produce your goods and products in the good old USA. It's very simple! **5/11/2019 13:55**

I won the 2016 Election partially based on no Tax Returns while I am under audit (which I still am) and the voters didn't care. Now the Radical Left Democrats want to again relitigate this matter. Make it a part of the 2020 Election! **5/11/2019 18:32**

So now the Radical Left Dems don't talk about Collusion anymore because the Mueller Report said there was No Collusion they only want to talk about Obstruction even though there was No Obstruction or No Crime - except for the crimes committed by the other side! **5/11/2019 18:44**

I think that China felt they were being beaten so badly in the recent negotiation that they may as well wait around for the next election 2020 to see if they could get lucky & have a Democrat win - in which case they would continue to rip-off the USA for $500 Billion a year.... (1/2) **5/11/2019 22:18**

....The only problem is that they know I am going to win (best economy & employment numbers in U.S. history & much more) and the deal will become far worse for them if it has to be negotiated in my second term. Would be wise for them to act now but love collecting BIG TARIFFS! (2/2) **5/11/2019 22:18**

I was NOT going to fire Bob Mueller and did not fire Bob Mueller. In fact he was allowed to finish his Report with unprecedented help from the Trump Administration.

Actually lawyer Don McGahn had a much better chance of being fired than Mueller. Never a big fan! **5/11/2019 22:39**

"The Democrats have nothing. Just want to distract from this President. The FBI was not doing its job the State Department was covering things up everyday for Hillary. At the end of the day they're fearful of what they did and should be fearful. This is a tough..... (1/2) **5/12/2019 10:33**

....President who is willing to have the battle and we have a great Attorney General who is willing to lead the battle and they are going to get to the bottom of it." @EdRollins @ LouDobbs (2/2) **5/12/2019 10:33**

Think of it. I became President of the United States in one of the most hard fought and consequential elections in the history of our great nation. From long before I ever took office I was under a sick & unlawful investigation concerning what has become known as the Russian.... (1/2) **5/12/2019 11:04**

....Hoax. My campaign was being seriously spied upon by intel agencies and the Democrats. This never happened before in American history and it all turned out to be a total scam a Witch Hunt that yielded No Collusion No Obstruction. This must never be allowed to happen again! (2/2) **5/12/2019 11:04**

Big attacks on Republicans and Conservatives by Social Media. Not good! **5/12/2019 17:12**

We are right where we want to be with China. Remember they broke the deal with us & tried to renegotiate. We will be taking in Tens of Billions of Dollars in Tariffs from China. Buyers of product can make it themselves in the USA (ideal) or buy it from non-Tariffed countries... **5/12/2019 21:06**

"Just another abuse of power in a long series of abuses of power by the Democrats that began during the Obama Administration continued through the Mueller FBI operation & now the baton has been passed to Jerry Nadler to continue to abuse power to harass President Trump.. **5/13/2019 2:00**

I say openly to President Xi & all of my many friends in China that China will be hurt very badly if you don't make a deal because companies will be forced to leave China for other countries. Too expensive to buy in China. You had a great deal almost completed & you backed out! **5/13/2019 10:49**

Bernie Sanders "The Economy is doing well and I'm sure I don't have to give Trump any credit - I'm sure he'll take all the credit that he wants." Wrong Bernie the Economy is doing GREAT and would have CRASHED if my opponent (and yours) Crooked Hillary Clinton had ever won!
5/13/2019 13:59

Democrat Rep. Tlaib is being slammed for her horrible and highly insensitive statement on the Holocaust. She obviously has tremendous hatred of Israel and the Jewish people. Can you imagine what would happen if I ever said what she said and says? **5/13/2019 14:09**

There is no reason for the U.S. Consumer to pay the Tariffs which take effect on China today. This has been proven recently when only 4 points were paid by the U.S. 21 points by China because China subsidizes product to such a large degree. Also the Tariffs can be..... **5/13/2019 15:55**

Under my Administration we are restoring @NASA to greatness and we are going back to the Moon then Mars. I am updating my budget to include an additional $1.6 billion so that we can return to Space in a BIG WAY! **5/13/2019 21:34**

Wishing former President Jimmy Carter a speedy recovery from his hip surgery earlier today. He was in such good spirits when we spoke last month - he will be fine!
5/13/2019 22:31

I met Marine Sgt. John Peck a quadruple amputee who has received a double arm transplant at Walter Reed in 2017. Today it was my honor to welcome John (HERO) to the Oval with his wonderful wife Jessica. He also wrote a book that I highly recommend "Rebuilding Sergeant Peck." https://t.co/eiNnHcEU7x **5/13/2019 23:15**

China buys MUCH less from us than we buy from them by almost 500 Billion Dollars so we are in a fantastic position. Make your product at home in the USA and there is no Tariff. You can also buy from a non-Tariffed country instead of China. Many companies are leaving China..... **5/14/2019 10:31**

When the time is right we will make a deal with China. My respect and friendship with President Xi is unlimited but as I have told him many times before this must be a great deal for the United States or it just doesn't make any sense. We have to be allowed to make up some..... (1/2) **5/14/2019 11:16**

....of the tremendous ground we have lost to China on Trade since the ridiculous one sided formation of the WTO. It will all happen and much faster than people think! (2/2)
5/14/2019 11:16

Today marks the one-year anniversary of the opening of the United States Embassy in Jerusalem Israel. Our beautiful embassy stands as a proud reminder of our strong relationship with Israel and of the importance of keeping a promise and standing for the truth. **5/14/2019 16:27**

The golden era of American energy is now underway! https://t.co/gEmhoMlLoc **5/15/2019 0:25**

The courage & sacrifice of our heroes is the reason our flag stands tall our hearts beat with pride and our Country remains one people one family and one NATION UNDER GOD. Today we thank you we honor you & we forever cherish the memory of our Fallen Men and Women in Blue! https://t.co/ARHYgDVi3M **5/15/2019 18:20**

We stand firmly strongly and proudly with the incredible men and women of law enforcement. You do not hear it nearly enough but Americans across this Country love you support you and respect you more than you could possibly know! #PeaceOfficersMemorialDay https://t.co/T0qB5zN7WG **5/15/2019 18:56**

The Fake News Washington Post and even more Fake News New York Times are writing stories that there is infighting with respect to my strong policy in the Middle East. There is no infighting whatsoever.... (1/2) **5/15/2019 19:10**

....Different opinions are expressed and I make a decisive and final decision - it is a very simple process. All sides views and policies are covered. I'm sure that Iran will want to talk soon. (2/2) **5/15/2019 19:10**

The Dems are getting another beauty to join their group. Bill de Blasio of NYC considered the worst mayor in the U.S. will supposedly be making an announcement for president today. He is a JOKE but if you like high taxes & crime he's your man. NYC HATES HIM! **5/16/2019 12:33**

.@BilldeBlasio is the worst Mayor in the history of New York City - he won't last long! https://t.co/NyYntsX573

5/16/2019 22:11

All people that are illegally coming into the United States now will be removed from our Country at a later date as we build up our removal forces and as the laws are changed. Please do not make yourselves too comfortable you will be leaving soon!

5/17/2019 10:51

DRAIN THE SWAMP! **5/17/2019 11:00**

MAKE AMERICA GREAT AGAIN! **5/17/2019 11:01**

New Fox Poll: 58% of people say that the FBI broke the law in investigating Donald J. Trump. @foxandfriends

5/17/2019 11:05

My Campaign for President was conclusively spied on. Nothing like this has ever happened in American Politics. A really bad situation. TREASON means long jail sentences and this was TREASON! **5/17/2019 11:11**

Will Jerry Nadler ever look into the fact that Crooked Hillary deleted and acid washed 33000 emails AFTER getting a most powerful demand notice for them from Congress?

5/17/2019 12:16

It now seems the General Flynn was under investigation long before was common knowledge. It would have been impossible for me to know this but if that was the case and with me being one of two people who would become president why was I not told so that I could make a change?

5/17/2019 14:35

With all of the Fake and Made Up News out there Iran can have no idea what is actually going on! **5/17/2019 16:53**

Consumer Sentiment in the month of May is the highest in 15 years. Very nice! @FoxNews **5/17/2019 22:49**

Courts & Dems in Congress neither of which have a clue are trying to FORCE migrants into our Country! OUR COUNTRY IS FULL OUR DETENTION CENTERS HOSPITALS & SCHOOLS ARE PACKED. Crazy! **5/18/2019 22:33**

As most people know and for those who would like to know I am strongly Pro-Life with the three exceptions - Rape Incest and protecting the Life of the mother - the same position taken by Ronald Reagan. We have come very far in the last two years with 105 wonderful new..... (1/3)

5/19/2019 3:37

....for Life in 2020. If we are foolish and do not stay UNITED as one all of our hard fought gains for Life can and will rapidly disappear! (3/3) **5/19/2019 3:37**

....Federal Judges (many more to come) two great new Supreme Court Justices the Mexico City Policy and a whole new & positive attitude about the Right to Life. The Radical Left with late term abortion (and worse) is imploding on this issue. We must stick together and Win.... (2/3)

5/19/2019 3:37

For all of the Fake News Sunday Political Shows whose bias & dishonesty is greater than ever seen in our Country before please inform your viewers that our Economy is setting records with more people employed today than at any time in U.S. history our Military which.... (1/2)

5/19/2019 12:49

....Conditions drug prices down for first time in 51 years (& soon will drop much further) Right to Try protecting your 2nd Amendment big Tax & Reg Cuts 3.2 GDP Strong Foreign Policy & much much more that nobody else would have been able to do. Our Country is doing GREAT! (2/2)

5/19/2019 12:49

Never a fan of @justinamash a total lightweight who opposes me and some of our great Republican ideas and policies just for the sake of getting his name out there through controversy. If he actually read the biased Mueller Report "composed" by 18 Angry Dems who hated Trump....

5/19/2019 13:55

Watched some of the Fake News Political Shows this morning and continue to be amazed at how every question is asked in the most negative way. The Mainstream Media should be ashamed of itself - But the good news is that the USA is wise to your game of dishonesty and deception!

5/19/2019 18:50

With the wonderful College University and other Graduations taking place all over the USA there has never been a better time than now to graduate. Best jobs market ever great housing and financing. Go out there work hard & have a GREAT life. You deserve it. Congratulations!

5/19/2019 19:48

If Iran wants to fight that will be the official end of Iran. Never threaten the United States again!

5/19/2019 20:25

Hard to believe that @FoxNews is wasting airtime on Mayor Pete as Chris Wallace likes to call him. Fox is moving more and more to the losing (wrong) side in covering the Dems. They got dumped from the Democrats boring debates and they just want in. They forgot the people..... **5/19/2019 21:15**

The Failing New York Times (it will pass away when I leave office in 6 years) and others of the Fake News Media keep writing phony stories about how I didn't use many banks because they didn't want to do business with me. WRONG! It is because I didn't need money. Very old **5/20/2019 11:20**

Looks like Bernie Sanders is history. Sleepy Joe Biden is pulling ahead and think about it I'm only here because of Sleepy Joe and the man who took him off the 1% trash heap President O! China wants Sleepy Joe BADLY! **5/20/2019 14:08**

Just returned to the beautiful @WhiteHouse after a great evening in Pennsylvania! https://t.co/wMeh9k9knv
5/21/2019 2:06

I am very disappointed that Mexico is doing virtually nothing to stop illegal immigrants from coming to our Southern Border where everyone knows that because of the Democrats our Immigration Laws are totally flawed & broken... (1/2) **5/21/2019 16:16**

...Mexico's attitude is that people from other countries including Mexico should have the right to flow into the U.S. & that U.S. taxpayers should be responsible for the tremendous costs associated w/this illegal migration. Mexico is wrong and I will soon be giving a response! (2/2)
5/21/2019 16:16

Great news for Republicans: Fred Keller has just won the hard fought for Pennsylvania Congressional contest in a LANDSLIDE over 70% of the vote. Thanks to the thousands who showed up for the Rally last night. Congratulations to Fred and his wonderful family! **5/22/2019 2:20**

PRESIDENTIAL HARASSMENT! **5/22/2019 10:03**

Much of the Wall being built at the Southern Border is a complete demolition and rebuilding of old and worthless barriers with a brand new Wall and footings. Problem is the Haters say that is not a new Wall but rather a renovation. Wrong and we must build where most needed.... **5/22/2019 11:22**

As I have long been saying and has now been proven out this is a Witch Hunt against the Republican Party and myself and it was the other side that caused the problem not us! **5/22/2019 15:15**

So sad that Nancy Pelosi and Chuck Schumer will never be able to see or understand the great promise of our Country. They can continue the Witch Hunt which has already cost $40M and been a tremendous waste of time and energy for everyone in America or get back to work.... **5/22/2019 17:01**

....In the meantime my Administration is achieving things that have never been done before including unleashing perhaps the Greatest Economy in our Country's history.... **5/22/2019 17:01**

....Democrat leadership is tearing the United States apart but I will continue to set records for the American People - and Nancy thank you so much for your prayers I know you truly mean it! **5/22/2019 17:02**

In a letter to her House colleagues Nancy Pelosi said: "President Trump had a temper tantrum for us all to see." This is not true. I was purposely very polite and calm much as I was minutes later with the press in the Rose Garden. Can be easily proven. It is all such a lie! **5/23/2019 2:28**

Zero is getting done with the Democrats in charge of the House. All they want to do is put the Mueller Report behind them and start all over again. No Do-Overs! **5/23/2019 2:31**

The Democrats are getting nothing done in Congress. All of their effort is about a Re-Do of the Mueller Report which didn't turn out the way they wanted. It is not possible for them to investigate and legislate at the same time. Their heart is not into Infrastructure lower..... (1/2) **5/23/2019 11:56**

....drug prices pre-existing conditions and our great Vets. All they are geared up to do six committees is squander time day after day trying to find anything which will be bad for me. A pure fishing expedition like this never happened before & it should never happen again! (2/2) **5/23/2019 11:56**

The Democrats have become known as THE DO NOTHING PARTY! **5/23/2019 11:58**

I was extremely calm yesterday with my meeting with Pelosi and Schumer knowing that they would say I was raging which they always do along with their partner the Fake News Media. Well so many stories about the meeting use the Rage narrative anyway - Fake & Corrupt Press! **5/23/2019 14:13**

Congratulations to Prime Minister @NarendraModi and his BJP party on their BIG election victory! Great things are in store for the US-India partnership with the return of PM Modi at the helm. I look forward to continuing our important work together! **5/23/2019 17:13**

"Today at the request and recommendation of the Attorney General of the United States President Donald J. Trump directed the intelligence community to quickly and fully cooperate with the Attorney General's investigation into surveillance activities.... (1/3) **5/24/2019 0:19**

....Today's action will help ensure that all Americans learn the truth about the events that occurred and the actions that were taken during the last Presidential election and will restore confidence in our public institutions." @PressSec (3/3) **5/24/2019 0:19**

....during the 2016 Presidential election. The Attorney General has also been delegated full and complete authority to declassify information pertaining to this investigation in accordance with the long-established standards for handling classified information.... (2/3) **5/24/2019 0:19**

"PELOSI STAMMERS THROUGH NEWS CONFERENCE" https://t.co/1OyCyqRTuk **5/24/2019 1:09**

Wow! CNN Ratings are WAY DOWN record lows. People are getting tired of so many Fake Stories and Anti-Trump lies. Chris Cuomo was rewarded for lowest morning ratings with a prime time spot - which is failing badly and not helping the dumbest man on television Don Lemon!

5/24/2019 3:19

When is Twitter going to allow the very popular Conservative Voices that it has so viciously shut down back into the OPEN? IT IS TIME! **5/24/2019 3:29**

"If they try to Impeach President Trump who has done nothing wrong (No Collusion) they will end up getting him re-elected" @LindseyGrahamSC Impeachment is for High Crimes and Misdemeanors. There were no High Crimes and Misdemeanors except for those committed by the other side! **5/24/2019 12:19**

I don't know why the Radical Left Democrats want Bob Mueller to testify when he just issued a 40 Million Dollar Report that states loud & clear & for all to hear No Collusion and No Obstruction (how do you Obstruct a NO crime?) Dems are just looking for trouble and a Do-Over!

5/24/2019 12:34

Just spoke to Prime Minister @ NarendraModi where I congratulated him on his big political victory. He is a great man and leader for the people of India - they are lucky to have him!

5/24/2019 18:00

Departed the @WhiteHouse and am now on Air Force One with the First Lady heading to Japan and looking forward to honoring on behalf of the United States His Majesty the Emperor of Japan. I will also be discussing Trade and Military with my friend Prime Minister @AbeShinzo. https://t.co/uwEjQNbEXE **5/24/2019 19:01**

Mitch McConnell and our Republican Senators have been very solid and strong. We have accomplished a great deal together in particular with our Courts 107 Federal Judges....
5/24/2019 20:56

In Alaska with our GREAT TROOPS departing shortly for Japan! https://t.co/9a72TMftpN **5/25/2019 0:38**

Can't believe that Rolling Thunder would be given a hard time with permits in Washington D.C. They are great Patriots who I have gotten to know and see in action. They love our Country and love our Flag. If I can help I will!
5/25/2019 7:32

Getting ready to land in Japan with First Lady Melania. We look forward to seeing everyone soon! **5/25/2019 7:48**

Another activist Obama appointed judge has just ruled against us on a section of the Southern Wall that is already under construction. This is a ruling against Border Security and in favor of crime drugs and human trafficking. We are asking for an expedited appeal! **5/25/2019 19:35**

In addition to great incompetence and corruption The Smollett case in Chicago is also about a Hate Crime. Remember "MAGA COUNTRY DID IT!" That turned out to be a total lie had nothing to do with "MAGA COUNTRY." Serious stuff and not even an apology to millions of people!
5/25/2019 20:43

North Korea fired off some small weapons which disturbed some of my people and others but not me. I have confidence that Chairman Kim will keep his promise to me & also smiled when he called Swampman Joe Biden a low IQ individual & worse. Perhaps that's sending me a signal?
5/26/2019 1:32

Great morning of golf with Prime Minister @AbeShinzo at Mobara Country Club in Chiba Japan!
https://t.co/EZeJ8znS51 **5/26/2019 4:07**

Great progress being made in our Trade Negotiations with Japan. Agriculture and beef heavily in play. Much will wait until after their July elections where I anticipate big numbers! **5/26/2019 4:39**

Tonight in Tokyo Japan at the Ryōgoku Kokugikan Stadium it was my great honor to present the first-ever U.S. President's Cup to Sumo Grand Champion Asanoyama. Congratulations! A great time had by all thank you @ AbeShinzo!! https://t.co/nwwxJl6KXH **5/26/2019 11:48**

Thank you @JPN_PMO @AbeShinzo! #POTUSinJapan https://t.co/fWToB1XotG
5/26/2019 12:26

"Why doesn't the press apologize to President Trump for the Russian Collusion Delusion?" @marklevinshow @ JudgeJeanine How about the Dems also? **5/26/2019 12:40**

The Great Patriots of Rolling Thunder WILL be coming back to Washington D.C. next year & hopefully for many years to come. It is where they want to be & where they should be. Have a wonderful time today. Thank you to our great men & women of the Pentagon for working it out! **5/26/2019 12:53**

Congratulations to the Great (and my friend) Roger Penske on winning his 18th (UNBELIEVABLE!) Indianapolis 500. I am in Japan very early in the morning but I got to watch Simon drive one of the greatest races in the history of the sport. I will see them both & TEAM at the WH! **5/26/2019 20:48**

.@ianbremmer now admits that he MADE UP "a completely ludicrous quote" attributing it to me. This is what's going on in the age of Fake News. People think they can say anything and get away with it. Really the libel laws should be changed to hold Fake News Media accountable!
5/27/2019 8:57

Impeach for what having created perhaps the greatest Economy in our Country's history rebuilding our Military taking care of our Vets (Choice) Judges Best Jobs Numbers Ever and much more? Dems are Obstructionists! https://t.co/NrTIxU9ZnA **5/27/2019 9:10**

Hoping things will work out with Israel's coalition formation and Bibi and I can continue to make the alliance between America and Israel stronger than ever. A lot more to do! **5/27/2019 15:24**

Anyone associated with the 1994 Crime Bill will not have a chance of being elected. In particular African Americans will not be able to vote for you. I on the other hand was responsible for Criminal Justice Reform which had tremendous support & helped fix the bad 1994 Bill! **5/27/2019 22:35**

I will be making two stops this morning in Japan to visit with our Great Military then a quick stop in Alaska and back to D.C. Meetings with Prime Minister Abe went very well and getting to spend time with the new Emperor and Empress of Japan was a great honor! **5/27/2019 22:57**

GOD BLESS THE USA https://t.co/Y8HRT6wnWZ **5/28/2019 12:39**

I was actually sticking up for Sleepy Joe Biden while on foreign soil. Kim Jong Un called him a "low IQ idiot" and many other things whereas I related the quote of Chairman Kim as a much softer "low IQ individual." Who could possibly be upset with that? **5/28/2019 21:58**

Back from Japan after a very successful trip. Big progress on MANY fronts. A great country with a wonderful leader in Prime Minister Abe! **5/29/2019 0:22**

Republicans cannot allow themselves to again lose the Senate seat in the Great State of Alabama. This time it will be for Six Years not just Two. I have NOTHING against Roy Moore and unlike many other Republican leaders wanted him to win. But he didn't and probably won't..... (1/2) **5/29/2019 11:40**

...If Alabama does not elect a Republican to the Senate in 2020 many of the incredible gains that we have made during my Presidency may be lost including our Pro-Life victories. Roy Moore cannot win and the consequences will be devastating....Judges and Supreme Court Justices! (2/2)
5/29/2019 11:40

Nothing changes from the Mueller Report. There was insufficient evidence and therefore in our Country a person is innocent. The case is closed! Thank you. **5/29/2019 15:37**

How do you impeach a Republican President for a crime that was committed by the Democrats? WITCH-HUNT!
5/30/2019 0:32

I was not informed about anything having to do with the Navy Ship USS John S. McCain during my recent visit to Japan. Nevertheless @FLOTUS and I loved being with our great Military Men and Women - what a spectacular job they do! **5/30/2019 0:59**

The Greatest Presidential Harassment in history. After spending $40000000 over two dark years with unlimited access people resources and cooperation highly conflicted Robert Mueller would have brought charges if he had ANYTHING but there were no charges to bring! **5/30/2019 11:21**

Russia Russia Russia! That's all you heard at the beginning of this Witch Hunt Hoax...And now Russia has disappeared because I had nothing to do with Russia helping me to get elected. It was a crime that didn't exist. So now the Dems and their partner the Fake News Media..... (1/2) **5/30/2019 11:57**

....say he fought back against this phony crime that didn't exist this horrendous false accusation and he shouldn't fight back he should just sit back and take it. Could this be Obstruction? No Mueller didn't find Obstruction either. Presidential Harassment! (2/2) **5/30/2019 11:57**

Robert Mueller came to the Oval Office (along with other potential candidates) seeking to be named the Director of the FBI. He had already been in that position for 12 years I told him NO. The next day he was named Special Counsel - A total Conflict of Interest. NICE! **5/30/2019 15:34**

Very sad to hear the news on the passing of my friend Senator Thad Cochran. He was a real Senator with incredible values - even flew back to Senate from Mississippi for important Healthcare Vote when he was desperately ill. Thad never let our Country (or me) down! **5/30/2019 16:27**

Yesterday Border Patrol agents apprehended the largest group of illegal aliens ever: 1036 people who illegally crossed the border in El Paso around 4am. Democrats need to stand by our incredible Border Patrol and finally fix the loopholes at our Border! https://t.co/6K1rlUzorM **5/30/2019 21:16**

The Navy put out a disclaimer on the McCain story. Looks like the story was an exaggeration or even Fake News - but why not everything else is! **5/30/2019 22:23**

On June 10th the United States will impose a 5% Tariff on all goods coming into our Country from Mexico until such time as illegal migrants coming through Mexico and into our Country STOP. The Tariff will gradually increase until the Illegal Immigration problem is remedied.. (1/2)

5/30/2019 23:30

....at which time the Tariffs will be removed. Details from the White House to follow. (2/2) **5/30/2019 23:30**

Mexico has taken advantage of the United States for decades. Because of the Dems our Immigration Laws are

BAD. Mexico makes a FORTUNE from the U.S. have for decades they can easily fix this problem. Time for them to finally do what must be done! **5/31/2019 13:30**

In order not to pay Tariffs if they start rising companies will leave Mexico which has taken 30% of our Auto Industry and come back home to the USA. Mexico must take back their country from the drug lords and cartels. The Tariff is about stopping drugs as well as illegals! **5/31/2019 14:27**

90% of the Drugs coming into the United States come through Mexico & our Southern Border. 80000 people died last year 1000000 people ruined. This has gone on for many years & nothing has been done about it. We have a 100 Billion Dollar Trade Deficit with Mexico. It's time! **5/31/2019 14:41**

As we celebrate LGBT Pride Month and recognize the outstanding contributions LGBT people have made to our great Nation let us also stand in solidarity with the many LGBT people who live in dozens of countries worldwide that punish imprison or even execute individuals.... (1/2) **5/31/2019 19:12**

....on the basis of their sexual orientation. My Administration has launched a global campaign to decriminalize homosexuality and invite all nations to join us in this effort! (2/2) **5/31/2019 19:12**

I will be announcing my Second Term Presidential Run with First Lady Melania Vice President Mike Pence and Second Lady Karen Pence on June 18th in Orlando Florida at the 20000 seat Amway Center. Join us for this Historic Rally! Tickets: https://t.co/1krDP2oQvG **5/31/2019 20:35**

Washington Post got it wrong as usual. The U.S. is charging 25% against 250 Billion Dollars of goods shipped from China not 200 BD. Also China is paying a heavy cost in that they will subsidize goods to keep them coming devalue their currency yet companies are moving to..... **6/1/2019 20:37**

...travesty that is taking place in allowing millions of people to easily meander through their country and INVADE the U.S. not to mention the Drugs & Human Trafficking pouring in through Mexico. Are the Drug Lords Cartels & Coyotes really running Mexico? We will soon find out! **6/1/2019 20:37**

When you are the "Piggy Bank" Nation that foreign countries have been robbing and deceiving for years the word TARIFF is a beautiful word indeed! Others must treat the United States fairly and with respect - We are no longer the "fools" of the past! **6/1/2019 22:20**

People have been saying for years that we should talk to Mexico. The problem is that Mexico is an "abuser" of the United States taking but never giving. It has been this way for decades. Either they stop the invasion of our Country by Drug Dealers Cartels Human Traffickers.... (1/2) **6/2/2019 11:44**

....Coyotes and Illegal Immigrants which they can do very easily or our many companies and jobs that have been foolishly allowed to move South of the Border will be brought back into the United States through taxation (Tariffs). America has had enough! (2/2) **6/2/2019 11:44**

NO COLLUSION NO OBSTRUCTION NO NOTHING! "What the Democrats are trying to do is the biggest sin in the impeachment business." David Rivkin Constitutional Scholar. Meantime the Dems are getting nothing done in Congress. They are frozen stiff. Get back to work much to do!

6/2/2019 12:30

I never called Meghan Markle "nasty." Made up by the Fake News Media and they got caught cold! Will @CNN @ nytimes and others apologize? Doubt it! **6/2/2019 12:44**

Mexico is sending a big delegation to talk about the Border. Problem is they've been "talking" for 25 years. We want action not talk. They could solve the Border Crisis in one day if they so desired. Otherwise our companies and jobs are coming back to the USA! **6/2/2019 18:19**

Democrats can't impeach a Republican President for crimes committed by Democrats. The facts are "pouring" in. The Greatest Witch Hunt in American History! Congress go back to work and help us at the Border with Drug Prices and on Infrastructure. **6/2/2019 23:43**

Hearing word that Russia Syria and to a lesser extent Iran are bombing the hell out of Idlib Province in Syria and indiscriminately killing many innocent civilians. The World is watching this butchery. What is the purpose what will it get you? STOP! **6/2/2019 23:49**

BIG NEWS! As I promised two weeks ago the first shipment of LNG has just left the Cameron LNG Export Facility in Louisiana. Not only have thousands of JOBS been created in USA we're shipping freedom and opportunity abroad!
6/3/2019 1:44

.@SadiqKhan who by all accounts has done a terrible job as Mayor of London has been foolishly "nasty" to the visiting President of the United States by far the most important ally of the United Kingdom. He is a stone cold loser who should focus on crime in London not me...... (1/2)

6/3/2019 7:51

....Kahn reminds me very much of our very dumb and incompetent Mayor of NYC de Blasio who has also done a terrible job - only half his height. In any event I look forward to being a great friend to the United Kingdom and am looking very much forward to my visit. Landing now! (2/2)
6/3/2019 7:51

Just arrived in the United Kingdom. The only problem is that @CNN is the primary source of news available from the U.S. After watching it for a short while I turned it off. All negative

& so much Fake News very bad for U.S. Big ratings drop. Why doesn't owner @ATT do something? **6/3/2019 10:37**

I believe that if people stoped using or subscribing to @ ATT they would be forced to make big changes at @CNN which is dying in the ratings anyway. It is so unfair with such bad Fake News! Why wouldn't they act. When the World watches @CNN it gets a false picture of USA. Sad! **6/3/2019 10:50**

London part of trip is going really well. The Queen and the entire Royal family have been fantastic. The relationship with the United Kingdom is very strong. Tremendous crowds of well wishers and people that love our Country. Haven't seen any protests yet but I'm sure the.... (1/2) **6/3/2019 17:41**

....Fake News will be working hard to find them. Great love all around. Also big Trade Deal is possible once U.K. gets rid of the shackles. Already starting to talk! (2/2) **6/3/2019 17:41**

Russia has informed us that they have removed most of their people from Venezuela. **6/3/2019 17:44**

As a sign of good faith Mexico should immediately stop the flow of people and drugs through their country and to our Southern Border. They can do it if they want! **6/3/2019 18:11**

Just had a big victory in Federal Court over the Democrats in the House on the desperately needed Border Wall. A big step in the right direction. Wall is under construction! **6/4/2019 18:09**

Can you imagine Cryin' Chuck Schumer saying out loud for all to hear that I am bluffing with respect to putting Tariffs on Mexico. What a Creep. He would rather have our Country fail with drugs & Immigration than give Republicans a win. But he gave Mexico bad advice no bluff! **6/5/2019 0:04**

Washed up psycho @BetteMidler was forced to apologize for a statement she attributed to me that turned out to be totally fabricated by her in order to make "your great president" look really bad. She got caught just like the Fake News Media gets caught. A sick scammer! **6/5/2019 0:30**

Plagiarism charge against Sleepy Joe Biden on his ridiculous Climate Change Plan is a big problem but the Corrupt Media will save him. His other problem is that he is drawing flies not people to his Rallies. Nobody is showing up I mean nobody. You can't win without people! **6/5/2019 5:55**

I kept hearing that there would be "massive" rallies against me in the UK but it was quite the opposite. The big crowds which the Corrupt Media hates to show were those that gathered in support of the USA and me. They were big & enthusiastic as opposed to the organized flops! **6/5/2019 6:01**

Could not have been treated more warmly in the United Kingdom by the Royal Family or the people. Our relationship has never been better and I see a very big Trade Deal down the road. "This trip has been an incredible success for the President." @IngrahamAngle **6/5/2019 8:02**

If the totally Corrupt Media was less corrupt I would be up by 15 points in the polls based on our tremendous success with the economy maybe Best Ever! If the Corrupt Media was actually fair I would be up by 25 points. Nevertheless despite the Fake News we're doing great! **6/5/2019 8:17**

As we approach the 75th Anniversary of D-Day we proudly commemorate those heroic and honorable patriots who gave their all for the cause of freedom during some of history's darkest hours. #DDay75 https://t.co/hjTkdM7VcN **6/5/2019 12:18**

Immigration discussions at the White House with representatives of Mexico have ended for the day. Progress is being made but not nearly enough! Border arrests for May are at 133000 because of Mexico & the Democrats in Congress refusing to budge on immigration reform. Further... (1/2) **6/5/2019 22:42**

....talks with Mexico will resume tomorrow with the understanding that if no agreement is reached Tariffs at the

5% level will begin on Monday with monthly increases as per schedule. The higher the Tariffs go the higher the number of companies that will move back to the USA! (2/2)

6/5/2019 22:42

A big and beautiful day today! **6/6/2019 5:57**

Heading over to Normandy to celebrate some of the bravest that ever lived. We are eternally grateful! #DDay75thAnniversary #DDay75 https://t.co/rg15c32Gow

6/6/2019 7:38

So sorry to hear about the terrible accident involving our GREAT West Point Cadets. We mourn the loss of life and pray for the injured. God Bless them ALL! **6/6/2019 16:36**

HAPPY BIRTHDAY to our great @VP Mike Pence! https://t.co/k2fmu5bR5R **6/7/2019 14:44**

Nervous Nancy Pelosi is a disgrace to herself and her family for having made such a disgusting statement especially since I was with foreign leaders overseas. There is no evidence for such a thing to have been said. Nervous Nancy & Dems are getting Zero work done in Congress.... (1/2)

6/7/2019 16:57

...and have no intention of doing anything other than going on a fishing expedition to see if they can find anything on me - both illegal & unprecedented in U.S. history. There was no Collusion - Investigate the Investigators! Go to work on Drug Price Reductions & Infrastructure! (2/2) **6/7/2019 16:57**

For all of the money we are spending NASA should NOT be talking about going to the Moon - We did that 50 years ago. They should be focused on the much bigger things we are doing including Mars (of which the Moon is a part) Defense and Science! **6/7/2019 17:38**

Dow Jones has best week of the year! **6/7/2019 21:43**

I am pleased to inform you that The United States of America has reached a signed agreement with Mexico. The

Tariffs scheduled to be implemented by the U.S. on Monday against Mexico are hereby indefinitely suspended. Mexico in turn has agreed to take strong measures to.... (1/2)

6/8/2019 0:31

....stem the tide of Migration through Mexico and to our Southern Border. This is being done to greatly reduce or eliminate Illegal Immigration coming from Mexico and into the United States. Details of the agreement will be released shortly by the State Department. Thank you! (2/2) **6/8/2019 0:31**

Mexico will try very hard and if they do that this will be a very successful agreement for both the United States and Mexico!

6/8/2019 11:02

MEXICO HAS AGREED TO IMMEDIATELY BEGIN BUYING LARGE QUANTITIES OF AGRICULTURAL PRODUCT FROM OUR GREAT PATRIOT FARMERS!

6/8/2019 12:03

Nervous Nancy Pelosi & the Democrat House are getting nothing done. Perhaps they could lead the way with the USMCA the spectacular & very popular new Trade Deal that replaces NAFTA the worst Trade Deal in the history of the U.S.A. Great for our Farmers Manufacturers & Unions!

6/8/2019 13:43

Everyone very excited about the new deal with Mexico!

6/8/2019 13:47

I would like to thank the President of Mexico Andres Manuel Lopez Obrador and his foreign minister Marcelo Ebrard together with all of the many representatives of both the United States and Mexico for working so long and hard to get our agreement on immigration completed!A3431

6/8/2019 14:20

Watched MSNBC this morning just to see what the opposition was saying about events of the past week. Such

lies almost everything they were saying was the opposite of the truth. Fake News! No wonder their ratings along with CNN are WAY DOWN. The hatred Comcast has is amazing!
6/8/2019 23:25

I know it is not at all "Presidential" to hit back at the Corrupt Media or people who work for the Corrupt Media when they make false statements about me or the Trump Administration. Problem is if you don't hit back people believe the Fake News is true. So we'll hit back! **6/9/2019 4:08**

.....there is not we can always go back to our previous very profitable position of Tariffs - But I don't believe that will be necessary. The Failing @nytimes & ratings challenged @ CNN will do anything possible to see our Country fail! They are truly The Enemy of the People! **6/9/2019 12:26**

Another false report in the Failing @nytimes. We have been trying to get some of these Border Actions for a long time as have other administrations but were not able to get them or get them in full until our signed agreement with Mexico. Additionally and for many years.... **6/9/2019 12:26**

Twitter should let the banned Conservative Voices back onto their platform without restriction. It's called Freedom of Speech remember. You are making a Giant Mistake!
6/9/2019 12:45

If President Obama made the deals that I have made both at the Border and for the Economy the Corrupt Media would be hailing them as Incredible & a National Holiday would be immediately declared. With me despite our record setting Economy and all that I have done no credit!
6/9/2019 13:26

....No Obstruction. The Dems were devastated - after all this time and money spent ($40000000) the Mueller Report was a disaster for them. But they want a Redo or Do Over. They are even bringing in @CNN sleazebag attorney John Dean. Sorry no Do Overs - Go back to work! **6/9/2019 22:50**

For two years all the Democrats talked about was the Mueller Report because they knew that it was loaded up with 13 Angry Democrat Trump Haters later increased to 18. But despite the bias when the Report came out the findings were No Collusion and facts that led to........ **6/9/2019 22:50**

We have fully signed and documented another very important part of the Immigration and Security deal with Mexico one that the U.S. has been asking about getting for many years. It will be revealed in the not too distant future and will need a vote by Mexico's Legislative body!.. (1/2) **6/10/2019 10:31**

....We do not anticipate a problem with the vote but if for any reason the approval is not forthcoming Tariffs will be reinstated! (2/2) **6/10/2019 10:31**

When will the Failing New York Times admit that their front page story on the the new Mexico deal at the Border is a FRAUD and nothing more than a badly reported "hit job" on me something that has been going on since the first day I announced for the presidency! Sick Journalism **6/10/2019 11:09**

Can't believe they are bringing in John Dean the disgraced Nixon White House Counsel who is a paid CNN contributor. No Collusion - No Obstruction! Democrats just want a do-over which they'll never get! **6/10/2019 18:17**

I have been briefed on the helicopter crash in New York City. Phenomenal job by our GREAT First Responders who are currently on the scene. THANK YOU for all you do 24/7/365! The Trump Administration stands ready should you need anything at all. **6/10/2019 18:52**

Despite the Phony Witch Hunt we will continue to MAKE AMERICA GREAT AGAIN! Thank you!! https://t.co/MXuiolM745 **6/10/2019 23:01**

PRESIDENTIAL HARASSMENT! **6/11/2019 11:51**

The United States has VERY LOW INFLATION a beautiful thing! **6/11/2019 12:10**

Maria Dagan Steve Stuart V - When you are the big "piggy bank" that other countries have been ripping off for years (to a level that is not to be believed) Tariffs are a great negotiating tool a great revenue producers and most importantly a powerful way to get...... **6/11/2019 12:50**

Beautiful afternoon in Iowa. Thank you to all of our Nation's Farmers. May God bless you and may God Bless America! https://t.co/VYA2bSzMWf **6/12/2019 1:21**

"Someone should call Obama up. The Obama Administration spied on a rival presidential campaign using Federal Agencies. I mean that seems like a headline to me?" @ TuckerCarlson It will all start coming out and the Witch Hunt will end. Presidential Harassment! **6/12/2019 4:28**

Wow! Just got word that our June 18th Tuesday ANNOUNCEMENT in Orlando Florida already has 74000 requests for a 20000 seat Arena. With all of the big events that we have done this ticket looks to be the "hottest" of them all. See you in Florida! **6/12/2019 12:40**

The Fake News has never been more dishonest than it is today. Thank goodness we can fight back on Social Media. Their new weapon of choice is Fake Polling sometimes referred to as Suppression Polls (they suppress the numbers). Had it in 2016 but this is worse..... **6/12/2019 12:46**

.....The Fake (Corrupt) News Media said they had a leak into polling done by my campaign which by the way and despite the phony and never ending Witch Hunt are the best numbers WE have ever had. They reported Fake numbers that they made up & don't even exist. WE WILL WIN AGAIN! **6/12/2019 12:46**

General Michael Flynn the 33 year war hero who has served with distinction has not retained a good lawyer he has retained a GREAT LAWYER Sidney Powell. Best Wishes and Good Luck to them both! **6/13/2019 10:21**

"Congress cannot Impeach President Trump (did nothing wrong) because if they did they would be putting themselves above the law. The Constitution provides criteria for Impeachment - treason bribery high crimes & misdemeanors. Unless there is compelling evidence Impeachment... **6/13/2019 11:03**

I meet and talk to "foreign governments" every day. I just met with the Queen of England (U.K.) the Prince of Wales the P.M. of the United Kingdom the P.M. of Ireland the President of France and the President of Poland. We talked about "Everything!" Should I immediately.... (1/2) **6/13/2019 13:23**

....call the FBI about these calls and meetings? How ridiculous! I would never be trusted again. With that being said my full answer is rarely played by the Fake News Media. They purposely leave out the part that matters. (2/2) **6/13/2019 13:23**

After 3 1/2 years our wonderful Sarah Huckabee Sanders will be leaving the White House at the end of the month and going home to the Great State of Arkansas.... (1/2) **6/13/2019 20:10**

....She is a very special person with extraordinary talents who has done an incredible job! I hope she decides to run for Governor of Arkansas - she would be fantastic. Sarah thank you for a job well done! (2/2) **6/13/2019 20:10**

HAPPY BIRTHDAY to our GREAT @USArmy. America loves you! #ArmyBday https://t.co/MyypBVGMoW **6/14/2019 17:03**

The dishonest media will NEVER keep us from accomplishing our objectives on behalf of our GREAT AMERICAN PEOPLE! #MAGA https://t.co/e36YM4QCEx **6/14/2019 19:15**

All in for Senator Steve Daines as he proposes an Amendment for a strong BAN on burning our American Flag. A no brainer! **6/15/2019 12:51**

LONDON needs a new mayor ASAP. Khan is a disaster - will only get worse! https://t.co/n7qKl3BbD2 **6/15/2019 18:47**

The Corrupt News Media is totally out of control - they have given up and don't even care anymore. Mainstream Media has ZERO CREDIBILITY - TOTAL LOSERS! **6/15/2019 19:04**

He is a national disgrace who is destroying the City of London! https://t.co/l3qcUS17jh **6/15/2019 23:17**

I enjoyed my interview with @GStephanopoulos on @ ABC. So funny to watch the Fake News Media try to dissect & distort every word in as negative a way as possible. It will be aired on Sunday night at 8:00 P.M. and is called "President Trump: 30 Hours" (which is somewhat....

6/16/2019 0:51

.....the first 2 1/2 years of his Presidency including the fact that we have one of the best Economies in the history of our Country. It is called Earned Media. In any event enjoy the show! **6/16/2019 0:51**

Do you believe that the Failing New York Times just did a story stating that the United States is substantially increasing Cyber Attacks on Russia. This is a virtual act of Treason by a once great paper so desperate for a story any story even if bad for our Country..... **6/16/2019 1:15**

Florida Governor Ron DeSantis just signed Bill banning Sanctuary Cities in State & forcing all law enforcement agencies to cooperate with Federal Immigration authorities. Bill prohibits local Gov't from enacting Sanctuary policies that protect undocumented immigrants...@FoxNews

6/16/2019 4:51

....More and more states want to do this but their governors and leaders don't have the courage to do so. The politics will soon mandate however because people from California

& all over the land are demanding that Sanctuary Cities be GONE. No illegals Drugs or Trafficking! **6/16/2019 4:51**

Yesterday was the Radical Left Democrats big Impeachment day. They worked so hard to make it something really big and special but had one problem - almost nobody showed up. "The Media admits low turnout for anti-Trump rallies." @FoxNews "All around the Country people are....... **6/16/2019 11:39**

A poll should be done on which is the more dishonest and deceitful newspaper the Failing New York Times or the Amazon (lobbyist) Washington Post! They are both a disgrace to our Country the Enemy of the People but I just can't seem to figure out which is worse? The good.....

6/16/2019 13:39

.....news is that at the end of 6 years after America has been made GREAT again and I leave the beautiful White House (do you think the people would demand that I stay longer? KEEP AMERICA GREAT) both of these horrible papers will quickly go out of business & be forever gone! **6/16/2019 13:39**

Happy Father's Day to all including my worst and most vicious critics of which there are fewer and fewer. This is a FANTASTIC time to be an American! KEEP AMERICA GREAT!

6/16/2019 13:55

https://t.co/9T5ONuGW28 **6/16/2019 16:58**

When will the Fake News Media start asking Democrats if they are OK with the hiring of Christopher Steele a foreign agent paid for by Crooked Hillary and the DNC to dig up "dirt" and write a phony Dossier against the Presidential Candidate of the opposing party......... **6/16/2019 20:36**

Almost 70% in new Poll say don't impeach. So ridiculous to even be talking about this subject when all of the crimes were committed by the other side. They can't win the election fairly! **6/16/2019 21:23**

Rep. Alexandria Ocasio-Cortez. "I think we have a very real risk of losing the Presidency to Donald Trump." I agree and that is the only reason they play the impeach card which cannot be legally used! **6/16/2019 22:55**

Big Rally tomorrow night in Orlando Florida looks to be setting records. We are building large movie screens outside to take care of everybody. Over 100000 requests. Our Country is doing great far beyond what the haters & losers thought possible - and it will only get better! **6/17/2019 12:00**

Only Fake Polls show us behind the Motley Crew. We are looking really good but it is far too early to be focused on that. Much work to do! MAKE AMERICA GREAT AGAIN! **6/17/2019 12:07**

Next week ICE will begin the process of removing the millions of illegal aliens who have illicitly found their way into the United States. They will be removed as fast as they come in. Mexico using their strong immigration laws is doing a very good job of stopping people....... (1/2) **6/18/2019 1:20**

....long before they get to our Southern Border. Guatemala is getting ready to sign a Safe-Third Agreement. The only ones who won't do anything are the Democrats in Congress. They must vote to get rid of the loopholes and fix asylum! If so Border Crisis will end quickly! (2/2) **6/18/2019 1:20**

Thousands of people are already lined up in Orlando some two days before tomorrow nights big Rally. Large Screens and food trucks will be there for those that can't get into the 25000 capacity arena. It will be a very exciting evening! Make America Great Again! **6/18/2019 1:39**

Only a few people showed up for the so-called Impeachment rallies over the weekend. The numbers were anemic no spirit no hope. More importantly No Collusion No Obstruction! **6/18/2019 5:10**

The Fake News doesn't report it but Republican enthusiasm is at an all time high. Look what is going on in Orlando Florida right now! People have never seen anything like it (unless you play a guitar). Going to be wild - See you later! **6/18/2019 11:30**

Had a very good telephone conversation with President Xi of China. We will be having an extended meeting next week at the G-20 in Japan. Our respective teams will begin talks prior to our meeting. **6/18/2019 13:39**

Together we are breaking the most sacred rule in Washington Politics: we are KEEPING our promises to the American People. Because my only special interest is YOU! #Trump2020 https://t.co/bYyK6sOrak **6/19/2019 1:52**

In the ultimate act of moral cowardice not one Democrat Candidate for president - not a single one - has stood up to defend the incredible men and women of ICE and Border Patrol. They don't have the character the virtue or the spine! #Trump2020 https://t.co/oULNnVtxmW **6/19/2019 2:04**

Don't ever forget - this election is about YOU. It is about YOUR family YOUR future & the fate of YOUR COUNTRY. We begin our campaign with the best record the best results the best agenda & the only positive VISION for our Country's future! #Trump2020 https://t.co/Vmu28hKQh6 **6/19/2019 2:13**

The Dems are very unhappy with the Mueller Report so after almost 3 years they want a Redo or Do Over. This is extreme Presidential Harassment. They gave Crooked Hillary's people complete Immunity yet now they bring back Hope Hicks. Why aren't the Dems looking at the..... (1/2) **6/19/2019 14:18**

....33000 Emails that Hillary and her lawyer deleted and acid washed AFTER GETTING A SUBPOENA FROM CONGRESS? That is real Obstruction that the Dems want no part of because their hearings are RIGGED and a disgrace to our Country! (2/2) **6/19/2019 14:18**

If I didn't have the Phony Witch Hunt going on for 3 years and if the Fake News Media and their partner in Crime the Democrats would have played it straight I would be way up in the Polls right now - with our Economy winning by 20 points. But I'm winning anyway! **6/19/2019 15:09**

So sad that the Democrats are putting wonderful Hope Hicks through hell for 3 years now after total exoneration by Robert Mueller & the Mueller Report. They were unhappy with result so they want a Do Over. Very unfair & costly to her. Will it ever end? Why aren't they....... (1/2) **6/19/2019 19:48**

....asking Hillary Clinton why she deleted and acid washed her Emails AFTER getting a subpoena from Congress? Anybody else would be in jail for that yet the Dems refuse to even bring it up. Rigged House Committee (2/2) **6/19/2019 19:48**

Congratulations to President Lopez Obrador — Mexico voted to ratify the USMCA today by a huge margin. Time for Congress to do the same here! **6/19/2019 23:01**

Iran made a very big mistake! **6/20/2019 14:15**

S&P closes at Record High! https://t.co/C5nOXIQ7EJ **6/20/2019 22:22**

Just revealed that the Failing and Desperate New York Times was feeding false stories about me & those associated with me to the FBI. This shows the kind of unprecedented hatred I have been putting up with for years with this Crooked newspaper. Is what they have done legal?... **6/21/2019 12:19**

President Obama made a desperate and terrible deal with Iran - Gave them 150 Billion Dollars plus I.8 Billion Dollars in CASH! Iran was in big trouble and he bailed them out. Gave them a free path to Nuclear Weapons and SOON. Instead of saying thank you Iran yelled..... (1/3) **6/21/2019 13:03**

....On Monday they shot down an unmanned drone flying in International Waters. We were cocked & loaded to retaliate last night on 3 different sights when I asked how many will die. 150 people sir was the answer from a General. 10 minutes before the strike I stopped it not.... (2/3)

6/21/2019 13:03

....proportionate to shooting down an unmanned drone. I am in no hurry our Military is rebuilt new and ready to go by far the best in the world. Sanctions are biting & more added last night. Iran can NEVER have Nuclear Weapons not against the USA and not against the WORLD! (3/3)

6/21/2019 13:03

The people that Ice will apprehend have already been ordered to be deported. This means that they have run from the law and run from the courts. These are people that are supposed to go back to their home country. They broke the law by coming into the country & now by staying.

6/22/2019 12:30

When people come into our Country illegally they will be DEPORTED!

6/22/2019 12:32

Iran cannot have Nuclear Weapons! Under the terrible Obama plan they would have been on their way to Nuclear in a short number of years and existing verification is not acceptable. We are putting major additional Sanctions on Iran on Monday. I look forward to the day that..... (1/2)

6/22/2019 18:56

....Sanctions come off Iran and they become a productive and prosperous nation again - The sooner the better! (2/2)
6/22/2019 18:56

At the request of Democrats I have delayed the Illegal Immigration Removal Process (Deportation) for two weeks to see if the Democrats and Republicans can get together and work out a solution to the Asylum and Loophole problems at the Southern Border. If not Deportations start!
6/22/2019 18:56

I never called the strike against Iran “BACK” as people are incorrectly reporting I just stopped it from going forward at this time! **6/22/2019 22:58**

I want to give the Democrats every last chance to quickly negotiate simple changes to Asylum and Loopholes. This will fix the Southern Border together with the help that Mexico is now giving us. Probably won’t happen but worth a try. Two weeks and big Deportation begins! **6/23/2019 12:13**

Wonderful Church service at Camp David. Thank you!
6/23/2019 13:20

When our Country had no debt and built everything from Highways to the Military with CASH we had a big system of Tariffs. Now we allow other countries to steal our wealth treasure and jobs - But no more! The USA is doing great with unlimited upside into the future! **6/23/2019 14:46**

China gets 91% of its Oil from the Straight Japan 62% & many other countries likewise. So why are we protecting the shipping lanes for other countries (many years) for zero compensation. All of these countries should be protecting their own ships on what has always been.... (1/2)
6/24/2019 12:08

....a dangerous journey. We don’t even need to be there in that the U.S. has just become (by far) the largest producer of Energy anywhere in the world! The U.S. request for Iran is very simple - No Nuclear Weapons and No Further Sponsoring of Terror! (2/2) **6/24/2019 12:08**

Despite a Federal Reserve that doesn't know what it is doing - raised rates far too fast (very low inflation other parts of world slowing lowering & easing) & did large scale tightening $50 Billion/month we are on course to have one of the best Months of June in US history... **6/24/2019 12:53**

Stock Market is heading for one of the best months (June) in the history of our Country. Thank you Mr. President!
6/25/2019 12:11

Iran leadership doesn't understand the words "nice" or "compassion" they never have. Sadly the thing they do understand is Strength and Power and the USA is by far the most powerful Military Force in the world with 1.5 Trillion Dollars invested over the last two years alone.. (1/2)
6/25/2019 14:42

....Iran's very ignorant and insulting statement put out today only shows that they do not understand reality. Any attack by Iran on anything American will be met with great and overwhelming force. In some areas overwhelming will mean obliteration. No more John Kerry & Obama! (2/2)
6/25/2019 14:42

Presidential Harassment! **6/26/2019 2:34**

Women's soccer player @mPinoe just stated that she is "not going to the F...ing White House if we win." Other than the NBA which now refuses to call owners owners (please explain that I just got Criminal Justice Reform passed Black unemployment is at the lowest level... (1/3) **6/26/2019 14:42**

....invited Megan or the team but I am now inviting the TEAM win or lose. Megan should never disrespect our Country the White House or our Flag especially since so much has been done for her & the team. Be proud of the Flag that you wear. The USA is doing GREAT! (3/3) **6/26/2019 14:42**

....in our Country's history and the poverty index is also best number EVER) leagues and teams love coming to the White House. I am a big fan of the American Team and

Women's Soccer but Megan should WIN first before she TALKS! Finish the job! We haven't yet.... (2/3) **6/26/2019 14:42**

"I have been in office for many years the Military is very important to me and at no time in my professional life has the U.S. Military been as strong as it is right now." Thank you @LindseyGrahamSC **6/26/2019 21:17**

Why aren't the Democrats in the House calling Comey Brennan Clapper Page and her FBI lover (whose invaluable phone records were illegally deleted) Crooked Hillary Podesta Ohr (and Nellie) the GPS Fusion characters Christopher Steele the DNC (& their missing server)....
6/26/2019 22:47

BORING!
6/27/2019 1:35

.@NBCNews and @MSNBC should be ashamed of themselves for having such a horrible technical breakdown in the middle of the debate. Truly unprofessional and only worthy of a FAKE NEWS Organization which they are!
6/27/2019 2:06

Just stopped in Alaska and said hello to our GREAT troops! https://t.co/oLYn1mpaVm **6/27/2019 2:33**

I look forward to speaking with Prime Minister Modi about the fact that India for years having put very high Tariffs against the United States just recently increased the Tariffs even further. This is unacceptable and the Tariffs must be withdrawn! **6/27/2019 3:47**

Thank you @MSNBC real professionals! @chucktodd @ maddow https://t.co/7ZCkcUQ4yA **6/27/2019 9:36**

Seems totally ridiculous that our government and indeed Country cannot ask a basic question of Citizenship in a very expensive detailed and important Census in this case for

2020. I have asked the lawyers if they can delay the Census no matter how long until the..... (1/2) **6/27/2019 17:37**

.....United States Supreme Court is given additional information from which it can make a final and decisive decision on this very critical matter. Can anyone really believe that as a great Country we are not able the ask whether or not someone is a Citizen. Only in America! (2/2) **6/27/2019 17:37**

Bipartisan Humanitarian Aid Bill for the Southern Border just passed. A great job done by all! Now we must work to get rid of the Loopholes and fix Asylum. Thank you also to Mexico for the work being done on helping with Illegal Immigration - a very big difference! **6/27/2019 22:22**

All Democrats just raised their hands for giving millions of illegal aliens unlimited healthcare. How about taking care of American Citizens first!? That's the end of that race! **6/28/2019 1:37**

The Stock Market went up massively from the day after I won the Election all the way up to the day that I took office because of the enthusiasm for the fact that I was going to be President. That big Stock Market increase must be credited to me. If Hillary won - a Big Crash! **6/28/2019 9:12**

I am in Japan at the G-20 representing our Country well but I heard it was not a good day for Sleepy Joe or Crazy Bernie. One is exhausted the other is nuts - so what's the big deal?

6/28/2019 9:26

54% in Poll! I would be at 75% (with our great economy maybe the best ever) if not for the Phony Witch Hunt and the Fake News Media! **6/28/2019 22:41**

After some very important meetings including my meeting with President Xi of China I will be leaving Japan for South Korea (with President Moon). While there if Chairman Kim of North Korea sees this I would meet him at the Border/ DMZ just to shake his hand and say Hello(?)! **6/28/2019 22:51**

Thank you #G20OsakaSummit https://t.co/9FCqSuR5Bp **6/29/2019 10:11**

I had a great meeting with President Xi of China yesterday far better than expected. I agreed not to increase the already existing Tariffs that we charge China while we continue to negotiate. China has agreed that during the negotiation they will begin purchasing large..... **6/29/2019 22:32**

....again with China as our relationship with them continues to be a very good one. The quality of the transaction is far more important to me than speed. I am in no hurry but things look very good! There will be no reduction in the Tariffs currently being charged to China. **6/29/2019 22:32**

I am in South Korea now. President Moon and I have "toasted" our new Trade Deal a far better one for us than that which it replaced. Today I will visit with and speak to our Troops - and also go to the the DMZ (long planned). My meeting with President Moon went very well! **6/29/2019 22:35**

The highly respected Farm Journal has just announced my Approval Rating with our great Farmers at 74% and that despite all of the Fake & Corrupt News that they are forced to endure. Farmers have been unfairly treated for many years - and that is turning around FAST! **6/30/2019 0:07**

The leaders of virtually every country that I met at the G-20 congratulated me on our great economy. Many countries are having difficulties on that score. We have the best economy anywhere in the world with GREAT & UNLIMITED potential looking into the future! **6/30/2019 0:29**

Leaving South Korea after a wonderful meeting with Chairman Kim Jong Un. Stood on the soil of North Korea an important statement for all and a great honor!

6/30/2019 10:21

JULY 2019 - SEPTEMBER 2019

★★★★★★★★★★★★★★★★★★★★★★★★★★★

Despite all of the United State's economic indicators being positive, with the markets soaring and jobs being plentiful, attacks against Trump increase from "The Squad." These four women become the leaders, along with Senator Bernie Sanders, of the socialist wing of the Democratic Party. Boris Johnson becomes prime minister of the U.K., ensuring that BREXIT will finally happen. In a major victory for Trump, the Supreme Court allows construction of the wall on the southern border. As the shooting in El Paso kills twenty-two, issues involving the 2nd Amendment escalate, further dividing Americans. The list of Democratic contenders for the presidency reaches twenty-four before Senator Kirsten Gillibrand (D-NY) leads the way and drops out. Spearheading repeated investigations concerning President Trump and his associates, Reps. Adam Schiff (D-CA) and Jerry Nadler (D-NY) become household names.

So many amazing things happened over the last three days. All or at least most of those things are great for the United States. Much was accomplished! **7/1/2019 3:17**

Congratulations to Prime Minister Abe of Japan for hosting such a fantastic and well run G-20. There wasn't a thing that was missing or a mistake that was made. PERFECT! The people of Japan must be very proud of their Prime Minister. **7/1/2019 15:02**

It is very hard and expensive to live in New York. Governor Andrew Cuomo uses his Attorney General as a bludgeoning tool for his own purposes. They sue on everything always in search of a crime. I even got sued on a Foundation which took Zero rent & expenses & gave away... **7/1/2019 16:10**

That's right The Trump Foundation gave away 100% plus with Zero rent or expenses charged and has been being sued by Cuomo and New York State for years - another part of the political Witch Hunt. Just in case anyone is interested - Clinton Foundation never even looked at! **7/1/2019 16:37**

It was great being with Chairman Kim Jong Un of North Korea this weekend. We had a great meeting he looked really well and very healthy - I look forward to seeing him again soon.... **7/1/2019 22:16**

People are fleeing New York like never before. If they own a business they are twice as likely to flee. And if they are a victim of harassment by the A.G. of the state like what they are doing to our great NRA which I think will move quickly to Texas where they are loved..... **7/2/2019 11:21**

As most people are aware according to the Polls I won EVERY debate including the three with Crooked Hillary Clinton despite the fact that in the first debate they modulated the sound on me and got caught. This crew looks somewhat easier than Crooked but you never know? **7/2/2019 11:38**

The Economy is the BEST IT HAS EVER BEEN! Even much of the Fake News is giving me credit for that! **7/2/2019 11:50**

Big 4th of July in D.C. "Salute to America." The Pentagon & our great Military Leaders are thrilled to be doing this & showing to the American people among other things the strongest and most advanced Military anywhere in the World. Incredible Flyovers & biggest ever Fireworks! **7/2/2019 14:25**

Robert Mueller is being asked to testify yet again. He said he could only stick to the Report & that is what he would and must do. After so much testimony & total transparency this Witch Hunt must now end. No more Do Overs. No Collusion No Obstruction. The Great Hoax is dead! **7/2/2019 14:51**

Thanks to "Phantom Fireworks" and "Fireworks by Grucci" for their generosity in donating the biggest fireworks show Washington D.C. has ever seen. CEO's Bruce Zoldan and Phil Grucci are helping to make this the greatest 4th of July celebration in our Nations history! **7/2/2019 22:05**

A very sad time for America when the Supreme Court of the United States won't allow a question of "Is this person a Citizen of the United States?" to be asked on the #2020 Census! Going on for a long time. I have asked the Department of Commerce and the Department of Justice.... (1/2) **7/3/2019 2:33**

....to do whatever is necessary to bring this most vital of questions and this very important case to a successful conclusion. USA! USA! USA! (2/2) **7/3/2019 2:33**

Iran was violating the 150 Billion Dollar (plus 1.8 Billion Dollar in CASH) Nuclear Deal with the United States and others who paid NOTHING long before I became President - and they have now breached their stockpile limit. Not good! **7/3/2019 4:06**

Our July 4th Salute to America at the Lincoln Memorial is looking to be really big. It will be the show of a lifetime!
7/3/2019 12:16

We have the greatest economy anywhere in the world. We have the greatest military anywhere in the world. Not bad!
7/3/2019 12:27

The cost of our great Salute to America tomorrow will be very little compared to what it is worth. We own the planes we have the pilots the airport is right next door (Andrews) all we need is the fuel. We own the tanks and all. Fireworks are donated by two of the greats. Nice! **7/3/2019 14:30**

Congratulations to Navy Seal Eddie Gallagher his wonderful wife Andrea and his entire family. You have been through much together. Glad I could help! **7/3/2019 14:47**

The News Reports about the Department of Commerce dropping its quest to put the Citizenship Question on the Census is incorrect or to state it differently FAKE! We are absolutely moving forward as we must because of the importance of the answer to this question. **7/3/2019 15:06**

Our Border Patrol people are not hospital workers doctors or nurses. The Democrats bad Immigration Laws which could be easily fixed are the problem. Great job by Border Patrol above and beyond. Many of these illegals aliens are living far better now than where they..... (1/2) **7/3/2019 19:31**

.....came from and in far safer conditions. No matter how good things actually look even if perfect the Democrat visitors will act shocked & aghast at how terrible things are. Just Pols. If they really want to fix them change the Immigration Laws and Loopholes. So easy to do! (2/2)
7/3/2019 19:31

.....Now if you really want to fix the Crisis at the Southern Border both humanitarian and otherwise tell migrants not to come into our country unless they are willing to do so legally and hopefully through a system based on Merit. This way we have no problems at all! **7/3/2019 19:31**

If Illegal Immigrants are unhappy with the conditions in the quickly built or refitted detentions centers just tell them not to come. All problems solved!

7/3/2019 20:22

Mexico is doing a far better job than the Democrats on the Border. Thank you Mexico! **7/3/2019 20:23**

Iran has just issued a New Warning. Rouhani says that they will Enrich Uranium to "any amount we want" if there is no new Nuclear Deal. Be careful with the threats Iran. They can come back to bite you like nobody has been bitten before! **7/3/2019 20:33**

Today's Stock Market is the highest in the history of our great Country! This is the 104th time since the Election of 2016 that we have reached a NEW HIGH. Congratulations USA! **7/4/2019 3:44**

So important for our Country that the very simple and basic "Are you a Citizen of the United States?" question be allowed to be asked in the 2020 Census. Department of Commerce and the Department of Justice are working very hard on this even on the 4th of July! **7/4/2019 11:20**

HAPPY 4TH OF JULY! **7/4/2019 11:23**

People are coming from far and wide to join us today and tonight for what is turning out to be one of the biggest celebrations in the history of our Country SALUTE TO AMERICA an all day event at the Lincoln Memorial culminating with large scale flyovers of the most modern..... (1/2) **7/4/2019 12:41**

....and advanced aircraft anywhere in the World. Perhaps even Air Force One will do a low & loud sprint over the crowd. That will start at 6:00P.M. but be there early. Then at 9:00 P.M. a great (to put it mildly) fireworks display. I will speak on behalf of our great Country! (2/2) **7/4/2019 12:41**

Great news for the Republican Party as one of the dumbest & most disloyal men in Congress is "quitting" the Party. No Collusion No Obstruction! Knew he couldn't get the nomination to run again in the Great State of Michigan. Already being challenged for his seat. A total loser! **7/4/2019 13:05**

Looks like a lot of people already heading to SALUTE TO AMERICA at Lincoln Memorial. It will be well worth the trip and wait. See you there at 6:00 P.M. Amazing music and bands. Thank you ARMY! **7/4/2019 18:03**

Been fully briefed on earthquake in Southern California. All seems to be very much under control! **7/4/2019 19:24**

Weather looking good clearing rapidly and temperatures going down fast. See you in 45 minutes 6:30 to 7:00 P.M. at Lincoln Memorial! **7/4/2019 21:57**

A great crowd of tremendous Patriots this evening all the way back to the Washington Monument! #SaluteToAmerica 🇺🇸 https://t.co/nJghdfqlhX **7/5/2019 0:28**

JOBS JOBS JOBS! https://t.co/lWqvRNJDOW **7/5/2019 14:28**

"Record 157005000 Employed; 19th Record of Trump Era" https://t.co/syROOk1UOb **7/5/2019 14:30**

Happy Birthday to our great United States @SecretService! https://t.co/RMgiPGnudZ **7/5/2019 21:47**

Strong jobs report low inflation and other countries around the world doing anything possible to take advantage of the United States knowing that our Federal Reserve doesn't have a clue! They raised rates too soon too often & tightened while others did just the opposite.... (1/2) **7/6/2019 3:24**

....As well as we are doing from the day after the great Election when the Market shot right up it could have been even better - massive additional wealth would have been created & used very well. Our most difficult problem is not our competitors it is the Federal Reserve! (2/2) **7/6/2019 3:24**

Our Country is the envy of the World. Thank you Mr. President! https://t.co/2h8mvu16YX **7/6/2019 12:11**

Joe Biden is a reclamation project. Some things are just not salvageable. China and other countries that ripped us off for years are begging for him. He deserted our military our law enforcement and our healthcare. Added more debt than all other Presidents combined. Won't win! **7/6/2019 12:45**

Sleepy Joe Biden just admitted he worked with segregationists and separately has already been very plain about the fact that he will be substantially raising everyone's taxes if he becomes president. Ridiculously all Democrats want to substantially raise taxes! **7/7/2019 13:03**

Last year was the first in 51 years where prescription drug prices actually went down but things have been and are being put in place that will drive them down substantially. If Dems would work with us in a bipartisan fashion we would get big results very fast! **7/7/2019 13:13**

Congratulations to the U.S. Women's Soccer Team on winning the World Cup! Great and exciting play. America is proud of you all!

7/7/2019 19:11

The Fake News Media in particular the Failing @nytimes is writing phony and exaggerated accounts of the Border Detention Centers. First of all people should not be entering our Country illegally only for us to then have to care for them. We should be allowed to focus on ..... (1/3) **7/7/2019 19:48**

....brought up not them) because the Dems won't change the Loopholes and Asylum. Big Media Con Job! (3/3)

7/7/2019 19:48

....United States Citizens first. Border Patrol and others in Law Enforcement have been doing a great job. We said there was a Crisis - the Fake News & the Dems said it was "manufactured." Now all agree we were right but they always knew that. They are crowded (which we..... (2/3)

7/7/2019 19:48

We are building the Wall now but the reason the badly needed Wall wasn't approved in the Republican controlled House and Senate was that we had a very slim majority in the Senate & needed 9 Democrat votes. They were totally unwilling to give Wall votes to us want Open Borders!

7/7/2019 21:09

Watching @FoxNews weekend anchors is worse than watching low ratings Fake News @CNN or Lyin' Brian Williams (remember when he totally fabricated a War Story trying to make himself into a hero & got fired. A very dishonest journalist!) and the crew of degenerate......

7/7/2019 23:50

Impossible to believe that @FoxNews has hired @ donnabrazile the person fired by @CNN (after they tried to hide the bad facts & failed) for giving Crooked Hillary Clinton the questions to a debate something unimaginable. Now she is all over Fox including Shep Smith by far....

7/8/2019 3:17

Brilliant Constitutional Lawyer Dr. John Eastman said the Special Prosecutor (Mueller) should have NEVER been appointed in the first place. The entire exercise was fundamentally illegal. The Witch Hunt should never happen to another President of the U.S. again. A TOTAL SCAM! https://t.co/5sRAMhHAR8 **7/8/2019 16:40**

I have been very critical about the way the U.K. and Prime Minister Theresa May handled Brexit. What a mess she and her representatives have created. I told her how it should be done but she decided to go another way. I do not know the Ambassador but he is not liked or well.... (1/2) **7/8/2019 18:31**

....thought of within the U.S. We will no longer deal with him. The good news for the wonderful United Kingdom is that they will soon have a new Prime Minister. While I thoroughly enjoyed the magnificent State Visit last month it was the Queen who I was most impressed with! (2/2) **7/8/2019 18:31**

The wacky Ambassador that the U.K. foisted upon the United States is not someone we are thrilled with a very stupid guy. He should speak to his country and Prime Minister May about their failed Brexit negotiation and not be upset with my criticism of how badly it was... **7/9/2019 11:48**

Outrage is growing in the Great State of Minnesota where our Patriots are now having to fight for the right to say the Pledge of Allegiance. I will be fighting with you! @ foxandfriends **7/9/2019 12:18**

Food Stamp participation hits 10 year low. Wow! @OANN **7/9/2019 12:42**

India has long had a field day putting Tariffs on American products. No longer acceptable! **7/9/2019 12:44**

....Why would Kentucky ever think of giving up the most powerful position in Congress the Senate Majority Leader for a freshman Senator with little power in what will hopefully be the minority party. We need Mitch in the Senate to Keep America Great!! **7/10/2019 0:13**

A truly great patriotic & charitable man Bernie Marcus the co-founder of Home Depot who at the age of 90 is coming under attack by the Radical Left Democrats with one of their often used weapons. They don't want people to shop at those GREAT stores because he contributed.... (1/2) **7/10/2019 1:30**

....to your favorite President me! These people are vicious and totally crazed but remember there are far more great people ("Deplorables") in this country than bad. Do to them what they do to you. Fight for Bernie Marcus and Home Depot! (2/2) **7/10/2019 1:30**

So now the Obama appointed judge on the Census case (Are you a Citizen of the United States?) won't let the Justice Department use the lawyers that it wants to use. Could this be a first? **7/10/2019 1:44**

Word just out that I won a big part of the Deep State and Democrat induced Witch Hunt. Unanimous decision in my favor from The United States Court of Appeals For The Fourth Circuit on the ridiculous Emoluments Case. I don't make money but lose a fortune for the honor of..... (1/2) **7/10/2019 15:06**

....serving and doing a great job as your President (including accepting Zero salary!). (2/2) **7/10/2019 15:06**

I was just informed by Marillyn Hewson CEO of Lockheed Martin of her decision to keep the Sikorsky Helicopter Plant in Coatesville Pennsylvania open and humming! We are very proud of Pennsylvania and the people who work there.... (1/2) **7/11/2019 0:06**

....Thank you to Lockheed Martin one of the USA's truly great companies! (2/2) **7/11/2019 0:06**

Democrats had to quickly take down a tweet called "Kids In Cages Inhumane Treatment at the Border" because the horrible picture used was from the Obama years. Very embarrassing! @foxandfriends **7/11/2019 12:08**

Dow just hit 27000 for first time EVER! **7/11/2019 14:52**

Do you believe this kind of bravery? Amazing drug seizure. WATCH! https://t.co/M1KKBFic4A **7/12/2019 2:29**

Wow @CNN RATINGS HAVE CRASHED. LOST ALL CREDIBILITY! **7/12/2019 13:01**

Leaving the Great State of Ohio! https://t.co/WTLC1fFzWl **7/13/2019 1:13**

House Minority Leader Kevin McCarthy is a far superior leader than was Lame Duck Speaker Paul Ryan. Tougher smarter and a far better fundraiser Kevin is already closing in on 44 Million Dollars. Paul's final year numbers were according to Breitbart "abysmal." People like..... (1/2)
7/13/2019 21:19

....Paul Ryan almost killed the Republican Party. Weak ineffective & stupid are not exactly the qualities that Republicans or the CITIZENS of our Country were looking for. Right now our spirit is at an all time high far better than the Radical Left Dems. You'll see next year! (2/2) **7/13/2019 21:19**

94% Approval Rating in the Republican Party an all time high. Ronald Reagan was 87%. Thank you! **7/13/2019 21:21**

So interesting to see "Progressive" Democrat Congresswomen who originally came from countries whose governments are a complete and total catastrophe the worst most corrupt and inept anywhere in the world (if they even have a functioning government at all) now loudly...... (1/3)

7/14/2019 12:27

....it is done. These places need your help badly you can't leave fast enough. I'm sure that Nancy Pelosi would be very happy to quickly work out free travel arrangements! (3/3)
7/14/2019 12:27

....and viciously telling the people of the United States the greatest and most powerful Nation on earth how our government is to be run. Why don't they go back and help fix the totally broken and crime infested places from which they came. Then come back and show us how.... (2/3)
7/14/2019 12:27

Friday's tour showed vividly to politicians and the media how well run and clean the children's detention centers are. Great reviews! Failing @nytimes story was FAKE! The adult single men areas were clean but crowded - also loaded up with a big percentage of criminals...... (1/2) **7/14/2019 13:45**

.....Sorry can't let them into our Country. If too crowded tell them not to come to USA and tell the Dems to fix the Loopholes - Problem Solved! (2/2) **7/14/2019 13:45**

Think what it would be without the 3 year Witch Hunt and Fake News Media in partnership with the Democrats! https://t.co/KBtI7wde0F **7/14/2019 18:31**

So sad to see the Democrats sticking up for people who speak so badly of our Country and who in addition hate Israel with a true and unbridled passion. Whenever confronted they call their adversaries including Nancy Pelosi "RACIST." Their disgusting language..... (1/2) **7/15/2019 0:02**

....and the many terrible things they say about the United States must not be allowed to go unchallenged. If the Democrat Party wants to continue to condone such disgraceful behavior then we look even more forward to seeing you at the ballot box in 2020! (2/2) **7/15/2019 0:02**

We are doing great Economically as a Country Number One despite the Fed's antiquated policy on rates and tightening. Much room to grow! **7/15/2019 2:17**

China's 2nd Quarter growth is the slowest it has been in more than 27 years. The United States Tariffs are having a major effect on companies wanting to leave China for non-tariffed countries. Thousands of companies are leaving. This is why China wants to make a deal.... (1/2) **7/15/2019 10:43**

....with the U.S. and wishes it had not broken the original deal in the first place. In the meantime we are receiving Billions of Dollars in Tariffs from China with possibly much more to come. These Tariffs are paid for by China devaluing & pumping not by the U.S. taxpayer! (2/2) **7/15/2019 10:43**

When will the Radical Left Congresswomen apologize to our Country the people of Israel and even to the Office of the President for the foul language they have used and the terrible things they have said. So many people are angry at them & their horrible & disgusting actions! **7/15/2019 10:54**

If Democrats want to unite around the foul language & racist hatred spewed from the mouths and actions of these very unpopular & unrepresentative Congresswomen it will be interesting to see how it plays out. I can tell you that they have made Israel feel abandoned by the U.S.
7/15/2019 11:42

"We all know that AOC and this crowd are a bunch of Communists they hate Israel they hate our own Country they're calling the guards along our Border (the Border Patrol Agents) Concentration Camp Guards they accuse people who support Israel as doing it for the Benjamin's.... (1/3) **7/15/2019 13:58**

....What does it mean for America to have free Healthcare for Illegal Immigrants no criminalization of coming into our Country - See how that works for controlling Immigration! They talk about Israel like they're a bunch of thugs not victims of the entire region. They wanted... (2/3) **7/15/2019 13:58**

.....to impeach President Trump on DAY ONE. Make them the face of the future of the Democrat Party you will destroy the Democrat Party. Their policies will destroy our Country!" @LindseyGrahamSC Need I say more? (3/3) **7/15/2019 13:58**

Here we go with the Fake Polls. Just like what happened with the Election against Crooked Hillary Clinton. ABC NBC CNN @nytimes @washingtonpost they all got it wrong on purpose. Suppression Polls so early? They will never learn!
7/15/2019 14:49

We will never be a Socialist or Communist Country. IF YOU ARE NOT HAPPY HERE YOU CAN LEAVE! It is your choice and your choice alone. This is about love for America. Certain people HATE our Country.... **7/15/2019 21:08**

....Detention facilities are not Concentration Camps! America has never been stronger than it is now – rebuilt Military highest Stock Market EVER lowest unemployment and more people working than ever before. Keep America Great! **7/15/2019 21:08**

....They are anti-Israel pro Al-Qaeda and comment on the 9/11 attack "some people did something." Radical Left Democrats want Open Borders which means drugs crime human trafficking and much more.... **7/15/2019 21:08**

The Dems were trying to distance themselves from the four "progressives" but now they are forced to embrace them. That means they are endorsing Socialism hate of Israel and the USA! Not good for the Democrats! **7/15/2019 21:26**

The Obama Administration built the Cages not the Trump Administration! DEMOCRATS MUST GIVE US THE VOTES TO CHANGE BAD IMMIGRATION LAWS. **7/15/2019 21:43**

MAKE AMERICA GREAT AGAIN!
7/15/2019 21:56

"The best economy in our lifetime!" @IngrahamAngle **7/16/2019 2:03**

The Democrat Congresswomen have been spewing some of the most vile hateful and disgusting things ever said by a politician in the House or Senate & yet they get a free pass and a big embrace from the Democrat Party. Horrible anti-Israel anti-USA pro-terrorist & public..... (1/2) **7/16/2019 11:20**

.....shouting of the F...word among many other terrible things and the petrified Dems run for the hills. Why isn't the House voting to rebuke the filthy and hate laced things they have said? Because they are the Radical Left and the Democrats are afraid to take them on. Sad! (2/2) **7/16/2019 11:20**

"Billionaire Tech Investor Peter Thiel believes Google should be investigated for treason. He accuses Google of working with the Chinese Government." @foxandfriends A great and brilliant guy who knows this subject better than anyone! The Trump Administration will take a look!

7/16/2019 11:46

If you come after the President the Country the Flag - he's going to defend himself. What the squad doesn't like is that Donald Trump is enforcing the very laws that are on the books that were put there by Congress." Jason Chaffetz. Also buy Jason's great new book POWER GRAB!

7/16/2019 12:00

Our Country is Free Beautiful and Very Successful. If you hate our Country or if you are not happy here you can leave!

7/16/2019 12:17

Those Tweets were NOT Racist. I don't have a Racist bone in my body! The so-called vote to be taken is a Democrat con game. Republicans should not show "weakness" and fall into their trap. This should be a vote on the filthy language statements and lies told by the Democrat..... (1/2)

7/16/2019 13:59

.....Congresswomen who I truly believe based on their actions hate our Country. Get a list of the HORRIBLE things they have said. Omar is polling at 8% Cortez at 21%. Nancy Pelosi tried to push them away but now they are forever wedded to the Democrat Party. See you in 2020! (2/2)

7/16/2019 13:59

Kevin McCarthy @GOPLeader "The President's Tweets were not Racist. The controversy over the tweets is ALL POLITICS. I will vote against this resolution." Thank you Kevin!

7/16/2019 15:11

Yesterday it was my great honor to host our third annual Made in America Showcase at the @WhiteHouse.... https://t.co/mBha7Qprr9 **7/16/2019 22:05**

So great to see how unified the Republican Party was on today's vote concerning statements I made about four Democrat Congresswomen. If you really want to see statements look at the horrible things they said about our Country Israel and much more. They are now the top most... (1/2) **7/17/2019 3:05**

....visible members of the House Democrats who are now wedded to this bitterness and hate. The Republican vote was 187-4. Wow! Also this was the first time since 1984 that the Speaker of the House was ruled Out of Order and broke the Rules of the House. Quite a day! (2/2) **7/17/2019 3:05**

"In America if you hate our Country you are free to leave. The simple fact of the matter is the four Congresswomen think that America is wicked in its origins they think that America is even more wicked now that we are all racist and evil. They're entitled to their..... (1/3) **7/17/2019 11:18**

....they are destroying the Democrat Party. I'm appalled that so many of our Presidential candidates are falling all over themselves to try to agree with the four horsewomen of the apocalypse. I'm entitled to say that they're Wack Jobs." Louisiana Senator John Kennedy (3/3) **7/17/2019 11:18**

...opinion they're Americans. Now I'm entitled to my opinion & I just think they're left wing cranks. They're the reason there are directions on a shampoo bottle & we should ignore them. The "squad" has moved the Democrat Party substantially LEFT and..... (2/3) **7/17/2019 11:18**

The Democrats in Congress are getting nothing done not on drug pricing not on immigration not on infrastructure not on nothing! Sooo much opportunity yet all they want to do is go "fishing." The American people are tired of the never ending Witch Hunt they want results now! **7/17/2019 11:20**

Big Rally tonight in Greenville North Carolina. Lots of great things to tell you about including the fact that our Economy is the best it has ever been. Best Employment & Stock Market Numbers EVER. I'll talk also about people who love and hate our Country (mostly love)! 7:PM **7/17/2019 12:46**

After a ten year search the so-called "mastermind" of the Mumbai Terror attacks has been arrested in Pakistan. Great pressure has been exerted over the last two years to find him!

7/17/2019 14:16

New Poll: The Rasmussen Poll one of the most accurate in predicting the 2016 Election has just announced that "Trump" numbers have recently gone up by four points to 50%. Thank you to the vicious young Socialist Congresswomen. America will never buy your act! #MAGA2020 **7/17/2019 14:30**

GOD BLESS THE USA https://t.co/w6FenobnlR **7/17/2019 16:18**

See you tonight North Carolina! #MAGA2020 https://t.co/rqOwEkTtqQ **7/17/2019 19:35**

The United States House of Representatives has just overwhelmingly voted to kill the Resolution on Impeachment 332-95-1. This is perhaps the most ridiculous and time consuming project I have ever had to work on. Impeachment of your President who has led the.... (1/2)

7/17/2019 22:24

....Greatest Economic BOOM in the history of our Country the best job numbers biggest tax reduction rebuilt military and much more is now OVER. This should never be allowed to happen to another President of the United States again! (2/2) **7/17/2019 22:24**

The Republican Party is the Party for ALL Americans. We are the Party of the American Worker the American Family & the American Dream. This is the proud banner the Republican Party will carry into the Republican National Convention next summer in the great city of Charlotte NC! https://t.co/T39INpON8N **7/18/2019 1:42**

Just returned to the White House from the Great State of North Carolina. What a crowd and what great people. The enthusiasm blows away our rivals on the Radical Left. #2020 will be a big year for the Republican Party! **7/18/2019 3:51**

A lot of bad things are happening in Puerto Rico. The Governor is under siege the Mayor of San Juan is a despicable and incompetent person who I wouldn't trust under any circumstance and the United States Congress foolishly gave 92 Billion Dollars for hurricane relief much.... (1/2) **7/18/2019 14:54**

....of which was squandered away or wasted never to be seen again. This is more than twice the amount given to Texas & Florida combined. I know the people of Puerto Rico well and they are great. But much of their leadership is corrupt & robbing the U.S. Government blind! (2/2) **7/18/2019 14:54**

Most of the MS-13 Gang members indicted & arrested in L.A. were illegal aliens 19 of 22. They are said to have killed many people in the most brutal fashion. They should never have been allowed in our Country for so long 10 years. We have arrested and deported thousands.... (1/2) **7/18/2019 15:10**

....of gang members in particular MS-13. ICE and Border Patrol are doing a great job! (2/2) **7/18/2019 15:10**

Today @FLOTUS Melania and I were honored to welcome members of Team USA to the @WhiteHouse for a great celebration of their success during the 2019 @ SpecialOlympics @WorldGamesAD! Congratulations @ specialolyUSA! #Cheer4USA https://t.co/m7PcT6N1KO **7/18/2019 22:14**

I am pleased to announce that it is my intention to nominate Gene Scalia as the new Secretary of Labor. Gene has led a life of great success in the legal and labor field and is highly respected not only as a lawyer but as a lawyer with great experience.... **7/19/2019 0:22**

It is amazing how the Fake News Media became "crazed" over the chant "send her back" by a packed Arena (a record) crowd in the Great State of North Carolina but is totally calm & accepting of the most vile and disgusting statements made by the three Radical Left Congresswomen... **7/19/2019 12:16**

Just spoke to @KanyeWest about his friend A$AP Rocky's incarceration. I will be calling the very talented Prime Minister of Sweden to see what we can do about helping A$AP Rocky. So many people would like to see this quickly resolved! **7/19/2019 20:01**

You can add 10% or 15% to this number. Economy doing better than EVER before! https://t.co/o59vl5tzXn **7/20/2019 11:18**

Just had a very good call with @SwedishPM Stefan Löfven who assured me that American citizen A$AP Rocky will be treated fairly. Likewise I assured him that A$AP was not a flight risk and offered to personally vouch for his bail or an alternative.... (1/2) **7/20/2019 13:52**

....Our teams will be talking further and we agreed to speak again in the next 48 hours! (2/2) **7/20/2019 13:52**

Economic numbers reach an all time high the best in our Country's history. Great to be a part of something so good for so many! **7/20/2019 22:56**

I will help Angel Mom (and great woman) Mary Ann Mendoza with Twitter. I know Mary Ann from the beginning and she should never be silenced. She is a winner who has lost so much her child. Twitter if you're watching please do what you have to do NOW! @foxandfriends **7/21/2019 10:40**

The Great State of West Virginia is producing record setting numbers and doing really well. When I became President it was practically shut down and closed for business. Not anymore! **7/21/2019 10:54**

Presidential Harassment! **7/21/2019 11:59**

MAKE AMERICA GREAT AGAIN! **7/21/2019 12:00**

I don't believe the four Congresswomen are capable of loving our Country. They should apologize to America (and Israel) for the horrible (hateful) things they have said. They are destroying the Democrat Party but are weak & insecure people who can never destroy our great Nation!
7/21/2019 12:07

Congratulations to Bibi @Netanyahu on becoming the longest serving PM in the history of Israel. Under your leadership Israel has become a technology powerhouse and a world class economy.... (1/2) **7/21/2019 20:33**

....Most importantly you have led Israel with a commitment to the values of democracy freedom and equal opportunity that both our nations cherish and share! (2/2) **7/21/2019 20:33**

....Based on the comments made by Senator Schumer he must have seen how dangerous & bad for our Country the Border is. It is not a "manufactured crisis" as the Fake News Media & their Democrat partners tried to portray. He said he wants to meet. I will set up a meeting ASAP! **7/22/2019 2:16**

Senator Chuck Schumer has finally gone to the Southern Border with some Democrat Senators. This is a GREAT thing! Nearby he missed a large group of Illegal Immigrants trying to enter the USA illegally. They wildly rushed Border Patrol. Some Agents were badly injured.... **7/22/2019 2:16**

The Mainstream Media is out of control. They constantly lie and cheat in order to get their Radical Left Democrat views out their for all to see. It has never been this bad. They have gone bonkers & no longer care what is right or wrong. This large scale false reporting is sick! **7/22/2019 12:37**

Fake News Equals the Enemy of the People! **7/22/2019 12:38**

Highly conflicted Robert Mueller should not be given another bite at the apple. In the end it will be bad for him and the phony Democrats in Congress who have done nothing but waste time on this ridiculous Witch Hunt. Result of the Mueller Report NO COLLUSION NO OBSTRUCTION!... **7/22/2019 12:53**

....But the questions should be asked why were all of Clinton's people given immunity and why were the text messages of Peter S and his lover Lisa Page deleted and destroyed right after they left Mueller and after we requested them(this is Illegal)? **7/22/2019 12:53**

Going with First Lady to pay our respects to Justice Stevens. Leaving now! **7/22/2019 14:32**

The "Squad" is a very Racist group of troublemakers who are young inexperienced and not very smart. They are pulling the once great Democrat Party far left and were against humanitarian aid at the Border...And are now against ICE and Homeland Security. So bad for our Country! **7/22/2019 14:48**

I am pleased to announce that a deal has been struck with Senate Majority Leader Mitch McConnell Senate Minority Leader Chuck Schumer Speaker of the House Nancy Pelosi and House Minority Leader Kevin McCarthy - on a two-year Budget and Debt Ceiling with no poison pills.... **7/22/2019 21:44**

....This was a real compromise in order to give another big victory to our Great Military and Vets! **7/22/2019 21:44**

When we rip down and totally replace a badly broken and dilapidated Barrier on the Southern Border something which cannot do the job the Fake News Media gives us zero credit for building a new Wall. We have replaced many miles of old Barrier with powerful new Walls! **7/22/2019 23:16**

"I completely read the entire Mueller Report and do you know what I concluded after reading both Volume 1 and Volume 2? There is no there there. NO THERE THERE! We completely wasted everybody's time and taxpayer's money." @trish_regan **7/23/2019 2:38**

Newest Poll: Only 11% in favor of starting ridiculous impeachment hearings. Well let's see: We have the Best Economy in History the Best Employment Numbers in History Most People Working in History Highest Stock Market in History Biggest Tax and Regulation Cuts in History.. (1/2) **7/23/2019 11:25**

....Best and Newest Military (almost totally rebuilt from the depleted military I took over) in History Best V.A. in History (Choice) and MUCH MUCH MORE. Gee let's impeach the President. The "Squad" (AOC Plus 3) and other Dems suffer from Trump Derangement Syndrome. Crazy! (2/2)

7/23/2019 11:25

Congratulations to Boris Johnson on becoming the new Prime Minister of the United Kingdom. He will be great!

7/23/2019 11:29

KEEP AMERICA GREAT! **7/23/2019 11:43**

Guatemala which has been forming Caravans and sending large numbers of people some with criminal records to the United States has decided to break the deal they had with us on signing a necessary Safe Third Agreement. We were ready to go. Now we are looking at the "BAN".... (1/2)

7/23/2019 12:23

....Tariffs Remittance Fees or all of the above. Guatemala has not been good. Big U.S. taxpayer dollars going to them was cut off by me 9 months ago. (2/2) **7/23/2019 12:23**

In 2016 I almost won Minnesota. In 2020 because of America hating anti-Semite Rep. Omar & the fact that Minnesota is having its best economic year ever I will win the State! "We are going to be a nightmare to the President" she say. No AOC Plus 3 are a Nightmare for America! **7/23/2019 12:51**

Leaving for Turning Point USA. Will be speaking to some of the greatest and smartest young people on the planet. See you there! **7/23/2019 14:06**

I was saddened to learn of the recent passing of Bob Morgenthau a truly great man! Bob served as a Naval Officer in World War II was an extraordinary US Attorney Manhattan District Attorney and always a warrior for our Country that he loved so dearly.... **7/23/2019 18:43**

Just got back only to hear of a last minute change allowing a Never Trumper attorney to help Robert Mueller with his testimony before Congress tomorrow. What a disgrace to our system. Never heard of this before. VERY UNFAIR SHOULD NOT BE ALLOWED. A rigged Witch Hunt! **7/23/2019 23:32**

So Robert Mueller has now asked for his long time Never Trumper lawyer to sit beside him and help with answers. What's this all about? His lawyer represented the "basement server guy" who got off free in the Crooked Hillary case. This should NOT be allowed. Rigged Witch Hunt! **7/24/2019 2:29**

So Democrats and others can illegally fabricate a crime try pinning it on a very innocent President and when he fights back against this illegal and treasonous attack on our Country they call It Obstruction? Wrong! Why didn't Robert Mueller investigate the investigators? **7/24/2019 10:50**

It was NEVER agreed that Robert Mueller could use one of his many Democrat Never Trumper lawyers to sit next to him and help him with his answers. This was specifically NOT agreed to and I would NEVER have agreed to it. The Greatest Witch Hunt in U.S. history by far! **7/24/2019 11:03**

So why didn't the highly conflicted Robert Mueller investigate how and why Crooked Hillary Clinton deleted and acid washed 33000 Emails immediately AFTER getting a SUBPOENA from the United States Congress? She must have GREAT lawyers! **7/24/2019 11:43**

NO COLLUSION NO OBSTRUCTION! **7/24/2019 11:55**

KEEP AMERICA GREAT! **7/24/2019 12:10**

It has been reported that Robert Mueller is saying that he did not apply and interview for the job of FBI Director (and get turned down) the day before he was wrongfully appointed Special Counsel. Hope he doesn't say that under oath in that we have numerous witnesses to the...
7/24/2019 12:18

"This has been a disaster for the Democrats and a disaster for the reputation of Robert Mueller." Chris Wallace @ FoxNews **7/24/2019 14:11**

"Mueller was asked whether or not the investigation was impeded in any way and he said no." In other words there was NO OBSTRUCTION. @KatiePavlich @FoxNews
7/24/2019 14:51

I would like to thank the Democrats for holding this morning's hearing. Now after 3 hours Robert Mueller has to subject himself to #ShiftySchiff - an Embarrassment to our Country! **7/24/2019 17:04**

TRUTH IS A FORCE OF NATURE!
7/24/2019 19:33

Thank you Rep. @Jim_Jordan! https://t.co/w9tF8xur44
7/25/2019 0:52

"Yesterday changed everything it really did clear the President. He wins." @ainsleyearhardt "It changed everything in favor of the President who said all along this investigation is rooted in nothing. Mueller was exposed as being best friends with Comey. Today you say..... (1/2)
7/25/2019 11:06

...impeachment you have a Party of one. It's over." @ kilmeade "Nancy said Jerry please sit down. Very bad idea. We discovered that after putting so much time & energy into the Mueller Report it turns out Mueller didn't know what was in his Report." @SteveDoocy @foxandfriends (2/2) **7/25/2019 11:06**

Fox Poll say best Economy in DECADES! **7/25/2019 11:54**

President Trump's Approval Rating on Economy is at 52% a 4 point jump. Fox Poll @foxandfriends Shouldn't this be at 100%? Best stock market economy and unemployment numbers ever! Most people working within U.S. ever! Low interest rates very low inflation! Country doing great!
7/25/2019 12:07

We love our Law Enforcement Officers all around this great Country. What took place in NYC with water being tossed on NYPD officers was a total disgrace. It is time for @NYCMayor @BilldeBlasio to STAND UP for those who protect our lives and serve us all so well... (1/2) **7/25/2019 18:03**

...What took place was completely unacceptable and will not be tolerated. Bill de Blasio should act immediately! (2/2)
7/25/2019 18:03

Very disappointed in Prime Minister Stefan Löfven for being unable to act. Sweden has let our African American Community down in the United States. I watched the tapes of A$AP Rocky and he was being followed and harassed by troublemakers. Treat Americans fairly! #FreeRocky
7/25/2019 21:19

Give A$AP Rocky his FREEDOM. We do so much for Sweden but it doesn't seem to work the other way around. Sweden should focus on its real crime problem! #FreeRocky

7/25/2019 21:24

I am pleased to announce the House has passed our budget deal 284-149. Great for our Military and our Vets. A big thank you! **7/25/2019 23:25**

.@FoxNews is at it again. So different from what they used to be during the 2016 Primaries & before - Proud Warriors! Now new Fox Polls which have always been terrible to me (they had me losing BIG to Crooked Hillary) have me down to Sleepy Joe. Even considering..... (1/2) **7/26/2019 13:58**

....the fact that I have gone through a three year vicious Witch Hunt perpetrated by the Lamestream Media in Collusion with Crooked and the Democrat Party there can be NO WAY with the greatest Economy in U.S. history that I can be losing to the Sleepy One. KEEP AMERICA GREAT! (2/2) **7/26/2019 13:58**

There may or may not be National Security concerns with regard to Google and their relationship with China. If there is a problem we will find out about it. I sincerely hope there is not!!! **7/26/2019 14:02**

Apple will not be given Tariff waiver or relief for Mac Pro parts that are made in China. Make them in the USA no Tariffs! **7/26/2019 15:25**

France just put a digital tax on our great American technology companies. If anybody taxes them it should be their home Country the USA. We will announce a substantial reciprocal action on Macron's foolishness shortly. I've always said American wine is better than French wine!

7/26/2019 16:32

The WTO is BROKEN when the world's RICHEST countries claim to be developing countries to avoid WTO rules and get special treatment. NO more!!! Today I directed the U.S. Trade Representative to take action so that countries stop CHEATING the system at the expense of the USA!

7/26/2019 18:29

Wow! Big VICTORY on the Wall. The United States Supreme Court overturns lower court injunction allows Southern Border Wall to proceed. Big WIN for Border Security and the Rule of Law!

7/26/2019 22:37

Rep Elijah Cummings has been a brutal bully shouting and screaming at the great men & women of Border Patrol about conditions at the Southern Border when actually his Baltimore district is FAR WORSE and more dangerous. His district is considered the Worst in the USA...... (1/2)

7/27/2019 11:14

....As proven last week during a Congressional tour the Border is clean efficient & well run just very crowded. Cumming District is a disgusting rat and rodent infested mess. If he spent more time in Baltimore maybe he could help clean up this very dangerous & filthy place (2/2)

7/27/2019 11:14

Why is so much money sent to the Elijah Cummings district when it is considered the worst run and most dangerous anywhere in the United States. No human being would want to live there. Where is all this money going? How much is stolen? Investigate this corrupt mess immediately!

7/27/2019 11:24

Consideration is being given to declaring ANTIFA the gutless Radical Left Wack Jobs who go around hitting (only non-fighters) people over the heads with baseball bats a major Organization of Terror (along with MS-13 & others). Would make it easier for police to do their job! **7/27/2019 19:55**

The Dems are now coming out of shock from the terrible Mueller performance and are starting to spin impeachment all over again. How sick & disgusting and bad for our Country are they. What they are doing is so wrong but they do it anyway. Dems have become the do nothing Party! **7/27/2019 20:24**

Democrats don't care about Border Security. They refuse to give the votes necessary to fix the Loopholes and Asylum. Would be so easy! They want Open Borders which means CRIMECRIMECRIME! **7/27/2019 21:10**

Elijah Cummings spends all of his time trying to hurt innocent people through "Oversight." He does NOTHING for his very poor very dangerous and very badly run district! Take a look.... #BlacksForTrump2020 https://t.co/seNVESZUht **7/27/2019 21:35**

We gave Nadler and his Trump hating Dems the complete Mueller Report (we didn't have to) and even Mueller himself but now that both were a total BUST they say it wasn't good enough. Nothing will ever be good enough for them. Witch Hunt! **7/27/2019 21:55**

NO COLLUSION NO OBSTRUCTION TOTAL EXONERATION. DEMOCRAT WITCH HUNT! **7/27/2019 22:15**

.@RepCummings why don't you focus on your district!? https://t.co/F3Ej0Z21PZ **7/28/2019 1:50**

....Robert Mueller's testimony and the Mueller Report itself was a disaster for this illegal Democrat inspired Witch Hunt. It is an embarrassment to the USA that they don't know how to stop. They can't help themselves they are totally lost they are Clowns! **7/28/2019 3:28**

"One of the biggest things to come out of Mueller's testimony was the fact that when he was asked was there ANYTHING that impeded your investigation the answer was

a clear unequivocal NO." Misty Marris @FoxNews True but many other great "exonerating" things came out.....
7/28/2019 3:28

So sad that Elijah Cummings has been able to do so little for the people of Baltimore. Statistically Baltimore ranks last in almost every major category. Cummings has done nothing but milk Baltimore dry but the public is getting wise to the bad job that he is doing! **7/28/2019 3:35**

"If it weren't for Donald Trump we would never know how corrupt these Democrats are we would never know for sure that there was a Deep State. Now we know it." @ JudgeJeanine **7/28/2019 10:56**

Someone please explain to Nancy Pelosi who was recently called racist by those in her own party that there is nothing wrong with bringing out the very obvious fact that Congressman Elijah Cummings has done a very poor job for his district and the City of Baltimore. Just take... (1/2)
7/28/2019 11:28

....a look the facts speak far louder than words! The Democrats always play the Race Card when in fact they have done so little for our Nation's great African American people. Now lowest unemployment in U.S. history and only getting better. Elijah Cummings has failed badly! (2/2)
7/28/2019 11:28

Speaking of failing badly has anyone seen what is happening to Nancy Pelosi's district in San Francisco. It is not even recognizeable lately. Something must be done before it is too late. The Dems should stop wasting time on the Witch Hunt Hoax and start focusing on our Country!
7/28/2019 11:39

"Elijah Cummings has had his chance to address it (crime & conditions in Baltimore) for decades and he hasn't gotten it done." @PeteHegseth @foxandfriends How can he get it done when he just wants to use his Oversight Committee to hurt innocent people and divide our Country! **7/28/2019 12:12**

There is nothing racist in stating plainly what most people already know that Elijah Cummings has done a terrible job for the people of his district and of Baltimore itself. Dems always play the race card when they are unable to win with facts. Shame!

7/28/2019 18:35

If racist Elijah Cummings would focus more of his energy on helping the good people of his district and Baltimore itself perhaps progress could be made in fixing the mess that he has helped to create over many years of incompetent leadership. His radical "oversight" is a joke! **7/28/2019 19:18**

Under the Trump Administration African American unemployment is the lowest (best) in the history of the United States. No President has come close to doing this before! I also created successful Opportunity Zones. Waiting for Nancy and Elijah to say "Thank you Mr. President!" **7/28/2019 19:34**

I am pleased to announce that highly respected Congressman John Ratcliffe of Texas will be nominated by me to be the Director of National Intelligence. A former U.S. Attorney John will lead and inspire greatness for the Country he loves. Dan Coats the current Director will.... (1/2)
7/28/2019 20:45

....be leaving office on August 15th. I would like to thank Dan for his great service to our Country. The Acting Director will be named shortly. (2/2) **7/28/2019 20:45**

I have known Al for 25 years. Went to fights with him & Don King always got along well. He "loved Trump!" He would ask me for favors often. Al is a con man a troublemaker always looking for a score. Just doing his thing. Must have intimidated Comcast/NBC. Hates Whites & Cops! https://t.co/ZwPZaOFWfN **7/29/2019 10:30**

Baltimore under the leadership of Elijah Cummings has the worst Crime Statistics in the Nation. 25 years of all talk no action! So tired of listening to the same old Bull...Next Reverend Al will show up to complain & protest. Nothing will get done for the people in need. Sad! **7/29/2019 10:49**

Al Sharpton would always ask me to go to his events. He would say "it's a personal favor to me." Seldom but sometimes I would go. It was fine. He came to my office in T.T. during the presidential campaign to apologize for the way he was talking about me. Just a conman at work! **7/29/2019 11:26**

Crazy Bernie Sanders recently equated the City of Baltimore to a THIRD WORLD COUNTRY! Based on that statement I assume that Bernie must now be labeled a Racist just as a Republican would if he used that term and standard! The fact is Baltimore can be brought back maybe...... (1/2) **7/29/2019 12:46**

....even to new heights of success and glory but not with King Elijah and that crew. When the leaders of Baltimore want to see the City rise again I am in a very beautiful oval shaped office waiting for your call! (2/2) **7/29/2019 12:46**

The Republican Party has a new STAR his name is Daniel Cameron (@djaycameron) and he is running for Attorney General of the Commonwealth of Kentucky.... **7/29/2019 20:28**

Just remember the Iranians never won a war but never lost a negotiation! **7/29/2019 20:40**

Senator Cindy Hyde-Smith is doing a GREAT JOB for the people of Mississippi and fully supports our #MAGA Agenda. Cindy is tough on Crime Strong on the Border and Illegal Immigration.... **7/29/2019 22:24**

Elijah Cummings never even went to the Southern Border and then he screams at the very good people who despite

Congresses failure to fix the Loopholes and Asylum make it work (crossings are way down and the Wall is being built). Even with zero Dem help Border getting strong! **7/30/2019 1:34**

Baltimore's numbers are the worst in the United States on Crime and the Economy. Billions of dollars have been pumped in over the years but to no avail. The money was stolen or wasted. Ask Elijah Cummings where it went. He should investigate himself with his Oversight Committee! **7/30/2019 1:45**

"I don't know what it's going to take. A lot of Democratic run cities all over America look like this it's not just Baltimore unfortunately." Kimberly Klacik Baltimore journalist Remember Vote for Trump what the h.... do you have to lose? Best unemployment numbers! **7/30/2019 2:46**

China is doing very badly worst year in 27 - was supposed to start buying our agricultural product now - no signs that they are doing so. That is the problem with China they just don't come through. Our Economy has become MUCH larger than the Chinese Economy is last 3 years.... **7/30/2019 11:09**

Wow! Morning Joe & Psycho ratings have really crashed. Very small audience. People are tired of hearing Fake News delivered with an anger that is not to be believed. Sad when the show was sane they helped get me elected. Thanks! Was on all the time. Lost all of its juice! **7/30/2019 12:11**

Just reminded my staff that Morning Joe & Psycho were with me in my room at their request the night I won New Hampshire. Likewise followed me to other states.... **7/30/2019 13:52**

We should immediately pass Voter ID @Voteridplease to insure the safety and sanctity of our voting system. Also Paper Ballots as backup (old fashioned but true!). Thank you! **7/30/2019 16:41**

Wow! A federal Judge in the Southern District of N.Y. completely dismissed a lawsuit brought by the Democratic

National Committee against our historic 2016 campaign for President. The Judge said the DNC case was "entirely divorced" from the facts yet another total & complete.... (1/2) **7/30/2019 23:26**

....vindication & exoneration from the Russian WikiLeaks and every other form of HOAX perpetrated by the DNC Radical Democrats and others. This is really big "stuff" especially coming from a highly respected judge who was appointed by President Clinton. The Witch Hunt Ends! (2/2) **7/30/2019 23:26**

Such a great victory in court yesterday on the Russian Hoax the greatest political scam in the history of our Country. TREASON! Hopefully the Attorney Generel of the United States and all of those working with him will find out in great detail what happened. NEVER AGAIN!!!! **7/31/2019 14:08**

If I hadn't won the 2016 Election we would be in a Great Recession/Depression right now. The people I saw on stage last night & you can add in Sleepy Joe Harris & the rest will lead us into an economic sinkhole the likes of which we have never seen before. With me only up! **7/31/2019 14:20**

"The lesser of two Socialists is still a Socialist!" Senator John Kennedy of Louisiana **7/31/2019 14:36**

CNN's Don Lemon the dumbest man on television insinuated last night while asking a debate "question" that I was a racist when in fact I am "the least racist person in the world." Perhaps someone should explain to Don that he is supposed to be neutral unbiased & fair..... (1/2)

7/31/2019 15:31

....or is he too dumb (stupid} to understand that. No wonder CNN's ratings (MSNBC's also) have gone down the tubes

- and will stay there until they bring credibility back to the newsroom. Don't hold your breath! (2/2) **7/31/2019 15:31**

The Prosecutors who lost the case against SEAL Eddie Gallagher (who I released from solitary confinement so he could fight his case properly) were ridiculously given a Navy Achievement Medal. Not only did they lose the case they had difficulty with respect.... **7/31/2019 19:58**

The Radical Left Dems went after me for using the words "drug-infested" concerning Baltimore. Take a look at Elijah C. https://t.co/E08ngbcw3d **7/31/2019 21:59**

Thank you Bill say hello to our GREAT VETERANS! https://t.co/toDqIAIQ54 **7/31/2019 22:43**

Very low ratings for the Democratic Debate last night — they're desperate for Trump! **7/31/2019 23:06**

The cages for kids were built by the Obama Administration in 2014. He had the policy of child separation. I ended it even as I realized that more families would then come to the Border! @CNN **8/1/2019 1:46**

The people on the stage tonight and last were not those that will either Make America Great Again or Keep America Great! Our Country now is breaking records in almost every category from Stock Market to Military to Unemployment. We have prosperity & success like never before.. (1/2) **8/1/2019 4:05**

...It will soon be time to choose to keep and build upon that prosperity and success or let it go. We are respected again all around the world. Keep it that way! I said I will never let you down and I haven't. We will only grow bigger better and stronger TOGETHER! (2/2) **8/1/2019 4:05**

China Iran & other foreign countries are looking at the Democrat Candidates and "drooling" over the small prospect that they could be dealing with them in the not too distant future. They would be able to rip off our beloved

USA like never before. With President Trump NO WAY!
8/1/2019 14:24

BIG RALLY tonight in Cincinnati Ohio. See you there! P.S. Our Country is doing GREAT! **8/1/2019 14:44**

Beautiful evening in Cincinnati Ohio tonight — with GREAT American Patriots! #KAG2020 https://t.co/wDN5B4Gp87
8/2/2019 1:18

Really bad news! The Baltimore house of Elijah Cummings was robbed. Too bad! **8/2/2019 11:58**

Kim Jong Un and North Korea tested 3 short range missiles over the last number of days. These missiles tests are not a violation of our signed Singapore agreement nor was there discussion of short range missiles when we shook hands. There may be a United Nations violation but.. (1/2)
8/2/2019 15:05

....Chariman Kim has a great and beautiful vision for his country and only the United States with me as President can make that vision come true. He will do the right thing because he is far too smart not to and he does not want to disappoint his friend President Trump! (2/2) **8/2/2019 15:05**

A$AP Rocky released from prison and on his way home to the United States from Sweden. It was a Rocky Week get home ASAP A$AP! **8/2/2019 17:41**

Our great Republican Congressman John Ratcliffe is being treated very unfairly by the LameStream Media. Rather than going through months of slander and libel I explained to John how miserable it would be for him and his family to deal with these people.... (1/2) **8/2/2019 18:06**

....John has therefore decided to stay in Congress where he has done such an outstanding job representing the people of Texas and our Country. I will be announcing my nomination for DNI shortly. (2/2) **8/2/2019 18:06**

Nice to see that one of my best pupils is still a giant Trump fan. Steve joined me after I won the primaries but I loved working with him! https://t.co/jRpmdrGYTB **8/2/2019 20:50**

Countries are coming to us wanting to negotiate REAL trade deals not the one sided horror show deals made by past administrations. They don't want to be targeted for Tariffs by the U.S. **8/3/2019 12:41**

Terrible shootings in ElPaso Texas. Reports are very bad many killed. Working with State and Local authorities and Law Enforcement. Spoke to Governor to pledge total support of Federal Government. God be with you all!

8/3/2019 20:10

Today's shooting in El Paso Texas was not only tragic it was an act of cowardice. I know that I stand with everyone in this Country to condemn today's hateful act. There are no reasons or excuses that will ever justify killing innocent people.... (1/2)

8/4/2019 4:19

....Melania and I send our heartfelt thoughts and prayers to the great people of Texas. (2/2) **8/4/2019 4:19**

The FBI local and state law enforcement are working together in El Paso and in Dayton Ohio. Information is rapidly being accumulated in Dayton. Much has already be learned in El Paso. Law enforcement was very rapid in both instances. Updates will be given throughout the day!

8/4/2019 12:13

God bless the people of El Paso Texas. God bless the people of Dayton Ohio. **8/4/2019 12:16**

Today I authorized the lowering of the flags to half-staff at all Federal Government buildings in honor of the victims of

the tragedies in El Paso Texas and Dayton Ohio.... (1/2)
8/4/2019 19:49

....The flags at the White House will be lowered today through Thursday August 8. Melania and I are praying for all those impacted by this unspeakable act of evil! (2/2)
8/4/2019 19:49

We cannot let those killed in El Paso Texas and Dayton Ohio die in vain. Likewise for those so seriously wounded. We can never forget them and those many who came before them. Republicans and Democrats must come together and get strong background checks perhaps marrying.... (1/2)
8/5/2019 10:54

....this legislation with desperately needed immigration reform. We must have something good if not GREAT come out of these two tragic events! (2/2) **8/5/2019 10:54**

The Media has a big responsibility to life and safety in our Country. Fake News has contributed greatly to the anger and rage that has built up over many years. News coverage has got to start being fair balanced and unbiased or these terrible problems will only get worse! **8/5/2019 11:32**

China dropped the price of their currency to an almost a historic low. It's called "currency manipulation." Are you listening Federal Reserve? This is a major violation which will greatly weaken China over time! **8/5/2019 12:12**

Based on the historic currency manipulation by China it is now even more obvious to everyone that Americans are not paying for the Tariffs – they are being paid for compliments of China and the U.S. is taking in tens of Billions of Dollars! China has always.... (1/2) **8/5/2019 15:58**

....used currency manipulation to steal our businesses and factories hurt our jobs depress our workers' wages and harm our farmers' prices. Not anymore! (2/2) **8/5/2019 15:58**

Today I am also directing the Department of Justice to propose legislation ensuring that those who commit hate crimes and mass murders face the DEATH PENALTY - and that this capital punishment be delivered quickly decisively and without years of needless delay. https://t.co/BDXdpelK7F **8/5/2019 17:10**

"Did George Bush ever condemn President Obama after Sandy Hook. President Obama had 32 mass shootings during his reign. Not many people said Obama is out of Control. Mass shootings were happening before the President even thought about running for Pres." @kilmeade @foxandfriends **8/6/2019 10:47**

Massive amounts of money from China and other parts of the world is pouring into the United States for reasons of safety investment and interest rates! We are in a very strong position. Companies are also coming to the U.S. in big numbers. A beautiful thing to watch! **8/6/2019 12:00**

As they have learned in the last two years our great American Farmers know that China will not be able to hurt them in that their President has stood with them and done what no other president would do - And I'll do it again next year if necessary! **8/6/2019 12:36**

Will be going to Dayton Ohio and El Paso Texas tomorrow to meet with First Responders Law Enforcement and some of the victims of the terrible shootings. **8/6/2019 20:57**

"California is trying to meddle with a ballot in order to oppose President Trump and it's clearly something California is not allowed to do. It violates the right of the Republican Party or any party to choose its leaders under the Free Speech clause and under the 14th..... **8/7/2019 3:41**

Beto (phony name to indicate Hispanic heritage) O'Rourke who is embarrassed by my last visit to the Great State of Texas where I trounced him and is now even more embarrassed by polling at 1% in the Democrat Primary should respect the victims & law enforcement - & be quiet! **8/7/2019 3:57**

South Korea has agreed to pay substantially more money to the United States in order to defend itself from North Korea. Over the past many decades the U.S. has been paid very little by South Korea but last year at the request of President Trump South Korea paid $990000000.. (1/2)

8/7/2019 10:21

...Talks have begun to further increase payments to the United States. South Korea is a very wealthy nation that now feels an obligation to contribute to the military defense provided by the United States of America. The relationship between the two countries is a very good one! (2/2)

8/7/2019 10:21

"Trump Urges Unity Vs. Racism" was the correct description in the first headline by the Failing New York Times but it was quickly changed to "Assailing Hate But Not Guns" after the Radical Left Democrats went absolutely CRAZY! Fake News - That's what we're up against... **8/7/2019 10:32**

"Meanwhile the Dayton Ohio shooter had a history of supporting political figures like Bernie Sanders Elizabeth Warren and ANTIFA." @OANN I hope other news outlets will report this as opposed to Fake News. Thank you!

8/7/2019 10:58

"Three more Central Banks cut rates." Our problem is not China - We are stronger than ever money is pouring into the U.S. while China is losing companies by the thousands to other countries and their currency is under siege - Our problem is a Federal Reserve that is too..... **8/7/2019 12:46**

Just left Dayton Ohio where I met with the Victims & families Law Enforcement Medical Staff & First Responders. It was a warm & wonderful visit. Tremendous enthusiasm & even Love. Then I saw failed Presidential Candidate (0%) Sherrod Brown & Mayor Whaley totally..... (1/2) **8/7/2019 19:48**

....misrepresenting what took place inside of the hospital. Their news conference after I left for El Paso was a fraud. It bore no resemblance to what took place with those incredible people that I was so lucky to meet and spend time with. They were all amazing!o (2/2) **8/7/2019 19:48**

Watching Fake News CNN is better than watching Shepard Smith the lowest rated show on @FoxNews. Actually whenever possible I turn to @OANN! **8/7/2019 19:55**

The people I met today in Dayton are the finest anywhere! https://t.co/sBxKZWExcR **8/7/2019 20:25**

I don't know who Joaquin Castro is other than the lesser brother of a failed presidential candidate (1%) who makes a fool of himself every time he opens his mouth. Joaquin is not the man that his brother is but his brother according to most is not much. Keep fighting Joaquin! **8/8/2019 0:23**

Leaving El Paso for the White House. What GREAT people I met there and in Dayton Ohio. The Fake News worked overtime trying to disparage me and the two trips but it just didn't work. The love respect & enthusiasm were there for all to see. They have been through so much. Sad! **8/8/2019 0:31**

The Dems new weapon is actually their old weapon one which they never cease to use when they are down or run out of facts RACISM! They are truly disgusting! They even used it on Nancy Pelosi. I will be putting out a list of all people who have been so (ridiculously) accused! **8/8/2019 0:48**

Incredible afternoon in El Paso Texas. We love you and are with you all the way! https://t.co/pTNhHapx86 **8/8/2019 1:43**

My time spent in Dayton and El Paso with some of the greatest people on earth. Thank you for a job well done! https://t.co/TNVDGhxOpo **8/8/2019 3:02**

Just watched a world class loser Tim O'Brien who I haven't seen or spoken to in many years & knows NOTHING about me except that he wrote a failed hit piece book about me 15 years ago. Fired like a dog from other jobs? Saw him on Lyin' Brian Williams Trump Slam Show. Bad TV.... (1/2)
8/8/2019 4:20

....I am so amazed that MSNBC & CNN can keep putting on over and over again people that have no idea what I am all about and yet they speak as experts on "Trump." Same people since long before the 2016 Election and how did that work out for the Haters and Losers. Not well! (2/2)

8/8/2019 4:20

As your President one would think that I would be thrilled with our very strong dollar. I am not! The Fed's high interest rate level in comparison to other countries is keeping the dollar high making it more difficult for our great manufacturers like Caterpillar Boeing..... **8/8/2019 14:38**

Iran is in serious financial trouble. They want desperately to talk to the U.S. but are given mixed signals from all of those purporting to represent us including President Macron of France.... (1/2) **8/8/2019 17:51**

....I know Emmanuel means well as do all others but nobody speaks for the United States but the United States itself. No one is authorized in any way shape or form to represent us! (2/2) **8/8/2019 17:51**

I am pleased to inform you that the Honorable Joseph Maguire current Director of the National Counterterrorism Center will be named Acting Director of National Intelligence effective August 15th. Admiral Maguire has a long and distinguished.... **8/8/2019 23:12**

....mentally ill or deranged people. I am the biggest Second Amendment person there is but we all must work together for the good and safety of our Country. Common sense things can be done that are good for everyone! (2/2)

8/9/2019 12:03

Serious discussions are taking place between House and Senate leadership on meaningful Background Checks. I have also been speaking to the NRA and others so that their very strong views can be fully represented and respected. Guns should not be placed in the hands of..... (1/2)

8/9/2019 12:03

Liberal Hollywood is Racist at the highest level and with great Anger and Hate! They like to call themselves "Elite" but they are not Elite. In fact it is often the people that they so strongly oppose that are actually the Elite. The movie coming out is made in order.... (1/2) **8/9/2019 18:44**

....to inflame and cause chaos. They create their own violence and then try to blame others. They are the true Racists and are very bad for our Country! (2/2) **8/9/2019 18:44**

Maggie Haberman of the Failing @nytimes reported that I was annoyed by the lack of cameras inside the hospitals in Dayton & El Paso when in fact I was the one who stated very strongly that I didn't want the Fake News inside & told my people NOT to let them in. Fake reporting! **8/10/2019 11:40**

In a letter to me sent by Kim Jong Un he stated very nicely that he would like to meet and start negotiations as soon as the joint U.S./South Korea joint exercise are over. It was a long letter much of it complaining about the ridiculous and expensive exercises. It was..... (1/2) **8/10/2019 11:58**

....also a small apology for testing the short range missiles and that this testing would stop when the exercises end. I look forward to seeing Kim Jong Un in the not too distant future! A nuclear free North Korea will lead to one of the most successful countries in the world! (2/2) **8/10/2019 11:58**

Never has the press been more inaccurate unfair or corrupt! We are not fighting the Democrats they are easy we are fighting the seriously dishonest and unhinged Lamestream Media. They have gone totally CRAZY. MAKE AMERICA GREAT AGAIN!

8/10/2019 12:07

Got to see by accident wacko comedian Bill Maher's show - So many lies. He said patients in El Paso hospital didn't want to meet with me. Wrong! Had really great meetings with numerous patients. Said I was on vacation. Wrong! Long planned fix up of W.H. stay here rather than.. (1/2)

8/10/2019 21:48

....cause big disruption by going to Manhattan. Working almost all of the time including evenings. Don't have to be in W.H. to do that...And sooo many other false statements. He is right about one thing though. I will win again in 2020. Otherwise he pays 95% in taxes! (2/2) **8/10/2019 21:48**

Think how wonderful it is to be able to fight back and show to so many how totally dishonest the Fake News Media really is. It may be the most corrupt and disgusting business (almost) there is! MAKE AMERICA GREAT AGAIN!

8/10/2019 22:27

Joe Biden just said "We believe in facts not truth." Does anybody really believe he is mentally fit to be president? We are "playing" in a very big and complicated world. Joe doesn't have a clue!

8/10/2019 22:44

Anthony Scaramucci who was quickly terminated (11 days) from a position that he was totally incapable of handling now seems to do nothing but television as the all time expert on "President Trump." Like many other so-called television experts he knows very little about me..... (1/2)

8/11/2019 2:47

.....other than the fact that this Administration has probably done more than any other Administration in its first 2 1/2 years of existence. Anthony who would do anything to come back in should remember the only reason he is on TV and it's not for being the Mooch! (2/2) **8/11/2019 2:47**

So funny to watch Little Donny Deutsch on TV with his own failing show. When I did The Apprentice Donny would call

me (along with @ErinBurnett & others) and BEG to be on that VERY successful show. He had the TV "bug" & I would let him come on though he (& Erin) had very little..
8/11/2019 21:33

Many incredible things are happening right now for our Country. After years of being ripped off by other nations on both Trade Deals and the Military things are changing fast. Big progress is being made. America is respected again. KEEP AMERICA GREAT! **8/11/2019 21:42**

Scaramucci who like so many others had nothing to do with my Election victory is only upset that I didn't want him back in the Administration (where he desperately wanted to be). Also I seldom had time to return his many calls to me. He just wanted to be on TV! **8/12/2019 19:31**

I thought Chris was Fredo also. The truth hurts. Totally lost it! Low ratings @CNN https://t.co/yBpGjt4N1T **8/13/2019 12:38**

Would Chris Cuomo be given a Red Flag for his recent rant? Filthy language and a total loss of control. He shouldn't be allowed to have any weapon. He's nuts! **8/13/2019 14:04**

Many are blaming me and the United States for the problems going on in Hong Kong. I can't imagine why?
8/13/2019 17:11

Our Intelligence has informed us that the Chinese Government is moving troops to the Border with Hong Kong. Everyone should be calm and safe! **8/13/2019 17:17**

It always happens! When a Conservative does even a fraction of what Chris Cuomo did with his lunatic ranting raving & cursing they get destroyed by the Fake News. But when a Liberal Democrat like Chris Cuomo does it Republicans immediately come to his defense. We never learn! **8/13/2019 20:41**

No debate on Election Security should go forward without first agreeing that Voter ID (Identification) must play a very strong part in any final agreement. Without Voter ID it is all so meaningless! **8/14/2019 0:46**

Great day in the incredible Commonwealth of Pennsylvania today with the amazing energy workers construction workers and craft workers who make America run - and who make America PROUD. No one in the world does it better than YOU! https://t.co/jfWGYjzwkm **8/14/2019 1:23**

Tremendous amounts of money pouring into the United States. People want safety! **8/14/2019 16:42**

We are winning big time against China. Companies & jobs are fleeing. Prices to us have not gone up and in some cases have come down. China is not our problem though Hong Kong is not helping. Our problem is with the Fed. Raised too much & too fast. Now too slow to cut.... **8/14/2019 19:21**

Good things were stated on the call with China the other day. They are eating the Tariffs with the devaluation of their currency and "pouring" money into their system. The American consumer is fine with or without the September date but much good will come from the short..... (1/2)
8/14/2019 22:32

..deferral to December. It actually helps China more than us but will be reciprocated. Millions of jobs are being lost in China to other non-Tariffed countries. Thousands of companies are leaving. Of course China wants to make a deal. Let them work humanely with Hong Kong first! (2/2)
8/14/2019 22:32

I know President Xi of China very well. He is a great leader who very much has the respect of his people. He is also a good man in a "tough business." I have ZERO doubt that if President Xi wants to quickly and humanely solve the Hong Kong problem he can do it. Personal meeting? **8/14/2019 22:59**

It would show great weakness if Israel allowed Rep. Omar and Rep.Tlaib to visit. They hate Israel & all Jewish people & there is nothing that can be said or done to change their minds. Minnesota and Michigan will have a hard time putting them back in office. They are a disgrace! **8/15/2019 13:57**

Representatives Omar and Tlaib are the face of the Democrat Party and they HATE Israel! **8/15/2019 16:38**

Walmart a great indicator as to how the U.S. is doing just released outstanding numbers. Our Country unlike others is doing great! Don't let the Fake News convince you otherwise. **8/15/2019 20:18**

Great news! Tonight we broke the all-time attendance record previously held by Elton John at #SNHUArena in Manchester New Hampshire! https://t.co/GHvFBkA2KZ **8/16/2019 2:52**

Israel was very respectful & nice to Rep. Rashida Tlaib allowing her permission to visit her "grandmother." As soon as she was granted permission she grandstanded & loudly proclaimed she would not visit Israel. Could this possibly have been a setup? Israel acted appropriately! **8/16/2019 22:26**

Rep. Tlaib wrote a letter to Israeli officials desperately wanting to visit her grandmother. Permission was quickly granted whereupon Tlaib obnoxiously turned the approval down a complete setup. The only real winner here is Tlaib's grandmother. She doesn't have to see her now! **8/16/2019 22:37**

Like it or not Tlaib and Omar are fast becoming the face of the Democrat Party. Cortez (AOC) is fuming not happy about this! **8/16/2019 22:43**

I donate 100% of my President's salary $400000 back to our Country and feel very good about it! https://t.co/cX8Op2qyw7

8/16/2019 22:52

Having dinner tonight with Tim Cook of Apple. They will be spending vast sums of money in the U.S. Great! **8/16/2019 23:04**

Biggest crowd EVER according to Arena people. Thousands outside trying to get in. Place was packed! Radical Left Dems & their Partner LameStream Media saying Arena empty. Check out pictures. Fake News. The Enemy of the People! https://t.co/KkZWspM93a **8/17/2019 3:11**

Major consideration is being given to naming ANTIFA an "ORGANIZATION OF TERROR." Portland is being watched very closely. Hopefully the Mayor will be able to properly do his job!

8/17/2019 14:04

The Failing New York Times in one of the most devastating portrayals of bad journalism in history got caught by a leaker that they are shifting from their Phony Russian Collusion Narrative (the Mueller Report & his testimony were a total disaster) to a Racism Witch Hunt..... **8/18/2019 12:22**

....."Journalism" has reached a new low in the history of our Country. It is nothing more than an evil propaganda machine for the Democrat Party. The reporting is so false biased and evil that it has now become a very sick joke...But the public is aware! #CROOKEDJOURNALISM **8/18/2019 12:22**

With all that this Administration has accomplished think what my Poll Numbers would be if we had an honest Media which we do not! **8/18/2019 12:26**

MAKE AMERICA GREAT AGAIN! **8/18/2019 12:34**

We are doing very well with China and talking! **8/18/2019 18:27**

Juan Williams at @FoxNews is so pathetic and yet when he met me in the Fox Building lobby he couldn't have been nicer as he asked me to take a picture of him and me for his family. Yet he is always nasty and wrong! **8/18/2019 19:15**

House Democrats want to take action against Israel because it is fighting back against two (maybe four) people that have said unthinkably bad things about it & the Israeli people. Dems have such disdain for Israel! What happened? AOC Plus 4 is the new face of the Democrat Party!
8/18/2019 22:03

Thank you @TedCruz I couldn't agree more! https://t.co/MGq0xXin0s **8/18/2019 22:50**

The New York Times will be out of business soon after I leave office hopefully in 6 years. They have Zero credibility and are losing a fortune even now especially after their massive unfunded liability. I'm fairly certain they'll endorse me just to keep it all going! **8/18/2019 23:57**

Great cohesion inside the Republican Party the best I have ever seen. Despite all of the Fake News my Poll Numbers are great. New internal polls show them to be the strongest we've had so far! Think what they'd be if I got fair media coverage! **8/19/2019 12:21**

Anthony Scaramucci is a highly unstable "nut job" who was with other candidates in the primary who got shellacked & then unfortunately wheedled his way into my campaign. I barely knew him until his 11 days of gross incompetence-made a fool of himself bad on TV. Abused staff... **8/19/2019 13:19**

Our Economy is very strong despite the horrendous lack of vision by Jay Powell and the Fed but the Democrats are trying to "will" the Economy to be bad for purposes of the 2020 Election. Very Selfish! Our dollar is so strong that it is sadly hurting other parts of the world... **8/19/2019 15:26**

Wow Report Just Out! Google manipulated from 2.6 million to 16 million votes for Hillary Clinton in 2016 Election! This was put out by a Clinton supporter not a Trump Supporter! Google should be sued. My victory was even bigger than thought! @JudicialWatch **8/19/2019 15:52**

Spoke to my two good friends Prime Minister Modi of India and Prime Minister Khan of Pakistan regarding Trade

Strategic Partnerships and most importantly for India and Pakistan to work towards reducing tensions in Kashmir. A tough situation but good conversations! **8/19/2019 23:43**

I promise not to do this to Greenland! https://t.co/O3DdyVU6HA **8/20/2019 0:07**

Sorry I don't buy Rep. Tlaib's tears. I have watched her violence craziness and most importantly WORDS for far too long. Now tears? She hates Israel and all Jewish people. She is an anti-Semite. She and her 3 friends are the new face of the Democrat Party. Live with it!

8/20/2019 15:42

CONGRATULATIONS @EricTrump and @LaraLeaTrump on the birth of Carolina Dorothy Trump. So proud! https://t.co/eSIrFzOzmR **8/20/2019 20:00**

Denmark is a very special country with incredible people but based on Prime Minister Mette Frederiksen's comments that she would have no interest in discussing the purchase of Greenland I will be postponing our meeting scheduled in two weeks for another time.... (1/2) **8/20/2019 23:51**

....The Prime Minister was able to save a great deal of expense and effort for both the United States and Denmark by being so direct. I thank her for that and look forward to rescheduling sometime in the future! (2/2) **8/20/2019 23:51**

"Thank you to Wayne Allyn Root for the very nice words. "President Trump is the greatest President for Jews and for Israel in the history of the world not just America he is the best President for Israel in the history of the world...and the Jewish people in Israel love him.... **8/21/2019 11:34**

So Germany is paying Zero interest and is actually being paid to borrow money while the U.S. a far stronger and more important credit is paying interest and just stopped (I hope!) Quantitative Tightening. Strongest Dollar in History very tough on exports. No Inflation!..... **8/21/2019 13:56**

For the record Denmark is only at 1.35% of GDP for NATO spending. They are a wealthy country and should be at 2%. We protect Europe and yet only 8 of the 28 NATO countries are at the 2% mark. The United States is at a much much higher level than that.... (1/2) **8/21/2019 17:32**

....Because of me these countries have agreed to pay ONE HUNDRED BILLION DOLLARS more - but still way short of what they should pay for the incredible military protection provided. Sorry! (2/2) **8/21/2019 17:32**

Henry Ford would be very disappointed if he saw his modern-day descendants wanting to build a much more expensive car that is far less safe and doesn't work as well because execs don't want to fight California regulators. Car companies should know.... **8/21/2019 23:01**

It was my honor to sign a Presidential Memorandum facilitating the cancellation of student loan debt for 25K of our most severely disabled Veterans. With today's order we express the everlasting love & loyalty of a truly grateful Nation. God bless our Vets & God Bless America! https://t.co/MMMsX3RDQM **8/22/2019 0:20**

94% Approval Rating within the Republican Party. Thank you! **8/23/2019 10:49**

Our Country has lost stupidly Trillions of Dollars with China over many years. They have stolen our Intellectual Property at a rate of Hundreds of Billions of Dollars a year & they want to continue. I won't let that happen! We don't need China and frankly would be far.... **8/23/2019 14:59**

....your companies HOME and making your products in the USA. I will be responding to China's Tariffs this afternoon. This is a GREAT opportunity for the United States. Also I am ordering all carriers including Fed Ex Amazon UPS and the Post Office to SEARCH FOR & REFUSE.... (1/2) **8/23/2019 14:59**

....all deliveries of Fentanyl from China (or anywhere else!). Fentanyl kills 100000 Americans a year. President Xi said this would stop - it didn't. Our Economy because of our gains in the last 2 1/2 years is MUCH larger than that of China. We will keep it that way! (2/2) **8/23/2019 14:59**

For many years China (and many other countries) has been taking advantage of the United States on Trade Intellectual Property Theft and much more. Our Country has been losing HUNDREDS OF BILLIONS OF DOLLARS a year to China with no end in sight.... **8/23/2019 21:00**

Just spoke with President @JairBolsonaro of Brazil. Our future Trade prospects are very exciting and our relationship is strong perhaps stronger than ever before. I told him if the United States can help with the Amazon Rainforest fires we stand ready to assist!

8/23/2019 22:04

For all of the Fake News Reporters that don't have a clue as to what the law is relative to Presidential powers China etc. try looking at the Emergency Economic Powers Act of 1977. Case closed! **8/24/2019 3:58**

When I looked up to the sky and jokingly said "I am the chosen one" at a press conference two days ago referring to taking on Trade with China little did I realize that the media would claim that I had a "Messiah complex." They knew I was kidding being sarcastic and just.... (1/2)

8/24/2019 15:00

....having fun. I was smiling as I looked up and around. The MANY reporters with me were smiling also. They knew the TRUTH...And yet when I saw the reporting CNN MSNBC and other Fake News outlets covered it as serious news & me thinking of myself as the Messiah. No more trust! (2/2)

8/24/2019 15:00

"Face It You Probably Got A Tax Cut!" This was a New York Times headline and it is very true. If Republicans take back the House and keep the Senate and Presidency one of our first acts will be to approve a major middle income Tax Cut! Democrats only want to raise your taxes! **8/24/2019 15:15**

The Media is destroying the Free Press! Mark Levin. So True! **8/24/2019 23:08**

Before I arrived in France the Fake and Disgusting News was saying that relations with the 6 others countries in the G-7 are very tense and that the two days of meetings will be a disaster. Just like they are trying to force a Recession they are trying to "will" America into.. **8/25/2019 5:41**

....bad Economic times the worse the better anything to make my Election more difficult to win. Well we are having very good meetings the Leaders are getting along very well and our Country economically is doing great - the talk of the world! **8/25/2019 5:41**

The question I was asked most today by fellow World Leaders who think the USA is doing so well and is stronger than ever before happens to be "Mr. President why does the American media hate your Country so much? Why are they rooting for it to fail?" **8/25/2019 17:30**

In France we are all laughing at how knowingly inaccurate the U.S. reporting of events and conversations at the G-7 is. These Leaders and many others are getting a major case study of Fake News at it's finest! They've got it all wrong from Iran to China Tariffs to Boris! **8/25/2019 23:10**

All Trump Haters and Lovers must watch. Thank you Steve Hilton! https://t.co/QaSkw8IWNz **8/26/2019 6:12**

The story by Axios that President Trump wanted to blow up large hurricanes with nuclear weapons prior to reaching shore is ridiculous. I never said this. Just more FAKE NEWS! **8/26/2019 9:25**

Just wrapped up a great meeting with my friend Prime Minister @NarendraModi of India at the #G7Summit in Biarritz France! https://t.co/q0NOnEcjFO **8/26/2019 12:26**

Just returned to Washington from France and the very successful G-7 only to find that the Fake News is still trying to perpetuate the phony story that I wanted to use Nuclear weapons to blow up hurricanes before they reach shore. This is so ridiculous never happened! **8/27/2019 2:30**

I have gotten to know President @jairbolsonaro well in our dealings with Brazil. He is working very hard on the Amazon fires and in all respects doing a great job for the people of Brazil - Not easy. He and his country have the full and complete support of the USA! **8/27/2019 14:30**

Axios (whatever that is) sat back and said GEEEEE let's see what can we make up today to embarrass the President? Then they said "why don't we say he wants to bomb a hurricane that should do it!" The media in our Country is totally out of control! **8/27/2019 23:30**

Can you believe it? I'm at 94% approval in the Republican Party and have Three Stooges running against me. One is "Mr. Appalachian Trail" who was actually in Argentina for bad reasons.... (1/2) **8/27/2019 23:36**

....Another is a one-time BAD Congressman from Illinois who lost in his second term by a landslide then failed in radio. The third is a man who couldn't stand up straight while receiving an award. I should be able to take them! (2/2) **8/27/2019 23:36**

So interesting to read and see all of the free and interesting advice I am getting on China from people who have tried to handle it before and failed miserably - In fact they got taken to the cleaners. We are doing very well with China. This has never happened to them before! **8/28/2019 12:06**

Would be very hard for Jeremy Corbyn the leader of Britain's Labour Party to seek a no-confidence vote against New Prime Minister Boris Johnson especially in light of the fact that Boris is exactly what the U.K. has been looking for & will prove to be "a great one!" Love U.K. **8/28/2019 13:36**

....I don't want to Win for myself I only want to Win for the people. The New @FoxNews is letting millions of GREAT people down! We have to start looking for a new News Outlet. Fox isn't working for us anymore! **8/28/2019 14:03**

Puerto Rico is one of the most corrupt places on earth. Their political system is broken and their politicians are either Incompetent or Corrupt. Congress approved Billions of Dollars last time more than anyplace else has ever gotten and it is sent to Crooked Pols. No good!.... **8/28/2019 14:45**

The Wall is going up very fast despite total Obstruction by Democrats in Congress and elsewhere! https://t.co/12tIW3aNQP https://t.co/2nFIEFppho **8/28/2019 17:48**

Thank you for the support as we MAKE AMERICA GREAT AGAIN! https://t.co/qKgwRMSgcf **8/28/2019 19:10**

A sad day for the Democrats Kirsten Gillibrand has dropped out of the Presidential Primary. I'm glad they never found out that she was the one I was really afraid of!

8/28/2019 22:26

There has never been a time in the history of our Country that the Media was so Fraudulent Fake or Corrupt! When the "Age of Trump" is looked back on many years from now I only hope that a big part of my legacy will be the exposing of massive dishonesty in the Fake News! **8/29/2019 0:35**

Crazy Lawrence O'Donnell who has been calling me wrong from even before I announced my run for the Presidency even being previously forced by NBC to apologize which he did while crying for things he said about me & The

Apprentice was again forced to apologize this time.....
8/29/2019 11:31

The totally inaccurate reporting by Lawrence O'Donnell for which he has been forced by NBC to apologize is NO DIFFERENT than the horrible corrupt and fraudulent Fake News that I (and many millions of GREAT supporters) have had to put up with for years. So bad for the USA!
8/29/2019 11:47

Perhaps never in the history of our Country has someone been more thoroughly disgraced and excoriated than James Comey in the just released Inspector General's Report. He should be ashamed of himself! **8/29/2019 18:05**

The disastrous IG Report on James Comey shows in the strongest of terms how unfairly I and tens of millions of great people who support me were treated. Our rights and liberties were illegally stripped away by this dishonest fool. We should be given our stolen time back? **8/30/2019 12:28**

...Yes I am currently suing various people for violating their confidentiality agreements. Disgusting and foul mouthed Omarosa is one. I gave her every break despite the fact that she was despised by everyone and she went for some cheap money from a book. Numerous others also!
8/31/2019 12:58

MAKE AMERICA GREAT AGAIN which is happening and then KEEP AMERICA GREAT! **8/31/2019 13:09**

Being scolded by failed former "Intelligence" officials like James Clapper on my condolences to Iran on their failed Rocket launch. Sadly for the United States guys like him Comey and the even dumber John Brennan don't have a clue. They really set our Country back.... **8/31/2019 19:06**

Pray for the people in the Bahamas. Being hit like never before Category 5. Almost 200 MPH winds. **9/1/2019 19:35**

The Amazon Washington Post did a story that I brought racist attacks against the "Squad." No they brought racist attacks against our Nation. All I do is call them out for the horrible things they have said. The Democrats have become the Party of the Squad! **9/2/2019 12:09**

The LameStream Media has gone totally CRAZY! They write whatever they want seldom have sources (even though they say they do) never do "fact checking" anymore and are only looking for the "kill." They take good news and make it bad. They are now beyond Fake they are Corrupt.. **9/2/2019 12:22**

The incompetent Mayor of London Sadiq Khan was bothered that I played a very fast round of golf yesterday. Many Pols exercise for hours or travel for weeks. Me I run through one of my courses (very inexpensive). President Obama would fly to Hawaii. Kahn should focus on.... (1/2) **9/3/2019 14:48**

...."knife crime" which is totally out of control in London. People are afraid to even walk the streets. He is a terrible mayor who should stay out of our business! (2/2) **9/3/2019 14:48**

"I am so tired of hearing the rationalization of the Left in the country because they hate Donald Trump. Inexplicably and without foundation they choose to hate America. The Democrats have truly become the party of hate." @ LouDobbs **9/4/2019 1:04**

"To declassify is so important because if this were a Democrat President or a Democrat Candidate that was spied on the way President Trump was spied on this would be a scandal that would make Watergate look like nothing. Illegal spying..... **9/4/2019 1:39**

"Absolutely nothing is more important than going back & getting to the bottom of the origins of the investigation. We had an administration using America's Spying Apparatus to spy on a political opponent at the height of a presidential election. Those are all known undisputed... **9/5/2019 0:49**

Bad "actress" Debra The Mess Messing is in hot water. She wants to create a "Blacklist" of Trump supporters & is being accused of McCarthyism. Is also being accused of being a Racist because of the terrible things she said about blacks and mental illness. If Roseanne Barr.... (1/2) **9/5/2019 13:15**

....said what she did even being on a much higher rated show she would have been thrown off television. Will Fake News NBC allow a McCarthy style Racist to continue? ABC fired Roseanne. Watch the double standard! (2/2)
9/5/2019 13:15

Thank you to Bahamian Prime Minister Hubert Minnis for your very gracious and kind words in saying that without the help of the United States and me their would have been many more casualties. I give all credit to FEMA the U.S. Coast Guard & the brave people of the Bahamas..
9/7/2019 10:39

"In 22 years of patrolling our Southern Border I have never seen Mexico act like a true Border Security Partner until President Trump got involved and now they are stepping up to the plate and doing what they need to do." Brandon Judd National Border Patrol **9/7/2019 13:14**

Unbeknownst to almost everyone the major Taliban leaders and separately the President of Afghanistan were going to secretly meet with me at Camp David on Sunday. They were coming to the United States tonight. Unfortunately in order to build false leverage they admitted to.. **9/7/2019 22:51**

....only made it worse! If they cannot agree to a ceasefire during these very important peace talks and would even kill 12 innocent people then they probably don't have the power to negotiate a meaningful agreement anyway. How many more decades are they willing to fight? **9/7/2019 22:51**

WE ARE BUILDING THE WALL...
https://t.co/OQQaag2ZUW **9/8/2019 16:56**

When all of the people pushing so hard for Criminal Justice Reform were unable to come even close to getting it done they came to me as a group and asked for my help. I got it done with a group of Senators & others who would never have gone for it. Obama couldn't come close.... **9/9/2019 3:11**

94% Approval Rating in the Republican Party a record. Thank you! **9/9/2019 11:29**

I know nothing about an Air Force plane landing at an airport (which I do not own and have nothing to do with) near Turnberry Resort (which I do own) in Scotland and filling up with fuel with the crew staying overnight at Turnberry (they have good taste!). NOTHING TO DO WITH ME **9/9/2019 13:43**

I informed John Bolton last night that his services are no longer needed at the White House. I disagreed strongly with many of his suggestions as did others in the Administration and therefore.... **9/10/2019 15:58**

BIG NIGHT FOR THE REPUBLICAN PARTY. CONGRATULATIONS TO ALL! **9/11/2019 2:38**

Today and every day we pledge to honor our history to treasure our liberty to uplift our communities to live up to our values to prove worthy of our heroes and above all to NEVER FORGET. #Honor911 https://t.co/3xbEvl92py **9/11/2019 17:23**

The Wall is going up very fast despite total Obstruction by Democrats in Congress and elsewhere! https://t.co/2nFIEFppho **9/12/2019 3:26**

It is expected that China will be buying large amounts of our agricultural products! **9/12/2019 12:45**

"We can't beat him so lets impeach him!" Democrat Rep. Al Green **9/12/2019 14:07**

How do you impeach a President who has helped create perhaps the greatest economy in the history of our Country? All time best unemployment numbers especially for Blacks Hispanics Asians & Women. More people working

today than ever before. Rebuilt Military & Choice for Vets...
9/13/2019 12:58

While I like the Vaping alternative to Cigarettes we need to make sure this alternative is SAFE for ALL! Let's get counterfeits off the market and keep young children from Vaping! **9/13/2019 22:35**

Who the hell is Joy-Ann Reid? Never met her she knows ZERO about me has NO talent and truly doesn't have the "it" factor needed for success in showbiz. Had a bad reputation and now works for the Comcast/NBC losers making up phony stories about me. Low Ratings. Fake News!
9/14/2019 13:04

MAKE AMERICA GREAT AGAIN!
9/14/2019 13:09

KEEP AMERICA GREAT! **9/14/2019 13:10**

The Taliban has never been hit harder than it is being hit right now. Killing 12 people including one great American soldier was not a good idea. There are much better ways to set up a negotiation. The Taliban knows they made a big mistake and they have no idea how to recover! **9/14/2019 19:02**

Brett Kavanaugh should start suing people for libel or the Justice Department should come to his rescue. The lies being told about him are unbelievable. False Accusations without recrimination. When does it stop? They are trying to influence his opinions. Can't let that happen! **9/15/2019 13:47**

I am fighting the Fake (Corrupt) News the Deep State the Democrats and the few remaining Republicans In Name Only (RINOS who are on mouth to mouth resuscitation) with the help of some truly great Republicans and others. We are Winning big (150th Federal Judge this week)!
9/15/2019 18:20

Based on the attack on Saudi Arabia which may have an impact on oil prices I have authorized the release of oil from the Strategic Petroleum Reserve if needed in a to-be-determined amount.... **9/15/2019 21:55**

Saudi Arabia oil supply was attacked. There is reason to believe that we know the culprit are locked and loaded depending on verification but are waiting to hear from the Kingdom as to who they believe was the cause of this attack and under what terms we would proceed! **9/15/2019 22:50**

PLENTY OF OIL! **9/15/2019 22:50**

They failed on the Mueller Report they failed on Robert Mueller's testimony they failed on everything else so now the Democrats are trying to build a case that I enrich myself by being President. Good idea except I will and have always expected to lose BILLIONS of DOLLARS.. **9/16/2019 14:01**

I call for the Resignation of everybody at The New York Times involved in the Kavanaugh SMEAR story and while you're at it the Russian Witch Hunt Hoax which is just as phony! They've taken the Old Grey Lady and broken her down destroyed her virtue and ruined her reputation... **9/16/2019 22:40**

The New York Times is now blaming an editor for the horrible mistake they made in trying to destroy or influence Justice Brett Kavanaugh. It wasn't the editor the Times knew everything. They are sick and desperate losing in so many ways! **9/17/2019 23:58**

Terrence K. Williams "You can't impeach Trump for being a winner!" **9/18/2019 12:21**

I have just instructed the Secretary of the Treasury to substantially increase Sanctions on the country of Iran! **9/18/2019 12:53**

All Polls and some brand new Polls show very little support for impeachment. Such a waste of time especially with sooo much good that could be done including prescription drug price reduction healthcare infrastructure etc. **9/19/2019 1:42**

GREAT progress on the Border Wall! https://t.co/TvOYxgsBSv **9/19/2019 2:05**

Another Fake News story out there - It never ends! Virtually anytime I speak on the phone to a foreign leader I understand that there may be many people listening from various U.S. agencies not to mention those from the other country itself. No problem! **9/19/2019 14:47**

....Knowing all of this is anybody dumb enough to believe that I would say something inappropriate with a foreign leader while on such a potentially “heavily populated” call. I would only do what is right anyway and only do good for the USA! **9/19/2019 14:47**

Presidential Harassment! **9/19/2019 14:51**

Because of my Administration drug prices are down for the first time in almost 50 years — but the American people need Congress to help. I like Sen. Grassley’s drug pricing bill very much and it’s great to see Speaker Pelosi’s bill today. Let’s get it done in a bipartisan way! **9/19/2019 21:42**

Oh no really big political news perhaps the biggest story in years! Part time Mayor of New York City @BilldeBlasio who was polling at a solid ZERO but had tremendous room for growth has shocking dropped out of the Presidential race. NYC is devastated he’s coming home! **9/20/2019 12:02**

I want to express my gratitude to America’s magnificent @FLOTUS for tonight’s exquisite evening where we celebrated more than a century of loyal and devoted friendship between 🇺🇸 🇦🇺 Both of our nations are blessed by uncommon courage unfailing commitment and unyielding character! https://t.co/i61cHCZYlD **9/21/2019 4:11**

Will be in Houston to be with my friend. Will be a great day in Texas! https://t.co/SqdOZfqd2b **9/22/2019 14:39**

The USA Loves India! https://t.co/xlfnWafxpg

9/22/2019 19:03

Just leaving the Great State of Ohio for New York and a few big days at the United Nations. Your Country will be well represented! **9/23/2019 0:06**

This is the real corruption that the Fake News Media refuses to even acknowledge! https://t.co/FCvUtWA33j

9/23/2019 19:37

94% approval rating in the Republican Party. Thank you!

9/23/2019 22:44

She seems like a very happy young girl looking forward to a bright and wonderful future. So nice to see! https://t.co/1tQG6QcVKO **9/24/2019 3:36**

I am currently at the United Nations representing our Country but have authorized the release tomorrow of the complete fully declassified and unredacted transcript of my phone conversation with President Zelensky of Ukraine.... (1/2) **9/24/2019 18:12**

....You will see it was a very friendly and totally appropriate call. No pressure and unlike Joe Biden and his son NO quid pro quo! This is nothing more than a continuation of the Greatest and most Destructive Witch Hunt of all time! (2/2)

9/24/2019 18:12

The Democrats are so focused on hurting the Republican Party and the President that they are unable to get anything done because of it including legislation on gun safety lowering of prescription drug prices infrastructure etc. So bad for our Country! **9/24/2019 18:52**

Such an important day at the United Nations so much work and so much success and the Democrats purposely had to ruin and demean it with more breaking news Witch Hunt garbage. So bad for our Country! **9/24/2019 21:08**

Pelosi Nadler Schiff and of course Maxine Waters! Can you believe this? **9/24/2019 21:11**

They never even saw the transcript of the call. A total Witch Hunt! **9/24/2019 21:14**

PRESIDENTIAL HARASSMENT! **9/24/2019 21:17**

Secretary of State Pompeo recieved permission from Ukraine Government to release the transcript of the telephone call I had with their President. They don't know either what the big deal is. A total Witch Hunt Scam by the Democrats! **9/24/2019 22:22**

There has been no President in the history of our Country who has been treated so badly as I have. The Democrats are frozen with hatred and fear. They get nothing done. This should never be allowed to happen to another President. Witch Hunt!

9/25/2019 11:24

Will the Democrats apologize after seeing what was said on the call with the Ukrainian President? They should a perfect call - got them by surprise! **9/25/2019 13:17**

I have informed @GOPLeader Kevin McCarthy and all Republicans in the House that I fully support transparency on so-called whistleblower information but also insist on transparency from Joe Biden and his son Hunter on the millions of dollars that have been quickly and easily.... (1/2)

9/25/2019 20:17

....taken out of Ukraine and China. Additionally I demand transparency from Democrats that went to Ukraine and attempted to force the new President to do things that they wanted under the form of political threat. (2/2) **9/25/2019 20:17**

One of our best fundraising days EVER! https://t.co/zohH8Xm5ak **9/26/2019 2:46**

So cute! Her father is under siege for no reason since his first day in office! https://t.co/8wtB3H4fth **9/26/2019 11:06**

THE GREATEST SCAM IN THE HISTORY OF AMERICAN POLITICS! **9/26/2019 11:24**

THE DEMOCRATS ARE TRYING TO DESTROY THE REPUBLICAN PARTY AND ALL THAT IT STANDS FOR. STICK TOGETHER PLAY THEIR GAME AND FIGHT HARD REPUBLICANS. OUR COUNTRY IS AT STAKE! **9/26/2019 12:41**

Adam Schiff has zero credibility. Another fantasy to hurt the Republican Party! **9/26/2019 16:48**

Liddle' Adam Schiff who has worked unsuccessfully for 3 years to hurt the Republican Party and President has just said that the Whistleblower even though he or she only had second hand information "is credible." How can that be with zero info and a known bias. Democrat Scam! **9/26/2019 18:13**

The President of Ukraine said that he was NOT pressured by me to do anything wrong. Can't have better testimony than that! As V.P. Biden had his son on the other hand take out millions of dollars by strong arming the Ukrainian President. Also looted millions from China. Bad! **9/26/2019 23:02**

To show you how dishonest the LameStream Media is I used the word Liddle' not Liddle in discribing Corrupt Congressman Liddle' Adam Schiff. Low ratings @CNN purposely took the hyphen out and said I spelled the word little wrong. A small but never ending situation with CNN! **9/27/2019 11:02**

Rep. Adam Schiff fraudulently read to Congress with millions of people watching a version of my conversation with the President of Ukraine that doesn't exist. He was

supposedly reading the exact transcribed version of the call but he completely changed the words to make it... (1/2)
9/27/2019 12:29

...sound horrible and me sound guilty. HE WAS DESPERATE AND HE GOT CAUGHT. Adam Schiff therefore lied to Congress and attempted to defraud the American Public. He has been doing this for two years. I am calling for him to immediately resign from Congress based on this fraud! (2/2)
9/27/2019 12:29

Iran wanted me to lift the sanctions imposed on them in order to meet. I said of course NO!
9/27/2019 13:23

Rep. Adam Schiff totally made up my conversation with Ukraine President and read it to Congress and Millions. He must resign and be investigated. He has been doing this for two years. He is a sick man!
9/27/2019 13:29

The Democrats are now to be known as the DO NOTHING PARTY!
9/27/2019 13:32

Sounding more and more like the so-called Whistleblower isn't a Whistleblower at all. In addition all second hand information that proved to be so inaccurate that there may not have even been somebody else a leaker or spy feeding it to him or her? A partisan operative?
9/27/2019 13:42

If that perfect phone call with the President of Ukraine Isn't considered appropriate then no future President can EVER again speak to another foreign leader!
9/27/2019 15:24

I AM DRAINING THE SWAMP! https://t.co/U7WxKrO6Kx
9/27/2019 19:41

Voter I.D. is the best way. Go for it Doug! https://t.co/DOHtwP2u59
9/28/2019 4:09

Can you imagine if these Do Nothing Democrat Savages people like Nadler Schiff AOC Plus 3 and many more had a Republican Party who would have done to Obama what the Do Nothings are doing to me. Oh well maybe next time!
9/28/2019 12:16

PRESIDENTIAL HARASSMENT! **9/28/2019 12:34**

MAKE AMERICA GREAT AGAIN! **9/28/2019 12:35**

KEEP AMERICA GREAT! **9/28/2019 12:35**

They are trying to stop ME because I am fighting for YOU! https://t.co/xiw4jtjkNl **9/28/2019 21:14**

How do you impeach a President who has created the greatest Economy in the history of our Country entirely rebuilt our Military into the most powerful it has ever been Cut Record Taxes & Regulations fixed the VA & gotten Choice for our Vets (after 45 years) & so much more?...
9/28/2019 22:00

The Whistleblower's complaint is completely different and at odds from my actual conversation with the new President of Ukraine. The so-called "Whistleblower" knew practically NOTHING in that those ridiculous charges were far more dramatic & wrong just like Liddle' Adam Schiff..
9/28/2019 22:30

It is disgraceful what the Do Nothing Democrats are doing (the Impeachment Scam) but it is also disgraceful what they are NOT doing namely the USMCA vote Prescription Drug Price Reduction Gun Safety Infrastructure and much more!
9/29/2019 1:53

The only people that don't like my conversation with the new Ukrainian President are those that heard Rep. Adam Schiff read a made up and totally fraudulent statement to the House and public words that I did not say but that he fabricated (& admitted to this fabrication). Sick! **9/29/2019 2:00**

Like every American I deserve to meet my accuser especially when this accuser the so-called "Whistleblower" represented a perfect conversation with a foreign leader in a totally inaccurate and fraudulent way. Then Schiff made up what I actually said by lying to Congress...... (1/3)

9/29/2019 22:53

His lies were made in perhaps the most blatant and sinister manner ever seen in the great Chamber. He wrote down and read terrible things then said it was from the mouth of the President of the United States. I want Schiff questioned at the highest level for Fraud & Treason..... (2/3)

9/29/2019 22:53

....In addition I want to meet not only my accuser who presented SECOND & THIRD HAND INFORMATION but also the person who illegally gave this information which was largely incorrect to the "Whistleblower." Was this person SPYING on the U.S. President? Big Consequences! (3/3)

9/29/2019 22:53

"All that's swirling around us now is Impeachment. We talk about it day and night it's what's on the news there is NOTHING that has turned up that is Impeachable. Our founding fathers set impeachment to be extremely rare. We need to get good stuff done. Let the people vote....

9/30/2019 0:22

"State Department has stepped up Hillary Clinton Email probe." @foxandfriends You mean the 33000 Emails that she has deleted and acid washed so they can never be found even though she said that all 33000 pertained only to her daughter's wedding and her Yoga!

9/30/2019 0:30

"Nancy Pelosi and the Democrats can't put down the Impeachment match. They know they couldn't beat him in 2016 against Hillary Clinton and they're increasingly aware of the fact that they won't win against him in 2020 and Impeachment is the only tool they have to get....

9/30/2019 1:11

The Greatest Witch Hunt in the history of our Country!

9/30/2019 11:39

Rep. Adam Schiff illegally made up a FAKE & terrible statement pretended it to be mine as the most important part of my call to the Ukrainian President and read it aloud to Congress and the American people. It bore NO relationship to what I said on the call. Arrest for Treason?

9/30/2019 12:12

WHO CHANGED THE LONG STANDING WHISTLEBLOWER RULES JUST BEFORE SUBMITTAL OF THE FAKE WHISTLEBLOWER REPORT? DRAIN THE SWAMP!

9/30/2019 12:43

Very simple! I was looking for Corruption and also why Germany France and others in the European Union don't do more for Ukraine. Why is it always the USA that does so much and puts up so much money for Ukraine and other countries? By the way the Bidens were corrupt! **9/30/2019 13:58**

The Fake News Media wants to stay as far away as possible from the Ukraine and China deals made by the Bidens. A Corrupt Media is so bad for our Country! In actuality the Media may be even more Corrupt than the Bidens which is hard to do!

9/30/2019 14:03

OCTOBER 2019 - DECEMBER 2019

★★★★★★★★★★★★★★★★★★★★★★★★★★

As the unemployment rate drops to 3.5 percent, a fifty-year low, based on an anonymous whistleblower's report, House Democrats become committed to impeaching President Trump over a telephone conversation with Ukrainian President Zelensky. The impeachment charge alleges that Trump illegally asked for a quid pro quo. With Rep. Adam Schiff (D-CA) leading the impeachment investigation, this story dominates the news and Trump's tweets. Much of the work of Congress comes to a standstill. The leader of ISIS, Abu Bakr al-Baghdadi, is killed, essentially ending the threat of the Caliphate. Despite the stock markets hitting record highs, the House votes two articles of impeachment against President Trump. Speaker Pelosi delivers the articles just before Christmas.

Today I was proud to sign the Autism CARES Bill! We support research for Americans with Autism and their families. You are not forgotten we are fighting for you! https://t.co/syyaLR0sNq **10/1/2019 1:18**

So if the so-called "Whistleblower" has all second hand information and almost everything he has said about my "perfect" call with the Ukrainian President is wrong (much to the embarrassment of Pelosi & Schiff) why aren't we entitled to interview & learn everything about.... **10/1/2019 13:19**

Why isn't Congressman Adam Schiff being brought up on charges for fraudulently making up a statement and reading it to Congress as if this statement which was very dishonest and bad for me was directly made by the President of the United States? This should never be allowed! **10/1/2019 15:00**

As I learn more and more each day I am coming to the conclusion that what is taking place is not an impeachment it is a COUP intended to take away the Power of the.... (1/2)

10/1/2019 23:41

....People their VOTE their Freedoms their Second Amendment Religion Military Border Wall and their God-given rights as a Citizen of The United States of America! (2/2) **10/1/2019 23:41**

The Greatest Witch Hunt in the history of our Country! https://t.co/7moLU6UTcE **10/2/2019 0:20**

I won the right to be a presidential candidate in California in a major Court decision handed down yesterday. It was filed against me by the Radical Left Governor of that State to tremendous Media hoopla. The VICTORY however was barely covered by the Fake News. No surprise! **10/2/2019 12:51**

Massive sections of The Wall are being built at our Southern Border. It is going up rapidly and built to the highest standards and specifications of the Border Patrol experts. It is actually an amazing structure! Our U.S. Military is doing a GREAT job. **10/2/2019 13:06**

Congressman Adam Schiff should resign for the Crime of after reading a transcript of my conversation with the President of Ukraine (it was perfect) fraudulently fabricating a statement of the President of the United States and reading it to Congress as though mine! He is sick! **10/2/2019 14:16**

Now the press is trying to sell the fact that I wanted a Moat stuffed with alligators and snakes with an electrified fence and sharp spikes on top at our Southern Border. I may be tough on Border Security but not that tough. The press has gone Crazy. Fake News! **10/2/2019 15:02**

All of this impeachment nonsense which is going nowhere is driving the Stock Market and your 401K's down. But that is exactly what the Democrats want to do. They are willing to hurt the Country with only the 2020 Election in mind! **10/2/2019 15:19**

Adam Schiff should only be so lucky to have the brains honor and strength of Secretary of State Mike Pompeo. For a lowlife like Schiff who completely fabricated my words and read them to Congress as though they were said by me to demean a First in Class at West Point is SAD! **10/2/2019 15:39**

The Do Nothing Democrats should be focused on building up our Country not wasting everyone's time and energy on BULLSHIT which is what they have been doing ever since I got overwhelmingly elected in 2016 223-306. Get a better candidate this time you'll need it! **10/2/2019 15:48**

DEMOCRATS WANT TO STEAL THE ELECTION! #KAG2020 https://t.co/hz6fWLId3L **10/2/2019 23:41**

The U.S. won a $7.5 Billion award from the World Trade Organization against the European Union who has for many years treated the USA very badly on Trade due to Tariffs Trade Barriers and more. This case going on for years a nice victory! **10/3/2019 10:00**

Schiff is a lowlife who should resign (at least!). https://t.co/nGp9aFP3rX **10/3/2019 12:09**

95% Approval Rating in the Republican Party and record setting fundraising that has taken place over the past two weeks. Thank you! **10/3/2019 17:16**

ELECTION INTERFERENCE! **10/3/2019 19:27**

There wasn't ANYTHING said wrong in my conversation with the Ukrainian President. This is a Democrat Scam! **10/3/2019 20:32**

DRAIN THE SWAMP! https://t.co/N3FaZ5Dkjq **10/3/2019 20:53**

As the President of the United States I have an absolute right perhaps even a duty to investigate or have investigated CORRUPTION and that would include asking or suggesting other Countries to help us out!

10/4/2019 1:04

AOC is a Wack Job! https://t.co/LU3hleek0c **10/4/2019 1:27**

We are simultaneously fighting the Fake News Media and their partner the Democrat Party. Always tough to beat the "Press" but people are beginning to see how totally CORRUPT they are and it makes our job a whole lot easier! **10/4/2019 1:35**

Nancy Pelosi today on @GMA actually said that Adam Schiffty Schiff didn't fabricate my words in a major speech before Congress. She either had no idea what she was saying in other words lost it or she lied. Even Clinton lover

@GStephanopoulos strongly called her out. Sue her?
10/4/2019 2:20

As President I have an obligation to end CORRUPTION even if that means requesting the help of a foreign country or countries. It is done all the time. This has NOTHING to do with politics or a political campaign against the Bidens. This does have to do with their corruption! **10/4/2019 12:16**

Breaking News: Unemployment Rate at 3.5% drops to a 50 YEAR LOW. Wow America lets impeach your President (even though he did nothing wrong!).
10/4/2019 12:47

I have just officially nominated Poland for entry into the Visa Waiver Program. With this decades long-awaited announcement we are in the final steps of the process which when complete would grant Polish nationals visa-free business and tourism travel to the U.S. & vice versa.
10/4/2019 22:02

LYIN' SHIFTY SCHIFF! https://t.co/vSZgFz9flS **10/4/2019 22:15**

"It isn't often I get angry at the dirty politics of the Democrats in Congress but this time I am enraged and hope this impeachment charade will backfire on Reps. Pelosi & Schiff & the Democrats. I have read thoroughly the telephone conversation between Trump & the President...
10/5/2019 2:25

The so-called Whistleblower's account of my perfect phone call is "way off" not even close. Schiff and Pelosi never thought I would release the transcript of the call. Got them by surprise they got caught. This is a fraud against the American people! **10/5/2019 13:58**

Somebody please wake up Mitt Romney and tell him that my conversation with the Ukrainian President was a congenial and very appropriate one and my statement on

China pertained to corruption not politics. If Mitt worked this hard on Obama he could have won.
Sadly he choked! **10/5/2019 14:06**

Mitt Romney never knew how to win. He is a pompous "ass" who has been fighting me from the beginning except when he begged me for my endorsement for his Senate run (I gave it to him) and when he begged me to be Secretary of State (I didn't give it to him). He is so bad for R's!
10/5/2019 14:17

Not only are the Do Nothing Democrats interfering in the 2020 Election but they are continuing to interfere in the 2016 Election. They must be stopped! **10/5/2019 18:33**

I'm hearing that the Great People of Utah are considering their vote for their Pompous Senator Mitt Romney to be a big mistake. I agree! He is a fool who is playing right into the hands of the Do Nothing Democrats!
#IMPEACHMITTROMNEY **10/5/2019 19:06**

So Crooked Hillary Clinton can delete and acid wash 33000 emails AFTER getting a Subpoena from the United States Congress but I can't make one totally appropriate telephone call to the President of Ukraine? Witch Hunt! **10/5/2019 19:25**

The first so-called second hand information "Whistleblower" got my phone conversation almost completely wrong so now word is they are going to the bench and another "Whistleblower" is coming in from the Deep State also with second hand info. Meet with Shifty. Keep them coming!
10/6/2019 1:17

95% Approval Rating in Republican Party. Thank you!
10/6/2019 13:24

It is INCREDIBLE to watch and read the Fake News and how they pull out all stops to protect Sleepy Joe Biden and his thrown out of the Military son Hunter who was handed $100000 a month (PlusPlus) from a Ukrainian based company even though he had no experience in energy...
(1/2) **10/6/2019 14:58**

The Biden family was PAID OFF pure and simple! The fake news must stop making excuses for something that is totally inexcusable. Sleepy Joe said he never spoke to the Ukrainian company and then the picture came out where he was playing golf with the company boss and Hunter..... (2/2)
10/6/2019 16:42

DRAIN THE SWAMP! **10/6/2019 20:13**

Unemployment Rate just dropped to 3.5% the lowest in more that 50 years. Is that an impeachable event for your President?
10/6/2019 23:39

Nancy Pelosi knew of all of the many Shifty Adam Schiff lies and massive frauds perpetrated upon Congress and the American people in the form of a fraudulent speech knowingly delivered as a ruthless con and the illegal meetings with a highly partisan "Whistleblower" & lawyer... (1/2) **10/7/2019 2:27**

....This makes Nervous Nancy every bit as guilty as Liddle' Adam Schiff for High Crimes and Misdemeanors and even Treason. I guess that means that they along with all of those that evilly "Colluded" with them must all be immediately Impeached! (2/2) **10/7/2019 2:27**

The United States was supposed to be in Syria for 30 days that was many years ago. We stayed and got deeper and deeper into battle with no aim in sight. When I arrived in Washington ISIS was running rampant in the area. We quickly defeated 100% of the ISIS Caliphate..... (1/2)
10/7/2019 11:40

I was elected on getting out of these ridiculous endless wars where our great Military functions as a policing operation to the benefit of people who don't even like the USA. The two most unhappy countries at this move are Russia & China because they love seeing us bogged..... (2/2)
10/7/2019 15:20

As I have stated strongly before and just to reiterate if Turkey does anything that I in my great and unmatched wisdom consider to be off limits I will totally destroy and obliterate the Economy of Turkey (I've done before!). They must with Europe and others watch over... (1/2) **10/7/2019 15:38**

....the captured ISIS fighters and families. The U.S. has done far more than anyone could have ever expected including the capture of 100% of the ISIS Caliphate. It is time now for others in the region some of great wealth to protect their own territory. THE USA IS GREAT! (2/2) **10/7/2019 15:38**

I would love to send Ambassador Sondland a really good man and great American to testify but unfortunately he would be testifying before a totally compromised kangaroo court where Republican's rights have been taken away and true facts are not allowed out for the public.... **10/8/2019 13:23**

I think that Crooked Hillary Clinton should enter the race to try and steal it away from Uber Left Elizabeth Warren. Only one condition. The Crooked one must explain all of her high crimes and misdemeanors including how & why she deleted 33000 Emails AFTER getting "C" Subpoena! **10/8/2019 14:06**

Someone please tell the Radical Left Mayor of Minneapolis that he can't price out Free Speech. Probably illegal! I stand strongly & proudly with the great Police Officers and Law Enforcement of Minneapolis and the Great State of Minnesota! See you Thursday Night! **10/8/2019 14:31**

Hasn't Adam Schiff been fully discredited by now? Do we have to continue listening to his lies? **10/8/2019 16:06**

Gasoline Prices in the State of California are MUCH HIGHER than anywhere else in the Nation ($2.50 vs. $4.50). I guess those very expensive and unsafe cars that they are mandating just aren't doing the trick! Don't worry California relief is on the way. The State doesn't get it! **10/9/2019 1:57**

The United States has spent EIGHT TRILLION DOLLARS fighting and policing in the Middle East. Thousands of our Great Soldiers have died or been badly wounded. Millions

of people have died on the other side. GOING INTO THE MIDDLE EAST IS THE WORST DECISION EVER MADE.....
10/9/2019 12:14

The so-called Whistleblower before knowing I was going to release the exact Transcript stated that my call with the Ukrainian President was "crazy frightening and completely lacking in substance related to national security." This is a very big Lie. Read the Transcript! **10/9/2019 12:43**

Crooked Hillary should try it again! https://t.co/UjfIpZp1FA
10/9/2019 14:10

Only 25 percent want the President Impeached which is pretty low considering the volume of Fake News coverage but pretty high considering the fact that I did NOTHING wrong. It is all just a continuation of the greatest Scam and Witch Hunt in the history of our Country! **10/9/2019 16:27**

So pathetic to see Sleepy Joe Biden who with his son Hunter and to the detriment of the American Taxpayer has ripped off at least two countries for millions of dollars calling for my impeachment - and I did nothing wrong. Joe's Failing Campaign gave him no other choice! **10/9/2019 17:55**

From the day I announced I was running for President I have NEVER had a good @FoxNews Poll. Whoever their Pollster is they suck. But @FoxNews is also much different than it used to be in the good old days. With people like Andrew Napolitano who wanted to be a Supreme....
10/10/2019 13:08

Big day of negotiations with China. They want to make a deal but do I? I meet with the Vice Premier tomorrow at The White House. **10/10/2019 13:49**

The joint statement released with President Bolsonaro in March makes absolutely clear that I support Brazil beginning the process for full OECD membership. The United States stands by that statement and stands by @ jairbolsonaro. This article is FAKE NEWS! https://t.co/Hym9ZATHjt **10/11/2019 0:03**

A GREAT evening in Minneapolis Minnesota with incredible American Patriots. THANK YOU! https://t.co/b3UQEoOwPq
10/11/2019 2:37

Over the next 13 months we are going to fight with all of our heart and soul - and we are going to win the Great State of Minnesota in 2020! #TrumpMinneapolis #KAG2020 https://t.co/c3FQnrPJWr **10/11/2019 2:49**

Good things are happening at China Trade Talk Meeting. Warmer feelings than in recent past more like the Old Days. I will be meeting with the Vice Premier today. All would like to see something significant happen! **10/11/2019 13:49**

WHERE'S HUNTER? **10/12/2019 2:58**

So funny to watch Steve Kerr grovel and pander when asked a simple question about China. He chocked and looks weak and pathetic. Don't want him at the White House!
10/12/2019 3:25

The deal I just made with China is by far the greatest and biggest deal ever made for our Great Patriot Farmers in the history of our Country. In fact there is a question as to whether or not this much product can be produced? Our farmers will figure it out. Thank you China! **10/12/2019 14:09**

So now they are after the legendary "crime buster" and greatest Mayor in the history of NYC Rudy Giuliani. He may seem a little rough around the edges sometimes but he is also a great guy and wonderful lawyer. Such a one sided Witch Hunt going on in USA. Deep State. Shameful!
10/12/2019 15:11

The Endless Wars Must End! **10/12/2019 21:20**

The same people that got us into the Middle East Quicksand 8 Trillion Dollars and many thousands of lives (and millions of lives when you count the other side) are now fighting to keep us there. Don't listen to people that haven't got a clue. They have proven to be inept! **10/13/2019 4:06**

Where's Hunter? He has totally disappeared! Now looks like he has raided and scammed even more countries! Media is AWOL. **10/13/2019 14:15**

We have become a far greater Economic Power than ever before and we are using that power for WORLD PEACE! **10/13/2019 14:32**

CHINA HAS ALREADY BEGUN AGRICULTURAL PURCHASES FROM OUR GREAT PATRIOT FARMERS & RANCHERS! **10/13/2019 21:50**

"Congressman Adam Schiff who when seeing the REAL Ukraine phone call Transcript decided he'd better make up one of his own. 'I'm going to say this only SEVEN times so you better listen good. I want you to MAKE UP DIRT ON MY POLITICAL OPPONENT UNDERSTAND LOTS OF IT AND..... **10/13/2019 22:16**

Somebody please explain to Chris Wallace of Fox who will never be his father (and my friend) Mike Wallace that the Phone Conversation I had with the President of Ukraine was a congenial & good one. It was only Schiff's made up version of that conversation that was bad! **10/14/2019 0:10**

"Serial killers get more Due Process than the Democrats give to the President of the United States." @marklevinshow **10/14/2019 0:34**

Former Democrat Senator Harry Reid just stated that Donald Trump is very smart much more popular than people think is underestimated and will be hard to beat in the 2020 Election. Thank you Harry I agree! **10/14/2019 10:54**

The same people who got us into the Middle East mess are the people who most want to stay there! **10/14/2019 11:40**

Happy Columbus Day! **10/14/2019 12:06**

Wow! Hunter Biden is being forced to leave a Chinese Company. Now watch the Fake News wrap their greasy and very protective arms around him. Only softball questions of him please! **10/14/2019 16:18**

America First! **10/14/2019 17:26**

After defeating 100% of the ISIS Caliphate I largely moved our troops out of Syria. Let Syria and Assad protect the Kurds and fight Turkey for their own land. I said to my Generals why should we be fighting for Syria.... **10/14/2019 19:10**

Shifty Schiff now seems to think they don't need the Whistleblower who started the whole Scam. The reason is that the Whistleblower has lost all credibility because the story is so far from the facts on the Transcript. Also the second Whistleblower is no longer even mentioned! **10/15/2019 0:17**

A big scandal at @ABC News. They got caught using really gruesome FAKE footage of the Turks bombing in Syria. A real disgrace. Tomorrow they will ask softball questions to Sleepy Joe Biden's son Hunter like why did Ukraine & China pay you millions when you knew nothing? Payoff? **10/15/2019 0:21**

"Project Veritas-Obtained Undercover Videos Highlight Jeff Zucker's (@CNN) Campaign To Destroy Trump. Videos Reveal @CNN's BIAS!" @TuckerCarlson @FoxNews Does this sound like a good or even great lawsuit? **10/15/2019 0:51**

Democrats are allowing no transparency at the Witch Hunt hearings. If Republicans ever did this they would be excoriated by the Fake News. Let the facts come out from the charade of people most of whom I do not know they are interviewing for 9 hours each not selective leaks. **10/15/2019 13:40**

Just out: MEDIAN HOUSEHOLD INCOME IS AT THE HIGHEST POINT EVER EVER EVER! How about saying it this way IN THE HISTORY OF OUR COUNTRY! Also MORE PEOPLE WORKING TODAY IN THE USA THAN AT ANY TIME IN HISTORY! Tough numbers for the Radical Left Democrats to beat! Impeach the Pres. **10/15/2019 15:32**

Now that we have found out that @CNN is a virtual fraud rumor has it that Jeff Zucker will be resigining momentarily?
10/15/2019 18:04

Shifty Adam Schiff wants to rest his entire case on a Whistleblower who he now says can't testify & the reason he can't testify is that he is afraid to do so because his account of the Presidential telephone call is a fraud & totally different from the actual transcribed call... **10/16/2019 2:21**

Looks good to me! https://t.co/3aHn7y3Zxl **10/16/2019 3:15**

We now have the greatest Economy in history! https://t.co/8fLOejOpxH **10/16/2019 3:22**

You would think there is NO WAY that any of the Democrat Candidates that we witnessed last night could possibly become President of the United States. Now you see why they have no choice but to push a totally illegal & absurd Impeachment of one of the most successful Presidents!
10/16/2019 11:10

95% Approval Rating in the Republican Party. Thank you! Just won two Congressional Seats in North Carolina & a Governors runoff in Louisiana which Republicans should now win! Because of Impeachment Fraud we will easily take back the House add in the Senate & again win Pres!
10/16/2019 11:25

Our record Economy would CRASH just like in 1929 if any of those clowns became President! **10/16/2019 11:29**

Republicans are totally deprived of their rights in this Impeachment Witch Hunt. No lawyers no questions no transparency! The good news is that the Radical Left Dems have No Case. It is all based on their Fraud and Fabrication!
10/16/2019 11:46

Senator Rand Paul just wrote a great book "The Case Against Socialism" which is now out. Highly recommended - as America was founded on LIBERTY & INDEPENDENCE - not government coercion domination & control. We were

born free and will stay free as long as I am your President!
10/16/2019 18:05

FAKE NEWS! https://t.co/ta8ii8yetP **10/16/2019 21:17**

Do you think they like me? https://t.co/TDmUnJ8HtF
10/16/2019 22:21

Nervous Nancy's unhinged meltdown! https://t.co/RDeUI7sfe7
10/16/2019 22:29

Nancy Pelosi needs help fast! There is either something wrong with her "upstairs" or she just plain doesn't like our great Country. She had a total meltdown in the White House today. It was very sad to watch. Pray for her she is a very sick person! **10/17/2019 0:00**

"This President is the most patriotic President I've seen in many years. He is going to do what is good for Americans." Congressman Brian Babin Texas. Thank you Brian!
10/17/2019 0:12

THANK YOU you Dallas Texas. See you tomorrow night at the American Airlines Center! #TRUMP2020 https://t.co/fbtzlbroQi **10/17/2019 0:44**

"What has happened here with the Anthony Wiener laptop the Server all of the Emails between Huma Abedin and Hillary Clinton the deleted Clinton Emails - what is going on?" @LouDobbs Joe D & Victoria T! **10/17/2019 0:58**

Hope all House Republicans and honest House Democrats will vote to CENSURE Rep. Adam Schiff tomorrow for his brazen and unlawful act of fabricating (making up) a totally phony conversation with the Ukraine President and U.S. President me. Most have never seen such a thing!
10/17/2019 1:14

"About 500000 human beings were killed in Syria while Barack Obama was president & leading for a "political settlement" to that civil war. Media has been more outraged in the last 72 hours over our Syria policy than they were at any point during 7 years of slaughter." BuckSexton
10/17/2019 4:29

I am the only person who can fight for the safety of our troops & bring them home from the ridiculous & costly Endless Wars and be scorned. Democrats always liked that position until I took it. Democrats always liked Walls until I built them. Do you see what's happening here? **10/17/2019 4:39**

My warmest condolences to the family and many friends of Congressman Elijah Cummings. I got to see first hand the strength passion and wisdom of this highly respected political leader. His work and voice on so many fronts will be very hard if not impossible to replace! **10/17/2019 12:54**

Great news out of Turkey. News Conference shortly with @VP and @SecPompeo. Thank you to @RTErdogan. Millions of lives will be saved! **10/17/2019 17:29**

This deal could NEVER have been made 3 days ago. There needed to be some "tough" love in order to get it done. Great for everybody. Proud of all! **10/17/2019 18:03**

This is a great day for civilization. I am proud of the United States for sticking by me in following a necessary but somewhat unconventional path. People have been trying to make this "Deal" for many years. Millions of lives will be saved. Congratulations to ALL!

10/17/2019 18:13

Just arrived at the American Airlines Center in Dallas Texas. Will be out shortly as we wait for more of you to get in! #TRUMP2020 https://t.co/TB2baAFoBK **10/18/2019 0:21**

The radical left tolerates no dissent it permits no opposition it accepts no compromise and it has absolutely no respect for the will of the American People. They are coming after me because I am fighting for YOU! #TrumpRallyDallas #KAG2020 https://t.co/OthKwS1bud **10/18/2019 2:57**

Democrats are now the party of high taxes high crime open borders late-term abortion socialism and blatant corruption. The Republican Party is the party of the American Worker the American Family and the American Dream! #KAG2020 https://t.co/qXB198T5cM **10/18/2019 3:39**

Can you believe I am doing this important work for our Country and have to deal with Corrupt Adam Schiff and the Do Nothing Democrats at the same time? It was not intended to be this way for a President! **10/18/2019 15:51**

Think of how many lives we saved in Syria and Turkey by getting a ceasefire yesterday. Thousands and thousands and maybe many more! **10/18/2019 23:25**

Corrupt Congressman Adam Schiff is angry that Ambassadors that he thought would be good for his fraudulent Witch Hunt are turning out to be good for me - some really good! He's got all meetings locked down no transparency only his illegal leaks. A very dishonest sleazebag! **10/19/2019 1:28**

Susan Rice who was a disaster to President Obama as National Security Advisor is now telling us her opinion on what to do in Syria. Remember RED LINE IN THE SAND? That was Obama. Millions killed! No thanks Susan you were a disaster. **10/19/2019 2:59**

#StopTheCoup **10/19/2019 12:32**

Crooked Hillary Clinton just called the respected environmentalist and Green Party candidate Jill Stein a "Russian Asset." They need a Green Party more than ever after looking at the Democrats disastrous environmental program! **10/19/2019 19:47**

I thought I was doing something very good for our Country by using Trump National Doral in Miami for hosting the G-7 Leaders. It is big grand on hundreds of acres next to MIAMI INTERNATIONAL AIRPORT has tremendous ballrooms & meeting rooms and each delegation would have... (1/2)
10/20/2019 1:18

.....its own 50 to 70 unit building. Would set up better than other alternatives. I announced that I would be willing to do it at NO PROFIT or if legally permissible at ZERO COST to the USA. But as usual the Hostile Media & their Democrat Partners went CRAZY! (2/2) **10/20/2019 1:18**

So now Crooked Hillary is at it again! She is calling Congresswoman Tulsi Gabbard "a Russian favorite" and Jill Stein "a Russian asset." As you may have heard I was called a big Russia lover also (actually I do like Russian people. I like all people!). Hillary's gone Crazy!
10/20/2019 2:41

Pelosi is now leading a delegation of 9 including Corrupt Adam Schiff to Jordan to check out Syria. She should find out why Obama drew The Red Line In the Sand & then did NOTHING losing Syria & all respect. I did something 58 missiles. One million died under Obama's mistake!
10/20/2019 20:28

This Scam going on right now by the Democrats against the Republican Party and me was all about a perfect phone call I had with the Ukrainian President. He's already stated NO PRESSURE! Where is the Whistleblower or the 2nd Whistleblower or the "informant?" All gone..... **10/20/2019 21:45**

Censure (at least) Corrupt Adam Schiff! After what he got caught doing any pol who does not so vote cannot be honest....are you listening Dems? **10/21/2019 12:31**

Doral in Miami would have been the best place to hold the G-7 and free but too much heat from the Do Nothing Radical Left Democrats & their Partner the Fake News Media! I'm surprised that they allow me to give up my $400000 Plus Presidential Salary! We'll find someplace else! **10/21/2019 13:17**

So some day if a Democrat becomes President and the Republicans win the House even by a tiny margin they can impeach the President without due process or fairness or any legal rights. All Republicans must remember what they are witnessing here - a lynching. But we will WIN! **10/22/2019 11:52**

Thank you Republicans. 185 out of 185 present voted for "US" last night. Really good! **10/22/2019 11:54**

95% Approval Rating in the Republican Party. Thank you! **10/22/2019 11:57**

Good news seems to be happening with respect to Turkey Syria and the Middle East. Further reports to come later! **10/22/2019 22:18**

Republicans are going to fight harder than ever to win back the House because of what the Do Nothing Democrats have done to our Country! **10/23/2019 11:36**

Where's the Whistleblower? **10/23/2019 12:40**

The Never Trumper Republicans though on respirators with not many left are in certain ways worse and more dangerous for our Country than the Do Nothing Democrats. Watch out for them they are human scum! **10/23/2019 17:48**

It would be really great if the people within the Trump Administration all well-meaning and good (I hope!) could stop hiring Never Trumpers who are worse than the Do Nothing Democrats. Nothing good will ever come from them! **10/23/2019 19:01**

The Federal Reserve is derelict in its duties if it doesn't lower the Rate and even ideally stimulate. Take a look around the World at our competitors. Germany and others are actually GETTING PAID to borrow money. Fed was way too fast to raise and way too slow to cut! **10/24/2019 14:20**

Thank you to House Republicans for being tough smart and understanding in detail the greatest Witch Hunt in American History. It has been going on since long before I even got Elected (the Insurance Policy!). A total Scam! **10/24/2019 14:28**

Where is the Whistleblower and why did he or she write such a fictitious and incorrect account of my phone call with the Ukrainian President? Why did the IG allow this to happen? Who is the so-called Informant (Schiff?) who was so inaccurate? A giant Scam! **10/25/2019 1:52**

"Donald J. Trump is an absolutely historic President already in less than 3 years in office. His record is there for everyone to look at & to examine and compare. This is an illegitimate effort to overthrow a President not a formal Impeachment inquiry." @LouDobbs Thank you Lou **10/25/2019 12:54**

To Tim: The Button on the IPhone was FAR better than the Swipe! **10/25/2019 22:39**

Democrats just announced that they no longer want the Whistleblower to testify. But everything was about the Whistleblower (they no longer want the second Whistleblower either) which they don't want because the account of my call bore NO RELATIONSHIP to the call itself..... **10/25/2019 23:30**

My lawyers should sue the Democrats and Shifty Adam Schiff for fraud! **10/25/2019 23:33**

"General Michael Flynn's attorney is demanding that charges be immediately dropped after they found that FBI Agents manipulated records against him. They say that James Clapper told a reporter to "take a kill shot at Flynn. This has been a complete setup of Michael Flynn.... **10/26/2019 11:02**

Had a beautiful dinner last night at Camp David in celebration of the 10th Wedding Anniversary of Ivanka and Jared. Attended by a small number of family and friends it could not have been nicer. Camp David is a special place. Cost of the event will be totally paid for by me! **10/26/2019 11:21**

I can't believe that Nancy Pelosi's District in San Francisco is in such horrible shape that the City itself is in violation of many sanitary & environmental orders causing it to owe the Federal Government billions of dollars - and all she works on is Impeachment..... **10/26/2019 11:29**

The Ukraine investigation is just as Corrupt and Fake as all of the other garbage that went on before it. Even Shifty Schiff got caught cheating when he made up what I said on the call! **10/26/2019 11:44**

Badly failing presidential candidate @KamalaHarris will not go to a very wonderful largely African American event today because yesterday I recieved a major award at the same event for being able to produce & sign into law major Criminal Justice Reform legislation which will.. **10/26/2019 12:18**

The Fake Washington Post keeps doing phony stories with zero sources that I am concerned with the Impeachment scam. I am not because I did nothing wrong. It is the other side including Schiff and his made up story that are concerned. Witch Hunt continues! **10/26/2019 14:41**

Where's the Whistleblower? **10/26/2019 14:43**

Something very big has just happened!
10/27/2019 1:23

As Diwali commences @FLOTUS Melania and I wish those observing the Festival of Lights a blessed and happy celebration! #HappyDiwali https://t.co/LGXkUzMJil
10/27/2019 10:21

Thank you to @MarthaRaddatz and @TerryMoran for a job well done! https://t.co/mcHjqX1K2L **10/27/2019 21:24**

The S&P just hit an ALL TIME HIGH. This is a big win for jobs 401-K's and frankly EVERYONE! Our Country is doing great. Even killed long sought ISIS murderer Al-Baghdadi. We are stronger than ever before with GREAT upward potential. Enjoy! **10/28/2019 13:41**

We have declassified a picture of the wonderful dog (name not declassified) that did such a GREAT JOB in capturing and killing the Leader of ISIS Abu Bakr al-Baghdadi! https://t.co/PDMx9nZWvw
10/28/2019 20:02

Can you believe that Shifty Adam Schiff the biggest leaker in D.C. and a corrupt politician is upset that we didn't inform him before we raided and killed the #1 terrorist in the WORLD!? Wouldn't be surprised if the Do Nothing Democrats Impeach me over that! DRAIN THE SWAMP!! **10/28/2019 21:22**

The only crimes in the Impeachment Hoax were committed by Shifty Adam Schiff when he totally made up my phone conversation with the Ukrainian President and read it to Congress together with numerous others on Shifty's side. Schiff should be Impeached and worse! **10/29/2019 3:58**

How many more Never Trumpers will be allowed to testify about a perfectly appropriate phone call when all anyone has to do is READ THE TRANSCRIPT! I knew people were listening in on the call (why would I say something inappropriate?) which was fine with me but why so many? **10/29/2019 12:47**

95% Approval Rating in the Republican Party a record. Thank you! **10/29/2019 13:20**

Just confirmed that Abu Bakr al-Baghdadi's number one replacement has been terminated by American troops. Most likely would have taken the top spot - Now he is also Dead!

10/29/2019 13:29

Nervous Nancy Pelosi is doing everything possible to destroy the Republican Party. Our Polls show that it is going to be just the opposite. The Do Nothing Dems will lose many seats in 2020. They have a Death Wish led by a corrupt politician Adam Schiff! **10/29/2019 15:14**

The Greatest Economy in American History! **10/30/2019 11:38**

A Federal Judge is allowing the Nick Sandman libel suit to move forward against the thoroughly disgusting Washington Post (which is no longer available at the White House!). He could now have a good chance of winning. Go Nick! **10/30/2019 12:26**

Yesterday's Never Trumper witness could find NO Quid Pro Quo in the Transcript of the phone call. There were many people listening to the call. How come they (including the President of Ukraine) found NOTHING wrong with it. Witch Hunt! **10/30/2019 12:59**

Thank you Daily Wire. Very cute recreation but the "live" version of Conan will be leaving the Middle East for the White House sometime next week! https://t.co/Z1UfhxsSpT **10/31/2019 4:36**

"Now is the time for Republicans to stand together and defend the leader of their party against these smears. It would be one thing if there were any indication of an underlying crime but there is not-not in the transcripts and not in the secret witness testimony that..... **10/31/2019 12:20**

READ THE TRANSCRIPT! **10/31/2019 13:29**

The Impeachment Hoax is hurting our Stock Market. The Do Nothing Democrats don't care! **10/31/2019 14:57**

The Greatest Witch Hunt In American History!

10/31/2019 15:31

While the Do Nothing Democrats FAIL the American People and continue the Impeachment Scam my Administration will continue to deliver REAL RESULTS as seen over the past month below! https://t.co/dxjHusgiFX **10/31/2019 22:44**

1600 Pennsylvania Avenue the White House is the place I have come to love and will stay for hopefully another 5 years as we MAKE AMERICA GREAT AGAIN but my family and I will be making Palm Beach Florida our Permanent Residence. I cherish New York and the people of.....

11/1/2019 1:32

Wow a blowout JOBS number just out adjusted for revisions and the General Motors strike 303000. This is far greater than expectations. USA ROCKS! **11/1/2019 12:52**

ISIS has a new leader. We know exactly who he is!

11/1/2019 13:38

Stock Market up BIG! Record highs for S&P 500 and NASDAQ. Enjoy! **11/1/2019 14:08**

I love New York but New York can never be great again under the current leadership of Governor Andrew Cuomo (the brother of Fredo) or Mayor Bill DeBlasio. Cuomo has weaponized the prosecutors to do his dirty work (and to keep him out of jams) a reason some don't want to be...

11/1/2019 21:11

Republicans have never been more unified than they are right now! The Dems are a mess under the corrupt leadership of Nervous Nancy Pelosi and Shifty Adam Schiff!

11/1/2019 21:40

Oh no Beto just dropped out of race for President despite him saying he was "born for this." I don't think so! **11/1/2019 21:51**

You can't Impeach someone who hasn't done anything wrong! **11/1/2019 22:48**

The Whistleblower must come forward to explain why his account of the phone call with the Ukrainian President was so inaccurate (fraudulent?). Why did the Whistleblower deal with corrupt politician Shifty Adam Schiff and/or his committee? **11/1/2019 23:16**

A great new book by Howie Carr "What Really Happened How Donald J. Trump Saved America From Hillary Clinton" is on sale now. Howie is a talented New England force who was there at the very beginning! **11/2/2019 16:26**

The Whistleblower has disappeared. Where is the Whistleblower? **11/2/2019 20:57**

The Governor of California @GavinNewsom has done a terrible job of forest management. I told him from the first day we met that he must "clean" his forest floors regardless of what his bosses the environmentalists DEMAND of him. Must also do burns and cut fire stoppers..... **11/3/2019 14:11**

The Whistleblower got it sooo wrong that HE must come forward. The Fake News Media knows who he is but being an arm of the Democrat Party don't want to reveal him because there would be hell to pay. Reveal the Whistleblower and end the Impeachment Hoax! **11/3/2019 14:33**

Many people listened to my phone call with the Ukrainian President while it was being made. I never heard any complaints. The reason is that it was totally appropriate I say perfect. Republicans have never been more unified and my Republican Approval Rating is now 95%! **11/3/2019 16:40**

The Angry Majority! **11/3/2019 16:41**

I hope everyone in the Great State of Virginia will get out and VOTE on Tuesday in all of the local and state elections to send a signal to D.C. that you want lower taxes a strong Military Border & 2nd Amendment great healthcare and must take care of our Vets. VOTE REPUBLICAN **11/3/2019 20:18**

False stories are being reported that a few Republican Senators are saying that President Trump may have done a quid pro quo but it doesn't matter there is nothing wrong with that it is not an impeachable event. Perhaps so but read the transcript there is no quid pro quo! **11/4/2019 0:59**

Great! But how do you know it was a "mistweet?" May be something with deep meaning! https://t.co/OOEXMCgQLp **11/4/2019 11:38**

What I said on the phone call with the Ukrainian President is "perfectly" stated. There is no reason to call witnesses to analyze my words and meaning. This is just another Democrat Hoax that I have had to live with from the day I got elected (and before!). Disgraceful! **11/4/2019 12:06**

The Whistleblower gave false information & dealt with corrupt politician Schiff. He must be brought forward to testify. Written answers not acceptable! Where is the 2nd Whistleblower? He disappeared after I released the transcript. Does he even exist? Where is the informant? Con! **11/4/2019 12:50**

95% Approval Rating in the Republican Party. Thank you! **11/4/2019 12:58**

Stock Market hits RECORD HIGH. Spend your money well! **11/4/2019 13:45**

Read the Transcript! **11/4/2019 14:51**

All-Time High for Stock Market and all the Fake News wants to talk about is the Impeachment Hoax! **11/4/2019 15:09**

My son @DonaldJTrumpJr is coming out with a new book "Triggered: How the Left Thrives on Hate and Wants to Silence Us" – available tomorrow November 5th! A great new book that I highly recommend for ALL to read. Go order it today! **11/4/2019 17:39**

This is the time for Mexico with the help of the United States to wage WAR on the drug cartels and wipe them off the face of the earth. We merely await a call from your great new president! **11/5/2019 13:28**

So sad to see what is happening in New York where Governor Cuomo & Mayor DeBlasio are letting out 900 Criminals some hardened & bad onto the sidewalks of our rapidly declining because of them city. The Radical Left Dems are killing our cities. NYPD Commissioner is resigning! **11/5/2019 14:05**

95% Approval Rating in the Republican Party. Thank you! https://t.co/Z0VHUIAwMD **11/6/2019 1:02**

Thank you to Kurt Volker U.S. Envoy to Ukraine who said in his Congressional Testimony just released "You asked what conversations did I have about that quid pro quo et cetra. NONE because I didn't know there was a quid pro quo." Witch Hunt! **11/6/2019 13:17**

Stock Markets (all three) hit another ALL TIME & HISTORIC HIGH yesterday! You are sooo lucky to have me as your President (just kidding!). Spend your money well!

11/6/2019 13:30

Years ago when Media was legitimate people known as "Fact Checkers" would always call to check and see if a story was accurate. Nowadays they don't use "Fact Checkers" anymore they just write whatever they want! **11/7/2019 5:06**

Bill Barr did not decline my request to talk about Ukraine. The story was a Fake Washington Post con job with an "anonymous" source that doesn't exist. Just read the

Transcript. The Justice Department already ruled that the call was good. We don't have freedom of the press!
11/7/2019 12:28

Read the Transcript! **11/7/2019 13:47**

Based on the information released last night about the Fake Whistleblowers attorney the Impeachment Hoax should be ended IMMEDIATELY! There is no case except against the other side! **11/7/2019 14:00**

It was just explained to me that for next weeks Fake Hearing (trial) in the House as they interview Never Trumpers and others I get NO LAWYER & NO DUE PROCESS. It is a Pelosi Schiff Scam against the Republican Party and me. This Witch Hunt should not be allowed to proceed! **11/7/2019 15:16**

The Amazon Washington Post and three lowlife reporters Matt Zapotosky Josh Dawsey and Carol Leonnig wrote another Fake News story without any sources (pure fiction) about Bill Barr & myself. We both deny this story which they knew before they wrote it. A garbage newspaper!
11/7/2019 15:27

Stock Market up big today. A New Record. Enjoy!
11/7/2019 15:43

STATEMENT FROM PRESIDENT DONALD J. TRUMP https://t.co/EktztHfLk6 **11/8/2019 0:08**

I will be announcing the winners of the #MAGACHALLENGE and inviting them to the @WhiteHouse to meet with me and perform. Good luck! https://t.co/3PYzOvYz17
11/8/2019 17:19

Fake News is reporting that I am talking to Mark Burnett about doing a big show perhaps The Apprentice after the presidency which I would assume they mean in 5 years. This is not true never had such a conversation don't even have time to think about it. False reporting! **11/9/2019 11:41**

Just finished reading my son Donald's just out new book "Triggered." It is really good! He along with many of us was very unfairly treated. But we all fight back and we always win!

1/9/2019 15:37

PRESIDENTIAL HARASSMENT! **11/9/2019 17:49**

I recommend that Nervous Nancy Pelosi (who backed up Schiff's lie) Shifty Adam Schiff Sleepy Joe Biden the Whistleblower (who miraculously disappeared after I released the transcript of the call) the 2nd Whistleblower (who also disappeared) & the I.G. be part of the list!

11/9/2019 18:52

Thank you to LSU and Alabama for a great game!

11/10/2019 0:40

ABC is as bad as the rest of them. Journalistic standards are nonexistent today. The press is so dishonest that we no longer have Freedom of the Press! https://t.co/nzF31cLYw7

11/10/2019 16:12

Corrupt politician Adam Schiff wants people from the White House to testify in his and Pelosi's disgraceful Witch Hunt yet he will not allow a White House lawyer nor will he allow ANY of our requested witnesses. This is a first in due process and Congressional history! **11/10/2019 18:58**

The call to the Ukrainian President was PERFECT. Read the Transcript! There was NOTHING said that was in any way wrong. Republicans don't be led into the fools trap of saying it was not perfect but is not impeachable. No it is much stronger than that. NOTHING WAS DONE WRONG!

11/10/2019 19:43

HAPPY VETERANS DAY! **11/11/2019 13:42**

Shifty Adam Schiff will only release doctored transcripts. We haven't even seen the documents and are restricted from (get this) having a lawyer. Republicans should put out their own transcripts! Schiff must testify as to why he MADE UP a statement from me and read it to all! **11/11/2019 14:20**

Today we come together as one Nation to salute the Veterans of the United States Armed Forces – the greatest warriors ever to walk on the face of the Earth. Our Veterans risked everything for us. Now it is our duty to serve and protect THEM every day of our lives! https://t.co/vC3UGvWF9S **11/11/2019 19:28**

Where is the Whistleblower who gave so much false information? Must testify along with Schiff and others! **11/11/2019 20:26**

Read the Transcript. It is PERFECT! **11/11/2019 22:10**

Schiff is giving Republicans NO WITNESSES NO LAWYER & NO DUE PROCESS! It is a totally one sided Witch Hunt. This can't be making the Democrats look good. Such a farce! **11/11/2019 23:18**

In order to continue being the most Transparent President in history I will be releasing sometime this week the Transcript of the first and therefore most important phone call I had with the President of Ukraine. I am sure you will find it tantalizing! **11/11/2019 23:35**

I will be releasing the transcript of the first and therefore more important phone call with the Ukrainian President before week's end! **11/12/2019 11:31**

Economy is BOOMING. Seems set to have yet another record day! **11/12/2019 11:32**

"This ridiculous Impeachment is a travesty it's not an inquiry. Just read the transcript." @LouDobbs **11/13/2019 1:34**

"The circus is coming to town. The corrupt compromised coward & congenital liar Adam Schiff Show on Capital Hill brought to you by his raging psychotic Democrats & the top allies in the Media Mob. Everything you're going to see in the next two weeks is rigged..... **11/13/2019 3:33**

"Millions of Americans will see what a partisan sham this whole thing is." Rush Limbaugh @foxandfriends Also why is corrupt politician Schiff allowed to hand over cross examination to a high priced outside lawyer. Did that lawyer ever work for me which would be a conflict? **11/13/2019 12:03**

READ THE TRANSCRIPT! **11/13/2019 13:30**

Wow! Was just told that my son's book "Triggered" is Number One on The New York Times Bestseller List. Congratulations Don!

11/14/2019 3:47

.@RepRatcliffe asked the two "star" witnesses "where is the impeachable event in that call?" Both stared straight ahead with a blank look on their face remained silent & were unable to answer the question. That would be the end of a case run by normal people! - but not Shifty! **11/14/2019 11:54**

Hit New Stock Market record again yesterday the 20th time this year with GREAT potential for the future. USA is where the action is. Companies and jobs are coming back like never before! **11/14/2019 13:44**

Walmart announces great numbers. No impact from Tariffs (which are contributing $Billions to our Treasury). Inflation low (do you hear that Powell?)! **11/14/2019 14:32**

Where's the Fake Whistleblower? **11/14/2019 15:39**

Everywhere Marie Yovanovitch went turned bad. She started off in Somalia how did that go? Then fast forward to Ukraine where the new Ukrainian President spoke unfavorably about her in my second phone call with him. It

is a U.S. President's absolute right to appoint ambassadors.
11/15/2019 15:01

We have vacancies in various departments because we do not want or need as many people as past administrations (and save great cost) and also the Democrats delay the approval process to levels unprecedented in the history of our Country! **11/15/2019 16:21**

Stock Market up big. New and Historic Record. Job jobs jobs! **11/15/2019 16:34**

So they now convict Roger Stone of lying and want to jail him for many years to come. Well what about Crooked Hillary Comey Strzok Page McCabe Brennan Clapper Shifty Schiff Ohr & Nellie Steele & all of the others including even Mueller himself? Didn't they lie?.... **11/15/2019 17:13**

#NewHoaxSameSwamp https://t.co/GIg9R9TxeO
11/16/2019 2:39

Dow hits 28000 - FIRST TIME EVER HIGHEST EVER! Gee Pelosi & Schitt have a good idea "lets Impeach the President." If something like that ever happened it would lead to the biggest FALL in Market History. It's called a Depression not a Recession! So much for 401-K's & Jobs!
11/16/2019 15:18

Visited a great family of a young man under major surgery at the amazing Walter Reed Medical Center. Those are truly some of the best doctors anywhere in the world. Also began phase one of my yearly physical. Everything very good (great!). Will complete next year. **11/17/2019 5:09**

Our great Farmers will recieve another major round of "cash" compliments of China Tariffs prior to Thanksgiving. The smaller farms and farmers will be big beneficiaries. In the meantime and as you may have noticed China is starting to buy big again. Japan deal DONE. Enjoy! **11/17/2019 16:08**

Where is the Fake Whistleblower? **11/17/2019 20:12**

Never has the Republican Party been so united as it is now. 95% A.R. This is a great fraud being played out against the American people by the Fake News Media & their partner the Do Nothing Democrats. The rules are rigged by Pelosi & Schiff but we are winning and we will win! **11/18/2019 12:29**

Nancy Pelosi just stated that "it is dangerous to let the voters decide Trump's fate." @FoxNews In other words she thinks I'm going to win and doesn't want to take a chance on letting the voters decide. Like Al Green she wants to change our voting system. Wow she's CRAZY! **11/19/2019 5:15**

NASDAQ UP 27% THIS YEAR ALONE! **11/19/2019 14:03**

I agree but in the end we will win and save our Country from certain destruction! https://t.co/CPjdxq5hXT **11/20/2019 0:10**

A great day for Republicans a great day for our Country! **11/20/2019 1:06**

Nancy Pelosi will go down as the least productive Speaker of the House in history. She is dominated by AOC Plus 3 and the Radical Left. Mexico and Canada after waiting for 6 months to be approved are ready to flee - and who can blame them? Too bad! **11/20/2019 13:29**

Impeachment Witch Hunt is now OVER! Ambassador Sondland asks U.S. President (me): "What do you want from Ukraine? I keep hearing all these different ideas & theories. What do you want? It was a very abrupt conversation. He was not in a good mood. He (the President) just said"... **11/20/2019 18:57**

Today I opened a major Apple Manufacturing plant in Texas that will bring high paying jobs back to America. Today Nancy Pelosi closed Congress because she doesn't care about American Workers! **11/20/2019 23:18**

If this were a prizefight they'd stop it! **11/20/2019 23:38**

The Republican Party and me had a GREAT day yesterday with respect to the phony Impeachment Hoax & yet when I got home to the White House & checked out the news coverage on much of television you would have no idea they were reporting on the same event. FAKE & CORRUPT NEWS! **11/21/2019 12:32**

I never in my wildest dreams thought my name would in any way be associated with the ugly word Impeachment! The calls (Transcripts) were PERFECT there was NOTHING said that was wrong. No pressure on Ukraine. Great corruption & dishonesty by Schiff on the other side! **11/21/2019 13:08**

The Navy will NOT be taking away Warfighter and Navy Seal Eddie Gallagher's Trident Pin. This case was handled very badly from the beginning. Get back to business! **11/21/2019 13:30**

I have been watching people making phone calls my entire life. My hearing is and has been great. Never have I been watching a person making a call which was not on speakerphone and been able to hear or understand a conversation. I've even tried but to no avail. Try it live! **11/21/2019 14:27**

Iran has become so unstable that the regime has shut down their entire Internet System so that the Great Iranian people cannot talk about the tremendous violence taking place within the country.... **11/21/2019 17:54**

SCHIFF'S "FACT" WITNESSES! https://t.co/Pab2y1BVoN **11/22/2019 2:35**

"Former FBI Employee Accused of Altering FISA Documents." Hello here we go! @foxandfriends **11/22/2019 12:05**

"The support for Impeachment is not there. I think the Democrats will have to come up with a new game plan." @ jasoninthehouse @FoxNews **11/23/2019 2:28**

Adam Schiff will be compelled to testify should the Democrats decide despite the fact that my presidential conversations were totally appropriate (perfect) to go forward with the Impeachment Hoax. Polls have now turned very strongly against Impeachment! **11/23/2019 15:17**

95% Approval Rate in the Republican Party a record! Thank you! **11/23/2019 22:57**

Nancy Pelosi Adam Schiff AOC and the rest of the Democrats are not getting important legislation done hence the Do Nothing Democrats. USMCA National Defense Authorization Act Gun Safety Prescription Drug Prices & Infrastructure are dead in the water because of the Dems! **11/24/2019 12:30**

Polls have now turned very strongly against Impeachment especially in swing states. 75% to 25%. Thank you! **11/24/2019 12:34**

The Impeachment Scam is driving Republican Poll Numbers UP UP UP! Thank you Shifty. **11/24/2019 22:01**

Democrats going back to their Districts for Thanksgiving are getting absolutely hammered by their constituents over the phony Impeachment Scam. Republicans will have a great #2020 Election! **11/24/2019 22:42**

I was not pleased with the way that Navy Seal Eddie Gallagher's trial was handled by the Navy. He was treated very badly but despite this was completely exonerated on all major charges. I then restored Eddie's rank. Likewise large cost overruns from past administration's..... **11/24/2019 23:32**

Support for Impeachment is dropping like a rock down into the 20's in some Polls. Dems should now get down to work and finally approve USMCA and much more! **11/25/2019 12:54**

Another new Stock Market Record. Enjoy! **11/25/2019 15:05**

“DOW NASDAQ S&P 500 CLOSE AT RECORD HIGHS” https://t.co/q8luuuUGjb **11/25/2019 22:25**

I will always protect our great warfighters. I’ve got your backs! **11/26/2019 11:33**

When the Military rips down an old & badly broken Border Wall in an important location & replaces it with a brand new 30 ft. high Steel & Concrete Wall Nancy Pelosi says we are not building a Wall. Wrong and it is going up fast. Brandon Judd just gave us great marks! @FoxNews **11/26/2019 11:53**

The D.C. Wolves and Fake News Media are reading far too much into people being forced by Courts to testify before Congress. I am fighting for future Presidents and the Office of the President. Other than that I would actually like people to testify. Don McGahn’s respected.... **11/26/2019 15:43**

THANK YOU FLORIDA! #KAG2020 https://t.co/mNB4KMEj9u **11/27/2019 3:09**

GOD BLESS THE U.S.A.! #MAGAhttps://t.co/CYkQGHAgcx **11/27/2019 14:45**

New Stock Market Record today AGAIN. Congratulations USA! **11/27/2019 22:09**

95% Approval Rating in the Republican Party. Thank you! **11/27/2019 22:11**

HAPPY THANKSGIVING! https://t.co/2GoxJEk6fN **11/28/2019 13:21**

I thought Newsweek was out of business? https://t.co/3ro4eSJloo

11/29/2019 1:25

Just returned to the United States after spending a GREAT Thanksgiving with our Courageous American Warriors in Afghanistan! https://t.co/b2vgY5BH6z **11/29/2019 14:06**

I will be representing our Country in London at NATO while the Democrats are holding the most ridiculous Impeachment hearings in history. Read the Transcripts NOTHING was done or said wrong! The Radical Left is undercutting our Country. Hearings scheduled on same dates as NATO! **11/30/2019 23:38**

"Schiff's impeachment hearings wasting time when Congress must do real work" https://t.co/4lb9bWrVRL **12/1/2019 1:28**

On World AIDS Day The First Lady and I express our support for those living with HIV/AIDS and mourn the lives lost. We reaffirm our commitment to end the HIV/AIDS epidemic.... **12/1/2019 18:31**

Breaking News: The President of Ukraine has just again announced that President Trump has done nothing wrong with respect to Ukraine and our interactions or calls. If the Radical Left Democrats were sane which they are not it would be case over! **12/2/2019 13:53**

The Republican Party has NEVER been so united! This Impeachment Scam is just a continuation of the 3 year Witch Hunt but it is only bringing us even closer together! **12/2/2019 17:56**

When Lisa Page the lover of Peter Strzok talks about being "crushed" and how innocent she is ask her to read Peter's "Insurance Policy" text to her just in case Hillary loses. Also why were the lovers text messages scrubbed after he left Mueller. Where are they Lisa? **12/2/2019 18:07**

Just landed in the United Kingdom heading to London for NATO meetings tomorrow. Prior to landing I read the Republicans Report on the Impeachment Hoax. Great job! Radical Left has NO CASE. Read the Transcripts. Shouldn't even be allowed. Can we go to Supreme Court to stop? **12/2/2019 22:30**

Mini Mike Bloomberg has instructed his third rate news organization not to investigate him or any Democrat but to go after President Trump only. The Failing New York Times thinks that is O.K. because their hatred & bias is so great they can't even see straight. It's not O.K.! **12/2/2019 23:11**

The United States of America supports the brave people of Iran who are protesting for their FREEDOM. We have under the Trump Administration and always will! **12/3/2019 15:33**

Too bad. We will miss you Kamala! https://t.co/QQd9SiFc0y **12/3/2019 23:25**

Great progress has been made by NATO over the last three years. Countries other than the U.S. have agreed to pay 130 Billion Dollars more per year and by 2024 that number will be 400 Billion Dollars. NATO will be richer and stronger than ever before.... **12/4/2019 14:26**

The Fake News Media is doing everything possible to belittle my VERY successful trip to London for NATO. I got along great with the NATO leaders even getting them to pay $130 Billion a year more & $400 Billion a year more in 3 years. No increase for U.S. only deep respect! **12/4/2019 22:36**

When I said in my phone call to the President of Ukraine "I would like you to do US a favor though because our country has been through a lot and Ukraine knows a lot about it." With the word "us" I am referring to the United States our Country. I then went on to say that...... **12/5/2019 3:50**

The Do Nothing Democrats had a historically bad day yesterday in the House. They have no Impeachment case and are demeaning our Country. But nothing matters to them they have gone crazy. Therefore I say if you are going to impeach me do it now fast so we can have a fair.... (1/2) **12/5/2019 13:01**

.....trial in the Senate and so that our Country can get back to business. We will have Schiff the Bidens Pelosi and many more testify and will reveal for the first time how corrupt our system really is. I was elected to "Clean the Swamp" and that's what I am doing! (2/2) **12/5/2019 13:01**

Nancy Pelosi just had a nervous fit. She hates that we will soon have 182 great new judges and sooo much more. Stock Market and employment records. She says she "prays for the President." I don't believe her not even close. Help the homeless in your district Nancy. USMCA?
12/5/2019 16:49

Republican Approval Rating = 95%. Thank you! **12/5/2019 17:38**

The story today that we are sending 12000 troops to Saudi Arabia is false or to put it more accurately Fake News!
12/6/2019 3:27

Where's the Fake Whistleblower? Where's Whistleblower number 2? Where's the phony informer who got it all wrong? **12/6/2019 3:32**

Do not believe any article or story you read or see that uses "anonymous sources" having to do with trade or any other subject. Only accept information if it has an actual living name on it. The Fake News Media makes up many "sources say" stories. Do not believe them! **12/6/2019 12:43**

Stock Markets Up Record Numbers. For this year alone Dow up 18.65% S&P up 24.36% Nasdaq Composite up 29.17%. "It's the economy stupid." **12/6/2019 13:16**

GREAT JOBS REPORT! **12/6/2019 14:57**

Without the horror show that is the Radical Left Do Nothing Democrats the Stock Markets and Economy would be even better if that is possible and the Border would be closed to the evil of Drugs Gangs and all other problems! #2020 **12/6/2019 16:00**

JOBS JOBS JOBS! https://t.co/QCtWgld2RW **12/6/2019 20:19**

Fake News @CNN is reporting that I am "still using personal cell phone for calls despite repeated security warnings." This is totally false information and reporting. I haven't had a personal cell phone for years. Only use government approved and issued phones. Retract! **12/7/2019 0:23**

Why is the World Bank loaning money to China? Can this be possible? China has plenty of money and if they don't they create it. STOP! **12/7/2019 0:28**

Read the Transcripts! Also see where I say "us" (our Country) as opposed to "me" (meaning me) and where I then say that the Attorney General (of the United States) will call you. People still remember Schiff's made up and fraudulent version of my conversation. Witch Hunt! **12/7/2019 17:13**

While the world is not doing well economically our Country is doing better perhaps than it has ever done before. Jobs Jobs Jobs! **12/7/2019 17:21**

Our Economy is the envy of the World! **12/7/2019 18:55**

Less than 48 hours before start of the Impeachment Hearing Hoax on Monday the No Due Process Do Nothing Democrats are believe it or not changing the Impeachment Guidelines because the facts are not on their side. When you can't win the game change the rules! **12/8/2019 15:29**

I got NATO countries to pay 530 Billion Dollars a year more and the U.S. less and came home to a Fake News Media that mocked me. Didn't think that was possible! **12/8/2019 19:59**

I.G. report out tomorrow. That will be the big story! **12/8/2019 20:18**

"No president in American history has been treated like this." @marklevinshow **12/9/2019 1:37**

Read the Transcripts! **12/9/2019 15:47**

I don't know what report current Director of the FBI Christopher Wray was reading but it sure wasn't the one given to me. With that kind of attitude he will never be able to fix the FBI which is badly broken despite having some of the greatest men & women working there! **12/10/2019 12:16**

To Impeach a President who has proven through results including producing perhaps the strongest economy in our country's history to have one of the most successful presidencies ever and most importantly who has done NOTHING wrong is sheer Political Madness! #2020Election **12/10/2019 12:37**

America's great USMCA Trade Bill is looking good. It will be the best and most important trade deal ever made by the USA. Good for everybody - Farmers Manufacturers Energy Unions - tremendous support. Importantly we will finally end our Country's worst Trade Deal NAFTA! **12/10/2019 14:32**

Nadler just said that I "pressured Ukraine to interfere in our 2020 Election." Ridiculous and he knows that is not true. Both the President & Foreign Minister of Ukraine said many times that there "WAS NO PRESSURE." Nadler and the Dems know this but refuse to acknowledge! **12/10/2019 14:56**

WITCH HUNT! **12/10/2019 14:56**

Shifty Schiff a totally corrupt politician made up a horrible and fraudulent statement read it to Congress and said those words came from me. He got caught was very embarrassed yet nothing happened to him for committing this fraud. He'll eventually have to answer for this! **12/10/2019 15:07**

On my way to Hershey Pennsylvania for a rally. See everyone soon. I love Hershey chocolate! https://t.co/bDUYBK8KRc **12/10/2019 22:36**

THANK YOU PENNSYLVANIA! With your help your devotion and your drive we are going to keep on working we are going to keep on fighting and we are going to keep ON WINNING! We are ONE movement ONE people ONE family and ONE GLORIOUS NATION UNDER GOD! https://t.co/g64HD9yL9N **12/11/2019 1:47**

Wow! All of our priorities have made it into the final NDAA: Pay Raise for our Troops Rebuilding our Military Paid Parental Leave Border Security and Space Force! Congress - don't delay this anymore! I will sign this historic defense legislation immediately! **12/11/2019 15:17**

They spied on my campaign! https://t.co/sOotkhk5fw **12/11/2019 19:12**

"New Polls Say Most Americans Oppose Impeachment." @ foxandfriends I did nothing wrong. This will be the first Impeachment ever where there was no crime. They don't even allege a crime. Crazy! **12/12/2019 11:51**

So ridiculous. Greta must work on her Anger Management problem then go to a good old fashioned movie with a friend! Chill Greta Chill! https://t.co/M8ZtS8okzE
12/12/2019 12:22

Getting VERY close to a BIG DEAL with China. They want it and so do we! **12/12/2019 14:35**

Dems Veronica Escobar and Jackson Lee purposely misquoted my call. I said I want you to do us (our Country!) a favor not me a favor. They know that but decided to LIE in order to make a fraudulent point! Very sad. **12/12/2019 15:40**

I also have constantly asked "Why aren't Germany France and other European countries helping Ukraine more? They are the biggest beneficiaries. Why is it always the good ol' United States?" The Radical Left Do Nothing Democrats never mention this at their phony hearing! **12/12/2019 16:05**

Nancy Pelosi just got duped in an interview to admitting that she has been working on impeaching me for "two and a half years." In other words she lied. This was the Radical

Left Do Nothing Democrats plan all along long before the Ukraine phone call. Impeachment Hoax! **12/13/2019 3:53**

Looking like a big win for Boris in the U.K.! **12/13/2019 4:06**

Congratulations to Boris Johnson on his great WIN! Britain and the United States will now be free to strike a massive new Trade Deal after BREXIT. This deal has the potential to be far bigger and more lucrative than any deal that could be made with the E.U. Celebrate Boris!
12/13/2019 6:08

The Republicans House members were fantastic yesterday. It always helps to have a much better case in fact the Dems have no case at all but the unity & sheer brilliance of these Republican warriors all of them was a beautiful sight to see. Dems had no answers and wanted out! **12/13/2019 11:51**

My Approval Rating in the Republican Party is 95% a Record. Thank you! #2020Election **12/13/2019 11:53**

Poll numbers have gone through the roof in favor of No Impeachment especially with Swing States and Independents in Swing States. People have figured out that the Democrats have no case it is a total Hoax. Even Pelosi admitted yesterday that she began this scam 2 1/2 years ago! **12/13/2019 12:01**

The Do Nothing Democrats have become the Party of lies and deception! The Republicans are the Party of the American Dream! **12/13/2019 12:05**

The Republican Party is more united now than at any time in its history - by far! **12/13/2019 12:07**

How do you get Impeached when you have done NOTHING wrong (a perfect call) have created the best economy in the history of our Country rebuilt our Military fixed the V.A. (Choice!) cut Taxes & Regs protected your 2nd A created Jobs Jobs Jobs and soooo much more? Crazy! **12/13/2019 13:42**

The Wall Street Journal story on the China Deal is completely wrong especially their statement on Tariffs. Fake News. They should find a better leaker! **12/13/2019 14:06**

We have agreed to a very large Phase One Deal with China. They have agreed to many structural changes and massive purchases of Agricultural Product Energy and Manufactured Goods plus much more. The 25% Tariffs will remain as is with 7 1/2% put on much of the remainder.... **12/13/2019 15:25**

"This whole process has been rigged from the start." @RepDLesko **12/13/2019 17:38**

It's not fair that I'm being Impeached when I've done absolutely nothing wrong! The Radical Left Do Nothing Democrats have become the Party of Hate. They are so bad for our Country! **12/14/2019 0:38**

"The FBI declares in a court filing that it has absolutely no records of disciplinary action against any lawyers in Russia Fisa Case despite 17 acts of misconduct. There is nothing noble about their leadership. FISA Court appears to be either corrupt or incompetent." @LouDobbs **12/14/2019 2:13**

25 Million Evangelical Christians are not registered to vote. We are working hard to get them registered! @robertjeffress @LouDobbs **12/14/2019 2:27**

After watching the disgraceful way that a wonderful man @BrettKavanaugh was treated by the Democrats and now seeing first hand how these same Radical Left Do Nothing Dems are treating the whole Impeachment Hoax I

understand why so many Dems are voting Republican!
12/14/2019 13:07

Chuck Schumer sat for years during the Obama Administration and watched as China ripped off the United States. He & the Do Nothing Democrats did NOTHING as this $ carnage took place. Now without even seeing it he snipes at our GREAT new deal with China. Too bad Cryin' Chuck! **12/14/2019 19:09**

The last time I spoke to Debbie Dingell was her call thanking me for granting top memorial and funeral service honors for her then just departed husband long time Congressman John Dingell. Now I watch her ripping me as part of the Democrats Impeachment Hoax. Really pathetic!
12/14/2019 23:26

Hard to believe that @FoxNews will be interviewing sleazebag & totally discredited former FBI Director James Comey & also corrupt politician Adam "Shifty" Schiff. Fox is trying sooo hard to be politically correct and yet they were totally shut out from the failed Dem debates! **12/15/2019 0:10**

Both Commiecast MSNBC & Fake News CNN are watching their Ratings TANK. Fredo on CNN is dying. Don't know why @FoxNews wants to be more like them? They'll all die together as other outlets take their place. Only pro Trump Fox shows do well. Rest are nothing. How's Shep doing?
12/15/2019 0:47

Congratulations to Tiger and the entire U.S. Team on a great comeback and tremendous WIN. True Champions! https://t.co/wyjBAgoF7J **12/15/2019 4:53**

As bad as the I.G. Report is for the FBI and others and it is really bad remember that I.G. Horowitz was appointed by Obama. There was tremendous bias and guilt exposed so obvious but Horowitz couldn't get himself to say it. Big credibility loss. Obama knew everything! **12/15/2019 18:01**

So now Comey's admitting he was wrong. Wow but he's only doing so because he got caught red handed. He

was actually caught a long time ago. So what are the consequences for his unlawful conduct. Could it be years in jail? Where are the apologies to me and others Jim?
12/15/2019 18:34

Approval Rating in Republican Party = 95% a Record! Overall Approval Rating = 51%. Think of where I'd be without the never ending 24 hour a day phony Witch Hunt that started 3 years ago! **12/15/2019 19:14**

Because Nancy's teeth were falling out of her mouth and she didn't have time to think! https://t.co/rx3pcyofip
12/15/2019 22:11

I look very much forward to debating whoever the lucky person is who stumbles across the finish line in the little watched Do Nothing Democrat Debates. My record is so good on the Economy and all else including debating that perhaps I would consider more than 3 debates.....
12/16/2019 14:25

New Stock Market high! I will never get bored of telling you that - and we will never get tired of winning! **12/16/2019 17:41**

Congressman Jeff Van Drew is very popular in our great and very united Republican Party. It was a tribute to him that he was able to win his heavily Republican district as a Democrat. People like that are not easily replaceable!
12/17/2019 5:44

Impeachment Poll numbers are starting to drop like a rock now that people are understanding better what this whole Democrat Scam is all about! **12/17/2019 14:51**

Would be sooo great if the Fed would further lower interest rates and quantitative ease. The Dollar is very strong against other currencies and there is almost no inflation. This is the time to do it. Exports would zoom! **12/17/2019 15:12**

Wow! "In a stunning rebuke of the FBI the FISA court severly chastised the FBI for the FISA abuses brought to light in the recent Inspector General's Report. There were at least 17 significant errors." @FoxNews Statement by the Court was long and tough. Means my case was a SCAM! **12/17/2019 23:14**

Democrat "leadership" despite their denials are putting tremendous pressure on their members to vote yes on this ridiculous Impeachment. If they vote yes it will be much easier for Republicans to win in 2020! **12/17/2019 23:48**

Good marks and reviews on the letter I sent to Pelosi today. She is the worst! No wonder with people like her and Cryin' Chuck Schumer D.C. has been such a mess for so long - and that includes the previous administration who (and now we know for sure) SPIED on my campaign. **12/18/2019 3:54**

So if Comey & the top people in the FBI were dirty cops and cheated on the FISA Court wouldn't all of these phony cases have to be overturned or dismissed? They went after me with the Fake Dossier paid for by Crooked Hillary & the DNC which they illegally presented to FISA... **12/18/2019 4:10**

Can you believe that I will be impeached today by the Radical Left Do Nothing Democrats AND I DID NOTHING WRONG! A terrible Thing. Read the Transcripts. This should never happen to another President again. Say a PRAYER!
12/18/2019 12:34

Thank you! https://t.co/YewSIzHxBM **12/18/2019 15:42**

"The evidence has to be overwhelming and it is not. It's not even close." Ken Starr Former Independent Counsel
12/18/2019 16:14

In the end here nothing happened. We don't approach anything like the egregious conduct that should be necessary before a President should be removed from office. I believe that a President can't be removed from

office if there is no reasonable possibility that the Senate..
12/18/2019 16:38

SUCH ATROCIOUS LIES BY THE RADICAL LEFT DO NOTHING DEMOCRATS. THIS IS AN ASSAULT ON AMERICA AND AN ASSAULT ON THE REPUBLICAN PARTY!!!!

12/18/2019 17:44

Thank you Michigan I am on my way. See everybody soon! #KAG https://t.co/GP9SbH67CN **12/18/2019 22:56**

100% Republican Vote. That's what people are talking about. The Republicans are united like never before! **12/19/2019 12:31**

"The Senate shall set the time and place of the trial." If the Do Nothing Democrats decide in their great wisdom not to show up they would lose by Default! **12/19/2019 13:22**

PRESIDENTIAL HARASSMENT! **12/19/2019 13:30**

I got Impeached last night without one Republican vote being cast with the Do Nothing Dems on their continuation of the greatest Witch Hunt in American history. Now the Do Nothing Party want to Do Nothing with the Articles & not deliver them to the Senate but it's Senate's call! **12/19/2019 14:10**

Pelosi feels her phony impeachment HOAX is so pathetic she is afraid to present it to the Senate which can set a date and put this whole SCAM into default if they refuse to show up! The Do Nothings are so bad for our Country!
12/19/2019 16:07

The great USMCA Trade Deal (Mexico & Canada) has been sitting on Nancy Pelosi's desk for 8 months she doesn't even know what it says & today after passing by a wide margin in the House Pelosi tried to take credit for it. Labor

will vote for Trump. Trade deal is great for USA!
12/19/2019 23:55

So after the Democrats gave me no Due Process in the House no lawyers no witnesses no nothing they now want to tell the Senate how to run their trial. Actually they have zero proof of anything they will never even show up. They want out. I want an immediate trial! **12/20/2019 0:16**

The House Democrats were unable to get even a single vote from the Republicans on their Impeachment Hoax. The Republicans have never been so united! The Dem's case is so bad that they don't even want to go to trial! **12/20/2019 0:36**

The reason the Democrats don't want to submit the Articles of Impeachment to the Senate is that they don't want corrupt politician Adam Shifty Schiff to testify under oath nor do they want the Whistleblower the missing second Whistleblower the informer the Bidens to testify! **12/20/2019 1:56**

I will be signing our 738 Billion Dollar Defense Spending Bill today. It will include 12 weeks Paid Parental Leave gives our troops a raise importantly creates the SPACE FORCE SOUTHERN BORDER WALL FUNDING repeals "Cadillac Tax" on Health Plans raises smoking age to 21! BIG! **12/20/2019 14:19**

Had a very good talk with President Xi of China concerning our giant Trade Deal. China has already started large scale purchaes of agricultural product & more. Formal signing being arranged. Also talked about North Korea where we are working with China & Hong Kong (progress!). **12/20/2019 15:24**

I guess the magazine "Christianity Today" is looking for Elizabeth Warren Bernie Sanders or those of the socialist/communist bent to guard their religion. How about Sleepy Joe? The fact is no President has ever done what I have done for Evangelicals or religion itself! **12/20/2019 18:18**

Just had a great call with the President of Brazil @ JairBolsonaro. We discussed many subjects including Trade. The relationship between the United States and Brazil has never been Stronger! **12/20/2019 21:09**

Nancy Pelosi is looking for a Quid Pro Quo with the Senate. Why aren't we Impeaching her?

12/20/2019 21:28

We are getting MS-13 gang members and many other people that shouldn't be here out of our Country! https://t.co/Cfk4iIBVTQ **12/20/2019 22:41**

"It's time to put House Democrats on trial." @IngrahamAngle **12/21/2019 3:16**

Last year I signed legislation that gives our Veterans CHOICE through private providers and at urgent care facilities! Today we fully funded this $10 billion a year effort that gets our brave Veterans care quickly and close to home. **12/21/2019 3:30**

Honored to finally put an end to the "Widow's Tax" and ensure that our surviving military spouses receive their full benefits. The spouses and families of our fallen heroes have suffered enough and WE must do everything in our power to ease the burden. **12/21/2019 3:31**

Broke all time Stock Market Record again today. 135 times since my 2016 Election Win. Thank you! **12/21/2019 4:43**

Last night I was so proud to have signed the largest Defense Bill ever. The very vital Space Force was created. New planes ships missiles rockets and equipment of every kind and all made right here in the USA. Additionally we got Border Wall (being built) funding. Nice! **12/21/2019 19:38**

Crazy Nancy wants to dictate terms on the Impeachment Hoax to the Republican Majority Senate but striped away all Due Process no lawyers or witnesses on the Democrat Majority House. The Dems just wish it would all end. Their case is dead their poll numbers are horrendous!

12/22/2019 20:18

Melania and I send our warmest wishes to Jewish people in the United States Israel and across the world as you commence the 8-day celebration of Hanukkah. https://t.co/WgQyO9qxSs **12/22/2019 20:21**

The Democrats and Crooked Hillary paid for & provided a Fake Dossier with phony information gotten from foreign sources pushed it to the corrupt media & Dirty Cops & have now been caught. They spied on my campaign then tried to cover it up - Just Like Watergate but bigger! **12/22/2019 22:14**

Pelosi gives us the most unfair trial in the history of the U.S. Congress and now she is crying for fairness in the Senate and breaking all rules while doing so. She lost Congress once she will do it again!

12/23/2019 13:38

Nancy Pelosi who has already lost the House & Speakership once & is about to lose it again is doing everything she can to delay the zero Republican vote Articles of Impeachment. She is trying to take over the Senate & Cryin' Chuck is trying to take over the trial. No way!.... **12/23/2019 22:13**

Wouldn't it be reasonable to assume that Republicans in the Senate should handle the Impeachment Hoax in the exact same manner as Democrats in the House handled their recent partisan scam? Why would it be different for Republicans than it was for the Radical Left Democrats?

12/23/2019 23:25

NASDAQ UP 72.2% SINCE OUR GREAT 2016 ELECTION VICTORY! DOW UP 55.8%. The best is yet to come!

12/23/2019 23:58

STOCK MARKET CLOSES AT ALL-TIME HIGH! What a great time for the Radical Left Do Nothing Democrats to Impeach your favorite President especially since he has not done anything wrong! **12/24/2019 0:17**

What the Democrats are doing is "Obstruction of the Senate. It's wrong Constitutionally it's wrong morally and it's wrong politically." @AlanDersh @seanhannity @dbongino I agree and so does the public! **12/24/2019 2:31**

Everything we're seeing from Speaker Pelosi and Senator Schumer suggests that they're in real doubt about the evidence they've brought forth so far not being good enough and are very very urgently seeking a way to find some more evidence. The only way to make this work is to.. **12/24/2019 12:10**

The ONLY reason we were able to get our great USMCA Trade Deal approved was because the Do Nothing Democrats wanted to show that they could approve something productive in light of the fact that all they even think about is impeachment. She knows nothing about the USMCA Deal! **12/24/2019 13:25**

187 new Federal Judges have been confirmed under the Trump Administration including two great new United States Supreme Court Justices. We are shattering every record! Read all about this in "The Long Game" a great new book by @senatemajldr Mitch McConnell. Amazing story! **12/24/2019 22:32**

MERRY CHRISTMAS!

12/25/2019 12:26

2019 HOLIDAY RETAIL SALES WERE UP 3.4% FROM LAST YEAR THE BIGGEST NUMBER IN U.S. HISTORY. CONGRATULATIONS AMERICA! **12/25/2019 20:32**

Governor Gavin N has done a really bad job on taking care of the homeless population in California. If he can't fix the problem the Federal Govt. will get involved! https://t.co/2z8zM37PUA **12/25/2019 22:29**

Wow. It's all a giant SCAM! https://t.co/e7ZCOVe98F **12/25/2019 23:04**

Why should Crazy Nancy Pelosi just because she has a slight majority in the House be allowed to Impeach the President of the United States? Got ZERO Republican votes there was no crime the call with Ukraine was perfect with "no pressure." She said it must be "bipartisan... **12/26/2019 3:12**

The Radical Left Do Nothing Democrats said they wanted to RUSH everything through to the Senate because "President Trump is a threat to National Security" (they are vicious will say anything!) but now they don't want to go fast anymore they want to go very slowly. Liars! **12/26/2019 12:18**

Nancy Pelosi's District in California has rapidly become one of the worst anywhere in the U.S. when it come to the homeless & crime. It has gotten so bad so fast - she has lost total control and along with her equally incompetent governor Gavin Newsom it is a very sad sight! **12/26/2019 12:59**

"Nancy Pelosi has no leverage over the Senate. Mitch McConnell did not nose his way into the impeachment process in the House and she has no standing in the Senate." Brad Blakeman. Crazy Nancy should clean up her filthy dirty District & help the homeless there. A primary for N? **12/26/2019 13:21**

Despite all of the great success that our Country has had over the last 3 years it makes it much more difficult to deal with foreign leaders (and others) when I am having to constantly defend myself against the Do Nothing Democrats & their bogus Impeachment Scam. Bad for USA! **12/26/2019 14:36**

Russia Syria and Iran are killing or on their way to killing thousands of innocent civilians in Idlib Province. Don't do it! Turkey is working hard to stop this carnage. **12/26/2019 15:25**

"Trump stock market rally is far outpacing past US presidents" https://t.co/lFegwHMLGr 12/26/2019 20:41

California leads the nation by far in both the number of homeless people and the percentage increase in the homeless population - two terrible stats. Crazy Nancy should focus on that in her very down district and helping her incompetent governor with the big homeless problem! 12/26/2019 23:53

I guess Justin T doesn't much like my making him pay up on NATO or Trade! https://t.co/sndS7YvIGR 12/27/2019 0:03

The movie will never be the same! (just kidding) https://t.co/FogquK1ei7 12/27/2019 0:07

"Democrats repeatedly claimed impeachment was an urgent matter but now Nancy Pelosi uses stall tactics to obstruct the Senate." @replouiegohmert @HeyTammyBruce @FoxNews It's all part of the Impeachment Hoax! 12/27/2019 4:27

Speaker Pelosi and Chuck Schumer's drive to try and rig the trial against the President is misplaced. There is no factual basis for the Articles of Impeachment that passed the House. This President will be exonerated." William McGinley @foxandfriends 12/27/2019 14:28

Thank YOU Indian Country for being such an IMPORTANT part of the American story! I recently signed 3 bills to support tribal sovereignty.... 12/27/2019 16:37

So interesting to see Nancy Pelosi demanding fairness from @senatemajldr McConnell when she presided over the most unfair hearing in the history of the United States Congress! 12/27/2019 20:43

Wow Crazy Nancy what's going on? This is big stuff! https://t.co/hoHSERKgh9 12/28/2019 2:31

Nancy this just doesn't seem right! https://t.co/0fmQj79DLX 12/28/2019 4:28

Now that wasn't very nice was it? https://t.co/RHEriGdEQO
12/28/2019 4:41

California and New York must do something about their TREMENDOUS Homeless problems. They are setting records! If their Governors can't handle the situation which they should be able to do very easily they must call and "politely" ask for help. Would be so easy with competence! **12/28/2019 13:33**

I want to thank Rush Limbaugh for the tremendous support he has given to the MAKE AMERICA GREAT AGAIN Movement and our KEEP AMERICA GREAT Agenda! He is a major star who never wavered despite the Fake News Hits he has had to endure. His voice is far bigger than theirs! **12/28/2019 21:06**

So sad to see that New York City and State are falling apart. All they want to do is investigate to make me hate them even more than I should. Governor Cuomo has lost control and lost his mind. Very bad for the homeless and all! **12/28/2019 21:14**

Any answers Nancy? https://t.co/CBb9tlXiue **12/29/2019 12:57**

Crazy Nancy Pelosi should spend more time in her decaying city and less time on the Impeachment Hoax! https://t.co/enoZZFxxmg **12/29/2019 14:55**

The anti-Semitic attack in Monsey New York on the 7th night of Hanukkah last night is horrific. We must all come together to fight confront and eradicate the evil scourge of anti-Semitism. Melania and I wish the victims a quick and full recovery.

12/29/2019 19:10

Thank you to highly respected Jewish leader Dov Hikind for his wonderful statements about me this morning on @ foxandfriends. **12/30/2019 14:28**

Our prayers are with the families of the victims and the congregation of yesterday's church attack. It was over in 6 seconds thanks to the brave parishioners who acted to protect 242 fellow worshippers. Lives were saved by these heroes and Texas laws allowing them to carry arms!

12/31/2019 0:57

The Democrats will do anything to avoid a trial in the Senate in order to protect Sleepy Joe Biden and expose the millions and millions of dollars that "Where's" Hunter & possibly Joe were paid by companies and countries for doing NOTHING. Joe wants no part of this mess! **12/31/2019 11:16**

Iran killed an American contractor wounding many. We strongly responded and always will. Now Iran is orchestrating an attack on the U.S. Embassy in Iraq. They will be held fully responsible. In addition we expect Iraq to use its forces to protect the Embassy and so notified! **12/31/2019 12:02**

Armed congregants quickly stopped a crazed church shooter in Texas. If it were not for the fact that there were people inside of the church that were both armed and highly proficient in using their weapon the end result would have been catastrophic. A big THANK YOU to them! **12/31/2019 13:53**

President Putin of Russia called to thank me and the U.S. for informing them of a planned terrorist attack in the very beautiful city of Saint Petersburg. They were able to quickly apprehend the suspects with many lives being saved. Great & important coordination! **12/31/2019 14:06**

I will be signing our very large and comprehensive Phase One Trade Deal with China on January 15. The ceremony will take place at the White House. High level representatives of China will be present. At a later date I will be going to Beijing where talks will begin on Phase Two! **12/31/2019 14:16**

To those many millions of people in Iraq who want freedom and who don't want to be dominated and controlled by Iran this is your time! **12/31/2019 15:44**

Read the Transcripts! **12/31/2019 17:34**

Remember when Pelosi was screaming that President Trump is a danger to our nation and we must move quickly. They didn't get one Republican House vote and lost 3 Dems. They produced no case so now she doesn't want to go to the Senate. She's all lies. Most overrated person I know! **12/31/2019 17:42**

The U.S. Embassy in Iraq is & has been for hours SAFE! Many of our great Warfighters together with the most lethal military equipment in the world was immediately rushed to the site. Thank you to the President & Prime Minister of Iraq for their rapid response upon request.... (1/2) **12/31/2019 21:19**

....Iran will be held fully responsible for lives lost or damage incurred at any of our facilities. They will pay a very BIG PRICE! This is not a Warning it is a Threat. Happy New Year! (2/2) **12/31/2019 21:19**

The Anti-Benghazi! **12/31/2019 21:38**

The Fake News said I played golf today and I did NOT! I had meeting in various locations while closely monitoring the U.S. Embassy situation in Iraq which I am still doing. The Corrupt Lamestream Media knew this but not surprisingly failed to report or correct! **12/31/2019 22:11**

JANUARY 2020 - FEBRUARY 2020

★★★★★★★★★★★★★★★★★★★★★★★★★★★

While Iran threatens the U.S. militarily, Trump promises that they will never be allowed to have nuclear weapons. The news shifts its attention from the House of Representatives to the Senate. This is where the impeachment trial against President Trump is scheduled to be held, with Chief Justice John Roberts presiding. Senate Democrats attempt to add witnesses but are voted down by the controlling Republicans. Voting strictly on party lines, except for Mitt Romney (R-UT), Trump is acquitted.

HAPPY NEW YEAR! **1/1/2020 1:30**

Best equipment & finest military in the World. On site quickly! https://t.co/cDUtqFLLYB **1/2/2020 1:32**

Sohrab Ahmari New York Post "The Trump Campaign raised $10 million in the two days following the impeachment (Scam) vote. It seems the Democrats have shot themselves in the foot in one more way. They set up a process they know is not going to lead to the Presidents removal &... **1/2/2020 13:42**

A lot of very good people were taken down by a small group of Dirty (Filthy) Cops politicians government officials and an investigation that was illegally started & that SPIED on my campaign. The Witch Hunt is sputtering badly but still going on (Ukraine Hoax!). If this.... (1/2) **1/2/2020 13:58**

....had happened to a Presidential candidate or President who was a Democrat everybody involved would long ago be in jail for treason (and more) and it would be considered the CRIME OF THE CENTURY far bigger and more sinister than Watergate! (2/2) **1/2/2020 13:58**

Iran never won a war but never lost a negotiation!

1/3/2020 12:44

General Qassem Soleimani has killed or badly wounded thousands of Americans over an extended period of time and was plotting to kill many more...but got caught! He was directly and indirectly responsible for the death of millions of people including the recent large number.... (1/2) **1/3/2020 13:54**

....of PROTESTERS killed in Iran itself. While Iran will never be able to properly admit it Soleimani was both hated and feared within the country. They are not nearly as saddened as the leaders will let the outside world believe. He should have been taken out many years ago! (2/2) **1/3/2020 13:54**

The United States has paid Iraq Billions of Dollars a year for many years. That is on top of all else we have done for them. The people of Iraq don't want to be dominated & controlled by Iran but ultimately that is their choice. Over the last 15 years Iran has gained more.... (1/2) **1/3/2020 15:09**

....and more control over Iraq and the people of Iraq are not happy with that. It will never end well! (2/2) **1/3/2020 15:09**

Christopher Bedford The Federalist Senior Editor. "There is NOTHING NEW in these Emails at all that's been discovered. It's exactly what we knew before which is that the White House & political figures wanted to cut off aid Trump wanted to question aid to a number of.... **1/3/2020 17:27**

95% Approval Rating in the Republican Party. Thank you! **1/4/2020 14:57**

As hard as I work & as successful as our Country has become with our Economy our Military & everything else it is ashame that the Democrats make us spend so much time & money on this ridiculous Impeachment Lite Hoax. I should be able to devote all of my time to the REAL USA!

1/4/2020 22:16

Iran is talking very boldly about targeting certain USA assets as revenge for our ridding the world of their terrorist leader who had just killed an American & badly wounded many others not to mention all of the people he had killed over his lifetime including recently.... (1/3) **1/4/2020 22:52**

....targeted 52 Iranian sites (representing the 52 American hostages taken by Iran many years ago) some at a very high level & important to Iran & the Iranian culture and those targets and Iran itself WILL BE HIT VERY FAST

AND VERY HARD. The USA wants no more threats! (3/3) **1/4/2020 22:52**

....hundreds of Iranian protesters. He was already attacking our Embassy and preparing for additional hits in other locations. Iran has been nothing but problems for many years. Let this serve as a WARNING that if Iran strikes any Americans or American assets we have..... (2/3) **1/4/2020 22:52**

They attacked us & we hit back. If they attack again which I would strongly advise them not to do we will hit them harder than they have ever been hit before! https://t.co/ql5RfWsSCH **1/5/2020 4:53**

The United States just spent Two Trillion Dollars on Military Equipment. We are the biggest and by far the BEST in the World! If Iran attacks an American Base or any American we will be sending some of that brand new beautiful equipment their way...and without hesitation!

1/5/2020 5:11

These Media Posts will serve as notification to the United States Congress that should Iran strike any U.S. person or target the United States will quickly & fully strike back & perhaps in a disproportionate manner. Such legal notice is not required but is given nevertheless! **1/5/2020 20:25**

"The reason they are not sending the Articles of Impeachment to the Senate is that they are so weak and so pathetic." @LindseyGrahamSC @MariaBartiromo The great Scam continues. To be spending time on this political Hoax at this moment in our history when I am so busy is sad! **1/6/2020 13:37**

The Impeachment Hoax just a continuation of the Witch Hunt which started even before I won the Election must end quickly. Read the Transcripts see the Ukrainian President's strong statement NO PRESSURE - get this done. It is a con game by the Dems to help with the Election! **1/6/2020 14:32**

Congress & the President should not be wasting their time and energy on a continuation of the totally partisan Impeachment Hoax when we have so many important matters pending. 196 to ZERO was the Republican House vote & we got 3 Dems. This was not what the Founders had in mind! **1/6/2020 14:39**

IRAN WILL NEVER HAVE A NUCLEAR WEAPON!

1/6/2020 14:48

The homeless situation in Los Angeles San Francisco and many other Democrat Party run cities throughout the Nation is a state and local problem not a federal problem.... (1/2) **1/6/2020 23:50**

....If however the city or state in question is willing to acknowledge responsibility and politely asks for help from the Federal Government we will very seriously consider getting involved in order to make those poorly run Democrat Cities Great Again! (2/2) **1/6/2020 23:50**

We love Australia! https://t.co/BFPCNS81YR **1/7/2020 11:44**

Great interview with @GOPLeader Kevin McCarthy on @ foxandfriends. "There was no urgency with the Articles of Impeachment because there was no case." **1/7/2020 13:27**

Had a very good meeting with @kbsalsaud of Saudi Arabia. We discussed Trade Military Oil Prices Security and Stability in the Middle East! **1/7/2020 19:05**

All is well! Missiles launched from Iran at two military bases located in Iraq. Assessment of casualties & damages taking place now. So far so good! We have the most powerful and well equipped military anywhere in the world by far! I will be making a statement tomorrow morning. **1/8/2020 2:45**

Pelosi doesn't want to hand over The Articles of Impeachment which were fraudulently produced by corrupt politicians like Shifty Schiff in the first place because after all of these years of investigations and persecution they show no crimes and are a joke and a scam! **1/9/2020 12:21**

PRESIDENTIAL HARASSMENT! **1/9/2020 12:30**

Hope that all House Republicans will vote against Crazy Nancy Pelosi's War Powers Resolution. Also remember her "speed & rush" in getting the Impeachment Hoax voted on & done. Well she never sent the Articles to the Senate. Just another Democrat fraud. Presidential Harassment! **1/9/2020 13:20**

Breaking News: The Fifth Circuit Court of Appeals just reversed a lower court decision & gave us the go ahead to build one of the largest sections of the desperately needed Southern Border Wall Four Billion Dollars. Entire Wall is under construction or getting ready to start! **1/9/2020 13:46**

U.S. Cancer Death Rate Lowest In Recorded History! A lot of good news coming out of this Administration. **1/9/2020 15:00**

STOCK MARKET AT ALL-TIME HIGH! HOW ARE YOUR 401K'S DOING? 70% 80% 90% up? Only 50% up! What are you doing wrong? **1/9/2020 15:47**

Happy National Law Enforcement Appreciation Day! #LESM https://t.co/kNN3RetVvs **1/9/2020 17:59**

95% Approval Rating in the Republican Party. Thank you! **1/9/2020 22:49**

Heading to Toledo Ohio for first Rally of the year. Tremendous crowd. Here we go for a big 2020 Win! **1/9/2020 22:55**

Under my administration we will NEVER make excuses for America's enemies - we will never hesitate in defending American lives - and we will never stop working to defeat

Radical Islamic Terrorism! https://t.co/022PjwhHjs
1/10/2020 2:04

Democrats are now the party of high taxes high crime open borders late-term abortion socialism and blatant corruption. The Republican Party is the party of the American Worker the American Family and the American Dream! #KAG2020 https://t.co/05XRX2odxN **1/10/2020 2:15**

Wow! Thank you Greg. Hope I live up to your expectations. https://t.co/jBWn1ksGo4 **1/10/2020 12:55**

Great interview this morning by @foxandfriends with some of the fantastic people who attended the big Rally last night in Toledo Ohio. Thank you. Such amazing energy! **1/10/2020 13:04**

"11000 points gained in the Dow in the 3 years since the Election of President Trump. Today it may hit 29000. That has NEVER happened before in that time frame. That has added 12.8 Trillion Dollars to the VALUE of American Business." @Varneyco @FoxNews The best is yet to come! **1/10/2020 15:08**

"I've been doing this for 40 years and I've never seen anything like this (Economy)." @Varneyco @foxandfriends **1/10/2020 15:11**

She will go down as perhaps the least successful Speaker in U.S. History! https://t.co/aTCkFW3pr4 **1/10/2020 15:37**

Will be interviewed tonight by Laura @IngrahamAngle at 10pmE on @FoxNews. Enjoy! **1/10/2020 23:32**

"FBI Director apologizes for FISA Errors (of which there were far to many to be a coincidence!)." @FoxNews Chris what about all of the lives that were ruined because of the so-called "errors?" Are these "dirty cops" going to pay a big price for the fraud they committed? **1/11/2020 13:38**

Where have the Radical Left Do Nothing Democrats gone when they have spent the last 3 days defending the life of

Qassem Soleimani one of the worst terrorists in history and the father of the roadside bomb? He was also looking to do big future damage! Dems are "unhinged." **1/11/2020 14:07**

New polling shows that the totally partisan Impeachment Hoax is going nowhere. A vast majority want the Do Nothing Democrats to move on to other things now! **1/11/2020 14:15**

Nancy Pelosi will go down as the absolute worst Speaker of the House in U.S. history! **1/11/2020 14:17**

Now the Radical Left Do Nothing Democrats are asking @senatemajldr Mitch McConnell to do the job that they were unable to do. They proved NOTHING but my total innocence in the House despite the most unfair & biased hearings in the history of Congress. Now they demand fairness! **1/11/2020 14:29**

95% Approval Rating in the Republican Party a record. 53% Approval Rating overall (can we add 7 to 10 percent because of the Trump "thing?"). Thank you! **1/11/2020 14:35**

The powerful Trump Wall is replacing porous useless and ineffective barriers in the high traffic areas requested by Border Patrol. Illegal crossing are dropping as more and more Wall is being completed! #BuildingTheWall https://t.co/2kdHNSMM04 **1/11/2020 21:13**

To the brave long-suffering people of Iran: I've stood with you since the beginning of my Presidency and my Administration will continue to stand with you. We are following your protests closely and are inspired by your courage.
1/11/2020 21:46

The government of Iran must allow human rights groups to monitor and report facts from the ground on the ongoing protests by the Iranian people. There can not be another massacre of peaceful protesters nor an internet shutdown. The world is watching. **1/11/2020 22:11**

I hope the House and Senate Democrats in particular watch this. It is a classic. Thank you to @JudgeJeanine Pirro! https://t.co/O8P9J0CArF **1/12/2020 4:12**

Congratulations to the Great State of Tennessee. You've got yourselves a fantastic football team. Big WIN last night! **1/12/2020 13:13**

To the leaders of Iran - DO NOT KILL YOUR PROTESTERS. Thousands have already been killed or imprisoned by you and the World is watching. More importantly the USA is watching. Turn your internet back on and let reporters roam free! Stop the killing of your great Iranian people! **1/12/2020 13:48**

John Kerry got caught essentially admitting that funds given ridiculously to Iran were used to fund attacks on the USA. Only a complete fool would have given that 150 Billion Dollars Plus to Iran. They then went on a Middle East Rampage! @foxandfriends @PeteHegseth **1/12/2020 14:06**

Why did Nervous Nancy allow corrupt politician Shifty Schiff to lie before Congress? He must be a Witness and so should she! **1/12/2020 16:13**

Why should I have the stigma of Impeachment attached to my name when I did NOTHING wrong? Read the Transcripts! A totally partisan Hoax never happened before. House Republicans voted 195-0 with three Dems voting with the Republicans. Very unfair to tens of millions of voters!

1/12/2020 16:40

You can't make this up! David Kris a highly controversial former DOJ official was just appointed by the FISA Court to oversee reforms to the FBI's surveillance procedures. Zero credibility. THE SWAMP! @DevinNunes @MariaBartiromo @FoxNews **1/12/2020 18:41**

Wow! Crazy Bernie Sanders is surging in the polls looking very good against his opponents in the Do Nothing Party. So what does this all mean? Stay tuned! **1/12/2020 19:02**

Many believe that by the Senate giving credence to a trial based on the no evidence no crime read the transcripts "no pressure" Impeachment Hoax rather than an outright dismissal it gives the partisan Democrat Witch Hunt credibility that it otherwise does not have. I agree! **1/12/2020 19:55**

National Security Adviser suggested today that sanctions & protests have Iran "choked off" will force them to negotiate. Actually I couldn't care less if they negotiate. Will be totally up to them but no nuclear weapons and "don't kill your protesters." **1/12/2020 23:46**

Mini Mike Bloomberg is spending a lot of money on False Advertising. I was the person who saved Pre-Existing Conditions in your Healthcare you have it now while at the same time winning the fight to rid you of the expensive unfair and very unpopular Individual Mandate.....
1/13/2020 13:39

Bernie Sander's volunteers are trashing Elizabeth "Pocahontus" Warren. Everybody knows her campaign is dead and want her potential voters. Mini Mike B is also trying but getting tiny crowds which are all leaving fast. Elizabeth is very angry at Bernie. Do I see a feud brewing?
1/13/2020 15:25

The Democrats and the Fake News are trying to make terrorist Soleimani into a wonderful guy only because I did what should have been done for 20 years. Anything I do whether it's the economy military or anything else will be

scorned by the Rafical Left Do Nothing Democrats!
1/13/2020 15:47

Wow! The wonderful Iranian protesters refused to step on or in any way denigrate our Great American Flag. It was put on the street in order for them to trample it and they walked around it instead. Big progress! **1/13/2020 15:53**

The Fake News Media and their Democrat Partners are working hard to determine whether or not the future attack by terrorist Soleimani was "imminent" or not & was my team in agreement. The answer to both is a strong YES. but it doesn't really matter because of his horrible past! **1/13/2020 16:09**

Really Big Breaking News (Kidding): Booker who was in zero polling territory just dropped out of the Democrat Presidential Primary Race. Now I can rest easy tonight. I was sooo concerned that I would someday have to go head to head with him!

1/13/2020 16:13

"We demand fairness" shouts Pelosi and the Do Nothing Democrats yet the Dems in the House wouldn't let us have 1 witness no lawyers or even ask questions. It was the most unfair witch-hunt in the history of Congress! **1/13/2020 17:31**

I stand stronger than anyone in protecting your Healthcare with Pre-Existing Conditions. I am honored to have terminated the very unfair costly and unpopular individual mandate for you! **1/13/2020 23:58**

Thank you to Rick Scott. This Impeachment Hoax is an outrage! https://t.co/HYfBmtYMqF **1/14/2020 5:25**

On my way to Milwaukee Wisconsin for a #TrumpRally. Look forward to see you all soon! https://t.co/L97KjEc9GW **1/14/2020 23:16**

We are helping Apple all of the time on TRADE and so many other issues and yet they refuse to unlock phones used by killers drug dealers and other violent criminal elements. They will have to step up to the plate and help our great Country NOW! MAKE AMERICA GREAT AGAIN. **1/14/2020 23:36**

Cryin' Chuck Schumer just said "The American people want a fair trial in the Senate." True but why didn't Nervous Nancy and Corrupt politician Adam "Shifty" Schiff give us a fair trial in the House. It was the most lopsided & unfair basement hearing in the history of Congress!

1/14/2020 23:45

GOD BLESS THE U.S.A.! https://t.co/xi2yTS5fY1 **1/15/2020 2:43**

Former National Security Adviser for President Obama said "President Trump was absolutely correct" in taking out terroristist leader Soleimani. Thank you General Jones! **1/15/2020 3:18**

Prime Minister of the United Kingdom @BorisJohnson stated "We should replace the Iran deal with the Trump deal." I agree! **1/15/2020 4:32**

I agree with him on this 100%. But why would anyone vote Democrat? We are setting all time records with the economy! https://t.co/trTemE8iUz **1/15/2020 6:13**

Here we go again another Con Job by the Do Nothing Democrats. All of this work was supposed to be done by the House not the Senate! **1/15/2020 15:33**

One of the greatest trade deals ever made! Also good for China and our long term relationship. 250 Billion Dollars will be coming back to our Country and we are now in a great position for a Phase Two start. There has never been anything like this in U.S. history! USMCA NEXT! **1/16/2020 13:41**

Cryin' Chuck Schumer is saying privately that the new China Trade Deal is unbelievable which it is but publicly he knocks it whenever possible. That's politics but so bad for our great Country! **1/16/2020 13:59**

"There is no crime here. I just think this whole thing should be rejected out of hand. I wouldn't waste a minute of taxpayer dollars or time on this. Entertaining this Impeachment is a joke." Laura Ingraham @IngrahamAngle @FoxNews **1/16/2020 15:04**

The farmers are really happy with the new China Trade Deal and the soon to be signed deal with Mexico and Canada but I hope the thing they will most remember is the fact that I was able to take massive incoming Tariff money and use it to help them get through the tough times! **1/16/2020 15:14**

I JUST GOT IMPEACHED FOR MAKING A PERFECT PHONE CALL!

1/16/2020 20:39

See you tomorrow! #CHAMPS https://t.co/ud1PVpx1zK **1/17/2020 0:22**

PROMISES MADE PROMISES KEPT! #KeepAmericaGreat2020 🇺🇸 https://t.co/CheEfoFUBT **1/17/2020 1:41**

"Years from now when we look back at this day nobody's going to remember Nancy's cheap theatrics they will remember though how President Trump brought the Chinese to the bargaining table and delivered achievements few ever thought were possible." @IngrahamAngle @ FoxNews **1/17/2020 13:33**

Mini Mike Bloomberg ads are purposely wrong - A vanity project for him to get into the game. Nobody in many years has done for the USA what I have done for the USA including the greatest economy in history rebuilding our military biggest ever tax & regulation cuts & 2nd A! **1/17/2020 14:12**

Getting ready to meet the LSU Tigers the National Champions. Great Coach great Team great School. Very exciting! **1/17/2020 15:17**

They are rigging the election again against Bernie Sanders just like last time only even more obviously. They are bringing him out of so important Iowa in order that as a Senator he sit through the Impeachment Hoax Trial. Crazy Nancy thereby gives the strong edge to Sleepy... **1/17/2020 15:35**

Heading to Florida for big Republican Party event. New Stock Market Record. Jobs in USA at all-time high! **1/17/2020 20:10**

Your 2nd Amendment is under very serious attack in the Great Commonwealth of Virginia. That's what happens when you vote for Democrats they will take your guns away. Republicans will win Virginia in 2020. Thank you Dems! **1/17/2020 22:22**

The so-called "Supreme Leader" of Iran who has not been so Supreme lately had some nasty things to say about the United States and Europe. Their economy is crashing and their people are suffering. He should be very careful with his words! **1/17/2020 22:22**

CONGRATULATIONS! #GeauxTigers https://t.co/Axc9ezAdar **1/18/2020 0:57**

A great day at the White House for our National Champions the LSU Tigers! https://t.co/0sbotFsMO7 **1/18/2020 13:09**

Tremendous surge in new housing construction in December 16.9% biggest in many years! **1/18/2020 13:19**

"Day after day really good news on the economy. By the way this didn't just happen by accident it's the result of a lot of the policies that Donald Trump has put into place. Obviously the Tax Cut and now we have these two BIG trade deals." @StephenMoore Great future growth!
1/18/2020 13:33

"Trade Deals Drive Stocks To Record Highs." @FoxNews
1/18/2020 13:35

95% Approval Rating in the Republican Party A Record. Thank You! **1/18/2020 22:56**

They are taking the Democrat Nomination away from Crazy Bernie just like last time. Some things never change! **1/18/2020 22:58**

Another Fake Book by two third rate Washington Post reporters has already proven to be inaccurately reported to their great embarrassment all for the purpose of demeaning and belittling a President who is getting great things done for our Country at a record clip. Thank you! **1/18/2020 23:16**

A massive 200 Billion Dollar Sea Wall built around New York to protect it from rare storms is a costly foolish & environmentally unfriendly idea that when needed probably won't work anyway. It will also look terrible. Sorry you'll just have to get your mops & buckets ready! **1/18/2020 23:18**

....BUT THE BEST IS YET TO COME! **1/19/2020 0:52**

"Nancy Pelosi said it's not a question of proof it's a question of allegations! Oh really?" @JudgeJeanine @FoxNews What a disgrace this Impeachment Scam is for our great Country! **1/19/2020 2:12**

I will be going to Austin Texas. Leaving soon. Always like (love!) being in the Lone Star State. Speaking to our great Farmers. They hit "paydirt" with our incredible new Trade Deals: CHINA JAPAN MEXICO CANADA SOUTH KOREA and many others! **1/19/2020 17:44**

I have never seen the Republican Party as Strong and as Unified as it is right now. Thank you!

1/19/2020 18:24

Now Mini Mike Bloomberg is critical of Jack Wilson who saved perhaps hundreds of people in a Church because he was carrying a gun and knew how to use it. Jack quickly killed the shooter who was beginning a rampage. Mini is against the 2nd A. His ads are Fake just like him! **1/19/2020 21:12**

"In the House the President got less due process than the 9-11 terrorists got. This is a corrupt process?" Mark Levin @marklevinshow "Very much so!" @RepDougCollins @ FoxNews **1/20/2020 1:16**

The Democrat Party in the Great Commonwealth of Virginia are working hard to take away your 2nd Amendment rights. This is just the beginning. Don't let it happen VOTE REPUBLICAN in 2020! **1/20/2020 15:43**

They didn't want John Bolton and others in the House. They were in too much of a rush. Now they want them all in the Senate. Not supposed to be that way! **1/20/2020 15:47**

Cryin' Chuck Schumer is now asking for "fairness" when he and the Democrat House members worked together to make sure I got ZERO fairness in the House. So what else is new? **1/20/2020 15:52**

USA! USA! USA! **1/20/2020 17:04**

...And they say you can add 7% to 10% to all Trump numbers! Who knows? https://t.co/Ta09xrAqUd

1/20/2020 18:53

It was exactly three years ago today January 20 2017 that I was sworn into office. So appropriate that today is also MLK jr DAY. African-American Unemployment is the LOWEST in the history of our Country by far. Also best Poverty Youth and Employment numbers ever. Great! **1/20/2020 19:59**

I will NEVER allow our great Second Amendment to go unprotected not even a little bit! **1/20/2020 20:12**

Heading to Davos Switzerland to meet with World and Business Leaders and bring Good Policy and additional Hundreds of Billions of Dollars back to the United States of America! We are now NUMBER ONE in the Universe by FAR!! **1/21/2020 0:59**

"It's about the Economy stupid" except when it comes to Trump. The fact is the Fake News Media hates talking about the Economy and how incredible it is! **1/21/2020 1:45**

THE BEST IS YET TO COME! https://t.co/YBMOBurdHQ
1/21/2020 1:59

READ THE TRANSCRIPTS!
1/21/2020 19:08

Making great progress in @Davos. Tremendous numbers of companies will be coming or returning to the USA. Hottest Economy! JOBS JOBS JOBS! **1/22/2020 6:48**

They are taking the nomination away from Bernie for a second time. Rigged! **1/22/2020 13:26**

"Not the Senate's job to mop up the mess made in the House by the Democrats. Biden admitted that he went to Ukraine and did the Quid Pro Quo." @SteveScalise @ FoxNews **1/22/2020 16:17**

One of the many great things about our just signed giant Trade Deal with China is that it will bring both the USA & China closer together in so many other ways. Terrific working with President Xi a man who truly loves his country. Much more to come! **1/22/2020 18:03**

"NO PRESSURE" **1/22/2020 19:58**

See you on Friday...Big Crowd! https://t.co/MFyWLG4HFZ
1/22/2020 22:04

Sorry if you come you will be immediately sent back!
https://t.co/Ba9kmD6HD0 **1/22/2020 22:13**

The Democrat House would not give us lawyers or not one witness but now demand that the Republican Senate produce the witnesses that the House never sought or even asked for? They had their chance but pretended to rush. Most unfair & corrupt hearing in Congressional history!
1/23/2020 12:52

No matter what you give to the Radical Left Do Nothing Democrats it will never be enough! **1/23/2020 12:54**

"This is all about undermining the next Election." Liz Peek @ FoxNews **1/23/2020 16:15**

The Democrats don't want a Witness Trade because Shifty Schiff the Biden's the fake Whistleblower(& his lawyer) the second Whistleblower (who vanished after I released the Transcripts) the so-called "informer" & many other Democrat disasters would be a BIG problem for them!
1/23/2020 18:18

"The Democrats have now conceded that President Trump has not committed a crime." @AriFleischer **1/23/2020 20:26**

Democrats are going to destroy your Social Security. I have totally left it alone as promised and will save it! **1/23/2020 21:08**

Crazy Bernie takes the lead in the Democrat Primaries but it is looking more and more like the Dems will never allow him to win! Will Sleepy Joe be able to stumble across the finish line? **1/23/2020 21:08**

"He's got to explain this. How did Hunter Biden get a billion and a half dollars (from China) to invest when he'd been in

business for 60 days?" @LindseyGrahamSC @FoxNews
1/24/2020 11:42

The Impeachment Hoax is interfering with the 2020 Election - But that was the idea behind the Radical Left Do Nothing Dems Scam attack. They always knew I did nothing wrong!
1/24/2020 12:50

More than anything else the Radical Left Do Nothing Democrats like AOC Omar Cryin' Chuck Nervous Nancy & Shifty Schiff are angry & "deranged" over the fact that Republicans are up to 191 Federal Judges & Two Great New Supreme Court Justices. Don't blame me blame Obama!
1/24/2020 15:37

READ THE TRANSCRIPTS! **1/24/2020 16:16**

The Do Nothing Democrats just keep repeating and repeating over and over again the same old "stuff" on the Impeachment Hoax. They want to use up ALL of their time even though it is the wrong thing to do. They ought to go back to work for our great American people! **1/24/2020 16:56**

China has been working very hard to contain the Coronavirus. The United States greatly appreciates their efforts and transparency. It will all work out well. In particular on behalf of the American People I want to thank President Xi! **1/24/2020 21:18**

After consultation with our Great Military Leaders designers and others I am pleased to present the new logo for the United States Space Force the Sixth Branch of our Magnificent Military! https://t.co/TC8pT4yHFT

1/24/2020 21:31

The Great @LouDobbs: "People know after 3 years of this President the most historic President in our Country's history that there is no one who can touch what he's done in 3 years foreign policy domestic policy you name it it's amazing. Just to have the guts not to be..... **1/25/2020 13:59**

"I like President Trump's Tweets (Social Media) I like everything about him...and this Ukraine stuff the trial the impeachment this isn't t about Ukraine. Donald Trump has committed the two unpardonable sins in the eyes of the Democrats. He beat Hillary Clinton in 2016 and.. **1/25/2020 14:19**

Our case against lyin' cheatin' liddle' Adam "Shifty" Schiff Cryin' Chuck Schumer Nervous Nancy Pelosi their leader dumb as a rock AOC & the entire Radical Left Do Nothing Democrat Party starts today at 10:00 A.M. on @FoxNews @ OANN or Fake News @CNN or Fake News MSDNC! **1/25/2020 14:37**

Any fair minded person watching the Senate trial today would be able to see how unfairly I have been treated and that this is indeed the totally partisan Impeachment Hoax that EVERYBODY including the Democrats truly knows it is. This should never be allowed to happen again! **1/25/2020 18:41**

"You don't come to court and ask for witnesses after you've already presented your case unless you know your case is not working. I think their real motivation is for them to keep this President busy. We're doing a great job on the economy we're building our military look..... **1/25/2020 21:57**

Iranian Foreign Minister says Iran wants to negotiate with The United States but wants sanctions removed. @FoxNews @OANN No Thanks! **1/26/2020 0:16**

All Democrats should watch this! https://t.co/WFK33pR0Lv **1/26/2020 2:15**

The Impeachment Hoax is a massive election interference the likes of which has never been seen before. In just two hours the Radical Left Do Nothing Democrats have seen their phony case absolutely shredded. Shifty is now exposed for illegally making up my phone call & more! **1/26/2020 13:09**

Shifty Adam Schiff is a CORRUPT POLITICIAN and probably a very sick man. He has not paid the price yet for what he has done to our Country! **1/26/2020 13:20**

Sleepyeyes Chuck Todd of Meet the Corrupt Press just had a "totally" softball interview with conman Adam Schiff never even calling Shifty out on his fraudulent statement to Congress where he made up ALL of the words of my conversation with the Ukrainian President! FAKE NEWS **1/26/2020 16:07**

95% Approval Rating in the Republican Party. Thank you! 191 Federal Judges (a record) and two Supreme Court Justices approved. Best Economy & Employment Numbers EVER. Thank you to our great New Smart and Nimble REPUBLICAN PARTY. Join now it's where people want to be! **1/26/2020 16:24**

Majority of people say "the U.S. Senate already has enough information!" @FoxNews **1/26/2020 20:01**

Nothing done wrong READ THE TRANSCRIPTS! **1/26/2020 20:39**

Reports are that basketball great Kobe Bryant and three others have been killed in a helicopter crash in California. That is terrible news! **1/26/2020 20:48**

Kobe Bryant despite being one of the truly great basketball players of all time was just getting started in life. He loved his family so much and had such strong passion for the future. The loss of his beautiful daughter Gianna makes this moment even more devastating.... (1/2)
1/26/2020 23:54

.....Melania and I send our warmest condolences to Vanessa and the wonderful Bryant family. May God be with you all! (2/2) **1/26/2020 23:54**

I NEVER told John Bolton that the aid to Ukraine was tied to investigations into Democrats including the Bidens. In fact he never complained about this at the time of his very public termination. If John Bolton said this it was only to sell a book. With that being said the... **1/27/2020 5:18**

The Democrat controlled House never even asked John Bolton to testify. It is up to them not up to the Senate! **1/27/2020 11:57**

READ THE TRANSCRIPTS! **1/27/2020 13:42**

Schiff must release the IG report without changes or tampering which is said to be yet further exoneration of the Impeachment Hoax. He refuses to give it. Does it link him to Whistleblower? Why is he so adamant? **1/27/2020 14:40**

We are in very close communication with China concerning the virus. Very few cases reported in USA but strongly on watch. We have offered China and President Xi any help that is necessary. Our experts are extraordinary! **1/27/2020 14:56**

Don Lemon the dumbest man on television (with terrible ratings!). https://t.co/iQXCc7lvCt **1/28/2020 5:26**

Really pathetic how @FoxNews is trying to be so politically correct by loading the airwaves with Democrats like Chris Van Hollen the no name Senator from Maryland. He has been on forever playing up the Impeachment Hoax. Dems wouldn't even give Fox their low ratings debates.... **1/28/2020 15:44**

Are you better off now than you were three years ago? Almost everyone say YES! **1/28/2020 15:47**

The Fed should get smart & lower the Rate to make our interest competitive with other Countries which pay much

lower even though we are by far the high standard. We would then focus on paying off & refinancing debt! There is almost no inflation-this is the time (2 years late)!
1/28/2020 15:55

Heading to New Jersey. Big Rally in fact Really Big Rally!
1/28/2020 22:16

It's amazing what I've done the most of any President in the first three years (by far) considering that for three years I've been under phony political investigations and the Impeachment Hoax! KEEP AMERICA GREAT! **1/28/2020 22:23**

If you want your children to inherit the blessings that generations of Americans have fought and died to secure— then we must devote everything we have toward victory in 2020. Only this way can we save the America we love - and drain the Washington Swamp once and for all! https://t.co/5NeC0mFWfU **1/29/2020 1:41**

No matter how many witnesses you give the Democrats no matter how much information is given like the quickly produced Transcripts it will NEVER be enough for them. They will always scream UNFAIR. The Impeachment Hoax is just another political CON JOB!
1/29/2020 2:25

Why didn't John Bolton complain about this "nonsense" a long time ago when he was very publicly terminated. He said not that it matters NOTHING! **1/29/2020 5:07**

For a guy who couldn't get approved for the Ambassador to the U.N. years ago couldn't get approved for anything since "begged" me for a non Senate approved job which I gave him despite many saying "Don't do it sir" takes the job mistakenly says "Libyan Model" on T.V. and.. **1/29/2020 12:28**

Remember Republicans the Democrats already had 17 witnesses we were given NONE! Witnesses are up to the House not up to the Senate. Don't let the Dems play you!
1/29/2020 12:56

On the Iraq War Resolution being voted on tomorrow in the House of Represenatives we are down to 5000 soldiers and going down and I want everyone Republican and Democrat to vote their HEART! **1/29/2020 15:33**

With Votes in the House tomorrow Democrats want to make it harder for Presidents to defend America and stand up to as an example Iran. Protect our GREAT COUNTRY!
1/29/2020 23:59

Nancy Pelosi wants Congress to take away authority Presidents use to stand up to other countries and defend AMERICANS. Stand with your Commander in Chiefs!
1/29/2020 23:59

"Schiff blasted for not focusing on California homeless." @ foxandfriends His District is in terrible shape. He is a corrupt pol who only dreams of the Impeachment Hoax. In my opinion he is mentally deranged! **1/30/2020 15:39**

Just landed in Michigan. Car companies and many others are building and expanding here. Great to see! **1/30/2020 20:34**

BIGGEST TRADE DEAL EVER MADE the USMCA was signed yesterday and the Fake News Media barely mentioned it. They never thought it could be done. They have zero credibility! **1/30/2020 20:37**

Working closely with China and others on Coronavirus outbreak. Only 5 people in U.S. all in good recovery.
1/30/2020 22:04

This November we are going to defeat the Radical Socialist Democrats and win the Great State of Iowa in a Historic Landslide! #KAG2020 https://t.co/jYIbSdyGjU **1/31/2020 2:54**

THE BEST IS YET TO COME! https://t.co/SOn6wRV9Zs **1/31/2020 4:22**

Nadler ripped final argument away from Schiff thinks Shifty did a terrible job. They are fighting big time! https://t.co/L2qTV9pWiL **1/31/2020 14:25**

The Radical Left Do Nothing Democrats keep chanting "fairness" when they put on the most unfair Witch Hunt in the history of the U.S. Congress. They had 17 Witnesses we were allowed ZERO and no lawyers. They didn't do their job had no case. The Dems are scamming America! **1/31/2020 21:06**

Democrats = 17 Witnesses. Republicans = 0 Witnesses. **1/31/2020 23:05**

No matter what you give to the Democrats in the end they will NEVER be satisfied. In the House they gave us NOTHING! **2/1/2020 0:13**

Congratulations to @loudobbs Number One. Lou has shown the Fake News what happens when you cover "America's Greatest President" fairly & objectively! #MAGA #KAG https://t.co/68b0vPvmNd **2/1/2020 13:14**

Trump poll numbers are the highest since election despite constant phony Witch Hunts! Tens of thousands of people attending rallies (which the Fake News never mentions) to see "The Greatest Show On Earth". Fun because USA is WINNING AGAIN! https://t.co/L14hDtx6cT **2/1/2020 13:42**

Getting a little exercise this morning! https://t.co/fyAAcbhbgk **2/1/2020 16:14**

Such a great common sense question. Crazy! https://t.co/i13tgw24wN **2/1/2020 21:53**

The Radical Left Do Nothing Democrats don't want justice when pushing the Impeachment Hoax they only want to destabilize the Republican Party so they can do better in the 2020 election & that includes the House & Senate. They are playing with the people by taking it this far! **2/2/2020 5:04**

Mini Mike is part of the Fake News. They are all working together. In fact Bloomberg isn't covering himself (too boring to do) or other Dems. Only Trump. That sounds fair! It's all the Fake News Media and that's why nobody believes in them any more. **2/2/2020 5:10**

Many of the ads you are watching were paid for by Mini Mike Bloomberg. He is going nowhere just wasting his money but he is getting the DNC to rig the election against Crazy Bernie something they wouldn't do for @CoryBooker and others. They are doing it to Bernie again 2016. **2/2/2020 5:17**

Mini Mike is now negotiating both to get on the Democrat Primary debate stage and to have the right to stand on boxes or a lift during the debates. This is sometimes done but really not fair! **2/2/2020 5:25**

ENJOY THE GAME USA OUR COUNTRY IS DOING GREAT!

2/2/2020 23:13

I promised to restore hope in America. That includes the least among us. Together let's KEEP AMERICA GREAT! Text TRUMP to 88022 if you liked our Super Bowl ad! https://t.co/Lgjt53B7QX **2/2/2020 23:56**

Congratulations to the Kansas City Chiefs on a great game and a fantastic comeback under immense pressure. We are proud of you and the Great State of Missouri. You are true Champions! **2/3/2020 3:27**

Hope you liked this! https://t.co/y1j2Wf6J4p **2/3/2020 5:25**

I hope Republicans & the American people realize that the totally partisan Impeachment Hoax is exacty that a Hoax. Read the Transcripts listen to what the President & Foreign Minister of Ukraine said ("No Pressure"). Nothing will ever satisfy the Do Nothing Radical Left Dems! **2/3/2020 16:42**

Republicans in Iowa go out and Caucus today. Your great Trade Deals with China Mexico Canada Japan South Korea and more are DONE. Great times are coming after waiting for decades for our Farmers Ranchers Manufacturers and ALL. Nobody else could have pulled this off! **2/3/2020 16:51**

MAKE AMERICA GREAT AGAIN!
2/3/2020 16:52

KEEP AMERICA GREAT! **2/3/2020 16:52**

Where's the Whistleblower? Where's the second Whistleblower? Where's the Informer? Why did Corrupt politician Schiff MAKE UP my conversation with the Ukrainian President??? Why didn't the House do its job? And sooo much more! **2/3/2020 17:03**

Many people do not know what a great guy & fantastic political talent the great Rush Limbaugh is. There is nobody like him. Looking for a speedy recovery for our friend! https://t.co/GRTt56BjEu **2/4/2020 3:20**

Big WIN for us in Iowa tonight. Thank you! **2/4/2020 4:27**

The Democrat Caucus is an unmitigated disaster. Nothing works just like they ran the Country. Remember the 5 Billion Dollar Obamacare Website that should have cost 2% of that. The only person that can claim a very big victory in Iowa last night is "Trump". **2/4/2020 11:33**

When will the Democrats start blaming RUSSIA RUSSIA RUSSIA instead of their own incompetence for the voting disaster that just happened in the Great State of Iowa? **2/4/2020 14:22**

The Democrat Party in Iowa really messed up but the Republican Party did not. I had the largest re-election vote in the history of that great state by far beating President Obama's previous record by a lot. Also 97% Plus of the vote! Thank you Iowa! **2/4/2020 14:34**

Market up big today on very good economic news. JOBS JOBS JOBS! **2/4/2020 15:52**

My Approval Rating in the Republican Party = 95% a record! Big Iowa win. Approval Rating overall = 53% a new high. With our great Economy and other major successes would be 20 points higher without the phony Witch Hunts and Hoaxes??? **2/4/2020 15:59**

It was a great and triumphant evening for our Country. Thank you for all of the nice remarks and wonderful reviews of my State of the Union Speech. It was my great honor to have done it! **2/5/2020 12:59**

"The Democrats want to run a Country and they can't run a Caucus." Brad Blakeman @FoxNews Iowa is a complete disaster for the Dems. They should bring in Mini Mike Bloomberg ASAP! **2/5/2020 15:22**

I will be making a public statement tomorrow at 12:00pm from the @WhiteHouse to discuss our Country's VICTORY on the Impeachment Hoax! **2/5/2020 22:07**

INDEX